List of Contributors

JASPER BRENER — *University of Hull, Hull, England*

MARGARET J. CHRISTIE — *Department of Psychology, University of Bradford, West Yorkshire, England*

R. P. FLETCHER — *Department of Psychology, University of York, Heslington, York, England*

ANTHONY GALE — *Department of Psychology, University of Southampton, Southampton, England*

JAMES H. GEER — *Department of Psychology, State University of New York at Stony Brook, Stony Brook, New York, USA.*

ALBERTO GRIGNOLO — *University of North Carolina, North Carolina, USA.*

FRANCIS K. GRAHAM — *University of Wisconsin, Wisconsin, USA.*

JOHN D. HAINES — *Medical Research Council, Clinical Psychiatry Unit, Graylingwell Hospital, Chichester, England*

J. RICHARD JENNINGS — *University of Pittsburgh School of Medicine, Western Psychiatric Institute and Clinic, Pittsburgh, Pennsylvania, USA.*

LAVERNE C. JOHNSON — *Naval Regional Medical Center, Department of the Navy, San Diego, California, USA.*

BEATRICE C. LACEY — *Fels Research Institute, Wright State University School of Medicine, USA.*

JOHN I. LACEY — *Fels Research Institute, Wright State University School of Medicine, USA.*

PETER J. LANG — *University of Wisconsin, Madison, Wisconsin, USA.*

v

ALAN W. LANGER   *University of North Carolina, North Carolina, USA.*

L. N. LAW   *Department of Psychology, Institute of Psychiatry, University of London, London, England*

A. B. LEVEY   *Medical Research Council, Clinical Psychiatry Unit, Graylingwell Hospital, Chichester, England*

KATHLEEN C. LIGHT   *University of North Carolina, North Carolina, USA.*

TIM LOBSTEIN   *University of London, London, England.*

DAVID T. LYKKEN   *Department of Psychiatry, University of Minnesota, Minneapolis, Minnesota, USA.*

JAMES A. MCCUBBIN   *University of North Carolina, North Carolina, USA.*

COLIN J. MACKAY   *Health and Safety Executive, London, England*

IRENE MARTIN   *Department of Psychology, Institute of Psychiatry, University of London, London, England.*

PAUL A. OBRIST   *University of North Carolina, North Carolina, USA.*

KIERON P. O'CONNOR   *Department of Psychology, Institute of Psychiatry, University of London, London, England*

PHYLLIS J. OSTER   *Department of Psychology, Washington University, Behavior Research Laboratories at Malcolm Bliss Mental Health Center, St. Louis, Missouri, USA*

TERENCE W. PICTON   *Departments of Medicine and Experimental Psychology, University of Ottawa, Ontario, Canada*

D. P. REDMOND   *Department of Military Medical Psychophysiology, Forest Glen Annex, Walter Reid Army Medical Center, Washington DC, USA*

Techniques in Psychophysiology

Edited by

IRENE MARTIN
Department of Psychology, Institute of Psychiatry, London

and

PETER H. VENABLES
Department of Psychology, University of York

JOHN WILEY & SONS
Chichester · New York · Brisbane · Toronto

British Library Cataloguing in Publication Data:

Techniques in psychophysiology.
  1. Psychology, Physiological—Technique
  I. Martin, Irene
  II. Venables, Peter Henry
  612'.8   QP360   79-42925

ISBN 0 471 27637 5

Typeset by Preface Ltd., Salisbury, Wilts. and printed by
Page Bros. (Norwich) Ltd., Norwich.

M. D. RUGG	*Department of Psychology, University of St. Andrews, Fife, Scotland.*
B. McA. SAYERS	*Engineering in Medicine Laboratory, Imperial College, University of London, London, England*
DAVID A. T. SIDDLE	*Department of Psychology, University of Southampton, Southampton, England*
DAVID SMITH	*Department of Psychology, University of Southampton, Southampton, England*
ANDREW STEPTOE	*Department of Psychology, St. George's Hospital Medical School, Jenner Wing, London, England*
JOHN A. STERN	*Department of Psychology, Washington University, Behavior Research Laboratories at Malcolm Bliss Mental Health Center, St. Louis, Missouri, USA*
ALBERT J. TAHMOUSH	*Department of Military Medical Psychophysiology, Forest Glen Annex, Walter Reid Army Medical Center, Washington DC, USA*
GRAHAM TURPIN	*Department of Pharmacology, Institute of Psychiatry, University of London, London, England*
PETER H. VENABLES	*Department of Psychology, University of York, Heslington, York, England*
RONALD S. WILSON	*University of Louisville, Louisville, Kentucky, USA.*
DAVID D. WOODMAN	*Medicinal Research Centre, Beecham Research Laboratories, Harlow, England*

Contents

Preface

In this book, as in our previous manual, we are concerned with methods of psychophysiological measurement on the intact human person. During the past decade psychophysiology has flourished; newer recording techniques and methods of analysis have developed and understanding of relevant physiological mechanisms has increased. The various chapters attempt to reflect this growth in knowledge and to indicate the shifts in interest and preoccupation with different research problems which have taken place.

The general availability of adequate commercial equipment has lessened the need for extensive and detailed circuits to be given in the text for the 'do-it-yourself' technician. Standardization of recording may still be some way off, but in many areas there is a general consensus of opinion about optimal recording techniques. However, there is still a need to weigh up the pros and cons of the many available systems, and to understand the consequences of different recording methodologies.

There has also been a rapid growth in methods of data analysis. This has been due in part to the increased use of computers but it also reflects greater awareness of the large amount of information obtained in our recordings, much of which had to be ignored in the era of painstaking hand measurement from pen and ink charts. Thus a set of factors is considered in this book which previously received little mention but which are current preoccupations; given that the data have been collected to our satisfaction, the next step is to consider the methods of measurement and analysis which are available and the criteria by which we can judge them.

Our two goals have therefore been:

(1) To examine what information is available to ensure good basic recordings of physiological activity when it is recorded from the body surface of the intact individual. This involves review of available measurement techniques, methods of placement and of calibration, artifacts, and such relevant operating characteristics of equipment as time constants, filters, and gain.
(2) To discuss how we can go about analysing recorded waveforms. This involves a consideration of the topography of the waveform and its response elements such as onset latency; of frequency

xi

components; and of the kinds of scales which should be applied. Authors discuss these and related matters such as the question of baselines, pre and post stimulus values and their relationships, and nomenclature. Some contributors refer to the difficulties in specifying response shape in certain systems, and discuss the role of a standard presentation of data and the relationship of observed measures to the physiology of the system. Subsequent chapters examine in a more detailed discussion the general problems of measurement.

The book does not deal with substantive problems like the measurement of arousal or stress, or the status of the concept of emotion. It is avowedly technique oriented. However, we have widened our view of techniques to include a chapter on biochemical methods and another on self-report techniques. Early workers frequently commented upon the bias of psychophysiologists towards rather few response systems and the neglect of others. The initial focusing on electrodermal activity has already given way to a wider interest in cortical and cardiovascular activity. We are now growing aware of the background of biochemical activity which is much more difficult to assess, especially in the form of continuously recorded activity to which we have been accustomed. However, there are some simpler techniques which psychophysiologists might well incorporate, and these are described. So far as self-report techniques are concerned, it now seems evident that one real but neglected view on physiological activity is the subject's own perception of internal events. A chapter is devoted to the examination of these methods.

The role of the computer in data analysis is far more sophisticated that a decade ago. Many of the chapters which deal with individual response systems indicate the range of methods of analysis which have been applied to the recorded activity. Some requirements are adequately met by computer programs which are widely available. In the situation which many of us at present find ourselves in, that is with small Departmental computer systems, we are able to explore techniques which permit the visual presentation of data in a variety of forms, the editing of response waveforms, and the application of automatic scoring systems. Some of these are illustrated in the chapters describing response detection and analysis and the use of computers in psychophysiological research.

The endpoints of our recordings are responses which we treat as waveforms containing information. In choosing our instruments and in selecting appropriate methods of analysis certain criteria have therefore to be recognized. Always important is the extent to which the physiological response represents the psychological situation in which it was observed, and lends itself to psychological interpretation. At the same time we have to bear in mind the physiological events represented. Thus, many of those researchers who use psychophysiological techniques to try to elucidate psychological concepts like attention and emotion are at the same time keenly aware of the complexities of physiological activity occurring beneath their recording electrodes.

We are grateful to the authors for keeping to what was a complex brief. The authors in Part 1 were asked to examine and evaluate the current status of recording techniques in their respective areas; to consider methods of data analysis; to refer to the physiological background of the response where appropriate but to avoid a review of substantive research findings. The authors in Part 2 were asked to present a general description of the problems of recording, measurement, and analysis, independently of any specific response system; and to consider the handling of psycho-physiological data in a general sense—the setting up of a laboratory, the use of small laboratory computers, the appropriateness of different measurement units, and the general problems of response detection and analysis.

Our intention was that the contents would both serve as an introduction for the novice and as a review of current practice for more experienced workers. In practice this has proved difficult and in some areas the nature of the material has dictated the level of sophistication which can be assumed. Most authors have provided a *vade mecum* of their fields, as well as practical details of recording techniques.

Readers will note the inclusion of a glossary in addition to the usual list of abbreviations. In reading the texts as they were received, it seemed that a glossary might prove useful. The use of technical terms often gives rise to difficulties, sometimes because there are exact definitions which we are unsure about, and sometimes because they are used in different ways by different groups of workers. To illustrate with two examples: 'acceleration' is used by cardiac investigators to denote an increase in heart rate but is also used by others in a more mathematical sense; 'time constant' has a precise mathematical definition but is frequently used in a very specific way by psychophysiologists. Thus there is sometimes a common usage and a technical usage, and some of the definitions given may reflect more common usage within psychophysiology.

Authors were circulated with lists of terms taken from manuscripts with the request that they supply definitions wherever possible. They responded swiftly and generously, and we acknowledge with thanks all the authors named in the list of contents who were so obliging, and in addition Ray Hilbert, Mathematician of the Naval Regional Medical Center at San Diego, USA. The contributions were mostly non-overlapping, but occasionally two kinds of explication were received and where this has occurred both are given. We hope that there are not too many errors or inaccuracies; if there are, we as Editors must accept responsibility and apologise in advance. We would appreciate corrections which could perhaps be incorporated in some future glossary for psychophysiologists, should the present one prove useful.

Grey Walter, in a foreword to *EEG Technology* (Cooper, Osselton and Shaw, 1969) commented that thirty years ago taking an EEG was fun. 'In fact, one didn't "take" an EEG, one struggled to wrest some sort of a record from a home-made rig of noisy valves, leaky batteries, fragile oscilloscopes and bulky cameras; the chance of everything working properly at the same time was small and it was all very strenuous, often exasperating, but always fun.'

Perhaps for the less technically skilled it was also enormously frustrating. Those days are largely behind us, and we are now in an era where breakdowns in equipment are relatively rare and computers—though not infallible—open up vast possibilities of analysis.

Yet, as many of us who have monitored data through pen and ink recorders, magnetic tape recorders, through small Departmental computers and on to large-scale 'number-crunchers' will testify, the most exciting part of our work very often resides in watching the record as it comes straight off our human subject or from the averager. What can it tell us? At whatever level of technical sophistication we work we can all acquire what Darwin has termed 'the habit of minute observation'.

As psychophysiologists we are fortunate that we have an abundance of data for observation! This book is about ensuring that the data are collected well and observed minutely.

January, 1979

IRENE MARTIN,
Institute of Psychiatry,
University of London,
London

PETER H. VENABLES,
University of York,
York

Reference

Cooper, R., Osselton, J. and Shaw, J. C. (1969). *EEG Technology*, 1st ed., Butterworth, London.

Part 1

Recordings of Specific Response Systems

Techniques in Psychophysiology
Edited by I. Martin and P.H. Venables
© 1980, John Wiley & Sons Ltd.

CHAPTER 1

Electrodermal Activity

P. H. VENABLES AND M. J. CHRISTIE

B

1.0 INTRODUCTION

A survey of practice in electrodermal measurement carried out by Tursky and O'Connell in 1966 reported an alarming range of disparate techniques then in use and a disenchantment with the results of recordings of electrodermal activity because of difficulty in obtaining reliable measurements.

This state of affairs had been earlier deplored by McCleary (1950) who in reviewing the status of work on electrodermal activity regretted the ignorance which then existed regarding the fundamental mechanisms on which the phenomena were based.

Thus, although work in the area had begun in the 1880s with the pioneering studies of Féré (1888) and Tarchanoff (1889) and had continued with some success up to the 1960s (see historical review by Neumann and Blanton, 1970) it has probably only been in the last twenty years that energetic attempts to perfect procedures of measurement based on an understanding of underlying physiology have been made. This is probably a somewhat unfair statement in the light of work undertaken by Darrow from the 1920s onwards (see Gullickson, 1973), but it is realistic to say that his work probably had less impact than it deserved on the diversity of practice or data which were reviewed by Tursky and O'Connell and by McCleary.

During the past decade there has been a move towards a consensus of opinion about the appropriate measurement techniques to use to the extent that is now almost possible to propose a standard set of procedures which may be generally acceptable. Such standardization of techniques makes possible the interchangeability of results from laboratory to laboratory with the consequent greater confidence in interpretation of data that can ensue.

Thus, this chapter should be seen as a development of earlier attempts to present the principles of electrodermal measurement (e.g., Edelberg and Burch, 1962; Montagu and Coles, 1966, 1968; Edelberg, 1967, 1972a; Venables and Martin, 1967a; Lykken and Venables, 1971; Venables and Christie, 1973; Grings, 1974) and therefore as a consolidation of the experience represented in this earlier material. There is little doubt that there are still many loose ends and some of these will become apparent in later pages. It is, however, at least helpful that they are indeed apparent and not, as before, embedded in so much error variance that it was not possible to detect points that needed clearing up.

Perhaps the major change which has taken place over the past decade or two has been the demonstration of the value of taking into account parameters of electrodermal activity other than tonic level and amplitude of response. There is undoubtedly some controversy (e.g., Bundy, 1977) over the extent to which the temporal aspects of a response, e.g. the latency, rise time and recovery, are independent of each other and of the magnitude measures but there does appear to be evidence which suggests that for heuristic purposes it is important at this time to treat the components of responses as independent.

The move towards standardization of techniques and the expansion in the number of variables that can be measured from a record of electrodermal activity have gone along with a development of knowledge of the role of peripheral mechanisms underlying the measured activity and this has been reflected in increasing complexity of electrical models to represent the function of the skin.

Nevertheless there are still wide areas of uncertainty resulting in part from a still inadequate understanding of the nature and function of peripheral mechanisms at active sites on the palmar and plantar surfaces of hand and foot. There is also an incomplete knowledge of the local and central innervation of these peripheral mechanisms.

The lack of knowledge is to some extent a result of the lack of use or the non-availability of suitable animal models. The extensive work of Wang (e.g., 1964), for instance, was based on the cat as a physiological preparation. Unfortunately, while we may accept the pointers which his work has produced as far as central mechanisms are concerned, the peripheral physiology of the cat food-pad is very unlike that of the human palm or sole and this means that for some important aspects of function one cannot extrapolate from cat to man.

The peripheral mechanisms in sub-human primates approximate more closely to those of man. However, work on these animals is comparatively rare. The best known is perhaps that of Pribram and his colleagues (Bagshaw, Kimble and Pribram, 1965; Kimble, Bagshaw and Pribram, 1965). A colony of large primates is, however, increasingly expensive to maintain and the recent report of Levy, Igarashi, Ledet and Reshke (1977) that the electrodermal response of the squirrel monkey appears to show close similarities to that of man may offer possibilities for future investigation.

At this time it is possible to see three levels of interest in and usage of electrodermal measurement. There are those, probably increasingly rare, who view an electrodermal response as no more than any other behavioural response and who on that account are not very interested in mechanisms that underly it, any more, for instance, than in the physiological mechanisms giving control of a limb. A second and probably majority group are again mainly users of electrodermal measurement, but in wishing to understand what they are measuring, and in particular in wishing to place the measured activity in the widest context, they take account of available knowledge of peripheral and central mechanisms. The third class of workers, whose numbers are very few, are other than mere users of the techniques and are actively engaged in understanding both the physiological mechanisms involved and the physical techniques involved in measuring their activity.

Another, more recent, area of activity is the application of computer techniques in electrodermal measurement. Measurement from paper chart recordings is undoubtedly feasible (in a way, for instance, that EEG averaged evoked responses are not) and in some cases quicker, overall, to accomplish than computer analysis techniques. However, the more general availability of minicomputers in psychophysiological laboratories enables large numbers of electrodermal records to be scored more readily than by hand once the appropriate software has been written and hence provides particular economies in large-scale studies.

However, possibly the greatest benefit in the use of computers is that standard definitions of response criteria have to be used (see Chapters 11 and 13) and the scoring procedure is thereby made more objective.

In summary, in this chapter it is the intention to present, in a fairly didactic fashion, an up to date guide to the measurement and analysis of electrodermal activity, based as far as possible on investigated principles but also pointing out where shortcomings in our knowledge still leave room for no more than 'best guess' decisions. Although measurement of electrodermal variables is perhaps one of the technically easiest psychophysiological variables, workers do appear to find difficulties at certain stages. For that reason some procedures may appear to be rather tediously spelt out and because of this the cognoscenti are advised to indulge in judicious skipping.

2.0 TERMINOLOGY

2.1 Introduction

From the earliest times, two different forms of electrodermal activity have been recognized. The most common, *exosomatically* recorded activity—involving the passage of a current through the skin—is associated with the name of Féré (1888) and activity is measured in terms of the resistance of (or conductance of) the tissue to the current. The less commonly used *endosomatic* recording of activity is due originally to Tarchanoff (1889, 1890) and involves the measurement of potential difference between two points on the skin surface. Normally one of these, the active site, is on a palmar or plantar surface and the other reference point is on an abraded, and hence low resistance to body interior, non-palmar site.

The two types of electrodermal activity although having some parallels are not identical and may yield different results.

Over the years the terminology used in describing electrodermal activity has not always reflected the types of measurement used nor indeed the different aspects, tonic or phasic, of those measurements. Thus, the most widely known term, galvanic skin response (GSR), which is perhaps most properly used to indicate the phasic response of the skin measured exosomatically has sometimes been used in other ways, as has the other previously common term, psychogalvanic response (PGR). There have, however, been a number of attempts to produce alternative terminologies with resultant increasing confusion. A suggestion to create a degree of order from this situation was made in 1967 by the Society of Psychophysiological Research (Brown, 1967) and then extended by Venables and Martin (1967a), Lykken and Venables (1971) and Venables and Christie (1973). With these developments as a basis a somewhat more extensive set of definitions is proposed here.

2.2 Proposals

What the proposals cited above lacked was a general term for electrodermal activity not necessarily defining whether or not it was endosomatically or exosomatically measured. To take account of this it is proposed, following Edelberg (1972a), that the terms

    electrodermal activity,   EDA
    electrodermal response,   EDR
    electrodermal level,   EDL

are used in contexts where the general nature of the area is being discussed.

Following directly from the suggestions of the Society for Psychophysiological Research nomenclature committee it is proposed that the terms

skin conductance response, SCR
skin resistance response,   SRR
skin potential response,   SPR

are used to indicate phasic activity in the relevant context.

In parallel with this terminology

skin conductance level, SCL
skin resistance level,   SRL
skin potential level,   SPL

are used when indicating tonic levels of activity from which responses arise.

These proposals assume that exosomatic activity is measured as a resultant of the passage of direct current through skin tissue. If, however, an alternating electrical source is used then the appropriate terminology would be

skin impedance response, SZR
skin admittance response, SYR
skin impedance level,   SZL
skin admittance level,   SYL

These terms enable the type of response or level to be defined. There are also, however, other components of response which require definition and terminology.

The SCR, for instance, in addition to the amplitude of response is characterized by three temporal measures: latency, rise time and recovery. There is less conventional authority on which to rely in the abbreviation of these aspects but the following are suggested:

latency   lat
rise time   ris. t
recovery time rec. t

However, where the last item is conventionally measured as a half-time value the abbreviation, rec. t/2, may be considered appropriate. If recovery is measured in terms of the time constant, rec. tc, then $tc/t/2 = 1.43$ (Edelberg, 1971). It is also suggested that the term amplitude, SCR amp, is used when the size of the response is particularly indicated. Figure 1.1 shows in diagrammatic form the components of response which have been outlined.

A further need for definition arises when describing average values of size of response. Two possibilities occur; firstly, the mean size of response

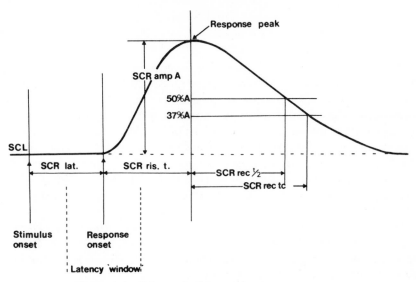

Figure 1.1   Schematic skin conductance response

may be calculated on all occasions *on which a response was given*. Following, for instance, Prokasy and Kumpfer (1973) it is proposed that the term *amplitude* is used in this instance. In contrast, where the mean size of response is calculated over all occasions *on which a response might be given* (i.e. over all stimulus occasions), so that zero values are entered into the average on those occasions on which a response does not occur, then it is proposed that the term mean *magnitude* is used. The occasions on which it is more appropriate to use amplitude or magnitude will be discussed later (Section 9.4).

In the case of the SPR, the shape of the response may be uniphasic negative, biphasic or, more rarely, uniphasic positive and sometimes triphasic; there seems no alternative to providing an unambiguous description of the component of the response in this instance.

Finally, perhaps the greatest variety of descriptions have been given to those fluctuations of EDA which have the appearance of responses but which nevertheless cannot be associated with a particular identifiable, external stimulus. However, physiologically a stimulus must have occurred at some level and hence the term *non-specific response* (NS), as used for instance by Kimmel and Hill (1961), Katkin (1965), Miller and Shmavonian (1965), Katkin and McGubbin (1969), appears to be appropriate and it is suggested that unless made clear by the context NS could be used as a prefix, as in NS.SCR.

3.0 UNITS

3.1 Skin conductance

In Section 5.4 it is shown that it is realistic to think of the principal effector mechanism in SC measurement as sweat glands arranged as resistors in parallel. Resistors in parallel are additive in terms of their reciprocals, that is, in terms of conductances. For this reason it is appropriate to measure exosomatic EDA as SCL and SCR. Units of conductance are mhos. However, because of the range of values normally obtained for SCL and SCR (see Section 5.3) it is more convenient to express SC in terms of micromhos (μmhos) (1 μmho = 1/1MΩ). (The SI unit of conductance is the siemen, and SC data should thus be expressed in terms of microsiemens. However, this unit does not appear to have been widely accepted in the psychophysiological literature and in this chapter it is proposed to use the better known micromho.) If exosomatic EDA has been measured using an alternating current source then it is appropriate to measure impedance in ohms and admittance in μmhos.

In addition to the greater physiological reality of measuring exosomatic activity in terms of conductance values there are other advantages. Lader (1970) presents data measured in both conductance and resistance units showing the decline in electrodermal activity which results from atropinization of the palmar surface. In the case of the conductance data the decline is orderly, whereas data expressed in resistance terms fluctuate more randomly. A further advantage is shown by Lykken and Venables (1971). As will be discussed in Section 7.1.3, it is convenient to separate measures of tonic level, SCL, from measures of phasic activity, SCR, by 'backing off' the SCL and thereby being able to measure SCR amp at a greater gain. It is found in practice that the number of resettings of the backing off control when measuring conductance is about half that needed when measuring in resistance terms.

3.2 Skin potential

Skin potential, both SPL and SPR, is conveniently measured in terms of millivolts (mV). Normally the polarity of the measured potential difference (p.d.) at the two electrode sites is negative at the palm but because this is not always so the polarity of the p.d. should be stated.

3.3 Normality of distribution

Data reviewed by Edelberg (1972a) suggest that transformation of conductance is unnecessary as conductance is reasonably normally distributed and such transformations as conversion to log conductance values over-correct for skewness.

However, the number of subjects giving rise to the data on which these statements are made is small and no material is presented on the temporal components of SCR.

Three sets of data are presented here to examine deviations from normality in SC data shown as figures for skewness and kurtosis. The first set of data, presented in Tables 1.1 and 1.2, is from a fairly large

Table 1.1. Mean, median, mode, variance, skewness, and kurtosis values of SCL and log SCL, SCR amp, and log SCR amp, in 5 age samples

Age	Mean	Median	Mode	Variance	Skewness	Kurtosis	N
SCL							
5	3.597	3.020	1.500	6.085	1.729	4.635	127
10	2.613	1.810	2.500	3.613	1.408	1.857	126
15	2.825	2.190	1.440	4.126	1.624	2.786	126
20	2.935	2.360	1.426	4.328	1.350	1.426	128
25	3.223	2.180	1.260	6.444	1.392	1.272	128
Total	3.040	2.350	1.110	5.009	1.568	2.908	635
log SCL							
5	0.461	0.480	0.176	0.088	−0.258	−0.128	127
10	0.305	0.258	0.398	0.110	−0.622	1.720	126
15	0.351	0.340	0.158	0.090	−0.131	−0.004	126
20	0.364	0.373	−0.149	0.096	−0.171	−0.308	128
25	0.387	0.338	0.100	0.107	0.095	−0.513	128
Total	0.374	0.371	0.045	0.100	−0.237	0.279	635
SCR amp							
5	0.430	0.300	0.200	0.226	3.367	14.895	106
10	0.455	0.300	0.500	0.228	2.150	5.375	109
15	0.495	0.340	0.250	0.268	2.238	6.107	114
20	0.549	0.350	0.150	0.385	2.819	10.117	106
25	0.668	0.440	0.250	0.539	2.850	10.403	104
Total	0.518	0.350	0.250	0.332	2.892	11.456	539
log SCR amp							
5	−0.543	−0.523	−0.699	0.158	−0.149	0.425	106
10	−0.560	−0.523	−0.301	0.222	−0.414	0.116	109
15	−0.517	−0.469	−0.602	0.207	−0.230	−0.446	114
20	−0.475	−0.456	−0.824	0.203	−0.198	−0.132	106
25	−0.377	−0.357	−0.602	0.193	−0.258	−0.009	104
Total	−0.496	−0.456	−0.602	0.200	−0.252	−0.038	539

Data collected from sample of 640 Mauritian subjects using bipolar placement of 0.125 cm^2 area Ag/AgCl electrodes on left fore and middle fingers. Electrolyte 0.5% KCl in agar. Constant voltage 0.5 V.SCR to 90 dB noise, 4 s duration, 5 ms rise time.

Table 1.2. Mean, median, mode, variance, skewness, and kurtosis values of SCR lat., reciprocal SCR lat., log SCR lat., SCR ret. t/2, reciprocal SCR rec. t/2, log SCR rec. t/2, in 5 age groups. (Data from same source as Table 1.1.)

Age	Mean	Median	Mode	Variance	Skewness	Kurtosis	N
SCR lat							
5	1.472	1.405	1.200	0.139	1.592	3.196	111
10	1.647	1.507	1.400	0.175	0.994	0.345	110
15	1.822	1.755	1.600	0.161	1.164	1.165	116
20	1.811	1.731	1.600	0.149	0.864	0.875	109
25	1.754	1.638	1.600	0.165	0.868	0.342	113
Total	1.702	1.613	1.600	0.174	0.917	0.630	559
recip SCR lat.							
5	0.715	0.713	0.833	0.023	−0.194	−0.193	111
10	0.642	0.666	0.714	0.021	0.016	−0.258	110
15	0.572	0.561	0.556	0.012	−0.085	−0.127	116
20	0.576	0.585	0.625	0.014	0.856	2.749	109
25	0.599	0.620	0.625	0.016	0.139	−0.358	113
Total	0.620	0.623	0.625	0.020	0.320	0.021	559
log SCR lat.							
5	0.156	0.147	0.079	0.010	0.837	0.802	111
10	0.204	0.177	0.146	0.011	0.517	−0.313	110
15	0.251	0.249	0.204	0.008	0.628	0.185	116
20	0.249	0.235	0.204	0.008	0.122	0.834	109
25	0.233	0.210	0.204	0.009	0.368	−0.329	113
Total	0.219	0.206	0.204	0.010	0.308	−0.138	559
SCR rec. t/2							
5	3.252	2.500	1.500	4.827	1.676	3.117	61
10	4.324	4.433	1.500	6.480	0.293	−0.332	38
15	3.844	3.044	3.000	4.296	0.969	−0.755	39
20	4.879	4.525	6.000	6.312	0.671	0.401	47
25	4.851	4.500	2.000	7.428	0.842	0.785	35
Total	4.144	3.750	1.500	6.081	0.890	0.598	220
recip SCR rec. t/2							
5	0.448	0.400	0.667	0.090	2.506	10.937	61
10	0.493	0.224	0.167	0.676	4.756	25.568	38
15	0.348	0.330	0.333	0.040	1.250	1.496	39
20	0.332	0.221	0.167	0.230	5.614	34.920	47
25	0.354	0.222	0.154	0.290	5.250	29.540	35
Total	0.398	0.252	0.500	0.243	5.953	45.148	220
log SCR rec. t/2							
5	0.429	0.398	0.176	0.072	0.115	−0.006	61
10	0.524	0.649	0.179	0.138	−0.302	1.830	38
15	0.523	0.484	0.477	0.057	−0.143	−0.628	39
20	0.617	0.656	0.778	0.082	−1.550	4.381	47
25	0.604	0.653	0.301	0.093	−1.443	4.153	35
Total	0.530	0.572	0.176	0.090	−0.848	1.430	220

Table 1.3. Mean, median, mode, variance, skewness, and kurtosis values of SCL, SCR amp, lat. and rec. t/2 under log and reciprocal transformations.

	Mean	Median	Mode	Variance	Skewness	Kurtosis	N
SCL	2.383	2.050	1.360	2.447	1.800	5.518	1761
log SCL	0.288	0.312	0.134	0.086	-0.714	2.716	1761
SCR amp	0.296	0.200	0.250	0.122	4.150	35.763	1145
log SCR amp	-0.774	-0.699	-0.602	0.247	-0.322	-0.396	1145
SCR lat.	1.488	1.427	1.500	0.150	1.303	2.233	1161
recip. SCR lat.	0.712	0.711	0.667	0.026	0.027	-0.547	1161
log SCR lat.	0.160	0.150	0.176	0.011	0.561	0.149	1161
SCR rec. t/2	4.113	3.045	1.000	10.348	1.391	2.521	678
recip. SCR t/2	0.540	0.333	1.000	0.701	7.173	72.136	678
log SCR t/2	0.470	0.479	0.100	0.148	-0.580	0.312	678

Data collected from a sample of 1800 3-year-old children (Venables, 1978) using bipolar placement of 0.125 cm^2 area Ag/AgCl electrodes on left fore and middle fingers. Electrolyte 0.5% KCl in agar. Constant voltage 0.5 V. SCR to 90 dB noise, 4 s duration, 5 ms rise time.

Table 1.4. Mean, median, mode, variance, skewness, and kurtosis values of SCL, SCR amp, lat, ris. t, rec. t/2 under log and reciprocal transformations

	Mean	Median	Mode	Variance	Skewness	Kurtosis	N
SCL	3.612	3.000	2.120	6.102	1.834	5.412	65
log SCL	0.465	0.477	0.326	0.086	-0.243	-0.097	65
SCR amp	0.365	0.242	0.050	0.155	2.166	5.808	45
log SCR amp	-0.646	-0.617	-1.301	0.187	0.192	-0.859	45
SCR lat.	1.896	1.879	1.900	0.122	0.920	1.712	45
recip. SCR lat.	0.544	0.531	0.526	0.009	0.458	1.006	45
log SCR lat.	0.271	0.274	0.279	0.006	0.228	0.781	45
SCR ris. t	2.184	2.012	1.700	0.413	0.516	-0.660	45
recip. SCR ris. t	0.498	0.498	0.588	0.022	0.776	1.348	45
log SCR ris. t	0.321	0.303	0.230	0.016	-0.005	-0.572	45
SCR rec. t/2	3.971	2.400	2.100	25.118	2.991	8.173	42
recip. SCR rec. t/2	0.439	0.417	0.476	0.063	1.562	5.008	42
log SCR rec. t/2	0.442	0.380	0.322	0.100	1.486	2.823	42

Data collected from a sample of 65 18–75-year old adults using bipolar placement of 0.125 cm^2 area Ag/AgCl electrodes on left fore and middle fingers. Electrolyte 0.5% KCl in agar. Constant voltage 0.5 V. SCR to 75 dB, 1000 Hz tone, 1 s duration, 25 ms rise and fall time.

cross-sectional study (Venables and coworkers, 1979) and allows the examination of the consistency of results obtained from five age groups from age 5–25 years. Table 1.3 represents data collected from a very large sample of 3 year olds using the same techniques as those employed in the cross-sectional study (Venables, 1978) and Table 1.4 presents data using slightly different stimulus conditions on an adult sample, age range 18–75, having the sort of sample size more usually encountered in psychophysiological experiments. The data in Tables 1.1, 1.2, and 1.3 are from a non-white population in tropical conditions and the data in Table 1.4 are from a white European sample. Consistency of results over the disparate samples therefore gives strength to recommendations which arise. Unfortunately, SCR rise time was not measured in the first two samples so that the data on this variable in Table 1.3 are not confirmed by material from the other samples.

3.3.1 SCL

The data from the three samples show a high degree of comparability and in each case log conversion produces a very marked fall in skewness and kurtosis.

3.3.2 SCR amp

The data again show a high degree of consistency across samples, the distribution in all cases being very peaky. Log conversion again reduces both this leptokurtosis and also the skew. It should be noted in this instance that log conductance change is the variable calculated rather than change in log conductance. Preliminary analysis of these data showed no reduction in skewness or kurtosis with the use of this latter measure over and above that with untransformed conductance change. Figures 1.2 and 1.3 present for comparison histograms of the data for the total N of 539 in Table 1.1 on SCR amp and log SCR amp. The improvement in normality of distribution is clearly shown in this graphic representation.

3.3.3 SCR lat.

In addition to log conversion it was thought worthwhile in this instance and with the other temporal measures to examine the effect of reciprocal conversion as this represents data in terms of speed rather than time. In the case of SCR lat there is a consistent indication of a small advantage in the use of either reciprocal or log conversion but the effect is not very marked.

Techniques in Psychophysiology

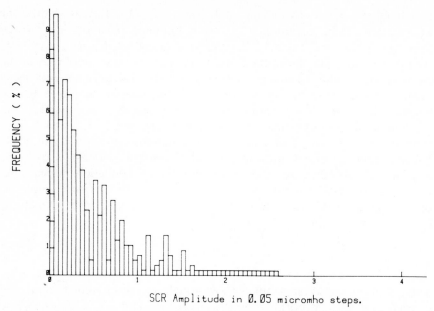

Figure 1.2   Histogram of SCR values (data from Table 1.1)

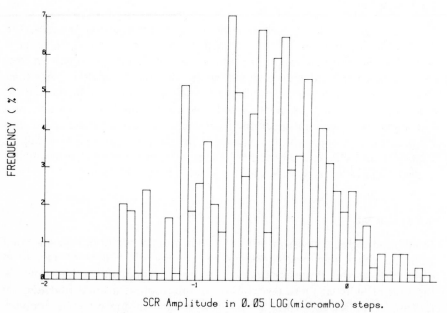

Figure 1.3   Histogram of $\log_{10}$ SCR values

$$1 \, \mu \, mho = \frac{1}{10^6}$$

$$.05 \, \mu mho = \frac{1}{10^6} \times .05$$

$$R = \frac{10^6}{.05} = \frac{10^8}{5}$$

$$= 20 \, M\Omega \, !!$$

$$R = \frac{10^6}{.05} = \frac{10^8}{5}$$

$$= 20 \, M\Omega. \, ??$$

$$1 \mu mho = \frac{1}{10^6}$$

$$\frac{1}{10^6} \times .05 = \frac{.05}{10^6} = \frac{5}{10^6 \times 10^2}$$

$$\frac{1}{2 \times 10^3} = \frac{.5 \times 10^{-3}}{10^6} \qquad = \frac{5/10^2}{10^6}$$

$$= \frac{.5 \times 10^3}{10^6}$$

$$= \frac{5}{10^4}$$

$$R = \frac{10^4}{5} = 2 \times 10^3$$

3.3.4 SCR ris. t

On the basis of the data presented in Table 1.4 there appears to be no very strong basis for the conversion of this variable although log conversion does reduce skewness.

3.3.5 SCT. t/2

There is a very strong indication that reciprocal conversion of data for this variable is contra-indicated. Log conversion does result in improvement in some data but this is not consistent.

In summary, therefore, there appears to be a good case for log conversion of SCL and SCR amp data, but no very strong indication that it is worthwhile converting the temporal variables from measurement in seconds.

It should be noted that the advocacy of the use of log conductance for SCL and SCR amp is in no way based on a presupposition of physiological appropriateness, in the same way as the use of conductance is based on the notion of parallel conducting pathways in the skin, but rather on the greater statistical appropriateness of normally distributed data. These points are discussed in greater detail in Chapter 12.

The analyses in Tables 1.1 to 1.4 have used amplitude data (see Section 2.0); that is, no zero values were included. If, however, magnitude values of SCR amp are to be analysed using log conversion it is obviously necessary to avoid the log of zero and consequently it is a sensible convention to add 1 to all conductance values representing SCR amp and to express data in terms of log $(1 + x)$.

Examination of SPL data suggests that there is no need for transformation. Data on 1183 subjects from the sample of 1800 which form the population from which the SC data in Table 1.2 are taken provide figures of -0.897 for skewness and 1.164 for kurtosis for the distribution of SPL.

4.0 CHARACTERISTICS OF OBSERVED ELECTRODERMAL PHENOMENA

As in the case of the previous section where terminology is proposed, the description of electrodermal phenomena already presupposes their measurement by particular techniques and the descriptions of these techniques are to appear later in the chapter. Nevertheless, it does seem appropriate to present some descriptions at this stage so that the reader is fully aware of what is being discussed.

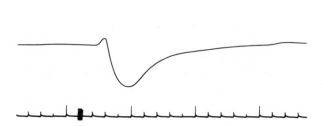

Figure 1.4   Comparison of conventional polygraph write
out of SC and SP data

4.1 Conventions of write-out

The tradition amongst neurophysiologists is that data should be recorded
'negative-up', thus in the case of SPR the uniphasic negative response or
the initial negative component of the biphasic response should be in the
upward direction. Similarly, increasing negativity of SPL should be shown
as an upward deflection of pen write-out. In general, increasing negativity
of SPL is consonant with increasing 'arousal' and this would also be
indicated by increasing SCL. It is thus reasonable to suggest that increases
in conductance should be recorded upwards and therefore increases in
resistance downwards. Figure 1.4 shows parallel recordings of SC and SP
which follow these conventions.

4.2 Identification of responses

Because of the lability of EDA in some subjects it is difficult on some
occasions to identify elicited responses in the presence of a large number
of non-specifics.

Identification of responses using latency criteria is probably the safest
method to use. Some authors have used a fairly wide latency 'window',
identifying responses where the latency falls between 1 and 5 seconds.
While the lower value is probably reasonable it is suggested that the
higher value is too high and a 'window' of 1 to 3 seconds is probably
adequately conservative for most purposes. Figure 1.1 indicates this latency
window. Stern and Walrath (1977) propose a slightly different method

which is to identify a modal latency for each subject and then to accept responses ±0.5 s around this value. They also propose a more conservative narrowing of this range of −0.25 s to +0.5 s around the modal latency. The value of Stern and Walrath's approach is that it does enable a conservative identification of responses to be made where SCR lat is somewhat atypical, for instance, because of age or abnormal status.

4.3 Expected values

The values quoted can only be used as general indications; SCL and SCR amp, for instance, vary with the electrode size, electrolyte concentration, and type of electrode medium. SPL and SPR vary with electrolyte concentration and medium.

4.3.1 Skin conductance level, SCL

Values will depend on electrode size. However, earlier recommendations (Lykken and Venables, 1971; Venables and Christie, 1973) that measurements should be reported in terms of specific conductance (i.e. in μmhos cm^{-2}) appear to be inappropriate in the light of recent data (see Section 6.2.2) suggesting that conductance values do not vary in a linear fashion with electrode area.

Values are also related to electrolyte type and concentration; for instance, an electrolyte containing saturated sodium chloride will produce SCLs about three times as large as an electrolyte employing physiological levels of NaCl. The proposals in this chapter are to use electrodes of around 0.5 cm^2 and physiological levels of saline electrode. The range of expected values of SCL with these in a bipolar placement (i.e. both electrodes on active sites) will probably be from 1 to 40 μmhos or 0 to 1.6 log μmhos.

4.3.2 Skin conductance response, SCR

As with SCL, SCR amp values depend on area of electrode and type of electrolyte. However, using the electrode/electrolyte type suggested above, it is expected the values of SCR amp will have a maximum value of 2–3 μmhos, 0.3–0.47 log μmhos. Minimum values, of course, depend on system gain (see Section 9.3 for a discussion of non-responsivity). No data suggest that the temporal variables SCR lat, ris. t and rec. t are affected by electrode size or electrolyte type.

The range of expected SCR latency values is from 1.3 to 2.5 s (see Section 4.2 above.) Rise time will have expected values of from 1 to 2.5 s and half recovery time (rec. t/2) will range from about 1 to 15 or more

Table 1.5. Typical equivalent values for SCL, log SCL, and SRL; SCR amp, log SCR amp, and SRR amp

SCL (μmho)	1	2	3	4	5	10	15	20	40
log SCL (log μmho)	0	0.30	0.47	0.60	0.70	1.00	1.17	1.30	1.60
SRL (kΩ)	10^3	5×10^2	3.3×10^2	2.5×10^2	2.0×10^2	1×10^2	66	50	25
SCR amp (μmho)	0.01	0.02	0.05	0.10	0.20	0.50	1.0	2.0	
log SCR amp (log μmho)	−2.0	−1.69	−1.30	−1.0	−0.69	−0.30	0	0.30	
SRR amp (kΩ)[a]	0.10	0.20	0.50	1.0	1.96	4.76	9.09	16.6	
SRR amp (kΩ)[b]	0.02	0.05	0.125	0.25	0.50	1.22	2.38	4.54	

(a) SRR amp from SRL at 100 kΩ.
(b) SRR amp from SRL at 50 kΩ (see text).

seconds depending on stimulus intensity, situational and subject characteristics, and time since last response. Table 1.5 shows some typical equivalent figures for level and response data measured in terms of SC, log SC and SR, the latter figure being given for those who are more accustomed to using this variable. Two equivalent values from SRR amp are given, one assuming an SRL at $100\,k\Omega$, the other at $50\,k\Omega$. The difference between these two sets of values illustrates the point that conductance and resistance response measures are *not* equivalent at different tonic levels.

4.3.3 Skin potential level, SPL

Values depend upon concentration and type of electrolyte used, but not on electrode size. However, with physiological levels of saline, expected values will range from $+10\,mV$ to $-70\,mV$, the polarity being that at the palmar site.

4.3.4 Skin potential response, SPR

Measurement of the amplitude of SPR is not feasible as it is generally the result of two opposing potential sources and it is never possible to tell how the amplitude of one component is affected by the other. Even in the case of an apparent uniphasic response this may be modified by a hidden opposite polarity response.

The latency of the initial negative component is about 300 ms shorter than that of SCR lat (Patterson, unpublished data).

5.0 PERIPHERAL MECHANISMS RESPONSIBLE FOR ELECTRODERMAL PHENOMENA

5.1 Eccrine sweat glands

Two forms of sweat gland are found in the human gland; these are denoted as apocrine and eccrine, the distinction between the two being delineated by Schiefferdecker (1917, 1922). Apocrine glands are of little apparent importance in the production of electrodermal phenomena; they are not under nervous control but secretion is stimulated by circulating adrenaline. The distribution of apocrine glands is local to such specific sites as the axillae and the mons pubis.

In contrast the distribution of eccrine sweat glands is widespread over the body surface. Regional differences in density are found; Weiner and Hellman (1960) give figures of not less than $2000/cm^2$ on palm and sole of foot, $200–300/cm^2$ in the axillae and $100–200/cm^2$ on the trunk. Eccrine sweat glands are involved in thermoregulatory control but this role is only normally seen at palmar and plantar sites when the ambient temperature exceeds 30 °C. Darrow (1933) has suggested that the role of eccrine sweat glands at palmar and plantar sites is more concerned with grasping behaviour than with evaporative cooling. Palmar eccrine sweating as an accompaniment of a motor response may form the basis for secretion as a response to what have been called psychic stimuli but what are possibly best described as orienting or signal stimuli. All eccrine sweat glands have the property of responding to both thermal and signal stimuli. Although it was thought that the threshold for elicitation of sweating at the palm and sole was lower for psychic stimuli than at other areas of the body, work by Allen, Armstrong and Roddie (1973) suggests that sweat output due to mental arithmetic is evident in all body areas and is roughly proportional to the number of sweat glands in each region.

Innervation of eccrine glands is solely via the sympathetic branch of the autonomic nervous system; however, the postganglionic synapse is cholinergic, having acetylcholine, rather than the usual sympathetic neurotransmitter nor-adrenaline. Eccrine sweat gland activity may be initiated locally by intradermal injections of acetylcholine or cholinomimetics and inhibited by local treatment with an anti cholinergic agent. Grice and Bettley (1966) have reported inactivation with topical applications of poldine methosulphate, and Lader (1970), Lader and Montagu (1962) and Venables and Martin (1967b) have shown similar inactivation with the iontophoresis of atropine and hyoscyamine.

The discharge of sweat at the skin surface is, in part, a product of pulsatile contraction of a myoepithelial spiral chain surrounding the sweat duct. In each individual gland this pulsatile discharge has a frequency of 12–21 Hz (Nicolaidis and Sivadjian, 1972). The myoepithelial 'squeezing' of the duct has the effect not only of discharging sweat at the skin surface but also increasing ductal hydraulic pressure favouring ductal reabsorption. The neuro-transmitter responsible for innervation of the myoepithelial chain has not been satisfactorily determined; however, Goodall (1970) has suggested that the innervation is adrenergic.

Sweat discharged at the skin surface is hypotonic while sweat at the point of secretion at the base of the duct is slightly hypertonic with respect to plasma. An active reabsorption process is suggested as being responsible for this difference and the limited capacity of the process is inferred from the fact that NaCl content of sweat reaching the surface increases with increased rate of secretion. Two reabsorption systems are suggested (see Fowles and Venables, 1970; Venables and Christie, 1973, and Fowles, 1974 for detailed reviews), one at a dermal and the other at an epidermal level. Schultz and coworkers (1965) provide evidence that sodium is actively absorbed in the dermal portion and that this process is accompanied by a lumen negative potential relative to interstitial fluid; a similar potential is also found in the epidermal portion of the duct even when the lower dermal mechanism is experimentally isolated by insulating oil. The evidence that these systems are sodium pumps is given by the demonstration that sub-cutaneous injections of g-strophanthin, a sodium pump inhibitor, results in an increased concentration of NaCl in surface sweat. Slegers (1967) provides a mathematical basis for a model of two ductal reabsorption mechanisms and suggests that NaCl is absorbed in the proximal (dermal) portion of the duct while the epidermal mechanism provides a final control where sodium can be exchanged for potassium or hydrogen ions. Fowles (1974) makes the point that the epidermal portion of the duct is concerned with the reabsorption of water as well as NaCl and that as such is likely to be more conductive.

The relevance of presenting this material is that it suggests that at least three conducting pathways may be present in the sweat duct, through the secretory, and the dermal and epidermal absorption systems. Furthermore, the latter two are certainly associated with sources of electrical potential (see Section 5.4). Thus, while it may be convenient to think of sweat glands as conducting pathways through relatively nonconducting dermal and epidermal tissue, these conducting pathways are by no means simple in function or characteristics.

5.2 The epidermis

For some purposes it is useful to think of the eccrine sweat glands as set in a sheet of epidermal membrane having different physiological and electrical characteristics from the glands themselves. This distinction may however be too simplified and the possibility of membrane functions being ascribable to the epidermal ductal portion of the sweat glands should not be dismissed. On the palms of the hands and the soles of the feet it is convenient to divide the epidermis into four layers. The innermost living layer is the stratum germinativum or mucous layer and the outer layer composed of dead cells is the stratum corneum. In between these are two layers, the stratum granulosum and the stratum lucidum. On palmar and plantar surfaces the whole epidermis is thicker than elsewhere and it is only in these areas where the stratum lucidum can be clearly seen. Because of the characteristic electrical properties of palm and sole it has been suggested that the stratum lucidum may be the membrane responsible for the non-sudorific aspects of this activity; however, it is possible that it is the greater thickness of the epidermis and particularly the stratum corneum that may be involved. What is certainly important is that the stratum corneum be considered as a reservoir of moisture and electrolytes. We thus have the possibility when, for instance, SP is being measured that the potential generated is a junction potential due to the contact of the external electrolyte and the electrolytes in the stratum corneum or that the activity is a membrane potential resulting from differences in electrolytes inside and ouside the semipermeable stratum lucidum or similar structure.

5.3 The skin as a site of electrical activity

It is not the purpose of this section to give a detailed discussion of the electrophysiological properties of the skin as this has been presented by, for instance, Edelberg (1971), Venables and Christie (1973) and Fowles (1974); rather, this material is introduced here to make the point that the skin cannot be considered as a simple system and that inevitably there will be interrelationships betweeen all aspects of electrodermal activity. If, for instance, as seems to be the case, an SCR is initiated by the occurrence of secretory activity, what happens subsequently is affected by the state of the skin, in particular the hydration of the stratum corneum and the fullness of the sweat duct at the time of secretion. It is likely that a different electrodermal response will be produced if the amount of secretion is small and in the environment of an empty duct, so that perhaps only the dermal reabsorption mechanism is brought into play, as against a large secretory response occurring when the ducts are full and the stratum corneum inundated with water and electrolytes. In this latter instance the epidermal ductal reabsorption mechanism is likely to be activated and an alternative electrical pathway established.

It has been suggested, for instance by Fowles (1974) and by Venables and Christie (1973), that ductal reabsorption is a function of electrolyte concentration in sweat, and hydrostatic pressure in the duct. The electrolyte concentration reaching the epidermal ductal system is in part a function of secretory flow as the dermal reabsorption system is rate limited; equally the hydrostatic pressure is a function of amount of secretion and because there may be ductal poral closure when the stratum corneum is hydrated (Fowles and Venables, 1970), the hydrostatic pressure is in part a function of past secretion of sweat and of course external conditions. As stated in Section 5.1, discharge of sweat is also accomplished by ductal squeezing due to myoepithelial contraction and thus another factor triggering reabsorption is brought into play. These factors alone are not able completely to explain electrical activity of the reabsorption system as the extent of this activity is probably under the control of aldosterone (see Venables and Christie, 1973, p. 25, for a review of relevant material).

The outcome of such considerations would appear to be that some extension of our understanding of relevant mechanisms may result from the manipulation of external factors, such as current flow in exosomatic measurement, type of electrolyte, particularly in endosomatic measurement, and the use of different electrolyte media to control epidermal hydration. On the other hand, attempts may be made to examine the effect of factors in the function of the skin, for instance by the elimination of secretory activity by the iontophoresis of anticholinergics. However, the approach of examining the statistical interrelation of aspects of activity under standard conditions is also valid and in combination with results from more manipulative approaches capable of increasing understanding of the electrodermal system. Because of the complexity of mechanisms it is likely that in the present state of knowledge the appropriate approach is a statistical one and that the best that can be done is to gather data using techniques which vary as little as possible from laboratory to laboratory. To some extent, as stated earlier, these techniques are based on experiment but in other instances are due to 'best guesses' or even prejudice.

5.4 Electrical models of the skin

As is undoubtedly apparent from the previous section, our knowledge of the electrical activity of the skin is imperfect and hence the attempt to present electrical equivalent circuits necessarily premature. Nevertheless, for heuristic purposes and to guide measurement techniques it is worthwhile presenting two circuits as summaries of what has already been said and as a partial basis for the sections which follow.

The simplest model which is undoubtedly useful for some purposes is that presented in Figure 1.5 and follows that originally given by Montagu and Coles (1966). Resistors r_1–r_n represent sweat ducts capable of being switched into and out of the circuit depending on their activity. These resistors in parallel are themselves in parallel with R_p representing the resistance of the stratum corneum. R_s represents a resistance largely in the dermis and body core. The inclusion of the capacitor C follows the work of Tregear (1966) and Lykken (1971) whose results indicated the necessity of the inclusion of a capacitative element in the equivalent skin circuit.

It is, of course, the model in Figure 1.5 which is important in the justification of the use of conductance rather than resistance measurement of SC (see Section 3.1).

Support for the model comes particularly from the work of Thomas and Korr (1957) whose data show a linear relation between the number of active sweat glands and conductance. These authors' measurements suggest values of from 3 to 20 MΩ for the resistance of a single sweat gland and a value of from 3 to 10 MΩ for R_p.

Figure 1.6 shows an equivalent circuit due to an elaboration by Fowles (1974) of a circuit originally presented by Edelberg (1968); it takes

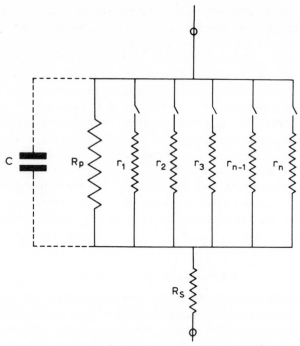

Figure 1.5   Electrical model of the skin; after Montagu and Coles (1966)

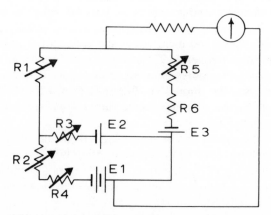

Figure 1.6   Electrical model of the skin; after Fowles (1974)

account of the factors briefly outlined in Sections 5.1 and 5.2 and may be seen as an elaborated version of a circuit involving R_p, R_s, and one of the sweat gland resistors, for example r_1 in Figure 1.5.

In Figure 1.6, R_5 is in part equivalent to R_p in Figure 1.5 but is that element of epidermal resistance particularly isolated in the stratum corneum which varies with hydration. R_6 also in part contributes to R_p in Figure 1.5 and is intended to represent the resistance of the barrier layer discussed in Section 5.2, possibly the stratum lucidum.

R_1 and R_2 represent the resistance of the sweat gland duct and vary with the height of the column of sweat; they are thus equivalent to one of the resistors, e.g. r_1 in Figure 1.5, which instead of being switched as in Figure 1.5 are considered in this elaborated model as being variable. R_1 and R_2 are shown separately and represent resistance of the epidermal and dermal portions of the duct respectively. R_3 and R_4 represent the resistance of the epidermal and dermal duct wall and in particular of the reabsorption mechanisms discussed in Section 5.1. Since these mechanisms as discussed earlier are also potential sources, these sources are represented by E_1 and E_2, the direction of the potential being duct lumen negative. E_3 is the potential discussed in Section 5.2 as the junction or membrane potential generated due to the meeting of external electrolyte with electrolytes in the skin surface.

A detailed discussion of the operation of the model is given in Fowles (1974) and reference will again be made to aspects of it later in this chapter. It should, however, be emphasized that it is at this stage little more than a description of aspects of electrodermal mechanisms which may, with differing degrees of certainty be known to exist. At this stage of our knowledge it would not be possible to build the model with any degree of confidence because only suggestions can be made about the values of the elements and only guesses can be made about the dynamic relations between them. It must also be recognized that R_1, R_2, R_3, E_1, and E_2 represent the mechanisms in a single sweat gland and as stated in Section 5.1 there are approximately 2000 glands per square centimetre on the palmar surface. The measured conductance or potential is thus obviously best thought of as some complex average function of sweat glands and epidermal mechanisms whose combined action should be analysed statistically.

6.0 ELECTRODES AND ELECTROLYTES

The elements in the process of measurement of EDA which are necessary to consider are: skin site and its preparation, electrodes and electrolytes, skin conductance 'coupler', pre and main polygraph amplifiers, output in terms of paper chart, analogue or digital tape recording, and possible computer analysis. This section considers the first three.

6.1 Electrode sites

From what has been said earlier, and indeed by tradition, palmar and plantar areas are the choices for electrodermal recording. Rickles and Day (1968) surveyed electrodermal activity from 14 non-palmar sites. They indicate that with the exception of sites on the foot all other sites may be disregarded as substitutes for the palm 'since all of the sites demonstrated long periods of inactivity while the palm was responding to specific stimuli or exhibiting spontaneous activity'. On the foot, palmar-like activity was found to extend from the sole to include hypomalleolar areas (underneath the ankle) and may thus be useful under conditions where it is undesirable to use the hands for measuring EDA and when a plantar site could not be used as the subject is standing. Edelberg (1967) also presents a survey of possible sites and shows that the hypomalleolar site is particularly useful. He states, 'the site is on the medial side of the foot over the *abductor hallucis* muscle adjacent to the plantar surface and mid-way between the first phalange and a point directly beneath the ankle'. Furthermore, he shows that SCL is 1.26 and SCR amp 1.70 times as great at this site than a palmar finger site taken as reference. This site on the shaft of the foot allows the electrodes to be fixed fairly easily.

However, it is only exceptionally that non-palmar sites tend to be used and a decision has to be made about where on the palm it is best to place electrodes.

The points to be considered are: (a) relative ease of fixing and non-susceptibility to disturbance by movement, (b) size of available area, (c) likely freedom from scarring, (d) relative electrodermal activity.

With regard to the last point, Edelberg's (1967) data show that non-finger sites, the thenar and hypothenar eminence, and the centre of the palm are slightly more responsive than the fingers having SCL 1.21 and SCR 1.38 times as great as finger sites. However, these differences are small and easily compensated by amplification and are therefore not in themselves points in consideration as to siting.

The centre of the palm is a particularly difficult site on which to fix electrodes firmly and is prone to movement as the hand flexes. The thenar and hypothenar eminences are less likely to produce movement artifacts and have large surface areas but it is relatively difficult to fix electrodes to them firmly. Electrodes may be fixed firmly to the fingers and there is relative freedom from movement artifacts from electrodes on these sites. The main disadvantage is the small area available, this particularly being

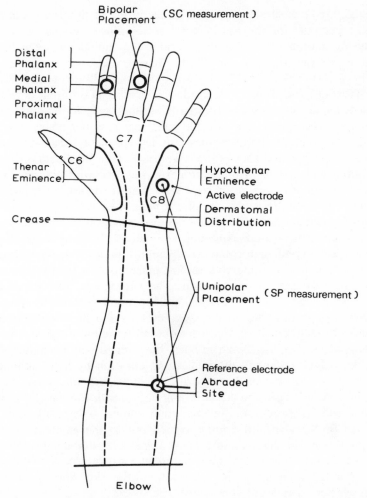

Figure 1.7 Suggested palmar electrode sites for measuring SC and SP

the case with women and children. In spite of this latter disadvantage this site has been used as standard by the authors for many studies and the data in Tables 1.1, 1.2, 1.3, and 1.4 were collected using finger sites, and miniature Beckman electrodes. (The question of electrode size will be discussed in Section 6.2.2.)

Figure 1.7 shows the sites used for the recording of SC and SP. The medial phalanges of the fore and middle fingers are suggested (following

Edelberg, 1967) as sites for the bipolar recording of SC (see Section 6.2.3 for the arguments for the use of bipolar recording). As shown on Figure 1.7, the dermatomal distribution separates the thumb from the fore and middle and from the ring and little fingers; because of the evidence (Christie and Venables, 1972), shown more markedly in some individuals than others, of asynchrony of electrodermal activity in different dermatomal areas it is important to choose finger sites in the same dermatomal area for bipolar SC recording. The medial phalanges rather than the distal phalanges are chosen because they are less prone to scarring than the proximal phalanges and also as the effect of moving the fingers is less. For SP a unipolar arrangement of electrodes is required with one electrode on an active and another on an inactive site. What is measured is a potential difference between the active site and a neutral or reference site. Bipolar recording at two active sites would, of course, result in no or little potential difference being measured. Although in Figure 1.7 the active electrode is shown on the hypothenar eminence it could equally well be placed on a finger site. The inactive reference is best placed over a lightly abraded site on the volar surface of the forearm. The site shown, two thirds of the distance from the wrist to elbow, is in general electrically non-active (whereas sites nearer the wrist sometimes are) and abrasion may not be necessary. In children there appears to be no potential difference between abraded and non-abraded forearm sites; however, the more mature skin of adults does show potential differences and abrasion by light rubbing with fine sandpaper or by a dental drill produces the necessary electrical neutrality. In no case should abrasion be carried too far or a wound potential will be produced. Sandpapering should only produce a slight reddening of the skin and drilling carried out to the extent that a small shiny pit is seen in the skin surface by transverse illumination. No blood should be drawn. Practice on the experimenter's own arm is recommended as essential apprenticeship. No abrasion of the skin surface should, of course, ever be carried out at an active site.

If both SC and SP are measured then the reference site for SP may be used to earth or ground the subject. If SC only is measured then it may be possible to obtain a good recording without grounding but if any difficulty is encountered then grounding on a similar abraded site as that used for the reference electrode in SP recording should be used. If other channels of psychophysiological measurement are to be recorded then only one point of grounding should be employed preferably nearest to the site of the variable with the smallest signal. Consequently, if EEG is measured then the grounding should be at the head and care should be taken to record SP with an amplifier with neither input grounded (i.e. floating with respect to earth).

6.1.1 Preparation of site

An element in the determination of SC and SP is the hydration and electrolyte concentration of the skin surface. Carrie and Heemeyer (1936) showed that the concentration of NaCl on the skin surface rises linearly with time since the last wash. Venables and Martin (1967a) report as a result of informal investigation that no marked differences in SC are apparent as a result of washing electrode sites with distilled water, ether or acetone; however, a marked fall in SC was noted after washing with soap and water. As some subjects will come to the laboratory having washed their hands and some not, it appears a wise standardizing procedure to have all subjects wash their hands with soap and water immediately before the start of an experiment.

6.2 Electrodes

Whereas in the past a variety of electrode types has been used in electrodermal measurement there is now almost complete standardization on the use of silver/silver chloride (Ag/AgCl) electrodes. Electrodes of this type are in a class known as reversible electrodes and consist of a metal in contact with a solution of its own ions. Lowest values of bias and polarization potentials are found with reversible electrodes. Bias potentials are important in SP measurement and are measured by placing a pair of electrodes in a solution of electrolyte of the same type and concentration used in the electrolyte medium. It is usual for SP work to choose electrodes with a bias potential of under 1 mV. Commercial electrodes are available which have stated bias potentials of less than 250 μV. It is a standard finding that electrodes having low initial bias potentials also show less potential drift over time so that selection for the former characteristic tends to ensure good drift performance.

Polarization potentials result from a passage of current and are thus important in SC work. They are potentials arising at the interface between electrode and electrolyte, due either to an energy barrier in the oxidation reduction interaction at the electrode surface or to a limitation placed upon ion transfer by the rate of diffusion of ions to or from the interface. Silver/silver chloride electrodes have a low polarization potential, and if in doubt this may be checked by the use of a technique outlined by Edelberg (1967, p. 7).

Silver/silver chloride disc electrodes may be made in the average psychological laboratory workshop and with care in construction electrodes with bias potentials of 250 μV or less and polarization potentials of 5 mV or less are feasible. Details of construction of this type of electrode are

given in Venables and Christie (1973, p. 107). Bearing in mind that
99.99% pure silver has to be used in construction and the making of
electrodes makes considerable demands on technicians' time, it may be
more economical to consider the purchase of commercially made
electrodes. Beckman 'biopotential' electrodes which employ a silver/silver
chloride pellet have bias potentials of less than 250 μV and are stated to
have polarization potentials as low as 5 μV and are thus entirely
satisfactory from this point of view for the measurement of both types of
EDA.

6.2.1 Care of electrodes

When electrodes are not in current use they should be thoroughly cleaned
and stored in dry conditions. Before usage they should be soaked for at
least 24 hours in a solution of electrolyte of the type and concentration
which is used in the electrolyte paste. This allows adequate time for the
electrolyte to penetrate into the interstices of the porous electrode surface
and for local reaction to take place which might otherwise cause instability.
There is probably some advantage in shorting together the leads of the
electrodes during this soaking process as the current generated by local
reactions may then flow and equilibrium be achieved.

It is very important when cleaning electrodes that nothing other than a
jet of water from a tap or wash bottle be used to remove electrolyte paste;
no vigorous cleaning particularly with metallic materials should be
undertaken.

6.2.2 Size of electrodes

Lykken and Venables (1971) stated very categorically, 'Since conductance
varies directly with effective electrode area, all measurements should be
reported in terms of specific conductances, i.e., in micromhos per square
centimetre.' They advocate that this should be done by a method that
assumes a *linear* relation between electrode area and conductance.
Unfortunately, there are few studies available which actually examine this
relationship. Edelberg and Burch (1962), for instance, showed that SCL
and SCR amp varied directly with electrode area when they altered the
latter by varying the number of 0.389 cm electrode sites arranged in
parallel. Venables and Patterson (unpublished study) showed when
comparing SC values obtained using miniature and standard Beckman
electrodes that the data obtained did not fit the relation which would be

expected from a linear relation between SC and area and in particular that the linear relation when extrapolated did not pass through the origin of the axes as would be predicted. Because of this, Mitchell and Venables (to be published) undertook a more formal study using standard 1 cm² electrodes but varying the effective electrode area by the use of masks of decreasing size. The preliminary results from this study indicate a non-monotonic relation between SCL or SCR and electrode area with a tendency for there to be no increase in conductance values as electrode size increases beyond 0.8 cm². This is not a result of 'overhang' of the electrode when attempting to place too large an electrode on a finger site, as the same effect is obtained when using an adequately sized hypothenar site.

The implications of these findings are that because of the uncertainty of the relation between area and SCL and SCR amp it is not advisable to express these values in terms of specific conductance by making a linear conversion. Until it is possible to give an accurate description of the function relating electrode size and SC values the latter should be given in terms of the actual electrode size used. There is no suggestion from the data so far available that temporal components of SCR vary with electrode size.

The quotation at the head of this section talks of 'effective electrode area' and this was shown by Blank and Finesinger (1946) to be that area of skin covered by electrode plus that covered by excess electrolyte or surface sweat.

Two methods appear to be effective in maintaining electrode size constant. If the electrode (e.g. of the disc electrode type described in Venables and Christie, 1973) has a fairly hard well-defined rim then if this is applied quite firmly and used with a viscous electrolyte, little seepage is observed and the electrode area remains effectively constant. The second method is to use a mask formed from double-sided adhesive tape with a hole punched in it of the appropriate size. Commercially available masks formed of very flexible tape and with good adhesive qualities serve the dual purpose of masking the electrode site and holding the electrode in place and their use is to be recommended. Under certain circumstances, where hand movement is expected, additional fixing with adhesive tape on top of the electrode is also suggested. It should be noted that the relative error due to seepage of electrolyte depends on initial electrode or mask size. For example, 1 mm of seepage with a 0.4 cm diameter electrode (the size of the effective electrode area of the miniature Beckman electrode) results in an increase of effective electrode area to 2.25 times its original size while with the standard 1 cm diameter electrode the increase is only 1.13 times. This clearly suggests that to minimize error electrode size should be the largest possible compatible with area of skin site available.

In the case of SP recording there is no evidence for effect of electrode size on any of the variables recorded.

6.2.3 Bipolar versus unipolar placement of electrodes

In Section 6.1 bipolar placement of electrodes on the medial phalanges of two fingers is advocated. The reasons for this proposal are several: (a) with the constant voltage method of measurement of conductance (see Section 7.1) the threshold of non-linearity of voltage/current relationship (see Section 7.1.2) is not exceeded if a voltage of 0.5 V is impressed across a *single* site. With bipolar placement the impressed voltage is divided approximately equally across each site, thus if required the impressed voltage may be doubled with consequent improvement in signal and freedom from endosomatic contamination; (b) the use of two active sites gives changes in conductance that are twice those using a unipolar site; (c) there is no need for abrasion of the skin as is required under the inactive site with unipolar placement.

6.3 Electrolytes and electrolyte media

In contrast to other psychophysiological measures where the principal aim is to transduce most effectively the electrical signal arising from some underlying source (e.g. the heart in EKG or the muscles in EMG) and the electrolyte is therefore chosen with maximum conductivity properties in mind, in the case of the measurement of electrodermal activity the electrolyte interacts in a major way with the tissue over which it is placed to produce the electrodermal phenomena which are measured.

It is important that the electrolyte should be compatible with the biological system in which it is in contact and for that reason either NaCl or KCl are the electrolytes of choice. Edelberg, Greiner and Burch (1960), for instance, demonstrated that multivalent ions such as Ca^2, Zn^2 or Al^3 have a potentiating effect on SC and a decreasing effect on SP dependent on the effective size of the ion.

The electrolyte should have approximately equivalent concentration to the sweat or electrolyte concentration of the stratum corneum with which it comes into contact. It has already been stated that due to reabsorption of NaCl in sweat ducts the concentration of sweat will vary widely. Rothman (1954, Chap. 7) reports that the NaCl concentration in human sweat varies from 0.015 to 0.06 M. On this basis Edelberg (1967) recommends that an appropriate electrolyte solution is 0.05 M NaCl. This contains 0.29 g NaCl per 100 ml of water. Edelberg suggests that the electrolyte concentration will not be greatly altered by sweating under the electrode and that the specific resistance of such a solution being of the order of 200 Ω/cm is low enough not to provide a source of artefact.

Venables and Sayer (1963) adopted a recommendation of Rein (1929) that potassium chloride was most suitable for skin potential measurement and after empirical studies with different concentrations of this electrolyte recommended that the use of 0.5 g/100 ml was a concentration which produced a distribution of potentials over a useful working range and with few subjects exhibiting positive potentials at the hand (0.5 g/100 ml KCl is equivalent to 0.067 M solution). Data from Edelberg, Greiner, and Burch (1960) suggest that the use of KCl minimizes electrodermal responses in comparison to NaCl; nevertheless, the use of 0.5 KCl has been used as a standard in the authors' laboratories for many years for both SP and SC measurements and the data, for instance, in Tables 1.1 to 1.4 have been obtained with its use.

In summary, while it is probably reasonable to suggest that not very different results will be obtained using 0.05 M NaCl or 0.067 M KCl, for any experimenter starting from scratch and wishing to adopt a standard procedure NaCl might be used for SC measurement and KCl for SP measurement.

It is very important to emphasize that most commercially available electrode media are produced for EEG or EKG use and contain saturated saline solutions which are *not* suitable for electrodermal measurement, in spite of their apparent convenience.

Venables and Sayer (1963) at the same time as suggesting 0.5 g/100 ml KCl as the saline content of a suitable electrolyte suggested the use of 2 g agar-agar per 100 ml solution as the medium of the paste. Similarly, Edelberg (1967) advocates the use of starch paste made at the concentration of 6 g of corn starch per 100 ml solution of electrolyte. In both cases the keeping properties are not good and the consistency tends to be somewhat variable. Nevertheless, these media are relatively easy to make in the laboratory and have been used as standards over many years so that their characteristics are known. Both agar-agar and starch paste media should be stirred continuously while being brought just to the boil but while Edelberg (1967, p. 11) recommends that the starch paste should be put into containers and capped after 30 s boiling, Venables and Martin (1967a, p. 84) found that lumpiness resulted with their agar-agar medium unless stirring continued while the solution cooled. A simple slow speed mechanical stirrer with plastic (not metal) paddles is invaluable for this process.

Lykken and Venables (1971) suggested the use of a commercial neutral ointment, 'Unibase', base as an electrolyte medium. Miller (1968) indicates that 1.2 g NaCl dissolved in 100 ml water and mixed with 295 g Unibase produces a 0.05 M electrolyte. In 1971 when Lykken and Venables advocated the use of either agar or Unibase electrolyte media they were thought to be equivalent in use; however, subsequent experimentation has shown that this is not so.

Fowles and Schneider (1974) showed in general that both SCL and SCR amp obtained from agar based electrolytes showed a decline in values whereas with Unibase as the electrolyte medium (while maintaining the same saline concentration) there was no decline of SCL or SCR amp during the course of an experiment. At the end of their paper Fowles and Schneider ask, 'Will the real SCR please stand up?' There is, of course, no real answer. The effects of hydration with agar based electrolytes are suggested by the authors to be due to poral closure (see Section 5.3) but it is not really possible to say that the apparently potentiated SCL and SCR amp due to the use of Unibase is 'real'.

In 1968, Edelberg, for research purposes, used polyethylene glycol as an electrode medium as it was capable of maintaining skin hydration at a level equivalent to that of skin exposed to air with a relative humidity of 65%. Glycol cannot, however, be used for normal recording purposes as it tends to seep beyond the defined area of the electrode and create difficulties with adhesive tape holding the electrodes.

Recently Fowles and Schneider have carried out experiments on the use of four types of electrolyte media: glycol, Unibase, agar, and a Unibase/glycol mixture. The last item was made by mixing 100 ml of polyethylene glycol (mol. wt. 400–600) with 100 g of Parke-Davis Unibase and with 0.76 g KCl added to this mixture until the mixture assumed the consistency of cold cream and all of the KCl crystals were dissolved.

The results using SP measurement favoured the use of Unibase/glycol. SPR amp (pos) was higher than with any other electrolyte and declined little over time. SPL with Unibase/glycol was intermediate between those obtained with glycol and Unibase alone and was maintained unchanging over time.

For SC measurement, however, SCL was lower with Unibase/glycol than with agar although the level was fairly constant over time, and for SCR amp again the amplitude was lower than with agar although fairly constant over time.

Fowles and Schneider suggest that Unibase/glycol may be considered as the preferred electrolyte for SP measurement but indicate that the mixture is not particularly desirable for SC measurement. Their work suggests that different electrolyte media may emphasize (or de-emphasize) the particular components of the peripheral mechanism (for instance, as summarized in Figure 1.5) and therefore different media could possibly be important for different purposes.

At this juncture it is clear that: (a) further studies of different electrolyte media need to be carried out under working rather than experimental conditions, preferably in parallel with more conventional, standard electrolyte systems; and (b) that what has been done so far indicates the very powerful role of what had been thought of as 'just a jelly' and consequently we cannot afford to be cavalier in our choice of different media.

7.0 APPARATUS

It is unfortunately still true that many manufacturers of commercial polygraph equipment do not provide adequate means of measuring skin conductance, although in most cases skin potential phenomena may be readily recorded using standard high sensitivity d.c. pre-amplifiers. For this reason it is necessary to introduce appropriate circuitry for the measurement of SC and to discuss some of the underlying principles on which these circuits are based.

7.1 Skin conductance measurement

In Sections 3.1 and 5.4 the case for measurement of exosomatic EDA in skin conductance rather than skin resistance terms has already been made. It is possible, and indeed is frequently done, to measure EDA in terms of skin resistance and subsequently to make conversion to conductance values by taking reciprocals. Not only is this undesirable because of the increased labour involved and because of the possibility of introducing errors but it is also less desirable from an electrophysiological point of view (see Section 7.1.2) and also for the reason discussed in Section 3.1, that more adjustment of the 'backing-off' control (see Section 7.1.3) is required when measuring resistance.

7.1.1 Constant voltage versus constant current systems

Measurement of either resistance or conductance employs basically the same simple voltage divider circuit. The difference in the two cases lies in the values of the two resistance elements in the divider. In either case the basic principle involved is that of Ohm's law and the important caveat is the extent to which the law applies to the biological part of the circuit, that is, the current pathway between the two electrodes represented by R_s in Figures 1.8(a) and 1.8(b). (See Section 7.1.2.) In the case of Figure 1.8(a) where resistance is being measured by a 'constant' current system, R_A is large with respect to R_s, the subject resistance. Ohm's law may be written as $R = V/I$, where R is resistance, I is the current flowing in the circuit, and V is the potential difference across R. In this case the relevant potential difference is across R_s, that is, across the two electrodes on the skin surface. If I is constant then R is directly proportional to V. This voltage is

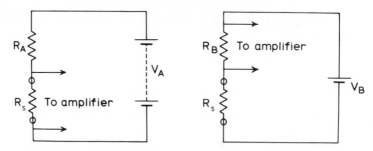

Figure 1.8   Schematic circuits to illustrate: (a) constant current; and (b) constant voltage methods of measuring SC

the signal which is then fed to the polygraph pre-amplifier to provide output via the main amplifer to pen, tape recorder or computer.

A circuit such as that of Figure 1.8(a) is a passive voltage divider and current through the circuit remains *relatively* constant because R_A is large in comparison with R_s. If for instance $R_A = 10$ MΩ and $V_A = 100$ V the current flowing in the circuit will be 9.99 μA if the subject resistance R_s is a low value, e.g. 10 kΩ (= 100 μmho) and 9.75 μA if R_s is high, e.g. 250 kΩ (= 4 μmho). Thus there is only a small variation in current over the range of R_s values likely to be encountered in practice.

In Figure 1.8(b) where conductance is measured by a 'constant' voltage circuit formed by the passive voltage divider, R_B, and R_s, R_B is small in relation to R_s and consequently the amount of potential dropped across it is small in relation to the relatively constant voltage appearing across the subject R_s.

If $V_B = 0.5$ V and $R_B = 100$ Ω, then the voltage across the subject varies from 0.4950 to 0.4998 V as R_s varies from 10 kΩ to 250 kΩ. It is this principle which has been successfully employed in the practical circuits outlined first in Lykken (1968) and presented in slightly elaborated forms in Lykken and Venables (1971) and Venables and Christie (1973). The main disadvantage of this type of circuit is that the signal to be fed to the polygraph, i.e. the potential difference across the signal resistor R_B, is relatively small and requires that the pre-amplifier of the polygraph be run at a high gain which may produce, under adverse circumstances, a rather 'noisy' output.

In 1977, Lowry published *active* circuitry for the measurement of skin resistance and skin conductance where instead of constant current or constant voltage being maintained within limits by the judicious choice of resistive values in a voltage divider as outlined above, control of current or voltage is exercised by the use of an operational amplifier. Figure 1.9 shows such a circuit for the measurement of skin conductance. As before

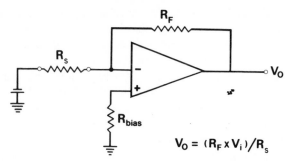

Figure 1.9 'Active' circuit for measuring SC; after Lowry (1977)

R_s is the subject resistance; variation in this alters the current fed to the summing node of the operational amplifier as determined by $I = V_i \times 1/R_s$; that is, the current is a direct function of conductance. The amplifier then produces an output voltage V_o such as to extract the same current (I) through R_F, the feedback resistor. This output V_o will thus be a direct function of $1/R_s$, the subject conductance. The possible error, the current through this bias resistor, R_{bias}, is constant and additive and is minimized by appropriate selection of values.

Lowry (1977) provides a working circuit to measure SR and SC based on operational amplifiers as the critical elements in an active circuit. However, because in this chapter the measurement of conductance only is advocated, a working circuit having some of the same useful design features as the Lykken and Venables' (1971) passive circuitry but incorporating Lowry's principles is provided in the Appendix.

7.1.2 The skin as an ohmic resistor

Arguments for the measurement of EDA in SC units and for its direct measurement by constant voltage circuitry have been made earlier. The discussion in the preceding section demands that the subject resistor R_s in the circuits in Figures 1.7 and 1.8 behaves like a true ohmic resistor; that is, it does not alter its value with the passage of current, or, if thought of in terms of Ohm's law, maintains a direct linear relation between V and I.

This consideration is important in the choice of constant current or constant voltage circuitry. The advocacy of the constant current type of circuit and hence the direct measurement of SR was supported by data provided by Edelberg, Greiner and Burch (1960) which showed that Ohm's law was only valid in measurement of EDA for current densities of less than 10 μA/cm^2. Beyond this limit, as Grings (1953) had previously shown, SRL and SRR decreased as current density increased. Edelberg (1967), however, showed that the limiting current density depended on individual subject's resistance. Ss with R_s of a low value could tolerate current densities as high as 75 μA/cm^2 before non-linearity became evident; on the other hand, Ss with R_s of a high value showed non-linearity with current densities of 4 μA/cm^2. The explanation for these findings would appear to be that individual sweat glands can carry a limited current before they show non-linearity. When the subject has a low R_s there are many sweat glands active per unit area and a large total current can be carried by the many parallel pathways. However, with a high R_s only a few sweat glands are available as current pathways and the point of non-linearity is thus exceeded with only a small total current. With a constant voltage system, the voltage across each sweat gland remains the same and the current through individual glands remains constant, the total current being dependent on the number of glands which are active.

In 1967, Edelberg reported that voltage/current curves were linear below an impressed voltage level of 0.8 V across a single active site, and on the basis of these data suggests the adoption of 0.5 V across a single site to avoid both time-variant and time-invariant non-linearity. This proposal is adopted in the practical circuit shown in the Appendix.

As indicated above non-linearity of voltage/current curves is a function of current density at electrode sites. In order to reduce current density electrodes should thus be as large as is practicable. This is a further reason in addition to those discussed in Section 6.2.2 for making the recommendation although as suggested at that point it appears that 0.8 cm^2 might be considered as a maximum size.

7.1.3 The simultaneous measurement of SCL and SCR

SCL typically has a larger value than the largest SCR amp. If the gain of the recording system is set at a value to enable the SCL to be accommodated within the full scale of the paper write out or the maximum tolerable voltage of recorder or computer, then SCR amp will appear as a small fraction of that output and be measured only with limited accuracy. One solution which has been suggested to overcome this has been to record SCL using a directly coupled amplifier and SCR amp using a resistance/capacity coupled amplifier at a higher gain. The main disadvantage of this system is that two channels of recording are required. The other more commonly used alternative is to suppress that voltage output from, for instance, the signal resistor in the circuit in Figure 1.8(b) which is proportional to SCL thereby allowing SCR amp to be recorded at greater gain from an artificial zero baseline. Following the principle· introduced by Lowry's (1977) circuitry, the insertion of this 'backing-off', 'bucking' or 'suppression' voltage may be introduced at a later stage than the input and in the practical circuit shown in the Appendix it is introduced as a signal to the opposite side of a differential amplifier from that into which the SCR amp signal is introduced.

The disadvantage of this system is that the operator has to be alert to changes in SCL which might lead the record to deviate outside the range of pen excursion, and to make the necessary adjustments to the backing-off control and note these down in the course of carrying out what may be an otherwise complex experiment.

An automatic voltage suppressor to undertake this task has been devised by Simon and Homoth (1978) and a version of their circuit to work with the modified Lowry active constant voltage circuit is shown in the Appendix. Difficulty arises with computer analysis of SC data when changes in the backing-off control have to be accounted for in the calculation of final values of SC in the course of a total recording. It is possible to note from the paper record when changes in backing-off are made and to record their magnitude and to insert these values by teletype. However, with the use of the automatic backing-off circuit a means of measuring its status at regular intervals is required and this is incorporated in the practical circuit in the Appendix. The principle employed is that of representing the state of the backing-off control as a pulse appearing at a specified time. This value may then be sampled by the computer and the value automatically included as part of the digitized recording.

7.2 Skin potential measurement

As stated in Section 4.3.3, the range of SPLs to be measured is expected to be from about +10 to −70 mV at the palm with respect to an active forearm site.

Although the source of SP is complex (see Figure 1.6), it is possible to represent skin potential as a voltage source (V_s) in series with an internal or source resistance (R_s). When the skin is intact under both the active palmar electrode and the reference or forearm site (see Section 6.1) the source resistance is of the order of 1 MΩ. The measurement of SP therefore involves the same principles as the measurement of any potential from a high resistance source. Figure 1.10 shows the essential features of the circuit involved. If the input resistance of the pre-amplifier used for measuring SP is of the order of 1 MΩ then the value of SP which will be measured at the polygraph wll be half V_s. This is, of course, because the p.d. V_s is distributed half across R_s, the source resistance, and half across R_A, the input resistance of the amplifier.

Two steps may be taken to improve this situation. Firstly, R_s may be reduced by abrasion of the skin under the reference electrode. This not

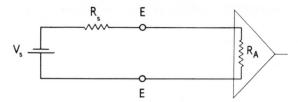

Figure 1.10   Schematic circuit to illustrate factors in measuring SP

only produces a zero reference point against which palmar potential may be measured but also reduces the source resistance, R_s, to a value of about 100 kΩ. With a 1 MΩ input impedance amplifier this reduces the error of measurement of V_s from 50% to 10%. The second step to improve matters involves an increase in the value of the effective input resistance of the amplifier. There is no reason why this cannot be done by the use of an amplifier having better characteristics than the relatively standard polygraph pre-amplifier. Commercially produced probes with very high input resistance are available. On the other hand, if it is required to measure SPR as well as SPL, then the same problem as with the separation of SCR and SCL is encountered (see Section 7.1.3) and it is convenient to back-off or buck SPL and measure SPR at a higher amplifier gain. Most commercially available polygraph pre-amplifiers have a backing-off control by which SPL is opposed by an equal and opposite potential so that SPR may be recorded around an arbitrary pen zero, the value of the knob setting to achieve this pen zero being noted on the paper record. The effect of backing-off is to reduce current flow in the circuit and hence lessen the proportion of V_s which is dropped across R_s, the source resistance. Even if the operation is rather inaccurate in the adjustment of the backing-off control and there is a mismatch of potential of 5 mV, the apparent input resistance will be as high as 10 MΩ (with an actual R_A of 1 MΩ) and error of measurement will fall to 1%. Details of the calculation of the effective input resistance of an amplifier with backing-off control and the percentage accuracy of measurement are given in Venables and Martin (1967a, p. 88).

Difference between the temperature of hand and forearm electrode sites can give rise to measured differences in potential due to electrothermal mechanisms. Errors of about 2.mV are possible from this source and if it appears important to correct for this degree of error then a circuit for its automatic compensation is available in Venables and Sayer (1963).

8.0 EFFECTS OF PHYSICAL VARIABLES

8.1 Environmental variables

This subject is treated at length by Venables and Christie (1973) in Section VA. However, data have recently become available which provide additional material on the effect of climatic variables on SC. These data are derived from the work in Mauritius which has already been referred to in Tables 1.1, 1.2, and 1.3.

Two lessons were derived from this study. The first was concerned with a decision about the temperature at which to run the laboratory in Mauritius. In a temperate European climate the aim to run the laboratory at 70 °F (21 °C) had in general resulted in a reasonable degree of responsivity and reported subject comfort. At this temperature virtually no Mauritian subject responded electrodermally and there were complaints of feeling cold in spite of the fact that the mean external temperature was only some 3 °F warmer. It was decided to run the laboratory at 86 °F (30 °C) and this resulted in more normal levels of responsivity and no complaints of discomfort. Although this experience is with a rather unusual sub-tropical environment the general lesson does appear to underline the necessity to run a psychophysiological laboratory at a temperature rather higher than that suggested for normal office conditions and certainly much higher than mean ambient external conditions.

Table 1.6 shows the mean temperature and humidity conditions achieved in the laboratory and the external conditions of temperature, humidity, and pressure which were recorded. Laboratory temperature was controlled automatically by an air conditioning system while humidity was controlled by manual operation of a dehumidifier. The comparability of data from the two studies which were carried out in successive years should be noted in relation to the data in Table 1.7.

Table 1.6. Environmental variables in the study (a) of 1800 3-year old children, and (b) of 640 subjects age 5–25 years

	Mean		Standard deviation	
Study	(a)	(b)	(a)	(b)
Outside temperature (°C)	22.98	22.89	3.14	2.42
Outside humidity (%RH)	76.96	71.27	11.99	9.88
Outside pressure (mb)	967.56	967.96	6.63	2.97
Lab. temperature (°C)	30.00	29.52	1.44	0.56
Lab. humidity (%RH)	51.85	50.09	4.21	3.14

Techniques in Psychophysiology

Table 1.7. Relation of skin conductance variables to environmental variables in different age groups

Age	Variable	Outside temperature	Outside humidity	Outside pressure
3 (n = 1800)	SCL			
	SCR amp			
	SCR lat.			
	SCR rec. t/2			
5 (n = 128)	SCL			
	SCR amp			
	SCR lat.		+	
	SCR rec. t/2			−
10 (n = 128)	SCL		+	
	SCR amp	−		
	SCR lat.		−	
	SCR rec. t/2			−
15 (n = 128)	SCL		+	
	SCR amp		+	
	SCR lat.			
	SCR rec. t/2	−	+	
20 (n = 128)	SCL	+		−
	SCR amp			
	SCR lat.	−		+
	SCR rec. t/2	−	+	
25 (n = 128)	SCL	+		−
	SCR amp	−		−
	SCR lat.	−		
	SCR rec. t/2	−		+

+ entered in cell when majority of correlations for that variable are positive and greater than 0.2.
− when majority are negative and greater than 0.2.

This table represents a summary of a large amount of data in the form of 60 possible values of SCL, SCR amp, lat., and rec. t/2 for each of the 2440 subjects tested.

No correlations greater than 0.2 were recorded for any environmental variable for the 3-year olds and no correlations greater than 0.2 were recorded between laboratory temperature and humidity and the SC variables for any of the subject groups. The data in Table 1.7 do, however, suggest that for subjects aged up to and including adolescence there is an important relation with humidity but that for the older subjects temperature is a relevant variable; there is too some consistency with the correlation between SC variables and pressure.

The important point to note, however, is that these correlations are with the external environmental conditions and not with the laboratory conditions. Thus control has to be statistical rather than by physical control of the laboratory environment. It should also be noted that while the entries in Table 1.7 are for correlations greater than 0.2 which, of course, are significant for the numbers involved, none is greater than 0.4 and consequently no more than 16% of the variance is accounted for by these factors. It is also necessary to point out again that these data were collected in circumstances not usually encountered in areas where the majority of psychophysiological work is carried out; nevertheless, they do point to the need to be aware of the relevance of these variables.

8.2 Skin temperature

Early workers, for instance Floyd and Keele (1936), showed that SRR exhibited a longer latency, smaller amplitude, and longer recovery at a cool than a warm site.

Table 1.8. Relation of skin temperature to skin conductance variables

	SCL	SCR amp	SCR lat.	SCR ris. t	SCR rec. t/2
r	0.02	0.00	−0.30	−0.18	−0.20

More recently Maulsby and Edelberg (1960) confirmed the reported negative relation of latency to temperature and also showed that rise time decreased as skin temperature increased. These authors also showed that SRL increases as a function of cooling the skin. Table 1.8 provides some recent data on 260 11-year old children which give partial confirmation of these results. Again the main effect is with latency although that with rise time is significant although small. The relation of skin temperature with SCL and SCR amp is notably absent.

9.0 INTERPRETATION OF RESULTS

9.1 Skin conductance: relative independence of SCR component measures

As indicated in the introduction to this chapter the change in usage of skin conductance data which has taken place over the last twenty years has been particularly in the measurement of components of responsivity other than SCR amp. The temporal measures—SCR lat., ris. t, and rec.t/2—have been used as indices in their own right to relate to other aspects of behaviour.

Perhaps the greatest interest has been shown in SCR rec.t/2. On the one hand, this is because of the work of Edelberg (1970, 1972b) who suggested that shortness of SCR recovery could be thought of as a measure of goal orientation which was relatively independent of other SCR component measures. On the other hand, the findings of Mednick and Schulsinger (1968), Mednick (1974), Mednick and coworkers (1978) indicated that shortness of SCR rec.t/2 was predictive of schizophrenic breakdown, and Ax and Bamford (1970) and Gruzelier and Venables (1972) showed that it was characteristic of adult schizophrenics. Venables (1974) attempted a reconciliation of the position of Edelberg and that of the work on schizophrenics by suggesting that shortness of SCR rec.t/2 was indicative of 'openness to the environment'.

This work, on the whole, has tended to accord a separate status to SCR recovery. This position has recently been questioned by Bundy (1973, 1977), Bundy and Fitzgerald (1975), and by Edelberg and Muller (1977).

Essentially what these authors have shown is that recovery time appears to be a function of the extent and closeness in time of previous responses and is consequently not independent of other measures. This is hardly surprising when the summary model (Figure 1.6) of the determinants of EDA is considered together with the discussion presented in Section 5.4 of the interrelatedness of the different components of the model. What does need careful consideration is the extent of the degree of relatedness of recovery to other measures, so that the *relative* independence of the measure may be understood.

Bundy and Fitzgerald (1975) provide data from five subjects showing that the correlation between SCR rec.t/2 and time since previous response ranged from 0.13 to 0.87. When a formula was used which weighted size (amp) of and interval (i) from the two previous responses ($S = amp_1/i_1 + amp_2/i_2$) then the correlations between the index X and SCR rec.t/2 ranged between 0.52 and 0.91.

Edelberg and Muller (1977) also provide data to support Bundy's findings by showing that the correlations between Bundy's 'X' index and recovery ranged from -0.14 to 0.84 for 20 within-subject correlations and that the pooled within-subject correlation of 0.37 was highly significant.

While Edelberg uses these results to cast doubt on his previous views about the independence of separate secretory and epidermal effector mechanisms they are not essentially in conflict with a modified view attributable to Fowles (e.g., 1974) which ascribes more importance to the hydration of the corneum. The point at issue, however, is that while the data provided by Bundy and Fitzgerald (1975) give a mean correlation between the X index and recovery of 0.76, and thus explain 58% of the variance, Edelberg's data suggest that previous responsivity explains only 14% of the variance and consequently leaves much to be explained by other factors.

Both Bundy and Fitzgerald's (1975) and Edelberg and Muller's (1977) data are in the form of within-subject correlations. Lockhart and Lieberman (1976), however, present comparable between-subject correlations on a single response to shock across 110 subjects showing a correlation of 0.437 between elapsed time since the previous response and SCR rec.t/2, and also 0.413 between elapsed time and SCR ris.t, these two component measures themselves intercorrelating 0.777. Lockhart and Lierberman's data thus suggest that less than 20% of the variance of recovery is explained by the time since the previous response, a figure comparable to that of Edelberg and Muller.

While Bundy and Fitzgerald have emphasized the influence of the context of earlier responding on present electrodermal activity, another viewpoint is concerned with the examination of the independence of the components of SCR from one another.

Table 1.9 presents between-subject correlations from three studies. The data (a) and (c) are from the study of 1800 Mauritian 3-year olds and have previously been presented in Table 1.3. Data (b) are from Lockhart and Lieberman (1976), referred to above, and data (d) are from 260 11-year olds in Copenhagen and have not previously been presented. Data (a) and (b) are presented for comparison, as (a) is from response to an intense auditory stimulus and (b) to a shock; on the other hand, (c) and (d) may be compared as responses to the same mild auditory stimulus but from two very different samples. Two other indices than those which have so far been used are presented here; these are SCR 'recovery rate' calculated as μmhos recovered per second during the $\frac{1}{2}$ recovery time—in other words, the slope of the recovery limb of the SCR—and secondly SCR 'recruitment' calculated as μmhos gained per second during rise time. Data on recovery rate are included particularly because this index has been used by, for instance, Mednick and coworkers (1978) as a predictor of schizophrenic breakdown.

The data in Table 1.9 shows a reasonably high degree of consistency across studies and across stimulus conditions.

The table should be examined in relation to data presented by Lockhart (1972) and Lockhart and Lieberman (1975) where they suggest that the correlation between components of SCR change in size and possibly direction according to the type of stimulus and stimulus situation which elicits the response. For instance, they suggest strong correlations between latency and amplitude, rise time and amplitude, and recovery and amplitude under 'orienting' conditions, only weak relations between these

Table 1.9. Matrix of correlations of skin conductance variables from four sources: SCL and SCR amp in terms of absolute conductance values

	SCR amp	SCR lat.	SCR ris. t	SCR rec. t/2	SCR rec. rate	SCR recruitment
SCL	0.24[a]	−0.08	–	−0.18	0.20	–
	0.62[b]	−0.18	−0.33	−0.32	−0.10	–
	0.23[c]	−0.07	–	−0.12	0.27	–
	0.33[d]	−0.14	−0.01	−0.12	0.34	0.47
SCR amp		−0.21	–	0.29	0.29	–
		−0.14	−0.18	0.00	0.15	–
		−0.18	–	0.20	0.45	–
		−0.12	0.17	0.12	0.67	0.86
SCR lat.			–	−0.13	−0.11	–
			0.30	0.27	−0.14	–
			–	−0.08	−0.08	–
			0.25	0.18	−0.16	−0.18
SCR ris. t				–	–	–
				0.77	−0.08	–
				–	–	–
				0.54	−0.18	−0.13
SCR rec. t/2					−0.23	–
					−0.25	–
					−0.30	–
					−0.23	−0.02
SCR rec. rate						–
						–
						–
						0.80

(a) Data collected from a sample of 1800 3-year old children in Mauritius (Venables, 1978). SCR to 90 dB noise, 4 s duration, 5 ms rise time.
(b) Data from Lockhart and Lieberman (1976) from sample of 123 subjects. SCR to electrotactual stimulus (SCR amp measured in $(\mu\text{mhos})^{1/2}$).
(c) Data from same source as (a). SCR to 75 dB 1000 Hz tone. 1 s duration, 25 ms rise and fall time.
(d) Data from a source of 260 11-year old children in Copenhagen. SCR to 75 dB 1000 Hz tone 1 s duration 25 ms rise and fall time.

Data from samples (a), (c) and (d) using bipolar placement of 0.125 cm² Ag/AgCl electrodes on left fore and middle fingers. Electrolyte 0.5% KCl in agar. Constant voltage 0.5 V.

variables being shown under 'defensive' conditions with strong stimulation. They suggest, however, that the latency–rise time and latency–recovery correlations are weak under orienting and strong under defensive conditions. Table 1.9 provides no evidence to back the first of these statements and slight evidence for the second. The Lockhart position was examined by analysis of data collected in Copenhagen shown, in part, in line (d) of Table 1.9.

Correlations between SCR amp, SCR lat., SCT ris.t, SCR rec.t/2 were calculated from data from seven different stimulus conditions, separately for males and females, and for three clinically different groups of children. All correlations were converted to z coefficients and an analysis of variance conducted using z coefficients as variables for the factors, stimulus type, sex, and group. In no case was there any evidence of a difference in correlation between variables being due to the factors listed or their interactions. Under the conditions within this study, therefore, the type of stability shown in Table 1.9 is supported.

Because of the recommendations made in Section 3.3.1 that SCL and SCR amp should be measured in log units, it was considered appropriate to examine the effect of this transformation on intercomponent correlations and this is presented in Table 1.10 where data from three sources are listed. The major change which appears to occur as a result of this transformation is the consistent alteration of sign and size of the correlation between recovery time and recovery rate.

What both the data in Table 1.9 and Table 1.10 suggest is the apparent relative independence of SCR rec.t/2 from all components of SCR other than rise time; thus, in a manner slightly different from that of Bundy's indicating the separate status of this measure. Also important is the comparatively high correlation between SCR rec.t/2 and SCR ris.t. One major difficulty in the use of the former variable is that it is often difficult to measure, if, for instance, a NS.SCR sometimes occurs before ½ recovery takes place. However, if a response is present it is usually possible to measure its rise time and consequently values for this variable, which may be equivalent to recovery time in their relation to external variables, may more often be available.

The second point to note is the independence of latency from the other purely temporal measures. There is a general indication, particularly when log values are taken, that larger amplitude responses have shorter latencies. The other consistent finding is that amplitude and level are moderately positively related.

As far as the 'secondary' indices, recruitment, and recovery rate, are concerned, the important point to note is their large relation to amplitude when the measures from which they are in part derived, rise time and recovery time, are more independent of amplitude.

Techniques in Psychophysiology

Table 1.10. Matrix of correlations of skin conductance variables from three sources: SCL and SCR amp in terms of log conductance

	log SC amp	SCR lat.	SCR ris. t	SCR rec. t/2	SCR rec. rate	SCR recruitment
	0.37[a]	−0.15	–	−0.19	0.07	–
log SCL	0.49[b]	−0.30	–	−0.11	0.18	–
	0.46[c]	−0.14	−0.40	−0.33	0.06	0.24
		−0.31	–	0.31	0.49	–
log SCR amp		−0.24	–	0.36	0.51	–
		−0.58	0.00	0.13	0.68	0.87
			–	−0.13	−0.11	–
SCR lat.			–	−0.14	−0.08	–
			0.17	−0.07	−0.27	−0.37
				–	–	–
SCR ris. t				–	–	–
				0.56	0.45	0.41
					0.46	–
SCR rec. t/2					0.46	–
					0.40	0.29
						–
SCR rec. rate						–
						0.88

(a) Data collected from a sample of 1800 3-year old children in Mauritius (Venables, 1978). SCR to 90 dB noise 4 s duration, 5 ms rise time.
(b) Data collected from sample of 640 subjects age range 5–25 years (Venables and coworkers, 1979). SCR to 90 dB noise, 4 s duration, 5 ms rise time.
(c) Data collected from sample of 65 18–75-year old adults. SCR to 75 dB, 1000 Hz tone, 1 s duration, 25 ms rise and fall time.

Data from all samples using bipolar placement of 0.125 cm^2 Ag/AgCl electrodes on left fore and middle fingers. Electrolyte 0.5% KCl in agar. Constant voltage 0.5 V.

The data presented in Tables 1.9 and 1.10 are across-subject correlations of SCR components resulting from single stimuli. Somewhat different material is presented by Martin and Rust (1976) where mean values over stimulus trials are used to provide *across*-subject correlations, and also pooled values of *within*-subject correlations are given. Table 1.11 gives extracted data from Martin and Rust's paper in a form comparable to those in Tables 1.9 and 1.10.

Two comparisons are of interest. The first of these is that between the between-subject correlations on single response data in Table 1.9 (data sets (a) and (b) for comparable stimulus intensity) and the between-subject correlations on mean data (row (a)) in Table 1.11. The correlations

Table 1.11. Matrix of correlations of skin conductance variables showing values of between and pooled within subject correlations from the same study

	SCR amp	SCR lat.	SCR ris. t	SCR rec. t/2
SCL*	(a) 0.62 (b) 0.08	−0.18 0.02	−0.30 −0.23	−0.27 −0.23
SCR amp		−0.55 −0.37	−0.39⎫ 0.62⎭	−0.43⎫ 0.41⎭
SCR lat.			0.60⎫ −0.40⎭	0.74⎫ −0.29⎭
SCR ris. t				0.80 0.65

Data from Martin and Rust (1976): (a) between subject correlations, (b) pooled within subject correlations. Responses to 21 95 dB, 1000 Hz, 1 s tones. $N = 84$.
*SCL measured as square root conductance.

between SCL and SCR variables are consistent between the two data sets; where the data do differ is in the strong relation between SCR amp and the temporal components in the Martin and Rust data not shown in Table 1.9, and the strong relation between SCR lat. and the other temporal components, where latency, as has been indicated above, appears as an independent variable in the other studies. Two explanations are possible: one is the difference between the use of mean and single response data; the second is that the Martin and Rust data fit with the expectations of correlations between latency and rise time, and latency and recovery for defensive responses to high intensity stimuli suggested by Lockhart and Lieberman (1975) which were reviewed earlier.

The second comparison to be noted is between the two sets of data in Table 1.11 where brackets have been inserted to indicate where between- and pooled within-subject correlations provide markedly different results. Some discussion of these discrepancies is given in Martin and Rust (1976).

The importance of the comparison of the data presented in Tables 1.9, 1.10, and 1.11 is that, while consistency of data is obtainable when the type of statistical procedure is the same, superficially comparable methods do not necessarily produce the same result and thus the statements which are made as a result have to be treated with caution.

9.2 Skin conductance: comparability of tonic measures

Silverman, Cohen and Shmavonian (1959), on the basis of data presented in the form of a scatter plot, show that changes in SRL tend to be accompanied by changes in the number of non-specifics (NS.SCRs) in the direction that falls in SRL are related to increases in the number of NS.SCRs. These data are cited as indicating that both SRL and numbers of NS.SCRs may be used as measures of 'arousal'. Surwillo and Quilter (1965) provide data to show that behavioural indications of vigilance were related to numbers of NS.SCRs in a positive fashion. On the basis of these and other results Depue and Fowles (1973), for instance, reviewing data on arousal in schizophrenics have suggested that NS.SCR frequency may be a measure of 'arousal'.

The position is not, however, clear; Kimmel and Hill (1961) showed that while changes in SCL appeared to be appropriate indicants of response to stress, NS frequency did not behave as predicted. Katkin (1965) concluded after a study in which SCL and NS frequency were used as 'autonomic indicants of stress' that the indices reflected different phenomena, and Miller and Shmavonian (1965) in replicating Katkin's study also showed a divergence of SCL and NS frequency variables as indications of tonic arousal.

The data of Martin and Rust (1976) referred to in the previous section indicate that the association between the two measures is not high. They give a between-subject correlation between SCL and NS frequency of 0.27 and a pooled within-subject correlation of 0.15 between the same variables. Clearly on the basis of these data there is no case for considering the two measures, which have on occasions been thought of as equivalent measures of tonic activity, as being interchangeable.

9.3 Skin conductance: definition of non-responsivity

In the field of work on patient subjects, some have been classified as skin conductance non-responders (cf. Venables, 1977). This class of subjects apparently forms a considerable proportion of the adult schizophrenic population and clearly the establishment of criteria for non-responsivity is essential. Similarly, in studies on habituation it is important to establish when the subject has ceased to respond.

The difficulty lies in the possibility that on the one hand there may be a state of true non-response and on the other hand a response may exist but be too small for it to be measured using the equipment available.

Two points are of concern in this issue. The first is the differences in criterion level for presence of a response which have been used by workers measuring SR or SC; the second is whether there is a relationship between amplitude or response and pre-stimulus level, in other words whether the law of initial values (LIV) holds for electrodermal activity and consequently whether non-responsivity as defined will vary according to the pre-stimulus level from which a response might be measured.

These points are taken up in detail by O'Gorman (1978) who shows: (a) that different conventional changes of EDA have been used as criteria for responsivity by workers using conductance units (e.g. Gruzelier and Venables, 1972: 0.05 μmho) or resistance units (e.g. Zahn, 1976: 0.4 kΩ); and (b) that the comparability of these units varies according to the pre stimulus level from which they are measured, not on account of the operation of LIV but because of the way in which SCR and SRR are measured; this point is already illustrated in Table 1.5.

The issue of whether LIV operates in EDA data is unresolved. Bull and Gale (1974) indicate that there are subject differences in the evidence for LIV, and they concur with Hord, Johnson and Lubin (1964) in showing that SC and SR measures provide different evidence for the operation of the law.

Recently Edelberg (1978) has suggested that whether or not this law operates and its direction depends on the temporal spacing of stimuli and the responses to them. Clearly at this stage there is no consensus in the data available, but the awareness of factors determining non-responsivity (or size of response) is essential in examining the data from any experiment.

9.4 Amplitude versus magnitude measures of SCR

In Section 2.2 amplitude and magnitude were defined. In the former case the average size of response is calculated as the mean of all non-zero values. In the case of magnitude all occasions on which a response might be given, that is on which stimuli are presented, are used and consequently zeros may enter the calculation. On the basis of what has been said in the previous section on the difficulties of defining non-responsivity it might be suggested that the magnitude measure is to be advocated as although zeros may be used in the calculation of the mean they might sensibly be thought of as small but finite values whereas arbitrary omission of these responses in the calculation of amplitude depends on the definition of a non-response.

A further argument for the use of magnitude as the preferred measure is that the same N is used as a basis for each mean and consequently when calculating correlations between responses for entry into a matrix for further analysis the N underlying each cell is comparable.

Arguments against the use of the magnitude measure have, however, been made by Prokasy and Kumpfer (1973) insofar as this variable confounds frequency and response size which do not always co-vary.

This issue is again one on which there are arguments on both sides and while no absolute resolution is possible the difference between the two measures needs to be kept in mind.

10.0 APPENDIX: A SYSTEM FOR SKIN CONDUCTANCE MEASUREMENT

The following description is presented not so much because it is thought of as outlining a 'perfect' system but rather because it does embody certain principles which have been introduced earlier and provides a somewhat 'modular' approach that may be instrumented either whole or in part. The description here is a condensed version of that given in Fletcher and coworkers (1979, in preparation).

10.1 Introduction

The system consists of an 'active' skin conductance measurement coupler, working with an automatic 'backing-off' device, recording through a conventional polygraph to provide a paper record output and with input either directly into a computer or via intermediate storage on an analog recorder to provide edited automatic data output.

Figure 1.11 shows the elements of the system from the subject input to the output to the computer. At the left-hand side of the figure, input from the subject electrodes is into the active SC coupler which is shown in detail in Figure 1.13. The differential output of this coupler with the 'man/auto' switch in the manual position is fed into the polygraph input, after suitable attenuation to achieve compatibility with the polygraph input characteristics. One side of the coupler output is fed to the auto backing-off or suppression device (Simon and Homoth, 1978). The output from that device with the man/auto switch in the auto position is fed into one side of the polygraph differential input so as to provide a polygraph record in which SCL is automatically suppressed (see Section 7.1.3). The output from the auto-suppression device is also available after suitable amplification and buffering as a pulse to be read by the computer. In order that gain of the system may be known by the computer a standard pulse of calibration voltage is fed into the upper differential input line to the polygraph. Finally, so that a record of skin temperature may be made without the necessity of employing a further polygraph channel for a slowly changing variable, output from a suitable transducer amplifier (e.g. Trolander, 1967, p. 107) is also available as a pulse to the computer.

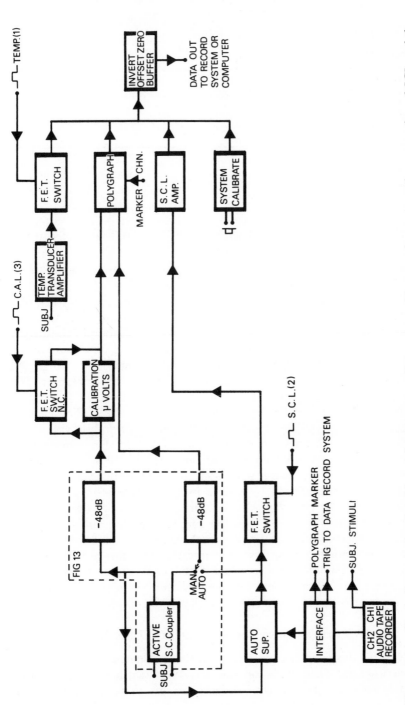

Figure 1.11 Block diagram of active skin conductance recording system with manual or automatic suppression of SCL and the elicitation of temperature, SCL, and calibration pulses for computer analysis

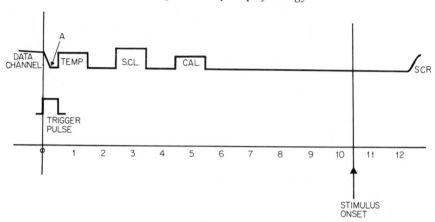

Figure 1.12   Timing of pulses for temperature, SCL, and calibration of system

Figure 1.12 shows the timing of the data outputs. The sequence starts
with a trigger pulse, either initiated manually or, as shown on Figure 1.11,
from a tape recording in which the stimulus is recorded on one track of a
stereo tape recorder and a trigger pulse is recorded on the other track. In
the system presented here the interval between the initiation of the trigger
pulse and the onset of the stimulus is 10.5 s. This allows for the collection
of 5 s of pre stimulus data after the data on temperature, SCL and
calibration (to calculate gain) have been presented to the computer. The
auto-suppression circuit is initiated from the leading edge of the trigger
pulse and the SCL is referred to baseline at A before the trailing edge of
the trigger pulse initiates the 'temp' pulse (Figure 1.12) and provides a 1 s
pulse on the data channel whose amplitude indicates skin temperature.
This is followed 1 second later by the pulse to the FET switch which
samples the state of the auto-suppression output and presents a pulse on
the data channel indicating SCL. After a further second a 0.5 μmho pulse
is introduced into the polygraph thus enabling the output of the polygraph
to be assessed in terms of the polygraph gain setting. The initiating trigger
pulse also provides a pulse to the polygraph marker pen and to the timing
channel of the data recording system if intermediate storage is used prior
to computer analysis. In order to establish the gain setting of the recorder
and computer input a manually operated system for injecting a pulse of
known size is provided by the element labelled 'system calibrate'.

10.2 Active skin conductance coupler (Figure 1.13)

The circuit for this coupler is derived from that presented by Lowry (1977)
but it incorporates some of the operating features that have been found to
be useful with the passive circuit described by Venables and Christie

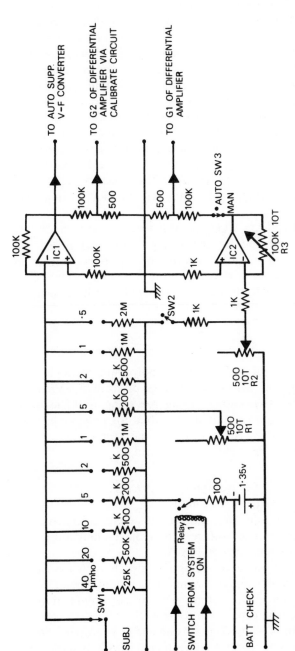

Figure 1.13 Active skin conductance coupler (modified from Lowry, 1977) with suppression, calibration and attenuation for direct connection to differential pre-amplifier. Output to automatic suppression voltage to frequency convertor 100 mV per μmho. Output to G2 of pre-amplifier positive going for conductance increase of 250 μV per μmho

R_1 = subject volts
R_2 = suppression calibration
R_3 = zero suppression
SW1 = select subject or dummy subject
SW2 = suppression cal
SW3 = man/auto suppression

(1973). These features enable dummy subjects of 1, 2, 5, 10, 20, and 40 μmhos to be connected in place of an actual subject by the operation of SW1 and conductance values of 0.5, 1, 2, and 5 μmhos to be added by means of press-button switches during the course of recording. The resistors providing these dummy subject conductances or the actual subject are equivalent to Rs in the schematic active circuit shown in Figure 1.9. IC1, a 748 amplifier, is equivalent to the operational amplifier in Figure 1.9; R_F and R_{bias} in that circuit have the value of 100 kΩ. The output of the amplifier appears across a pair of resistors to provide 100 mV per μmho to operate the auto-suppression system and 250 μV per μmho as output to the polygraph (i.e. the 48 dB attenuation shown in Figure 1.12). The choice of output to match a particular recording system may of course be made by a suitable choice of values of the pair of resistors. The resistors R_2, R_3, and the network around IC2, another 748 amplifier, provide a manually operated suppression system.

The 1.35 V mercury cell and the 100 Ω resistor together with the 500 Ω ten-turn potentiometer R_1 provide for the voltage appearing across the subject to be set at 0.5 V in accordance with the recommendations in Section 7.1.2. The subject voltage is switched on in the circuit shown by a voltage appearing across relay 1 from the polygraph with which the coupler is used.

10.2.1 Calibration

The procedure outlined is for use with a polygraph with a d.c. pre-amplifier having a range of sensitivity settings of from 5 mV/cm to 0.01 mV/cm; a typical sensitivity setting during recording is 0.5 mV/cm. The calibration procedure should be suitably modified for polygraphs with other sensitivities. Steps 1 to 3 are to calibrate the voltage across the subject; steps 4 and 5 calibrate the suppression control.

(1) Select sensitivity setting of polygraph of 5 mV/cm.
(2) Select dummy subject value of 20 μmho.
(3) Switch on coupler and adjust R_1, subject volts control, to achieve a pen deflection of 1 cm. The voltage across the dummy subject is then 0.5 V and the subject current 10 μA.
(4) Select dummy subject value of 40 μmho; switch on suppression circuit, SW2; turn zero suppression ten-turn potentiometer R_3 to maximum, i.e. 10 on dial. Return pen to zero deflection by adjusting the suppression calibration control R_2.
(5) Select 'subject' with a subject not connected; i.e. open circuit. Return zero suppression control to zero and check that the pen gives zero deflection.

With steps 4 and 5 the zero suppression control is calibrated to give 4 μmho per turn of the potentiometer; i.e. the scale value should be multiplied by 4. Other values of suppression control may, of course, be used; e.g. if step 4 were used with 10 μmho as the dummy subject value the zero suppression control would be in terms of 1 μmho per turn.

The following coupler sensitivities are achieved with the selected polygraph sensitivity settings.

Polygraph (mV/cm)	Coupler (μmho/cm)
5	20
1	4
0.5	2
0.1	0.4
0.05	0.2
0.01	0.04

10.3 Automatic skin conductance suppression

The detailed circuit for the auto-suppression device is given by Simon and Homoth (1978); the principle is, however, shown in Figure 1.14. The input to the device is from the 100 mV/μmho level for the SC coupler. This input enters a voltage to frequency (VF) converter which provides an output to a counter and a memory proportional to SCL. The output from the VF converter which is counted is the number of pulses occurring during a 20 ms epoch, this epoch being timed from 50 Hz mains frequency. The digital content of the memory is thus proportional to SCL and is available for conversion to an analog voltage by the digital to analog (DA) converter. This analog voltage is used to suppress SCL in a manner analogous to that of the manual suppression circuit on the coupler. The action of a trigger pulse to the control unit from the tape recorder (or

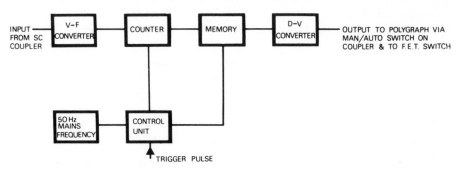

Figure 1.14 Block diagram of automatic suppression system (after Simon and Homoth, 1979)

other means of presenting stimuli to the subject) resets the counter and takes a new sample of SCL via the VF converter. In addition to rezeroing the baseline of the SC recording the output of the DA converter is available to be sampled by the second pulse shown in Figure 1.13 to provide a pulse proportional to SCL for the computer to read.

10.4 Computer analysis

The system described consists of three parts: (1) a procedure for sampling data, (2) a program for inserting suppression and polygraph gain figures if these have not been recorded automatically by the system outlined in the previous sections, and (3) a system for analysing and logging the sampled data.

The time structure of the sampling process for one trial is shown in Figure 1.15; this accords with the timing of pulses shown in Figure 1.12 but also indicates the times taken up by sampling and writing to disk (on a PDP 11/40 system).

The computer starts listening for a trigger one second before it is due to arrive; following the appearance of the trigger, temperature, suppression and gain calibration signals are sampled and stored, after 5.5 s (5 s pre stimulus) 500 samples at 20 Hz are initiated giving 5 s of pre and 20 s of post stimulus data. Data are written to disk after which the computer 'goes to sleep' until one second before the next trigger is due. The program is interactive in that on initiation it asks the experimenter for a user identification code and a subject code; after this it asks for details of trials and their timing and if necessary searches the user's running disk for the details of the inter trial intervals in use for the experiment in question. Finally a question is asked about the speed at which the FM tape recording is being run if intermediate storage is used, the possibilities of 1×, 2×, and 4× being available; 4× would, of course, normally be used. The program offers the possibility of sampling three data channels at the same time thus allowing the bilateral recording of SC and a channel of SP data. The output written to file is in the form of: (1) subject number, (2) trial

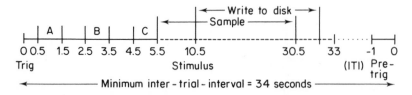

Figure 1.15 Timing of SC data collection. A is skin temperature sampling window, B is suppression voltage sampling window and C is 0.5 micromho calibrating signal (gain)

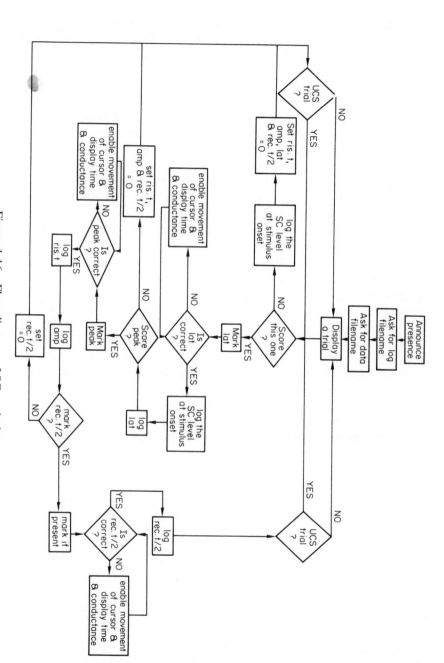

Figure 1.16 Flow diagram of SC analysis system

number, (3) system calibration signal, (4) temperature, (5) suppression, (6) gain, followed by 500 data points of signal. This is the form which the third part of the system expects. If items 3, 4, 5, and 6 are not automatically recorded then a second program is available for inserting them via teletype.

The third part of the system is interactive via a dynamic display on a GT40 graphics system associated with the PDP 11/40 computer. The user is provided with a hand-held box by which he can answer 'yes/no' questions by pressing an appropriate button and move a cursor by a potentiometer knob. Two versions of the systems are available, one for dealing with single channel recordings and the second for scoring with both channels of a bilateral recording at the same time. The data are displayed trial by trial from stimulus onset to 20 s post stimulus. Following the earlier input sampling processes, the data are displayed directly in micromhos and seconds.

The flow diagram in Figure 1.16 outlines the operation of the system. The value of the latency of response is established by searching over a window from 1–3 s post stimulus. The search is made by starting at 3 seconds and working backwards, a method which has proved more error free than working in the opposite direction. When the point of inflection indicating the latency value is found it is marked and the program asks if it is satisfactory; an answer 'no' allows the user to enter the manual mode and place the cursor at a point he considers to be correct. The peak amplitude is then sought and marked automatically, and so on. At each marking stage the user has the option of entering the manual mode if the automatically marked point appears wrong due, for instance, to a noisy trace. The program allows for the scoring of single responses from a single stimulus presentation or double responses from a dual stimulus presentation, i.e. to CS and UCS in a conditioning paradigm.

Typically a 50 trial bilateral recording with 6 embedded double stimulus trials making 112 possible responses can be scored and logged in approximately 5 minutes. The output of the scoring process is a file containing values of SCL, SCR lat., amp, ris.t and rec.t/2 for each response.

REFERENCES

Allen, J. A., Armstrong, J. E., and Roddie, I. C. (1973). The regional distribution of emotional sweating in man. *J. Physiol.* (Lond.), **235**, 749–59.

Ax, A. F., and Bamford, J. L. (1970). The GSR recovery limb in chronic schizophrenia. *Psychophysiology*, **7**, 145–7.

Bagshaw, M. H., Kimble, D. P., and Pribram, K. H. (1965). The GSR of monkeys during orienting and habituation and after ablation of the amygdala hippocampus and infero temporal cortex. *Neuropsychologia*, **3**, 111–19.

Blank, I. H., and Finesinger, J. E. (1946). Electrical resistance of the skin. *Archs. Neurol. Psychiat., Chicago,* **56**, 544–57.

Brown, C. C. (1967). A proposed standard nomenclature for psycholophysiological measures. *Psychophysiology,* **4**, 260–4.

Bull, R., and Gale, A. (1974). Does the law of initial value apply to the galvanic skin response? *Biol. Psychol.,* **1**, 213–28.

Bundy, R. S. (1973). The effect of previous responses on the skin conductance recovery limb. *Paper presented to a meeting of the Society for Psychophysiological Research, Galveston, Texas.*

Bundy, R. S. (1977). Electrodermal activity as a unitary phenomenon. *Paper presented to the meeting of the Society of Psychophysiological Research, Philadelphia.*

Bundy, R. S., and Fitzgerald, H. E. (1975). Stimulus specificity of electrodermal recovery time: an examination and reinterpretation of the evidence. *Psychophysiology,* **12**, 406–11.

Carrie, C., and Heemeyer, R. (1936). Untersuchungen über die chemischen Substanzen auf der Haut II Über das Vorkommen von Kochsalz und Cholesterin auf der Haut. *Archs. Derm. Syph. (Berlin),* **173**, 606–11.

Christie, M. J. and Venables, P. H. (1972). Site, state, and subject characteristics of palmar skin potential levels. *Psychophysiology,* **9**, 645–9.

Darrow, C. W. (1933). The functional significance of the galvanic skin reflex and perspiration on the backs and palms of the hands. *Psychol. Bull.,* **30**, 712.

Depue, R. A., and Fowles, D. C. (1973). Electrodermal activity as an index of arousal in schizophrenics. *Psychol. Bull.,* **79**, 233–8.

Edelberg, R. (1967). Electrical properties of the skin. In C. C. Brown (Ed.), *Methods in Psychophysiology,* Williams and Wilkins, Baltimore.

Edelberg, R. (1968). Biopotentials from the skin surface: the hydration effect. *Ann. New York Acad. Sci.,* **148**, 252–62.

Edelberg, R. (1970). The information content of the recovery limb of the electrodermal response. *Psychophysiology,* **6**, 527–39.

Edelberg, R. (1971). Electrical properties of the skin. In H. R. Elder (Ed.), *A Treatise on the Skin,* Vol. 1. Wiley, New York.

Edelberg, R. (1972a). The electrodermal system. In N. S. Greenfield and R. A. Sternbach (Eds), *Handbook of Psychophysiology.* Holt, New York.

Edelberg, R. (1972b). Electrodermal recovery rate, goal-orientation, and aversion. *Psychophysiology,* **9**, 512–20.

Edelberg, R. (1978). A new look at the initial value effect in the measurement of skin conductance response amplitude. *Paper presented to the 18th Annual Meeting of the Society for Psychophysiological Research, Madison.*

Edelberg, R., and Burch, N. R. (1962). Skin resistance and galvanic skin response. *Archs. Gen. Psychiat.,* **7**, 163–9.

Edelberg, R., Greiner, T., and Burch, N. R. (1960). Some membrane properties of the effector in the galvanic skin response. *J. Appl. Physiol.,* **15**, 691–6.

Edelberg, R., and Muller, M. (1977). The status of the electrodermal recovery measure: a caveat. *Paper presented to the 17th Annual Meeting of the Society for Psychophysiological Research, Philadelphia.*

Féré, C. (1888). Note sur des modifications de la résistance électrique sous l'influence des excitations sensorielles et des émotions. *C. R. Séanc. Soc. Biol., Ser. 9,* **5**, 217–9.

Fletcher, R. P., O'Riordan, P. W., Spaven, D., and Venables, P. H. (1979). A system for skin conductance measurement. In preparation.

Floyd, W. F., and Keele, C. A. (1936). Further observations on changes of potential and EMF recorded from human skin. *J. Physiol. (Lond.)*, **86**, 23P–25P.

Fowles, D. C. (1974). Mechanisms of electrodermal activity. In R. F. Thompson and M. M. Patterson (Eds), *Methods in Physiological Psychology. Vol. 1: Bioelectric Recording Techniques. Part C: Receptor and Effector Processes*, Academic Press, New York.

Fowles, D. C., and Venables, P. H. (1970). The effects of epidermal hydration and sodium reabsorption on palmar skin potential. *Psychol. Bull.*, **73**, 363–78.

Fowles, D. C., and Schneider, R. E. (1974). Effects of epidermal hydration on skin conductance responses and levels. *Biol. Psychol.*, **2**, 67–77.

Goodall, McC. (1970). Innervation and inhibition of eccrine and apocrine sweating in man. *J. Clin. Pharmacol.*, **10**, 235–46.

Grice, K. A., and Bettley, F. R. (1966). Inhibition of sweating by poldine methosulphate (Nacton). *Br. J. Derm.*, **78**, 453–64.

Grings, W. W. (1953). Methodological considerations underlying electrodermal measurement. *J. Psychol.*, **35**, 271–82.

Grings, W. W. (1974). Recording of electrodermal phenomena. In R. F. Thompson and M. M Patterson (Eds), *Methods in Physiological Psychology. Vol. 1: Bioelectric Recording Techniques. Part C: Receptor and Effector Processes*, Academic Press, New York.

Gruzelier, J. H., and Venables, P. H. (1972). Skin conductance orienting activity in a heterogenous sample of schizophrenics. Possible evidence of limbic dysfunction. *Journal of Nervous and Mental Disease*, **155**, 277–87.

Gullickson, G. R. (Ed.) (1973). *The Psychophysiology of Darrow*, Academic Press, New York.

Hord, D. J., Johnson, L. G., and Lubin, A. (1964). Differential effect of the law of initial value (LIV) on autonomic variables. *Psychophysiology*, **1**, 79–87.

Katkin, E. S. (1965). Relationship between manifest anxiety and two indices of autonomic response to stress. *J. Personality Social Psychol.*, **2**, 324–33.

Katkin, E. S., and McGubbin, R. J. (1969). Habituation of the orienting response as a function of individual differences in anxiety and autonomic lability. *J. Abnorm. Psychol.*, **74**, 54–60.

Kimble, D. P., Bagshaw, M. H., and Pribram, K. H. (1965). The GSR of monkeys during orienting and habituation after selective partial ablations of the cingulate and frontal cortex. *Neuropsychologia*, **3**, 121–8.

Kimmel, H. D., and Hill, F. A. (1961). A comparison of two electrodermal measures of response to stress. *J. Comp. Physiol. Psychol.*, **54**, 395–7.

Lader, M. H. (1970). The unit of quantification of the GSR. *J. Psychosom. Res.*, **14**, 109–10.

Lader, M. H., and Montagu, J. D. (1962). The psycho-galvanic reflex: a pharmacological study of the peripheral mechanism. *J. Neurol. Neurosurg. Psychiat.*, **25**, 126–33.

Levy, J. K., Igarashi, M., Ledet, J. C., and Reschke, M. F. (1977). Electrodermal response in the squirrel monkey. *Percept. Mot. Skills*, **45**, 943–8.

Lockhart, R. A. (1972). Interrelations between amplitude, latency, rise time and the Edelberg recovery measure of the galvanic skin response. *Psychophysiology*, **9**, 437–42.

Lockhart, R. A., and Lieberman, W. (1975). A new model for understanding the GSR waveform. *Paper presented to the Annual Convention of the Western Psychological Association, Sacramento*.

Lockhart, R. A., and Lieberman, W. (1976). Factor structure of the electrodermal response. *Paper presented to the Society for Psychophysiological Research, San Diego*.

Lowry, R. (1977). Active circuits for the direct linear measurement of skin resistance and conductance. *Psychophysiology*, **14**, 329–31.

Lykken, D. T. (1968). Neuropsychology and psychophysiology in personality research. In E. F. Borgatta and W. W. Lambert (Eds), *Handbook of Personality Theory and Research*, Chap. 7, Rand McNally, Chicago.

Lykken, D. T. (1971). Square wave analysis of skin impedance. *Psychophysiology*, **7**, 262–75.

Lykken, D. T., and Venables, P. H. (1971). Direct measurement of skin conductance: a proposal for standardization. *Psychophysiology*, **8**, 656–72.

Martin, I., and Rust, J. (1976). Habituation and structure of the electrodermal system. *Psychophysiology*, **13**, 554–62.

Maulsby, R. L., and Edelberg, R. (1960). The interrelationship between the galvanic skin response, basal resistance, and temperature. *J. Comp. Physiol. Psychol.*, **53**, 475–9.

McCleary, R. A. (1950). The nature of the galvanic skin response. *Psychol. Bull.*, **47**, 97–117.

Mednick, S. A. (1974). Electrodermal recovery and psychopathology. In S. A. Mednick, F. Schulsinger, J. Higgins, and B. Bell (Eds), *Genetics, Environment and Psychopathology*, North Holland, Amsterdam.

Mednick, S. A., and Schulsinger, F. (1968). Some pre-morbid characteristics related to breakdown in children with schizophrenic mothers. In D. Rosenthal and S. S. Kety (Eds), *The Transmission of Schizophrenia*, Pergamon, New York, pp. 267–91.

Mednick, S. A., Schulsinger, F., Teasdale, T. W., Schulsinger, H., Venables, P. H., and Rock, D. R. (1978). Schizophrenia in high-risk children: sex difference in pre-disposing factors. In G. Serban (Ed.), *Cognitive Defects in the Development of Mental Illness*. Brunner/Mazel, New York. Chap. 9, pp. 169–97.

Miller, L. H., and Shmavonian, B. H. (1965) Replicability of two GSR indices as a function of stress and cognitive activity. *J. Personality Soc. Psychol.*, **2**, 753–6.

Miller, R. D. (1968). Silver–silver chloride electrodermal electrodes. *Psychophysiology*, **5**, 92–6.

Montagu, J. D., and Coles, E. M. (1966). Mechanism and measurement of the galvanic skin response. *Psychol. Bull.*, **65**, 261–79.

Montagu, J. D., and Coles, E. M. (1968). Mechanism and measurement of the galvanic skin response: an addenum. *Psychol. Bull.*, **69**, 74–6.

Neumann, E., and Blanton, R. (1970). The early history of electrodermal research. *Psychophysiology*, **6**, 453–75.

Nicolaidis, S., and Sivadjian, J. (1972). High frequency pulsatile discharge of human sweat glands: myoepithelial mechanism. *J. Appl. Physiol.*, **32**, 86–90.

O'Gorman, J. (1978). Method of recording: a neglected factor in the controversy over bimodality of electrodermal response in schizophrenic samples. *Schizophrenia Bull.*, **4**, 150–2.

Prokasy, W. F., and Kumpfer, K. L. (1973). Classical conditioning. In W. F. Prokasy and D. C. Raskin (Eds), *Electrodermal Activity in Psychological Research*. Academic Press, New York. Chap. 3

Rein, H. (1929). Die Elekrophysiologie der Haut. In J. Jadassohn (Ed.), *Handbuch der Haut und Geschelechtkrankheiten I. Part 2*. Springer: Berlin. Chap. 6 pp. 43–91.

Rickles, W. .H., and Day, J. L. (1968). Electrodermal activity in non palmar sites. *Psychophysiology*, **4**, 421–35.

Rothman, S. (1954). *Physiology and Biochemistry of the Skin*. University of Chicago Press, Chicago.

Schiefferdecker, P. (1917). Die Hautdrusen des Menschen und det Saugetiere ihre biologische und rassenanatomische Bedeutung, sowie die Muscularis sexualis. *Biol. Zbl.*, **37**, 534–62.

Schiefferdecker, P. (1922). Die Hautdrüsen des Menschen und det Säugetiere, ihre biologische und rassenanotomische Bedeutung, sowie die Muscularis sexualis. *Zool. Stuttgart*, **27**, 1–154.

Schultz, I., Ullrich, K. J., Frömter, E., Holzgreve, H., Frick, A., and Hegel, U. (1965). Mikropunktion und elektrische Potentialmessung an Schweißdrusen des Menschen. *Pflügers Arch. ges. Physiol.*, **284**, 360–72.

Silverman, A. J., Cohen, S. I., and Shmavonian, B. M. (1959). Investigations of psycho-physiologic relationships with skin resistance measures. *Journal of Psychosomotic Research*, **4**, 65–87.

Simon, W. R., and Homoth, R. W. G. (1978). An automatic voltage suppressor for the measurement of electrodermal activity. *Psychophysiology*, **15**, 502–5.

Slegers, J. F. S. (1967). A mathematical approach to the two step reabsorption hypothesis. *Mod. Probl. Pediatrics*, **10**, 74–88.

Stern, J. A., and Walrath, L. C. (1977). Orienting responses and conditioning of electrodermal responses. *Psychophysiology*, **14**, 334–42.

Surwillo, W. W., and Quilter, R. E. (1965). The relation of frequency of spontaneous skin potential responses to vigilance and age. *Psychophysiology*, **1**, 272–6.

Tarchanoff, J. (1889). Décharges électriques dans la peau de l'homme sous l'influence de l'excitation des organes des sens et de différentes formes d'activité psychique. *C. R. Séanc. Soc. Biologie, Ser. 9*, **41**, 447–51.

Tarchanoff, J. (1890) Über de galvanischen Erscheinungen an der Haut des Menschen bei Reizung der Sinnesorgane und Dei verscheidenen Formen der Psychischen Tätigkeit, *Pflügers Arch. ges. Physiol.*, **46**, 46–55.

Thomas, P. E., and Korr, I. M. (1957). Relationship between sweat gland activity and electrical resistance of the skin. *J. Appl. Physiol.*, **10**, 505–10.

Tregear, R. T. (1966). *Physical Functions of the Skin*. Academic Press, London.

Trolander, H. W. (1967). The measurement of biological temperatures. In C. C. Brown (Ed.), *Methods in Psychophysiology*, Williams and Wilkins Baltimore. Chap. 4.

Tursky, B., and O'Connell, D. N. (1966). Survey of practice in electrodermal measurement. *Psychophysiology*, **2**, 237–40.

Venables, P. H. (1974). The recovery limb of the skin conductance response in 'high risk' research. In S. A. Mednick, F. Schulsinger, J. Higgins, and B. Bell (Eds), *Genetics, Environment and Psychopathology*. North Holland, Amsterdam.

Venables, P. H. (1977). The electrodermal physiology of schizophrenics and children at risk for schizophrenia: Current controversies and developments. *Schizophrenia Bull.*, **3**, No. 1, 28–48.

Venables, P. H. (1978). Psychophysiology and psychometrics. *Psychophysiology*, **15**, 302–15.

Venables, P. H., and Christie, M. J. (1973). Mechanisms, instrumentation, recording techniques and quantification of responses. In W. F. Prokasy and D. C. Raskin (Eds), *Electrodermal Activity in Psychological Research*. Academic Press, New York. Chap. 1.

Venables, P. H., Fletcher, R. P., Mednick, S. A., Schulsinger, F., and Cheeneebash, R. (1979). Aspects of development of electrodermal and cardiac activity between 5 and 25 years. In preparation.

Venables, P. H., and Martin, I. (1967a). Skin resistance and skin potential. In P. H. Venables and I. Martin (Eds), *A Manual of Psychophysiological Methods*. North Holland, Amsterdam. Chap. 2.

Venables, P. H. and Martin, I. (1967b). The relation of palmar sweat gland activity to level of skin potential and conductance. *Psychophysiology,* **3**, 302–11.

Venables, P. H., and Sayer, E. (1963). On the measurement of skin potential. *Br. J. Psychol.,* **54**, 251–60.

Wang, G. H. (1964). *Neural Control of Sweating.* University of Wisconsin Press, Madison.

Weiner, J. S., and Hellman, K. (1960). The sweat glands. *Biol. Rev.,* **35**, 141–86.

Zahn, T. P. (1976). On the bimodality of the distribution of electrodermal orienting responses in schizophrenic patients. *J. Nerv. Ment. Dis.,* **162**, 195–9.

D

Techniques in Psychophysiology
Edited by I. Martin and P. H. Venables
© 1980, John Wiley & Sons Ltd.

CHAPTER 2

Non-invasive Measurement of Peripheral Vascular Activity

J. R. JENNINGS, A. J. TAHMOUSH, & D. P. REDMOND

1 INTRODUCTION

A primary function of the cardiovascular system is the exchange of nutrients and waste products for each cell of the body. An increase in the metabolic demands of any group of cells requires a balanced cardiovascular response so that a local increase in blood flow occurs without compromising the blood supply of other areas. Thus, the metabolic requirements imposed by an action, such as hurling a missile, will be associated with a supportive cardiovascular adjustment. The significance of such a necessary concomitance between cardiovascular regulation and behaviour has long been recognized (e.g. Roy and Sherrington, 1890; Cannon, 1939; Sokolov, 1963); however, the accurate measurement of vascular responses in man is a continuing challenge.

In this chapter, we will review the major non-invasive techniques available for the measurement of peripheral vascular activity. Discussions of invasive techniques may be found in Harper, Lorrimer and Thomas (1970) and in Hwang and Normann (1977). The photometric examination of vascular events, strain gauge and volumetric plethysmography, impedance plethysmography, and Doppler or ultrasound techniques will be reviewed. The photometric section is emphasized due to the widespread use of optical techniques among psychophysiologists, and the availability of new information based on recent investigations led by A. Tahmoush. Introductory sections discuss vascular physiology and measurement issues common to the techniques. The sections discussing specific techniques are arranged so that general information is presented first and more complex issues are presented later.

Psychophysiologists for the most part have employed photoplethysmography and used 'blood volume' and 'blood volume pulse' as dependent measures. Figure 2.1 illustrates a typical analog record showing these measures. The top channel shows blood volume, a direct current (d.c.) coupled recording at relatively low amplification. The bottom channel shows blood volume pulse, the same signal seen on the blood volume channel but amplified and filtered to eliminate slow changes in baseline. Both blood volume and blood volume pulse are frequently scaled in terms of millivolts or millimetres of chart deflection, arbitrary units with undetermined physiological significance. The use of these arbitrary and non-physiological units limits the interpretation of the optical measures, since plethysmography results cannot be compared between laboratories, individuals, or even within individuals on different occasions.

For the non-invasive measurement of vascular activity, the transfer function relating the measure of interest, e.g. blood flow, to the obtained index, e.g. millimetres of chart deflection, is unknown. Non-invasive measurement implies that a feature of the measure of interest is detected at the surface of the body. The non-invasive measures to be discussed are based on different features of the vascular events of interest: the photometric technique on optical features, the volume technique on distensibility features, the impedance technique on electrical features, and the Doppler technique on sound features. In no case is the relation precisely known between the feature as measured at the surface and the vascular event of interest. Thus, problems of calibration, and the issues raised by the use of indirect *indices* as opposed to direct measurements will receive central attention in this chapter.

An understanding of the general physiology of blood flow provides the necessary background for understanding non-invasive measurement techniques. In Figure 2.1, for example, the blood volume label implies that this signal measures the amount of blood in the area studied while the blood volume pulse label implies pulsatile changes in this volume. In fact, however, the photometric technique only measures changes in the optical

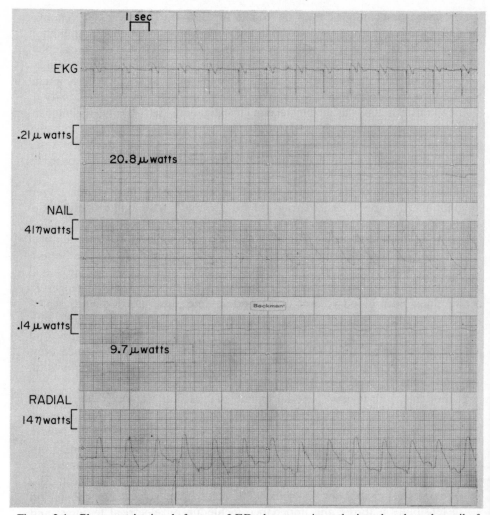

Figure 2.1   Photometric signals from an LED-phototransistor device placed on the nail of the third finger and over the radial artery at the wrist. The top tracing is an EKG signal. For each vascular site, the top tracing shows the d.c. signal at low gain; the lower tracing shows the pulsatile signal obtained by filtering low frequency components (TC = 1 s) and amplifying the signal. Calibrations are for light sensed in power units. See text

characteristics of the tissues in the measurement site. The relationship of the blood volume and blood volume pulse changes to the photometric signal must be either experimentally or theoretically examined. Thus, we will briefly discuss the physiology of blood flow to develop a context for the discussion of non-invasive techniques. Readers are referred to Burton (1972), Ruch and Patton (1974), or Guyton, Jones and Coleman (1973) for a more thorough treatment of basic physiology. A summary of psychophysiological investigations using plethysmography is also useful reading (Cook, 1974; Brown, 1967).

2 GENERAL PHYSIOLOGY OF BLOOD FLOW

2.1 Characteristics of blood flow

The heart pumps approximately 6 litres of blood per minute on the average, that is, during each stroke, or systole, about 75 millilitres of blood are forced from the left ventricle into the aorta (Guyton, Jones and Coleman, 1973). This volume of blood is distributed through a branching network of vessels decreasing in size, from large arteries to arterioles to capillaries, and thence back up in size to the large veins. The pulsatile component of flow is gradually attenuated, and virtually absent in the venous side of the circulation. On the arterial side, each systolic pulse wave is superimposed upon a changing but continuous level of flow, sustained by the elastic property of the large arteries. These arteries store a portion of the energy and volume of each cardiac ejection, releasing this during the post-ejective or diastolic phase of the cardiac cycle,

The determinants of the blood flow in this complex biological network of vessels are not precisely understood (Hwang and Normann, 1977). However, certain fundamental relationships are known for fluid flow through tube-shaped vessels, and these relations can be used here for a first approximation to understanding flow phenomena. Three principal factors determine the level of flow in an isolated vessel: first, pressure gradient along the length of the vessel; second, the radius of the vessel; and third, the viscosity of the fluid. Flow in the cardiovascular system is complicated by factors within the cardiovascular system but extrinsic to the isolated vessel. The volume and impetus of flow entering the isolated vessel depends upon the heart and the intervening vessels. The resistance to flow imposed by the vasculature beyond the vessel further affects the rate of flow. Since blood vessels are not rigid, flow is influenced by the intrinsic property of the vessel to expand with increasing pressure, and to recoil as pressure decreases. Flow is altered by this property, since with increasing pressure for instance, radius of the segment is increased (increasing flow) while volume and energy are 'absorbed' (decreasing the flow). In summary, primary relationships exist between flow, pressure, vessel radius, and fluid viscosity. These relationships are influenced by cardiac performance, the characteristics of both proximal and distal vascular beds, and the property of compliance. Since flow is both pulsatile and continuous in nature, these relationships are constantly changing throughout the cardiac cycle.

In physiologic systems, blood vessel *radius* exerts by far the most important regulating influence on vascular flow. Elastic and other connective tissue components of the vessel wall modulate the passive response of lumen size to pressure changes. These tissues may be altered by chronic effects such as disease and ageing. Of greatest interest to the psychophysiologist, however, is the active control of vascular diameter from innervated smooth muscle present to a significant degree in the smaller arteries, veins, and arterioles. Subject to both direct neural and neurohumoral stimulation, vascular smooth muscle provides the major control over regional distribution of blood flow. Small arteries, and to a greater extent, the (so-called) precapillary arterioles, control the entry of blood into particular organs, either by their constriction, or in some instances by their dilation (which allows blood to shunt directly from artery to vein, bypassing the capillaries). Both functions operate in the skin, and are particularly important to thermoregulation (Burton, 1972). The net effect of such vascular control on the arterial side of the capillaries is the peripheral resistance presented to the volume output of the heart, and hence, the regulation of the arterial blood pressure. Variation of vessel size on the venous side has more indirect effects on the circulation: venous circulation, especially that in the splanchnic bed, serves to some extent as a blood reservoir. The capacity of the venous bed modulates total blood volume and the rate at which blood returns to the heart. On a beat-to-beat basis, venous return affects both heart rate and stroke volume, and hence, blood pressure and total blood flow.

The neural regulation of circulation via control of vessel diameter is of primary concern to the psychophysiologist, and often, the main purpose of monitoring cardiovascular function is to obtain an index of autonomic nervous system function. The effects on cardiac performance and vascular smooth muscle of humoral substances, such as calcium, the catecholamines or angiotension and other vasoactive polypeptides, should not be neglected in assessing short-term regulation of circulation. Still, the sympathetic nervous system predominates as the mediator of abrupt alterations in systemic, regional, or segmental blood flow. Modulation of a continuous but rhythmically varying adrenergic vasoconstrictive tone is the main mechanism for response to numerous environmental stimuli. Sympathetic vasodilator nerve fibres exist, but are far less potent than vasoconstrictive ones, and are in general confined to the service of striated muscle bundles (Barcroft and Swan, 1953). Parasympathetic dilator fibres are thought to be restricted to specific organs, such as the salivary glands, genitalia, bladder and rectum (Burton, 1972). The investigator may thus find that evaluation of peripheral vascular flow is a useful index of sympathetic/adrenergic activity. He should remain alert, however, to the number of possible reservations upon neural interpretations of observed vascular changes. More detailed discussion of the integrated control of vasculature may be found in Mellander and Johansson (1968), Korner (1971), Rushmer (1976), and Ruch and Patton (1974).

Returning to another variable which influences flow, in Sir Isaac Newton's words, 'the lack of slipperiness between adjacent layers of fluid', the viscosity of fluids affects both the energy (or pressure) required to maintain a given volume flow, and the physical distribution of flow velocities within a vessel. Fluid near the walls of a vessel flows less rapidly than that in the centre, so that a velocity gradient occurs which is (ideally) parabolic in form. The presence of red blood cells, i.e. the hematocrit, greatly affects the viscous properties of blood. Furthermore, flow phenomena in turn affect the distribution of blood cells in the plasma, so that the hematocrit is not necessarily uniform throughout any vascular segment. For instance, cells tend to aggregate in the centre of larger vessels, flattening out the parabolic distribution of flow, and in small vessels, especially arterioles, plasma is relatively diluted and viscosity lessened by local factors. Finally, various degrees of turbulence may occur depending on flow velocity, viscosity, and the anatomical form (branches and constrictions) of vessels. All in all, the effects of viscosity are somewhat variable and subject to small changes in vessel size and pressure gradients. (See Burton, 1965 and 1972, for more detailed discussion.) For brief experiments involving either large vessels or vascular segments (e.g. forearm) such effects may be reasonably ignored. However, detailed examination of microscopic flow phenomena, influenced greatly by viscosity and cell distribution, may eventually provide more exact means of indirect measurement of blood flow regulation.

2.2 Flow waveforms at different sites

The appearance of any pulsatile flow waveform will depend largely on the site from which it is recorded and the particular measurement technique. Furthermore, changes in observed amplitudes, time intervals or waveforms are determined not only by local vascular or neuro-vascular events but may result from alterations elsewhere in the cardiovascular system. That is, such observations do not necessarily speak to the *mechanisms* of change.

The various techniques discussed in this chapter differ considerably in terms of the physical principles involved, and each measures different features of vascular events. From laboratory to laboratory, the response characteristics of transducing instruments, electronic filters, signal processors, and recorders may vary, giving rise to different waveforms. Finally, the elementary distinctions and relationships between vascular measures having similar waveshape should be borne in mind: pressure (dyn/cm^2); volume flow (cm^3/min); flow velocity (cm/s); flow acceleration

(cm/s^2). The following discussion surveys typical pulsatile waves in order to identify their basic morphology. Some of the more important physical influences on waveform will be mentioned.

2.2.1 Flow in arteries

Figure 2.2 presents a diagrammatic representation of four arterial waveforms displayed in relation to an electrocardiogram signal. The waveforms are drawn from McDonald (1974) and are based on ciné and electromagnetic flowmeter techniques applied to dog arteries and represent flow *velocity*. The four waveforms are from : (a) the ascending aorta as it leaves the left ventricle of the heart; (b) the abdominal aorta, a distal segment of less diameter than the descending aorta; (c) the femoral artery of the upper limb; and (d) the saphenous artery (a small artery in the hind limb). The radii of these vessels decrease from approximately 1 cm to less than $\frac{1}{4}$ cm; the amount of elastin in the walls of these arteries similarly declines (Burton, 1972).

All four waveforms show the pulsatile flow induced during each cardiac cycle. The initial steep upsweep of the curve reflects the sudden onset of flow caused by ventricular contraction and ejection of blood. The steepness of the upsweep depends primarily on the volume ejected by the heart and the elastic distention of the arterial system prior to the outflow of blood to the remaining vasculature. Flow begins to decrease after maximum pressure is achieved, but continues, due to the elastic recoil of the artery as well as ongoing ventricular ejection. The smooth decrease in flow is temporarily interrupted by the dicrotic notch, which marks the closure of the aortic valve and the end of cardiac systole. Thereafter; in diastole, the elasticity of the arterial system stores the energy of cardiac ejection, gradually releasing arterial volume through the capillaries into the veins.

Flow velocity comparisons between the four waveforms of Figure 2.2 show first a clear decrease of peak flow velocity with decreasing size, which is expected from the relationship of flow to vessel radius. The second feature of note is the decrease in the slope of the upsweep of the waveform. The systolic pressure wave is damped, due to the increasing influences of outflow and the different effects of the elasticity of the peripheral vessels. In the ascending aorta, flow quickly returns to a zero baseline as elastic recoil is transformed into flow. In the saphenous artery, the dissipation of the stored elastic energy in the arterial tree has led to flow continuing through virtually the whole cardiac cycle. Likewise, the dicrotic notch is less clearly marked.

Timing of the peripheral arrival of the pulse waves, relative to the ECG, defines the pulse propagation time. Indices based on this measure can be related to the elasticity of the system, the velocity of propagation being greater in the more rigid system. Since with greater pressure, vessels are

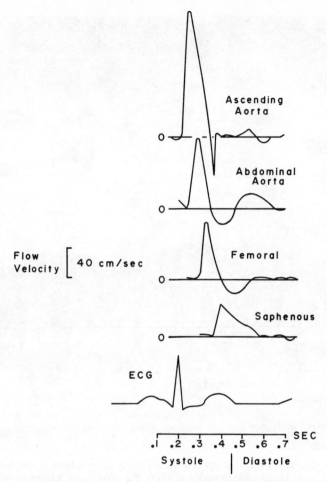

Figure 2.2 Idealized representation of the blood flow waveforms obtained at different vascular sites. The EKG signal is presented to illustrate the differences in time between cardiac events and vascular events at the different sites. The figure is based on recordings presented in McDonald (1974). (Used with permission of Edward Arnold Ltd)

more distended hence more rigid, Steptoe (1976) (see also Chapter 4) has proposed propagation time as an index of beat-by-beat blood pressure.

2.2.2 Vascular bed of the finger

The finger represents a common, but complex measurement site, compared to arterial sites. The sizes of the arterioles, capillaries, and venules involved are 20 micrometres or less in diameter, making direct invasive

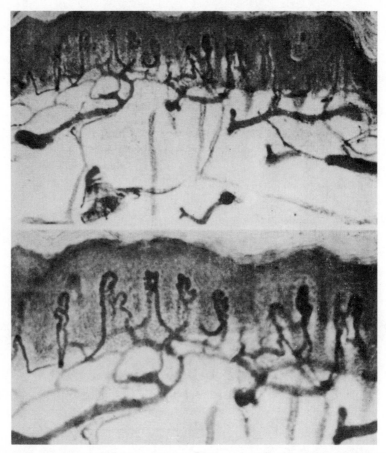

Figure 2.3   Vascular plexus of normal skin. These sections from tissue in which the vessels have been injected with carmine show the disposition of the capillary loops in the papillae, and the subadjacent horizontal vascular plexuses in the upper dermis with their ascending and descending communications. Upper ×65, Lower ×125. From Percival, Montgomery and Dodds (1962). (Used with permission of Churchill Livingstone)

measurement difficult. Figure 2.3 presents an anatomical section showing density and geometry of the vessels within the vascular bed of the finger pad. This figure suggests the difficulty of considering any non-invasive measure to involve any singular type of vessel—rather, any waveform is a complex composite reflecting from arterioles, capillaries, and venules. Note, nevertheless, that waveforms from the finger pad (Figure 2.1) are similar to those from the saphenous artery (Figure 2.2).

The finger pad is of interest to psychophysiologists because of the concentration of arterioles with ample sympathetic constrictor control. Thus, waveform variations observed in the finger are likely to reflect in large part local sympathetic activity. While changes in waveform are yet a function of cardiac changes (e.g. stroke volume), this difficulty may be resolved to some extent if concurrent measurements are taken at a larger vessel such as the radial artery. Radial artery signals should reflect cardiac changes fairly clearly, but should be differentially less sensitive to small vessel changes than waveforms derived from the finger pad (cf. Lawler and Obrist, 1974; Obrist and coworkers, 1974). A second advantage of such joint measurement is the computation of pulse wave propagation time (Steptoe, 1976).

2.3 Implications for measurement

The above brief discussion suggests a few obvious cautions concerning the controls necessary for plethysmographic measurement in the psychophysiology laboratory. First, anything which artificially changes the radii of vessels must be very carefully avoided. The clearest example of this are heavy transducers which distort the vascular bed. Second, position of the transducer may be critical when composite sites such as the finger are employed. Slight variations in site of measurement may produce significant variations in the composition of vessels assessed. Third, related cardiovascular changes, such as blood pressure and heart rate, should be assessed as well, since observed changes in a vascular measure cannot be interpreted as purely peripheral sympathetic vasomotor activity. Fourth, hydrostatic pressure variation due to position relative to the level of the heart must be controlled. Both posture and position of the measurement site must be constant. Fifth, temperature must be carefully observed. Extremes of temperature will vary blood viscosity; however, the more important concern is the neural regulation of blood flow *vis a vis* body temperature. Room temperature and humidity must be closely regulated and measurement devices must not induce temperature changes at the site of measurement. A final concern is movement. By definition indirect measurements are made from the skin surface. Movement of either the person or the device will invariably alter the signal measured.

3 DATA ACQUISITION AND COMPUTER SCORING

Although initial transduction and amplification of plethysmograph signals are technique specific, most investigators will obtain analog signals corresponding to blood volume (steady state or d.c. signal) and blood volume pulse (pulsatile or a.c. signal). The blood volume signal is amplified by a direct current amplifier while the same signal is amplified using a time constant in the range of 0.1 to 1.0 second for the blood volume pulse. The time constant eliminates slow, large magnitude changes in the pulse signal thus allowing high amplification. Chart speeds for polygraph recording depend on the use of the data. If the blood volume is of primary interest a chart speed of 1 mm/s is adequate but speeds of 5 to 10 mm/s are minimal for examination of blood volume pulse.

Scoring of blood volume requires only the measurement of voltage at times of interest. The interpretation of such measures is technique specific and often difficult. Investigators of blood volume should be particularly aware of the rhythmic changes in signal amplitude induced at the respiratory rate and at approximately half that rate by the so-called 'vasomotor' rhythm or Traube–Hering wave. Assessment of such rhythmic changes may prove to be a useful dependent variable as discussed in Chapter 3 of this volume.

Scoring of blood volume pulse most frequently compares features of the pulse before, during and after a stimulus event. Alternate assessment might involve stimulation induced changes in the respiratory and 'vasomotor' rhythms.

Extraction of features of plethysmograph waveforms for beat-by-beat analysis, for all practical purposes, requires computer assessment. Programs have been developed for these purposes. Descriptions of two systems are readily available. One is a system developed at NIH and described in Gilbert (1968). Another system was developed by Ax and is described in part in the previous edition of this volume (Ax, 1967). Detailed descriptions may be obtained from Dr Ax at NOVA University, Fort Lauderdale, Florida. These systems seem workable, although both are oriented to the concurrent collection of a large number of physiological parameters—the NIH programs for invasively collected cardiovascular data from dogs and Ax's system to variables often collected in psychophysiology.

We, primarily D. Redmond, are developing a combination hardware/software system that fits our particular needs. This system is oriented primarily to collection of EKG and multiple plethysmograph signals and is designed to do as much processing off line as possible. Briefly, the system is based on time relative to the R-wave of the EKG combined with sampling of the analog plethysmograph signal at a 1 kHz rate. Consistent changes in slopes are used to define five features of interest (cf. discussion of physiology of flow): (a) initiation of pulse rise; (b) peak pulse amplitude; (c) dicrotic notch; (d) peak first derivative; and (e) peak second derivative. At each of these five events, time from R-wave and voltage level is stored. In addition, two areas are computed, one between pulse rise and dicrotic notch and a second one between the dicrotic notch and subsequent pulse rise.

4 VOLUMETRIC AND STRAIN GAUGE PLETHYSMOGRAPHY*

4.1 General description

Plethysmography, in the strict meaning of the word, applies to the fullness or volume of an object. Volume and strain gauge techniques remain true to this definition. Volumetric measures of limbs were accurately taken well before the advent of electronic transducers and polygraphs (see Barcroft and Swan, 1953; Hyman and Windsor, 1961; Lombard and Pillsbury, 1902).

The basic principle of both volumetric and strain gauge techniques is straightforward. Under resting conditions blood provides the primary source of changes in the volume and girth of a limb. More specifically, changes in blood vessel diameter will occur: (a) due to changes in blood pressure and flow; and (b) due to direct neural influence on vessel walls. Volumetric changes in the limbs will reflect such changes in vessel size.

The volume technique senses change in limb volume by enclosing the limb and observing displacement of an enclosed medium, e.g. air or water. The strain gauge technique senses change in volume by measuring changes in limb girth. A mercury-in-rubber gauge is employed, which changes its electrical resistance when its length is changed. The brevity of this section does not reflect the importance of these techniques, but rather the availability of excellent papers (cited in context) describing the details of the methods.

4.2 Attachment and apparatus

The basic apparatus for volume plethysmography is a chamber which encloses the limb segment to be measured. Figure 2.4 illustrates plethysmographs constructed for the measurement of three different limb segments. The enclosed segment must be free to expand or contract; and thus change pressure or force in the medium inside the plethysmograph. For this reason, the junction between the limb and the plethysmograph is critical. An air or water tight seal must be maintained without constraining the limb. This has been generally accomplished by placing the limb segment in a thin rubber sleeve and then attaching the ends of this sleeve to the aperture(s) of the plethysmograph. An adjustable gasket may then be placed loosely around the limb to restrain the rubber sleeving in the case of the water filled plethysmograph. The sensitivity of air pressure to changes in temperature has led many investigators to prefer water filled plethysmographs which can be equipped with heating systems to produce a constant temperature medium. In practice air filled plethysmographs have

---

*The assistance of Dr Loring Rowell is gratefully acknowledged for providing an initial set of references and also critically reading an initial draft of this section.

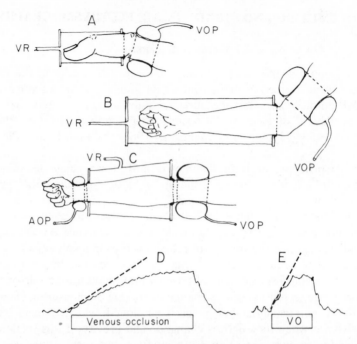

Figure 2.4   Types of plethysmographs are illustrated for measuring blood flow by venous occlusion. A, for finger (skin flow). B, for lower arm plus hand. C, for forearm alone (mostly muscle flow). D, typical record of the changes of volume when the veins are occluded in hand or forearm. E, typical record for the finger, where the venous reservoir is much smaller and a new steady state is reached in a few heartbeats. The broken line is the initial tangent from which the rate of arterial inflow is estimated. VR, connection to volume recorder. VOP, connection to supply of venous-occlusion pressure (e.g. 60 mm Hg). AOP, to arterial-occlusion pressure (e.g. 160 mm Hg). VO, venous occlusion. From Burton, A.C. (1972). *Physiology and Biophysics of the Circulation*, 2nd Edn. Copyright 1972 by Yearbook Medical Publishers Inc., Chicago. Reproduced with the permission of Yearbook Medical Publishers

been used primarily with small segments such as fingers and toes. While many volume recorders have been devised, diaphragm strain/pressure gauges are in common use (e.g. Stratham P23 series, Hewlitt Packard Model 270). Details of the construction of water filled plethysmographs may be found in Wood (1965), Greenfield, Whitney, and Mowbray (1963), and Abrahamson (1967). Air filled plethysmography is described in Lader (1967) and Burch (1977).

By substituting a measure of changes in girth of the limb for changes in volume, the size and clumsiness of the volumetric system may be avoided. In the seminal paper on strain gauge plethysmography, Whitney (1953) presents arguments suggesting that little accuracy is lost by replacing the volume plethysmograph with a mercury-in-rubber-type strain gauge. This type of gauge expands and contracts with changes in the segment, i.e. the force required to expand the gauge is minimal. The lengthening and shortening of the gauge changes the resistance of the mercury column encased in the rubber. This resistance change can then be recorded using a Wheatstone bridge or similar circuit.

The gauge circles the limb segment and is joined by a holder which may be adjusted to change the length and thus the tension of the gauge. The gauge must always be at some tension in order for changes in length of the gauge to be directly proportional to changes in electric resistance. Temperature compensation for the gauge is desirable in some situations (see Youdin and Reich, 1976). Whitney (1953) provides details of construction and application. Shapiro and Cohen (1965) have provided further suggestions for gauge construction.

4.3 Basis of measurement

Volume plethysmography assumes that measured volume changes in a segment are a direct function of blood volume changes in that segment. Blood volume changes must be transmitted through the tissue to produce corresponding changes in the plethysmograph medium. Information is not available concerning the transfer function relating blood volume changes to surface body volume changes. Problems of precision are ameliorated, however, as measurement of a whole segment provides an average estimate of blood volume, which can be expected to be more stable than estimates collected from small areas of tissue.

Strain gauge plethysmography grew out of volume plethysmography and assumes that an accurate measure of volume may be obtained from a measurement of girth. By making a number of reasonable assumptions, Whitney (1953) was able to derive volume from girth. As a derived volume measure, the strain gauge technique is clearly based on the same principles as the volumetric technique.

4.4 Calibration

Calibration of a volume plethysmograph is accomplished by injecting known volumes of medium into the plethysmograph and noting the response of the system. This calibrates the volume response and linearity of the system, but does not provide a physiological calibration in terms of blood flow or volume.

Calibration of the strain gauge involves defining an accurate and known relationship between limb girth and strain gauge length. This relationship is complicated by the constraining influence on limb girth exerted by the strain gauge. Whitney (1953) provides a thorough description of the calibration procedure. After an initial determination of length–resistance relationships, the gauge is mounted on the limb with a fixed distance separating the ends of the gauge. The gauge is then calibrated by decreasing this distance by a known amount, d. The galvanometer output is then related to this change in distance. Decreasing the distance between ends of the gauge has two effects: lengthening the gauge and compressing the tissue of the limb. The more compressible the tissue, the less lengthening will occur. Thus, the calibration takes into account the influences of the restraint on limb expansion induced by the gauge. Whitney expresses his measure as per cent variation in limb girth and presents arguments that this may simply be doubled to yield a per cent variation in limb volume. Some investigators have calibrated the gauge electrically or by length changes independent of tissue compressibility, but errors may result from such calibration (Greenfield, Whitney, and Mowbray, 1963; cf Strandness and Bell, 1965). As with the volume plethysmograph, the strain gauge calibration relates the presumed outcome of a vascular change, limb girth, to the output of an instrument. A direct calibration in terms of blood flow or volume is not usually performed.

4.5 Critique of the technique

Volume plethysmography is the oldest and most generally accepted of vascular measurement techniques. It is clearly the favoured measure of total segment blood volume. The major criticism of the technique is its cumbersomeness and the difficulty of maintaining airtight or watertight seals without unduly constraining the limb. As for all non-invasive techniques, the transfer function relating vascular change in the tissue to the measured index (in this case volume displacement) is not precisely known. Whitney (1953) and Landowne and Katz (1942) provide critical discussions of the technique.

Strain gauge plethysmography's primary advantage is the provision of a reasonably accurate estimate of limb volume using an easily applied and simply employed gauge. Like volume plethysmography, it has been widely used and has been shown to yield reproducible and meaningful results. Simplifying assumptions are necessary to relate girth to volume and to adequately account for tissue elasticity (Whitney, 1953); however, the assumptions appear to be useful and reasonable approximations to the actual situation.

4.6 Application

The primary application of both strain gauge and volume techniques has been as a measure of segmental blood flow using the venous occlusion method. This method attempts to isolate a limb segment using occluding cuffs so that only arterial inflow into the segment is measured. One or more pneumatic cuffs are used in conjunction with either a strain gauge or volume plethysmograph. Figure 2.4 illustrates pneumatic cuff placement with a volume plethysmograph for three measurement sites. The use of the cuffs may be illustrated by considering a hypothetical vascular measurement of the forearm (see Greenfield, 1960). As shown in Figure 2.4(C) an initial cuff, AOP, is placed distal to the plethysmograph and above the wrist. This cuff isolates the segment of interest. When inflated above maximum systolic pressure, vascular events in the hand are prevented from affecting the forearm measurement. A second cuff, VOP, is placed on the arm above the plethysmograph. When inflated to a pressure below systolic (50 to 100 mm of mercury), this cuff serves to occlude the venous return to the heart. A measure of blood flow is derived from the changes in volume of the forearm resulting from the inflow of blood with the venous return blocked. When calibrated, the plethysmograph record from either a volume or strain gauge transducer will reflect millilitres of flow per second per 100 ml of limb volume.

Sample venous occlusion records obtained for blood flow assessment are shown in Figure 2.4(D) and (E). Cuff occlusion above the plethysmograph (VOP) is indicated by the arrow and the record shows the expected increase in volume recorded by the plethysmograph. Blood flow is calculated by fitting a straight line, as indicated in the figure, to the initial segment of the volume rise. The slope of this line is the blood flow in ml/s. This figure is then related to the volume (ml) of tissue assessed by the plethysmograph to yield ml/100 ml/sec. The variety of records obtained and attendant problems of line fitting are discussed in Greenfield (1960). A frequently encountered problem not evident in Figure 2.4, is the occurrence of a cuff artifact, an initial signal increase due to the mechanics of cuff inflation (Lansdowne and Katz, 1942). Depending on the artifact appearance, the 3 or 4 seconds following the artifact are sometimes suitable for flow determination (Greenfield, Whitney and Mowbray, 1963).

The validity of the venous occlusion technique is generally accepted, although questions about the technique have been raised at various times. Rapid inflation of a cuff causes known changes in the vascular bed as congestion occurs (Lansdowne and Katz, 1942). By assessing blood flow over the initial beats after occlusion (see Figure 2.4), the venous occlusion technique attempts to minimize the influence of these physiologic reactions to the cuff. Investigators have been concerned about reflex reactions to cuff inflation (e.g. Gaskell and Burton, 1953); however, to date these concerns have not been shown to be well-founded (Greenfield, 1960). Raman, Van Huyse and Jageneau (1973) have suggested on the basis of an electromagnetic flowmeter comparison that the venous occlusion technique underestimates blood flow. Such comparisons must however be considered in relation to the difficulty of the comparison. The flowmeter measures flow velocity in a single artery. The flowmeter signal may be appropriately integrated over time but it remains unclear what volume of tissue the artery actually supplies, and whether it is the same as that assessed by the occlusion technique. Similar problems of specifying and relating measures based on different principles arise frequently when comparing vascular techniques. Exercise and environmental physiologists (e.g. Johnson, Brengelmann, and Rowell, 1976), have consistently found the venous occlusion technique to provide reliable and meaningful estimates of blood flow. Williams (e.g. Williams and coworkers, 1975) has successfully employed the venous occlusion technique to study changes in forearm flow during different cognitive tasks.

A second important application of volume plethysmography has been the study of venous congestion. Wood (1965) has discussed the use of a cuff (analogous to cuff VOP in Figure 2.4) inflated between 0 and 30 mm of mercury to observe changes in limb volume due to venous congestion. This method does not produce a measure of venous flow but a function relating congesting pressure to increasing volume of the veins. This function can then be used to index the state of the veins across conditions of interest.

Both strain gauge and volume plethysmographs may be employed without the use of occluding cuffs. This application allows the examination of beat to beat changes often of interest to psychophysiologists. Without occluding cuffs, however, arterial and venous events cannot be separated and capillary and venous events will significantly influence the vascular signal (Parrish and coworkers, 1963). As is the case with the photometric and impedance techniques, however, arguments can be made that pulse amplitudes or related features are an index of blood flow under certain conditions. The analytic separation of arterial and venous events may not be critical for certain topics, e.g. vascular changes associated with penile erection (Rosen and Keefe, 1978). Lader (1967) has discussed the use of volume plethysmography without cuffs.

5 PHOTOPLETHYSMOGRAPHY

5.1 General description

Optical techniques commonly used by psychophysiologists for the examination of vascular events were developed as alternatives to volumetric plethysmography. Since the optical signals appeared quite similar to those obtained by volumetric plethysmography, the optical techniques were referred to as photoplethysmography (the optical recording of changes in tissue volume). The term photometry may, however, be more appropriate for a technique which measures light rather than volume. In addition to being technically correct, photometry does not contain the physiological implications associated with the term photo-plethysmography.

As a measurement of light, the photometric examination of vascular events should be based on optical principles. However, optical properties of the transducer, of tissue, and of coupling of the transducer to the measurement site have not been taken into account by most investigators. The result has been a virtual standstill in the applicability of optical techniques since the pioneer work of Hertzman (Hertzman, 1937a; Hertzman, 1937b; Hertzman, 1938; Hertzman and Dillon, 1940; Hertzman and Roth, 1942; Hertzman, Randall and Jochim, 1946; Hertzman, Randall and Jochim, 1947). Ultimately, photometric results may be related to the scattering and absorbing properties of biologically heterogenous tissues (Longini and Zdrojkowski, 1968). Recent experimental data have suggested that the optical properties of blood vary with changes in blood flow (Moaveni, 1970; Pisharoty, 1971). Such results from biophysical investigations encourage further development of photometric techniques.

The transducers employed in photometry combine a light source, such as a tungsten lamp or light emitting diode, with a light detector, commonly a photoconductive cell or a phototransistor. Two configurations are generally used: when the light source and detector are adjacent to each other, light *backscattered* from the examination site is measured by the detector; when the faces of the light source and detector are placed on opposite sides of an examination site, light *transmitted* through the tissues is measured.

The amount of light measured by the detector depends upon: (a) the geometric relationship and optical characteristics of both light source and detector; (b) the spectrum, total amount, direction and spatial distribution of light emitted by the source; (c) the occurrence of boundary conditions* between either the light source or detector and the measurement site; (d) the sensitivity of the detector; and (e) the optical properties of the tissues in the measurement site. Since the only variables of interest are tissue optical properties related to vascular events, the photometric technique must be designed to minimize the number of confounding variables which may affect the light measured by the detector.

---

*A boundary condition occurs when the light passes through media of different refractive indices. At the optical boundary, the distribution of light in space may be dramatically altered.

5.2 Transducer attachment and recording apparatus

5.2.1 Transducer description

The photometric transducer employed for all the studies reported here is the light-emitting diode (LED), phototransistor device marketed as the STRT-850A by Sensor Technology.† The choice is not based on any known superiority of the STRT-850A as a photometric transducer, or on the non-availability of similar devices from other manufacturers. Rather, it is based on the extensive amount of optoelectronic data collected by this laboratory for the Sensor device. As a class, LED phototransistor devices may be superior to previously used optical transducers. Brown (1967) and Weinman (1967) have previously discussed other photometric transducers, e.g. the photoconductive cell.

The Sensor transducer is a small, compact, lightweight device which employs a source and adjacent detector. As illustrated in Figure 2.5, the Sensor transducer measures $4.45 \times 6.09 \times 4.49$ mm, with variation in each dimension of ± 0.35 mm (Figure 2.5), and weighs 0.4 g. The centres of the LED and the phototransistor (PT) are in the same plane and separated by 2.21 mm with a displacement variation of ± 0.13 mm. The LED measures 0.38×0.38 mm, and the phototransistor, 0.89×0.89 mm. A black plastic partition separates the two elements and extends to the transducer face so that light from the LED does not directly irradiate the phototransistor. The two components are encapsulated in a clear epoxy material (Hysol).

5.2.2 Attachment

The size and weight of the LED–phototransistor transducer permit attachment to virtually any skin site. Many investigators have ignored the difficult problems associated with attachment of photometric transducers to the skin surface. The common practice of taping a device to the skin or employing bulky housing units with spring tension produces significant alterations of the vascular bed at the measurement site. Attachment techniques should not lead to distortion or heating of the vascular area measured which would make physiological interpretation impossible. We have used three attachment techniques: a direct attachment to the skin; attachment to the fingers or toes with a holder; and attachment to the nail of the fingers or toes.

The direct attachment of the photometric transducer to the skin surface is shown in Figure 2.6. In order to minimize boundary conditions between the transducer and the skin, a thin layer of optical coupling medium is

†Sensor Technology, Inc., 21012 Lassen St, Chatsworth, Ca. 91311, USA.

PHYSICAL   DIMENSIONS   (mm)

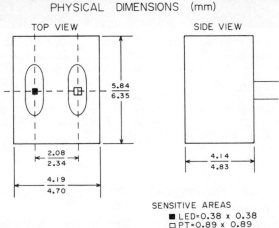

SENSITIVE AREAS
■ LED=0.38 x 0.38
□ PT=0.89 x 0.89

Figure 2.5   The Sensor Technology STRT–850A reflective
transducer. A photograph (upper) and the physical dimensions
(lower) of the transducer are presented

applied to the measurement site.* Stomaseal† is applied to the area
surrounding the measurement site. The face of the transducer rests directly
over the skin with the edges of the transducer adhering to the stomaseal.
Collodion is applied about the edges of the transducer to prevent any

*Dow Corning MDX 4-4210, Dow Corning Co., Midland, Michigan 48640, USA.
†Medical Products Division, Minnesota Mining and Manufacturing Co., St. Paul, Minn.
55701, USA.

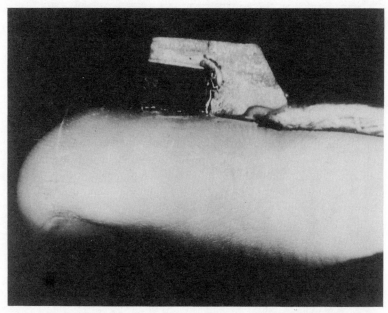

Figure 2.6 Sensor transducer attached to ventral surface of finger. Stomaseal has been placed along the edges of the transducer and collodion binds the transducer to the stomaseal. The clear material surrounding the transducer is a receptacle allowing different transducers to be 'plugged' into the same cable. Copyright © 1976, The Society for Psychophysiological Research. Reprinted with permission of the publisher from 'Characteristics of a light emitting diode-transistor photoplethysmograph', by A. J. Tahmoush, J. R. Jennings, A. L. Lee, S. Camp, and F. Weber, *Psychophysiology*, 1976, **13**, 357–62

displacement from the stomaseal. This technique permits continuous monitoring for several hours.

The direct application of the transducer to the skin applies an unknown amount of distortion to the measurement site. This distortion is insufficient to affect the vascular events in superficial arteries, but does affect the vascular events in cutaneous beds. If repeated applications of the transducer to the skin surface are required, distortion must be minimized in order to compare optical signals over several applications. Since we were unable to replicate optical signals from the finger pad on repeated applications with the stomaseal–collodion technique, finger and toe holders were designed. As shown in Figure 2.7, the finger is inserted above the body of the plexiglass holder (A), and two velcro straps (B) secure the finger in position. The ventral surface of the distal phalanx is available for application of the transducer (position C). The transducer (E), is attached

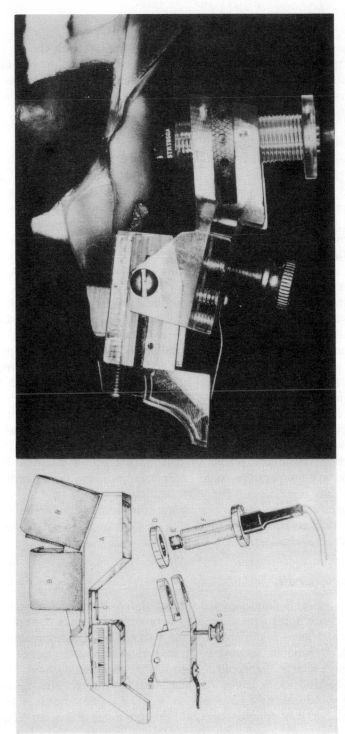

Figure 2.7 Finger holder for placement of Sensor transducer with a fixed alignment and controlled pressure. The body of the holder is indicated by A. B shows velcro straps. C is the opening in which the transducer is inserted. D is the ring which advances the transducer, E, on its threaded mount, F, into the opening C. Screw adjustments G control the angle of the transducer assembly while H controls the longitudinal axis of adjustment

to the plexiglass cylinder (F), and is positioned in contact with the finger surface by appropriate rotation of ring (D). Screw adjustments (G, H), permit alignment of the device with the curved contour of the skin surface. While the transducer is approaching the finger surface, light may be seen between the transducer and measurement site. Adequate placement is defined as the first position in which light is completely occluded by the finger surface–transducer interface.

Since the use of the holders requires considerable experience before reproducible placements are assured, we are currently exploring an alternative and simpler placement technique. For measurements of vascular events in a digital cutaneous site, the transducer is applied with stomaseal and collodion to the nail of the digit. Transducer application does not distort the underlying measurement site since the nail is relatively non-elastic. When transducers are simultaneously placed on the nail and finger surface, the signals are qualitatively similar in waveforms and exhibit similar changes to cold or auditory stimuli.

Heating of the measurement site is a potential problem which should be minimized in any attachment technique. Heat will tend to dilate the vasculature under study creating artificial measurements. Phototechniques using broad band (white) light characteristically produce significant heating which is often exacerbated by an attachment technique which prevents free air circulation. In the Sensor transducer, heat is produced by the passage of current through the LED and from the emission of infrared radiation. An unknown fraction of this heat is transferred to the tissue at the measurement site. In order to estimate possible temperature changes at a measurement site, a thermograph scan was performed immediately after the removal of a transducer placed on the finger for 30 minutes. No difference in surface temperature could be detected between the recording site and adjacent skin areas. Therefore, although some heating was probably imparted to the recording site by the transducer, the amount was either very small or its dissipation by the blood flow so fast that we were unable to detect local changes.

5.2.3 Recording apparatus

The recording apparatus employed for our studies is schematically shown in Figure 2.8. Since total light output is a function of LED current, a regulated current source is required for the LED. The phototransistor is employed with a variable resistor (R_E) in series with the emitter. A regulated supply voltage is applied across the phototransistor-resistor combination. The transistor current, I, which results from light striking the phototransistor produces a voltage across R_E. This photometric signal consists of a large d.c. component (2–5 V) and a small pulsatile a.c.

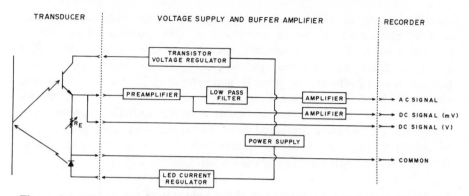

Figure 2.8 Block diagram of the circuit configuration employed with the Sensor LED-phototransistor device. Resistor R_E is varied between 1 and 3 kΩ to set phototransistor resistor gain

component (10–200 mV). The large d.c. component is buffered and recorded separately. The a.c. signal and small changes in the d.c. signal are amplified and recorded. Information and schematics are available for the voltage supply and buffer amplifier.*

5.3 Optical and electronic bases of the photometric measurement

5.3.1 Background

The optical characteristics of transducers are difficult to measure, and only a limited amount of information is available describing the characteristics of the light sources and detectors commonly employed. Brown (1967) and others have noted the broad spectrum of wavelengths emitted by the commonly used miniature tungsten light sources, and Weinman and his collaborators have examined the characteristics of the frequently used cadmium selenide photoconductive detectors (Weinman, Bicker, and Levy, 1960; Weinman and Manoach, 1962; Weinman, 1967; Weinman and Fine, 1972; Fine and Weinman, 1973; Weinman et al., 1977). Unfortunately, the output of the photoconductive cell is dependent on temperature and prior light exposure, as well as incident radiation (Weinman and Fine, 1972; Novelly, Perona and Ax, 1973).

The light emitting diode and phototransistor employed in the Sensor transducer are optoelectronic devices. The LED emits electromagnetic radiation as current flows through the diode, while the phototransistor converts the electromagnetic radiation striking the transistor into electrical

*Mr Alison Lee, Department of Military Medical Psychophysiology, Walter Reed Army Institute of Research, Washington, DC 20012, USA.

current. During the 1970s, a number of optoelectronic transducers became commercially available which combined a light emitting diode with a phototransistor. These transducers are inexpensive (costing. less than twenty dollars), and contain the necessary components required of a photometric transducer. A general understanding of the optoelectronic characteristics of the Sensor light source and detector is necessary for interpretation of the photometric signals obtained with this transducer. A qualitative treatment is presented here, and a more detailed presentation of the electronics can be found in most electrical engineering textbooks (Smith, 1971; Fitzgerald, Higginbotham and Grabel, 1967).

5.3.2 Optoelectronic characteristics of the light source

The LED in the Sensor transducer produces near-infrared light which is backscattered to excite the phototransistor. The optical characteristics of the LED have implications for the calibration and interpretation of photometric signals. For example, spectral distribution of emitted radiation is important as light of different wavelengths is not equally backscattered by tissue. In what follows, the light source spectrum, total light output of the LED, directional light distribution, and spatial light distribution will be discussed.

For the Sensor transducer, the light emitting diode is not directly accessible to optical measurements and the light source is defined as the face of the transducer above the light emitting diode. The LED employed in the Sensor device is a gallium arsenide crystal with an 'n' type tellurium doped region and a 'p' type zinc doped region. When current flows through the pn junction, kinetic energy is released in the form of electromagnetic radiation (photons). The wavelength of the radiation is determined by the energy band characteristics of the semiconductor material, and for the GaAs light emitting diode, the peak spectral output is at $0.94 \mu m$, with a bandwidth of $0.04 \mu m$. As seen in Figure 2.9, this is a good approximation to a monochromatic output; in comparison, tungsten emits a broad spectrum of wavelengths. Figure 2.9 also shows the close correspondence between the LED spectrum peak and the peak response characteristic of the silicon material used in the phototransistor.

Since the radiation emitted by the light source is a function of the current flowing through the LED, it is of importance to define the exact nature of this relationship. An understanding of this relationship is also important for calibration of the device and ultimately for estimates of the tissue area examined. A calibrated silicon photodiode–integrating sphere combination was employed to measure the total light output at five different currents for four devices.* The light source was positioned so that all the

*Optronic Laboratories, 7676 Fenton Street, Silver Spring, MD 20910, USA.

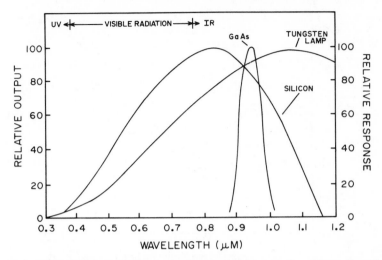

Figure 2.9   The relative spectral output of a tungsten lamp and a gallium arsenide light emitting diode is presented. The relative response of a silicon detector is presented for radiation in the ultraviolet (UV), visible, and infrared regions (IR)

emitted radiation entered the detector–sphere combination. As seen in Figure 2.10, a linear relationship was shown between forward current and total light output for the currents examined. From these curves, the current necessary to produce a given total light output can be calculated.

The total light output of itself is not sufficient to define the amount of light emitted to any given space. It is also necessary to determine the directional distribution of light leaving the source and spatial distribution of light energy on the surface of the source. For example, two light sources with the same total light output will produce different amounts of light at a given point in space if one emits a focused and the other a diffuse beam.

The directional distribution of light output for three light sources is presented in Figure 2.11. In this study, a reference Sensor phototransistor is used as the light detector. Each light source is placed 5 mm from the detector and optically aligned so that a maximum reading is obtained. The light emitting diode current for each device is arbitrarily set at 37 mA, and each light source is rotated in 5° increments from ± 50° of the normal.* As seen in Figure 2.11, the light source output is independent of angle when the source rotates from −30° to +20° from the normal. With larger rotations, the output decreases as the angle increases. The differences noted in the range of outputs between −20° to −50° and +20° to +50° is due to the asymmetrical location of the light emitting diode in the

*These measurements were performed in collaboration with Dr Edward Zalewski at the National Bureau of Standards.

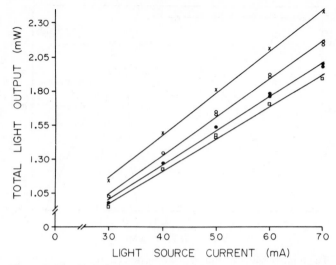

Figure 2.10   Relationship between light source current (mA) and total light output (mW) for four devices. The light source current is defined as the current flowing through the LED plus its biasing resistor. The light output is measured on each of three successive days for each current ($n = 3$)

transducer. The directional distribution of light output from each source is relatively similar. The voltage level offset noted between the distributions is probably due to differences in total light ouput from each source is sources.

As mentioned above, in addition to the directional distribution, the spatial distribution of light energy, i.e. the area from which light emanates, must also be measured to determine the amount of light projected in a given space. The pinhole imaging technique is employed to determine the spatial characteristics of the light source (see Tahmoush and coworkers, 1976a, 1976b). This technique involves placing an opaque screen containing a very small aperture midway between a light source and infrared film. According to geometric optics, the image formed on the photographic film should be identical to the area of the transducer light source which emits radiation. Since film exposure is proportional to the product of light intensity and time, a series of prints with progressively larger areas of film exposure were obtained by taking multiple pictures at progressively slower shutter speeds. With the largest area of film exposure defined as 100%, the relative amount of light emitted by different areas of the transducer light source can be determined.

The spatial distribution for a typical Sensor light source is shown in Figure 2.12 as a topographic display of the relative amount of light (as

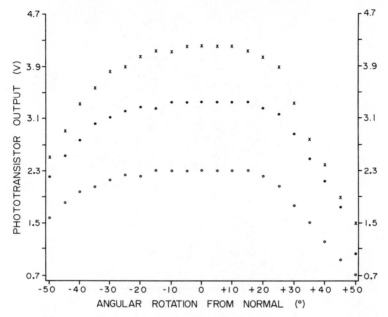

Figure 2.11   Angular distribution of light emitted by the Sensor light source. A reference phototransistor is employed to measure relative light intensity. Functions for three different LEDs are shown

indicated by the enclosing contours) radiating from within selected areas of the transducer light source. Approximately 75% of the light is emitted from an approximately circular area of radius 1.4 mm. Since the area of light emission is larger than the area of the light emitting diode, there is a significant amount of light scattering within the transducer. The topographic patterns of light output from three Sensor light sources are similar.

In summary, the Sensor light source has been shown to have the following optoelectronic properties: (a) the light spectrum approximates that of a monochromatic source; (b) the total light output is linearly related to the forward current over a wide range of LED currents; (c) the directional light distribution is similar across devices; and (d) the spatial light distribution is such that most of the light emanates from a small area.

5.3.3 Optoelectronic characteristics of the phototransistor

The properties of the transducer's detector must also be known before calibration is possible, and are important for interpretation of phostometric signals. Relationships will be examined between incident radiant flux and detector output, between the sensitivities of the different transducers, and

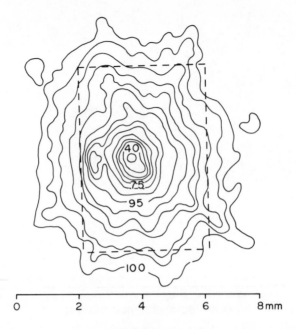

Figure 2.12 Light intensity topography of the face of the Sensor transducer. Numbered contours are the percentage of light output. The dashes outline the face of the transducer. Contours were obtained with a pinhole imaging technique (see text). Copyright © 1976, The Society For Psychophysiological Research. Reprinted with permission of the publisher from 'Characteristics of a light emitting diode-transistor photoplethysmograph', by A. J. Tahmoush, J. R. Jennings, A. L. Lee, S. Camp, and F. Weber, *Psychophysiology*, 1976, **13**, 357–62

between relative sensitivity and the angle at which light strikes the detector. Finally temperature and light exposure effects on detector output will be described.

The phototransistor in the Sensor device is a silicon npn transistor with a collector and an emitter which are n type semiconductors and a base which is a p type semiconductor. A photoelectrically generated current is induced by light energy striking the phototransistor. The relationship between transistor current, I, voltage across the transistor, V_{ce}, and incident radiant flux, Φ, striking the transistor was examined by using a Sensor LED with a known normal light output* as the source. The curves in Figure 2.13 are analogous to those of conventional npn transistors employed in the common emitter configuration.

*Optronic Laboratories, 7676 Fenton Street, Silver Spring, MD 20910, USA.

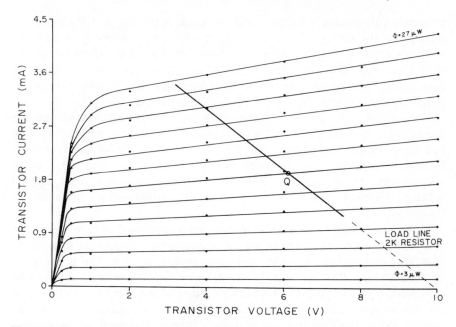

Figure 2.13 Phototransistor output current (I_c) as a function of supply voltage (V_{CE}), determined for thirteen different incident radiant flux (Φ) values. The solid diagonal line between the two axes is a load line for a resistance value (R_E) of 2 kΩ. Q is the operating point defined in the text

For a constant incident flux, e.g. 27 μW, the transistor current can be examined as a function of transistor voltage. When V_{ce} varies from 0–2 V there is a rapid increase in transistor current for any incident flux. For transistor voltages between 2–10 V and low incident flux, transistor current is relatively independent of transistor voltage. At higher incident flux, transistor current increases as voltage increases. This increase in transistor current may be due to changes in the thermally-generated current at the collector–base junction.

The basic relationship between incident light and transistor current is illustrated by the family of curves in Figure 2.13. In the determination of these curves, no resistor is included in the circuitry. For our specific application, however, a load resistor is placed in series with the emitter and the transistor is constrained to operate along the load line shown in Figure 2.13. This enables the measurement of transistor current in terms of voltage across the resistor.

The signal output of the phototransistor–resistor combination to radiant flux is expressed by the load line. With no incident flux, resistance is essentially infinite, the transistor current is essentially zero, and the entire supply voltage (10 V) is across the transistor. As incident flux increases, transistor current also increases and produces, according to Ohm's law, an increase in the voltage across the load resistor and conversely, a decrease in the voltage across the transistor. These changes are expressed by the load line. For example, at 15 μW of incident flux, the transistor is constrained to operate at point Q such that the supply voltage is proportioned between the transistor (6 V) and the load resistor (4 V).

The resistance value selected for each phototransistor–resistor combination is determined by the calibration procedure (Section 5.4). The operating range along the load line is restricted (solid line) so that transistor currents are between 1.0–3.5 mA. This operating range encompasses the range of photometric signals recorded from normal subjects (Section 5.7), and minimizes the nonlinearities inherent in transistors.

Photometric signals have traditionally been expressed in terms of a d.c. and an a.c. component, where the d.c. component corresponds to a steady state flux and the a.c. to small variations around the d.c. The relationship of steady-state flux to signal output may be determined by careful examination of Figure 2.13. Transistor voltage at any light flux is the value on the x-axis determined by the line drawn normal to it from the intersection of the load line and that flux. The signal output (voltage across the load resistor) is calculated as the difference between the supply voltage and the transistor voltage obtained above. In practice, the transistor characteristics shown in Figure 2.13 are not available, and the incident flux to signal output relationship is determined empirically.

Figure 2.14 shows the plot of steady-state flux against signal output for two transducers. Signal output was measured across the load resistor determined by the calibration procedure (see Section 5.4). The range of incident flux is that included within the operating section of the load line. The light source employed was a Sensor light emitting diode with a measured normal light output. These signals are analogous to the large d.c. component of the photometric signal illustrated in Figure 2.1 and schematically shown in Figure 2.8. A parabolic function best describes the relationship between incident flux and transistor output. Although the parabolic form is common to all detectors examined, the functions differ between transducers as suggested by Figure 2.14.

Pulsatile photometric signals similar to those obtained from subjects in Figures 2.1 and 2.22 require nanowatt pulsatile incident flux changes. These signals are 3 orders of magnitude less than the microwatt signals shown in the operating range of Figure 2.14. Hence, nanowatt changes in light should produce approximately linear changes in the output. It may be seen from Figure 2.14 that linear changes around an incident radiant flux of, e.g. 13 μW, will not show the same linear relation as changes around an incident flux of, e.g., 22 μW. These points are illustrated in the

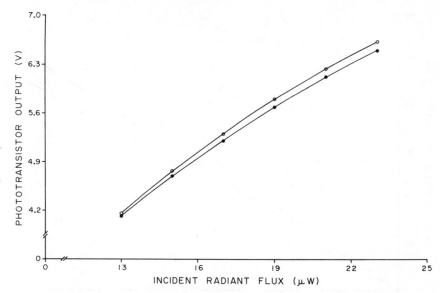

Figure 2.14 Phototransistor voltage output as a function of steady light flux in microwatts for two separate transducers. Parabolic approximations to the experimental points are shown. The range of incident flux approximates that observed for photometric measures in human volunteers

experimental data shown in Figure 2.15. Signal output is shown as a function of sinusoidal variation in incident flux around three levels of background flux. The slope of the linear relationship decreases as the non-varying incident flux increases, whereas the intercept is zero for each line. Therefore, the phototransistor response to sinusoidal variations in incident flux is dependent on the non-varying component of incident flux.

Since backscattered light from the measurement sites strikes the phototransistor at different angles, the relationship between signal output and the angle at which light strikes the detector was examined for three devices.* If the phototransistor is an ideal diffuse detector, the current response to a constant light source rotating about the detector would vary according to the cosine of the angle from the normal to the ray projected from the source to the detector. The relationship between transistor output and angle of irradiation is shown in Figure 2.16, in which the solid line is the function $3.5 \cos \theta$. For each transistor, the decrement in transistor output as the angle moves from the normal is greater than the cosine function, thus, the phototransistor does not behave as an ideal diffuse detector. Since the phototransistor is a silicon crystal, reflection from its

*These measurements were performed in collaboration with Dr Edward Zalewski at the National Bureau of Standards.

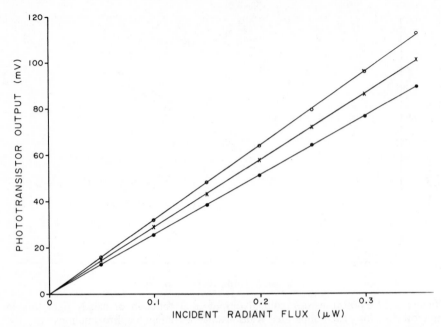

Figure 2.15 Phototransistor amplitude output (millivolts) as a function of amplitude changes in transient light flux (μW). From top to bottom, the lines are for 13, 17, and 21 microwatts of steady flux. Linear equations have been fitted to the data

surface probably accounts for the deviation from an ideal diffuse detector. In practice, this means that light entering the transistor normal to its surface will be disproportionately weighted in the transistor output.

Signal values from photoconductive detectors have been shown to be influenced by prior light exposure (e.g., Novelly, Perona, and Ax, 1973). Storage of the Sensor phototransistor in room light or in the dark does not, however, change the signal output (both a.c. and d.c. signals) when placed 3 mm from a reflecting surface (Tahmoush and coworkers, 1976a, 1976b).

Transistor sensitivity to temperature changes may affect the transistor incident flux responses described above. In order to examine the effect of environmental temperature on the transistor current, five devices were inserted into a constant temperature oil bath and the temperature varied from 24–40 °C. A change of 1 °C resulted in a mean change of approximately 4 mV (Tahmoush and coworkers, 1976a, 1976b). Since the d.c. signal for the finger of normal subjects is generally greater than 2 V, this change in phototransistor output with respect to temperature would be insignificant in most applications.

In summary, the signal output to the range of steady-state flux shown in Figure 2.14 is parabolic in form. As would be expected from this function,

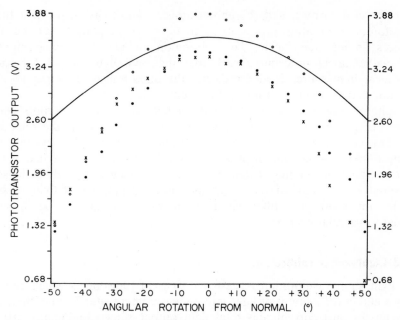

Figure 2.16   Phototransistor response to light at different angles of incidence. The response of an ideal diffuse detector is shown by the solid line. The three sets of data points are from different phototransistors. See text for methodology employed

the Sensor phototransistor has a linear response to small changes in incident flux about a fixed incident flux. The signal output to small changes in incident flux is dependent upon the steady-state flux. The signal output is influenced by the angle at which incident light strikes the detector but is not influenced by prior light exposure or significantly altered by commonly encountered changes in temperature.

5.4 Calibration

5.4.1 Background

A major deficiency in optical techniques for the examination of vascular events has been the absence of a calibration procedure. In order to compare the optical signals obtained with one transducer to those obtained with any other transducer, the optoelectronic characteristics of each transducer must be known. Section 5.3 described the similarities of the Sensor transducer with respect to: (a) light spectrum; (b) directional and spatial light distribution characteristics; and (c) phototransistor sensitivity to light incident at different angles. However, two important optoelectronic characteristics are not similar among transducers: (a) the total light output for a given forward current; and (b) phototransistor sensitivity to incident flux. Therefore, a calibration procedure is required to compensate for the differences among transducers. The calibration includes both experimental and mathematical procedures such that the total light output for each transducer light source is identical; and the phototransistor output is calibrated in terms of common units of incident radiant flux.

A photometric measurement based on light units (μW) permits comparison of photometric signals among transducers. However, the relationship between changes in photometric signals and vascular events still remains unknown. Definition of this relationship requires knowledge of the transfer function relating vascular events to changes in light intensity measured at the skin surface. Since the optical properties of living tissue are for the most part unknown, photometric units can not be directly related to vascular events.

5.4.2 Light source calibration

The light source calibration is designed to yield transducers which emit a known and equal amount of light into a measurement site. The relationship between forward current and total light output shown in Figure 2.10 is used to adjust the total light output for each light source. The linear relationship permits a simple adjustment in LED forward current to produce an arbitrarily chosen total light output. For our studies, we have operated the light source so that 1.5 mW of radiant flux are emitted. When this light enters a measurement site, radiant flux levels are obtained which are located within the operating range of the light detector (Figure 2.13).

Although it is preferable to have a quantitative forward current/total light output function for each light source, the measurements for this function require specialized optical equipment. An alternative procedure requires that one or a small number of light sources is calibrated and thereafter employed as the reference. If the forward current necessary to emit 1.5 mW total light output is experimentally determined for one device, a matching technique may be used so other sources are set to emit the same amount of radiation. For this procedure, we have employed a modified microscope and an arbitrarily chosen light detector as shown in Figure 2.17. The light detector is placed in the microscope stage holder and the reference light source is placed in the holder attached to the microscope support structure. The two devices are optically aligned by adjustment of the mechanical stage until a maximum detector signal is recorded with a digital voltmeter. The detector output to the calibrated reference light source (1.5 mW) at a known distance is determined. Light sources of unknown total light output can then be placed in the holder, replacing the reference source while maintaining the same distance

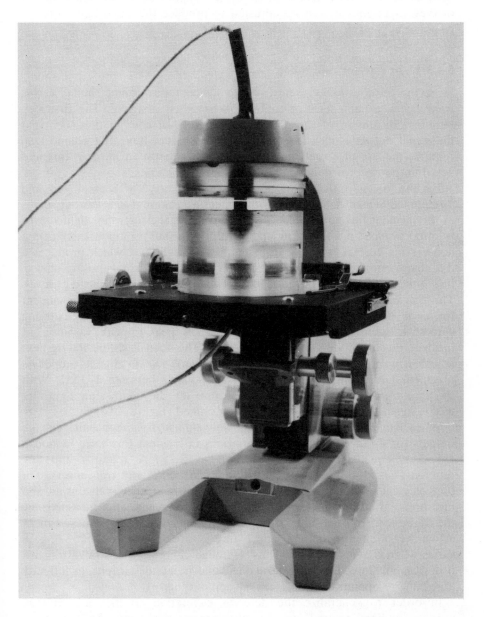

Figure 2.17 Student microscope modified to operate as an optical system allowing the three-dimensional alignment of transducers serving as light sources and receivers. Two transducers are shown mounted in the milled circular plexiglass

between source and detector. After optical alignment, the forward current of these light sources can be adjusted to produce the same light detector response as the reference source.

5.4.3 Light detector calibration

Since the phototransistor sensitivity to incident flux is not similar across transducers, a light detector calibration has been designed. The first step requires adjustment of the phototransistor–resistor combination such that the signal output is identical for a varying incident flux. The second step requires the use of a mathematical relationship between incident flux and signal output to provide a common scale of metric units.

For the first step, the microscope shown in Figure 2.17 is employed, and a reference Sensor light source with a measured normal light output serves as the incident flux source. A forward current to the reference light source is used which has two independently adjusted components: (a) a non-varying current resulting in a steady state light flux which produces a d.c. signal output; and (b) a sinusoidally varying current imposing an a.c. light output which varies signal output sinusoidally about the d.c. level. The non-varying forward current is adjusted so that the transistor current for each detector is identical, i.e. 2.25 mA. The sinusoidally varying current is then adjusted so that a $0.27 \, \mu\text{W}$ peak-to-peak variation of incident flux is produced at the detector. The load resistor, R_E, is next adjusted until a 100 mV peak to peak variation in signal output is obtained. Given this procedure, R_E usually varies between 1–3 kΩ. With the phototransistor–resistor combination thus set, the steady-state light flux to d.c. signal output function may be determined (Figure 2.14).

When five photometric transducers were adjusted as above, the voltage outputs for a range of sinusoidal variations in incident flux were identical. However, equalizing transistor currents at 2.25 mA requires imposing different steady state flux conditions in different transducers. In physiological use, light sources are set to a constant microwatt output and measurement site characteristics determine steady-state flux measured by the transducer. In brief, identical operating points cannot be achieved in an actual measurement situation, and Figure 2.15 demonstrates that a.c. gain varies when d.c. level varies. Thus, although calibration is straightforward if devices are forced to operate at the same transistor current, a difficulty arises due to operation at different current outputs.

In order to generalize the detector calibration so that a.c. voltage outputs obtained around any d.c. photometric signal may be compared, additional procedures must be performed. We are now testing three procedures: (a) an adjustment procedure in which a phototransistor with a base lead is employed as the light detector so that the detector is forced electrically to operate at a predetermined point; (b) a mathematical procedure in which the first derivative of the parabolic function relating signal output to steady-state incident flux is calculated and used to adjust for variations in the photometric transducer gain as the d.c. signal changes; and (c) an empirical procedure in which the a.c. gain to varying incident flux is determined at the d.c. signal observed during the physiological recordings. The empirically determined a.c. gain is multiplied with the a.c signal outputs to obtain photometric units. Functions such as those in Figure 2.15 will be obtained and can then be used as calibration curves for the specific a.c. signals observed in physiological measurements.

The calibration shown in some of the figures, e.g. Figure 2.1, was derived using the mathematical technique. A brief example will suffice to show the steps involved in deriving optical units. The technique is based on the experimentally determined parabolic function relating microwatts of incident steady-state flux to signal output of a particular transducer. The parabolic equation for one transducer in Figure 2.14 is:

$$V_0 = -1.095 + 0.412\Phi - 0.007\Phi$$

where V_0 is signal output and Φ is incident flux in microwatts on the phototransistor. The first derivative of a function at a point is the slope of the function at that point. For small changes along that function (i.e. $\Delta\Phi$ indicating small changes in light flux), this slope may be used to determine changes in V_0, signal output. For the device whose parabolic equation has just been presented, the derivative is expressed as:

$$V_0' = 0.412 - 0.014\Phi$$

Using the particular transducer from which the above equation is derived, both d.c. and a.c. signals obtained from a subject may be expressed in photometric units in the following way. The d.c. signal, in volts, is converted to microwatts by the relationship shown in Figure 2.14. The a.c. gain at this steady-state flux is determined by the derivative of the parabolic equation shown above. This a.c. gain in μW/mV is multiplied with the a.c. signal in mV to yield a.c. signals in μW photometric units.

In summary, the calibration procedure permits expression of signal output detected for any measurement site in photometric units, μW. Upon completion of the detector calibration procedure, it will be possible to compare transducer outputs for different measurement sites and different individuals.

5.5 Physiological basis of the photometric signal

The relationship between photometric signals and vascular events must be defined in order to make inferences about vascular events from the photometric data. It has generally been assumed that the d.c. component of the photometric signal is an index of total blood volume, and the a.c. component is an index of pulsatile changes in blood volume (Brown, 1967; Weinman, 1967). However, these assumptions have not been confirmed experimentally.

In an attempt to examine the physiological basis of the photometric signal, we have studied signals obtained with blood flow through an *in vitro* system (Figure 2.18). With this system, it is possible to examine the effects of changes in blood flow, red blood cell content, and vascular distensibility on the photometric signal. In addition, it is possible to compare the photometric signal to that obtained with an electromagnetic flowmeter.

The *in vitro* system consists of a Harvard infusion pump capable of producing either steady, pulsatile, or pulsatile flow about a steady flow. Rigid Tygon tubing is used to connect the components of the *in vitro* system. Statham pressure transducers are employed as shown in Figure 2.18 before and after the measurement site. The photometric transducer and an electromagnetic flowmeter are positioned in line with the direction of blood flow. The total system measures approximately one meter in length. The calibrated transducer is placed either on the rigid glass tubing or over an agar-encased dog artery. Outdated human blood is used for all the studies.

The general assumption that the a.c. photometric signal is an index of blood volume pulse may be tested by using a rigid glass cell in the system. If this assumption is valid, an a.c. photometric signal will not be observed in a rigid, non-distensible glass cell. As seen in Figure 2.19, a pulsatile a.c. signal does occur in the rigid system when a pulsatile change in blood flow is produced by the pump. The sinusoidal photometric signal is similar to that obtained with the electromagnetic flowmeter. Therefore, the a.c. component of the photometric signal is not exclusively an index of blood volume pulse.

In order to determine the basis of the a.c photometric signals obtained above, different fluids were examined using the *in vitro* system. When either hemolysed blood or plasma is pulsed through the glass cell, there is

IN VITRO SYSTEM

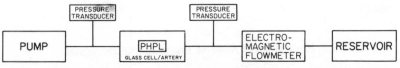

Figure 2.18 Block diagram of *in vitro* system for assessment of flow, pressure, and vessel compliance effects on the photometric signal

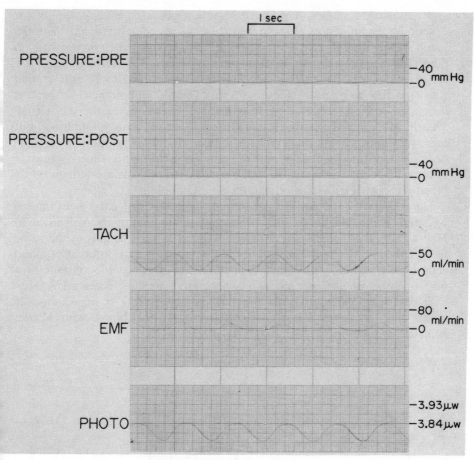

Figure 2.19 Pulsatile photometric signals obtained during pulsatile blood flow in the rigid glass system (Figure 2.18). Electromagnetic flowmeter (EMF), pressure (pre and post), and pump tachometer (TACH) signals are also displayed

no detectable pulsatile photometric signal. This suggests that the presence of red blood cells is necessary for the occurrence of a pulsatile photometric signal in a rigid system. Since the optical properties of blood have been shown to be dependent on blood flow (Moavini, 1970), the a.c. photometric signal may be an index of pulsatile blood flow. From theoretical considerations of red blood cells as light scattering objects, the orientation of red blood cells with flow changes may account for the a.c. photometric signals observed.

As previously discussed in the introduction, Section 2, the primary factors affecting blood flow are: pump output, viscosity, vessel diameter, and vessel distensibility. The *in vitro* system provides an opportunity for examining the influences of these factors on the photometric signal. With the pump output in the range of 0–100 ml/min, a small d.c. signal with no detectable a.c. component is observed for steady flow through the glass cell. The signal increases as steady flow increases from 1 to 10 ml/min, and then reaches a plateau (Figure 2.20). The d.c. photometric signal is dependent on the steady flow in a manner analogous to the a.c. signal. That is, variation of the d.c. signal with flow occurs with whole blood but not with either plasma or hemolysed blood. Additionally, the d.c. signal is dependent on the number of red cells present (Hct), and since viscosity is in turn dependent on hematocrit, the photometric signals are influenced by blood viscosity. Figure 2.20 illustrates all these points.

The relationship of vessel diameter to photometric signal was examined by varying the heights of the tubes containing the fluid. As shown in Figure 2.21, the d.c. signal is inversely related to tube heights at the same flow. This may be attributed to greater flow velocity and ordering of blood cells in the vessels with small diameters. Maintenance of constant flow across vessels of different diameters necessarily implies increased velocity with decreased diameters. Volume flow in Figure 2.21 is logarithmically scaled and linearizes the flow/signal functions for blood with known hematocrits seen in Figure 2.20.

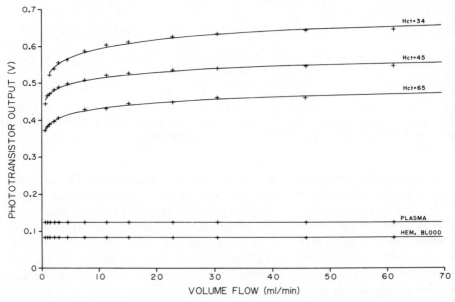

Figure 2.20 Phototransistor output as a function of steady or volume flow. Functions are shown for different hematocrits, plasma, and hemolyzed blood

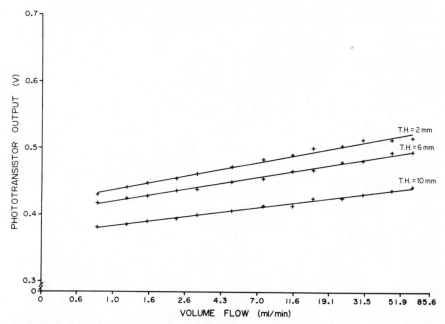

Figure 2.21 Signal output as a function of volume flow for glass tubes of three different heights (T.H.). Volume flow is logarithmically scaled. The system shown in Figure 2.18 was employed for these studies

Previous studies utilized rigid rather than compliant systems. The influence of vessel distensibility on photometric signals was examined with an agar-encased dog artery inserted in the *in vitro* system. Pulsatile signals resulted when whole blood was pulsed through the system. Figure 2.22 shows a typical pulsatile signal. Pulsatile signals were also obtained when either hemolyzed blood or plasma was used. Therefore, these studies have demonstrated that both ordering of red cells and vessel movement with flow contribute to the photometric signal.

These *in vitro* studies suggest that: (a) pulsatile photometric signals are possible in a rigid system and are dependent on the presence of red blood cells; (b) in a compliant system, vessel wall movement occurring with flow also contributes to the photometric signal; and (c) the d.c. signal is directly related to increased flow, inversely related to vessel diameter, and is dependent on blood viscosity.

The conclusions derived from the *in vitro* system may assist in interpretation of photometric signals from human subjects. Blood flow in superficial arteries is predominantly pulsatile. Signals from superficial arteries are comparable to those obtained in the compliant system. Blood flow in the finger bed is a combination of pulsatile and steady flow with

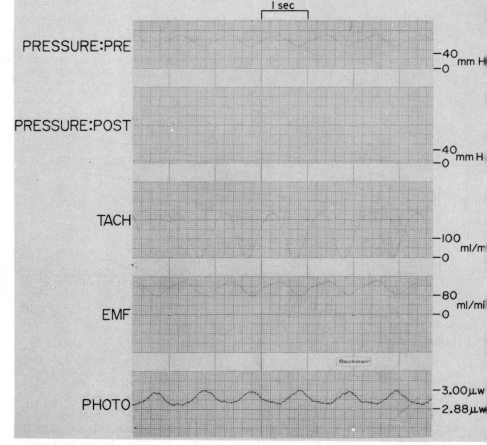

Figure 2.22   Pulsatile photometric signals obtained during pulsatile blood flow in a dog artery encased in agar (Figure 2.18). Electromagnetic flowmeter (EMF), pressure (pre and post), and pump tachometer (TACH) signals are also displayed

the pulsatile component predominating in the arterial circulation and the steady-state component predominant in the venous circulation. The *in vitro* studies suggest that arterial events in the finger bed contribute to the a.c. component and venous events contribute to the d.c. component of the photometric signal.

5.6 Critique

Many of the problems with previous optical devices have been discussed in the context of the advantages of the Sensor transducer. Problems such as bulk, heating of the tissue, and light history effects (e.g. Brown, 1967;

Novelly, Perona, and Ax, 1973) have been to a great extent eliminated. A continuing problem with optical techniques is the need for stable, replicable attachment. The use of an optical coupling medium and the attachment techniques described solve a portion of the attachment problem. Practice and care in attachment are, however, continuing necessities.

The absence of a photometric calibration system has been largely remedied by the work described. The detector calibration system remains to be completed, and further testing of the calibration system is necessary. In particular, the practical utility of the calibration for psychophysiological studies needs to be established.

As noted previously, an optical transducer with a base lead may be of importance for a convenient calibration procedure. Transducers designed for, rather than adapted for, photometry would be desirable.

The vascular area sampled by the Sensor transducer is undefined. We believe that only a limited cutaneous vascular bed directly below the device is studied. Evidence on the area assessed is not readily available, and studies probing this question should be initiated.

A related problem shared by most if not all vascular measurement techniques is the absence of a complete understanding of the physiological basis of the signal. Although *in vitro* studies have provided new insights into this basis of the photometric signal, these studies are only preliminary, and additional work is essential.

5.7 Applications

The small size of the photometric transducer makes possible the examination of vascular events in relatively homogeneous vascular beds. The a.c. photometric signal obtained by placement on several cutaneous areas is shown in Figure 2.23. The a.c. signals from the skin adjacent to the carotid artery, the cheek, and the skin over the temporal artery are illustrated. The pulsatile signals (time constant of 1 s) from the finger pad and carotid artery are similar in contour to those obtained from volumetric plethysmographs, impedance plethysmographs, and Doppler ultrasound techniques.

As seen in Figure 2.23, the pulsatile photometric signals obtained by placement on several cutaneous areas differ dramatically in both contour and amplitude. The a.c. signal from the skin adjacent to the carotid artery is barely detectable, and the signal from the cheek is small in amplitude without a recognizable dicrotic notch. The signal from the finger pad has an amplitude in the range of the carotid artery signal, with a dicrotic notch which is clearly defined and slightly lower on the down-slope than that of the carotid artery.

The skin adjacent to superficial blood vessels produces a very small a.c.

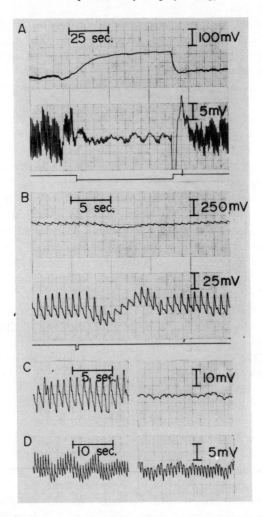

Figure 2.23   Photometric signals illustrating: (A) changes in the d.c. signal (upper) and a.c. signal (lower) from the finger pad during venous occlusion of the forearm (depressed section of the event marker); (B) changes in the d.c. and a.c. signals from the finger pad after an auditory tone 40 dB above threshold (even marker); (C) a.c. signals obtained from placement directly over (left) and adjacent to (right) carotid artery; and (D) a.c. signal obtained from placement over the temporal artery (left) and cheek (right). Time constant of 1 s for the a.c. signals. Copyright ©1976, The Society For Psychophysiological Research. Reprinted with permission of the publisher from 'Characteristics of a light emitting diode-transistor photoplethysmograph', by A. J. Tahmoush, J. R. Jennings, A. L. Lee, S. Camp, and F. Weber, *Psychophysiology*, 1976, **13**, 357–62

signal when compared to that obtained from placement over the artery. As seen in Figure 2.23, the pulsatile signal obtained from placement over the carotid artery, with vascular contributions from both the artery and the overlying skin, is dominated by vascular events occurring within the carotid artery. Therefore, the photometric technique provides a simple, non-invasive index of vascular events in superficial arteries.

The photometric signals are sensitive to physiological and psychological stimuli which affect vascular activity. During venous occlusion of the forearm with the sphygmomanometric pressure raised midway between the systolic and diastolic reading, there is a change in the d.c. signal accompanied by a decrease in the amplitude of the pulsatile signal from the finger pad (Figure 2.23). A transitory decrease in the d.c. signal associated with a decrease in the amplitude of the pulsatile signal occurs when an auditory tone 40 dB above threshold is presented (Figure 2.23).

The photometric pulsatile signal is also sensitive to procedures which alter sympathetic nervous system influences on the smooth muscle of small blood vessels. Post-ganglionic fibres from the stellate ganglion in the neck innervate the smooth muscle of blood vessels in the hand. When the stellate ganglion is surgically removed (stellate ganglionectomy) and the sympathetic nervous system innervation of the hand is interrupted, blood flow is increased. As seen in Figure 2.24, there is an eight-fold increase in the amplitude of the a.c. signal between measurements before and after sympathectomy. In the operated extremity, there is a two-fold change in the amplitude of the a.c. signal.

As illustrated above, available qualitative optical techniques provide a simple non-invasive measurement of vascular events. A quantitative methodology should result in greater applicability of optical techniques since it will be possible to compare vascular parameters obtained from the same subject over time or across subjects. As seen previously, this methodology is less simple and requires attention to details not considered in qualitative optical techniques. However, the advantages far outweigh the costs.

The optical measurement of blood flow is a powerful technique which has been seriously neglected by most biomedical engineers and physiologists. It is a relatively inexpensive technique when compared to electromagnetic flowmeters and ultrasound techniques. It permits simultaneous measurements of vascular signals from multiple sites.

The optical measurement of blood flow can be strengthened by additional information concerning the contribution of surrounding tissue to the optical signals. An optical model of tissue which permits predictions concerning the influence of changes in blood flow to changes in backscattered light is a major requirement for the future.

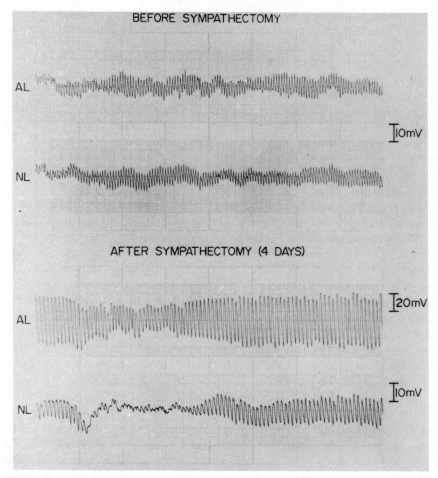

Figure 2.24   Photometric a.c. signals (TC = 1s) obtained before and after a unilateral sympathectomy performed for the relief of pain in the affected limb (AL). Signals from the non-affected limb (NL) are presented for comparison

6 IMPEDANCE PLETHYSMOGRAPHY

6.1 General description

Impedance plethysmography is a method of estimating blood volume pulse or volume flow which is based upon principles of electrical conductivity. Body fluids and tissues are, in a sense, ionic solutions and thus are conductors of electricity. Since blood is a conductive field, an increase in its volume should result in a measurable *decrease* in the electrical resistance, which, when it involves alternating current, is termed impedance.

By measuring impedance changes, volume changes may thus be inferred. As shown in Figure 2.24, if one juxtaposes simultaneously recorded volume plethysmograph tracings and *inverted* impedance tracings, remarkable congruence of the signals may be demonstrated (Brook and Cooper, 1957).

The quantitative and empirical relationships between resistance and volume apparent in this figure have been extensively discussed by such investigators as Nyboer, Kubicek, and VanDeWater. These positive relationships, as well as the theoretical and practical drawbacks, will be discussed in this section. More thorough surveys than can be presented here may be found in Nyboer (1970) and Markovich (1970).

6.2 Attachment and apparatus

6.2.1 Electrical relationships

Impedance (Z) is measured in ohms and is related to alternating voltage and current in the same way as resistance is related to direct current; that is, Ohm's law may be expressed as $E = IZ$ where I is the current and E is the voltage. This relationship allows impedance to be computed if a constant-current source is applied across a limb segment and variations in voltage are measured. Impedance assessment is complicated, however, by

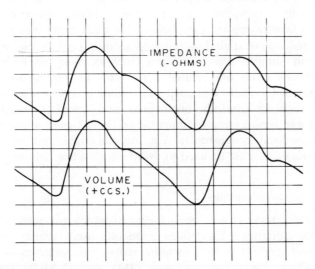

Figure 2.25 Concomitant volume and impedance plethysmographic waveforms taken from the same limb segments. The impedance waveform is inverted and scales adjusted to display similarity

the presence of three component factors: (a) 'pure' resistance, usually the quantity of primary interest; (b) capacitive reactance; and (c) inductive reactance. Capacitive reactance appears to be a particularly important quantity in biological tissue, while inductive effects are negligible (Hyman and coworkers, 1964). Fortunately, capacitive reactance may be minimized by the use of high-frequency (40 kilohertz or more) alternating current, which thus allows the primary assessment of the resistive component of impedance and simplifies the assessment of volume/impedance relationships. Capacitive reactance cannot be eliminated completely, however, and may become an important confounding influence when electrodes are attached improperly (Schwan, 1955).

6.2.2 Impedance apparatus

The expense of commercially available impedance devices increases with the degree of refinement. All produce amplified output signals which are usually directly compatible with standard recording instrumentation. Most provide both a separate direct-coupled or low-frequency output for recording of total or baseline segment impedance (Z_{total}), and a highly amplified a.c. coupled signal for transient or pulsatile changes (ΔX_{output}). The first derivative of the ΔZ_{output}, dZ/dt, is also often available. Some devices further provide for simultaneous recording of EKG which facilitates measurement of peripheral propagation time (PPT). A few devices may also internally compute a pulsatile impedance-to-volume or impedance-to-flow transform (see below) for each beat, or an average of beats, with analogue or digital outputs reported as 'cm^3' or 'cm^3/min'. Some models permit simultaneous recording from as many as eight pairs of sensor electrodes (with one source pair). This feature is useful for the study of regional blood flow phenomena (Hadjiev, 1972). The use of high frequencies requires carefully engineered and shielded instrumentation whose input and sensor circuitry must be precisely tuned, and if more than one system is used concurrently, e.g. on the right and left forearms, different frequencies must be used to avoid interference between sources.

6.2.3 Electrode considerations

Over the years, devices have been designed which variously utilize two, three, or four electrodes. Electrodes frequently used include circular spot electrodes and circumferential metallic strips, the latter made of steel, copper or silver, aluminium foil tape (3M), coated Mylar (duPont) or Velcro (Technit Confuzz). Electrodes are usually taped to the skin with conductive paste between the electrode and skin.

Figure 2.26(a) shows two-electrode (bipolar) and four-electrode

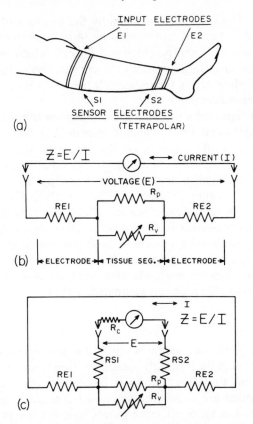

Figure 2.26(a) Electrode placement for calf segment. Sensor electrodes are omitted for bipolar methods. For volume equations (see text), the distance L is measured between E1 and E2 (bipolar) or S1 and S2 (tetrapolar). (b) Schematic of bipolar configuration. Voltage E is provided by the instrument, current I measured, and resistance (net R) computed. (c) Schematic of tetrapolar configuration. Current I is provided by the instrument, and E measured across sensor electrodes, with device in effect isolated by high impedance (R_c) of sensor circuitry

(tetrapolar) arrays with circumferential electrodes about the lower leg. In the bipolar arrangement, sensor electrodes (S_1 and S_2) are omitted; voltage (E) and current (I) are measured between the input electrodes (E_1 and E_2), the ratio, $E/I = Z$, computed, amplified, and recorded. In the tetrapolar arrangement, E_1 and E_2 provide a source of *constant* alternating current, while the voltage E is measured between sensor electrodes (S_1 and S_2).

Figures 2.26(b) and (c) schematize these two electrode arrangements. The leg segment is represented by resistors (R_p) arrayed in *parallel*; one of these is shown to be variable (R_v), representing the effect of pulsatile blood volume changes. The resistance imposed by the junction of the two excitor electrodes with the skin are represented by *series* resistance (R_{E1} and R_{E2}). The tetrapolar sensor circuitry (Figure 2.26(c)), which measures E, has a high input impedance (R_c), so that little current flows through the sensor electrodes. Thus, their series resistance (R_{S1} and R_{S2}) is negligible, in terms of affecting the measurement.

The last point represents the major advantage of tetrapolar over bipolar arrangements. Measured limb segment impedances are usually less than 200 Ω, and the pulsatile changes of the order of 0.1–0.2 Ω (or 0.1%) (Nyboer, 1970, pp. 72–81). Skin electrodes may constitute a series resistance of 500 Ω or more depending on the preparation, uniformity, and stability of application (Nyboer, 1970, p. 29). Thus, in bipolar plethysmography where series resistance affects the measured current, the recordings are more sensitive to contact factors, noise, and mechanical artifact. In tetrapolar arrays, current is held constant irrespective of series resistance, so that electrode artifact is less of a problem. Empirically, for reasons not clear, bipolar methods also tend to estimate pulse volume erroneously (Nyboer, Kreider and Hannapel, 1951).

6.2.4 Safety

Since impedance plethysmography is one of the few circumstances in which an electrical current is purposefully caused to flow through human subjects, particular attention to safety factors is incumbent upon the investigator. The currents applied are radio frequency (40–200 kHz), and the levels of current low (0.5–4 mA). Such currents are not known to be irritable or harmful in man or animals (Geddes and coworkers, 1969). Still, assurance is necessary against malfunction of the device, with current-limiting or other fail-safe features. Since any grounded instrument may provide a current path *vis a vis* some other device (e.g. EKG), a number of plethysmographs operate with batteries, fully isolated from ground (which may improve the signal quality as well).

6.3 Basis of measurement

The basic calculations relating impedance to volume (Nyboer, 1970) generally assume that the segment being measured is a perfect cylinder with length, L, and uniform cross-sectional area, A. In this manner, its *volume*, $V = A L$, and its *resistance*, $R = \rho L/A$ (where ρ is the resistivity of the conductor within the cylinder), may be simply related in terms of the distance, L, between the two sensor electrodes. If we allow Z to represent measured impedance (resistance):

$$V = \rho L^2/Z \tag{1}$$

If length is held constant, as in a limb segment defined by fixed electrode placements, two different measurements of impedance, Z_0 and Z_t, at time 0 and time t, reflect two different corresponding volumes, V_0 and V_t, or a change in volume, $\Delta V = V_0 - V_t$. The change in volume is related to the change in impedance ($\Delta Z = Z_0 - Z_t$) by the above equation:

$$\Delta V = V_0 - V_t = \frac{\rho L^2}{Z_0} - \frac{\rho L^2}{Z_t} = \frac{\rho L^2 (Z_t - Z_0)}{Z_0 Z_t} = \frac{\rho L^2 \Delta Z}{Z_0 Z_t} \tag{2}$$

For pulsatile changes where ΔZ is small with respect to the baseline, $Z_0 \simeq Z_t$. Thus,

$$\Delta V \cong - \frac{\rho L^1 \Delta Z}{Z_0^2} \tag{3}$$

Finally, if ΔV represents *pulse volume*, then *pulse volume flow* is related to heart rate (HR):

$$\text{Flow (cm}^3/\text{min)} = \Delta V.\text{HR} = \frac{\rho L^2 \Delta Z.\text{HR}}{Z^2} \tag{4}$$

These two equations are the fundamental relationships used by most investigators and commercial vascular computing devices to calculate volume/flow indices from impedance measurements.

6.4 Calibration

The electrical calibration of any impedance device is simple and usually available as a built-in feature of the device. Referring to Figure 2.26, calibration is achieved by inserting a known resistance in place of the limb segment between E_1 and E_2 for the bipolar electrode arrangement and between S_1 and S_2 for the tetrapolar arrangement. These electrical calibrations are then transformed into volume and flow measures using the assumptions and equations discussed. Note that this procedure does not provide a direct physiological calibration.

6.5 Critique of the technique

6.5.1 Current distribution and geometry

The practical derivation of impedance/volume relationships requires a number of approximations or assumptions which should be borne in mind by any user of impedance devices. These approximations are largely responsible for the empirical limitations of the method as a volumetric index (VanDenBerg and Alberts, 1954).

First, few, if any, body segments are true cylinders, even though a number of reports, and some commercial devices which compute volume data depend upon this assumption. A degree of geometric correction may be made in many cases, e.g. approximating the segment with a conical frustum. By this method, the circumference of both sensory electrodes, or a similar measurement, as well as the distance between them, are used in the computation (VanDenBerg and Alberts, 1954). Some instruments are supplied with correction coefficients for the geometry of the segment studied (Montgomery, 1976). In any event, a measure of actual segmental volume is necessary since for comparative purposes, flow data are often reported in terms of tissue volume (i.e. flow per 100 cm^3 tissue).

A second facilitating assumption involves the notion of *homogeneity* of the flow of electric current within the cross-sectional area, and along the length of the segment involved. Such uniformity is requisite if proportional or pulsatile volume changes are to be accurately measured independently of individual physiognomy, lead placement and movement. Actually, skin, muscle, connective tissue, relaxed and tense muscle, and blood all behave quite differently as conductors, and do so at different frequencies, so that no simple model of conductivity (such as Figure 2.26(b)) can entirely suffice (Schwan and Kay, 1956; Lofgren, 1951). Homogeneity of current appears less critical with tetrapolar methods, although in this instance, the separation of sensing from input electrodes is an important factor. Sensor electrode placement may be guided by the suggestion that current-field at the midpoint between source electrodes may be the most uniform (Nyboer, 1970). Schraibman and coworkers (1976b) have shown that spot source electrodes, well separated from sensor electrodes, give adequate results. Mathematical models accounting for current distribution factors have been discussed but not empirically confirmed in the engineering literature (Lehr, 1972; Geselowitz, 1971). The related assumption, that sensor measurements are independent of non-volumetric changes *outside* the segment studied, has been questioned by Krasner and Nardella (1972).

Finally, the resistivity of whole blood is assumed to be constant. The resistivity, ρ, must remain constant in the impedance/volume equation if calculated pulsatile volume changes are to be interpreted as due to the changing quantity of blood within the segment. The value usually given, 150 Ω cm, is derived from static, *in vitro* measurements (Nyboer, 1970, p. 89). However, blood resistivity has been shown to vary with a number of physiologic factors: hematocrit, temperature, shape of red cells, flow *velocity*, and orientation of red blood cells with respect to the axis of flow (Frewer, 1974; Liebman, Pearl and Bagno, 1962; Gollan and Namon, 1971; Visser and coworkers, 1976; Dellimore and Gosling, 1975).

Resistivity is thus complex, and may depend somewhat on the distribution of flow within segments, as for instance between the cooler but more constraining subdermal capillaries and the warmer and larger vessels of the interior. In brief, the assumption of constancy is questionable as resistivity is influenced by the dynamic events being measured.

6.5.2 Segmental flow considerations and estimations of ΔZ

Estimation of pulsatile blood flow for individual pulse curves poses certain problems. Any instantaneous change in segment volume (or impedance) is the net effect of four possible sources of flow: arterial inflow, arterial outflow, venous inflow, and venous outflow. If pulsatile (arterial) influx were measured independently of simultaneous efflux, the change in segment resistance (ΔZ) during the ascending phase of the pulse curve would provide an immediate measure not only of volume change, but of arterial inflow (Figure 2.27(a)). However, means of estimating an *effective* ΔZ have evolved for 'compensating' for simultaneous efflux of blood. In a series of *in vitro* stop-flow studies, Nyboer (1970, pp. 118–20) argues empirically for utilizing the extrapolation of the 'end systolic slope' to its y-intercept for this estimation (see Figure 2.27(b)); this method seems the most commonly used at present for peripheral measurements. Others, including Kubicek and his coworkers (1966) simultaneously record the first derivative (dZ/dt) of the analogue pulse waveform. In their computations, the *peak* (minimum) deflection of the derivative, $(dZ/dt)_{min}$, is multiplied by the total duration of systole (upsweep to dicrotic notch of the analogue waveform) to yield an estimate of ΔZ (see Figure 2.27(c)). Although the latter method is primarily used in thoracic impedance measurements (i.e. impedance cardiography) for estimates of cardiac output, the computation $dZ/dt \times T = \Delta Z$ has been used in peripheral measurements.

In experiments involving venous occlusion, impedance records may be treated in the same manner as volume of strain gauge records. Over a series of successive beats, the slope of the baseline shift may be related to blood flow in ml/s (Figure 2.27(d)) (Schraibman, Mott, and Naylor, 1975; Schraibman and coworkers, 1976a).

Irrespective of the theoretical basis for particular methods, calculating volume and flow changes from impedance data must rely ultimately on empirical evidence. Nyboer (1970) feels that impedance curves yield a reliable measure of segmental flow. Others argue that the method is limited in accuracy but may be useful in specified conditions or together with other methods (Schraibman and coworkers, 1976a; Hill, Jansen, and Fling, 1967; Brown and coworkers, 1975; Mount and VandeWater, 1975). Without resolving these issues, it is important, at least for each investigator

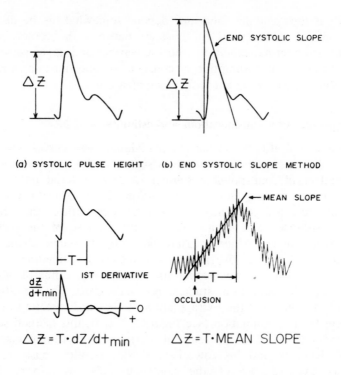

(a) SYSTOLIC PULSE HEIGHT   (b) END SYSTOLIC SLOPE METHOD

(c) IST DERIVATIVE METHOD   (d) VENOUS OCCLUSION

Figure 2.27   Methods for estimating pulsatile impedance change (ΔZ). (a) Pulsatile change in impedance recorded by calibrated measurement of pulse height. (b) End systolic slope method for compensating for outflow effects on pulsatile volume changes. (c) Peak first derivative method for computing net pulsatile impedance change, using duration (T) of systole. (d) Standard method for venous occlusion technique

to study and define carefully methods of computation, and to remain cognizant of their empirical limitations. The complexity of impedance plethysmography cannot be overemphasized. It is clear that most reports of successful practical applications come from investigators intimate with the mathematics, electronic theory, circulatory physiology involved, and the devices themselves. The complexity, which tends to narrow the margin of error, and the relative expense of the precise instruments preclude casual use of the impedance techniques. Where relatively crude measures are justified on clinical grounds, or where emphasis on quantitative interpretation is tempered by an understanding of the empirical limits of the method—impedance plethysmography promises to be quite useful (VanDenBerg and Alberts, 1954; Brook and Cooper, 1957).

6.6 Applications

There are important semi-quantitative applications of impedance plethysmography in clinical medicine and surgery, and this technology has been reviewed several times (Wheeler and Mullick, 1970; Allison, 1967; Brook and Cooper, 1957; Dean and Yao, 1976). In general, such applications concern the pathological impairment of peripheral circulation, e.g. large and small arterial occlusion and venous thrombosis. The presence of lesions may be confirmed, or the response to treatment (e.g. surgical bypass or anticoagulants) assessed, with the patient serving as his own control. The non-invasive character of the method is still its chief advantage, allowing frequent sampling or monitoring of the particular condition.

Other clinical and research applications involve the measurements of regional or organ blood flow. Selected lead placements can apparently yield specific data regarding renal (Allison, Sanchez and Langskoen, 1970), ocular (Cristini and coworkers, 1975), vestibular (Snow and Suga, 1975), and even dental circulation (Liebman and Cosenza, 1962). There is growing usage in neurology and neurophysiology with measurements of cerebral blood flow or rheoencephalography (Lovett Doust, 1977; Hadjiev, 1972).

Thoracic impedance, derived when leads are placed about the neck and at mid-torso level, has received considerable attention by Kubicek and others (Kubicek and coworkers, 1966; Sova, 1970; Baker and coworkers, 1971). A low-frequency component of waveform clearly reflects respiratory movement, and quantitative relationships between impedance and pulmonary volumetrics have been studied (Allison, Holmes, and Nyboer, 1964; Baker, Geddes and Hoff, 1965). The pulsatile component, now called the impedance cardiogram (ZCG), has been proposed as an index of stroke volume and cardiac output (see Miller and Horvath, 1978). A number of reports have shown reliable correlation between impedance-computed volumes and those derived from dye-dilution or other techniques (Denniston and coworkers, 1976; Handt, Farber and Szwed, 1977) but results are not always consistent (Bache, Harley and Greenfield, 1969; Lababidi and coworkers, 1970). Disagreement exists as to the sources of the observed complex thoracic impedance changes: aortic or pulmonary volume, flow, velocity or acceleration, or other dynamic factors (Brown et al. 1975; Kubicek et al. 1970; Witsoe and Kottke, 1967; Patterson, 1973). The ZCG does appear to provide data useful in terms of *timing* central circulatory events (Lababidi and coworkers, 1970).

The impedance pulse derived from peripheral sites is comparable with the pulse observed from air or water displacement volume measures taken simultaneously. The results from studies of finger pulsation are consistent, with high degrees of correlation: impedance-determined volumes are approximately 2/3 of the values calculated from volumetric data (Montgomery, 1976; VanDenBerg and Alberts, 1954). Similar comparative studies involving larger body segments such as the forearm or leg are less consistent, although in general, the relationship between volumes assessed by impedance and volumetric techniques is linear, and results with venous occlusion are comparable (Schraibman, Mott, and Naylor, 1975; Schraibman and coworkers, 1976a; 1976b; Brook and Cooper, 1957). Peripheral impedance measures are also comparable with other arterial flow measurement techniques, such as electromagnetic flowometry (VanDeWater and coworkers, 1971; Young and coworkers, 1967) and ultrasonic Doppler probes (Schraibman and coworkers, 1976a; 1976b). Mount and VanDeWater (1975) have proposed combining methods. Comparison with optical plethysmography has not been reported. If the quantitative precision of the method remains unestablished, impedance plethysmography may yet be used *in lieu* of other techniques in selected psychophysiologic applications, and has been recently applied in this manner by Gliner, Browe, and Horvath (1977) and Roessler and coworkers (1975).

7 DOPPLER ULTRASONIC FLOWOMETRY

7.1 General description

The possibility of acoustically measuring the velocity of fluids flowing through vessels or tubes has been the subject of vigorous research for almost forty years. As reviewed by Herrick (1977), ultrasonic devices for recording blood velocity were reported in the 1950s, and practical devices for non-invasive application in man were available by 1964 (Baker, 1964). The Doppler technique is based on reflected ultrasonic waves (echoes) altered by the movement of reflecting or backscattering surfaces. Directing ultrasonic energy at a blood vessel allows the assessment of the movement of blood cells, and provides an index of flow velocity, rather than blood volume or pressure. As a *quantitative* method for recording peripheral vascular phenomena, however, its use is as yet largely investigational and limited to selected circumstances. Compared to other methods described in this chapter, the technique is difficult to master, and expensive, so the present discussion is basic and brief. The reader is encouraged to consult recent reviews (Woodcock, 1975; Baker and Daigle, 1977), and follow developments in this field.

7.2 Attachment and apparatus

Figure 2.28 shows a Doppler probe positioned over a subcutaneous vessel, at an angle (θ) to the vessel, and coupled to the skin with a jelly. The core

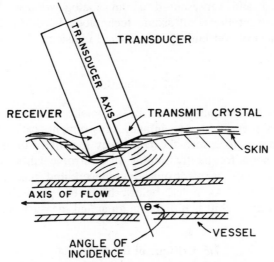

Figure 2.28   Doppler flowometry. Piezoelectric transducer transmits ultrasonic energy of fixed frequency, and receives 'echos' with frequency altered by moving particles (blood cells) according to rate of flow and angle of incidence (θ)

of the probe contains both the transmitter of sound energy and the receiver which senses the echoes or reflected sound energy. A piezoelectric crystal is used to transmit coherent, high-frequency soundwaves (1–10 MHz), and a similar crystal serves as receiver. Complex and expensive instruments are required to control the sound energy and to analyse the changes in reflected sound induced by movement of the blood.

7.3 Basis of measurement

Use of ultrasonic velocity-meters is based on two fundamental principles: first, a sound wave is reflected or backscattered by substances within its path; and second, if such substances are in motion, the frequency of backscattered energy is altered (Doppler shift) in relation to the velocity of motion. The frequency of the received sound differs from that transmitted (f_o) by the amount of Doppler shift (f_d), determined by V, the velocity of the blood cells and θ, the angle between the direction of transmitted sound and the direction of blood flow. Hence,

$$f_d = \frac{2f_0 V \cos \theta}{c} \tag{5}$$

where c is the velocity of sound in tissue. The Doppler shift frequency can be electronically measured, and with the angle θ known, the blood velocity

V is computed and represented as an analog voltage. Beyond these simplified representations, ultrasonic technology becomes quite complex, and is the subject of continuing research and revision.

7.4 Calibration

As noted previously, quantitative measurement of blood velocity using Doppler techniques is in its infancy. Instrument calibration may be achieved, however, to insure the consistent sensitivity of the instrument. Current instruments frequently employ an electronic calibration in which a 'Doppler phase shift' is electronically induced and resulting instrument output is calibrated. As noted below, however, precisely relating flow velocity and Doppler shift is difficult in an actual measurement situation.

7.5 Critique of the technique

A number of basic problems must be resolved before a quantitatively reliable and practical Doppler flowmeter becomes generally available. Some of the more important considerations will be listed here, without attempting to assess the current state of progress in each case. First, the actual angle of the transducing device to the vessel is difficult to measure precisely and to duplicate on different occasions. Next, the flow of red cells is non-uniform through any given cross section of vessel. Normally laminar blood flow varies considerably over each cardiac cycle and may change to turbulent flow in some circumstances. Indeed, flow in different areas may be in opposite directions at a given moment, especially during diastole (Strandness and coworkers, 1969). Consequently, it is necessary either to integrate the myriad of Doppler shifts presented to the receiver at any given moment, or to limit or focus the reception to a single, minute portion of the cross section. In this connection, controlling the size of the beam in relation to the diameter of the vessel may be required. With simple devices such as illustrated in Figure 2.28, discrimination of *direction* of flow is not straightforward, but requires complex methods of detection (Coghlan and Taylor, 1976).

Several sources of noise are inherent in the method, which may or may not be systematic and easily discriminated. For instance, motion of the walls of the vessel, occurring with each pulse, as well as adventitious movement of other tissues between transducer and the blood cells, will alter the output signal. Flow in other vessels near to that under study may interfere with the resolution of the device. At the frequencies involved, electromagnetic interference is always a possibility. And as suggested above, subtle movements of the transducer itself might be undetected, and will disturb the accuracy of the device. Finally, there remains doubt on the part of some investigators as to the safety, or at least as to our understanding of physiologic effects, of ultrasonic sound energies focused into the human organism.

7.6 Application

Given such an array of technical problems, the degree of current progress is impressive. It is interesting that refinements in technology, directed largely at solving some of the above problems, have led in their own right to further invention and novel applications of the general ultrasonic methodology. For instance, development of beaming, pulsing, and focusing techniques has provided a method for studying minute intravascular flow patterns *in vivo* (Strandness and Sumner, 1972). Measurement of vascular diameter is possible from a discrimination between vessel wall and fluid movement. Extension of the same discrimination may allow ultrasonic imaging of large vessels, or ultrasonic arteriography (Hokanson and coworkers, 1972). Furthermore, cross-sectional vessel area, measured by this technique, multiplied by velocity, yields a measure of volume flow (Arts and Roevros, 1972; McCarty and Woodcock, 1975).

Given the current practical limitations to quantitative ultrasonic methodology, several non-quantitative applications have become firmly established. Qualitative detection of the presence or absence of arterial wall motion and turbulent flow has led to a method of indirectly determining systolic and diastolic blood pressure during cuff deflation, and is perhaps more accurate than audio-acoustical methods (Stegall, Kardon, and Kemmerer, 1968). Recognition of turbulent flow secondary to localized arterial lesions or stenosis has been improved by this technique (Gosling and King, 1974). Fraser and coworkers (1976) by directing ultrasonic velocity probes to the suprasternal notch, have ascertained a varying parameter, 'peak systolic flow velocity', derived from flow in the aortic arch, which may be a useful index of left ventricular function.

As with impedance plethysmography, the largest area of application for ultrasonic techniques resides in semi-quantitative, clinical approaches, especially in vascular surgery (Dean and Yao, 1976). As the technology improves, both in terms of quantitative accuracy and economics, routine application in the psychophysiology laboratory will grow. At present, its application in combination with other vascular measurements, as suggested by Mount and VanDeWater (1975) is a most intriguing and immediate possibility.

8 COMPARISON OF VASCULAR MEASUREMENTS

None of the vascular measurement techniques surveyed is clearly superior to the others. Each technique depends on a set of simplifying assumptions which are known to only approximate true physiological conditions. The techniques clearly differ in the aspect of the vascular system which they measure, physical characteristics, and requirements for obtaining a signal from the body surface. A choice between vascular measures may be made by relating the characteristics of a technique to the vascular information required by an investigator. This section provides examples comparing the relative advantages of photo, volume, strain gauge, impedance, and Doppler techniques for particular measurement problems. The discussion will focus only on selection of a technique; desirable adjunctive measures, e.g. blood pressure, will not be discussed. Cost and availability are other obvious considerations not discussed.

8.1 Biofeedback treatment of Raynaud's disease

Raynaud's disease is an episodically occurring cyanosis of the digits induced by emotional stress or exposure to cold. Although the etiology of this condition is not known, the immediate cause of the cyanosis is constriction of cutaneous blood vessels. This constriction may be reversible if the lumen of the peripheral vessels were brought under the patient's control through biofeedback (e.g Surwit, 1973). Requirements of a vascular measure in this situation might be: (a) sensitivity to constriction and dilation of the cutaneous vasculature; (b) beat to beat sensitivity to allow timely feedback; (c) psychological acceptance by the patients; and (d) presuming multiple training sessions, a calibrated signal allowing session assessments of stability of improvement.

Although the depth of measurement has not been exactly defined, the phototechnique appears to be primarily sensitive to cutaneous changes when appropriately applied. The phototechnique also meets the three other requirements. If circulation in the digits is primarily cutaneous, the strain gauge and impedance techniques meet the requirements as well. The use of occluding cuffs would not be acceptable given requirements (b) and (c), although pre- and post-feedback measures of blood flow using the venous occlusion techniques might provide a useful criterion for success of the treatment. Volume techniques may not be acceptable to the patient and are generally difficult to operate given the acceptability of the other measures. Doppler ultrasound techniques are not suitable for cutaneous measures.

8.2 Stenosis, pregnancy, and thermal orienting

Three other hypothetical measurement situations will be briefly mentioned and an optimum technique suggested. The process of generating measurement requirements and discussing each technique will not be repeated.

Stenosis refers to the narrowing of an artery due to a variety of pathologic conditions. Early detection and localization is critical to optimal treatment. The Doppler technique is ideal for examining blood flow at different points along an artery, detecting turbulent flow, and imaging the artery wall.

Pregnancy is associated with an increase in blood volume and an attendant increase in the prevalence of varicose veins, an irreversible dilation of the veins. Suitable venous measurements for the assessment of treatment would be provided by a water-filled volume plethysmograph (Wood, 1965). Strain gauge and impedance techniques are sensitive to changes in the venous volume of limbs, but procedures for venous measurement are not well developed with these techniques.

Although vascular orienting responses to auditory and visual stimuli have been widely observed, responses to local thermal stimulation have not. The desire to study orienting responses both proximal and distal to the measurement site suggests that the phototechnique would be most useful. Its physical characteristics and sensitivity to the richly innervated arterioles justify this choice.

In summary, a variety of noninvasive techniques are available to assess peripheral vascular activity, i.e. the flow, pressure, and size of peripheral vessels. No one technique is a superior physiological measure, therefore, choice of technique depends on matching the requirements of an investigator with the characteristics of the technique. Once a technique is chosen, careful attention must be paid not only to the accurate use of that technique, but also to its interpretive validity in the context of the overall cardiovascular system.

REFERENCES

Abrahamson, D. I. (1967). *Circulation in the Extremities*, Academic Press, New York.

Allison, R. D. (1967). Clinical applications of impedance plethysmography. *Clin. Med.*, **74**, 33–41.

Allison, R. D., Holmes, E. L., and Nyboer, I. (1964). Volumetric dynamics of respiration as measured by electrical impedance plethysmography. *J. Appl. Physiol.*, **19**, 166–73.

Allison, R. D., Sanchez, S. A., and Langsjoen, P. H. (1970). The role of impedance plethysmography in the evaluation of renal vascular hypertension. *Ann. NY Acad. Sci.*, **170**, 768–92.

Arts, M. G. J., and Roevros, J. M. J. G. (1972). On the instantaneous measurement of blood flow by ultrasonic means. *Med. Biol. Eng.*, **10**, 23–34.

Ax, A. F. (1967). Electronic storage and computer analysis. In P. H. Venables and I. Martin (Eds), *A Manual of Psychophysiological Methods*, Wiley, New York. pp. 481–520.

Bache, R. J., Harley, A., and Greenfield, J. C. Jr (1969). Evaluation of thoracic impedance plethysmography as an indicator of stroke volume in man. *Am. J. Med. Sci.*, **258**, 100–13.

F

Baker, D. W. (1964). A sonic transcutaneous blood flowmeter. *Proc. 17th Annual Conf. on Engineering and Medical Biology*, p. 76.

Baker, D. W., and Daigle, R. E. (1977). Non-invasive ultrasonic flowmetry. In N. H. Hwang and N. A. Norman (Eds). *Cardiovascular Flow Dynamics and Measurements*, University Park Press, Baltimore. pp. 151–89.

Baker, L. E., Geddes, L. A., and Hoff, H. E. (1965). Quantitative evaluation of impedance spirometry in man. *Am. J. Med. Electron.*, **4**, 73.

Baker, L. E., Judy, W. V., Geddes, L. A., Langley, F. M., and Hill, D. W. (1971). The measurement of cardiac output by means of electrical impedance. *Cardiovasc. Res.*, **9**, 135–45.

Barcroft, H., and Swan, H. J. C. (1953). *Sympathetic Control of Human Blood Vessels*, Arnold, London.

Block, E. H. (1973). A quantitative study of the hemodynamics in the living microvascular system. *J. Appl. Physiol.*, **16**, 125–44.

Brook, D. L., and Cooper, P. (1957). The impedance plethysmogram. *Surgery*, **42**, 1061–70.

Brown, B. H., Pryce, W. I., Baumber, D., and Clark, R. G. (1975). Impedance plethysmography: Can it measure changes in limb blood flow? *Med. Biol. Engng*, **13**, 674–82.

Brown, C. C. (1967). The techniques of plethysmography. In C. C. Brown (Ed.), *Methods in Psychophysiology*, Williams and Wilkins, Baltimore. pp. 54–74.

Burch, G. E. (1977). The use of digital rheoplethysmography for the study of psychogenic and neurogenic factors in man. *Pavlovian J. Biol. Sci.*, **12**, 3–18.

Burton, A. C. (1965). Hemodynamics and the physics of circulation. In T. C. Ruch and H. D. Patton (Eds), *Physiology and Biophysics*, 19th edn, Saunders, Philadelphia.

Burton, A. C. (1972). *Physiology and Biophysics of the Circulation*, Yearbook Medical Publishers, Chicago.

Cannon, W. B. (1939). *Wisdom of the Body*, 2nd edn, W. W. Norton, New York.

Coghlan, B. A., and Taylor, M. G. (1976). Directional Doppler techniques for detection of blood velocities. *Ultrasound Med. & Biol.*, **2**, 181–8.

Cook, M. R. (1974). Psychophysiology of peripheral vascular changes. In P. A. Obrist, A. H. Black, J. Brener, and L. V. DiCara (Eds), *Cardiovascular Psychophysiology: Current Issues in Response Mechanisms, Biofeedback, and Methodology*. Aldine, Chicago. pp. 60–84.

Cristini, G., Meduri, R., Garbini, G. C., and Giovaninni, A. (1975). A new method for determining the blood quantity in the eye in a unit of time. *Albrecht von Graefes Arch. Klin. Ophthalmol.*, **197**, 1–11.

Dean, R. H., and Yao, I. S. (1976). Hemodynamic measurements in peripheral vascular disease. *Curr. Probl. Surg.*, **13**, 1–76.

Dellimore, J. W., and Gosling, R. G. (1975). Change in blood conductivity with flow rate. *Med. Biol. Engng*, **12**, 904–13.

Denniston, J. C., Maher, J. T., Reeves, J. T., Cruz, J. C., Cymerman, A., and Grover, R. F. (1976). Measurement of cardiac output by electrical impedance at rest and during exercise. *J. Appl. Physiol.*, **40**, 91–5.

Fine, S., and Weinman, J. (1973). The use of photoconductive cells in photoplethysmography. *Med. Biol. Engng*, **11**, 455–63.

Fitzgerald, A. E., Higginbotham, D. E., and Grabel, A. (1967). *Basic Electrical Engineering*, McGraw-Hill, New York.

Fraser, C. B., Light, L. H., Shinebourne, E. A., Buchthal, A., Healy, M. J. R., and Beardshaw, J. A. (1976). Transcutaneous aortovelography: reproducibility in adults and children. *Eur. J. Cardiol.*, **4**, 181–9.

Frewer, R. A. (1974). The electrical conductivity of flowing blood. *Biomed. Engng,* **9**, 552–55.

Gaskell, P., and Burton, A. C. (1953). Local postural vasomotor reflexes arising from the limb veins. *Circulation Res.,* **1**, 27–39.

Geddes, L. A., and Baker, L. E. (1975). *Principles of Applied Biomedical Instrumentation,* Wiley, New York.

Geddes, L. A., Baker, L. E., Moore, A. G., and Coulter, T. W. (1969). Hazards in the use of low frequencies for the measurement of physiologic events by impedance. *Med. Biol. Engng,* **7**, 289.

Geselowitz, D. B. (1971). An application of electrocardiographic lead theory to impedance plethysmography. *IEEE Trans. Biomed. Engng,* **BME-18**, 38–41.

Gilbert, D. B. (1968). Digital analysis of hemodynamic data. *NIH Technical Report No. 2.*

Gliner, J. A., Browe, A. C., and Horvath, S. M. (1977). Hemodynamic changes as a function of classical aversive conditioning in human subjects. *Psychophysiology,* **14**, 281–6.

Gollan, F., and Namon, R. (1971). Electrical impedance of pulsatile blood flow in rigid tubes and in isolated organs. *Ann. NY Acad. Sci.,* **170**, 568–75.

Gosling, R. G., and King, D. H. (1974). Arterial assessment by Doppler-shift ultrasound. *Proc. Res. Soc. Med.,* **67**, 447.

Greenfield, A. D. M. (1960). Venous occlusion plethysmography. In H. D. Bruner (Ed.), *Methods of Medical Research,* Vol. 8, Yearbook Medical Publishers, Chicago. pp. 293–301.

Greenfield, A. D. M., Whitney, R. J., and Mowbray, J. F. (1963). Methods for the investigation of peripheral blood flow. *Br. Med. Bull.,* **19**, 101–9.

Guyton, A. C., Jones, C. E., and Coleman, T. C. (1973). *Circulatory Physiology: Cardiac Output and its Regulation,* Saunders, Philadelphia.

Hadjiev, D. (1972). Impedance methods for investigation of cerebral circulation. *Prog. Brain Res.,* **35**, 25–85.

Handt, A., Farber, M. O., and Szwed, J. J. (1977). Intradialytic measurement of cardiac output thermodilution and impedance cardiography. *Clin. Nephrol.,* **7**, 61–4.

Harper, A. M., Lorimer, A. R., and Thomas, D. L. (1970). Methods of measuring blood flow. In C. Scurr and S. Feldman (Eds), *Scientific Foundations of Anesthesia,* F. A. Davis, Philadelphia. pp. 28–44.

Herrick, J. F. (1977). Background leading to the earliest ultrasonic blood flowmeters. *Med. Instrum.,* **11**, pp. 134–5.

Hertzman, A. B. (1937a). Photoelectric plethysmography of the fingers and toes in man. *Proc. Soc. Exp. Biol. Med.,* **37**, 529–34.

Hertzman, A. B. (1937b). Observations on the finger volume pulse recorded photoelectrically. *Am. J. Physiol.,* **19**, 334–5.

Hertzman, A. B. (1938). The blood supply of various skin areas as estimated by the photoelectric plethysmograph. *Am. J. Physiol.,* **124**, 328–40.

Hertzman, A. B., and Dillon, J. B. (1940). Distinction between arterial, venous and flow components in photoelectric plethysmography in man. *Am. J. Physiol.,* **130**, 177–85.

Hertzman, A. B., and Roth, L. W. (1942). The reactions of the digital artery and minute pad arteries to local cold. *Am. J. Physiol.,* **136**, 680–91.

Hertzman, A. B., Randall, W. C., and Jochim, K. E. (1946). The estimation of the cutaneous blood flow with the photoelectric plethysmograph. *Am. J. Physiol.,* **145**, 716–26.

Hertzman, A. B., Randall, W. C., and Jochim, K. E. (1947). Relations between cutaneous blood flow and blood content in the finger pad, forearm, and forehead. *Am. J. Physiol.*, **150**, 122–32.

Hill, R. V., Jansen, I. C., and Fling, J. L. (1967). Electrical impedance plethysmography: A critical analysis. *J. Appl. Physiol.*, **22**, 161–8.

Hokanson, D. E., Mozersky, D. J., Sumner, D. A., McLeod, F. D., Jr, and Standness, D. E., Jr (1972). Ultrasonic arteriography: a non-invasive method for arterial visualization. *Radiology*, **102**, 435.

Hwang, N. H. C., and Normann, N. A. (Eds), (1977). *Cardiovascular Flow Dynamics and Measurements*, University Park Press, Baltimore.

Hyman, C., Greeson, T., Clem, M., and Winsor, D. (1964). Capacitance plethysmograph method for separating blood flow in muscle and skin in the human forearm. *Am. Heart J.*, **68**, 508–14.

Hyman, C., and Winsor, T. (1961). History of plethysmography. *J. Cardiovasc. Surg.*, **2**, 506–12.

Johnson, J. M., Brengelmann, G. L., and Rowell, L. B. (1976). Interactions between local and reflex influences on human forearm skin blood flow. *J. Appl. Physiol.*, **41**, 826–31.

Korner, P. I. (1971). Integrative neural cardiovascular control. *Physiol. Rec.*, **51**, 312–67.

Krasner, J. L., and Nardella, P. C. (1972). Physiological correlates of impedance plethysmography. *Med. Electron. Data*, **3**, 76–80.

Kubicek, W. G., Karnegis, J. N., Patterson, R. P., Witsoe, D. A., and Mattson, R. H. (1966). Development and evaluation of an electrical impedance cardiac output system. *Aerospace Med.*, **37**, 1208–12.

Kubicek, W. G., Patterson, R. P., and Witsoe, D. A. (1970). Impedance cardiography as a noninvasive method of monitoring cardiac function and other parameters of the cardiovascular system. *Ann. NY Acad. Sci.*, **170**, 724–32.

Lababidi, Z., Ehmke, D. A., Durnin, R. E., Leaverton, P. E., and Lauer, R. M. (1970). The first derivative thoracic impedance wave form. *Circulation*, **41**, 651–8.

Lader, M. H. (1967). Pneumatic plethysmography. In P. H. Venables and I. Martin (Eds), *A Manual of Psychophysiological Methods*, Wiley, New York. pp. 159–63.

Landowne, M., and Katz, L. N. (1942). A critique of the plethysmographic methods of measuring blood flow in the extremities of man. *Am. Heart. J.*, **23**, 644–75.

Lawler, J. D., and Obrist, P. A. (1974). Indirect indices of contractible force. In P. A. Obrist, A. H. Black, J. Brener, and L. V. DiCara (Eds), *Cardiovascular Psychophysiology: Current Issues in Response Mechanisms, Biofeedback, and Methodology*, Aldine, Chicago. pp. 60–84.

Lee, A. L., Tahmoush, A. J. and Jennings, J. R. (1975). An LED-transistor photoplethysmograph. *IEEE Trans. Biomed. Engng*, **BME-22**, 248–50.

Lehr, J. (1972). A vector derivation useful in impedance plethysmographic field calculations. *IEEE Trans. Biomed. Engng*, **BME-19**, 156–7.

Liebman, F. M., and Cosenza, F. (1962). Study of blood flow in dental pulp by an electrical impedance technique. *Phys. Med. Biol.*, **7**, 167–76.

Liebman, F. M., Pearl, L., and Bagno, S. (1962). The electrical conductance properties of blood in motion. *Phys. Med. Biol.*, **7**, 177–94.

Lofgren, B. (1951). The electrical impedance of a complex tissue and its relation to changes in volume and fluid distribution. *Acta Physiol. Scand.*, **23**, 1–51.

Lombard, W. P. and Pillsbury, W. B. (1902). A new form of piston recorder and some of the changes of the volume of the finger which it records. *Am. J. Physiol.*, **7**, 186–200.

Longini, R. L. and Zdrojkowski, R. (1968). A note on the theory of backscattering of light by living tissue. *IEEE Trans. Biomed. Engng,* **BME-15**, 4–10.

Lovett Doust, J. W. (1977). Carotid-vertebral artery transit time in health and in neurological patients. *Dis. Nerv. Syst.,* **38**, 344–8.

McCarty, K., and Woodcock, J. P. (1975). Frequency modulated ultrasonic Doppler flowmeter. *Med. Biol. Engng.* **13**, 59–64.

McDonald, D. A. (1974). *Blood flow in arteries.* Edward Arnold, London.

Markovich, S. E. (Ed.) (1970). International Conference on Bioelectrical Impedance. *Ann. NY Acad. Sci.,* **170**, 407–836.

Mellander, S., and Johansson, B. (1968). Control of resistance exchange and capacitance functions in the peripheral circulation. *Pharmacol. Rev.,* **20**, 117–96.

Miller, J. C. and Horvath, S. M. (1978). Impedance cardiography. *Psychophysiology,* **15**, 80–91.

Moavini, M. K. (1970). A multiple scattering field theory applied to whole blood. *Ph.D. Thesis,* University of Washington, Seattle (University Microfilms, Ann Arbor, Michigan, No. 71-1004).

Montgomery, L. D. (1976). Comparison of an impedance device to a displacement plethysmograph for study of finger blood flow. *Aviation, Space, Environ. Med.,* **47**, 33–8.

Mount, B. E., and VanDeWater, J. M. (1975). Estimation of peripheral arterial blood flow non-invasively by combining blood velocity, blood pressure, and pulsatile volume measurements. *Angiology,* **26**, 165–71.

Novelly, R. A., Perona, P. J., and Ax, A. F. (1973). Photoplethysmography: System calibration and light history effects. *Psychophysiology,* **10**, 67–73.

Nyboer, J. (1970). *Electrical Impedance Plethysmography,* 2nd edn, Charles C. Thomas, Springfield.

Nyboer, J., Kreider, M. M. and Hannapel, L. (1951). Quantitative studies of electrical conductivity of the peripheral body segment. *Ann. Western Med. Surg.,* **11**, 1951.

Obrist, P. A., Lawler, J. E., Howard, J. L., Smithson, K. W., Martin, P. L. and Manning, J. (1974). Sympathetic influences on cardiac rate and contractibility during acute stress in humans. *Psychophysiology,* **11**, 405–27.

Parrish, D., Bray, R. A., Strandness, D. E., Jr, and Bell, J. W. (1968). Evidence for the venous origin of plethysmographic information. *J. Lab. Clin. Med.,* **62**, 943–8.

Patterson, R. P., Witsoe, D. A., From, A. H. L., and Kubicek, W. G. (1973). Studies on the cardiogenic origin of the thoracic electrical impedance change. (Abstract) *Proc. 26th Annual Conf. on Engineering and Medical Biology.* p. 69.

Percival, G. H., Montgomery, G. L., and Dodds, T. C. (1962). *Atlas of Histopathology of the Skin,* Williams and Wilkins, Baltimore.

Pisharoty, N. R. (1971). Optical scattering in blood. *Ph.D. Thesis,* Carnegie-Mellon University, Pittsburgh (University Mircofilms, Ann Arbor, Michigan, No. 71–24, 861).

Raman, E. R., Van Huyse, W. J., and Jageneau, A. H. (1973). Comparison of plethysmographic and electromagnetic flow measurements. *Phys. Med. Biol.,* **18**, 704–11.

Roessler, R., Bruch, H., Thum, L., and Collins, F. (1975). Physiologic correlates of affect during psychotherapy. *Am. J. Psychotherapy,* **29**, 26–36.

Rosen, R. C. and Keefe, F. J. (1978). The measurement of human penile tumescence. *Psychophysiology,* **15**, 366–76.

Roy, C. S., and Sherrington, C. S. (1890). On the regulation of the blood supply of the brain. *J. Physiol.,* **11**, 85–108.

Ruch, T. C. and Patton, H. D. (1974). *Physiology and Biophysics; Circulation ,
respiration, and fluid balance*, Saunders, Philadelphia.
Rushmer, R. F. (1976). *Cardiovascular Dynamics*, 4th edn, Saunders, Philadelphia.
Schraibman, I. G., Mott, D., and Naylor, G. P. (1975). Comparison of impedance
strain gauge plethysmography in the measurement of blood flow in the lower
limb. *Br. J. Surg.*, **62**, 909–12.
Schraibman, I. G., Naylor, G. P., Smith, K., Patel, P., and Charlesworth, D.
(1976a). Pulsatile changes of electrical impedance in the lower limb. *Br. J. Surg.*,
63, 907–9.
Schraibman, I. G., Mott, D., Naylor, G. P., and Charlesworth, D. (1976b).
Impedance plethysmography evaluation of a simplified system of electrodes for the
measurement of blood flow in the lower limb. *Br. J. Surg.*, **63**, 413–6.
Schwan, H. P. (1955). Electrical properties of body tissue and impedance
plethysmography. *IRE Trans. Med. Electron.*, **PGME-3**, 32.
Schwan, H. P., and Kay, C. F. (1956). Specific resistance of body tissues.
Circulation Res., **4**, 664–70.
Shapiro, A. and Cohen, H. D. (1965). The use of mercury capillary length gauges
for the measurement of the volume of thoracic and diaphragmatic components of
human respiration. *Transactions of the New York Academy of Sciences*, **27**,
634–49.
Smith, R. D. (1971). *Circuits, Devices, and Systems*, Wiley, New York.
Snow, J. B., Jr, and Suga, F. (1975). Control of the microcirculation of the inner
ear. *Otolaryogol. Clin. North Am.*, **8**, 455–66.
Sokolov, Y. N. (1963). *Perception and the Conditioned Reflex*, Macmillan, New
York.
Sova, I. (1970). Cardiac rheometry. *Ann. NY Acad. Sci.*, **170**, 577–93.
Stegall, H. F., Kardon, M. B., and Kemmerer, W. T. (1968). Indirect measurement
of arterial blood pressure by Doppler ultrasonic sphygmomanometry. *J. Appl.
Physiol.*, **25**, 793–98.
Steptoe, A. (1976). Blood pressure control: A comparison of feedback instructions
using pulse wave velocity measurements. *Psychophysiology* **13**, 528–35.
Strandness, D. E., and Bell, J. W. (1965). Peripheral vascular disease: Diagnosis
and objective evaluation using a mercury strain gauge. *Ann. Surg.*, **161**, *Suppl*,
1–35.
Strandness, D. E., Kennedy, J. W., Judge, T. P., and McLeod, F. J. (1969).
Transcutaneous direction flow detection. *Am. Heart J.*, **78**, 65.
Strandness, D. E., and Sumner, D. S. (1972). Noninvasive methods of studying
peripheral arterial function. *J. Surg. Res.*, **12**, 419–30.
Surwit, R. S. (1973). Biofeedback: A possible treatment of Raynaud's disease.
Sem. Psychiat., **5**, 483–9.
Tahmoush, A. J., Jennings, J. R., Camp, S., Lee, A. L., and Weber, F.
(1976a). Photoplethysmography. A quantitative approach. *Psychophysiology*, **13**,
163.
Tahmoush, A. J., Jennings, J. R., Lee, A. L., Camp, S., and Weber, F. (1976b).
Characteristics of a light emitting diode-transistor photoplethysmograph.
Psychophysiology, **13**, 357–62.
VanDenBerg, J., and Alberts, A. J. (1954). Limitations of electric impedance
plethysmograph. *Circulation Res.*, **44**, 333–9.
VanDeWater, J. M., Dmochowski, J. R., Dove, G. B., and Couch, N. P. (1971).
Evaluation of an impedance flowmeter in arterial surgery. *Surgery* **70**, 954.
Visser, K. R., Lamberts, R., Korsten, H. H. M., and Zijlstra, W. G. (1976).
Observations on blood flow related electrical impedance changes in rigid tubes.
Pflügers Arch. ges. Physiol., **366**, 289–91.

Weinman, J. (1967). Photoplethysmography. In P. H. Venables and I. Martin (Eds), *A Manual of Psychophysiological Methods*, Wiley, New York. pp. 185–217.

Weinman, J., Bicker, C., and Levy, D. (1960). Applications of a photoconductive cell to the study of peripheral circulation in limbs of animals and man. *J. Appl. Physiol.*, **15**, 317–20.

Weinman, J., and Fine, S. (1972). Detectivities of photoconductive and silicon p-i-n light sensors in photoplethysmography. *TIT J. Life Sci.*, **2**, 121–7.

Weinman, J., Hayat, A., and Raviv, G. (1977). Reflection photoplethysmography of arterial blood volume pulses. *Med. Biol. Engng Comput.*, **15**, 22–31.

Weinman, J., and Manoach, M. (1962). A photoelectric approach to the study of peripheral circulation. *Am. Heart J.*, **63**, 219–31.

Wheeler, H. B., and Mullick, S. C. (1970). Detection of venous obstruction in the leg by measurement of electrical impedance. *Ann. NY Acad. Sci.*, **170**, 804–11.

Whitney, R. J. (1953). The measurement of volume changes in human limbs. *J. Physiol. (Lond.)*, **121**, 1–27.

Williams, R. B., Bittker, T. E., Buchsbaum, M. S., and Wynne, L. C. (1975). Cardiovascular and neurophysiologic correlates of sensory intake and rejection. I: Effect of cognitive tasks. *Psychophysiology*, **12**, 427–33.

Witsoe, D. A., and Kottke, F. J. (1967). The origin of cardiogenic changes in thoracic electrical impedance. *Federation Proc.*, **26**, 595.

Wood, J. E. (1965). *The Veins, Normal and Abnormal Function*, Little, Brown and Co., Boston.

Woodcock, J. P. (1975). Development of the ultrasonic flowmeter. *Ultrasound Med. Biol.*, **2**, 11–18.

Youdin, M. and Reich, T. (1976). Mercury-in-rubber (Whitney) strain gauge: Temperature compensation and analysis of error caused by temperature drift. *Ann. Biomed. Engng*, **4**, 220–31.

Young, D. G., Jr, Cox, R. H., Stoner, E. K., and Erdman, W. J. (1967). Evaluation of quantitative impedance plethysmography for continuous blood flow measurement. *Am. J. Physiol. Med.*, **46**, 1450.

Techniques in Psychophysiology
Edited by I. Martin and P. H. Venables
© 1980, John Wiley & Sons Ltd.

CHAPTER 3

Measurement, Quantification, and Analysis of Cardiac Activity

DAVID A. T. SIDDLE AND GRAHAM TURPIN (Editors)

3.1 INTRODUCTION AND OVERVIEW

The purpose of this chapter is to outline and discuss the major problems associated with the use of measures of cardiac activity within psychophysiology. Four general areas are covered, and they include the measurement, quantification, analysis, and interpretation of cardiac data. Measurement problems concern the description of the basic recording apparatus necessary to monitor cardiac activity either within the laboratory or in extra-laboratory settings. These are reviewed briefly in the Introduction and discussed in greater detail in Section 3.3.1. In addition, the Introduction deals with special techniques and control procedures to be considered when cardiac activity is monitored from particular subject groups such as neonates or hyperkinetic children, or in extra-laboratory environments. There is also a brief review of the effects on cardiac activity of intersubject differences such as age, sex, and ethnic group.

The second major problem area concerns the quantification of the basic EKG waveform. Essentially, this involves the expression of the basic datum, the interbeat interval, in terms of its duration and sequential occurrence in real time. Section 3.3.2 is specifically concerned with the appropriateness of heart rate (HR) and heart period (HP) as measurement units, and with their expression in either real time (s) or organismic time (beats).

The third general area reviews problems associated with the analysis of cardiac data. Elliott (1970) has suggested that since cardiac data can be measured simply and reliably, they should display a high degree of cross-laboratory consistency. However, although there may be standardization with regard to the measurement of cardiac activity, there is a wide variety of analysis techniques. The purpose of this section is not to assess such techniques *per se*, but to examine some of the fundamental approaches and problems encountered in the analysis of cardiac data. The first question to be asked concerns the nature of the changes in cardiac activity to be examined. Originally, changes in either 'tonic level' or 'phasic response' were investigated. However, this distinction has become less clear with the recognition that tonic activity displays changes not only in terms of mean level, but also in terms of variability. Furthermore, cardiac variability is now of interest in its own right, since there are reliable patterns of cardiac variability associated with subject differences (Varni, Clarke, and Giddon, 1971; Porges, 1976) and with task demands (Sayers, 1975a). Moreover, the recent development of techniques for monitoring long-term changes in cardiac activity, particularly in extra-laboratory environments, has lead to a growing interest in this area. A discussion of the techniques available for the analysis of tonic activity and also a comparison of these techniques with those used to assess phasic changes can be found in Section 3.4.1.

Notwithstanding the above, the majority of psychophysiological investigations involve examination of stimulus-evoked short-term changes. Discussion of the analysis of such changes has been confined to two commonly encountered problems. The first concerns the effect of prestimulus level and variability on the one hand on the nature of the evoked cardiac response (ECR) on the other. This is dealt with in some depth in Section 3.4.2. The second problem concerns the statistical techniques available for evaluation of the ECR. The techniques discussed include the analysis of the cardiac response curve (CRC) using either repeated measures analysis of variance or multivariate techniques (Section 3.4.3). In addition, the Introduction contains some discussion of the analysis of temporal aspects of the ECR and of the use of response parameter analysis to examine individual components of the CRC.

The fourth area concerns the general use and interpretation of cardiac data in psychophysiology. This has been approached in two ways. First, the Introduction contains a brief résumé of the different uses and constructs which have evolved in relation to cardiac data in psychophysiology. The purpose here is to introduce the unfamiliar reader to the application of cardiac data within this area. Second, the physiological mechanisms responsible for changes in cardiac activity have been outlined. The rationale for this approach is the provision of a physiological context within which changes in cardiac activity may be interpreted. It can be argued that such a context may help in differentiating physiological factors from those of psychological relevance. Moreover, many of the current models of cardiac activity in psychophysiology emphasize the physiological nature of the response and highlight, therefore, the necessity for considering the role of physiological factors in the interpretation of the experiments on which the models are based. In this connection, Section 3.2 is concerned with the functional implications of phasic cardiac activity and includes summaries of two important models of cardiac activity and behaviour.

In addition to the four general areas described above, there is a section on the biofeedback and operant control of cardiac activity. Although other sections undoubtedly involve issues of importance for biofeedback control of cardiac activity, the extensive use of cardiac activity, both in the study of biofeedback control *per se* and in its clinical applications, indicated that this topic merited a separate contribution. Section 3.5 provides, therefore, an introduction to the specific problems associated with the application of biofeedback and operant control procedures to cardiac activity.

3.1.1 Psychological correlates

Cardiac activity has been used extensively as a psychophysiological measure, and its popularity may be traced to two factors. First, since the recording techniques arose from the older disciplines of medicine and physiology, they have been readily available for some time. Second, cardiac activity has long been associated with the concept of arousal. Cannon

(1929) put forward the idea of some generalized physiological response which accompanied the motivational changes elicited by a change in stimulation; this response was said to enhance or prepare the body's physiological state in order to facilitate increased behavioural drive. This particular interpretation of the arousal hypothesis has been termed 'energy mobilization' (Duffy, 1962). Since the heart was viewed as being intimately related to the regulation of metabolic requirements, the use of heart rate as an objective index of physiological arousal seemed entirely appropriate.

However, multiple response system recording soon began to suggest that there were differences in the pattern of physiological responses, and that these differences were a function of both individual differences between subjects (Malmo and Shagass, 1949) and the nature of the stimulus (Sternbach, 1960). More specifically, heart rate was shown to decelerate in response to simple stimuli (Darrow, 1929; Davis, Buchwald, and Frankmann, 1955) and to accelerate in response to intense or threatening stimuli (Sternbach, 1960), during periods of word association (Darrow, 1929) and during mental arithmetic (Blair and coworkers, 1959). Similarly, both accelerative and decelerative responses have been observed in classical conditioning paradigms (Wilson, 1969).

The bidirectional nature of cardiac changes posed problems for the simplistic arousal interpretation in which changes in cardiac activity were viewed only in terms of energy mobilization. Consequently, several alternative explanations were suggested in order to describe the relationship between cardiac activity and certain types of behaviour (e.g. Schachter, 1957). However, by far the most influential hypothesis concerning the 'directional fractionation' of cardiac activity was that of situational stereotypy (Lacey, 1967). Essentially, the original Lacey hypothesis related the directional fractionation of cardiac activity according to the type of situation in which stimulation occurred. It was argued that the situation may be appraised by the subject as one which required either environmental intake or environmental rejection; heart rate was said to decelerate in situations which required environmental intake, and to accelerate in situations in which environmental rejection was involved. However, the importance of this hypothesis was that it was not solely descriptive, but was extended to a functional explanation of the relationship between cardiac activity, cortical activity, and behaviour. The presence of cardiac deceleration was not just associated with environmental intake *per se*, but was said to be instrumental in the facilitation of sensory processing. Similarly, cardiac acceleration was said to lead to an inhibition of sensory processing. In support of this view, Lacey proposed a neurophysiological model by which cardiac and pressor responses indirectly altered cortical activity via a visceral afferent feedback loop mediated by the baroreceptors (Lacey, 1967, 1972). This emphasis on the active nature of cardiac activity has stimulated much research concerned with the relationships between various parameters of cardiac activity and performance on tasks involving some form of information processing (e.g. Higgins, 1971; Coles and Duncan-Johnson, 1975). Since the results of such studies have not provided unequivocal support for the Lacey hypothesis, and since a detailed review is beyond the scope of this introduction, the interested reader is referred to previous reviews (Elliott, 1972; J. I. Lacey and B. C. Lacey, 1974) and Section 3.2.2 of this chapter.

More recent experiments concerned with cardiac activity and performance have emphasized the importance of the task requirements which were inherent in much of the earlier work (e.g. Jennings and coworkers, 1971). In particular, the relationship between motor requirements and cardiac activity has been stressed, and the nature of this relationship can be contrasted with the active role ascribed to cardiac activity by Lacey. Specifically, it has been suggested that cardiac changes which accompany motor activity originate from an integrative mechanism which is common to the control of both cardiac activity and movement. The most elaborate hypothesis concerning somatic influences on cardiac activity has been proposed by Obrist and his colleagues (1974). Essentially, this hypothesis states that changes in cardiac activity reflect changes in the level of somatic movement. Increase in the general level of somatic activity is said to lead to an increase in the metabolic demand of the musculature, and this in turn, results in an increase in heart rate. The integration of the metabolic requirements of the musculature and level of cardiac activity has been termed cardiac–somatic coupling (Obrist, Lawler, and Gaebelein, 1974). However, Obrist has also argued that under certain conditions, specifically those related to active avoidance of aversive stimuli, cardiac–somatic coupling is dissociated, resulting in substantial increases in heart rate which are unrelated to the overt level of somatic activity. Once again, space limitations prevent a detailed review of the somatic coupling hypothesis; however, recent reviews are available (Obrist, 1976), along with a discussion of the current status of the hypothesis in Section 3.2.1 of this chapter.

As noted earlier, the purpose of this section is to illustrate the potential use of measures of cardiac activity in psychological research, and the above examples represent three distinct approaches to the problem. First, the use of cardiac activity in relation to the arousal hypothesis demonstrates its utility as a unidimensional index of psychological state. However, it appears that cardiac activity does not exhibit such a one-to-one relationship with other measures of arousal, either physiological or behavioural. Furthermore, cardiac responses have been shown to demonstrate short-term phasic changes of a bidirectional nature depending upon the nature of the stimulus. The second approach, the Lacey hypothesis, has attempted to resolve the problem of directional fractionation by identifying certain common elements within stimulus situations which are responsible for a particular cardiac change. This approach emphasizes the active role of cardiac activity as a possible intervening variable in psychological processes, especially those involved in information processing. The usefulness of such an hypothesis can be demonstrated by the work of Graham and Clifton (1966) who were concerned with the differentiation of orienting and defensive responses. These authors used the Lacey hypothesis in conjunction with a critical literature review, to identify the nature of both orienting and defensive responses. Not only did the literature substantiate the predicted directions in cardiac activity as a function of the nature of the stimulus, but the active role of cardiac activity suggested by Lacey was consistent with the functional significance of the responses as described by Sokolov (1963). Furthermore, it has been claimed by many workers who have examined the implications of Lacey's approach, that the original distinctions concerning situational stereotypy can be refined to include such psychological constructs as decision making (Coles and Duncan-Johnson, 1975), problem solving (Tursky, Schwartz and Crider, 1970), and affective appraisal (Gang and Teft, 1975) which it is said are sensitively linked to cardiac activity.

The third approach, the somatic coupling hypothesis, can be strongly contrasted with the previous two. This hypothesis concerns relationships between two physiological activities—somato-motor and cardiac. In this connection, Elliott (1974) has noted that if cardiac activity merely indexes changes in gross motor activity, its potential value for psychological research is minimal. However, there may be circumstances in which changes in the metabolic requirements of the musculature are of importance, and in those circumstances, the somatic-coupling hypothesis offers a sophisticated and specialized development of the earlier energy mobilization function associated with the arousal hypothesis. Moreover, even if the somatic-coupling hypothesis has limited predictive value for psychological theories, it does demonstrate a particular approach which is probably essential in the interpretation of other more psychologically relevant models of cardiac activity. Obrist (1976) has advocated what has been termed a psychobiological approach, and has stressed the importance of taking physiological considerations into account when reviewing the behaviour of particular peripheral physiological measures. The rationale of this approach rests upon the fact that a peripheral end organ effector such as the heart is under the influence of several intrinsic control systems which regulate its behaviour in accordance with homeostatic requirements. As such, the psychological effects on an effector probably represent only a small portion of the relevant influences. Thus, if a particular psychological source of variation is to be assessed accurately, it must be differentiated from other sources which are related to intrinsic homeostatic demands. The somatic–cardiac coupling hypothesis represents one of several sources of variance which must be identified in order to assess accurately the important psychological influences on cardiac activity. Several other sources of intrinsic regulation will be discussed in the next section.

The importance of the physiological control systems which are responsible for homeostatic regulation of cardiac activity has also been noted by Sayers (1975a), who has argued that the longer-term pattern of control of such systems may be a far better indicator of psychological influences than are short-term phasic changes in cardiac activity itself. His rationale for examining such changes arises from the statistical unreliability of phasic changes, and from the fact that if such changes occur, they are probably obscured or modified by homeostatic constraints. His approach, therefore, seeks to identify certain parameters of cardiac activity which represent homeostatic control mechanisms, and by this means, examine the effects of environmental events on the control processes. This approach is discussed in more detail in Section 3.4.1.

3.1.2 Cardiac physiology

The purpose of this section is to provide, via a brief résumé of cardiac physiology, a rationale for the use of heart rate or heart period as indices of cardiovascular dynamics, and to outline some of the levels of interaction between cardiac function and behaviour. As the models of cardiac–behavioural interaction become more complex (Obrist, 1976; Jennings and Wood, 1977; Lacey and Lacey, 1977), it is necessary to examine closely the physiological processes which underly changes in heart rate. However, since heart rate represents only one of a number of indices of cardiac function, it has become increasingly important to examine the general physiological mechanisms concerned with cardiovascular dynamics. This may well necessitate the evaluation of heart rate as an adequate index of cardiovascular control. Furthermore, investigation of the mechanisms responsible for heart rate and its regulation may help to identify the factors which influence changes in cardiac activity, especially those related to psychological events. Thus, the latter part of this section will deal specifically with both intrinsic and extrinsic factors which can affect cardiac function.

1.2.1 The structure and function of the heart

Essentially, the role of the heart within the cardiovascular system is that of a pump which supplies oxygenated blood to the tissues of the body in accordance with their metabolic requirements. In these terms, a comprehensive index of cardiac function would be one which described the rate of change in the volume of blood supplied to the tissues. However, since the cardiovascular system represents a closed loop, this hypothetical index is dependent on two factors. First, the volume of blood reaching the tissues is a function of the energy supplied to the system via the heart in its capacity as a pump, and second, the transfer of blood via the circulatory system depends on the peripheral resistance encountered. Accordingly, both of these factors must be assessed separately in order to derive some functional index of cardiovascular dynamics. The efficiency of the heart in supplying blood to the system can be expressed in terms of the volume of blood ejected from the heart at each contraction, i.e. the stroke volume, or as an integrated volume over some specified time period, i.e. cardiac output. Heart rate has also been used as an index of cardiac efficiency since if it is assumed that stroke volume remains constant, cardiac output will be related directly to heart rate. Thus, increases in heart rate should represent an increase in the volume of blood forced into the arterial circulation within a given amount of time. However, the assumption concerning stroke volume does not hold in all circumstances. On this basis, it is clear that heart rate represents only one aspect of cardiac output in that similar changes in heart rate can accompany different behavioural and physiological events. For example, an increase in heart rate can accompany either an increase or decrease in blood pressure depending on the overall status of the cardiovascular system.

The extent to which blood is forced into the arterial system can also be assessed by measurement of the height and velocity of the pressure wave which accompanies the expulsion of blood into the arterial vessels. However, changes in the characteristics of this wave may also be a function of the resistance encountered in the form of changes in the circumference of the arterial vessels. The techniques available for assessing such changes are discussed in the chapters on plethysmography and the measurement of blood pressure.

The structure of the mammalian heart consists essentially of four chambers, two ventricles and two atria. The ventricles represent the major muscular pumping chambers of the heart, and as such, are larger in terms of both volume and thickness than are the atria. The main function of the atria is to act as reservoirs for blood returning from the venous circulation prior to its reintroduction into the arterial circulation by the pumping action of the ventricles. Conceptually, the heart consists of two pumps, each of which is composed of one atria and one ventricle. These systems supply blood to the lungs (right ventricle and the pulmonary circulation) and to the rest of the body tissues (left ventricle and the systematic circulation). Because of its greater workload, the left ventricle is larger than the right.

The three main types of heart tissue are nodal tissue, Purkinje fibres, and the myocardium or heart muscle. The nodal tissue is instrumental in the origin and conduction of the excitatory depolarization which is responsible for cardiac contraction. It is found principally at three sites: the sinoatrial node (SA), the arteriventricular node (AV) and the bundles of His. The major site of spontaneously depolarizing cardiac tissue, or pacemaker, is the SA node. The Purkinje fibres represent a specialized conduction system associated with the rapid spread of depolarization throughout the ventricles. Finally, the myocardium constitutes the muscle fibres which are responsible for the contraction of the chambers of the heart. It should also be noted that the heart contains a network of blood vessels, the coronary vessels, which supply the tissues of the heart and also a series of specialized valves which regulate the flow of blood between the various chambers.

1.2.2 The cardiac cycle and its relationship with cardiac function and to the EKG

The contraction of the heart is initiated by a spread of depolarization from a pacemaker site to the myocardium which in turn undergoes contraction. The sequence of events which constitutes the cardiac cycle can be described with respect to either the course of electrical excitation or its resulting pressure/volume changes in the muscular chambers of the heart. The electrical events can be monitored either directly by recording the changes in current flow within the cardiac tissue using a unipolar electrode attachment to the cardiac tissues themselves, or indirectly by a surface-placed bipolar electrode configuration. It is the latter technique which gives rise to the EKG and is the one of major interest to the psychophysiologist. Similarly, the pressure changes which take place in the atria and ventricles can be monitored either directly, or indirectly by examination of their effect on the form and propagation of the transmitted pressure wave within the arterial system.

Initiation of the cardiac cycle commences with the spontaneous depolarization of the SA node which results in atrial contraction and an increase in pressure in both the atria and the ventricles; this gives rise to an inflow of blood from the former to the latter. This phase of depolarization corresponds to the P-wave within the EKG waveform. Excitation spreads to the AV node just prior to the termination of the P-wave and then travels through the bundles of His and the Purkinje system during the P–R segment. During this phase, the atria relax and this results in a relatively higher pressure within the ventricles. Ventricular depolarization and thus contraction is represented by the QRS complex and produces a rise in pressure within both the ventricles and the aorta. The subsequent relaxation of the ventricles and their repolarization are represented by the T-wave. The movement of blood between the various chambers of the heart is a result of pressure differences between the chambers and their associated vessels. This flow pattern is also modified by the presence of a series of valves located at junctions between the chambers. The inflow of blood to the heart is termed the diastolic phase, while the ejection of blood from the ventricles is termed the systolic phase of the cardiac cycle.

In summary, the cardiac cycle describes the sequence of events which is instrumental in the expulsion of blood into the arterial circulation. As was mentioned previously, this volume of blood (stroke volume) is a major determinant of both mean blood pressure within the system and also the amount of blood supplied to the tissues. The use of heart rate as an index of cardiac function, however, provides limited information concerning the nature of the cardiac cycle and its output. Heart rate, as it is usually defined, describes only the time interval between consecutive ventricular contractions as indicated by the R-wave of the EKG. As such, it represents only one factor which contributes to the determination of the cardiac cycle. Although there is often a positive relationship between heart rate and both stroke volume and cardiac output, this is not always the case. Other factors which relate to both the ventricular filling phase and the subsequent systole should also be considered. The most important of these is the amount of blood that is allowed to enter the ventricle during diastole, and this in turn is dependent on both the volume of blood returning from the venous circulation and the duration of the diastolic period. A second factor concerns the efficiency of ventricular contraction. The force developed by the ventricular myocardium and the subsequent amount of blood ejected is a function of the static muscle fibre length, the rate of dynamic contraction and the synchrony of the contractile units. Thus, there are several additional factors which can influence stroke volume and cardiac output, and these need to be considered when interpreting heart rate changes in relation to the overall pattern of cardiovascular dynamics.

1.2.3 Cardiac regulation

The cardiac cycle is influenced by several mechanisms which are responsible for the continuation of a stable steady-state level of performance and for the implementation of dynamic changes in performance brought about by changes in metabolic demand. The necessity for a steady state within the cardiovascular system has obvious importance, and it is not surprising that the regulation of cardiac function relies on control systems which operate at a higher level than does the intrinsic rhythmicity of the pacemaker. There are two main advantages of such a system. First, since the pacemaker represents a diverse population of cells, reliance upon such a system may result in a large degree of interbeat variability. Second, the ability of the heart to maintain an output which is sensitive to changes within the cardiovascular system as a whole requires some integrative mechanisms which can alter stroke volume. Such mechanisms are located within the cardiovascular system and as such, can be regarded as sources of intrinsic regulation. Similarly, mechanisms which bring about changes in stroke volume in relation to the metabolic requirements of the tissues must also exist. These changes may result from an actual change in metabolic demand or may even precede it in preparation for future activity. Thus, the input to this system is usually located external to the cardiovascular system and as such, may be described as extrinsic. The notion of both intrinsic and extrinsic control presupposes some form of effector mechanism which can bring about changes in the characteristics of the cardiac cycle. Indeed, the heart possesses a complex neural innervation and this is discussed below prior to a discussion of these actual control processes.

The neural innervation of the heart can be separated into two interactive inputs deriving from the sympathetic and parasympathetic branches of the autonomic nervous system. The sympathetic input consists of adrenergic fibres which originate in the spinal cord via the stellate and caudal cervical ganglia. Essentially, excitation of these inputs results in increases in blood pressure and heart rate which are associated with changes in both the myocardial contractile force and the pattern and duration of the cardiac cycle. More specifically, the greater contractile force results in a faster ejection of blood from the ventricles and this results in a shorter systolic phase and a subsequent increase in diastolic filling time. The net result of these changes is to ensure that stroke volume is maintained despite the rapid increase in heart rate (tachycardia). Furthermore, there appears to be, in the dog at least, some separation of the physical location for these two effects (Randall, 1977). The positive inotropic effect, or increased ventricular contractility, is associated primarily with stimulation of the left cardiac sympathetics, whereas the chronotropic, or increased heart rate response, appears to be more a function of right cardiac sympathetic stimulation.

The parasympathetic input consists of cholinergic fibres which originate from branches of the vagus nerve. Parasympathetic stimulation results in changes which are essentially antagonistic to sympathetic activity and results in a decrease in both heart rate and the contractile force of the myocardium. However, the exact nature of parasympathetic effects are dependent on two important variables. First, the magnitude of the effect is dependent on the time of arrival of vagal impulses with regard to the cardiac cycle. For example, Levy and colleagues (1969) have shown that there is an optimum interval between the onset of the P-wave and the onset of vagal stimulation for producing changes in interbeat interval. This

factor is of considerable importance in relation to both cycle time effects
(Jennings and Wood, 1977; Lacey and Lacey, Section 3.2.2 of this
Chapter) and the latency characteristics of vagally-induced cardiac
deceleration. Second, it has been demonstrated recently that neither
sympathetic not parasympathetic stimulation necessarily leads to mutually
antagonistic effects (Levy, 1971, 1977). Instead, sympathetic–parasympathetic
interactions have been described as examples of accentuated antagonism,
such that the degree of vagal cardio-inhibition is dependent on the background level of sympathetic activity. Thus, the greater the level of sympathetic activity, the greater will be the inhibitory effect for a given vagal
input. Interactions of this type may be of considerable importance for the
interpretation of both individual differences in reactivity and for the occurrence of paradoxical responses which may occur (Heilizer, 1975; Teichner,
1968).

Finally, a brief mention should be made of the origins of the cardiac
sympathetic and parasympathetic nerves. These origins were located
initially by isolation of the area within the central nervous system which is
responsible for both pressor and depressor effects on blood pressure. This
area, the medulla oblongata, was delineated further into centres which
were said to be responsible for sympathetic and parasympathetic
innervation of the heart. However, the classical model of cardiac regulation
which involves reciprocally-innervated excitatory and inhibitory centres has
been criticized recently. Specifically, it is argued that the physical location
of such centres is imprecise. More importantly perhaps, is the recent
recognition of the importance of the role of supramedullary structures in
cardiovascular control (Peiss, 1965).

Intrinsic control of the heart operates at two levels. First, the heart itself
exhibits a strong tendency to maintain an adequate stroke volume despite
changes in either the duration or extent of diastolic filling or systolic
contraction. This capacity has been termed autoregulation, and is believed
to depend on the intrinsic properties of the cardiac muscle. Since a detailed
discussion of these mechanisms is beyond the scope of this section, the
interested reader should consult the relevant reviews (Sarnoff and
coworkers, 1960; Berne and Levy, 1967). However, it should be
emphasized that the existence of these mechanisms implies the operation
of homeostatic constraints, and this may provide some physiological basis
for 'initial value' effects which are often demonstrated with cardiac data
(see Section 3.4.2).

The second level of operation of intrinsic control is concerned with the
integration of cardiac function in relation to the entire cardiovascular
system. For such a system to operate, there must be receptors present in
the circulatory system which are reflexively linked to the heart. Such
receptors have been identified and are broadly classified into two groups.

These are baroreceptors which are sensitive to changes in pressure within the cardiovascular system and the chemoreceptors which are sensitive to the concentration of pCO_2 and pO_2 in the blood. Both types of receptor are found within the carotid arteries and also in the aortic arch. There is also a third group, the pressoreceptors, which are located within the heart, and which are responsible for cardiovascular reflexes associated with the volume and pressure of the various cardiac chambers (Bard, 1968). However, it is the baroreceptors which are of prime interest to the psychophysiologist since changes in blood pressure probably occur more frequently in response to psychological stimuli than to changes in the chemical composition of the blood. Baroreceptors are said to stabilize blood pressure (Sleight, 1976) by reflexively slowing the heart in response to an increase in arterial blood pressure. Similarly, since a tonic level of baroreceptor discharge is always maintained, a fall in blood pressure results in a decrease in baroreceptor cardiac inhibition and a resulting increase in heart rate. The baroreceptor mechanism is important to psychophysiology for two reasons. First, it is possible that baroreceptors modify and attenuate cardiac responses which have been elicited by psychological stimuli. Second, the baroreceptors have been ascribed a specific role in the modification of cortical functioning by changes in heart rate (Lacey, 1972). This hypothesis is discussed in greater detail in Section 3.2.2.

There are many sources of externally-mediated changes in both cardiac function and the cardiovascular system as a whole. Detailed reviews are available concerning these influences which include postural change, exercise, temperature, somatic integration and emotional stress (Milnor, 1968; Berne and Levy, 1967; Cohen and MacDonald, 1974; Manning, 1977). Our purpose here is to examine only those influences of particular relevance to psychophysiology.

One of the most dominant influences on cardiac activity is respiration. Resting heart rate usually demonstrates a phasic cycling known as respiratory sinus arrhythmia and many authors have examined this feature in relation to the characteristics of the breathing pattern (Davies and Neilson, 1967; Manzotti, 1958), its implications for data quantification (see Section 3.4.2), and in relation to the effects of psychological variables (e.g. Piggott and coworkers, 1973). However, the central interest here concerns the mechanism responsible for the generation of these cyclic fluctuations. Melcher (1976) has reviewed this area recently and has suggested that the most important mechanism relies on low pressure atrial receptors that are located within the heart itself. These receptors are said ·to be responsive to the increased diastolic filling pressure which occurs as a function of changes in the intrathoracic pressure during respiration. Melcher has also suggested that during the acceleratory phase of respiratory sinus arrhythmia, there is an inhibition of the baroreceptor reflex which would normally accompany such an increase in heart rate. Furthermore, Davidson, Goldner, and McCloskey (1976) have demonstrated 'gating' of efferent vagal activity that is said to result from changes in the baroreceptor reflex gain which in turn, is related to respiratory phase. Such results might explain the observations by Gautier (1972) that cardiac decelerations could only be demonstrated during the expiratory phase of respiration. The possibility of respiratory linked vagal gating has major implications for cardiac psychophysiology, since the majority of stimulus-evoked cardiac responses are thought to be of a predominantly vagal origin (Obrist, Wood and Perez-Reyes, 1965). Similarly, alterations in the gain of the baroreceptor reflex may have implications for the Laceys' theory concerning sensorimotor behaviour.

Another form of physiological activity which has been associated with cardiac integration is that of movement or somatic activity. The most extreme example of cardio-somatomotor integration is seen in the cardiovascular response to exercise. Exertional behaviour is usually accompanied by an increase in cardiac output which results from an increased stroke volume and tachycardia (see Freyschuss, 1970). An alteration of baroreceptor reflex gain which results in lowered sensitivity (Cunningham and colleagues, 1972; Mancia and colleagues. 1978) also appears to accompany such changes. However, it has also been suggested that for less extreme forms of somatomotor activity, there is a reasonable degree of integration between the heart and the motor efferent system. This may be demonstrated by cardiac changes in relation to either muscular contraction (Freyschuss, 1970; Petro, Hollander and Bouman, 1970) or gross body movement (Obrist, 1976). The sources of mediation for such cardiovascular adjustments are obscure. However, Obrist (1976) has suggested that they may result from either proprioceptive feedback from the musculature or from some integrative mechanisms within the central nervous system which is common to both processes. The nature of cardiosomatic coupling is discussed in greater detail in Section 3.2.1. A more specialized form of cardiosomatic mechanisms can also be seen within specific muscle systems such as the cardio-ocular (Hayes, 1974) and the acoustic cardiac reflex (Hatton, Berg, and Graham, 1970).

Finally, some mention should be made of mechanisms which are responsible for short-term phasic changes in cardiac activity evoked by discrete stimuli. It appears that such responses are mediated primarily via the parasympathetic innervation of the heart (Obrist, Wood and Perez-Reyes, 1965; Fitzgerald, 1976; Dykman and Gantt, 1959). However, such generalizations should be made cautiously since Cohen (1974a) has demonstrated clearly the importance of sympathetic effects in classical conditioning in pigeons. Similarly, in situations involving aversive stimuli, there is a tendency for sympathetic dominance of cardiac function. This has been demonstrated in the aversive conditioning paradigm (Obrist and colleagues, 1972) and also in terms of cardiovascular changes in response to emotional stressors (Bond, 1943; Ulrych, 1969; Turpin and Siddle, 1978a).

Since identification of the relative sympathetic–parasympathetic contribution to cardiac responses is a central step for the understanding of cardiovascular mechanisms, some mention should be made of the procedures employed to determine these separate influences. First, there are the obvious invasive techniques for selectively disrupting the autonomic innervations. These may involve selective de-innervation (see Cohen, 1974b) or the use of pharmacological blocking agents (Obrist, Wood and Perez-Reyes, 1965). Both of the techniques, however, have obvious limitations for human psychophysiology and may also be too insensitive for certain animal preparations. Although non-invasive techniques are rare, some approaches have been suggested. Scher and his colleagues (1972) have suggested that the differential latency of cardiac responses to vagal and sympathetic stimulation may be used in this context. Matyas and King (1976) have also suggested that the T-wave amplitude may be viewed as a relative index of sympathetic activity. Similarly, Katona and Jih (1975) have argued that the relative changes in parasympathetic activity can be assessed by examination of the degree of respiratory sinus arrhythmia. This approach has been applied recently to psychophysiological data by Porges (1976). An alternative approach is to record several parameters of cardiac function in order to gain greater insight into the nature of changes which occur within the cardiac cycle. An example of this approach is the recording of the first differential of the carotid pulse and its use as an index of cardiac contractility (Lawler and Obrist, 1974). By assessing changes in cardiac contractility, these authors have suggested that vagally mediated increases in heart rate can be distinguished from sympathetic mediation.

3.1.3 Experimental design: subjects and their environment

1.3.1 Experimental setting and task requirements

The choice of measurement technique for cardiac activity depends on several factors which relate to the physical characteristics of the experimental paradigm. The first problem concerns the amount of movement that subjects are expected to make during the experimental session. Movement may bring about recording artifacts regardless of whether cardiac data are derived from the EKG or from a photoplethysmographic device. These artifacts arise either from movement of the cable connecting the electrodes to the preamplifier (Schneiderman,

Dauth and VanDercar, 1974) or from movement of the electrodes themselves.

The prevalence of movement artifact clearly depends on the type of experimental setting, e.g. EKG recording from aircraft pilots (Carruthers, Arguelles, and Mosovich, 1976) and on the ability of subjects to remain relatively still throughout the experimental session, e.g. recording from young children and neonates (Lewis, 1974). The optimal solution to the problem is to reduce the artifacts associated with connecting leads by adopting an indirect recording system which does not require a direct connection between the electrodes or transducer and the polygraph preamplifier. Two such systems are available, and they rely on either radiotelemetry to transmit the EKG signal to a receiver and preamplifier or on the use of a portable tape recorder such as Medilog (Oxford Instruments Company) which is attached to the subject and which records the EKG signals on tape for subsequent analysis (see Section 3.1.4). Obviously, in certain experimental situations where movement is restricted to a single limb (e.g. reaction time task), the occurrence of artifacts may be avoided by the use of an appropriate EKG electrode configuration.

A second major problem concerns whether cardiac activity is to be recorded in a laboratory or in the 'field'. If the latter is the case, problems arise from the physical restrictions on equipment size and from movement artifact from freely moving subjects. Again, the solution to these problems is the adoption of an indirect recording system. Aside from the reduction in movement artifact, both telemetry and Medilog possess advantages due to their compactness and flexibility with regard to power supply requirements. In fact, the successful application of these systems to cardiac measurement has resulted in the popular use of HR as a measure in many applied psychophysiological and ergonomic settings (e.g. Rolfe, 1973; Sayers, 1975a).

The final consideration concerning the experimental situation involves the possible influence of intrinsic variables such as temperature, humidity and posture on the data collected. Malmstrom (1971) and Norman and Melville (1972) have argued that such variables account for a substantial proportion of the variance associated with measures of 'resting heart rate'. More specifically, they cite reports which suggest that temperature (Kleitman and Ramsaroop, 1948), posture (Semler, 1965), smoking (Elliott and Thynsell, 1968), time of day (Luce, 1970), and time of the last meal (Grollman, 1929) can all affect the value of heart rate level. Whether such factors also affect phasic reactivity is difficult to assess since there have been no studies which specifically addressed this question. In summary, it would appear that where possible these variables should be controlled when measuring cardiac activity.

1.3.2 Subjects

There are several subject variables which should be considered in the measurement of cardiac activity. The first of these concerns the use of special techniques for animal (Schneiderman, Dauth and VanDercar, 1974) or neonatal (Lewis, 1974) recording. With regard to recording from neonates, there is a general problem of movement artifact, as well as specific problems concerning the inclusion of pacifiers, concealment of electrodes, and the monitoring of changes in arousal state. These more specific questions have been covered in previous reviews (Graham and Jackson, 1970; Lewis, 1974; Clifton and Nelson, 1976; Lipton, Steinschneider, and Richmond, 1961), and the general problem of movement artifact has already been dealt with here. The use of telemetry in neonatal research and the choice of appropriate electrode configurations have been discussed by Norman and Melville (1971) and Lewis (1974) respectively.

A second consideration relates to intrinsic variables such as sex, race and age, which, if uncontrolled, may contribute to the variance associated with measures of cardiac activity, and the aim here is to provide specific examples of group differences in cardiac activity. It should be noted, however, that although such differences may be demonstrated, they are not necessarily related to peripheral factors (as may be the case with electrodermal activity, Venables and Christie, 1973), but may reflect sex or racial differences in response to the experimental situation. Thus, caution should be exercised in generalizing from any particular study which might indicate group differences.

Few racial or ethnic differences in cardiac activity have been reported. Schachter and coworkers (1974) have reviewed a number of studies which indicate that resting HR level tends to be higher in black than white Americans, and higher in white Americans than in North American Indians. The higher levels in black Americans was also demonstrated by these authors in neonates matched for birth history and sociometric status. Schachter and coworkers (1975) also reported differences in the patterning of phasic responses; white newborns displayed greater cardiac deceleration than did black newborns. They also argued that these response differences were independent of differences in tonic level, and that they probably represented racial differences in cardiac regulation. However, there do not appear to be any similar reports of racial differences in reactivity within adult subjects, and it would be premature to extrapolate from the neonatal research to the typical adult experimental population.

Reported sex differences in cardiac activity are rare and tend to occur as incidental experimental findings. For example, Coles, Porges, and

Duncan-Johnson (1975) reported that males tended to demonstrate greater cardiac variability and larger cardiac deceleration to a reaction time warning stimulus than did females. Coles and coworkers (1975) interpreted these findings as suggesting greater cardiac plasticity in males than in females, and in support of this argument, cited a study by Young and Blanchard (1972) which demonstrated greater cardiac changes in males during instrumental cardiac conditioning. On the other hand, Duffy (1962) has suggested that greater cardiac variability is characteristic of women rather than men. The findings concerning phasic cardiac changes are also equivocal. McGuinness (1973) found no sex differences in terms of either initial response amplitude or in terms of number of responses to a series of tone presentations. In contrast, Hare and coworkers (1971) demonstrated differences in both the amplitude and direction of cardiac responses to visual stimuli. However, since some of the stimuli were of a highly affective nature, these differences may well represent differences in cognitive appraisal rather than in the underlying physiological mechanism.

The effect of age on cardiac activity is difficult to assess since there have been few studies which have included comparisons of cardiac activity from subjects spanning the age spectrum from birth to old age. However, it appears that for cardiac level at least, a distinction can be made between children and adults; adults seem to display lower HR levels than do children (Lawler, Obrist, and Lawler, 1976; Mills, Kunca, and Karrer, 1977). Similarly, Hellman and Stacey (1976) have reported a decrease in HR variability with increasing age in a group of subject aged 20 to 65 years. However, the effect of age on phasic activity is unclear. For example, developmental trends in phasic cardiac responses have been reported by Graham and colleagues (1970) and Sroufe (1971) respectively. On the other hand, Obrist and colleagues (1973) failed to show any developmental trends for either deceleration or acceleration. Differences between studies in terms of the age range used and the task requirements have undoubtedly contributed to such discrepancies.

In conclusion, it appears that such factors as sex, race, and age do affect cardiac activity. However, it should be pointed out that there are insufficient data to make general statements concerning the nature of these differences, especially in connection with phasic reactivity. Whether these differences are important in terms of error variance remains to be seen, and will undoubtedly depend on the range of such variables in the experimental sample. If this risk is great, error variance can be reduced either statistically or by the use of homogenous groups. However, the latter technique obviously leads to a restriction in the generality of the findings.

3.1.4 Measurement and quantification

1.4.1 Instrumentation

A variety of techniques has been used to measure cardiac activity and include the EKG, changes in the arterial pressure wave and changes in the pulse wave monitored at various sites within the peripheral circulatory system. Essentially, these techniques involve the measurement of the interbeat interval (IBI) between consecutive contractions of the heart. For laboratory work, the basic requirements consist of a transducer system, an amplifying system and a recording system. In the case of EKG measurement, the transducer usually takes the form of silver or stainless steel surface electrodes, while in the case of pulsatile measures, a photoplethysmographic device is employed. The amplifying system consists of a differential a.c. amplifier whose time constant is determined by the type of transducer. For EKG, a time constant of about 0.4 s is usually employed, whereas for pulsatile measures, a shorter time constant of about 0.03 to 0.1 s may be required if the baseline is to remain relatively constant. The choice of recording system depends largely on the method of quantification, and these considerations are discussed later. Basically, three techniques have been employed; raw IBI or heart rate are displayed on a chart recorder, digitized IBIs are presented on some form of visual display or raw IBI or heart rate are stored on magnetic tape for future processing, usually by a laboratory computer. A discussion of the instrumentation required for all the above techniques is presented in detail in Section 3.3.1.

It has already been noted that the type of subject tested and the task demands made upon subjects may determine the choice of recording technique. For example, since the EKG record is susceptible to muscle and movement artifacts, none of the standard electrode placements may be appropriate in situations where subjects are required to make motor responses. In such cases, either chest electrodes may be used (Chase, Graham, and Graham, 1968) or IBIs may be obtained from pulsatile measures. In the latter case, however, it should be noted that stimulation often produces changes in pulse amplitude, and this may raise difficulties in relation to the detection of IBIs. In this connection, Stern (1974) has shown that stimulation produces little change in pulse amplitude at the ear lobe, and has suggested the use of lobe plethysmography for reliable triggering.

However, if cardiac activity is to be monitored in extra-laboratory settings, it is necessary to include additional instrumention in order to overcome the problems of portability and movement artifact. There are two approaches to these problems. The first relies on the technique of radio telemetry which enables amplified signals from the transducer to be transmitted directly from the subject to an externally-located receiver. This obviously eliminates the need for the subject to be physically connected to the recording system via the usual leads. The common method of transmitting these signals is frequency modulation (FM). Here, the frequency and amplitude of the signal are used to modulate a carrier frequency produced by the transmitter, and this change in frequency is then decoded by the receiver and the original characteristics of the signal reconstructed. The actual frequency of the carrier is usually in the VHF waveband (100 MHz), although in certain situations such as in the use of telemetry in swimmers, a low frequency carrier (400 KHz) may be used (Frampton, Riddle, and Roberts, 1976). VHF systems possess an advantage in that they use the standard FM radio broadcast band and thus allow the use of commercially available receivers. Moreover, most telemetric transmitters have a range of only 20–50 feet and do not, therefore, interfere with radio broadcasts. However, if a greater distance is required, a more powerful transmitter must be used and the problem of interference with commercial radio becomes important. A detailed account of the uses of telemetry and some of the available circuits has been presented elsewhere (Schneiderman, Dauth, and VanDercar, 1974; Ko, 1970; Frampton, Riddle, and Roberts, 1976; Taggart, Gibbons, and Somerville, 1969).

The second approach uses a small cassette tape recorder which is worn by the subject and which records the amplified signals from the transducer. One example is the Medilog system (Oxford Instruments) which consists of a four channel cassette recorder capable of recording up to 24 hours of physiological data on one cassette. The portability of this machine is ensured by its compactness and by its battery power supply. The recorded physiological data are then played back via a replay machine, usually at much increased speed, into the usual data quantification system, e.g. minicomputer, where they can be processed according to the needs of the experimenter. The advantages of this system lie in its unlimited range of operation and in the fact that there are none of the interference problems which can be associated with radio telemetry. However, Frampton and colleagues have suggested that in physically active subjects, the tape recorder suffers from wow and flutter caused by high angular accelerations. Another consideration is that of cost in that radio telemetry instrumentation can be constructed by the experimenter, whereas the use of a miniature tape recorder relies on the availability of commercially produced systems. A recent example of the application of the Medilog system is described by Carruthers, Arguelles, and Mosovich (1976).

Regardless of which technique is employed to obtain the EKG or the pulsatile waveform, it is necessary to quantify the raw data in terms of the IBI or its reciprocal, heart rate. Although IBI data can be obtained by manual scoring of polygraph records (Hayes and Venables, 1972), most researchers feed the signal into a laboratory computer or record it on magnetic tape for subsequent computer analysis. In either case, this involves triggering of the computer laboratory peripheral system and, therefore, the detection of R-waves. Although the most common method of R-wave detection utilizes a Schmitt trigger (amplitude discriminator), a number of other techniques involving peak detectors, time windows and one-shot multivibrators have been employed (Schneiderman, Dauth, and VanDercar, 1974). If a laboratory computer is not available, the easiest way of measuring IBIs is by the use of a cardiotachometer (Brener, 1967). Essentially, this device produces a voltage output proportional in amplitude to the interval between successive R-waves. Although the IBI expressed in this way has usually been in terms of HR, a device which gives the raw IBI or HP output has been described recently (Shimizu, 1977). A detailed discussion of the instrumentation required for the quantification of IBIs can be found in Section 3.3.1.

A recent area of interest which also requires additional instrumentation is that of biofeedback control of cardiac activity. Both binary and analogue feedback have been employed, and in some work, binary feedback concerning whether each IBI was shorter or longer that the criterion duration was achieved by the use of logic circuits (Brener and Hothersall, 1966). Analogue feedback has been presented via a simple meter display (Blanchard, Young, and McLeod, 1972). More recent work with both types of feedback has utilized computer measurement, control, and feedback display (Lang and Twentyman, 1974). A review of these and other techniques associated with biofeedback research is presented in Section 3.5.

1.4.2 Quantification

Measurement of an IBI provides a measure of HP in milliseconds, while cardiotachometer output provides a measure of HR in beats per minute (bpm). Although it is often assumed that there is little difference between the two units, the transformation of IBIs to HR is a non-linear one, and as Graham and Jackson (1970) have noted, both measures cannot, therefore, have the same linear relationship with a third variable. The choice of HP or HR is a continuing issue, and while some authors (Graham and Jackson, 1970) have suggested that the non-linearity is only moderate and might not be of practical significance, others (Khachaturian and colleagues, 1972) have argued that if HR is used, the non-linearity may distort the IBI relationships within the original data. Similarly, Graham and Jackson (1970) have reported little difference in terms of skewness between HP and HR distributions, while Jennings, Stringfellow and M. Graham (1974) have reported that HP demonstrates fewer departures from linearity than does HR.

A second problem in the quantification of cardiac activity concerns the time base employed. If a real time base is used, an equal interval time dimension (usually 1 s) is employed, and the mean values of all full and partial IBIs during one interval are weighted according to the fraction of that interval occupied by each and expressed in terms of either HP or HR. This is known as second-by-second analysis. Alternatively, a beat-by-beat analysis employs what Graham and Jackson (1970) have termed 'organismic time' and quantifies cardiac activity for each successive beat of the heart. Clearly, the response curve obtained with the two methods may not be identical since subjects differ in terms of prestimulus level. Although cardiotachometer output is obviously more amenable to beat-by-beat analysis, second-by-second analysis facilitates the comparison of cardiac activity across events and across groups of subjects who may differ widely in terms of tonic cardiac level. Section 3.3.2 presents a detailed discussion of the second-by-second versus beat-by-beat issue as well as a consideration of the appropriate unit of measurement for cardiac activity, i.e. HP versus HR.

3.1.5 Analysis of cardiac data

1.5.1 Tonic level

Although there has been much recent interest in phasic cardiac activity, there are also many psychophysiological problems which involve the measurement of cardiac activity over relatively long time periods. In such circumstances, the experimenter may be interested in differences in tonic cardiac level between subjects as a function of say psychiatric diagnosis, or in differences within subjects as a function of task demands. One characteristic of experiments in which cardiac level is of interest is the large amount of data which is collected, and a major problem concerns the appropriate choice of statistic to represent such data. Although the simplest approach has been to sample cardiac activity at regular intervals (see Elliott, 1970), this is wasteful of data and ignores the fundamental nature of cardiac activity itself. Cardiac activity is essentially a time series composed of several different linear and cyclic trends. Moreover, the periodicity of these trends may be of several hours or seconds, and although some scoring procedures such as the method of mean cyclic maxima (Malmstrom, 1968) attempt to reduce the influence of this type of variability on the estimation of mean level, they ignore the possibility that cardiac variability itself might be a useful measure.

On the basis of this sort of argument, a number of techniques which attempt to take the time series nature of cardiac activity into account have been developed. Essentially, they are concerned with the variability exhibited within the cardiac record. They range from a simple estimation of the standard deviation of cardiac values which may take into account the serial dependence between successive beats (Varni, Clarke, and Giddon, 1971; Burdick, 1968, 1978; Luczak and Laurig, 1973), to sophisticated forms of waveform analysis which utilize either the autocorrelation function of the data or Fourier analysis. A detailed discussion of these techniques is presented in Section 3.4.1.

1.5.2 Phasic activity

Cardiac activity following presentation of a stimulus may be expressed along temporal and magnitudinal dimensions and the graphical representation of such activity may be termed the cardiac response curve (CRC). Although the shape of this curve, expressed in terms of either HR or HP is in itself sufficient to demonstrate the presence of stimulus-bound changes in cardiac activity (Wilson, 1974; Graham, Putnam, and Leavitt, 1975), the large between- and within-subjects variance associated with this method has precluded its widespread use. Instead, methods which are designed to differentiate pre- and poststimulus activity have been developed. An example of such a technique is the simple difference score in which the mean of a number of prestimulus beats or seconds is subtracted from each individual poststimulus beat or second. Such a differentiation results in a set of difference scores which represent the evoked cardiac response (ECR). However, the use of change or difference scores is a controversial matter in psychophysiological research in general, and there are two problems specifically related to the ECR. The first concerns the effect of prestimulus level (initial level) on poststimulus scores, while the second concerns the problem of the variability inherent in prestimulus cardiac activity.

With regard to the effect of initial level, numerous authors (Lacey, 1956; Block and Bridger, 1962; Clifton and Graham, 1968; Graham and Jackson, 1970) have suggested that Wilder's (1962) law of initial value operates in the case of cardiac activity. Essentially, this law posits a relationship between prestimulus level (X) and either poststimulus level (Y) or the difference score ($Y - X$). If such a relationship exists in a particular data set, methods for removing the dependence of $Y - X$ on X are of importance, and three techniques have been employed. The first involves the manipulation of X around a certain constant value within the experimental situation (Woodcock, 1971). The second, which is currently used by many authors, relies on the statistical adjustment of either Y or

$Y - X$ in terms of the degree of their dependency on X (Lacey, 1956; Benjamin, 1963, 1967). The third method utilizes a 'range-correction' procedure (Lykken, 1968; Lykken and Venables, 1971). None of these methods seems to be completely satisfactory and a discussion of their advantages and disadvantages is presented in Section 3.4.2.

The measurement of the ECR and the adjustment of difference scores in terms of their dependence on initial level presupposes reliable measurement of the prestimulus level. The mean of several prestimulus HR or HP values is used frequently, and would be adequate if cardiac activity was reasonably constant. However, as noted earlier, cardiac activity is composed of several different trends; the periodicity of the cyclic fluctuations may range from several hours (Halberg, 1969) to a few seconds (Sayers, 1975a). Trends with a relatively short periodicity are known as sinus arrhythmia, and are of some consequence for the quantification of the ECR, since it is possible for several cycles to occur during the duration of the normal analysis period. Although there are several sources of sinus arrhythmia (SA), respiratory sinus arrhythmia is usually the most dominant and consists of a resting cardiac waveform with a periodicity of about 3–12 s and a peak-to-trough amplitude of 2-20 bpm. Thus, a major difficulty in the quantification of the ECR concerns the differentiation of pre- and poststimulus data points which occur against a background of this waveform. In essence, the difficulty concerns the fact that poststimulus HR or HP represents a summation of any phasic response and the ongoing stimulus-irrelevant cardiac activity. Indeed, a number of studies have shown that the shape and variability of ECRs are determined, at least in part, by the direction of prestimulus level (Williams, Schachter and Tobin, 1967; Hart, 1975). It could be argued, of course, that the effects of SA are averaged out when data are collapsed across either subjects or trials. However, this does not seem to be the case, even in the case of a pseudostimulus (Turpin and Siddle, 1978b). Alternatively, it is possible to reduce response variability by presenting stimuli at a constant point with respect to the respiratory phase. However, although mean SA amplitude tends to correlate with mean respiratory cycle length, individual cycles do not show this correlation (Cort and colleagues, 1977). Thus, control of stimulus presentation within the respiratory phase will still leave some residual variability. Moreover, this procedure may not be experimentally convenient, particular when stimulus presentations have to be fixed in real time. A number of *post hoc* techniques which attempt to take the variability of prestimulus level into account are discussed in Section 3.4.2.

If we assume that pre- minus poststimulus difference scores have been reliably obtained and perhaps corrected for their dependency on initial level, the question arises as to how the data should be analysed. Two major approaches have emerged. The first involves analysis of the CRC, while the second involves response parameter analysis. Response curve analysis has usually involved analysis of variance with repeated measures. Wilson (1967) has identified the *F*-ratios to be tested in order to assess the reliability of poststimulus change scores across trials and groups, and also within subjects, trials, and groups. Additionally, he has drawn attention to the implications of the unequal variance–covariance matrices which are often present, and has stressed the importance of estimating epsilon, the correction factor for degrees of freedom, which is necessary in such situations. A detailed account of CRC analysis is provided in Section 3.4.3.

Response parameter analysis involves the selection of certain criterion indices of the response profile which are then scored individually for each subject (Woodcock, 1971; Lipton, Steinschneider, and Richmond, 1961; Lobstein, 1974). Since there is a wide range of ECR indices, a detailed account cannot be provided in this introduction. Instead, we would like to emphasize some of the problems that may be encountered in this form of analysis. The first derives from the lack of an expressed rationale for particular response indices. Indices can and should be derived on the basis of past knowledge of the stimulus and the experimental situation, observation of the response profile, or in terms of lack of ambiguity. The first criterion should be available for most experiments which are performed at present, and the predicted shape of the ECR should be clearly stated in the overall rationale of the experiment. If, for some reason, the situation is novel and no prediction concerning ECR shape can be made, *post hoc* examination of the group and individual CRCs will have to be made to select the appropriate response index. These curves should be examined in any case, even when a prediction has been made. The index should also be unambiguous in that the observed changes should be easily interpreted. For example, the 'peak-to-valley difference' index (Lang and Hnatiow, 1962) where habituation may represent a decrement in either the decelerative or the accelerative component does not seem to meet requirements of lack of ambiguity.

A second problem concerns the choice of beat or IBI sample size and the time base from which the index is to be chosen. Graham and Jackson (1970) have demonstrated the danger of unequal sample sizes when the index concerns a pre–poststimulus difference. Similarly, Lobstein (1974) has suggested that an initial level effect can be generated when the time bases for selection are mixed, e.g. the maximum decelerative beat within 4 s.

The last problem arises when polyphasic responses occur and only one of the response components is selected for analysis. The chosen index will represent change in only one direction; this results in a biased weighting of those ECRs which represent change in the opposite direction to the index

G

since they must receive either negative or zero scores (Graham and Jackson, 1970; Lewis, 1974). This problem can be overcome by using either multiple response indices in both directions or a response index which represents a maximum change in either direction. In this way, both accelerative and decelerative responses are equally weighted independently of the direction of change. Finally, it should be noted that response parameter analysis using individual indices derived from the CRC bears certain conceptual similarities to multivariate techniques such as Tucker's three-way factor analysis (see Section 3.4.3) which have recently been applied to cardiac data. Both techniques attempt to identify and analyse individual components of the CRC, as well as examining overall group differences between CRCs.

This introduction to the analysis of phasic cardiac activity has largely been confined to changes in response amplitude. Temporal measures of phasic cardiac change have seldom been undertaken. Presumably, this is due to the difficulties which are often encountered in specifying the exact profile of the CRC. When temporal measures have been extracted from the CRC, they have usually been associated with a response parameter analysis. For example, response latency was considered by Lipton, Steinschneider, and Richmond (1961) as the time from stimulus onset to peak response. Similarly, Chase (1965) defined latency in terms of the number of beats required to obtain maximum response level. Temporal measures other than latency have included response duration (Clifton and Graham, 1968) and return latency (Lipton, Steinschneider, and Richmond, 1961).

3.2 FUNCTIONAL IMPLICATIONS OF PHASIC CARDIAC ACTIVITY

3.2.1 The cardiac-behavioural interaction*

Paul A. Obrist, Alan W. Langer,
Alberto Grignolo, Kathleen C. Light and James A. McCubbin

The purpose of this section is to overview briefly our research, particularly that of the past five years, concerning cardiovascular behavioural interactions. This will include a disussion of what we believe the data tell us about how this interaction comes about and its significance to some current psychophysiological issues.

Acknowledgement. The research cited which was performed by the authors was supported by Grants MH-07995, National Institute of Mental Health and HL 18976, National Institutes of Health, United States Public Health Service.

2.1.1 Heart rate and somatic covariation

This work has been reviewed in several sources (Obrist and coworkers, 1970a; Obrist, Sutterer, and Howard, 1972; Obrist and coworkers, 1974a; Obrist, 1976). Therefore, only the major conclusions will be discussed.

In aversive paradigms where the subject has no control of the aversive events, such as classical conditioning, (e.g. Wood and Obrist, 1964) and in non-aversive paradigms which have some motivationally or emotionally significant consequences, such as the signalled RT task (Obrist, Webb, and Sutterer, 1969; Wood and Obrist, 1968), the heart rate (HR) changes observed, whether increases or decreases, are primarily under vagal control. Most importantly, when there is an increase in vagal excitation resulting in a decrease in HR, as is seen in humans in anticipation of unavoidable signalled aversive events, sympathetic excitatory effects are masked (Obrist, Wood and Perez-Reyes, 1965; Obrist and coworkers, 1970b; Obrist and Webb, 1967; Obrist and coworkers, 1974b). These vagally mediated HR effects are directionally related to somatomotor or striate muscular activity, including both subtle activities such as movements in and around the mouth, and more gross movements such as postural changes and struggling. This relationship was observed in children (Obrist and coworkers, 1973; Lawler, Obrist and Lawler, 1976), young adults (Obrist, 1968; Obrist and coworkers, 1970b; Obrist and coworkers, 1974b; Webb and Obrist, 1970), dogs (Obrist and Webb, 1967; Sutterer and Obrist, 1972; Webb and Obrist, 1967), and cats, who also demonstrate a concomitance between HR and electrical activity in the pyramidal tract (Howard and coworkers, 1974). Experimental manipulations which alter HR have a similar effect on somatomotor activity (e.g., see Obrist, 1968; Webb and Obrist, 1967, 1970). Other investigators have made similar observations (e.g., Elliott, 1974; Black and DeToledo, 1972; Roberts, 1974).

These various observations have led us to develop the position that this relationship between these vagally mediated HR changes and somatomotor activity is due to the manner in which cardiovascular and striate muscular activity is integrated within the central nervous system. This integration allows the cardiovascular system to adjust rapidly and efficiently to alterations in metabolic requirements associated with changes in striate muscular activity. This has been reviewed elsewhere (Obrist and coworkers, 1970a; Obrist and coworkers, 1974a). It has been further supported by recent observations that heart rate acceleration is still observed when humans are instructed either to tense or move an arm even though such is impossible because of experimentally induced local paralysis (Freyschuss, 1970) or nerve damage (Brucker and coworkers, 1975). Also, non-curarized rats shaped with operant contingencies to either increase or decrease HR demonstrate pronounced changes in O_2 consumption and ambulation consistent in direction with the HR changes (Brener, Phillips and Connally, 1977). Admittedly, one can make a better case for this causal relationship when there is a significant increase in metabolic activity such as when a dog struggles. Phasic anticipatory decreases in heart rate and somatic activity typically observed in humans are likely too small and brief in duration to result in any measurable change in either cardiac output (CO) or O_2 consumption. Yet vagal influences on the heart appear closely integrated with somatic activity. For example, at the onset of exercise, loss of vagal tone occurs within a beat (Rushmer, 1976). Also, we have observed in resting humans, momentary 3–4 beat increases in HR associated with such subtle activities as mouth movements (Obrist, 1968). Therefore, until an alternative or additional mechanism can be demonstrated, we are forced to maintain the position that under circumstances where a concomitance between vagally mediated HR and somatic activities are observed, it is because of this central integrating mechanism.

Finally, a brief word on the significance of the phasic anticipatory decreases in HR and somatic activity to behavioural processes. We have proposed that in non-aversive paradigms such as the signalled RT task, these phasic effects reflect attentional processes, i.e. task-irrelevant somatic activities cease. Heart rate decelerates because of the integrative mechanism. There is some evidence to support this (e.g. Obrist and coworkers, 1970b). In aversive paradigms, the significance is not clear. One possibility is that under conditions where escape or avoidance is not possible, recourse to immobility is protective, e.g. minimizes pain (see Obrist, Webb, and Sutterer, 1969). However, there is to our knowledge no definitive evidence on this possibility.

2.1.2 Sympathetic influences on the myocardium

A paradox that the previously described work did not resolve was why sympathetic influences were observed with respect to vasomotor and sudomotor activity (Obrist, Wood, and Perez-Reyes, 1965; Roberts, 1974) but not on the myocardium. It was in pursuit of this issue that we have shifted our efforts into a more complete appraisal of hemodynamic processes particularly as they relate to blood pressure control and the possible relevance of stress for the etiology of hypertension.

The first effort was to modify the aversive paradigm from one where the aversive events were inescapable or unavoidable to one where the aversive events were avoidable or controllable contingent on a subject's performance. A beta-adrenergic influence on the myocardium was now observed. Using a signalled RT shock avoidance paradigm, both HR and an indirect index of cardiac force were observed to anticipate the aversive stimulus, the receipt of which was made contingent on performance. Use of beta-adrenergic blockade verified that these phasic myocardial changes were sympathetic in origin (Obrist and coworkers, 1974b). Also, three measures of somatic activity were observed to be independent of the phasic cardiac events. As myocardial activity was increasing, somatic activity was decreasing. Finally, it should be noted that prior to when the sympathetic effect was observed, i.e. during the eight second foreperiod and immediately after response execution, both increases and decreases in HR were under vagal control. At this point, somatic activity did covary with HR. This also suggests that when the heart is primarily under vagal control as is true in classical conditioning and a non-aversive signalled RT task, as well as the foreperiod of this shock avoidance task, its control is integrated with somatic activity. Once sympathetic effects become manifest this integration breaks down.

The next question was why had a sympathetic influence on the myocardium now been demonstrated. There seemed to be two possibilities. One, the shock avoidance task was in some manner more stressful. Second, giving subjects some control over the aversive stimuli was somehow important. Several recent experiments bear on this (Obrist and coworkers, 1978). Only one study concerned the question of stress intensity. It was not conclusive.The problem here is the difficulty in operationalizing stress intensity. The second possibility, i.e. the availability of control, has been investigated now in three studies. The results of these are more conclusive. Here the focus was on tonic levels of myocardial activity, i.e. on the difference in myocardial activity between a resting baseline and that observed over the course of the stressor, which could range from 90 seconds to 20 minutes. This was because in the previous shock avoidance study (Obrist and coworkers, 1974b) tonic levels of activity were observed to increase appreciably at the onset of the RT task. This tonic increase was not observed in an earlier classical aversive conditioning study (Hastings and Obrist, 1967). In one experiment, the control parameter was manipulated using a biofeedback paradigm by leading one group of subjects to believe they had control of the aversive events (when in fact, they did not) in contrast to another group given no indications they had control. Initially, both measures of myocardial performance increased tonically, but increases were sustained only in subjects believing they had control. In a second study, two manipulations of the control variable were performed. One compared myocardial changes to stressors where no control was provided (i.e. the cold pressor and viewing a pornographic movie) to a stressor where control was actually provided (i.e. an unsignalled shock avoidance RT task). Much more pronounced increases in myocardial performance were observed with the avoidance task. Use of pharmacological blockade again verified that this was beta-adrenergic in origin. A second procedure was manipulating the difficulty of the avoidance task to determine if the sympathetic effect would be more prolonged under a condition where the task was sufficiently difficult to keep subjects engaged. This condition was compared to conditions where the task criterion was either very easy or impossible to master. Although under all three conditions, myocardial activity initially increased, it dissipated more rapidly under the conditions where the task was either too easy or too hard. Thus, once a subject realizes he either has perfect control or no control of the stressors, the beta-adrenergic effect dissipates.

Although these data indicate that the control dimension is significant, there is unquestionably more to the picture. One other significant variable appears to be a novelty or an uncertainty effect with respect to the nature of the stressors, e.g. what the shock will feel like. In the previous study where one group of subjects were not led to believe they had control of the aversive stimuli, half were given no prior experience with the shocks while half were. Those with no experience were much more reactive at the onset of the task. This effect was not observed with subjects led to believe they had control. Dogs show a similar effect when first exposed to aversive stressors (Obrist and coworkers, 1972). However, dogs typically struggle at this point which might be viewed as an attempt to control through escape. Another variable is individual differences in myocardial reactivity. This is clearly seen from the experiment (Obrist and coworkers, 1978) involving two no-control stressors and a control shock avoidance stressor. Averaged over all stressors, control resulted in an appreciably greater sympathetic influence on the heart. However, if one removes from the group the most myocardially reactive 25% of the subjects, the control condition is no longer significantly differentiated from the two no-control conditions on heart rate, and now is only modestly differentiated on the cardiac force measure.

2.1.3 Sympathetic activity—metabolic relevance

As previously noted, these sympathetic effects on the myocardium appear independent of concurrent somatic activity. This suggests that the beta-adrenergic effect is metabolically unwarranted particularly in those very reactive subjects where, for example, HR increases in excess of 40 bpm. This is of significance since such metabolically unwarranted effects could be the forerunner of pathological changes. That is to say, no one believes that exercise which in a healthy person results in a metabolically warranted adjustment is harmful to one's health. We have some recent data from a chronic dog preparation which bears on this. One can ascertain whether a given cardiovascular adjustment occurring to a behavioural stressor is metabolically warranted by assessing the relationship between CO and O_2 consumption as derived from arterial–venous (AV) oxygen differences in the following way. First, assess this relationship during treadmill exercise which results in a metabolically warranted adjustment and as such serves as a reference point for a given dog. Then, expose the dog to a shock avoidance task. Data have been collected on six dogs. In three, there was clear evidence of a metabolically unwarranted adjustment. Over a range of treadmill speeds both CO and the AV differences increased linearly as the intensity of exercise increased. However, during shock avoidance, this relationship broke down. Although the CO tended to increase to varying degrees, the AV difference or O_2 consumption failed to increase to the same degree as in exercise. In effect, the heart was pumping excessive amounts of blood relative to the metabolic requirements. Put another way, it was not adjusting efficiently as it commonly does during exercise. Although this effect was not pronounced in three other dogs and actually reversed in one, there was still a disruption in the relationship between CO and the AV difference which at this point is hard to fathom. If one looks at the relation of HR to the AV difference, which like the CO is directly related during exercise, the relationship was more clearly disrupted in all six dogs. That is, at comparable levels of HR, the O_2 consumption was less during stress than exercise.

2.1.4 Blood pressure control

A final issue to discuss concerns the control of blood pressure. We began to measure both the systolic (SBP) and diastolic (DBP) pressure non-invasively in humans when evaluating the control dimension using the cold pressor, film, and avoidance task. SBP was observed to be most elevated during the avoidance task and directly related to the magnitude of the myocardial effect. On the other hand, DBP increased least under this condition and tended to be inversely related to the magnitude of the myocardial effect. DBP in some subjects actually decreased below baseline momentarily at the onset of the avoidance task. This DPB effect can be interpreted as reflecting a beta-adrenergic effect on the vasculature producing vasodilation which results in little or no increase in total peripheral resistance. The SBP effect can be understood as reflecting a more forceful cardiac beat and an elevated CO. This was verified with respect to cardiac force in humans with pharmacological blockade where there was also observed an attenuation of the increase in SBP while the DBP was more increased. On the other hand, blockade had a minimal influence on both SBP and DBP during the cold pressor and film, indicating that myocardial influences on BP were less under these conditions. In dogs, we have directly measured the CO in three studies during shock avoidance and find it elevated particularly early in training or at the onset of a given bout of avoidance. Large individual differences are also found with more reactive dogs demonstrating a greater increase in both CO and BP (Lawler, Obrist, and Lawler, 1975). In a study just being completed, we have also now demonstrated a significant beta-adrenergic influence on the myocardium and SBP under these conditions.

One relevant aspect of these data is how they bear on the possible influence of stress in the etiology of hypertension. We are only beginning to get involved in this problem but a brief discussion of the issue seems appropriate. There is evidence to suggest that in the early stages of hypertension (i.e. borderline or labile hypertension) a significant number of such individuals demonstrate a heightened beta-adrenergic influence on the myocardium (see Obrist and coworkers, 1977). If a borderline or labile hypertension is in fact the precursor of a later more sustained and elevated blood pressure and if stress has some role in the etiology, then it would be expected that individuals who are most reactive myocardially under conditions which evoke maximal sympathetic influences on the heart (e.g. shock avoidance task) should have a higher and/or a more labile casual blood pressure under naturalistic or field conditions. Work in progress is now evaluating this possibility. It involves a difficult technology which is still being developed. For example, we are attempting to develop a means to measure pulse wave propagation time (PPT) in the field. PPT we have found to be highly related to SBP and sympathetic influences on the myocardium. Also, it is a non-encumbering procedure in that it does not disrupt the subject's activities.

In summary, our current research has shed additional light on the manner the cardiovascular system is influenced by the organism's interaction with its environment. It has also pointed the way by which a psychophysiological strategy might prove relevant in furthering our understanding of the hypertensive disease process.

3.2.2 Sensorimotor behaviour and cardiac activity*

Beatrice C. Lacey and John I. Lacey

Probably in the majority of psychophysiological investigations where multiple physiological recordings are made, it will be found that all measures change congruently, all changing in a sympathetic-like manner, or all showing a parasympathetic-like response. Quantitative analyses have

*Acknowledgement. This research was supported by a grant (MH 623) from the National Institute of Mental Health.

shown, however, that there are individual-specific and situational-specific variations in the pattern of response. In particular, blood pressure and heart rate may decrease while other simultaneously recorded variables, such as electrodermal and pupillary activity, show sympathetic-like changes (e.g. Lacey and coworkers, 1963; Lacey and Lacey, 1970; Libby, Lacey, and Lacey, 1973). To this phenomenon we have applied the term 'directional fractionation' to imply that different fractions of the autonomic nervous system may show different directions of response. We have found repeatedly that tasks which invoke an intention by the subject to note and detect environmental events produce such directional fractionation.

Our original formulation that bradycardia accompanies attention to simple environmental events was quickly followed by our observation that systematic beat-by-beat cardiac deceleration reliably appears in the foreperiod of simple reaction time tasks in anticipation of an imperative stimulus requiring a rapid motor response (Lacey and Lacey, 1970). The decelerations, which can be very large (40 beats per minute in an occasional subject), reach a nadir at the time of stimulation and response. They occur in a majority of individuals and trials, persist over time, increase with increased motivation, appear with diverse respiratory patterns, and are not secondary to hypertensive episodes (Nowlin, Thompson, and Eisdorfer, 1969). We have found repeatedly (e.g. Lacey and Lacey, 1970) a consistent, though typically low, correlation associating fast reaction times with large decelerations, a finding now widely, although not invariably, replicated (e.g. Connor and Lang, 1969; Duncan-Johnson and Coles, 1974; Holloway and Parsons, 1972; Obrist, Webb, and Sutterer, 1969).

Anticipatory cardiac deceleration is not restricted to the reaction time experiment. It has been found, for example, in time-estimation experiments (Johnson and May, 1969), in a task in which thinking the word 'stop' was substituted for an overt motor response (Schwartz and Higgins, 1971), and in a variety of other circumstances. Whether all such instances can be accommodated within a common interpretative framework is a problem for future exploration. In current work, we are focusing on the fact that cardiac deceleration precedes the emission of subject-initiated ('voluntary') motor responses in experiments in which the response is made to result in the instantaneous occurrence of signal stimuli. We first observed this phenomenon in subjects pressing a telegraph key on an operant (drl 15″ 1h 4″) schedule (Lacey and Lacey, 1970, 1973). In more recent experiments in our laboratory, deceleration was seen in advance of still another 'volitional' act—a self-initiated response which resulted in a tachistoscopic exposure (Lacey and Lacey, 1978). Figure 3.1 shows the anticipatory pattern of a typical subject in this experiment. At the top is a computer averaged cardiotachometric curve which shows that heart rate

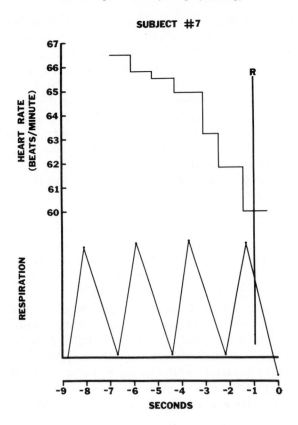

Figure 3.1 Computer-averaged curves for one typical subject showing deceleration in advance of self-initiated motor responses which resulted in a brief tachistoscopic stimulus, and lack of concomitant respiratory changes. 'R' is the time of the subject's response. Respiratory curve shows times of onset of inspiration (upwards deflection) and expiration (downwards deflection) and relative amplitude of chest movement. Copyright © 1978, The American Psychological Association. Reprinted with permission of the publishers from 'Two-way communication between the heart and the brain: Significance of time within the cardiac cycle' by B. C. Lacey and J. I. Lacey, *American Psychologist*, 1978, **33**, 99–113

is already decelerating six beats prior to the average time of motor response, labeled 'R' on the graph. The deceleration consists of a series of dynamic transients—changes in frequency that tend to increase successively in magnitude, beat-by-beat. This same temporal pattern is characteristic of response intention in drl experiments (Lacey and Lacey, 1970), and of the period preceding the imperative stimulus in reaction time experiments. The bottom trace in Figure 3.1 is a computer averaged respiratory curve which preserves both the amplitude and the timing of respiration. It illustrates the fact that the deceleratory pattern is not an artifact of respiratory change.

The various psychophysiological observations just outlined, when combined with an ever-growing neurophysiological literature showing cardiovascular modification of brain function and of peripheral function (for review see Lacey, 1967), have led us to speculate that decreases in heart 'rate and blood pressure facilitate both attention to external environmental events and sensorimotor integration. Increases in heart rate and blood pressure, on the other hand, degrade and hamper such behaviours. We have proposed that the mechanism underlying these effects is the inhibition of cortical and subcortical activity which results from stimulation of baroreceptors in the carotid sinus and aortic arch. Decreases in blood pressure and heart rate, by decreasing baroreceptor discharge per unit time, result in a relative lack of inhibition, effectively an 'excitation'.

Recent experiments have demonstrated such inhibitory effects at the cellular level. Coleridge, Coleridge, and Rosenthal (1976) showed that inflation of the carotid sinus results in prolonged inhibition of pyramidal cells in the motor cortex. Gahery and Vigier (1974) showed that stimulation of vago-aortic afferents (many of which are baroreceptor afferents) markedly reduced responses of single cells in the nucleus cuneatus to natural skin stimulation or to stimulation of cutaneous nerves. These two demonstrations are perhaps the most conclusive to date showing that baroreceptor activity exercises a regulatory effect on sensory and motor functions.

The first suggestive evidence in intact humans which supports the notion that cardiac deceleration may serve a regulatory role in behaviour was the demonstration of an association between fast reaction times and both large decelerations and slower proximal heart rate level. However, alternative explanations have been offered to account for these data. The most prominent of these holds that cardiac deceleration is coupled to a centrally pre-programmed somatic quieting during attentive states and reflects decreased metabolic demands. Its relationship to behaviour is held to be an indirect accompaniment of this quieting. We have argued against this viewpoint elsewhere (B. C. Lacey and J. I. Lacey, 1974; J. I. Lacey and B. C. Lacey, 1974), and exceptions to the notion of invariant cardiac–somatic coupling continue to appear (e.g. Bohlin and Graham, 1977; Cohen, 1973; Coles, 1974; Coles and Duncan-Johnson, 1975; Lawler, Obrist, and Lawler, 1976).

Other data from our laboratory provide additional instances of behaviourally related cardiac slowing which cannot be accounted for by such a concept. In three different kinds of experiments we have demonstrated an immediate slowing of heart rate which is systematically related to the timing within the cardiac cycle of meaningful sensorimotor events. In the first of these, a simple visual reaction time experiment with a four-second foreperiod (Lacey and Lacey, 1977) the effect was found on presentation of an imperative stimulus which required a rapid motor response. The results are seen in Figure 3.2 which shows the average heart period for a group of 66 subjects as a function of the decile of the cardiac cycle in which three events occurred. The three events were: a ready signal, an imperative stimulus, and a 'pseudo-event'. The pseudo-event was a control point during the intertrial interval, four seconds prior to the ready signal. The difference in height of the three curves reflects the facts that heart period increases (heart rate decreases) slightly in anticipation of the ready signal and that a larger deceleration occurs in anticipation of the imperative stimulus. However, the total magnitude of the deceleration from ready signal to imperative stimulus was markedly dependent on where in the cardiac cycle the stimulus happened to fall. This is due to the

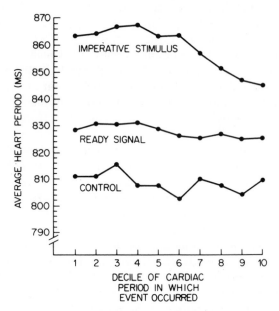

Figure 3.2 Relationship of concurrent heart period to relative cycle time of event occurrence. Ordinate is average of individual median heart periods. $N = 66$. Copyright © 1977, The Psychonomic Society, Inc. Reprinted with permission of the publishers from 'Change in heart period: A function of sensorimotor event timing within the cardiac cycle' by B. C. Lacey and J. I. Lacey, *Physiological Psychology*, 1977, **5**, 383–93

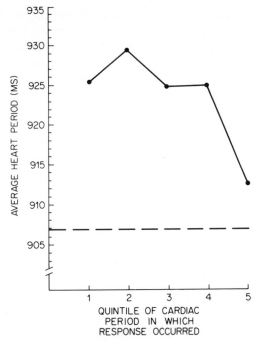

Figure 3.3   Relationship of concurrent heart period to relative cycle time of subject response. Dashed line indicates group average of median heart periods for the single preceding cardiac cycle. $N = 20$. Copyright © 1977, The Psychonomic Society, Inc. Reprinted with permission of the publishers from 'Change in heart period: A function of sensorimotor event timing within the cardiac cycle' by B. C. Lacey and J. I. Lacey, *Physiological Psychology*, 1977, **5**, 383–93

fact that stimuli presented early in the cardiac cycle prolonged the concurrent heart period more than stimuli presented later in the cycle. The decreasing linear trend over deciles was highly significant, $p < 10^{-8}$ by Ferguson's non-parametric trend test (Ferguson, 1965). There was a significant quadratic trend as well, $p < 0.01$. No significant trends were found for either the ready signal or the control point.

In a second experiment (Lacey and Lacey, 1977) in which anticipatory deceleration preceded response-intention, similar effects were found. Subjects, working at their own pace, self-initiated tachistoscopic exposures of a clock face on which all but one of 12 numerals were illuminated. The subject's task was to detect and report the missing numeral. Figure 3.3

shows the average heart period for a group of 20 subjects as a function of the quintile of the cardiac cycle in which the response occurred. The dashed line indicates the average heart period for the preceding cycle. Again, cardiac slowing was much greater when the event occurred early, rather than late in the cycle. The linear trend was significant, $p < 0.01$. When the response occurred late in the cycle, however, the subsequent cycle was prolonged, the more so the later the response. This effect is seen in Figure 3.4. The dashed line again indicates the pre-response heart period. When the response had been early in the response cycle, recovery towards higher heart rates had occurred by the subsequent cycle but the subsequent cycle

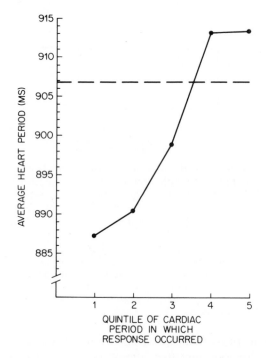

Figure 3.4 Relationship of subsequent heart period to relative cycle time of subject response. Dashed line indicates group average of median heart periods for the single cardiac cycle preceding the response. $N = 20$. Copyright © 1977, The Psychonomic Society, Inc. Reprinted with permission of the publishers from 'Change in heart period: A function of sensorimotor event timing within the cardiac cycle' by B. C. Lacey and J. I. Lacey, *Physiological Psychology*, 1977, **5**, 383–93

was considerably prolonged when response had been relatively late in the response cycle. The linear trend was significant, $p < 10^{-5}$.

These effects on heart rate are strikingly congruent with those found in acute animal experiments upon direct electrical stimulation of the vagus (Brown and Eccles, 1934; Dong and Reitz, 1970; Levy, Iano and Zieske, 1972; Levy and coworkers, 1969, 1970; Reid, 1969). Electrical stimulation of the vagus early in the cardiac cycle prolongs that cycle but has little effect on the subsequent cycles. Stimulation late in the cycle, however, fails to prolong that cycle, but prolongs the subsequent one, the more so the later the stimulation. The mechanism underlying this temporal dependency is discussed in the above referenced literature, and is reviewed by us elsewhere (Lacey and Lacey, 1977). Further analogies between our results and those of the animal studies are detailed in that article also. The mechanism, briefly described, starts with stimulation of the vagus which results in the release, following a latent period, of acetylcholine (ACh), the neurotransimtter substance which directly affects the sino-atrial node. Since ACh tends to decrease the slope of diastolic depolarization, its availability at the pacemaker early in diastole will prolong the cycle more than if ACh becomes available later in the cycle. However, since ACh is rapidly hydrolysed, it will be more effective in prolonging the subsequent cycle if it arrives late in a cycle than if it arrives earlier and thus has more time to be dissipated.

In our experiments, vagal stimulation is effected by cortically mediated, punctate sensorimotor events rather than by direct electrical techniques, but the same temporal dependencies are found. As we have also seen, a considerable proportion of the total anticipatory deceleration both in the reaction time experiment and in response-intention is thus attributable to the operation of this mechanism.

Still a third experimental design in which these temporal dependencies can be demonstrated is being used in current research in our laboratory. Some preliminary findings which extend and confirm the results presented here can be found in a recent article (Lacey and Lacey, 1978.)

Time within the cardiac cycle is not only an independent variable related to differential slowing of heart rate. It can be a dependent variable as well. We have shown that momentary heart rate level is effective in determining the cardiac cycle time of self-initiated responses. These results, which come from our studies of response intention, lend further support to the notion that cardiac slowing plays an instrumental role in the modification of behaviour, but they cannot be accommodated by, and so further weaken, the 'alternative' hypothesis.

The effect is illustrated in Figure 3.5 by the results of a single subject in a drl 15″ 1h 4″ experiment (Lacey and Lacey, 1978).

The heart rates, grouped into the quintiles shown on the abscissa, were

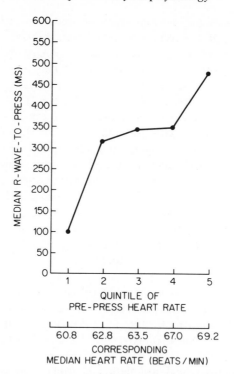

Figure 3.5 Showing for one subject the postponement of subject-initiated responses to increasingly later times within the cardiac cycle as immediately prevailing heart rate increased. The curve shows the empirical regression of central locations (medians) of distributions of elapsed times from the R-wave on central locations (medians) of successive heart-rate 'bands', i.e. successive fifths of the distribution of heart rates for the cardiac cycle immediately preceding the cycle in which the response occurred. Copyright © 1978, The American Psychological Association. Reprinted with permission of the publishers from 'Two-way communication between the heart and the brain: Significance of time within the cardiac cycle' by B. C. Lacey and J. I. Lacey, *American Psychologist*, 1978, **33**, 99–113

those for the cycle immediately preceding each of 60 'successfully' timed responses. This heart rate was uncontaminated by the motor response itself. The dependent variable on the ordinate is median elapsed time from R-wave to subject key press. This subject, then, displayed a strong tendency to respond later and later in the cardiac cycle as momentary heart rate level increased. For the entire group of 52 subjects the linear increasing trend was significant, $p < 10^{-3}$. These results were confirmed in the experiment on self-initiated tachistoscopic exposures. Again, subjects tended to respond later and later in the cardiac cycle with higher and higher pre-response heart rate levels. Certainly this must be taken as evidence that heart rate is of consequence for these kinds of behaviours. Why, however, the behaviour takes the precise form it does, why responses are emitted later and later in the cycle when momentary heart rate is relatively high, is a phenomenon yet to be explained.

Our early speculation, that as frequency of input (heart rate) to the baroreceptors increased, inhibitory baroreceptor activity in the early part of the cycle would be stronger and more prolonged, was based on an extrapolation from a report by Spickler and Kezdi (1967). These investigators had used a sine wave forcing function in studying baroreceptor outputs as a function of carotid sinus pulsation. The use of sine waves of pressure, however, confounds the effect of rate of rise and fall with the effect of frequency. Rise rates in particular are very important variables determining baroreceptor response. In our laboratory we are using a pump which provides a constant quasi-triangular waveform of pressure as an input to the carotid sinus, a technique which keeps rise time constant over all input frequencies. Our results with this technique do not support the notion of prolonged, baroreceptor discharge, displaced forward in time, with increasing frequency. We do find higher amplitude spikes per unit of time at higher pumping frequencies than at lower, a demonstration which is of consequence for a concept of increased inhibition at higher heart rate levels. But this, of itself, does not explain the occurrence of voluntary response at later times within the cycle as heart rate increases.

Our current thinking and research on this problem stems from our observation of the nature of the deceleratory pattern which precedes the emission of such responses and which is illustrated in Figure 3.1. The decelerations we have noted, are characterized by a series of dynamic transients, abrupt changes in frequency which become increasingly large. It seems a reasonable working hypothesis that baroreceptor discharge may vary as a function of such patterned dynamic changes. Preliminary results from acute cat experiments suggest that changes in frequency and the direction of such change do indeed make a difference in baroreceptor output. While it is far too early to generalize the nature of these differences and their relationship to the empirical data, we are hopeful that such studies will enable us to specify which aspects of the entire pattern of inputs are of consequence in modifying central nervous system activity.

3.3 MEASUREMENT AND QUANTIFICATION

3.3.1 The measurement of heart rate

Jasper Brener

The heart beat is a well-defined electromechanical event. Each mechanical cycle of the heart begins with the contraction of the atria. This results in blood being delivered from the atria to the ventricles. After a brief delay, the ventricles contract ejecting blood into the systemic and pulmonary arterial systems. This recurring rhythmic circulatory process is manifested peripherally in a number of different ways that render the activity of the heart readily amenable to peripheral detection. This section describes methods of transducing cardiac activity and illustrates the use of electronic circuitry in automatically analysing and recording various aspects of heart rate.

3.1.1 Methods of transduction

3.1.1.1 Electrocardiography

The most reliable method of monitoring cardiac activity from the moving subject is by recording the electrical potentials associated with myocardial activity (electrocardiography). The body acts as a volume conductor transmitting electrocardiac signals to the body surface.

The wave of depolarization that sweeps through the heart during its cycle starts at the apex of the right atrium (SA node) and terminates at the apex of the ventricles. Because the electrocardiac potential recorded from each part of the body surface reflects the state of polarization of that part of the heart it is electrically adjacent to, the largest change in electrical potential during the heart beat may be recorded between electrodes placed on the right arm and the left leg (limb lead II) which reflect two extremes on the axis of myocardial depolarization.

Human EKG signals recorded from standard limb leads are illustrated in Figure 3.6. It will be seen that the EKG signal is comprised of three principal waves. The P-wave is associated with atrial contraction and has a normal duration of 60–110 milliseconds (ms). The ventricular contraction is marked by the QRS complex which also has a normal duration of 60–110 ms. The P–R interval has a duration of 120–210 ms and values outside of this range generally indicate a conduction disorder. The T-wave is associated with ventricular repolarization and in some individuals its amplitude may approximate that of the R-wave in limb lead I. Various factors such as body type and posture influence the orientation of the heart and hence its mean axis of depolarization resulting in predictable changes in the form of the EKG.

The EKG may be recorded by attaching surface electrodes to the limbs or torso of a subject. Although the R-wave of the normal human EKG is relatively large in bioelectrical terms (1.5 mV) it is advisable to use a differential (push–pull) amplifier to reject common mode noise. Typically the EKG surface electrodes' impedance is in the order of 20 kΩ and hence the amplifier should have an input impedance of at least 1 MΩ. Most

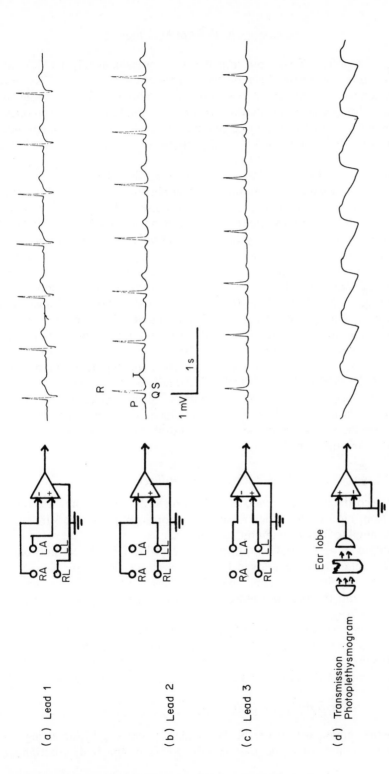

(a) Lead 1

(b) Lead 2

(c) Lead 3

(d) Transmission
Photoplethysmogram

Figure 3.6 Standard limb lead arrangements and recordings are shown in (a), (b), and (c). A photoplethysmographic record made concurrently with the EKG in (c) is displayed in (d)

modern bioamplifiers have input impedances of approximately 10 MΩ and so this is rarely a problem. Because the constituent waves of the EKG are low frequency, a long time constant (TC) about 0.4 s, is typically employed. The voltage gain requirements of the amplifier are also modest and a voltage gain factor of 2000 providing an amplified R-wave amplitude of 2–3 V will suffice for most recording purposes (Jernstedt and White, 1974).

The principal artifacts associated with recording the EKG result from: (i) high source impedance due to improper application of electrodes. This results in greater sensitivity to environmental noise and a slowly fluctuating baseline. (ii) Electrode movement due to electrodes being loosely attached causes large transients that may block the amplifier. Care should also be taken not to apply the electrodes too tightly if straps are used. This causes muscle tremor and cuts off the circulation in the part of the limb distal to the electrode strap. (iii) Skeletal muscle activity in the recording domain of the electrodes will result in electromyograph (EMG) artifacts. Since this EMG activity is predominantly of a higher frequency than the components of the EKG it may be filtered out. A low pass filter which attenuates frequencies greater than approximately 20 Hz will eliminate most EMG artifacts without significantly reducing the R-wave amplitude. In moving subjects it is preferable to attach electrodes to the chest. Beckman biopotential electrodes or equivalent are useful in this application. Reliable recordings from active subjects may be obtained by placing one electrode on the sternum, one below the left breast and placing the reference (earth) electrode below the right breast.

3.1.1.2 Pressure recordings

Pressure recordings only provide reliable cardiac data when they are taken directly from an arterial catheter. Surface recordings of the pressure pulse wave are suitable only in immobilized subjects.

The output of an arterial blood pressure transducer fed by an indwelling arterial cannula may be employed to obtain accurate heart rate data. Slow fluctuations in blood pressure may be filtered out by using an a.c. preamplifier and the pressure pulse waves counted using a Schmitt trigger (see Figure 3.7(a)).

If the subject's limb is immobilized, cardiac activity may be detected reliably by using a pressure transducer located on the skin surface above a major peripheral artery such as the radial artery or the carotid. However, any movement at the transducer site will cause a substantial artifact.

3.1.1.3 Photoplethysmographic recordings

The blood-pumping action of the heart may be sensed by detecting the pulsatile movement of blood past certain points of the body's periphery.

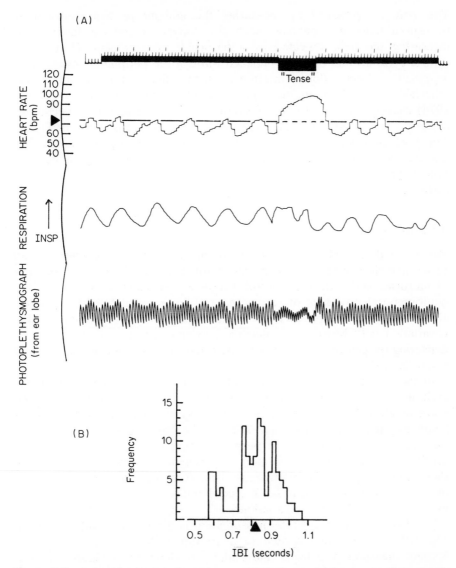

Figure 3.7   A beat-by-beat tachometer record is shown in the top tracing of (A) together with concurrent recording of respiration (chest circumference) and blood flow through the ear lobe (photoplethysmograph). During the 12 seconds marked by the broad downward deflection of the event pen, the subject was instructed to tense his biceps. It will be seen that this manoeuvre led to a pronounced increase in heart rate, irregularity in the pattern of respiration and a decrease in the amplitude of the photoplethysmograph. A close correlation between variations in respiration and heart rate (sinus arrhythmia) will also be observed. The histogram illustrated in (B) describes the distribution of the 127 IBIs that occurred during the period marked by the broad upward deflection of the event pen. The symbols indicate the mean heart rate associated with this heart rate sample

This may be achieved by measuring the amount of light transmitted through a limb or appendage such as a finger or the ear lobe or by measuring the light reflected by a particular area of skin. During the cardiac cycle arterial blood is impelled through the peripheral vessels. The increased blood flow interferes with light transmission and reflection, particularly in the *infrared* band (Tahmoush and coworkers, 1976) causing less light to be transmitted through the limb or reflected by the skin. This results in a phototransducer output as displayed in Figure 3.6(d) which resembles the pressure pulse wave. Photoplethysmographic transducers are sensitive to body movement artifacts and records derived from them also vary in amplitude with the respiratory cycle (see Figure 3.7(a).

3.1.2 Recording

Periodic and aperiodic changes in environmental and bodily conditions lead to predictable variations in heart rate through the mediation of a number of intrinsic and extrinsic control processes. A concise review of the neurohumoral processes of cardiac control is provided by Scher (1974). Responses of the respiratory and somatomuscular system display reliable covariation with heart rate reflecting a primary function of the heart in delivering oxygen from the lungs to the active tissues (Brener, Phillips, and Connally, 1977).

In the absence of any special conditions heart rate displays continuous cyclical variations. The durations of these heart rate cycles vary from approximately five seconds (sinus arrhythmia) through diurnal cycles of 24 hours to menstrual (Little and Zahn, 1974) and seasonal cycles. The short-term (phasic) changes in heart rate that are typically recorded in conditioning and similar laboratory experiments are superimposed upon these underlying cardiac biorhythms. Therefore the time frame employed in heart rate measurement is of crucial importance in the analysis and interpretation of heart rate variation.

The basic unit of heart rate measurement is the interbeat interval (IBI). The IBI is reciprocally related to heart rate (IBI (s) = 60/HR (bpm)). Various measures of a heart rate sample are depicted in Figure 3.7. The tachograph record (Figure 3.7(a)) provides an indication of heart rate equivalents of successive IBIs. A histogram representing the frequency of IBIs of different durations is provided in Figure 3.7(b). The mean heart rate associated with this sample is identified on each of these records to indicate the nature and magnitude of short-term variations in heart rate.

The circuits described in this section provide a means of automatically analysing and displaying the characteristics of heart rate that are of experimental interest.

3.1.2.1 Polygraph

The simplest and most conventional method of obtaining a permanent record is to display the output of the cardiac transducer and preamplifier on an oscillograph as in Figures 3.6 and 3.7(a). Although very time-consuming to quantify, continuous oscillographic records are frequently obtained by experimenters. The nature of the relationship between variations in heart rate and other measures of performance is often revealed by the use of a polygraph to provide continuous records of a number of dependent and independent variables. However, the quantification of heart rate from oscillographic records involves counting, measurement, and arithmetic calculation. It is also important to adopt appropriate procedures in estimating heart rate from cardiotachometer records (Thorne, Engel, and Holmblad, 1976). These time-consuming activities are obviated by the use of some basic instrumentation.

The circuits described below are all designed to quantify various aspects of heart rate. Although they are built from digital electronic components, functionally equivalent circuits may be built from analogue components. Highly precise measurement may be achieved with cheaper components but at the cost of more complex circuits using digital rather than analogue devices. Microprocessors and computers may also be used to good effect in achieving the functions described.

3.1.2.2 Pulse shaper

The purpose of pulse shaping is to transform a complex bioelectric signal into a discrete binary event. This is a necessary first step in the digital processing of heart rate information. Shaping of the EKG signal is most easily accomplished by using a voltage discriminator (Schmitt trigger) to sense the R-wave which is the highest voltage component of the EKG. The output state of the Schmitt trigger changes whenever its input voltage exceeds an adjustable criterion value (the trigger level). By setting the trigger level to an appropriate value, it is possible to obtain a discrete voltage change on each EKG complex. This pulse may then be 'stretched' to a width suitable for driving automatic counting circuits by arranging for it to fire a one-shot (monostable multivibrator). A pulse width of 20 milliseconds (ms) is suitable for most applications. A simple pulse shaping circuit is shown in Figure 3.8(a).

In particularly 'noisy' conditions such as when the subject is engaging in strenuous exercise, a filter may be employed to attenuate signals other than the EKG. Since the dominant frequency of the R-wave is in the region of 8 Hz (Boyd and Eadie, 1954) which is lower than the frequency of most EMG signals, the dominant source of noise, a low pass filter is

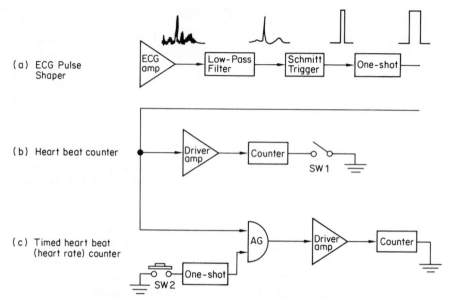

Figure 3.8   Shaping and counting EKG signals

indicated for this application. The filter is placed in the circuit prior to the Schmitt trigger.

3.1.2.3 Timing and counting heart beats

Deriving a uniform electrical pulse on each heart beat enables the use of standard electronic circuits to count and time the heart rate.

A simple electromechanical counter circuit is depicted in Figure 3.8(b). When the counter circuit is completed by closing the switch SW1, the counter total accumulates 1 on each heart beat. A power amplifier is provided to drive the one-shot logic pulse through the electromagnetic coil of the counter. Thus if the counter is reset and SW1 closed for 1 minute and then opened, the counter total will represent the number of heart beats in that minute.

Instead of operating the switch manually to enable the operation of the counter for a preset time, a logic 'and' gate may be inserted between the heart beat one-shot and the counter circuit. The gate may then be opened by a timing pulse thereby permitting heart beat pulses to activate the counter for the duration of the time interval. This arrangement is illustrated in Figure 3.8(c). In this circuit the timing interval is initiated by a momentary switch closure (SW2).

If heart beat counting is a primary operation in a more complex analysis process, it may be more convenient to count heart beats on electronic binary counters. For example an N-bit counter may be built from several SN 7493 4-bit binary counter integrated circuits (ICs) arranged in series.

3.1.2.4 IBI Histogram Compiler

Although mean heart rate measures are appropriate for certain analyses, measurement of heart rate variability is more useful for others. When measured on a beat-by-beat basis, the IBIs of a normal individual commonly vary by ±25% of the mean IBI over a period of one minute. An effective way of recording the dispersion of heart rates over a given time period is by means of an interbeat interval (IBI) histogram compiler of the sort illustrated in Figure 3.9. This instrument classifies each IBI according to its duration with the width of each category selected by the experimenter to provide the required resolution. The category width is determined by the frequency of the clock pulse generator (CPG). We have found a frequency of 50 Hz (20 ms IBI categories) to be adequate for most purposes.

Following the termination of each heart beat pulse (OS_1) the ring counter is reset to its initial condition by a short pulse (1 ms) delivered by OS_2. In this condition FF1 is in the $Q = 1$ state. The heart beat pulse also fires OS_3 which is adjusted to provide a pulse duration of just less than the subject's shortest IBI (300–700 ms). The inverted output of OS_3 disables the CPG for the duration of this pulse thereby ensuring that the ring counter is not triggered during the categorization of an IBI or in the period immediately following a heart beat when no further heart beats will occur. The duration of OS_3 determines the band width of the distribution's first category. Following the termination of the OS_3 pulse, the CPG is again enabled. It delivers pulses to the clock (CK) inputs of the ring counter. On each trigger pulse the next flip–flop in the sequence changes state from $Q = 0$ to $Q = 1$ and its preceding flip–flop reverts from the $Q = 1$ to the $Q = 0$ state. The final flip–flop in the ring counter is wired so that once it has changed state further clock pulses will not influence the condition of the ring counter. The Q output of each flip–flop provides the input to one leg of an associated 'and' gate (AG). The other input to each AG is fed from the normal output of OS_1 which delivers a 20 ms pulse on each heart beat. If a flip–flop is in the $Q = 1$ state when a heart beat occurs, its AG will deliver a 20 ms output pulse to the associated driver amplifier (DA) and counter resulting in that counter's total being increased by one. Following a criterion time interval or number of heart beats, the counter totals may be used to generate a histogram of the sort illustrated in Figure 3.7(b).

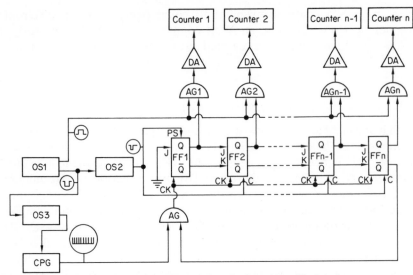

Figure 3.9   IBI Histogram compiler. (The devices identified below are necessary for constructing this curcuit and those illustrated in subsequent figures.)

Abbreviation

	Analog multiplier	107C	(Hybrid Systems Corp.)
AG	and gate	SN7400	(Texas Instruments)
CPG	clock pulse generator	555	(Signetics)
COMP	4-bit magnitude comparator	SN7485	(Texas Instruments)
DCU	decade counter	SN7490	(Texas Instruments)
DA convertor	digital-to-analog convertor	DAC-9-8	(Datel Systems Inc.)
DL	Quad. bistable latch	SN7475	(Texas Instruments)
FF	J–K flip–flops with present and clear	SN7476	(Texas Instruments)
OS	one-shot	SN74121	(Texas Instruments)

3.1.2.5   Classification of high, medium, and low heart rates

The circuit illustrated in Figure 3.10 functions to classify each IBI according to whether it is shorter than one preset criterion, t_1 (high heart rate), longer than another criterion, t_2 (low heart rate) or between the two criteria (medium heart rate). This arrangement is useful for recording purposes and also for immediate external feedback of short, medium, and long IBIs on a beat-by-beat basis.

On the occurrence of each heart beat pulse (OS_1) the number of clock pulses generated since the preceding heart beat is compared to two binary-coded decimal (BCD) numbers corresponding to the preset criteria t_1 and t_2. Criterion t_1 is set on the BCD thumbwheel switches SW_1 (units) and SW_2 (tens) and criterion t_2 on SW_3 and SW_4. The comparisons are accomplished by the use of two 8-bit magnitude comparators (COMP 1, 2

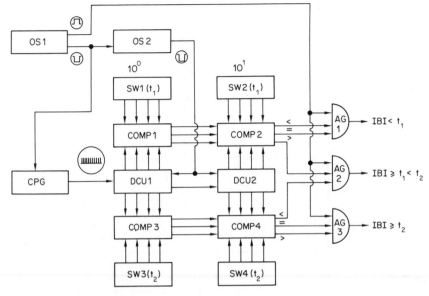

Figure 3.10 Tonic heart rate analyser

and COMP 3, 4) which receive one set of inputs from the DCUs and the other set from the BCD thumbwheel switches. The outputs of the comparators are fed to three 'and' gates (AGs) which each also receive an input from the heart beat one-shot (OS$_1$). If the IBI is shorter in duration than the time interval represented by the settings of SW$_1$ and SW$_2$ (t_1) and output is derived from AG1, if IBI $\geqslant t_1 < t_2$, the output occurs at AG2 and if IBI $\geqslant t_2$, the output occurs at AG3.

The CPG is inhibited during the operation of OS$_1$ following which OS$_2$ is fired to reset the DCUs for timing the interval to the next heart beat.

3.1.2.6 *Classification of phasic heart rate changes*

The circuit described above classifies heart rate on a beat-by-beat basis according to certain preset criteria. As such it may be viewed as a tonic heart rate analyser. Heart rate changes between its tonic limits in a step-wise fashion and in certain experimental applications it is of interest to know when the heart rate is increasing and when it is decreasing. Whether each IBI is equal to, less, or greater in duration than the preceding IBI may be determined by employing the circuit illustrated in Figure 3.11.

The principle of operation of this circuit is the same as that of the tonic level discriminator circuit illustrated in Figure 3.10 except that in the present case each IBI is compared with the IBI which immediately preceded it.

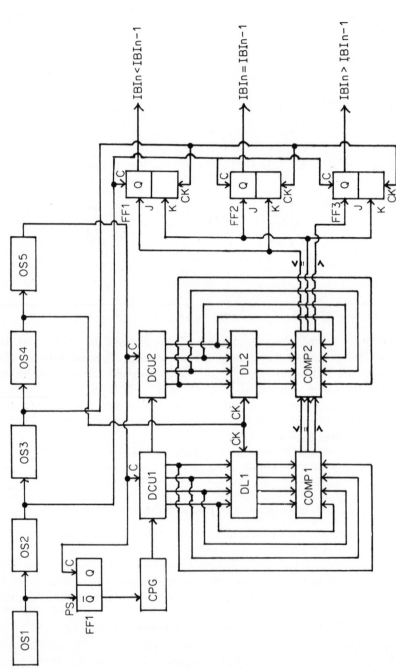

Figure 3.11   Phasic heart rate analyser

The number of clock pulses generated between successive heart beats is counted on the 8-bit counter (DCU1 and DCU2). Data latches (DL1 and DL2) are employed to remember the duration of the preceding IBI. On the occurrence of each heart beat the value of the current IBI is compared to the value of the preceding IBI using the comparators (COMP1 and COMP2).

Each heart beat pulse leads to the sequential firing of five one-shots (OSs 1–5). The CPG is inhibited via the Q output of FF1 which is set to low by the set pulse (PS) delivered by OS_1. The output of OS_2 clears FFs 2–4. When OS_3 delivers a pulse to the clock (CK) inputs of these flip–flops they change state according to the levels on the J and K inputs. The circuit is arranged to provide the following input/output relations:

	FF_2	FF_3	FF_4
$IBIn < IBIn - 1$ (HR increasing)	$Q = 1$	$Q = 0$	$Q = 0$
$IBIn = IBIn - 1$ (HR stable)	$Q = 0$	$Q = 1$	$Q = 0$
$IBIn > IBIn - 1$ (HR decreasing)	$Q = 0$	$Q = 0$	$Q = 1$

Following the comparison of $IBIn$ with $IBIn - 1$, OS_4 delivers a clock pulse to the data latches (DL1 and DL2) causing the data on the DCUs which contain the duration of $IBIn$ to be transferred to data latches. Finally OS_5 fires to reset the DCUs and disinhibit the CPG by clearing FF1. This commences the timing of $IBIn + 1$.

If the $<$ output of COMP2 is permitted to set and the $>$ output permitted to reset a flip–flop, the state of this flip–flop will provide an instantaneous binary indicator of whether the heart rate is increasing or decreasing. Using this circuit it is possible, for example, to count the number of heart rate fluctuations per unit time or to measure automatically the latency of a phasic heart rate increase or decrease. The resolution of this phasic heart rate discriminator is a function of the frequency of the CPG and the binary capacity of the counting, memory and comparison circuits.

3.1.2.7 Beat-by-beat tachometer

In preliminary examination of heart rate performance, the preferred method of display is as a beat-to-beat tachometer. Generally such records are displayed oscillographically where they provide an instantaneous and permanent record of the direction and magnitude of heart rate variations. The purpose of the circuit illustrated in Figure 3.12 is to express the instantaneous heart rate in terms of a directly-related voltage level.

As in the previous two circuits DCUs count the number of clock pulses

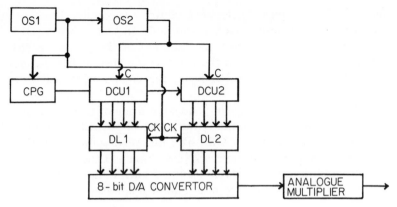

Figure 3.12   Beat-to-beat tachometer

generated between heart beats. On the occurrence of a heart beat, OS_1 inhibits the CPG and delivers a clock pulse to the data latches. This causes the contents of the DCUs (the interval separating the current heart beat from the immediately preceding heart beat) to be deposited in the data latches. On the trailing edge of the pulse from OS_1, OS_2 fires causing the DCUs to be reset for timing the interval to the next heart beat. The output of the data latches feed a digital-to-analogue (D/A) convertor which provides a d.c. voltage directly proportional to the IBI.

This voltage is reciprocally related to the instantaneous heart rate. Employing an analogue divider, a voltage that is directly related to the instantaneous heart rate may be derived. The output of the analogue divider may be used to drive an oscillograph or to provide the subject with continuous proportional feedback of heart rate on a beat-by-beat basis. By arranging for the output to drive a voltage-controlled oscillator an audible tone which varies in pitch as a direct function of instantaneous heart rate may be produced.

This circuit may be greatly simplified by substituting a period-to-voltage convertor (e.g. Ancom Model No. PV7) for the DCUs, data latches and D/A convertor. However, the circuit as described is compatible with the circuits illustrated in Figures 3.10 and 3.11 and all three circuits may be incorporated into a comprehensive system thereby minimizing redundancy.

3.3.2 Representing cardiac activity in relation to time*

Francis K. Graham

No clear consensus has been reached concerning which measure of cardiac activity, rate or period, should be followed through which kind of time, i.e.

Acknowledgement. This work was supported by the Grant Foundation and by a Research Scientist Award K5-21762 from the National Institute of Mental Health, Public Health Service, USA.

for successive beats or for successive real time. Either measure or either kind of time may be suitable, depending on the research problem and the resources available, but there are restrictions on the combinations of measure and time that are optimal.

3.2.1 Heart rate versus heart period

Rate and period are not interchangeable with regard to the consequences of measurement error or with regard to the statistical properties of their distributions. It is reasonable to determine, therefore, whether either of these factors favours use of one measure over the other.

3.2.1.1 Errors of measurement

Error may be introduced either by the recording system or through the process of digitizing the output of the recording system. The important consideration is whether the error is linear with rate or with period; if it is constant for one measure, it necessarily varies with the other. Error due to the recording system is often too small to be of practical significance but this is not always the case. If, for example, some component of the system is unable to follow large changes, it may be worthwhile to choose the measure, rate or period, with which the output is linear. A potentially larger source of error can occur in digitizing outputs. Even with automatic digitizing, error can be substantial if resolution is inadequate. Consider the consequences of using rate when real time is sampled in units of 0.01 s. While the error for period will be ±0.01 s for any period, the error for rate will range from +0.61 to −0.59 bpm when rate is 60 but will reach +3.85 to −3.66 bpm when rate is 150. Thus, the phasic heart rate response of an infant may be smaller than the error due to sampling. Resolution of at least ±1 ms is required if error is to remain less than 1 beat at rates typical of both adult and infant. The same considerations apply when digitizing is accomplished by manual reading of a polygraph record. If distance between R-waves of an electrocardiogram is read, error size depends on polygraph speed but will be constant for period and will increase with rate. Similarly, if the output of a cardiotachometer is linear with rate, reading error will increase with period: a constant error of 1 bpm in rate will be +2.68 to −2.65 ms for a 400-ms period and +16.95 to −16.39 ms for a 1000-ms period. Thus, unless measurement error is much smaller than the effects being studied, it will generally be advisable to select the measure for which error remains constant.

3.2.1.2 Statistical properties

The models underlying parametric statistical procedures commonly assume normality of distributions and homogeneity of variances. Since period and rate have a reciprocal relationship to one another and reciprocation is among the transformations used to provide data better fitting the model, it would not be surprising if one of the measures had more desirable statistical properties than the other. The question has been investigated in several studies (Graham and Jackson, 1970; Jennings, Stringfellow, and Graham, 1974; Khachaturian and coworkers, 1972) whose findings, along with new data, were recently reviewed by Graham (1979a). The answer varied depending on whether individuals or groups were studied, whether samples were from adult or infant subjects, and whether change or raw scores were used.

When samples were drawn from *individual-subject* data, a substantial percentage of distributions showed significant departures from normality and differences among sample variances showed highly significant heterogeneity. These findings held for both rate and period at both ages and neither measure had a consistent advantage with regard to distribution shape; rate showed somewhat less marked heterogeneity of variance.

When samples consisted of data from *groups* of subjects, statistical properties better met model assumptions. With raw scores, there were no skewed distributions for period data from adult subjects nor for rate data from infant subjects. Significant kurtosis was also virtually absent with either measure in either age group, and variance was homogeneous. With change scores, non-normality and variance heterogeneity were more frequent. While neither measure was more satisfactory than the other with adult data, rate showed less skew, less kurtosis, and less extreme variance differences than period when infants were the subjects.

Although rate had more satisfactory properties than period in all of the reports using infant data, Khachaturian and coworkers (1972) concluded that it was preferable to use period. The preference was based on an assumption that period is the 'raw data' with high speed electronic recording and that a transformation to rate must, therefore, be specially justified. As discussed in the preceding section, the output of recording systems may be linear with either measure and what is relevant is the constancy (and size) of the errors of measurement. Even if measurement error was constant with period in the recording–digitizing system used by Khachaturian and colleagues, a transformation to rate could not be said to introduce 'error' because it led 'to different conclusions about homogeneity of variance' (i.e. rate distributions were homogeneous in variance when period distributions based on the same data were not). To view a transformation that removes variance heterogeneity as introducing error is clearly not the view of transformations espoused in the statistical literature. The Khachaturian paper has also been cited as showing that period has a 'practical' advantage since transforming to rate may reduce the size of an evoked response. The statement is based on a computer simulation in which a constant difference between simulated periods was programmed and, as must necessarily be the case, reciprocals of the programmed values did *not* exhibit a constant difference. As Graham (1979a) pointed out, the simulated data are arbitrarily labelled and have no bearing on the issue; had the numbers simulating 'periods' been labelled 'rates', the effects of a reciprocal transformation would have been the same, but the conclusion would have been reversed.

Thus, the empirical evidence suggests that for adult group data, the degree of non-normality and non-heterogeneity present in either period or rate distributions will not violate assumptions of statistical tests when raw scores are used and may not when difference scores are analysed. For infant data, rate was found to be generally more satisfactory than period but, when raw score data based on groups of subjects were considered, variance was not significantly heterogeneous with either measure. Since *t*-tests and many analyses of variance are robust in the face of violations of assumptions, period can probably be safely employed in many analyses of infant group data. In both age samples, the most serious violations were observed when individual-subject data were analysed but such samples have limited generalizability to the commonly used research designs.

3.2.2 Changes in cardiac rate or period over time

The question of whether successive changes in cardiac activity should be followed in real time, as second by second, or in cardiac time, as beat by beat, has been considered from several points of view.

A consideration of *theoretical* interest is whether processes of a biological organism are more likely to be timed in terms of its own activities than by oscillations of a crystal and whether all biological processes are timed by the same mechanism. It seems unlikely, for example, that cognitive processes involving rapid neural response would be timed by a biological clock as slow as the cardiac cycle. How this issue is viewed affects a related issue. If cardiac activity is studied for a fixed number of beats, a smaller real-time sample will be obtained from individuals with rapid heart rates than from individuals with slow heart rates and the converse is true if activity is studied over fixed real time (Graham and Jackson, 1970; Buckley, 1979). Whether equality of the real-time or of the cardiac-time sample is desired will, of course, depend on whether the process studied is believed to vary with real or with cardiac time.

Another consideration is that of *preserving information*. If single beats are the basic timing unit, all of the information about cardiac events will be preserved but there will be a problem in coordinating cardiac and stimulus events. Should the beat in which stimulus onset falls be treated as part of

H

the response, part of the prestimulus baseline, omitted, or categorized separately (Buckley, 1979)? Triggering stimulus onset so that it is coincident with an R-wave can mitigate the problem but is not always appropriate and will not solve the problem when there is a fixed real-time interval between two stimuli, as in conditioning and reaction time paradigms. Since different subjects will have differing numbers of beats within a fixed time interval, averaging across subjects would require either omitting some portion of the real-time interval or allowing the number of observations contributing to the interval to vary.

If real-time units are employed, information about cardiac events can also be preserved, either by sampling cardiac activity at discrete points in time at a rate faster than the fastest cardiac rate or by estimating the activity *during* the real-time unit from the sum of whole and fractional beats that fall within the unit (Buckley, 1979). If the sampling rate is slower than the cardiac rate, responses will be attenuated and the attenuation will be greater with rapid than with slow responses. Coordinating stimulus and cardiac events is simpler with real-time than with cardiac-time units but the time unit immediately preceding stimulus onset may reflect response to the stimulus when onset falls early in the cardiac cycle (B. C. Lacey and J. I. Lacey, 1974). The effect can be made trivial if estimates of prestimulus cardiac activity are taken over a sufficiently long time period.

On *practical* grounds, beats as the basic unit have the major advantage that a beat-by-beat output can be directly recorded. Sampling at fixed real-time rates is nearly as convenient, but the method of counting whole and fractional beats within real-time units imposes a sizeable computational cost. The increased precision may not be worth its cost if cardiac change occurs slowly over a number of beats or seconds and if the number of subjects or trials is sufficiently large.

Finally, there is the question of *combining time units and cardiac activity measures*. Although all four of the possible combinations of rate and period with real-time and cardiac-time units have been employed, only two combinations yield unbiased estimates. Only when rate is estimated from real-time units and period from cardiac-time units will the average of unit estimates provide an unbiased estimate of a whole trial or sequence of observations (Graham, 1979b). For rate, the definition (beats/real time) imposes the constraint that subsets estimating rate must be equal in real time if their average is to yield the expected value for the whole set. Similarly, for period, the definition (real-time events/beat) requires that subset estimates be based on units containing equal numbers of beats. Under normal conditions, beats will not be equal in real-time and fixed real-time intervals will not contain the same number of whole and fractional beats. Although estimates of rate based on beats and estimates of period based on real time can be weighted so that they represent equal units of the appropriate scale and thus average (or sum) to the correct estimate, information is lost since such weighted subset scores have no variability. A more detailed discussion of estimation methods is given in Graham (1979b).

Whatever the time unit employed, it must be remembered that rate and period are non-linear transformations of one another and averaging non-linear transforms is not equivalent to transforming the average, e.g. transforming each cardiac period to a rate and averaging the rates will not yield the same value as averaging the cardiac periods and then transforming to a rate. Neither the mean nor sum of reciprocals equals the reciprocal of the mean or sum.

3.4 ANALYSIS

3.4.1 Pattern analysis of the heart rate signal*

B. McA. Sayers

4.1.1 Spontaneous fluctuations of heart rate

Several identifiable biological components contribute strongly to the pattern of heart rate fluctuations: 'thermal' vasomotor activity, blood pressure vasomotor activity, respiratory movements (including the influence of speaking). The first two of these components are autonomically mediated and are believed to originate in non-linear biological mechanisms (especially involving interfaces in the brain-stem) so they can interact with other components, as well as independently change character—perhaps spontaneously—regardless of applied disturbance. Spontaneous changes of this kind that occur with the passage of time, constitute non-stationarity of the underlying process generating the intervals between successive beats; abrupt changes of the running mean to a different sustained heart rate, and brief transients, are common. The nature and extent of any such non-stationarity needs to be explored before further analysis of any heart rate records, since recent experience with ambulatory monitoring studies shows that these effects are the rule rather than the exception.

Short-term mean interbeat interval (i.e. sample mean) can only be interpreted in the light of the scatter of individual intervals, which is influenced by the pattern of the interval sequence. It is also necessary to estimate

Acknowledgement. The research utilized in this section was supported by the Medical Research Council.

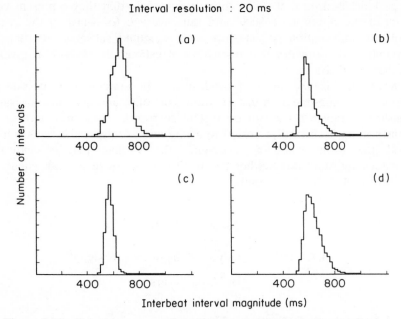

Figure 3.13 Four histograms of cardiac interval in one sequence from a single resting adult subject. Note the shape and variability

the probability density function (PDF) of the intervals in order to convert standard errors into confidence limits. This PDF (Figure 3.13) is strongly influenced by waveform features and is not often Gaussian; indeed the histogram is usually skewed and frequently bimodal. This fact militates against the use of Gaussian statistics and of simple tests (e.g. ANOVAR) based on it; spontaneous non-stationarity deteriorates the position further, both during stimulated changes and in the apparently resting state. However, this discussion will be restricted largely to the analysis of patterns that occur in the sequence of cardiac interbeat intervals.

4.1.2 Methods of heart rate analysis

The sequence of heart beats can be envisaged as a point-event sequence in which different beats are distinguished only by their times of occurrence. So heart rate can be considered in terms either of event-rate or of interbeat interval. However the various event-rate statistics of this kind of point process merely comprise transformations of interval-statistical measures (Sayers, 1970); interval statistics can therefore be treated as basic, and four kinds of change in any experimental situation can be considered:

(a) difference in mean interval between control and experimental records;
(b) difference in variance of interval;
(c) alterations of any trends in the interval sequence;
(d) pattern changes within the sequence.

4.1.2.1 Degrees of freedom

In respect of the first two types of measure, any spontaneous variability of the records must be quantifiable, and the degrees of freedom (DF) of the interval sequence in use must be estimated.

The significance of the DF concept in this situation is that DF specifies the number of independent observations in the statistical sample of intervals being considered. If the interval Fourier spectrum is non-uniform (as is demonstrated in Figure 3.14) the successive intervals are correlated to some extent—and so predictable.

Thus in principle, greater non-uniformity of the spectrum implies that the sample of intervals contains fewer independent observations, and so fewer DF. The observed DF will count for the ensemble variability of the mean value of an interval sample of given size (i.e. containing a given number of intervals); it may be estimated by the squared ratio of standard deviation (SD) estimated for the population to standard error of the mean in samples of given size. The other figure of DF, that refers to power or power-spectral variability—accounting for the ensemble variability of interval variance across a group of statistical samples comprised of interval sequences of say, length N—is generally somewhat (but not greatly) different, except for fully random sequences. This DF figure is estimated

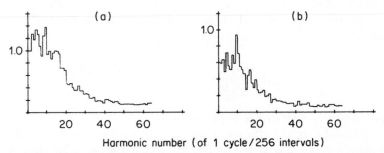

Figure 3.14 Mean relative amplitude spectrum of Fourier components of 256 interbeat interval sequences in an ensemble of 10 records (a), together with the ensemble standard deviation (b). There are virtually no discernible differences in pattern if each interval magnitude is replaced by its reciprocal, scaled to indicate 'instantaneous' rate

from the smoothed average power spectrum of the ensemble of intervals (Sayers, 1975b). It applies only when the variations between members of the ensemble differ merely due to statistical sampling variations, not due to sporadic or systematic biological changes. Indeed, the comparison of the variability of signal variance across the ensemble, by coefficient of variation = SD/mean of the variance, with the variability calculated as $2/(DF)^{1/2}$ from the degrees of freedom estimated from the smoothed average power spectrum, can be used as an indicator of heterogeneity in an ensemble of records (Sayers, 1975b).

In practice the average number of DF per interval in a sequence is between 0.1 and 0.3, so that interval sequences are highly redundant and the sample by sample variations relatively large.

4.1.2.2 Trends and non-stationarities

In respect of trends and non-stationarities in the interval sequence, definitions and tests are inherently arbitrary. The problem is that a specific low-frequency component in one record of a certain length may appear as a trend in the same record when this is truncated to part of its original length. However, the matter cannot be disregarded since it can influence much of the signal processing required in any analysis of patterns in the record.

Two kinds of test are available: the reverse-arrangement test (Bendat and Piersol, 1966) and those such as the Brown–Trigg trend test (Brown, 1962; Trigg, 1964; Lewis, 1971). Broadly speaking, the former test evaluates the number of reverse arrangements in an interval sequence (intervals that are smaller than an earlier reference interval value, that nevertheless occur later in the sequence; each interval in turn is used as the reference and the number of reverse arrangments are totalized as N_r).

The expected number and standard deviation for a sequence N are, respectively:

$$\bar{N}_r = \frac{N(N-1)}{4} \quad \text{and} \quad SD_{N_r} = \left[\frac{N(2N+5)(N-1)}{72} \right]^{\frac{1}{2}}$$

Bendat and Piersol (1966) give a table.

The principle of the Brown–Trigg test is to forecast new values of interval from earlier ones, and to test the running error of the forecast for the presence of excessive low-frequency power that would indicate a trend. The advantage of this approach is its reduced sensitivity to broad features of the Fourier spectrum of the spontaneous pattern, and the fact that this sensitivity can be further reduced by pre-filtering the input record.

4.1.2.3 Pattern analysis

Pattern changes in the sequence of cardiac interbeat intervals could originate in changes of posture, change of respiratory pattern or of activity that involves thoracic movement (speech, physical effort) and other sources of a continuing or repetitive kind; a change towards a specific recognizable pattern may occur, but any change might only lie in the emergence of recognizable different pattern features that could not be prescribed in advance. The choice of analysis techniques depends strongly upon such circumstances.

Pattern changes can be detected, located, characterized, and described by techniques such as Fourier spectral analysis, matched filtering, coherent averaging, or feature analysis. The simplest and most accessible methods depend on spectral analysis but both amplitude and phase spectra are required; procedures that use power spectra, omitting any consideration of the phases of individual Fourier components, are unduly restrictive. These methods rely partly on the recognition of significant differences in the amplitude spectral profile of the test and control interval sequences; statistical variability of spontaneous origin in the control sequence must thus be understood and quantified. On the other hand, broadly identifiable pattern features in any record are linked mainly with the phase spectrum, not the amplitude (or power) spectrum, so phase analysis is usually necessary if pattern features are of interest.

Numerically, the Fourier coefficients that describe any N-point record can be obtained by using the fast Fourier transform; efficient Fortran programs have been published by Monro (1976, 1977). If the record comprises a set of cardiac interbeat intervals the relevant Fourier components are harmonics of 1 cycle/N intervals, and if the record is stationary in the mean interval ($\overline{T}$), these components can be regarded as broadly equivalent to harmonics of 1 cycle in $N\overline{T}$, or $1/(N\overline{T})$ Hz. Some workers insist on attempting a regular interpolation of the interbeat interval record in the time domain, but whenever comparisons have been made, differences from the interval spectrum have been found to be trivial (Rompelman, Coenen and Kitney, 1977). It is usual in all cases, however, to taper the first and last 10 per cent of the record down to the mean interval value in order to avoid possibly abrupt discontinuities at the ends of the record (since these are implicitly linked up to make a repetitive record by virtue of conducting a Fourier analysis).

The interpretation of amplitude spectra is direct: large coefficients imply important spectral activity at the specific frequency (or its vicinity) for the record being analysed. But in order to allow generalization of the findings, the magnitudes of any large coefficients must be regarded in the light of their statistical fluctuations over an ensemble of such records. In the absence of this information, some indications can be obtained from the harmonic by harmonic fluctuations across the spectrum of the individual record. Large variations between components would not justify special attention to individual components or perhaps even to any small group of components; for any practical purposes, significant results depend on the existence of consistent effects over a band of components.

Power spectra, or more explicitly the distribution of total record variance amongst the available spectral components, emphasize the large-amplitude components at the expense of small-amplitude components and may therefore produce an unrealistic picture. So amplitude spectra may be preferred to power spectra in the analysis of interbeat interval records.

Phase spectra are subject to the effect of two contributions and one complicating factor. First, the 'shape' of a record contributes to, and of course reflects, its phase spectrum. Second the relative displacement of main features in the pattern, away from its most nearly symmetrical position, contributes an additional phase shift which is proportional to harmonic number and to the extent of displacement. The complication arises because phase angles outside the principal-angle range of $\pm 90°$ or $\pm 180°$ (depending upon the method of evaluation of angle) are 'wrapped-around' so as to fall inside the principal angle range (Sayers, 1975c). The phase pattern can be clarified by 'unwrapping'. The linear trend in phase angle due to any relative displacement of the pattern from its most nearly symmetrical position is then evident, and can be eliminated. Alternatively the original record can be 'rotated' on its length until the simplest phase pattern emerges.

Band selective filtering emphasizes wanted, at the expense of unwanted, Fourier components. It can be accomplished by numerical filtering as a direct operation on the input data value (Sayers, 1970; Lynn, 1977), or by operations on their Fourier series. It is important, in the latter case particularly, to avoid abrupt truncation of the transmitted spectral components at the edges of the pass-band, and to recognize that narrow-band filtering always generates an output with an oscillatory appearance. The main defence then against being misled into inferring that such components are significant is to seek for evidence of the apparent oscillation in the input record; and this can only be done reliably if the filter acts as a zero-phase shift system. (In the case of frequency domain operations this can be achieved by performing the same scaling operations on both sine and cosine coefficients.)

If the wanted pattern of cardiac interval is known, matched filtering (cross-correlation) can be used to detect the occurrence of the pattern (Sayers, 1970). This is rarely useful in the heart rate case. However, the complementary technique, coherent averaging, is useful; it requires that the times of occurrence of the pattern be known, and this is most readily met if the wanted pattern is the result of some detectable, or selectable, stimulus or disturbance. The stimulus instant is treated as response time: zero, in each case; the cardiac interval sequence that follows each stimulus is treated as one member of an ensemble and the ensemble mean and ensemble standard deviation is formed, for each post stimulus interval. The former is the coherent average; the latter specifies the scatter of the various responses and can be used to set confidence limits on the ensemble mean. Objective detection of the presence of a response can be based on a phase-analysis method as developed for sensory-evoked EEG responses by Sayers and Beagley (1974).

4.1.3.1 The basic statistics

Feature analysis relies upon the identification of pattern aspects like slope, maximum, minimum, or plateau. The distributions of magnitudes and locations of these features are estimated from the histograms constructed from an ensemble of observations so that for example, differences in the occurrence of these features in individual records or groups of records can be statistically evaluated. This approach is potentially of value in the heart-rate context in respect of stimulated patterns; a detailed account of the basic approach is given by Sayers, Nghia, and Mansourian (1978) in a different kind of study.

4.1.3 Examples of the techniques in use

4.1.3.1 The basic statistics

A typical 256-point segment of an interval sequence is shown in Figure 3.15. The sample mean interval value has been removed to show the fluctuations more clearly. Undoubtedly the fluctuations appear sporadic, but are certainly not random; this can be confirmed by the evident change of character shown in the centre record of this figure, which is a representation of the intervals in randomized order. Incidentally, a useful display of some interval properties is provided by a rank-ordering of the sequence of intervals, as shown in the lower curve. This gives information which could also be extracted from an interval histogram (as an estimate of interval probability density); but the rank-ordered curve lends itself to simple mathematical description, using say, a fitted third-order polynomial, by the slope of the straight line that best fits the central portion, or by the range of say, the central 80 per cent of values.

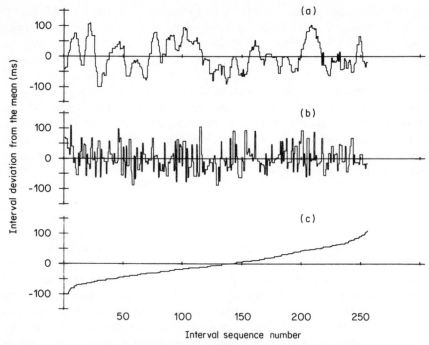

Figure 3.15 (a) 256-point sample from an interval sequence, expressed as deviations from the sample mean. (b) the interval sequence re-ordered randomly. (c) the same sequence rank-ordered, i.e. according to magnitude

4.1.3.2 Band-selective enhancement

The effect of band-selective filtering is shown in Figure 3.16, using the same 256-point segment of intervals as in Figure 3.15, but with its mean value retained (about 700 ms). The low-pass filtered signal (uniform transmission of d.c. plus the first 5 harmonics of the fundamental: 1 cycle per 256 intervals, i.e. about $1/180$ s $= 0.0056$ Hz, then tapered down to zero transmission at the 10th harmonic and above) is shown superimposed on the raw signal. The indicated activity is thought to link with that aspect of thermal regulation in the body mediated by adjustments of cutaneous blood flow and so, heat loss. The centre curve shows the result of using a band filter from H25–64 (plus a 5-harmonic taper each end) to include most of any broadly cyclic, stable patterns of respiratory activity. In fact this kind of filtered record does show (but in a distinctly non-proportional way) the broad features of respiratory activity. The top curve shows the so-called pressure-vasomotor activity (H15–25 plus tapers). Three separate burst of quasi-oscillatory patterns (Sayers, 1973) with a period in the vicinity of 14 intervals (about 10 s) are evident. Precise analysis of the

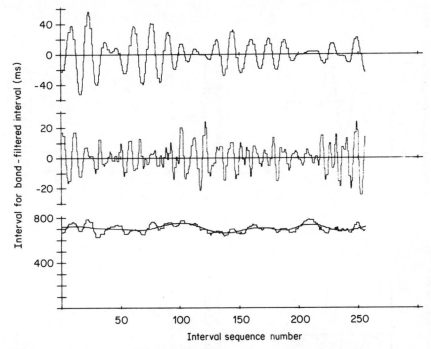

Figure 3.16   Band selective filtering. The bottom traces show the original interval sequence and its low-pass filtered (i.e. smoothed) form (passband from d.c. to the 5th harmonic, H5, of the fundamental Fourier frequency; 1 cycle/256 intervals, plus a taper down to H10, the 10th harmonic).

   The centre and top records are band filtered from H25–H64 and H15–H25 respectively, with a 5 harmonic taper each side, as before. The centre record purports selectively to emphasize the respiratory sinus arrhythmia contribution; the upper record provides evidence of pressure–vasomotor oscillations when these occur (see text)

'instantaneous' frequency and amplitude of these oscillations, and their changes with time, can be achieved by complex demodulation (Sayers, 1975b). Comparison of the top curves of Figures 3.15 and 3.16 will demonstrate that the strongly emphasized filtered patterns can actually be identified in the raw data. The presence and form of valid pattern components in the interval sequence can be identified by coherent-averaging suitable sequences of intervals (from the raw interval signal) utilising the peak locations of say, pressure-vasomotor fluctuations derived from the band-filtered signal as the fiducial points. The characteristics of the fluctuations are then obtained in a direct way, as shown in Figures 3.17(a) and (b), the former showing the extracted pattern of presumed vasomotor components, the latter those due to respiratory

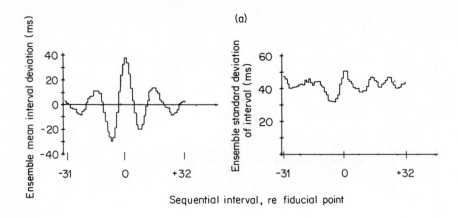

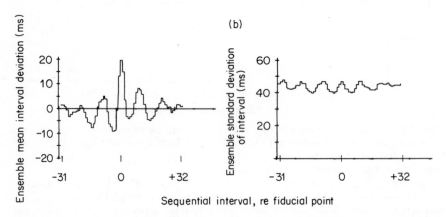

Figure 3.17   Coherent average of raw interval signal, using peaks of regular fluctuations in the band-filtered interval signal as a timemarker (fiducial point). Both ensemble mean (coherent average) and ensemble standard deviation are shown for interval deviations used

(a)   150 pressure–vasomotor components
(b)   250 respiratory components

activity. In this latter analysis, an appreciable range of respiratory periodic durations can be seen (compare Figure 3.16, centre curve), even when attention is restricted to bursts of roughly regular activity; for Figure 3.17(b) only long-period fluctuations were taken into account. In both cases the ensemble mean is shown as a deviation from the sequence mean interval from 31 intervals before, to 32 intervals after, the occurrence of a fiducial marker point.

4.1.3.3 *Interpretation and use of spectra*

The interpretation of spectral diagrams and some of the difficulties, are illustrated by the patterns in Figure 3.18(a). One of the quasi-oscillatory bursts has been extracted from the H16–24 filtered signal shown in Figure 3.16, and embedded in a constant level sequence. Analysis of the amplitude and phase spectrum of this signal is illuminating. First, the phase spectrum is complicated (Figure 3.18(a)) and difficult to interpret. But the complication originates wholly in the relative location of the oscillatory activity on the signal time-base, 256 intervals in length. When the signal is

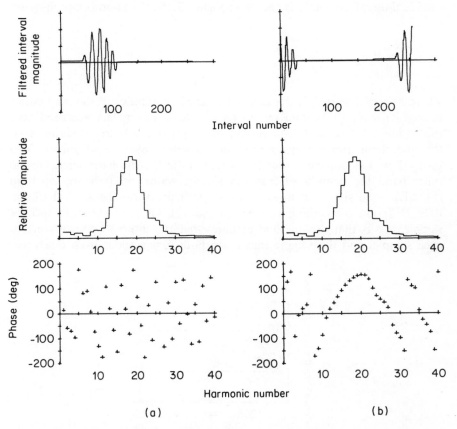

(a)　　　　　　　　　　　　　　　　(b)

Figure 3.18　(a) A short burst of pressure–vasomotor oscillation extracted from the signal in Figure 3.16 (top) and embedded in a 256-point zero field (top). Centre: the amplitude spectrum for the first 40 harmonics of 1 cycle per 256 intervals. Bottom: the phase spectrum for the first 40 harmonics. (b) The amplitude and phase spectrum of the pressure vasomotor burst, after optimally spinning the signal on its time base, as shown in the top record

displaced optimally along the time-base (any segment that is shifted off one end enters the other end, since the record is treated as cyclic for spectral purposes), the phase spectrum (Figure 3.18(b)) over the important spectral band becomes quite simple. It is then characteristic of the pattern itself, freed from any time-displacement component that is further confused by the effect of wrap-round of phase values into the principal angle range.

Ensemble analysis of a set of records can be used to define the degrees of freedom in respect of the interval sequence itself and of its instantaneous variance. The results can be used, with care, in estimating variability, and so the possible existence of responses to defined experimental disturbances. The smoothed power-spectral average of a cardiac interval ensemble is shown in Figure 3.19; the appropriate measure is:

$$\frac{2(\Sigma_{i=1}^{M}P_i)^2}{\Sigma_{i=1}^{M}P_i^2}$$

where $M = N/2$ and P_i is the power (squared amplitude) of the ith Fourier harmonic, from an N-point record ($N = 256$ here)—in fact averaged over the ensemble of records, and smoothed, to provide a better description of the underlying process generating the records. The data of Figure 3.19 give DF = 43.0 for the power (variance) in the first 64 harmonics. On the other hand the degrees of freedom for the sequence itself are equal to $(SD/SE)^2$—see above; in these records this figure varies between 0.15 and 0.29 DF/point, depending on the sample size chosen. The relevance of sample size is that this method assumes that the intervals contributing to each sample, and the sample mean, are both independent from one value

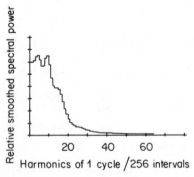

Figure 3.19 Smoothed spectral density of signal power in an ensemble of 256-point interval sequences from one subject, shown for harmonic 1 to 64

to the next. This is not true in cardiac interval records, and the various length patterns (e.g. vasomotor oscillations) that occur do influence the serial correlation dominantly when the sample size is, broadly speaking, comparable with their average extent (say, average half period).

4.1.3.4 Coherent averaging

Finally, the coherent averaging of response to stimulation is illustrated by the curve of Figure 3.20 which shows the deviation of successive intervals from the initial value following a disturbance, in this case due to short-duration speech messages uttered by an air traffic controller in the course of normal duty. The ensemble standard deviation of responses is also shown. (The double peak is due to the fact that some messages are followed by another after a few seconds.)

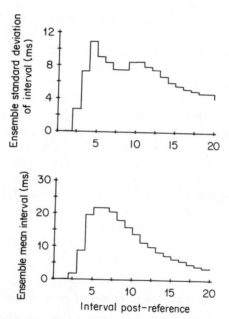

Figure 3.20   Coherent average (ensemble mean) and ensemble standard deviation of intervals linked to a recurrent disturbance (production of brief speech messages)

4.1.4 Conclusion

Pattern analysis of the heart rate or interval signal amounts to a specification of the main waveform features, a recognition of their occurrences, and a quantification of their individual features in specific instances. Its purpose is the detection of changes linked to defined disturbances, or the clarification of the nature or state of underlying biological mechanisms that affect the signal.

Analysis depends on various techniques, some of which have been discussed here; band-selective filtering, spectral analysis of the amplitudes and phases of the Fourier components of the signal, coherent averaging, matched filtering, and feature analysis are convenient and useful approaches. The relevant statistical aspects that need confirmation or evaluation are: the extent to which stationarity applies to the probability density estimate of the interval (or heart rate) variable or alternatively to its moments, and the estimated degrees of freedom in the statistical sample relating to the interval variable to its instantaneous power or spectral density of the power-measures that illuminate the spontaneous variability due to statistical sampling effects.

Two of the characteristics that recur in heart rate records are those due to respiratory movements of the thorax and those due to the pressure-vasomotor oscillations. These can be identified by band-selective filtering or by spectral analysis, and investigated in their ensemble average aspects (i.e. average recurrent behaviour) by coherent averaging the interval signal using oscillatory maxima in the band filtered records as fiducial points. The third contributory component is a labile unspecific fluctuation of low frequency, presumed to be of thermal-vasomotor origin.

Mental work load imposed on the subject has a discernable subject-dependent effect on the pattern of fluctuations, but not consistently on average heart rate; in essence, there is a relative increase in the low-frequency components of the interval spectrum. This effect originates in at least two causes—an alteration in breathing pattern (in a very subject dependent manner), partial entrainment of any pressure-vasomotor oscillations by respiratory activity, and perhaps a direct suppression of these oscillations.

3.4.2 Phase activity: the influence of prestimulus variability

Graham Turpin, Tim Lobstein, and David A. T. Siddle

As noted earlier in this chapter (Section 1.5.2), there are two major problems associated with the derivation of pre (X) minus post stimulus (Y) cardiac difference scores. The first involves the possibility that there is a dependency between such difference scores and the prestimulus level, while the second concerns the difficulty of differentiating pre and post stimulus values which occur against a background of the sinus arrhythmia (SA) waveform.

4.2.1 Initial level

The most commonly employed technique for removing tonic-phasic dependency has involved the statistical adjustment of $Y - X$ using analysis of covariance (ANCOVA). Although Benjamin (1963) proposed the use of ANCOVA for both between- and within-subjects adjustments, the test–retest reliability of individual regression coefficients has been found to be low, at least with neonate data (Clifton and Graham, 1968). Accordingly, between-subjects adjustments have been used most frequently, and the appropriate formula (Chase, Graham, and Graham, 1968; Stratton, 1970) is as follows:

$$D' = D - b_X (X - \bar{X})$$

where D' is the corrected difference score, D is the observed difference score, and b_X is the linear regression coefficient of $Y - X$ on X. However, the use of this formula implies several statistical assumptions which if not met, may invalidate the use of ANCOVA. First, the relationship between X and $Y - X$ must be linear. Although Graham and Jackson (1970) have reported that in the case of neonates, departures from linearity are few, higher-order trends have been reported for adult subjects (Lazarus, Speisman, and Mordkoff, 1963), and their possible occurrence should, therefore, be checked. Second, if a pooled estimate of the between-subjects regression coefficients is used, the homogeneity of these coefficients should be assessed (Stratton, 1970; Pomerleau-Malcuit, Malcuit, and Clifton, 1975). In this connection, it should be pointed out that the assumption of homogeneity will often be violated if the treatments result in different changes in pre stimulus cardiac activity (Evans and Anastasio, 1968). Even if this assumption is not violated, the presence of treatment effects on the covariate still poses problems for the interpretation of the adjusted variate means. Overall and Woodward (1977a, 1977b) have shown that if the treatment effects on the variate and covariate are independent, the adjusted variate mean represents a combination of the two independent effects. They have stated that in this case, the separate magnitudes of the two treatment effects cannot be estimated. It follows, therefore, that ANCOVA can only be used when the treatment effects on both the variate and covariate arise from a common underlying factor. In the case of cardiac activity, this requires assumptions concerning the source of tonic-phase dependency which at present cannot be made (see below).

The use of between-subjects adjustments for the correction of the dependency of $Y - X$ on X has also been criticized on other grounds (Block and Bridger, 1962; Lykken, 1968; Lykken and Venables, 1971). Essentially, their objections are based on the possibility that there are several sources of tonic-phasic dependency, some of which may represent *within-subjects* phenomena. Lykken and Venables (1971) have suggested four phenomena which may account for tonic-phasic relationships. These are: (a) choice of measurement units in that second-by-second and beat-by-beat analyses may reveal different tonic-phasic relationships, as may the use of either HP or HR; (b) the presence of intersubjects reactivity differences; (c) homeostatic ceiling effects; and (d) the effect of behavioural state upon the nature of stimulus-specific responses. Two of these have particular relevance for cardiac activity. Well-defined homeostatic constraints may lead to a within-subject relationship between X and $Y - X$, and the existence of such a relationship is well-documented (Libby, Lacey, and Lacey, 1973; Steinschneider and Lipton, 1965). Clearly, between-subjects adjustments will not remove, and may even distort, tonic-phasic dependency arising from such a source. Although within-subjects adjustments may seem more appropriate, they too must be treated with caution since the presence of ceiling effects often implies a non-linear relationship between X and $Y - X$.

The presence of an intersubject reactivity factor also has implications for the removal of a relationship between X and $Y - X$. Lykken (1968) and Lykken and Venables (1971) have argued that the most important source of a between-subjects tonic-phasic dependency, at least with regard to electrodermal activity, is the presence in both tonic level and phasic responses of a common reactivity factor. This may stem in part from structural and physiological differences which not only constitute a large source of error variance, but are also unrelated to the psychological variables of interest. The solution proposed by Lykken and Venables (1971) involves a range-correction procedure. It is argued that since an individual's range of responsiveness is constrained by structural and physiological factors, extraneous reactivity can be partialled out by expressing each evoked response as a ratio of that particular subject's range of responsiveness. However, in an experiment involving electric shock, Lykken (1972) has reported that range-corrected and untransformed accelerative responses yielded similar results. Although this suggests that range-corrected scores possess no advantage over untransformed scores for accelerative responses, general conclusions concerning the efficacy of range correction of cardiac data should perhaps be postponed until the effect of the procedure on decelerative responses has been investigated. Although several criticisms concerning the use of range correction have been discussed elsewhere (Siddle and coworkers, 1979), it should be noted that a major disadvantage of the technique for cardiac responses is that it can be employed only when a specific index of the response has been obtained.

In summary, any tonic-phasic dependency may be investigated using regression techniques. If such a dependency exists, it may be corrected by either covariance analysis or by range correction procedures. Both techniques rely on a number of assumptions which need to be considered prior to a choice of method. Of course, there may be circumstances (e.g. with clinical groups) in which correction for tonic-phasic dependency is undesirable.

4.2.2 Variability of prestimulus level

It was argued earlier (Section 1.5.2) that the variability inherent in cardiac activity, and particularly that attributable to SA, posed serious problems for reliable detection of the evoked cardiac response (ECR). Three approaches have been adopted to avoid these problems.

The first approach employs an extended prestimulus interval in an attempt to obtain a more reliable measure of the prestimulus level. For example, Engel (1960) used the mean of the ten highest prestimulus beats, while Opton, Rankin, and Lazarus (1965) employed the peak rate in a 10 s interval. While these procedures and other similar techniques (Malmstrom, 1968) probably reduce the variability of the sampled prestimulus level, they do not take into account the continuation into the poststimulus period of any regular cyclic fluctuation.

The second approach attempts to correct for SA and utilizes the SA waveform to make predictions about poststimulus activity in the absence of a stimulus. The technique has been termed the SA-corrected method (Turpin and Siddle, 1978b). The basis of the method is the determination of the period of the SA cycle immediately prior to stimulus presentation. This is expressed in terms of number of beats, T, and the last T prestimulus values are then employed to predict what poststimulus activity would have been in the absence of a stimulus. This is shown in Figure 3.21 in which the dashed line represents the predicted activity and the solid line the observed values. The shaded area represents the change in cardiac activity attributable to stimulation, and specific poststimulus values are obtained by subtracting each predicted beat from its corresponding observed beat. These scores can then be used for response curve analysis or for extracting specific response parameters.

The usefulness of the SA-corrected method has been demonstrated in two ways. First, Turpin and Siddle (1978b) have shown that when the technique is applied to pseudostimulus data, the predicted minus the observed poststimulus difference scores were significantly smaller than when each poststimulus beat was subtracted from the mean of the last four prestimulus beats. Moreover, there was also a reduction in variance across post stimulus beats. Second, these authors also showed that when the SA-corrected and mean difference methods were applied to data arising from an investigation of the effects of stimulus intensity on the

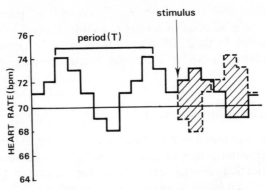

Figure 3.21 Hypothetical heart rate record demonstrating the application of the SA-corrected method. The solid line represents observed cardiac activity and the dashed line represents the predicted activity in the absence of stimulation. The hatched area represents the inferred stimulus-evoked changes. Copyright © 1978, North-Holland Publishing Company. Reprinted with permission of the publisher from 'Measurement of the evoked cardiac response: The problem of prestimulus variability' by G. Turpin and D. A. T. Siddle, *Biological Psychology*, **6**, 127–38

ECR, the proportion of the between-subjects error term sums of squares was 11% less for the former than for the latter. Wilson (1967) has argued that this error term represents idiosyncratic responses, and on this basis, it appears that ECRs derived using the SA-corrected method are more consistent across subjects.

Although the SA-corrected technique avoids many of the statistical assumptions which are necessary in the application of time series to cardiac data (see below), it does possess some limitations. The method relies on visual assessment of the periodicity of the SA waveform, and a technique of computer assessment would be an advantage. Perhaps more importantly, the use of prestimulus values for prediction purposes requires a relatively regular prestimulus pattern. In this respect, Cort and coworkers (1977) have reported that the SA waveform can vary considerably from one cycle to the next. Nevertheless, the simplicity of the SA-corrected method and its demonstrated usefulness (Turpin and Siddle, 1978b) suggest that it is worthy of further investigation.

Time series analysis has been applied to cardiac data by Jones and his colleagues (Jones, Crowell, and Kapuniai, 1969, 1970; Jones and co-workers, 1971). This approach regards cardiac data as a discrete stochastic process which can be expressed as a function of the dependency of the observations on time. The autoregressive model (AR) which has been employed expresses current observations in terms of the current disturbance and past observations. The general form of an autoregressive model of order 1, AR(1), is as follows:

$$z_t = \phi z_{t-1} + \delta + u_t$$

where in the case of cardiac data, ϕ is the autoregressive coefficient, δ is a constant, z_{t-1} is the previous cardiac value, and z_t is the predicted value. The term u_t is a random variate. The differences between observed and predicted values are taken to represent the stimulus-evoked activity. Such differences may also be expressed as a function of the standard error of the predicted value and presented as T values (Jones, Crowell, and Kapuniai, 1969). The original Jones, Crowell, and Kapuniai paper utilized a first-order model and later work has attempted to improve the estimation of the AR coefficients and to overcome, by adaptive estimation, the problem of changes in the individual parameters of the model. This is particularly important in view of the fact that the time series is often non-stationary across trials. Lobstein (1978) has advocated the use of a fourth- or fifth-order AR model on the basis of the fact that the residuals from the first-order model were found to be dependent upon time.

The effects of the application of time series analysis to ECRs is demonstrated in Figure 3.22, which shows the mean ECR to the first presentation of a brief 85 dB tone to six subjects under moderately noisy conditions (80 dB white noise) and six subjects in relatively quiet conditions (60 dB white noise). The upper graph shows responses presented as deviations from the prestimulus mean, while the lower graph shows responses presented as T values. The shaded areas show the extent of the standard errors around the most divergent points. Only the T values show a significant background noise effect (around the sixth poststimulus beat). The background noise effect became significant for the mean difference analysis only with the inclusion of responses to the second stimulus, i.e. when twice the number of observations were used (Lobstein, Webb, and Cort, 1978).

Although time series represents a statistically elegant approach to the problem of prestimulus variability, it is open to a number of criticisms. AR(1) has been applied to neonate data (Jones, Crowell, and Kapuniai, 1969) and has been used in an adaptive form which recomputes the autoregressive coefficient for each successive prediction (Jones, Crowell, and Kapuniai, 1970). Lobstein, Webb, and Cort (1978) found adult cardiac data to need as many as four coefficients, i.e. AR(4). for adequate description. The need to extend the AR model implies that an integrated moving average model (Box and Jenkins, 1970) might be usefully applied to cardiac data. A second criticism concerns the number of observations from which the coefficients are estimated. If a higher-order AR model is used, reliable estimation of the AR coefficients requires a relatively large number of observations (Montgomery and Johnson, 1976). However, Jones and coworkers (1971) and Lobstein, Webb, and Cort (1978) have employed only nine and ten prestimulus values respectively. This may produce unreliable AR coefficients which will lead to cumulative forecast errors. In order to overcome this difficulty, Jones and coworkers (1971)

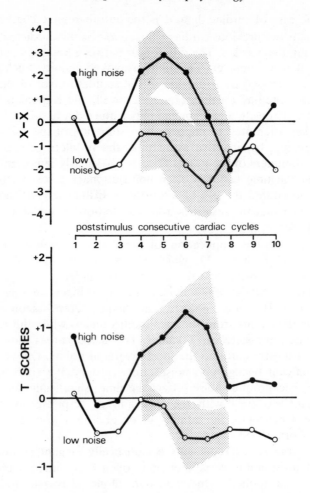

Figure 3.22 Comparison of ECRs for high and low background noise levels. The upper curves represent deviations from a mean pre stimulus value and the lower curves represent standardized deviations from predicted values (T values). Shaded areas show the standard errors of the more divergent points. Copyright 1978, The Society for Psychophysiological Research. Reprinted with permission of the publishers from 'Background noise and heart rate orienting: Response detection using time series analysis' by T. Lobstein, B. Webb, and J. Cort, *Psychophysiology*, 1978, **15**, 316–9

have advocated the use of observed poststimulus values for estimating subsequent poststimulus predictions. It should be pointed out, however, that the observed poststimulus beat may bear no relation to the prestimulus process from which the AR coefficients have been estimated, and may give rise to conservative or even erroneous estimates of response deviation.

On the basis of the above discussion, it would appear that although time series models are of potential use in the derivation of reliable ECRs a number of problems require further work. The most important of these concern the choice of time series model and the use of small prestimulus sample sizes.

One other approach which is closely related to time series should also be mentioned. This attempts to filter phasic fluctuations which are associated with the breathing pattern out of the cardiac waveform (Rickles, Chatoff, and Buchness, 1969; Womack, 1971). It differs from both the SA-corrected technique and autoregressive approaches in that stimulus-evoked cardiac activity that has resulted from changes in respiration may also be filtered out. Obviously, acceptance of such an approach requires more information concerning stimulus-evoked cardiac-respiratory interactions than is currently available. Moreover, the technique has not yet been applied to experimental psychophysiological data.

In summary, it is clear that the variability inherent in cardiac activity poses serious problems for the derivation of reliable ECRs, and methods which take prestimulus variability into account are obviously desirable. Although both the SA-corrected method and time series analysis attempt to do this, neither method is problem free. Nevertheless, the potential gain in terms of error variance reduction would seem to encourage more extensive investigation of the techniques.

3.4.3 Statistical analysis of phasic cardiac activity*

Ronald S. Wilson

Many autonomic variables undergo phasic changes in response to a stimulus and the direction and amplitude of these changes can be preserved by scoring at frequent intervals along the response curve. Phasic changes are particularly evident in cardiac data, where patterns of acceleration and deceleration may be tied to such processes as attention, expectancy, or habituation.

Repeated-measures analysis of variance is perhaps the most widely used statistical method for analysing cardiac data, in large part because of its availability, power, comparative simplicity, and sensitivity to the phasic properties of cardiac data. When properly employed, it can furnish a comprehensive and detailed picture of the systematic components in the response curve.

Acknowledgement. Preparation of this article was supported in part by research grants from the Office of Child Development, the National Science Foundation, and the National Institute of Child Health and Human Development.

A number of procedures drawn from analysis of variance have been developed for use with cardiac data, and the enabling computer programs have been compiled (Wilson, 1967, 1974; Wilson and Scott, 1970). The present section illustrates how several of these procedures may be employed, then briefly surveys several other statistical methods for analysing phasic cardiac data. Of necessity, the treatment here will be cursory in nature, and the cited references should be consulted for a fuller discussion of each design. A more general survey of statistical methods in psychophysiology may be found in Johnson and Lubin (1972).

In the examples to follow, a cardiac response curve (as defined by time scores for successive R–R intervals) is the subject of analysis—what its form may be, how it changes over trials, and how it varies between different treatment groups. The form of the curve and its manner of change are best appraised by the use of orthogonal polynomials, which reveal the different trend components in the curve. Trend analysis is a straightforward extension of repeated-measures ANOVA (Winer, 1971), and it partitions the variance in the response curve into linear, quadratic, cubic, and higher-order trends. The prominence of each trend reflects how strongly a particular phasic change is represented in the curve—a monophasic acceleration, for example, or a biphasic deceleration followed by acceleration.

For illustration we begin with the cardiac response data for four spaced conditioning trials, as shown in Figure 3.23.

The analysis first assesses the common trends evident in all four curves, and then evaluates the extent of change in the curves over successive trials. The results of the trend analysis performed on these response curves are presented in Table 3.1.

The linear and quadratic components were the most significant trends in the composite cardiac response curve during training (i.e. a single curve condensed from the four curves displayed in Figure 3.23). The linear component reflected the general acceleratory trend in R–R time over the 12 data points, while the quadratic component reflected the additional monophasic acceleration beginning at CS onset and gradually dissipating by the third data point following shock.

What were the specific changes in the form of the response curve from one trial to the next? The overall significance test of trials × R–R intervals was marginal, but a more exact test can be made by assessing the trial-to-trial differences in the size of each trend component. As shown in Table 3.1, the quadratic trend component changed significantly over trials, whereas the other trend components did not. When this is evaluated in references to the curves displayed in Figure 3.23, it appears evident that the quadratic component was most prominent on trial 1 and diminished over subsequent trials. The effect of shock anticipation and onset produced

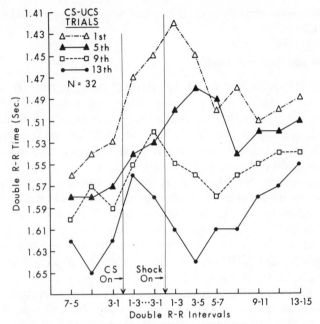

Figure 3.23 Cardiac response to tone CS and shock UCS on four conditioning trials. Copyright © 1974. The Society for Psychophysiological Research. Reprinted with permission of the publishers from 'Cardivar: The statistical analysis of heart rate data' by R. S. Wilson, *Psychophysiology*, 1974, **11**, 76–85

Table 3.1. Trend analysis of changes in cardiac response curve over trials

Source	F	DF
R–R intervals		(11/341)
linear trend	16.05^c	1/31
quadratic trend	7.98^b	1/31
cubic trend	4.22^a	1/31
quartic trend	4.25^a	1/31
Trials × R–R intervals		(33/1023)
differences in linear trend	0.70	3/93
differences in quadratic trend	5.09^b	3/93
differences in cubic trend	0.66	3/93
differences in quartic trend	1.77	3/93

$^a p < 0.05$
$^b p < 0.01$
$^c p < 0.001$

strong acceleration initially, but this effect was markedly weakened over repeated trials.

4.3.1 Trend analysis over trials

The above interpretation could be further strengthened by a second analysis in which the order of trials was taken into account. If E wished to confirm that the trend components changed systematically from the first to the last trial, as suggested by Figure 3.23, he might go one step further and apply a set of orthogonal polynomials to trials, since they constitute an ordered dimension of the analysis as well.

The mean squares for trials × R–R intervals would thus be partitioned into two-way trend components expressing the pattern of change over trials for each trend component in the response curve. The analysis applies linear and quadratic polynomials to the trials dimension for this analysis; and in the table below, the trend component for trials is listed first, while the trend component for R–R intervals (the response curve) is listed second. The results are shown in Table 3.2.

The one highly significant result was the linear reduction over trials in the magnitude of the quadratic trend component. It confirmed the earlier interpretation that the quadratic component was largest on trial 1, when reactivity was greatest, and that it diminished in roughly equal amounts between subsequent trials.

So from a point in the initial analysis where all that could be said was that the response curves changed from trial to trial in some marginally significant fashion the analysis now identifies exactly which trend

Table 3.2. Analysis of two-way trend components in trials × R–R intervals interaction

Source	F	DF
Trials × R–R intervals		(33/1023)
linear × linear	0.31	1/31
linear × quadratic	12.46[b]	1/31
linear × cubic	0.02	1/31
linear × quartic	4.11	1/31
quadratic × linear	0.09	1/31
quadratic × quadratic	0.15	1/31
quadratic × cubic	1.94	1/31
quadratic × quartic	0.09	1/31

[b]$p < 0.01$

component was changing in the response curve, and how the change progressed from trial to trial. It gives a much more detailed test of what is happening in the data and how it relates to the experimental variables of interest.

4.3.2 Comparison between groups

The analysis thus far has been for the one-group case; what about the case where E wants to make comparisons between two or more groups in the form of their response curves?

For illustration, data are presented in Figure 3.24, which display the response curves for three groups in a cardiac conditioning experiment.

A trend analysis can be performed on the composite curve for all three groups, but there is more interest in the curve differences between the groups. Applying the trend analysis to the group curves yielded the results shown in Table 3.3.

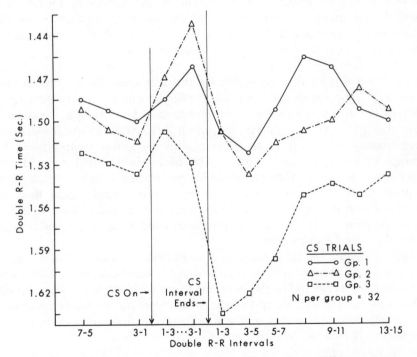

Figure 3.24 Cardiac response to tone CS for three different groups. Copyright © 1974, The Society for Psychophysiological Research. Reprinted with permission of the publishers from 'Cardivar: The statistical analysis of heart rate data' by R. S. Wilson, *Psychophysiology*, 1974, **11**, 76–85

Table 3.3. Trend analysis of differences between groups in form of
cardiac response curve

Source	F	DF
Groups × R–R intervals		(22/1023)
differences in linear trend	1.63	2/93
differences in quadratic trend	10.95[c]	2/93
differences in cubic trend	4.44[a]	2/93
differences in quartic trend	3.52[a]	2/93

[a]$p < 0.05$
[c]$p < 0.001$

There was a highly significant difference in quadratic trend for the groups × R–R intervals interaction, plus less significant differences for the cubic and quartic trends. An inspection of the curves in Figure 3.24 showed that group 3 appeared to be the primary contributor to the differences in quadratic trend, because of its substantial deceleration at CS onset and gradual recovery to pre-CS baseline.

Here again it would be desirable within the formal analysis to isolate the group that was primarily responsible for the difference. To accomplish this, a series of comparisons are specified between groups to identify the largest discrepancy in the size of the trend component. For example, suppose it were desired to verify whether the group differences in quadratic trend were contributed chiefly by the deviation of the group 3 curve from the average curve of groups 1 and 2. The comparison would be made by specifying a set of coefficients which weight groups 1 and 2 equally and contrast them with group 3. The contrast coefficients would then be combined with the quadratic trend values for each group, and the final test would determine whether this contrast accounted for a significant amount of the variance between groups.

The procedure is fully illustrated elsewhere (Wilson, 1974), and it confirmed that the specified contrast was highly significant ($p < 0.001$) and accounted for nearly all of the between-group variance in quadratic trend. When this can be interpreted in light of the separate treatment conditions for each group, it furnishes a much more precise indication of how each treatment affected the response curves.

4.3.3 Cautions

The analyses illustrated in this paper can provide a powerful method for appraising the dynamic properties of polyphasic cardiac responses. There are, however, certain restrictions and limitations which must be kept in mind when using these procedures. *E* should be familiar with the general assumptions of repeated-measures ANOVA, especially the covariance assumption, and how to make the epsilon correction if the covariances are not equal (cf. Wilson 1967, 1974). Further, the trend analysis of any response curve should include advance planning by *E* about how many data points to include in the curve, and which trend components are actually related to his hypothesis about the form and phasing of the response curve. In general, *E* should be able to give an explicit description of the expected form of the response and its point of origin and termination, as these relate to the experimental variables of interest.

4.3.4 Analysing individual differences

While the power of these procedures for group comparisons is evident, the shortcoming of analysis of variance is that it does not provide scores for individuals. If *E* wishes to scale his subjects on various dimensions of cardiac activity, an additional operation on the data is required.

There are three potentially useful scores that can be derived for each *S*. The first is a sustained activity score, which represents subject's tonic heart rate plus the cumulative changes induced throughout the experiment. In the present example it is given by the average of all R–R time scores for a subject, and for comparison purposes it can be transformed into a standard score.

The second score that can be calculated for each subject is a measure of reactivity or responsiveness to the experimental treatment. Reactivity is defined in terms of how far each subject deviates from his baseline, i.e. what is the magnitude of his response curve? Since polyphasic responses may occur, the proposed solution gives equal weight to changes in either direction, but in certain cases *E* may want to restrict his definition of change (e.g. only cardiac acceleration), and the calculations are changed accordingly. If desired, *E* may obtain a score for each trend component in a subject's response curve, reflecting how closely the trend approximates that subject's response.

The third score available for each subject is a measure of within-cell variance. Since this represents the residual variance after all systematic effects have been removed, it may be regarded as spontaneous fluctuation or non-specific variability that appears in the cardiac response curve.

It is worth emphasising that the three scores calculated for each subject by the methods outlined above are based on independent sources of variance, and may be said to represent three separate dimensions of cardiac activity; sustained activity, reactivity, and non-specific variability. Condensing the data into single scores for each subject also makes possible a comparison with other personality and behavioural measures. A fuller description may be found in Wilson (1967), and computer programs to implement these calculations are referenced in Wilson and Scott (1970).

4.3.5 Multivariate procedures

Several other procedures may be mentioned for the analysis of phasic cardiac data. The multivariate generalization of analysis of variance (MANOVA) is often recommended for repeated measures data since it does not include the assumption of equal covariance among the measures. It is more formidable in concept and in calculation than univariate ANOVA, and a good introduction to its logic and use with psychophysiological data may be found in Van Egeren (1973). The latter is also helpful in coordinating MANOVA with other multivariate procedures such as factor analysis and multiple discriminant functions.

Recently, a version of factor analysis has been employed to identify individual differences in the phasic cardiac response. This method isolates independent patterns of response by factoring the data matrix and then identifying those subjects who most closely match a given pattern. The latter is accomplished by condensing each subject's response curve into a smaller number of factor scores which are weighted according to their prominence in the subject's response curve.

The method is derived from a principal-components model developed by Tucker (1958), and it is applied directly to the data matrix rather than to the correlation matrix, thus retaining information about actual levels of response. A detailed exposition may be found in Van Egeren, Headrick and Hein (1972), and recent applications are described in Cleary (1974) and Jennings and Wood (1977).

3.5 ACQUIRED HEART RATE CONTROL IN HUMAN SUBJECTS: INSTRUCTIONS AND FEEDBACK*

Peter J. Lang

It was traditionally assumed that human heart rate was not directly altered through instruction and that plastic changes in heart rhythm could not be brought under instrumental control in either the animal or human subject laboratories (Kimble, 1961; Mowrer, 1947). However, over the last two decades this view has been under continuous assault by researchers (Miller, 1978) and there are now few students of the literature who would defend it unequivocally.

*Acknowledgement. Preparation of this paper was supported in part by National Institute of Mental Health Grant, MH-10993.

3.5.1 Operant conditioning

The basic paradigm for the instrumental conditioning of heart rate requires only that a specific change in heart rhythm be followed by a contingent reward or punishment. Studies of the rat by Miller and DiCara clearly illustrate this procedure (Miller and DiCara, 1967; DiCara and Miller, 1968). A Schmitt trigger is set to detect heart rate increases or decreases, and the appropriate event is followed by a stimulus to the 'reward' centre of the lateral, medial hypothalamus, or an aversive electric shock to the tail. Methods adapted from the animal laboratory were early employed by Shearn (1962) and Frazier (1966) in demonstrating instrumental heart rate control in man.

A key issue in this early research concerned the possibility that the viscus was not directly conditioned, but that heart rate changes were mediated through the coincident conditioning of somatomotor activity. Miller's group adopted the strategy of curarizing and artificially respirating animals in an effort to demonstrate the autonomic specificity of their conditioning procedure. Nevertheless, despite heroic efforts, reliable instrumental learning of heart rate changes have not been achieved in this preparation (Miller and Dworkin, 1974). Potential mediational artifacts are even more difficult to exclude in man, and no experiment purporting to show operant conditioning of cardiac function has yet met the exacting criteria raised by some methodologists (Katkin and Murray, 1968). At present most students of visceral learning eschew a narrow operant view of their work. They hold that organ changes inevitably result from an interaction of somatic and autonomic innervation in the intact human being. Thus, a shift in emphasis has taken place, with investigators now less preoccupied with mediation and more concerned with defining the relevant parameters and uncovering the mechanism of acquired visceral control (Beatty and Legewie, 1977; Birnbaumer and Kimmel, 1978).

3.5.2 Biofeedback

Biofeedback procedures are complex, involving many elements which are not found, or are less meaningfully interpreted, in the animal operant conditioning laboratory:

(1) *Instructions*. Subjects are generally told what to do (e.g. 'Increase your heart rate.'). While it was once held that not telling subjects that heart rate was the focus of the experiment facilitated learning, later research proved this to be false (Blanchard and coworkers, 1974). Furthermore, instructions may include information on how to accomplish the task (e.g. 'Try to keep the green light on') or limitations on the methods to be used (e.g. 'Keep your respiration regular').

(2) *Information on performance*. From the operant perspective, information about correct responses has been viewed as a contingent reinforcer. However, the information given human subjects is often quite elaborate, telling them not only that an appropriate response has been achieved, but the magnitude of success, or the amount by which the criterion was missed, or what the pattern of results has been over several trials.

(3) *Organ feedback*. This is information about the functioning of a visceral organ. In the operant paradigm performance and organ feedback are identical. However, in biofeedback studies with human subjects they are often separately manipulated. This is clearly illustrated in an early report by the Russian investigator Lisina (1958), on the 'conversion of involuntary into voluntary reactions'. In a first attempt, she was unable to increase arm vasodilation by the operant strategy of discontinuing shock when small volume increases occurred. However, her procedure was later successful when she provided 'additional afferentation', mobilizing the 'orienting-exploratory activity' of subjects. This exteroceptive information was provided by a light beam, controlled by the plethysmograph, that changed coincident with variations in the volume of the blood vessels. Performance feedback was insufficient for subjects to accomplish the task; organ feedback was necessary for response acquisition.

A great variety of feedback displays and learning procedures have been employed in research on heart rate control. Engel and his colleagues (Engel and Hansen, 1966; Engel, 1972) used an operant methodology. Changes in heart rate that exceeded a criterion (performance feedback) resulted in the illumination of a light display. Subjects were encouraged to keep the light on as much as possible and received monetary rewards proportional to their success at the task. Lang and associates (Hnatiow and Lang, 1965; Lang, Sroufe, and Hastings, 1967) employed a meter display in training heart rate stabilization. Brener's group (Brener and Hothersall, 1966; Brener, 1974) stressed the exteroceptive augmentation of visceral feedback. They provided subjects with continuous auditory signals, in which each heart interval generated a high or low tone, depending on whether that period had achieved or fallen short of a preset criterion for change. Shapiro, Tursky, and Schwartz (1970) provided light signals for each successful heart interval, and an interesting slide to view when enough criterion heart intervals had been accumulated. A good review of research on heart biofeedback is provided by Blanchard and Epstein (1978, pp. 16–53).

Because of differences in theoretical orientation, type of display, reinforcers, number and length of trials, and sessions, etc., it is not possible to directly compare experiments on heart rate control from different laboratories. In the interest of clarity of exposition this section will focus on one research program, recent work by Lang and colleagues, in which a great many parameters of heart rate control were explored in the same experimental environment. A working assumption of this research was that the acquisition of heart rate control represented a skill, and that the variables which modulate human performance or motor learning were also relevant to visceral control. The experiments described here were all administered by a small computer which presented instructions and feedback displays, controlled the timing and sequence of trials, and collected the physiological date (Lang, 1974, 1975).

3.5.3 Type and frequency of heart rate feedback

In a first series of studies, Lang and his colleagues undertook an exploration of the information properties of heart rate feedback and its effect on instructed cardiac speeding and slowing. Under feedback conditions subjects were presented with an oscilloscope display representing successive heart periods. Each heart cycle initiated a moving line, starting at the right which extended itself across the screen at a constant rate. In the standard program, this line was turned off by the next EKG cycle, a vertical marker was illuminated briefly at the terminus, and within microseconds a new line started across the screen. Thus, the lengths of successive horizontal lines were exactly proportional to the lengths of successive interbeat intervals.

The screen also contained a fixed, vertical line, running from the top to the bottom of the screen. This was the subject's target. If the subject was asked to speed his heart rate, his job was to terminate the horizontal line before it crossed the target. If his task was slowing, it was necessary for the sweep line to extend past the target for a success to be recorded. Each success was underscored for the subject by the appearance of the word GOOD on the screen, at the completion of a criterion heart period.

The target line was initially set at the subject's median interbeat interval determined at the beginning of the experiment, while the subject performed the assigned task (speed or slow) without feedback. The target was altered over trials according to a programmed shaping schedule, designed to prompt improved performance without making discouraging demands.

In a first experiment Lang and Twentyman (1974) assessed differences between the *complete* oscilloscope feedback, a *limited* feedback display, and a control task. The limited feedback consisted of only the word GOOD, which appeared on the screen whenever an interbeat interval met the criterion. From the perspective of performance information this was conceptualized as *binary* feedback. This version of the task could also be viewed as a simple instrumental learning paradigm—the word GOOD

I

serving as a modest reinforcer. The control task employed a display similar to the full, *analogue* display, except that the sweep lines were generated by a computer program according to a semi-random schedule, rather than by the subject's heart rhythm. Subjects were instructed to press a key aperiodically during display presentation, depending on the movement of the sweep lines relative to the target. When subjects pressed correctly, the word GOOD appeared on the screen. They were told that the procedure was a tracking task designed to assess attentiveness.

Subjects who were administered the full, analogue display showed a greater instructed increase in heart rate than did the subjects observing the binary display. The latter group did not differ in heart rate from control subjects. When instructed to slow heart rate, both feedback groups showed significantly more slowing than the control group. However, differences between the two feedback displays were not obtained for the slowing task.

Gatchel (1974) undertook a more extended evaluation of information feedback and heart rate control. The computer program used by Lang and Twentyman was modified such that the sweep lines could be made to terminate at any subsequent beat, not only the next systole. Gatchel compared four displays, varying in frequency of heart rate information feedback: (1) the analogue display from the previous study in which each sweep line represented a single interbeat interval; (2) a display in which the sweep line terminated at the fifth systole after the initiating beat; (3) a display with sweep lines proportional in length to successive units of ten interbeat intervals; (4) the tracking task.

When instructed to speed heart rate, subjects showed maximum performance when they received information every heart period, and progressively poorer performance with less frequent feedback. When assigned a heart rate slowing task, all feedback groups showed more deceleration than tracking subjects, but there were no significant differences among feedback groups. These studies indicated a close relationship between feedback information and performance when heart rate speeding was the assigned task, but failed to confirm the hypothesis that a slowing task would be sensitive to information characteristics of the feedback display.

In addition to information frequency, incentives have been shown to differentially affect speeding and slowing tasks. Lang and Twentyman (1976) rewarded subjects with money for heart rate increases and decreases, establishing a contract with subjects before the experiment in which each appearance of the word GOOD on the screen increased their total remuneration. A clear effect of incentive was noted for speeding, with individual subjects achieving sustained rates over 120 B/M for monetary reward. However, slowing was not significantly affected by incentives during feedback, and incentive subjects were only slightly better than no-incentive subjects in maintaining slowing performance when feedback was removed.

Consideration of the paradigm used in the above experiments suggested that the negative results for slowing may have been attributable to a procedural artifact. The program could be construed as reducing reinforcement with improved slowing performance. The rate at which the program presented feedback information was controlled by each subject's cardiac rhythm. Thus, as the subject slowed his heart rate (i.e. lengthened the period between successive systoles) the interval between sweep terminations necessarily became longer, reducing the frequency with which the word GOOD appeared. From this perspective, successful performance during slowing could be seen as leading to fewer reinforcement trials, while the reverse was true for speeding. In order to control for this variable, the program was modified to present information at regular, fixed intervals rather than at the termination of heart periods.

Twentyman and Lang (1977) studied heart rate speeding and slowing with different groups receiving feedback every heart period, and at fixed intervals of one second and six seconds. In the latter two displays, subjects observed successive horizontal lines which were proportional in length to their average heart rates during the immediately previous fixed time interval. Under these conditions, subjects were given no information about the time of occurrence of heart systoles.

The real-time display proved no more effective than the heart-time display in modifying slowing performance. When instructed to slow heart rate, information frequency had no effect on the amount of heart rate change. Furthermore, more frequent information did not prompt better performance on the speeding task, as it had when heart-time controlled the display. In fact, subjects who were administered heart information at the fixed rate closest to the best heart-time display (i.e. once per second) showed a deterioration in performance over sessions relative to subjects receiving feedback at slower rates. This curious finding was later replicated by Twentyman (1977). He explored a variety of display frequencies and demonstrated that the decline in performance only occurred when the fixed display rate was slightly slower than the normal human heart rate. He suggested that the display might come to 'drive' the heart (similar to EEG frequency driving), or that subjects might unconsciously match their own heart rhythm to the display frequency. Whatever the explanation of this phenomenon it is clear that a heart-time display can facilitate speeding in systematic ways while a real-time feedback of heart rate does not. An important difference between these two display types is that the former provides a signal coincident with the occurrence of systole. Information on rate which does not include this component is apparently less useful and can even have negative effects on performance.

3.5.4 Heart rate slowing: meditation or biofeedback?

In subsequent research an effort was made to bring slowing under instructional control through the manipulation of other variables than heart rate feedback. Jacobson (1938) early pointed out the relationship between levels of somatic muscle tension and cardiovascular activity. He proposed muscle relaxation training as a technique for achieving lowered level of visceral arousal.

Cuthbert (1976) compared heart rate feedback and muscle tension feedback as methods for producing instructed heart rate slowing. Following the method of Budzynski and Stoyva (1969), frontalis muscle activity was recorded, and for one group of subjects this signal controlled the feedback display. Thus, sweep lines represented the EMG integral: a shorter line, appearing with greater frequency was produced by higher muscle tension, and less frequent, longer sweep lines were occasioned by lowered tension. As with heart rate, a target was set at the subject's median, no-feedback performance level. A criterion response resulted in the word GOOD appearing on the screen. While the organization of physiological systems produced by the two methods of training was slightly different, heart rate and muscle tension feedback produced the same amount of heart rate slowing.

An alternative approach involved the application of specific cognitive strategies, instructions to think in certain ways, apply oneself to various mental rituals, or attend to specific body parts or functions. Thus, Cuthbert (1976) compared heart rate feedback and Benson's secularized meditation instructions, as procedures for reducing heart rate. In this latter method subjects are told to attend to their own breathing and repeat to themselves the word 'one' with each exhalation. They are further instructed to relax, take a passive attitude towards their thinking and not dwell on particular ideas or solve problems but to always return to the self-repetition and respiratory focus (Beary and Benson, 1974; Benson, Beary, and Carol, 1974). In Cuthbert's initial experiment this method produced a dramatic reduction in heart rate relative to the performance of feedback subjects. However, a subsequent effort to replicate this effect generated no difference in slowing between meditation and feedback groups (Cuthbert and Lang, 1976; Simons and Lang, 1977).

A careful analysis of experimental procedure led to the conclusion that the subjects in these two studies differed in their personal 'involvement' in the task. The initial experiment had been undertaken by a single investigator who developed a relationship with the subjects, reviewed their progress with them, and socially reinforced subjects for following instructions. The second experiment was a general laboratory project, involving several investigators, who performed their duties competently but more perfunctorily. Thus, a third study (Kristellar, 1978) was undertaken in which these two types of experimenter/subject relationships were systematically examined. Separate groups were trained to reduce heart rate using either feedback or meditation. Half of the subjects in each group participated in a high 'involvement' procedure and half in a low 'involvement' administration of the task. The results obtained originally, i.e. marked superiority for meditation, appeared again for high 'involvement' subjects; the findings for the low 'involvement' subjects were the same as the previous follow-up study, i.e. no difference between experimental conditions. It is of interest to note that the difference between feedback and meditation subjects under high 'involvement' was contributed to in part by poorer performance by the feedback group. Somehow the concern and encouragement of the experimenter facilitated meditation, but this same attitude appeared to inhibit the optimal use of feedback.

The above results should not be taken as a final comment on the effects of the experimenter/subject relationship on meditation and feedback procedures. In the Cuthbert experiment, subjects were regularly informed as to their general performance on the task, i.e. a scoreboard was presented periodically to all subjects, regardless of group, stating their current heart rate in beats/minute and amount of change from initial rest. When this scoreboard was dropped from the procedure, the effects of the 'involvement' variable changed radically. Feedback subjects now performed best under *high* involvement conditions. It appears that the interest and coaching of the experimenter was helpful only in the absence of knowledge of results. For meditation subjects the opposite was true: high involvement prompted less slowing than low involvement when subjects received no information on their progress in the task. Furthermore, the greatest decelerations that we have observed in any of these experiments were seen in meditation trained subjects under the *low* involvement condition.

3.5.5 Motivation and information

Consideration of this research prompts several conclusions. First of all, it is clear that for normal subjects there is a differential effect of training variables on heart rate speeding and slowing. Thus, speeding performance is highly responsive to display characteristics and the manipulation of feedback information, which readily come to control the subject's performance output. This is not to say that feedback is necessarily an optimal strategy for increasing heart rate (instructions to change heart rate through exercise produce at least equally large heart rate increases, see Johnson, 1977), but only that subjects placed in a feedback loop in which stimuli to a distance receptor are controlled by heart rate, show specific, predictable, and systematic changes in cardiac rhythm. As the study of fixed rate feedback indicated, these effects can be deleterious to an instructed performance, as well as facilitating, and subjects are not always aware of them (see also Lang, Sroufe, and Hastings, 1967).

Secondly, there is little evidence that subjects in a biofeedback loop, who are under instructions to slow heart rate, show performance changes that are a simple function of the feedback manipulation. In part, this is due to the energy cost of the information processing demanded by the feedback task. Such processing has unconditioned acceleratory effects on heart rate which are in competition with the goals of the procedure. Furthermore, an increase in motivation, with associated physiological arousal can potentially confound efforts at heart rate slowing. As we have seen, slowing performance is very vulnerable to subtle interactions between the apparent processing demands of the task, knowledge of results, and motivational variables. A similar phenomenon has been noted in the clinical literature. Elmer Green (Green, Green, and Walters, 1970) stresses the importance of a proper mental set, if feedback and relaxation therapies are to be effective. Patients are instructed to assume an attitude of 'passive volition'—to be interested in changing their physiology in the appropriate direction, but not to 'force' these changes. This appears to be an effort at instructional balancing of some of the interacting variables just discussed.

3.5.6 Conclusions and applications

It is clear that psychological variables have a considerable impact on instructed heart rate control. However, the individual's characteristic pattern of heart functioning is of at least equal importance. Several investigators have reported a relationship between heart rate on a biofeedback task and resting rate and variability at the beginning of an experimental session (Gatchel, 1974; Stephens, Harris, and Brady, 1972). Bell and Schwartz (1973) have noted that change with training does not exceed the normal daily variation heart rate, occasioned by routine stress or rest. Furthermore, there appear to be large individual differences in prior ability to control heart rate (Lang, 1975). Some subjects are 'autonomic' athletes, and modify physiological functions with apparent ease, after little or no training; others show no profit from extended exposure to feedback and instruction. There are some data suggesting a relationship between personality characteristics and heart rate control, e.g. Rotter internal–external scale (Roy and Lamb, 1974; Gatchel, 1975) or the subject's capacity to generate emotional imagery (Lang, 1979). Age and disease are also of significance. Lang and coworkers (1975) found that patients who had recovered from ischemic heart disease were unable to profit from feedback training; age-matched controls did better, but not as well as young, college students.

The use of biofeedback as a clinical tool is now widespread. However, the specific value of heart rate training is unclear. Gatchel (1979) has shown that heart rate biofeedback can reduce anxiety in a stress situation. Nevertheless, research reported here suggests that meditation or muscle relaxation training reduce arousal equally well, and these techniques are clearly more cost-efficient. Engel (1972) has demonstrated that arrhythmias can be modified in heart patients, but the training required is demanding and time consuming. Perhaps because of this and the effectiveness of anti-arrhythmic drugs, this method has not yet been widely used.

The most provocative applications of heart rate control methods have been in the laboratory, where they provide a new approach to the study of cardio–behavioural interactions. Thus, Lindholm (1975) examined the Laceys' hypothesis (Lacey and Lacey, 1970) of a causal relationship between heart rate and reaction time (RT). She trained subjects to produce specific patterns of acceleration or deceleration during the RT foreperiod, testing directly the hypothesis that they would generate different response latencies. Shapiro (1977) is currently using this methodology in examining the phenomenon of pain, elucidating the interaction of physiological arousal and verbal report of distress.

In summary, there is little question that heart rate can be brought under instructional control and that cardiac function is significantly altered when subjects become part of a biofeedback loop. Progress has been made in explicating the role of information and motivational variables. Procedures developed in this area have made an important contribution to the methodology of psychophysiology and they may yet be shown to have practical clinical significance. It is also true that our understanding of these phenomena is still limited and that much work needs to be done before a comprehensive theory of instructed heart rate control can evolve.

REFERENCES

Bard, P. (1968). Regulation of the systemic circulation. In: V. B. Mountcastle (Ed.) *Medical Physiology*, 12th ed. Mosby, St. Louis, pp. 178–208.

Beary, J. F. and Benson H. (1974). A simple psychophysiologic technique which elicits the hypometabolic changes of the relaxation response. *Psychosom, Med.,* **36**, 115–20.

Beatty, T. and Legewie, H. (Eds) (1977). *Biofeedback and Behaviour*, Plenum Press, New York.

Bell, I. R. and Schwartz, G. E. (1973). Voluntary control and reactivity in human heart rate. *Psychophysiology*, **12**, 339–48.

Bendat, J. S. and Piersol, A. G. (1966). *Measurement and Analysis of Random Data*, Wiley, New York.

Benjamin, L. S. (1963). Statistical treatment of the law of initial values in autonomic research: A review and recommendation. *Psychosom. Med.,* **25**, 556–66.

Benjamin, L. S. (1967). Facts and artifacts in using analysis of covariance to 'undo' the law of initial values. *Psychophysiology,* **4**, 187–202.

Benson, H., Heary, J. E., and Carol, M. P. (1974). The relaxation response. *Psychiatry,* **37**, 37–46.

Berne, R. M. and Levy, M. N. (1967). *Cardiovascular Physiology.* C. V. Mosby, St. Louis.

Birnbaumer, N. and Kimmel, H. D. (1978). *Biofeedback and self-regulation.* Lawrence Erlbaum Associates, Hillsdale, NJ.

Black, A. H. and DeToledo, L. (1972). The relationship among classically conditioned responses: Heart rate and skeletal behavior. In A. H. Black and W. F. Prokasy (Eds), *Classical conditioning II: Current Research and Theory.* Appleton-Century-Crofts, New York. pp. 290–311.

Blair, D. A., Glover, W. E., Greenfield, A. D. M., and Roddie, I. C. (1959). Excitation of cholinergic vasodilator nerves to human skeletal muscles during emotional stress. *J. Physiol.,* **148**, 633–47.

Blanchard, E. B., and Epstein, L. H. (1978). *A Biofeedback Primer.* Addison-Wesley, Reading, Mass.

Blanchard, E. B., Scott, R. W., Young, L. D., and Edmundson, E. B. (1974). Effect of knowledge of response on the self-control of heart rate. *Psychophysiology,* **11**, 251–64.

Blanchard, E. B., Young, L. D., and McLeod, P. G. (1972). Awareness of heart activity and self-control of heart rate. *Psychophysiology,* **9**, 63–8.

Block, J. D., and Bridger, W. H. (1962). The law of initial value in psychophysiology: A reformulation in terms of experimental and theoretical considerations. *Ann. NY Acad. Sci.,* **98**, 1229.

Bohlin, G., and Graham, F. K. (1977). Cardiac deceleration and reflex blink facilitation. *Psychophysiology,* **14**, 423–30.

Bond, D. D. (1943). Sympathetic and vagal interaction in emotional response of the heart rate. *Am. J. Physiol.,* **138**, 468–78.

Boyd, W. E., and Eadie, W. R. (1954). Continuous recording of human heart rate. *Electron. Engng,* **26**, 330–4.

Box, G. E. P., and Jenkins, G. M. (1970). *Time Series Analysis, Forecasting and Control.* Holden-Day, San Francisco.

Brener, J. (1967). Heart rate. In P. H. Venables and I. Martin (Eds), *A Manual of Psychophysiological Methods.* North Holland, London, pp. 103–31.

Brener, J. (1974). A general model of voluntary control applied to the phenomena of learned cardiovascular change. In P. A. Obrist, A. H. Black, J. Brener, and L. V. DiCara (Eds), *Cardiovascular Psychophysiology: Current Issues in Response Mechanisms, Biofeedback and Methodology.* Aldine, Chicago. pp. 365–91.

Brener, J., and Hothersall, D. (1966). Heart rate control under conditions of augmented sensory feedback. *Psychophysiology,* **3**, 23–7.

Brener, J. M., Phillips, K. C., and Connally, S. R. (1977). Oxygen consumption and ambulation during operant conditioning of heart rate increases and decreases in rats. *Psychophysiology,* **14**, 483–91.

Brown, G. L., and Eccles, J. C. (1934). The action of a single vagal volley on the rhythm of the heart beat. *J. Physiol. (Lond.),* **82**, 211–40.

Brown, R. G. (1969). *Smoothing, Forecasting and Prediction of Discrete Time Series.* Prentice-Hall, Englewood Cliffs, NJ.

Brucker, B., Dworkin, B. R., Eisenberg, L., Miller, N. E., and Pickering, T. G. (1975). Learned voluntary control of diastolic pressure and circulatory effects of attempted muscle contraction in severely paralyzed patients. *J. Physiol.,* **252**, 67P–68P.

Buckley, P. B. (1979). Issues in cardiac data reduction. *Psychophysiology*, in press.

Budzynski, T. H., and Stoyva, T. (1969). An instrument for producing deep muscle relaxation by means of analogue information feedback. *J. Appl. Behavior Anal.*, **2**, 231–7.

Burdick, J. A. (1968). Heart rate variability (CVT): Concurrent validity and test-retest reliability. *Percept. Mot. Skills*, **26**, 1001–2a.

Burdick, J. A. (1978). Heart rate, tonic cardiac variability and evaluation. *J. Psychosom. Res.*, **22**, 69–77.

Cannon, W. B. (1929). *Bodily Changes in Pain, Hunger, Fear and Rage*, Appleton, New York.

Carruthers, M., Arguelles, A. E., and Mosovich, A. (1976). Man in transit: Biochemical and physiological changes during intercontinental flights. *The Lancet*, **7967**, 977–81.

Chase, H. (1965). Habituation of an acceleratory cardiac response in neonates. *Unpublished Master's Thesis*, University of Wisconsin.

Chase, W. G., Graham, F. K., and Graham, D. T. (1968). Components of heart rate response in anticipation of reaction time and exercise tasks. *J. Exp. Psychol.*, **76**, 642–8.

Cleary, P. J. (1974). Description of individual differences in autonomic reactions. *Psychol. Bull.*, **81**, 934–44.

Clifton, R. K., and Graham, F. K. (1968). Stability of individual differences in heart rate activity during the newborn period. *Psychophysiology*, **5**, 37–50.

Clifton, R. K., and Nelson, M. N. (1976). Developmental study of habituation in infants: The importance of paradigm, response system and state. In T. J. Tighe and R. N. Leaton (Eds), *Habituation: Perspectives from Child Developmental, Animal Behaviour, and Neurophysiology*. Erlbaum, New Jersey. pp. 159–205.

Cohen, D. H. (1974a). The neural pathways and informational flow mediating a conditional autonomic response. In L. V. DiCara (Ed.), *Limbic and Autonomic Nervous Systems Research*. Plenum, New York. pp. 223–75.

Cohen, D. H. (1974b). Analysis of the final common path for heart rate conditioning. In P. A. Obrist, A. H. Black, J. Brener, and L. V. DiCara (Eds), *Cardiovascular Psychophysiology: Current Issues in Response Mechanism, Biofeedback and Methodology*. Aldine, Chicago. pp. 117–35.

Cohen, D. H., and MacDonald, R. K. (1974). A selective review of central and neural pathways involved in cardiovascular control. In P. A. Obrist, A. H. Black, J. Brener, and L. V DiCara (Eds), *Cardiovascular Psychophysiology: Current Issues in Response Mechanisms, Biofeedback and Methodology*, Aldine, Chicago. pp. 33–59.

Cohen, M. J. (1973). The relation between heart rate and electromyographic activity in a discriminated escape-avoidance paradigm. *Psychophysiology*, **10**, 8–20.

Coleridge, H. M,, Coleridge, J. C. G., and Rosenthal, F. (1976). Prolonged inactivation of cortical pyramidal tract neurones in cats by distension of the carotid sinus. *J. Physiol. (Lond.)*, **256**, 635–49.

Coles, M. G. H. (1974). Physiological activity and detection: The effects of attentional requirements and the prediction of performance. *Biol. Psychol.*, **2**, 113–25.

Coles, M. G. H., and Duncan-Johnson, C. C. (1975). Cardiac activity and information processing: The effect of stimulus significance, and detection and response requirements. *J. Exp. Psychol.: Hum. Percept. Perform.*, **1**, 418–28.

Coles, M. G. H., Porges, S. W., and Duncan-Johnson, C. C. (1975). Sex differences in performance and associated cardiac activity during a reaction time task. *Physiol. Psychol.*, **3**, 141–3.

Connor, W. H., and Lang, P. J. (1969). Cortical slow-wave and cardiac rate responses in stimulus orientation and reaction time conditions. *J. Exp. Psychol.*, **82**, 310–20.

Cort, J., Edholm, O. G., Lobstein, T., and Webb, R. (1977). Some observations on sinus arrhythmia. *J. Physiol.*, **268**, 21–2.

Cunningham, D. J. C., Petersen, E. S., Peto, R., Pickering, T. G., and Sleight, P. (1972). Comparison of the effect of different types of exercise on the baroreflex regulation of heart rate. *Acta Physiol. Scand.*, **86**, 444–55.

Cuthbert, B. N. (1976). Voluntary slowing of heart rate: A comparison of various techniques. Unpublished doctoral dissertation, University of Wisconsin, Madison.

Cuthbert, B. N., and Lang, P. J. (1976). Biofeedback and cardiovascular self-control. *Scand. J. Beh. Therapy*, **5**, 111–32.

Darrow, C. W. (1929). Electrical and circulatory responses to brief sensory and ideational stimuli. *J. Exp. Psychol.*, **12**, 267–300.

Davidson, N. S., Goldner, S., and McCloskey, D. I. (1976). Respiratory modulation of baroreceptor and chemoreceptor reflexes affecting heart rate and cardiac vagal efferent nerve activity. *J. Physiol.*, **259**, 523–30.

Davies, C. T. M., and Neilson, J. M. H. (1967). Sinus arrhythmia in man at rest. *J. Appl. Physiol.*, **22**, 947–55.

Davis, R. C., Buchwald, A. M., and Frankmann, R. W. (1955). Autonomic and muscular responses and their relation to simple stimuli. *Psychol. Monogr.*, **69**, 1–71.

DiCara, L. V., and Miller, N. E. (1968). Changes in heart rate instrumentally learned by curarized rats as avoidance responses. *J. Comp. Physiol. Psychol.*, **65**, 8–12.

Dong, E.Jr, and Reitz, B. A. (1970). Effect of timing of vagal stimulation on heart rate in the dog. *Circulation Res.*, **27**, 635–46.

Duffy, E. (1962). *Activation and Behavior*, Wiley, New York.

Duncan-Johnson, C. C., and Coles, M. G. H. (1974). Heart rate and disjunctive reaction time: The effects of discrimination requirements. *J. Exp. Psychol.*, **103**, 1160–8.

Dykman, R. A., and Gantt, W. H. (1959). The parasympathetic component of unlearned and acquired cardiac responses. *J. Comp. Physiol. Psychol.*, **52**, 163–7.

Elliott, R. (1970). Comment on the comparability of measures of heart rate in cross-laboratory comparisons. *J. Exp. Res. Personality*, **4**, 156–8.

Elliott, R. (1972). The significance of heart rate for behavior: A critique of Lacey's hypothesis. *J. Personality Soc. Psychol.*, **22**, 398–409.

Elliott, R. (1974). The motivational significance of heart rate. In P. A. Pbrist, A. H. Black, J. Brener, and L. V. DiCara (Eds), *Cardiovascular Psychophysiology: Current Issues in Response Mechanisms, Biofeedback and Methodology*, Aldine, Chicago, pp. 505–37.

Elliott, R., and Thynsell, R. V. (1968). Note on smoking and heart rate. *Psychophysiology*, **5**, 280–3.

Engel, B. T. (1960). Stimulus-response and individual response specificity. *Archs. Gen. Psychiat.*, **2**, 305–13.

Engel, B. T. (1972). Operant conditioning of cardiac function: A status report. *Psychophysiology*, **9**, 161–77.

Engel, B. T., and Hansen, S. P. (1966). Operant conditioning of heart rate slowing. *Psychophysiology*, **3**, 176–87.

Evans, S. H., and Anastasio, E. J. (1968). Misuse of analysis of covariance when treatment effect and covariate are confounded. *Psychol. Bull.*, **69**, 225–34.

Ferguson, G. A. (1965). *Nonparametric Trend Analyses*, McGill University Press, Montreal.

Fitzgerald, R. D. (1976). Involvement of vagal activity in the unconditioned heart rate responses of restrained rats. *Physiol. Beh.,* **17**, 785–8.

Frampton, C., Riddle, H. C., and Roberts, J. R. (1976). An ECG telemetry system for physiological studies on swimmers. *Biomed. Engng,* **11**, 87–90, 94.

Frazier, T. W. (1966). Avoidance conditioning of heart rate in humans. *Psychophysiology,* **3**, 188–202.

Freyschuss, V. (1970). Cardiovascular adjustments to somatomotor activation: The elicitation of increments in heart rate, aortic pressure and veno-motor tone with the initiation of muscle contraction. *Acta Physiol. Scand. Suppl.,* **342**, 1–63.

Gahery, Y., and Vigier, D. (1974). Inhibitory effects in the cuneate nucleus produced by vago-aortic afferent fibers. *Brain Res.,* **75**, 241–6.

Gang, M. J., and Teft, L. (1975). Individual differences in heart rate responses to affective sound. *Psychophysiology,* **12**, 423–6.

Gatchel, R. (1974). Frequency of feedback and learned heart rate control. *J. Exp. Psychol.,* **103**, 274–83.

Gatchel, R. J. (1975). Change over training sessions of relationships between locus of control and voluntary heart rate control. *Percept. Mot. Skills,* **40**, 424–6.

Gatchel, R. J. (1979). Biofeedback and the treatment of fear and anxiety. In R. J. Gatchel, and K. P. Price (Eds). *Clinical Applications of Biofeedback: Appraisal and Status*. Pergamon, Elmsford, NY, pp. 148–72.

Gautier, H. (1972). Respiratory and heart rate responses to auditory stimulations. *Physiol. Beh.,* **8**, 327–32.

Graham, F. K. (1978a). Normality of distributions and homogeneity of variance of heart rate and heart period samples. *Psychophysiology,* **15**, 487–91.

Graham, F. K. (1978b). Constraints on measuring heart rate and period sequentially through real and cardiac time, *Psychophysiology,* **15**, 492–5.

Graham, F. K., Berg, K. M., Berg, K. W., Jackson, J. C., Hatton, H. M., and Kantowitz, S. R. (1970). Cardiac orienting responses as a function of age. *Psychonom. Sci.,* **19**, 363–4.

Graham, F. K., and Clifton, R. K. (1966). Heart-rate change as a component of the orienting response. *Psychol. Bull.,* **65**, 305–20.

Graham, F. K., and Jackson, J. C. (1970). Arousal systems and infant heart rate responses. In H. W. Reese and L. P. Lipsitt (Eds), *Advances in Child Development and Behavior*, Vol. 5, Academic Press: New York. pp. 69–117.

Graham, F. K., Putman, L. E., and Leavitt, L. A. (1975). Lead-stimulation effects on human cardiac orienting and blink reflexes. *J. Exp. Psychol.,* **104**, 161–9.

Green, E. E., Green, A. M., and Walters, E. D. (1970). Voluntary control of internal states: Psychological and physiological. *J. Transpersonal Psychol.,* **11**, 1–26.

Grollman, A. (1929). Physiological variations in the cardiac output of man. III. The effect of the ingestion of food on the cardiac output, pulse rate, blood pressure and oxygen consumption of man. *Am. J. Physiol.,* **89**, 366–70.

Halberg, F. (1969). Chronobiology. *Ann. Rev. Physiol.,* **32**, 675–725.

Hare, R., Wood, K., Britain, S., and Frazelle, J. (1971). Autonomic responses to affective visual stimulation: Sex differences. *J. Exp. Res. Personality,* **5**, 233–41.

Hart, J. D. (1975). Cardiac response to simple stimuli as a function of the respiratory cycle. *Psychophysiology,* **12**, 634–6.

Hastings, S. E., and Obrist, P. A. (1967). Heart rate during conditioning in humans: Effects of varying the inter-stimulus (CS-UCS) interval. *J. Exp. Psychol.*, **74**, 431–42.

Hatton, H. M., Berg, W. K., and Graham, F. K. (1970). Effects of acoustic rise time on heart rate response. *Psychonom. Sci.*, **19**, 101–3.

Hayes, R. W. (1974). An oculo-cardiac factor in the heart rate deceleration component of the orientation response. *Biol. Psychol.*, **1**, 315–20.

Hayes, R. W., and Venables, P. (1972). An accurate, direct reading beat-by-beat, heart rate scale for measurement of the cardiac orientation reaction. *Psychophysiology*, **9**, 624–5.

Heilizer, F. (1975). The law of initial vale (LIV) and personality. *J. Gen. Psychol.*, **92**, 273–90.

Hellman, J. B., and Stacey, R. W. (1976). Variation of respiratory sinus arrhythmia with age. *J. Appl. Physiol.*, **41**, 734–8.

Higgins, J. D. (1971). Set and uncertainty as factors influencing anticipatory cardiovascular responding in humans. *J. Comp. Physiol. Psychol.*, **74**, 272–83.

Hnatiow, M., and Lang, P. J. (1965). Learned stabilization of cardiac rate. *Psychophysiology*, **1**, 330–6.

Holloway, F. A., and Parsons, O. A. (1972). Physiological concomitants of reaction time performance in normal and brain-damaged subjects. *Psychophysiology*, **9**, 189–98.

Howard, J. L., Obrist, P. A., Gaebelein, C. J., and Galosy, R. A. (1974). Multiple somatic measures and heart rate during classical aversive conditioning in the cat. *J. Comp. Physiol. Psychol.*, **87**, 228–36.

Jacobson, E. (1938). *Progressive Relaxation*, University of Chicago Press, Chicago

Jennings, J. R., Averill, J. R., Opton, E. M., and Lazarus, R. J. (1971). Some parameters of heart rate change: Perceptual versus motor task requirements, noxiousness, and uncertainty. *Psychophysiology*, **7**, 194–212.

Jennings, J. R., Stringfellow, J. C., and Graham, M. (1974). A comparison of the statistical distributions of beat-by-beat heart rate and heart period. *Psychophysiology*, **11**, 207–10.

Jennings, J. R., and Wood, C. C. (1977). Principal component separation of pre- and post-response effects on cardiac interbeat-intervals in a reaction time (RT) task. *Psychophysiology*, **14**, 89–90.

Jernstedt, G. C., and White, W. F. (1974). Cardiovascular response measures with simple integrated circuit amplifiers. *Psychophysiology*, **11**, 211–15.

Johnson, H. J., and May, J. R. (1969). Phasic heart rate changes in reaction time and time estimation. *Psychophysiology*, **6**, 351–8.

Johnson, L. C., and Lubin, A. (1972). On planning psychophysiological experiments: Design, measurement, and analysis. In N. S. Greenfield and R. A. Sternbach (Eds), *Handbook of Psychophysiology*. Holt, Rinehart and Winston, New York. pp. 125–58.

Johnson, D. (1977). Biofeedback, verbal instructions and the motor skills analogy. In T. Beatty and H. Legewie (Eds), *Biofeedback and Behavior*. Plenum, New York. pp. 331–41.

Jones, R. H., Crowell, D. H., and Kapuniai, L. E. (1969). Change detection model for serially correlated data. *Psychol. Bull.*, **71**, 352–8.

Jones, R. H., Crowell, D. H., and Kapuniai, L. E. (1970). Change detection model for serially correlated multivariate data. *Biometrics*, **26**, 269–80.

Jones, R. H., Crowell, D. H., Nakagawa, J. K., and Kapuniai, L. E. (1971). An adaptive method for testing for change in digitized cardiotachometer data. *IEEE Tras. Biomed. Engng*, **BME-18**, 360–5.

Katkin, E. S., and Murray, E. N. (1968). Instrumental conditioning of autonomically mediated behavior: Theoretical and methodological issues. *Psychol. Bull.,* **70**, 52–68.

Katona, P. G., and Jih, F. (1975). Respiratory sinus arrhythmia: Noninvasive measure of parasympathetic cardiac control. *J. Appl. Physiol.,* **39**, 801–5.

Khachaturian, Z. S., Kerr, J., Kruger, R., and Schachter, J. (1972). A methodological note: Comparison between period and rate data in studies of cardiac function. *Psychophysiology,* **9**, 539–45.

Kimble, G. A. (1961). *Hilgard and Marquis' Conditioning and Learning.* Appleton–Century–Crofts, New York.

Kleitman, N., and Ramsaroop, A. (1948). Periodicity in body temperature and heart rate. *Endocrinology,* **43**, 1–20.

Ko, W. H. (1970). Biotelemetry. In M. Clynes and J. H. Milsum (Eds), *Biomedical Engineering Systems.* McGraw-Hill, New York. pp. 65–79.

Kristellar, J. L. (1978). Biofeedback and meditation training of heart rate slowing: Information and motivation factors. Unpublished doctoral dissertation, University of Wisconsin, Madison.

Lacey, B. C., and Lacey, J. I. (1974). Studies of heart rate and other bodily processes in sensorimotor behavior. In P. A. Obrist, A. H. Black, J. Brener, and L. V. DiCara (Eds), *Cardiovascular Psychophysiology: Current Issues in Response Mechanisms, Biofeedback and Methodology.* Aldine, Chicago. pp. 538–64.

Lacey, B. C., and Lacey, J. I. (1977). Change in heart period: A function of sensorimotor event timing within the cardiac cycle. *Physiol. Psychol.,* **5**, 383–93.

Lacey, B. C., and Lacey, J. I. (1978). Two-way communication between the heart and the brain: Significance of time within the cardiac cycle. *Am. Psychol.,* **33**, 99–113.

Lacey, J. I. (1956). The evaluation of autonomic responses: Toward a general solution. *Ann. NY Acad. Sci.,* **67**, 123–64.

Lacey, J. I. (1967). Somatic response patterning and stress: Some revisions of activation theory. In M. H. Appley and R. Trumbull (Eds), *Psychological Stress: Issues in Research,* Appleton–Century–Crofts, New York. pp. 14–37.

Lacey, J. I. (1972). Some cardiovascular correlates of sensorimotor behaviour: Examples of visceral afferent feedback? In C. H. Hockman (Ed.), *Limbic System Mechanisms and Autonomic Function,* C. C. Thomas, Illinois.

Lacey, J. I., Kagan, J., Lacey, B. C., and Moss, H. A. (1963). The visceral level: Situational determinants and behavioral correlates of autonomic response patterns. In P. H. Knapp (Ed.), *Expression of the Emotions in Man,* International University Press, New York.

Lacey, J. I., and Lacey, B. C. (1970). Some autonomic-central nervous system interrelationships. In P. Black (Ed.), *Physiological Correlates of Emotion,* Academic Press, New York.

Lacey, J. I., and Lacey, B. C. (1973). Experimental association and dissociation of phasic bradycardia and vertex-negative waves: A psychophysiological study of attention and response-intention. *Electroenceph. Clin. Neurophysiol., Suppl.* 33, 281–5.

Lacey, J. I., and Lacey, B. C. (1974). On heart rate response and behavior: A reply to Elliott. *J. Personality Soc. Psychol.,* **30**, 1–18.

Lang, P. J. (1974). Learned control of human heart rate in a computer directed environment. In P. A. Obrist, A. H. Black, J. Brener, and L. V. DiCara (Eds), *Cardiovascular Psychophysiology: Current Issues in Response Mechanisms, Biofeedback and Methodology.* Aldine, New York. pp. 392–405.

Lang, P. J. (1975). Acquisition of heart rate control: Method, theory and clinical implications. In D. C. Fowles (Ed.), *Clinical Applications of Psychophysiology.* Columbia University Press, New York. pp. 167–91.

Lang, P. J. (1979). Emotional imagery and visceral control. In R. J. Gatchel and K. P. Price (Eds), *Clinical Application of Biofeedback: Appraisal and Status*, Pergamon, Elmsford, NY.

Lang, P. J., and Hnatiow, M. (1962). Stimulus repetition and the heart rate response. *J. Comp. Physiol. Psychol.*, **55**, 781–5.

Lang. P. J., Sroufe, L. A., and Hastings, J. E. (1967). Effects of feedback and instructional set on the control of cardiac rate variability. *J. Exp. Psychol.*, **75**, 425–31.

Lang, P. J., Troyer, W. G., Twentyman, C. T., and Gatchel, R. J. (1975). Differential effects of heart rate modification training on college students, older males, and patients with ischemic heart disease. *Psychosom. Med.*, **37**, 429–46.

Lang, P. J., and Twentyman, C. T. (1974). Learning to control heart rate: Binary vs analogue feedback. *Psychophysiology*, **11**, 616–29.

Lang, P. J., and Twentyman, C. T. (1976). Learning to control heart rate: Effects of varying incentive and criterion of success on past performance. *Psychophysiology*, **13**, 378–85.

Lawler, J. E., and Obrist, P. A. (1974). Indirect indices of contractile force. In P. A. Obrist, A. H. Black, J. Brener, and L. V. DiCara (Eds), *Cardiovascular Psychophysiology: Current Issues in Response Mechanisms, Biofeedback and Methodology*, Aldine, Chicago. pp. 85–92.

Lawler, J. E., Obrist, P. A., and Lawler, K. A. (1975). Cardiovascular function during pre-avoidance and post-avoidance in dogs. *Psychophysiology*, **12**, 4–11.

Lawler, K. A., Obrist, P. A., and Lawler, J. E. (1976). Cardiac and somatic response patterns during a reaction time task in children and adults. *Psychophysiology*, **13**, 448–55.

Lazarus, R. S., Speisman, J. C., and Mordkoff, A. F. (1963). The relationship between autonomic indicators of psychological stress: Heart rate and skin conductance. *Psychosom. Med.*, **25**, 19–30.

Levy, M. N. (1971). Sympathetic–parasympathetic interactions in the heart. *Circulation Res.*, **29**, 437–45.

Levy, M. N. (1977). Parasympathetic control of the heart. In W. C. Randall (Ed.), *Neural Regulation of the Heart*, Oxford University Press, New York. pp. 97–129.

Levy, M. N., Iano, T., and Zieske, H. (1972). Effects of repetitive bursts of vagal activity on heart rate. *Circulation Res.*, **30**, 186–95.

Levy, M. N., Martin, P. J., Iano, T., and Zieske, H. (1969). Paradoxical effect of vagus nerve stimulation on heart rate in dogs. *Circulation Res.*, **25**, 303–14.

Levy, M. N., Martin, P. J., Iano, T., and Zieske, H. (1970). Effects of single vagal stimuli on heart rate and atrioventricular conduction. *Am. J. Physiol.*, **218**, 1256–62.

Lewis, C. D. (1971). Statistical monitoring techniques. *Med. Biol. Engng*, **9**, 315–23.

Lewis, M. (1974). The cardiac response during infancy. In R. F. Thompson and M. M. Patterson (Eds), *Bioelectric Recording Techniques (Part C): Receptor and effector Processes*, Academic Press, New York. pp. 201–31.

Libby, W. L. Jr, Lacey, B. C., and Lacey, J. I. (1973). Pupillary and cardiac activity during visual attention. *Psychophysiology*, **10**, 270–94.

Lindholm, J. M. (1975). Heart rate control and reaction time performance in human subjects. Unpublished doctoral dissertation, University of Wisconsin, Madison.

Lipton, E. L. Steinschneider, A., and Richmond, J. B. (1961). Autonomic function in the neonate: III. Methodological considerations. *Psychosom. Med.,* **23**, 461–71.

Lisina, W. I. (1958). The role of orienting in the conversion of involuntary into voluntary reactions. In L. G. Voronin and coworkers. (Eds), *The Orienting Reflex and Exploratory Behavior*, Academy of Pedagogical Sciences, Moscow.

Little, B. C., and Zahn, T. P. (1974). Changes in mood and autonomic functioning during the menstrual cycle. *Psychophysiology*, **11**, 579–90.

Lobstein, T. (1974). Heart rate and skin conductance activity in schizophrenia. Unpublished doctoral dissertation, University of London.

Lobstein, T. (1978). Detection of transient responses in adult heart rate. *Psychophysiology*, **15**, 380–1.

Lobstein, T., Webb, B., and Cort, J. (1978). Background noise levels and heart rate orienting: Response detection using time series analysis. *Psychophysiology*, **15**, 316–19.

Luce, G. G. (1970). *Biological Rhythms in Psychiatry and Medicine*, US Department of Health, Education, and Welfare, Public Health Service Publication, No. 2088, Chevy Chase, Maryland.

Luczak, H., and Laurig, W. (1973). An analysis of heart rate variability. *Ergonomics*, **16**, 85–97.

Lykken, D. T. (1968). Neuropsychology and psychophysiology in personality research. In E. F. Borgatta and W. W. Lambert (Eds), *Handbook of Personality theory and Research*. Rand McNally, Chicago. pp. 413–509.

Lykken, D. T. (1972). Range correction applied to heart rate and to GSR data. *Psychophysiology*, **9**, 373–9.

Lykken, D. T., and Venables, P. H. (1971). Direct measurement of skin conductance: A proposal for standardization. *Psychophysiology*, **8**, 656–72.

Lynn, P. A. (1977). On-line digital filters for biological signals: Some fast designs for a small computer. *Med. Biol. Engng*, **15**, 534–540.

Malmo, R. B., and Shagass, C. (1949). Physiologic study of symptom mechanisms in psychiatric patients under stress. *Psychosom. Med.,* **11**, 25–9.

Malmstrom, E. J. (1968). The effects of prestimulus variability upon physiological reactivity scores. *Psychophysiology*, **5**, 149–65.

Malmstrom, E. J. (1971). Cross-laboratory comparability of heart rate measures: A reply to Elliott. *J. Exp. Res. Personality*, **5**, 151–4.

Mancia, G., Iannos, J., Jamieson, G. G., Lawrence, R. H., Sharman, P. R., and Ludbrook, J. (1978). Effect of isometric hand-grip exercise on the carotid sinus baroreceptor reflex in man. *Cl. Sci. Molec. Med.,* **54**, 33–7.

Manning, J. W. (1977). Intracranial mechanisms of regulation. In W. C. Randall (Ed.), *Neural Regulation of the Heart*, Oxford University Press, New York. pp. 189–209.

Manzotti, M. (1958). The effect of some respiratory manoeuvres on the heart rate. *J. Physiol.,* **144**, 541–57.

Matyas, T. A., and King, M. G. (1976). Stable T wave effects during improvement of heart rate control with biofeedback. *Physiol.Beh.,* **16**, 15–20.

McGuinness, D. (1973). Cardiovascular responses during habituation and mental activity in anxious men and women. *Biol. Psychol.,* **1**, 115–23.

Melcher, A. (1976). Respiratory sinus arrhythmia in man. *Acta Physiol. Scand, Suppl.* 435.

Miller, N. E. (1978). Biofeedback and visceral learning. *Ann. Rev. Psychol.,* **29**, 373–404.

Miller, N. E., and DiCara, L. V. (1967). Instrumental learning of heart rate changes in curarized rats: Shaping and specificity to discriminative stimulus. *J. Comp. Physiol. Psychol.*, **63**, 12–19.

Miller, N. E., and Dworkin, B. (1974). Visceral learning: Recent difficulties with curarized rats and significant problems for human research. In P. A. Obrist, A. H. Black, J. Brener, and L. V. DiCara (Eds), *Cardiovascular Psychophysiology: Current Issues in Response Mechanisms, Biofeedback and Methodology*, Aldine, Chicago. pp. 312–31.

Mills, R. T., Kunca, D., and Karrer, R. (1976). Heart rate as an index of visual stimulus complexity processing: A developmental study. *Psychophysiology*, **13**, 184–5.

Milnor, W. R. (1968). Normal circulatory function. In V. B. Mountcastle (Ed.), *Medical Physiology*, Vol. I, 12th ed, Mosby, St Louis. pp. 118–33.

Monro, D. M. (1976). Real discrete fast Fourier transform. Algorithm AS97. *Appl. Statist.*, **25**, 166–72.

Monro, D. M. (1977). A portable integer FFT in Fortran. *Comput. Progams Biomed.*, **7**, 267–72.

Montgomery, D. C., and Johnson, L. A. (1976). *Forecasting and Time Series Analysis*, McGraw-Hill, New York.

Mowrer, O. H. (1947). On the dual nature of learning: A reinterpretation of 'conditioning' and 'problem solving'. *Harvard Ed. Rev.*, **17**, 102–48.

Norman, A., and Melville, C. H. (1971). Potential applications of telemetred heart rate data to developmental psychology. *Devl. Psychol.*, **5**, 190–4.

Norman, A., and Melville, C. H. (1972). The comparability of cross-laboratory resting heart rate: A reply to Elliott. *Psychophysiology*, **9**, 443–9.

Nowlin, J. B., Thompson, L. W., and Eisdorfer, C. (1969). Cardiovascular response to reaction time performance. *Psychophysiology*, **5**, 568.

Obrist, P. A. (1968). Heart rate and somatic-motor coupling during classical aversive conditioning in humans. *J. Exp. Psychol.*, **77**, 180–93.

Obrist, P. A. (1976). The cardiovascular–behavioural interactions – as it appears today. *Psychophysiology*, **13**, 95–107.

Obrist, P. A., Gaebelein, C. J., Teller, E. S., Langer, A. W., Grignolo, A., Light, K. C., and McCubbin, J. A. (1978). The relationship between heart rate, carotid dP/dt, and blood pressure in humans as a function of the type of stress. *Psychophysiology*, **15**, 102–15.

Obrist, P. A., Howard, J. L., Lawler, J. E., Sutterer, J. R., Smithson, K. W., and Martin, P. L. (1972). Alterations in cardiac contractility during classical conditioning in dogs: Methodological and theoretical implications. *Psychophysiology*, **9**, 246–61.

Obrist, P. A., Howard, J. L., Lawler, J. E., Galosy, R., Meyers, K., and Gaebelein, C. J. (1974a). Cardiac–somatic interaction. In P. A Obrist, A. H. Black, J. Brener, and L. V. DiCara (Eds), *Cardiovascular Psychophysiology: Current Issues in Response Mechanisms, Biofeedback and Methodology*, Aldine, Chicago. pp. 136–62.

Obrist, P. A., Langer, A. W., Grignolo, A., Sutterer, J. R., Light, K. C., and McCubbin, J. A. (1977). Blood pressure control mechanisms and stress: Implications for the etiology of hypertension. In G. Onesti and C. R. Klimt (Eds), *Hypertension: Determinants, Complications and Intervention*, Grune and Stratton, New York.

Obrist, P. A., Lawler, J. E., and Gaebelein, C. J. (1974). A psychobiological perspective on the cardiovascular system. In L. V. DiCara (Ed.), *Limbic and Autonomic Nervous Systems Research*, Plenum, New York. pp. 311–34.

Obrist, P. A., Lawler, J. E., Howard, J. L., Smithson, K. W., Martin, P. L., and Manning, J. (1974b). Sympathetic influences on the heart in humans: Effects on contractility and heart rate of acute stress. *Psychophysiology*, **11**, 405–27.

Obrist, P. A., Sutterer, J. R., and Howard, J. L. (1972). Preparatory cardiac changes: A psychobiological approach. In A. H. Black and W. F. Prokasy (Eds), *Classical Conditioning II: Current Research and Theory*, Appleton–Century–Crofts, New York. pp. 312–40.

Obrist, P. A., Sutterer, J. R., Howard, J. L., Hennis, H. S., and Murrell, D. J. (1973). Cardiac–somatic changes during a simple reaction time task: A developmental study. *J. Exp. Child Psychol.*, **16**, 346–62.

Obrist, P. A., and Webb, R. A. (1967). Heart rate during conditioning in dogs: Relationship to somatic-motor activity. *Psychophysiology*, **4**, 7–34.

Obrist, P. A., Webb, R. A., and Sutterer, J. R. (1969). Heart rate and somatic changes during aversive conditioning and a simple reaction time task. *Psychophysiology*, **5**, 696–723.

Obrist, P. A., Webb, R. A., Sutterer, J. R., and Howard, J. (1970a). The cardiac–somatic relationship: Some reformulations. *Psychophysiology*, **6**, 569–87.

Obrist, P. A., Webb, R. A., Sutterer, J. R., and Howard, J. L. (1970b). Cardiac deceleration and reaction time: An evaluation of two hypotheses. *Psychophysiology*, **6**, 695–706.

Obrist, P. A., Wood, D. M., and Perez-Reyes, M. (1965). Heart rate during conditioning in humans: Effects of UCS intensity, vagal blockade and adrenergic block of vasomotor activity. *J. Exp. Psychol.*, **70**, 32–42.

Opton, E., Rankin, N. O., and Lazarus, R. S. (1965). A simplified method of heart rate measurement. *Psychophysiology*, **2**, 87–97.

Overall, J. E., and Woodward, J. A. (1977a). Common misconceptions concerning the analysis of covariance. *J. Multivariate Behav. Res.*, **12**, 171–85.

Overall, J. E., and Woodward, J. A. (1977b). Nonrandom assignment and the analysis of covariance. *Psychol. Bull.*, **84**, 588–594.

Peiss, C. N. (1965). Concepts of cardiovascular regulation: Past, present and future. In W. C. Randall (Ed.), *Nervous Control of the Heart*, Williams and Wilkins, Baltimore.

Petro, J. K., Hollander, A. P., and Bouman, L. N. (1970). Instantaneous cardiac acceleration in man induced by a voluntary muscle contraction. *J. Appl. Physiol.*, **29**, 794–8.

Piggott, L. R., Ax, A. F., Bamford, J. L. and Fetzner, J. M. (1973). Respiration sinus arrhythmia in psychotic children. *Psychophysiology*, **10**, 401–14.

Pomerleau-Malcuit, A., Malcuit, G., and Clifton, R. K. (1975). An attempt to elicit cardiac orienting and defense responses in the newborn to two types of facial stimulation. *Psychophysiology*, **12**, 527–35.

Porges, S. W. (1976). Peripheral and neurochemical parallels of psychopathology: A psychophysiological model relating autonomic imbalance to hyperactivity, psychopathy, and autism. In H. W. Reese (Ed.), *Advances in Child Development and Behavior*, Vol. 11, Academic Press, New York. pp. 35–65.

Randall, W. C. (1977). *Neural Regulation of the Heart*, Oxford University Press, New York. pp. 45–93.

Reid, J. V. O. (1969). The cardiac pacemaker: Effects of regularly spaced nervous input. *Am. Heart J.*, **78**, 58–64.

Rickles, W. H., Chatoff, B., and Buchness, R. (1969). Computer simulation of cardiorespiratory coupling: A non-averaging method for eliminating respiratory reflexes from heart responses. *Psychophysiology*, **5**, 588–9.

Roberts, L. E. (1974). Comparative psychophysiology of the electrodermal and cardiac control systems. In P. A. Obrist, A. H. Black, J. Brener, and L. V. DiCara (Eds), *Cardiovascular Psychophysiology: Current Issues in Response Mechanisms, Biofeedback and Methodology*. Aldine, Chicago. pp. 163–89.

Rolfe, J. H. (1973). Symposium on heart rate variability. *Ergonomics*, **16**, 1–112.

Rompelman, O., Coenen, A. J. R. M., and Kitney, R. I. (1977). Measurement of heart rate variability. Part 1 – Comparative study of heart rate variability analysis methods. *Med. Biol. Engng Comput.*, **15**, 233–9.

Roy, W. J., and Lamb, S. B. (1974). Locus of control and the voluntary control of heart rate. *Psychosom. Med.*, **36**, 180–2.

Rushmer, R. F. (1976). *Cardiovascular Dynamics*, Saunders, Philadelphia.

Sarnoff, S. J., Mitchell, J. H., Gilmore, J. P., and Remensnyder, J. P. (1960). Homeometric autoregulation in the heart. *Circulation Res.*, **8**, 1077–91.

Sayers, B. McA. (1970). Inferring significance from biological signals. In M. Clynes and J. H. Milsum (Eds), *Biomedical Engineering Systems*, McGraw-Hill, New York. pp. 84–164.

Sayers, B. McA. (1973). Analysis of heart rate variability. *Ergonomics*, **16**, 17–32.

Sayers, B. McA. (1975a). Physiological consequences of informational load and overload. In P. H. Venables and M. J. Christie (Eds), *Research in Psychophysiology*. Wiley, London. pp. 95–124.

Sayers, B. McA. (1975b). The analysis of biological signals. In J. M. Forsyth and J. Anderson (Eds), *Proceedings of the Medical Informatics Conference*. North-Holland, Amsterdam. pp. 11–15, 1171–9.

Sayers, B. McA. (1975c). Science and judgement in biological signal analysis. In G. F. Inbar (Ed.), *Signal Analysis and Pattern Recognition in Biomedical Engineering*. Wiley London. pp. 3–20.

Sayers, B. McA., and Beagley, H. A. (1974). Objective evaluation of auditory evoked EEG responses. *Nature*, **251**, 608–9.

Sayers, B. McA., Nghia, M. T. T., and Mansourian, P. G. (1978). Objective specification of the weight variable in weaning diarrhoeal disease of infants. *Med. Informatics*, **3**, 87–104.

Schachter, J. (1957). Pain, fear and anger in hypertensive and normotensives: A psychophysiological study. *Psychosom. Med.*, **19**, 17–29.

Schachter, J., Kerr, J. L., Wimberley, F. C., and Lachlin, J. M. (1974). Heart rate levels of black and white newborns. *Psychosom. Med.*, **36**, 513–24.

Schachter, J., Kerr, J. L., Wimberley, F. C., and Lachlin, J. M. (1975). Phasic heart rate responses: Different patterns in black and in white newborns. *Psychosom. Med.*, **37**, 326–32.

Scher, A. M. (1974). Control of cardiac output. In T. C. Ruch and H. D. Patton (Eds), *Physiology and Biophysics*, Vol. 2, Saunders, Philadelphia.

Scher, A. M., Ohm, W. W., Bumgarner, K., Boynton, R., and Young, A. C. (1972). Sympathetic and parasympathetic control of heart rate in the dog, baboon and man. *Fed. Proc.*, **31**, 1219–25.

Schneiderman, N., Dauth, G. W., and VanDercar, D. H. (1974). Electrocardiogram: Techniques and analysis. In R. F. Thompson and M. M. Patterson (Eds), *Bioelectric Recording Techniques (Part C): Receptor and Effector Processes*, Academic Press, New York. pp. 165–200.

Schwartz, G. E., and Higgins, J. D. (1971). Cardiac activity preparatory to overt and covert behavior. *Science*, **173**, 1144–6.

Semler, H. J. (1965). Radiotelemetry during cardiac exercise tests. In C. A. Caceres (Ed.), *Biomedical Telemetry*, Academic Press, New York. pp. 129–45.

Shapiro, D. (1977). A monologue on biofeedback and psychophysiology. *Psychophysiology*, **14**, 213–227.

Shapiro, D., Tursky, B., and Schwartz, G. E. (1970). Differentation of heart rate and systolic blood pressure in man by operant conditioning. *Psychosom. Med.,* **32**, 417–23.

Shearn, D. W. (1962). Operant conditioning of heart rate. *Science,* **137**, 530–1.

Shimizu, H. (1977). Digital cardiac meter with D.A. converter. *Psychophysiology,* **14**, 417–9.

Siddle, D. A. T., Turpin, G., Spinks, J. A., and Stephenson, D. (1979). Peripheral physiological measures. In H. M. Van Praag, M. H. Lader, O. J. Rafaelsen, and E. J. Sachar (Eds), *Handbook of Biological Psychiatry, Vol. 3, Brain Mechanisms and Abnormal Behaviour.* Marcel Dekker, New York, in press.

Simons, R., and Lang, P. J. (1977). The effects of meditation training and biofeedback on instructed heart rate slowing. Unpublished manuscript.

Sleight, P. (1976). Neurophysiology of the carotid sinus receptors in normal and hypertensive animals and man. *Cardiology,* **61**, *Suppl.* 1, 31–45.

Sokolov, E. N. (1963). *Perception and the Conditioned Reflex.* Pergamon, Oxford.

Spickler, W. J., and Kezdi, P. (1967). Dynamic response characteristics of the carotid sinus baroreceptors. *Am. J. Physiol.,* **212**, 472–6.

Sroufe, L. A. (1971). Effects of depth and rate of breathing on heart rate and heart rate variability. *Psychophysiology,* **8**, 648–55.

Steinschneider, A., and Lipton, E. L. (1965). Individual differences in autonomic responsivity. *Psychosom. Med.,* **27**, 446–56.

Stephens, J. H., Harris, A. H., and Brady, T. V. (1972). Large magnitude heart rate changes in subjects instructed to change their heart rates and given exteroceptive feedback. *Psychophysiology,* **9**, 283–5.

Stern, R. M. (1974). Ear lobe photoplethysmography. *Psychophysiology,* **11**, 73–5.

Sternbach, R. A. (1960). A comparative analysis of autonomic responses in startle. *Psychosom. Med.,* **22**, 204–10.

Stratton, D. M. (1970). The use of heart rate for the study of habituation in the neonate. *Psychophysiology,* **7**, 44–56.

Sutterer, J. R., and Obrist, P. A. (1972). Heart rate and general activity alterations in dogs during several aversive conditioning procedures. *J. Comp. Physiol. Psychol.,* **80**, 314–26.

Taggart, P., Gibbons, D. S., and Somerville, W. (1969). Some effects of motorcar driving on the normal and abnormal heart. *Br. Med. J.,* **4**, 130–4.

Tahmoush, A. J., Jennings, J. R., Lee, A. L., Camp, S., and Weber, F. (1976). Characteristics of a light emitting diode–transistor photoplethysmograph. *Psychophysiology,* **13**, 357–62.

Teichner, W. H. (1968). Interaction of behavioral and physiological stress reactions. *Psychol. Rev.,* **75**, 271–91.

Thorne, P. R., Engel, B. T., and Holmblad, J. B. (1976). An analysis of the error inherent in estimating heart rate from cardiotachometer records. *Psychophysiology,* **13**, 269–71.

Trigg, D. W. (1964). Monitoring a forecasting system. *Op. Res. Q.,* **15**, 271–4.

Tucker, L. R. (1958). Determination of parameters of a functional relation by factor analysis. *Psychometrika,* **23**, 19–23.

Turpin, G., and Siddle, D. A. T. (1978a). Cardiac and forearm plethysmographic responses to high intensity auditory stimulation. *Biol. Psychol.,* **6**, 267–82.

Turpin, G., and Siddle, D. A. T. (1978b). Measurement of the evoked cardiac response: The problem of prestimulus variability. *Biol. Psychol.,* **6**, 127–38.

Tursky, B., Schwartz, G. E., and Crider, A. (1970). Differential patterns of heart rate and skin resistance during a digit-transformation task. *J. Exp. Psychol.,* **83**, 451–7.

Twentyman, C. T. (1977). The effect of information frequency and feedback timing on instructed heart rate speeding. Unpublished doctoral dissertation. University of Wisconsin, Madison.

Twentyman, C. T., and Lang, P. J. (1977). Two experiments on the learned control of heart rate: Fixed time effects. See appendix A of Twentyman (1977).

Ulrych, M. (1969). Changes of general haemodynamics during stressful mental arithmetic and non-stressing quiet conversation and modification of the latter by beta-adrenergic blockade. *Clin. Sci.*, **36**, 453–61.

Van Egeren, L. F. (1973). Multivariate statistical analysis. *Psychophysiology*, **10**, 517–32.

Van Egeren, L. F., Headrick, M. W., and Hein, P. L. (1972). Individual differences in autonomic responses: Illustration of a possible solution. *Psychophysiology*, **9**, 626–33.

Varni, J. G., Clarke, E., and Giddon, D. B. (1971). Analysis of cyclic heart rate variability. *Psychophysiology*, **8**, 406–13.

Venables, P. H., and Christie, M. J. (1973). Mechanisms, instrumentation, recording techniques and quantification of responses. In W. F. Prokasy and D. C. Raskin (Eds), *Electrodermal activity in Psychological Research*. Academic Press, New York. pp. 1–124.

Webb, R. A., and Obrist, P. A. (1967). Heart rate during complex operant performance in the dog. *Proc. Am. Psychol. Assoc.*, 137–138.

Webb, R. A., and Obrist, P. A. (1970). The physiological concomitance of reaction time performance as a function of preparatory interval and preparatory interval series. *Psychophysiology*, **6**, 389–403.

Wilder, J. (1962). Basimetric approach (law of initial value) to biological rhythms. *Ann. NY. Acad. Sci.*, **98**, 1211–20.

Williams, T. A., Schachter, J., and Tobin, M. (1967). Spontaneous variation in heart rates: Relationship to the averaged evoked heart rate response to auditory stimuli in the neonate. *Psychophysiology*, **4**, 104–11.

Wilson, R. S. (1967). Analysis of autonomic reaction patterns. *Psychophysiology*, **4**, 125–42.

Wilson, R. S. (1969). Cardiac response: Determinants of conditioning. *J. Comp. Physiol. Psychol.*, **68**, *Monogr. Suppl.* 1, 1–23.

Wilson, R. S. (1974). CARDIVAR: The statistical analysis of heart rate data. *Psychophysiology*, **11**, 76–85.

Wilson, R. S., and Scott, K. K. (1970). Computer programs for autonomic research. *Behav. Sci.*, **15**, 380–5.

Winer, B. J. (1971). *Statistical Principles in Experimental Design*, 2nd Edn, McGraw-Hill, New York.

Womack, B. F. (1971). The analysis of respiratory sinus arrhythmia using spectral analysis and digital filtering. *IEEE Trans. Biomed. Engng*, **BME-18**, 399–409.

Wood, D. M., and Obrist, P. A. (1964). The effects of controlled and uncontrolled respiration on the conditioned heart rate response in human beings. *J. Exp. Psychol.*, **68**, 221–9.

Wood, D. M., and Obrist, P. A. (1968). Minimal and maximal sensory intake and exercise as unconditioned stimuli in human heart rate conditioning. *J. Exp. Psychol.*, **76**, 254–62.

Woodcock, J. M. (1971). Terminology and methodology related to the use of heart rate responsivity in infancy research. *J. Exp. Child Psychol.*, **11**, 76–92.

Young, L. D., and Blanchard, E. B. (1972). Sex differences in the ability to control heart rate. *Psychophysiology*, **9**, 667–8.

Techniques in Psychophysiology
Edited by I. Martin and P. H. Venables
© 1980, John Wiley & Sons Ltd.

CHAPTER 4

Blood Pressure*

ANDREW STEPTOE

* *Acknowledgements*. This work was supported by the Medical Research Council, UK. The author would like to thank Derek Johnston and Derek Bergel for their comments on earlier versions of this chapter, and Les Aylesbury for his assistance on technical points.

1 INTRODUCTION

Blood pressure is one of the most widely measured indices of physiological activity, and is of fundamental importance to clinical science. Consequently, much energy has been put into the development of techniques for indirect assessment. Blood pressure differs from many other psychophysiological variables in being of interest for its own sake, rather than for its relationship with inferred emotional states or autonomic activity.

This chapter does not set out to provide a general survey of non-invasive blood pressure measurement, since this has been successfully accomplished in Geddes' (1970) monograph. Rather it has been written with the special requirements of psychophysiology in mind. Certain characteristics, such as accurate, repeatable, bias free monitoring, are desirable in all settings, but some features are of particular interest to psychophysiologists:

(1)   The equipment and measurement operations should not be distracting or disturbing to subjects.
(2)   Measurement should be possible in typical laboratory settings—for example in the presence of noise or when subjects are carrying out other tasks.
(3)   Monitoring should be automatic.
(4)   The recording method should either be continuous or allow for frequent sampling. This is desirable both in order to index short term reactions and to coordinate readings with simultaneous measures of other physiological parameters.

Blood pressure is a general index of cardiovascular function, reflecting the overall state of the circulation rather than particular events or processes. Properly speaking, any reading of pressure should specify the site of measurement, since pressure drops progressively through the circulatory tree. The greatest proportion of this decrease (about 80%) occurs at the arteriolar level; the arteries themselves are primarily conducting vessels and present little resistance to flow. Thus in practice systemic arterial pressure is usually implied in blood pressure measurement, as this is an indicator of the blood supply available for the microcirculation. Nevertheless, it should be noted that there is some reduction in pressure within the arterial tree itself, so measurements from different sites are not strictly comparable.

Arterial pressure is the product of the cardiac output (determined by heart rate and ventricular stroke volume) and the resistance of the peripheral vessels. Apart from conduction, the arteries have an important function in smoothing the intermittent output from the heart into steady flow, and this is accomplished through the viscoelastic properties of the

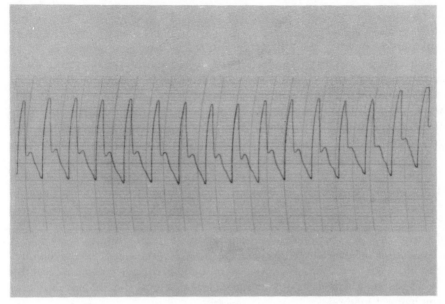

Figure 4.1   Blood pressure trace from left brachial artery

vessel walls. However pulses, albeit of a reduced size, are still observed in the arteries, and the different portions of the waveform reflect the phases of the cardiac contraction cycle. A typical arterial trace is shown in Figure 4.1—the maximum or systolic mirrors the peak pressure on contraction of the left ventricle, while the minimum (diastolic) occurs immediately before the pressure pulse reaches the measurement site. Ventricular systole precedes the arterial systolic pressure by an interval dependent on the distensibility of the vessels. Mean arterial pressure is commonly calculated as diastolic $+1/3$ pulse (systolic − diastolic) pressure.

The commonest method of indirect measurement is the auscultatory technique, described in Sections 3 and 4. Following the general adoption of the sphygmomanometer and cuff in the early years of the century, few major modifications were made in indirect methods for some 50 years. However, fresh incentives were provided firstly by aerospace medicine and subsequently by the requirements of areas such as anaesthesiology. In both of these fields, the need for continuous automated pressure monitoring is paramount. Many of the technical advances are refinements of auscultation, and will be described in Sections 3 and 4. More recently, dynamic methods based on pulse wave velocity measurement have been developed and validated. The psychophysiologist is thus now in a position to choose the system appropriate for the needs of particular experimental conditions.

2 DIRECT MEASUREMENT

The only completely accurate method of measuring arterial pressure is by monitoring directly from a major artery. A cannula is inserted into the vessel and is then coupled to a pressure transducer. External transducers connected with the measurement site by fluid filled manometers are commonly used, although care is required to ensure accurate transmission of the wave form. Catheter-tip transducers circumvent transmission problems, but are fragile and tolerate chronic inplantation only poorly (Krausman, 1975).

Although intra-arterial monitoring is employed in animal preparations, the procedure is seldom carried out in human psychophysiological studies. The method is not without dangers, since blood clots or damage to peripheral nerves can occur (Wyatt, Glares and Cooper, 1974). It should therefore never be undertaken without medical supervision. An additional disadvantage for experimental applications is that frequently repeated cannulation is unwise. However, the indirect measurement techniques described in the following sections stand or fall by their comparability with direct readings. Simultaneous monitoring is a critical part of the testing of any indirect method.

Readers interested in the technical aspects of direct pressure recording are referred to the discussions by Gabe (1972) and Geddes (1970). A valuable analysis of the psychological impact of cannulation has been made by Beamer and Shapiro (1973)

3 OCCLUSION METHODS

3.1 Principles of occlusion techniques

The basic operation underlying these methods is the application of an external occlusive pressure to a superficial artery, and the assessment of flow within the vessel during variation of this pressure. In the conventional procedure, the artery is initially collapsed by the imposition of pressure from the air-filled bag strapped around the limb in a non-distensible cuff. As the air escapes from the bag and the applied pressure is gradually reduced, a point arrives at which blood flow begins, since the systolic peaks exceed the external pressure level; this is taken to be the systolic pressure. When the cuff is further deflated, flow eventually becomes continuous throughout the cardiac cycle; this is the diastolic pressure. At a still lower cuff pressure, undisturbed flow is re-established in the vessel (Rushmer, 1976).

Although thigh cuffs are available, the usual site for occlusion is the brachial artery. Digital cuffs for monitoring systolic pressure from the finger have also been devised, and have enjoyed some use in psychophysiological experiments (Lenox and Lange, 1969; Brener and Kleinman, 1970). However, the level and lability of pressure at this site is not comparable with brachial values, making recordings difficult to interpret. Additionally, digital systems are very susceptible to movement artifact, while local vasoconstriction may contaminate measurements. Thus although monitoring from the finger is less uncomfortable than from the arm, the disadvantages outweigh any benefits. The following discussion will therefore be confined to recording from the upper arm.

3.2 The criteria for systolic and diastolic pressure

A number of methods exist for determining the criterion points for systolic and diastolic pressure, and the relation between these indices is shown schematically in Figure 4.2. Rive-Rocci estimated the systolic pressure by palpation, flow being indicated by a pulse distal to the cuff. The commoner auscultatory method was devised by Korotkoff (1905). Using a stethoscope, he found that sounds could be heard distal to the cuff, and that their quality changed in characteristic ways as the cuff was deflated. By perceiving the appropriate variations in sounds, Korotkoff claimed that the diastolic as well as the systolic pressure could be determined accurately. Conventionally, five sound phases are distinguished as the cuff pressure is reduced: (i) loud, snapping, staccato tones; (ii) succession of murmurs; (iii) thumping sounds, resembling phase (i) but rather less distinct; (iv) muffling or dulling of sounds; (v) disappearance of sounds.

Since Korotkoff's time, numerous comparisons of auscultation and

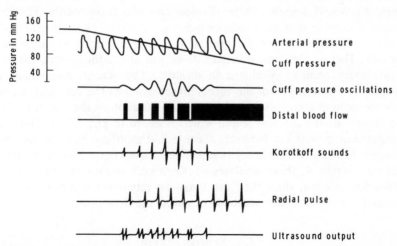

Figure 4.2 Schematic comparison of different indices used in the occlusion method to mark systolic and diastolic pressure

Table 4.1. Comparison of direct and indirect blood pressure measurements. Average difference (direct − indirect) in mm Hg

n	Systolic phase (i)	Diastolic phase (iv)	Diastolic phase (v)	Reference
50	5.4	−11.1	−6.6	Raftery and Ward (1968)
47	24.6	5.3	13.1	Holland and Humerfelt (1964)

directly monitored pressure have been carried out, not only to assess the accuracy of occlusion methods but also to establish reliable criteria for systolic and diastolic pressure. In particular, there has been a good deal of controversy about whether diastolic pressure is best indicated by phase (iv) or (v) sounds, and this can seriously affect the interpretation of clinical data (for example Short, 1975). Many of the earlier comparisons can be criticized for not taking readings simultaneously, or for using the standard sphygmomanometer which is prone to observer errors. But even the two well controlled studies summarized in Table 4.1 found widely different results. Some of the sources of error are discussed in the next section.

Although London and London (1967) considered the disappearance of Korotkoff sounds to be a more reliable criterion for diastolic pressure, there is a widespread preference for phase (iv) (muffling). McCutcheon and Rushmer (1967) carried out an experimental analysis of the sounds. Studies of flow with transcutaneous Doppler techniques indicated that the artery first remains open throughout the cardiac cycle at muffling. Furthermore, Korotkoff sounds can be divided into two components. The initial 'staccato' tapping that accompanies pulse wave arrival (systolic criterion) is produced by distention of the arterial wall as a jet of blood surges under the cuff. This acceleration transient drops out at muffling, since the vessel is no longer completely closed in diastole. The second component is a compression murmur from the turbulent jet distal to the occluded segment. This component increases in amplitude and duration as the cuff is deflated, and comprises the muffled sound which is heard in phase (iv). Thus there is a physical association between diastole and muffling, but not disappearance, of Korotkoff sounds (Kirkendall and coworkers, 1967). As will be seen in Section 4, these analyses of Korotkoff sounds are not solely of theoretical interest, since they can make an important contribution to the production of artifact-free methods of automatic detection.

3.3 Sources of error

It is evident from the numbers in Table 4.1, and from other work, that pressures measured by occlusion techniques can differ quite considerably from directly recorded levels. Indirect systolic pressures are too low, while diastolic values may be higher or lower than intra-arterial readings (Geddes, 1970). Some difference from direct recording is inherent in the occlusion method. True systolic must be higher than the applied pressure level in order that some blood may flow through the collapsed vessel (Figure 4.2). Conversely at diastolic levels, a muffled sound indicates that the acceleration transient has already disappeared. In both cases therefore, the accuracy of readings is intimately associated with the rate of cuff deflation, and the extent to which the applied pressure falls between each cardiac cycle (and potential Korotkoff sound). This problem is particularly pertinent to automated methods and will be discussed further in Section 4.3.

However, there are other sources of error and variability which can be avoided by the careful investigator.

3.3.1 Observer errors

The accuracy of auscultatory readings depends on the acuity and experience of the observer who must decide on which cardiac cycle the first Korotkoff sound or palpable pulse is present. Fukuda (1976) reported a study in which a quadrifurcated stethoscope enabled four observers to hear the same series of Korotkoff sounds simultaneously. The readings were normally distributed with a standard deviation of 1.36 mm. for systolic and 1.71 mm. for diastolic pressure. This variation can of course be enlarged if there are discrepancies in the interpretation of sounds. Rose, Holland, and Crowley (1964) noted two other sources of observer error: (a) terminal digit preference; observers tend to round off pressure readings, so that numbers ending in 0 or 5 are over-represented; (b) observer prejudice; there is a preference for conventional values (such as 120/80), and a tendency to avoid readings that are thought to divide 'populations'.

These sources of variation are largely eliminated in the automated systems described in Section 4. If readings are to be taken manually, then a sphygmomanometer that has been modified to prevent the observer from knowing the true level of mercury pressure during the estimation is valuable. Two such machines in common use are the random zero sphygmomanometer (Wright and Dore, 1970) and the London School of Hygiene instrument (Rose, Holland, and Crowley, 1964).

3.3.2 Procedural errors

The artery is not compressed directly, since an external pressure is applied to the whole limb. Care must therefore be taken to ensure complete transmission of pressure through the surrounding tissue. If the bag is too narrow or short, the pressure will not be reliably transmitted. Kirkendall's committee (Kirkendall and colleagues, 1967) recommended that the bag should be 20% wider than the diameter of the limb, and long enough to go more than half way round it; for the average adult, a bag 12–14 cm wide and 30 cm long is adequate. For obese people and those with very big arms, a larger bag is required, and a correction for arm circumference may have to be made (Khosla and Lowe, 1965).

Since the arteries and veins comprise an hydraulic system, the circulation is affected by the hydrostatic pressure. Thus if the arm is lowered, pressure will rise. Blood pressure should be measured at heart level, and this is ensured by placing the forearm opposite the fourth intercostal space. For other limb positions, a correction factor of 0.7 mm Hg per centimetre above or below the heart is appropriate (Kirkendall and colleagues, 1967). It should also be noted that difficulties can occur with the measurement of diastolic pressure by auscultation during physical exercise. Korotkoff sounds may continue down to zero pressure, and even if they do not, the accuracy of diastolic criteria is severely reduced (Karlefors, Nilson, and Westling, 1966).

4 AUTOMATED OCCLUSION METHODS

There are two major requirements for the automation of occlusion techniques: a system for inflating and deflating the cuff at prescribed rates together with a mechanism for detecting the pressure criteria reliably. A number of machines that fulfil these requirements have been commercially available for several years. However, Labarthe, Hawkins, and Remington (1973) tested five such devices and concluded that none were adequate replacements for manual auscultation. They further commented critically on the poor quality control and engineering, coupled with the high unit cost of these instruments. The intention is therefore not to make detailed comparisons of commercial systems, but to discuss the basic requirements of automation.

4.1 Pneumatic systems

Most automated pneumatic systems have been designed to mimic the operations involved in manual auscultation. The following sequence is thus followed: *Rapid inflation* of the cuff to a preset pressure level. This can be accomplished by a small air compressor or bottle of compressed gas controlled by a solenoid valve. The valve is closed when the applied pressure reaches a preset level. It is vital that safety features are incorporated to prevent inflation continuing to very high levels—a maximum pressure capability for the pump or else a relief valve will ensure this. *Slow deflation* of the cuff over the measurement range may be carried out by leaking the air through a small orifice valve. The release of pressure through a simple air leak of this type is exponential, so the rate at which pressure is reduced depends on the level. However, in practice the variation thereby incurred will be small. During this phase, the pressures at which systolic and diastolic criteria are triggered are detected by coupling either to a mercurial or an aneroid manometer. Alternatively a pressure gauge within the pneumatic system can be transduced to provide appropriate output. *Rapid deflation*: following the determination of blood pressure levels, the cuff is rapidly deflated to atmospheric pressure by releasing the air through a large orifice valve.

Some modifications have been made to this inflation–deflation cycle; for example, Katona and Bolvary (1975) describe the Medicor automatic sphygmomanometer, developed in Hungary, in which diastolic pressure is detected during inflation rather than deflation. The authors argue that the duration of the measurement cycle is thereby considerably reduced.

4.2 Detection of pressure criteria

Although Korotkoff microphones are commonly used to determine the criteria for systolic and diastolic pressure, other methods can be employed. Some of these are attractive, particularly under environmental conditions in which auscultatory techniques are not optimal.

4.2.1 Korotkoff sound detection

Inexpensive Korotkoff microphones are generally available, and these are either sewn into the cuff itself or else positioned distal to the occlusion. In both cases, the accurate positioning of the microphone is critical, and some adjustment may be required before a reliable signal is received. This is illustrated in figures collected by Hoobler, Oesterle, and Early (1976). Pressures were measured at the optimum locus of the microphone and then at various deviant positions. The differences from optimum locus readings are summarized in Table 4.2. Correct positioning can usually be ensured by placing the microphone over the palpable brachial pulse.

Table 4.2. Potential error from displacing microphone pickup. (From Hoobler, S. W., Oesterle, Betty, and Early, Harold (1976). Evaluation of a new automatic device for taking and recording blood pressures, *J. Lab. Clin. Med.*, **88**, 826–33)

BP deviation (mm Hg)	Deviation from optimum locus			
	Medial 2 cm	Lateral 2 cm	Above 2 cm	Below 2 cm
Systolic	−4	−3	−3	−3
Diastolic	+3	+1	−3	−3

For high fidelity reproduction of Korotkoff sounds, a microphone sensitive over the frequency range 20 to 300 Hz is adequate (Geddes, 1970). However, Korotkoff sounds are not specific—a sharp tap to the back of the hand, for example, produces a transient sound that is subjectively indistinguishable from them (McCutcheon and Rushmer, 1967). Broadband detection is thus beset with problems of artifactual triggering. Two ways of reducing this difficulty will be described.

Firstly, the microphone output can be filtered so that the critical frequencies associated with systolic and diastolic criteria are extracted. In resting subjects, the 'tapping' associated with systolic pressure (phase(i)) is due to frequencies in the 60 to 180 Hz range (McCutcheon and Rushmer, 1967). At muffling, the spectrum above 60 Hz is dramatically attenuated, with no frequencies above 150 Hz being present at all (McCutcheon, Baker, and Wiederhielm, 1969). Thus it appears that selective filtering of these higher frequencies will permit the detection of muffling as well as the phase (i) sounds. Ware and Kahn (1963), being specifically concerned with eliminating the noises generated during aircraft flight, employed 3 bandpass filters centred on 40, 90, and 150 Hz. On the other hand, Geddes (1970) recommended a broadband filter between 25 and 100 Hz, together with a filter peaking at 150 Hz. Multichannel filtering may not be necessary under all conditions, since a single filter centred on 90 or 100 Hz has been found adequate (Roman, Henry, and Meehan, 1965). It should be noted that in exercising subjects, the energy spectrum as a whole moves towards higher frequencies.

Secondly, artifactual triggering can be reduced by incorporating a form of time gating, so that Korotkoff sounds either have to be periodic, or will be accepted only if they follow the QRS complex of the ECG within a certain interval (Meldrum, 1976). Using the latter principle, Tursky, Shapiro, and Schwartz (1972) reject all microphone output that does not follow the QRS complex within 300 ms, while Geddes, Hoff, and Badger (1966) delay for 75 ms before sampling microphone output for 225 ms.

4.2.2   Other methods of detection

The use of transcutaneous transducers to detect the ultrasound frequency shifts associated with movement of the arterial wall under the cuff has gained widespread acceptance in recent years (Meldrum, 1976). The principle of 'ultrasound kineto-arteriography' is that if the ultrasound is reflected by a moving structure, it experiences a Doppler shift. The system is incorporated into the Arteriosonde range of pressure monitors. The accuracy of the method has been confirmed in comparisons with simultaneous intra-arterial recordings, although diastolic values tend to be somewhat lower than those indicated by the Korotkoff technique

(Hochberg and Salomon, 1971; Hoobler, Oesterle, and Early, 1976). Ultrasound may be useful to psychophysiologists when ambient noise levels are high, since the signal frequencies (300–500 Hz for an incident frequency of 8 MHz) are higher than those prominent in Korotkoff sounds. The method is, however, sensitive to movements because these can alter the distance between transducers and vessel (Greatorex, 1971).

As can be seen in Figure 4.2 both oscillations in the cuff pressure and the appearance of a distal pulse coincide with systolic pressure. These indices have been incorporated into automated instruments. Much of the doubt surrounding the accuracy of these criteria can be ascribed to human variability in perceiving pulsations, and will be reduced in automatic devices (Rogge and Meyer, 1967; Ramsay, and coworkers, 1977). Flanagan and Hull (1968) described a system by which pulsations in a cuff distal to the occlusion cuff are detected by heated thermistors. The small puffs of air cool the thermistors, leading to a transient change in resistance. The oscillations of cuff pressure are the basis of pressure detection in the Elag–Köln electronic sphygmomanometer (Ramsay and coworkers, 1977). Both principles are immune to ambient noise, although they are affected by movement of the limb. They are attractive for systolic monitoring, but the appropriate criteria for diastolic are still unclear (Geddes, 1970). Geddes and Newberg (1977) have recently demonstrated how the oscillometric method can be used to determine mean arterial pressure. Their system for detecting the amplitude of cuff oscillations may have considerable advantages for investigators interested in this parameter of blood pressure.

4.3 Accuracy and the recording of data

Assuming that the criterion detection method is sensitive, then accuracy is dependent on the rate of cuff deflation relative to the duration of the cardiac cycle. For example, if pressure is lost from the cuff at 5 mm/s and the pulse interval is 1 s (heart rate of 60 bpm), the system can be accurate only to ± 5 mm. A slower deflation rate provides a more accurate estimation, but on the other hand the measurement cycle will last longer, and the interval between systolic and diastolic readings is greater. The optimum rate will depend on the particular application, although pressure leak at less than 2–3 mm/s is unnecessary considering the limits in accuracy of occlusion methods. Prolongation of the measurement cycle can be avoided by making the maximum cuff pressure dependent on previous systolic readings; inflation to a level 20 mm above the previous systolic is sufficient unless a sudden rise is anticipated. Many commercial units are provided with an inflation control that can be set to the appropriate level.

In psychophysiological experiments, it may not be convenient to record blood pressures manually. Recording can be automated by coupling the pressure transducer in the pneumatic system to a chart, so that the trace mirrors the cuff cycle. The output of the criterion detection system, filtered and amplified by a standard a.c. preamplifier, can be superimposed or output on a second channel, and the systolic and diastolic pressures may subsequently be read off.

4.4 Continuous and semi-continuous systems

The occlusion methods described thus far provide at best one or two pressure estimations per minute. Recently, devices which permit more frequent sampling have been constructed, particularly for use in biofeedback experiments. Two distinct trends can be identified. On the one hand, the standard inflation–deflation cycle has been speeded up, so that the whole procedure is completed within a few seconds. On the other hand, sustained cuff inflation methods, operating on similar principles to lie detectors, have enabled pressure estimations to be made on several successive cardiac cycles. In both cases, the pressure criteria are detected by the methods discussed in Section 4.2; the modifications are in the coupling to sophisticated pneumatic systems. These instruments are designed to index either systolic or diastolic pressure, but not both simultaneously.

4.4.1 Rapid cycle tracking systems

In psychophysiological experiments, rapid cycle instruments have been used by Brener (1974) in a series of biofeedback experiments, and by Obrist (1976). The systolic pressure monitor operates by quickly inflating to a level just above the expected systolic, after which air is slowly leaked until a Korotkoff sound is detected. Rapid deflation then returns the bladder to atmospheric pressure. Since this cycle can be completed within about 10 s, several readings can be made each minute. Recently, P. A. Obrist, E. Shanks-Teller, and J. S. Hutcheson[*] compared this method with simultaneous intra-arterial recordings during a variety of manoeuvres. Correlations between the two were adequate, although the indirect method produced absolute values that were some 10–15 mm Hg below the direct.

The trade-off between frequency and accuracy of recordings becomes critical in fast cycle instruments. Frequency is also affected by the level to which the cuff inflates, and this is in turn influenced by the conditions in which measurement is required. For example, if transient depressor episodes occur, the deflation phase will continue for several extra cycles

---

[*] Unpublished manuscript: 'An evaluation of the reliability of an automated systolic blood pressure monitor'.

before systolic is reached. Since the system is reliant on only one Korotkoff sound, the elimination of artifactual triggering is especially pertinent. An adaptation of the same measurement principles for diastolic monitoring has been used in psychophysiological experiments by Brener (1974). However, no reliability studies have yet been published, although confidence limits of ± 3 mm Hg. have been reported (Lategola, Harrison, and Barnard, 1966).

4.4.2 Sustained inflation systems

One of the most highly developed semi-continuous pressure monitors is the constant cuff-pressure system devised by Tursky and his colleagues. This instrument has been described in detail elsewhere, so only a brief outline will be presented here (Tursky, Shapiro, and Schwartz, 1972; Tursky, 1974).

The operation of the monitor is summarized in Figure 4.3. The cuff is inflated to a level approximating systolic pressure and is maintained for several cardiac cycles. On each cycle, the presence or absence of Korotkoff sounds is detected by a microphone, and the machine counts the number of sounds compared with the total number of cardiac cycles. If 50% of QRS spikes on the ECG are followed by Korotkoff sounds, the cuff is by

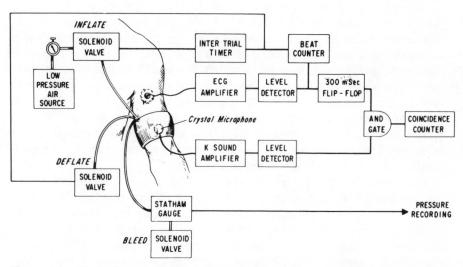

Figure 4.3 Block diagram of the constant cuff-pressure system (from Tursky, B., Shapiro, D., and Schwartz, G. (1972). Automated constant cuff-pressure system to measure average systolic and diastolic blood pressure in man. *IEEE Trans. Biomed. Engng*, BME–19, 274. Reproduced by permission of the Institute of Electrical and Electronics Engineering, Inc.)

K

definition inflated to median systolic pressure. Tursky and colleagues (1972) inferred from intra-arterial records that provided between 25% and 75% of possible ECG–Korotkoff sound coincidences are received, the cuff pressure lies within ± 2 mm of true systolic. The pressure is tracked by adjusting inflation level according to the percentage of possible Korotkoff sounds received; for example, when 75%–99% coincidence is recorded, the applied pressure is increased by 2 mm on the next trial. The occurrence of sounds on 0 or 100% of cycles suggests that a larger adjustment of cuff level is required to bring incidence back to 50%, so a change of ± 4 mm is made. This system has been used for many years in biofeedback experiments by Shapiro and his colleagues, where each inflation is commonly continued for 50 cardiac cycles (Shapiro, Tursky, and Schwartz, 1970; Shapiro, Schwartz, and Tursky, 1972).

It is evident from this description that the principles underlying measurement are rather different from those of standard occlusion. In the latter, the applied pressure is varied with respect to a (presumed) constant arterial level, while the reverse is true here. Simultaneous recordings of arterial pressure are thus required to demonstrate that the same relationship between Korotkoff sounds, arterial, and applied pressure exists. Such comparisons have been reported in only a single subject, and then only in resting conditions rather than in response to the stimuli commonly used in psychophysiological experiments.

Investigation of the dynamic response of the system is desirable as this aspect can cause some difficulty in interpreting the output of the instrument. Since monitoring is based solely on the direction of deviations in arterial pressure from inflation level, it is possible that the apparent time course of modifications may be distorted. For example, if systolic pressure lies 3 mm above cuff level for 90% of a trial, the system will report 90% coincidence. But the same is true if pressure is raised 10 mm above cuff level for a similar proportion of the trial. In both cases, inflation pressure will be increased by 2 mm on the next trial, and an identical change will be recorded. The system thus tends to smooth out pressure records, with rapid modifications being indexed as gradual responses.

This difficulty has been overcome in the recent development of a sustained inflation system in which the level of cuff pressure is adjusted within measurement periods according to changes in Korotkoff sounds (Elder and coworkers, 1977). During each inflation the cuff pressure is modified if sequences of consecutive sounds are detected: in the case of diastolic monitoring, such a sequence indicates that diastolic is higher than applied pressure, so the cuff is inflated until sounds disappear. In this way, the machine tracks arterial pressure with a lag of a few seconds and phasic distortion is reduced. The method is promising, and is currently being assessed against directly recorded arterial pressure.

4.4.3   Advantages and limitations of these methods

In 1957, Davis made an interesting analysis of the use of occlusion methods for continuous recording. The basic problem still remains, for while blood pressure is a dynamic index of circulatory function, occlusion techniques necessarily involve the prevention of normal circulation. The adaptations of cuff methods described in this section inevitably require the extension of a disturbed circulatory state.

Nevertheless, it is clear that substantial advances have been made in the techniques of automated occlusion. In terms of the pressure information provided a basic distinction can be made. Information is available on every cycle with sustained cuff methods, but is essentially of a binary nature, since it reflects whether arterial pressure is above or below inflation level. Alternatively, analogue output is available from fast tracking devices, but is only produced every few cycles. Comparison of these methods must take into account the nature of the pressure responses that are to be monitored. Tonic changes over an extended period, where brief excursions are not of interest, can be readily assessed by sustained inflation systems. But transient responses will be indexed more accurately with tracking methods. The latter also have the merit of being based upon well tried clinical practice.

All these systems rely on the appearance or disappearance of Korotkoff sounds for indicating diastolic pressure, principally because this is technically easier than the isolation of muffling (phase (iv)). Comparatively low diastolic readings are thus generated.

One final point deserves consideration. Sustained or repeated occlusion of the arm is uncomfortable for subjects, and can lead to tenderness over the cuff area. This factor may limit the length of experimental sessions and the duration of monitoring. Additionally it means that it is always clear to subjects exactly when pressure readings are being taken, and no covert monitoring is feasible. The disturbing nature of these methods may account for the fact that, in contrast with other recording methods, pressure levels do not always gradually fall as monitoring continues (Steptoe, 1977a). This point will be discussed further in Section 6.

5   DYNAMIC METHODS

The techniques described in this section do not involve gross circulatory disturbance. By sampling the dynamic state of the cardiovascular system, the limitations inherent in occlusion are removed. The most highly developed of dynamic methods is that based on pulse wave velocity measurement: other techniques have yet to come into general use.

5.1 Pulse wave velocity

Arterial pulse wave velocity (PWV) is the rate of propagation of the pressure pulse through the arterial system. The factors governing it were first delineated by analogy with the transmission of radial waves through thin walled tubes. The expression determined by Moens and by Korteweg (1875) describes the rate of pulse propagation in terms of the density of the enclosed fluid and the properties of the vessel walls. The equation was rewritten as a function of arterial distensibility by Bramwell and Hill (1922). It can be seen that PWV is related to the resting dimensions of the vessel (*V*) while varying inversely with the arterial distensibility ($\Delta V/\Delta P$). Because of the former, PWV can be used only as an index of distending pressure.

$$c^2 = \frac{\Delta P}{\Delta V} \cdot \frac{v}{\rho}$$

where

c = PWV in cm/s
ΔP = change in pressure in dyn/cm^2
ΔV = change in volume in cm^3
V = initial volume in cm^3
ρ = density of the blood in g/cm^3

PWV increases with distending pressure for two reasons. The first, which is unimportant within the physiological range, is that the volume of the vessel becomes greater as the pressure rises. Secondly, arterial distensibility is not a constant, because the arterial wall becomes stiffer and progressively more resistant to stretch as pressure increases (Bergel, 1961). Hence ΔV does not rise in proportion to ΔP. Over the range of distensibilities encountered in typical physiological conditions, an approximately linear relationship between changes in PWV and variations in pressure has been observed in both bench and clinical experiments (Bergel, 1972; Gribbin, Steptoe, and Sleight 1976). PWV permits an analogue estimation of pressure change to be made on every cardiac cycle.

A direct test of the sensitivity of PWV changes to variations in pressure within individuals was made by Gribbin, Steptoe, and Sleight (1976). PWV was monitored between brachial and radial sites while the transmural pressure over the arm was varied systematically. A wide range of subjects, aged from 8 to 80 years, and with resting mean arterial pressures from 75 to 150 mm Hg, were studied. Two important results emerged; firstly, the linear correlations between PWV and changes in transmural pressure were high in all cases ($r > 0.90$), confirming the validity of the measure.

Secondly, the regression coefficients were variable; thus the change in blood pressure indexed by an alteration in PWV differs between individuals. Nevertheless, the regression coefficients of the subgroup of normotensives under 45 years old were homogeneously distributed, suggesting that the relationship is not idiosyncratic but depends on the cardiovascular condition of individuals.

An alternative technique for monitoring PWV is to use the R-wave of the ECG as the proximal trigger. The pulse transit time (TT) between this and the foot of the radial systolic upstroke varies inversely with PWV and hence arterial pressure. This modification facilitates measurement since only a single stable pulse detector is required. However, the adaptation involves the inclusion of the cardiac pre-ejection period within the monitored interval, and under certain conditions variations of the intracardiac delay confound changes in pulse TT.

Steptoe, Smulyan, and Gribbin (1976) therefore carried out an experiment designed to determine the validity of this modification in the face of stimuli commonly encountered in psychophysiological settings. Five healthy young normotensives were studied on two occasions with simultaneous TT and direct brachial arterial pressure recordings. Highly reliable negative correlations ($r < 0.918$) between TT and mean arterial pressure were found during conditions such as mental arithmetic, isometric exercises, and the Valsalva manoeuvre. The relationship was disturbed on inhalation of the depressor drug amyl nitrite, since this agent leads to shortening of the isovolumic contraction time and hence the pre-ejection period. Linear correlations remained high on the retest of all individuals, while the regression coefficients differed significantly on the two occasions in only one individual. A further study was carried out with the same technique on five patients undergoing cardiac catheterization for medical purposes. TT was compared with pressure measured directly from the aorta during resting conditions and while Valsalva's manoeuvre was carried out. Reliable negative correlations were observed for four out of the five patients (r from -0.876 to -0.990). The final patient, a middle-aged man with ischaemic heart disease, was in atrial fibrillation, and this made measurements difficult to take.

It appears from these studies that TT can be used in most of the conditions commonly encountered in psychophysiological experiments without any loss of accuracy or reliability. TT correlated highly with both mean arterial and systolic pressure. It is not yet clear which parameter of blood pressure is reflected most accurately in PWV. As an instantaneous index it is clearly associated with the systolic upstroke, but at the same time the alterations in compliance of the arteries are a function of more tonic factors (Obrist and coworkers (1978)). Further research is required to elucidate this matter.

5.1.1 Measurement of PWV and TT

The studies described in the previous section utilized two different methods for measuring PWV. Gribbin, Steptoe, and Sleight (1976) monitored the pulse wave at two sites on the same major artery. External transducers are attached by elastic straps over the prominent brachial and radial pulses (Figure 4.4). 'Pixie' strain gauge transducers (Endevco Ltd), set in adjustable perspex mouldings, have been used successfully in our laboratory. These transducers accurately reflect the intra-arterial pressure pulse contour, as is seen in the recordings collected by Van der Hoeven, de Monchy, and Beneken (1973). Gribbin (1974) has demonstrated that the Pixie transducer produces a linear response for applied pressures up to 15 g/m^2, and accurate frequency responses up to 50 Hz. Photoelectric transducers with similar characteristics may be substituted, although precise positioning is rather more critical.

PMV is derived by measuring the delay between pulse arrivals at the two sites. It is important that measurements are made from the foot of the systolic upstroke, since peripheral wave reflections distort the amplitude and steepness of the upper portions of the waveform (McDonald, 1974). The alternative method of using only a single peripheral transducer, and measuring the delay from the electrical depolarization of the heart, has been found useful in psychophysiological experiments (Steptoe, Smulyan, and Gribbin, 1976; Steptoe, 1977b). However, since the precise duration of the intracardiac phase is unknown, and the length of the arterial segment cannot be measured with accuracy, the transformation of TT into PWV is perilous. It should be emphasized that in both methods very accurate detection of the interval between pulses is necessary. Since a 10 mm Hg. change in mean arterial pressure produces an alteration in pulse transit time of only about 10 ms, the margin of error must be small. Computer algorithms that detect the appropriate points of the waveforms while allowing for variations in signal amplitude and baseline level have been developed in our laboratory, but such corrections are less easy to make in hardwired systems.

Figure 4.4 Positioning of external transducers for measurment of pulse wave velocity
between the brachial and radial sites

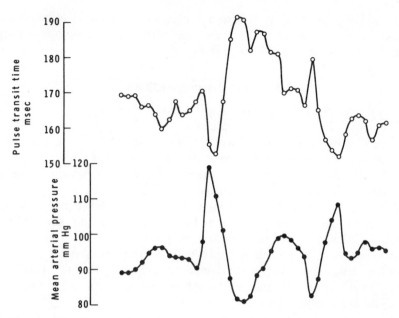

Figure 4.5 Changes in pulse transit time and mean arterial pressure during the Valsalva manoeuvre. For economical representation, each point is the average of values on two successive cardiac cycles

The PWV method satisfies several of the criteria for a measure suited to psychophysiology, as it produces analogue data on every cardiac cycle, while being undisturbing to subjects. Additionally changes in PWV respond rapidly to alterations in arterial pressure, permitting the monitoring of transient patterns. An example is shown in Figure 4.5, where the changes in TT and mean arterial pressure during Valsalva's manoeuvre are plotted.

However, a number of limitations should be emphasized. PWV is a measure of change only, so that absolute pressure level must be determined by conventional means. The slope of the relationship between PWV or TT and arterial pressure varies between individuals; the data cannot therefore be transformed into estimations of pressure change unless a regression slope is calculated for each subject. This may be done by inducing changes in pressure so that the parameters can be measured at various pressure levels. Finally, the monitoring of the interval between peripheral pulse arrivals is inherently preferable to the TT technique. This is because there are a variety of factors, such as physical exercise and vasoactive agents, that produce alterations in the pre-ejection period of cardiac contraction. These can be confounded with PWV variations, making the interpretation of the data difficult. PWV monitoring between arterial pulses is immune to this source of error, as external influences on the distensibility of large arteries are rare within the physiological range (Gow, 1972; Dobrin and Rovick, 1969).

5.2 Other dynamic methods

At several sites in the body, large arteries pass sufficiently close to the skin for pulsations to be readily detectable. If these pulsations could be transduced transcutaneously and without distortion of the vessel, a dynamic representation of circulatory state would be generated. Such a system would be an 'ideal' measurement device, being able to monitor pressure level continuously and without disturbance.

Unfortunately, this sort of instrument has yet to be developed, although some attempts have been made (e.g. Borkat, Kataoka and Silva, 1976). The chief difficulty is that the device must press on the skin at a constant pressure, so that a particular distortion at the mechanical interface accurately reflects a calibrated change in arterial pressure. However, progress in this area may lead to the solution of many of the problems of indirect measurement.

6. THE INTERPRETATION OF BLOOD PRESSURE RECORDINGS

6.1 Variability and measurement conditions

For the psychophysiologist, the variability of blood pressure and its sensitivity to measurement conditions is a mixed blessing. On the one hand, the reactivity of pressure in the presence of cognitive and emotional stimuli is of considerable interest in itself (e.g. Wolf and colleagues, 1948; Brod, 1971). At the same time, this susceptibility often constitutes an unwanted source of variance that can contaminate the interpretation of recordings unless attention is paid to the measurement conditions.

It is well established that an individual's pressure will vary widely both within and between occasions (Armitage and Rose, 1966; Armitage and coworkers, 1966). This is due in part to diurnal and other natural variations, and partly to the conditions of recording. Thus Dunne (1969) reported that pressure levels monitored during the first visit of hypertensive patients to the clinic were significantly reduced on subsequent visits. Smirk (1970) compared casual levels with those recorded after a night of sedated sleep in the hospital and repeated cuff measurements. Average falls in systolic of over 25 mm Hg were observed. Surwit and Shapiro (1977) noted that the pressures recorded by a physician during pretreatment assessment were considerably higher than those taken on other occasions or by other agents.

It can be anticipated that pressure will gradually fall within sessions irrespective of experimental conditions as the subject habituates to the setting. It is difficult precisely to specify the order of such changes, since they will vary between individuals and laboratories. It is advisable for the subject to have been resting quietly for 15–30 minutes before reading begins, and smoking should be avoided since it provokes transient pressor responses. Additionally, the gradual alteration of tonic level may be assessed by sampling baseline pressure periodically during the session as well as at the beginning. Analysis of pressure change from the initial level and a 'running baseline' can then be carried out (Steptoe, 1977b). If these effects are not considered, a misleading impression may be generated, with reductions being enhanced at the expense of pressure increases.

Reductions in pressure from one session to the next can also be expected. For example, before attempting to lower the systolic pressure of hypertensives with feedback, Benson and coworkers (1971) required patients to attend sessions of repeated measurement until they were fully adapted to the laboratory. Up to 16 sessions were necessary before pressure stopped falling between occasions. A similar effect has been

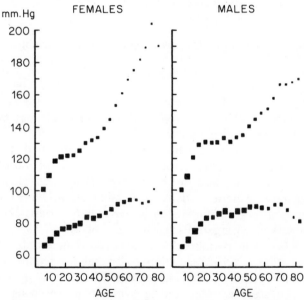

Figure 4.6 Normal values for systolic and diastolic blood pressure according to age and sex. The area of each square is inversely proportional to the standard error of the mean. (From Miall, W. E., and Oldham, P. D. (1963). The hereditary factor in arterial blood-pressure. *Br. Med. J.* 12 January. Reproduced by permission of British Medical Journal)

documented by Brady, Luborsky, and Kron (1974), who observed mean decreases in diastolic ranging from 4.0 to 33.9 mm over baseline sessions. Thus the introduction of any 'psychological treatment' at an earlier stage would have produced a spurious therapeutic effect, and this is a difficulty in interpreting many studies of the psychological management of hypertension (Steptoe, 1977c). Any investigation of the long-term influence of psychological interventions must also take the substantial effect of non-specific expectancy factors and placebo influences into account (Moutsos and coworkers, 1967; Goldring and coworkers, 1956; Steptoe, 1977c).

The psychophysiologist can anticipate that older subjects will have somewhat higher pressures than younger individuals, since levels tend to rise with age in industralized societies. This pattern is illustrated in Figure 4.6. The trend is, however, by no means universal, and there are a number of populations in the world who present little age-related change (Henry and Cassel, 1969). It is evident from Figure 4.6. that no one pressure level can be taken as a criterion for high blood pressure or hypertension (Pickering, 1968). The decision depends both on the age of the patient and the size of deviation from the norm.

6.2 Relation to other psychophysiological variables

Since arterial pressure is a general index of cardiovascular function, it is intimately dependent on other facets of the circulation and upon the metabolic requirements of the organism. Nor can blood pressure itself be taken as a unitary variable, as systolic and diastolic levels may be differentially associated with other parameters.

Heart rate and blood pressure are inversely related through the baroreceptor reflex, and thus a reduction in arterial pressure is rapidly compensated by an increase in heart rate (Rushmer, 1976). Under conditions such as exercise and aversive stimulation, however, the two parameters may increase simultaneously, so that no consistent pattern is universally observed, (Barger, Richards and coworkers, 1956; Herd, and coworkers, 1974). The peripheral resistance encountered by the cardiac output is a function of local regulation and metabolic requirements of the organs in question, while also being regulated by central vasomotor tone. Consequently, pressure is influenced by sympathetic vasoconstrictor fibres and by sympathomimetic agents (Folkow and Neil, 1971). It should be noted that the indexing of peripheral flow is confounded when pressure is monitored occlusively, as the distribution of the blood may be altered; thus Davies (1957) showed substantial increases in digit volume of the contralateral hand during application of only moderate pressures to the left arm.

Systolic and diastolic pressures are differentially associated with cardiac and peripheral circulatory variables. The former is influenced principally by the stroke volume and heart rate, modulated by the arterial distensibility. Diastolic depends on the rate and time over which blood flows out of the arterial tree; hence it is related to heart rate (a slow rate implying long pulse interval and extended diastole), and additionally to peripheral resistance. However, inferences from the differential modification of systolic and diastolic to possible neural mechanisms should be treated with the greatest caution, since many other factors are involved (Guyton, Coleman, and Granger, 1972).

7 AMBULATORY MONITORING

Development of methods for registering blood pressure in ambulating unrestricted subjects is of the greatest potential importance. The monitoring of antihypertensive treatments, diagnosis of transient circulatory disorders and the assessment of pressure levels outside the clinic are facilitated. For psychophysiologists, the study of pressure reactions in the conditions to which people are exposed in everyday life is one of the principal benefits.

Unfortunately, the most advanced and sophisticated ambulatory recordings require arterial cannulation; these have contributed a great deal of information about the circulation in health and disease (Littler and coworkers, 1972; Bevan, Honour, and Stott, 1969). Portable occlusion cuff devices, in which data are recorded with small tape recorders, commonly require the active participation of the patient in inflating the cuff and positioning the arm (Stott, 1977). However, Schneider and Cotisloe (1975) described a portable recorder incorporating a timer that initiates cuff inflation at 6 to 20 minute intervals. The device can thus generate and store data over several hours with a reported accuracy of 10 mm Hg. Pulse wave velocity methods have yet to be incorporated into ambulatory systems, but there is no reason why they should not operate successfully under these conditions.

8 CONCLUSIONS

It can be seen that techniques for recording blood pressure have advanced considerably in recent decades, and there is now no reason why it should not be included amongst the parameters commonly assessed in psychophysiological studies. The choice of method depends on the experimental conditions and the resources available. Discontinuous auscultation is adequate for settings in which readings are required less than about once every minute. The technique is simple, and equipment readily obtainable, although care must be taken to ensure that observer errors are not introduced. The more continuous monitors have sophisticated electronic features. PWV systems satisfy the criteria outlined in the introduction, and respond rapidly to changes in pressure. However, they are limited in application and involve complex signal processing. On the other hand, the automated cuff methods need simpler electronic analysis but can be disturbing to subjects. I would encourage the reader to select the system that can fulfil experimental requirements in the simplest and most economical way.

REFERENCES

Armitage, P., and Rose, G. A. (1966). The variability of measurements of casual blood pressure 1: Laboratory study. *Clin. Sci.,* **30**, 325–35.

Armitage, P., Fox, W., Rose, G. A., and Tinker, C. M. (1966). The variability of casual blood pressure 2: Survey experience. *Clin. Sci.,* **30**, 337–44.

Barger, A. C., Richards, V., Metcalfe, J., and Gunther, B. (1956). Regulation of the circulation during exercise. *Am. J. Physiol.,* **184**, 613–23.

Beamer, V., and Shapiro, A. P. (1973). Comparison of pressor and adrenergic responses derived from direct and indirect methods of cardiovascular testing. *Psychosom. Med.,* **35**, 112–120.

Benson, H., Shapiro, D., Tursky, B. and Schwartz, G. E. (1971) Decreased systolic blood pressure through operant conditioning techniques in patients with essential hypertension. *Science,* **173**, 740–2

Berger, D. H. (1961). The static elastic properties of the arterial wall. *J. Physiol.,* **156**, 445–57.

Bergel, D. H. (1972). The properties of blood vessels. In Y. C. Fung, N. Perrone, and M. Ankiler (Eds), *Biomechanics: its Foundations and Objectives.* Prentice-Hall, Englewood Cliffs. pp. 105–39.

Bevan, A. T., Honour, A. J., and Stott, F. H. (1969). Direct arterial pressure recording in unrestricted man. *Clin. Sci.,* **36**, 329–44.

Borkat, F. R., Kataoka, R. W., and Silva, J. (1976). An approach to the continuous non-invasive measurement of blood pressure. *Proc. San Diego Biomedical Symposium,* **15**, 9–12.

Brady, J. P., Luborsky, L., and Kron, R. E. (1974). Blood pressure reduction in patients with essential hypertension through metronome-conditioned relaxation. *Behaviour Therapy,* **5**, 203–9.

Bramwell, J. C., and Hill, A. V. (1922). The velocity of the pulse wave in man. *Proc. R. Soc.* **93**, 298–306.

Brener, J. (1974). A general model of voluntary control applied to the phenomena of learned cardiovascular change. In P. A. Obrist, A. H. Black, J. Brener, and L. V. DiCara (Eds), *Cardiovascular Psychophysiology: Current Issues in Response Mechanisms, Biofeedback and Methodology.* Aldine, Chicago. pp. 365–91.

Brener, J., and Kleinman, R. A. (1970). Learned control of decreases in systolic pressure. *Nature,* **226**, 1063–5.

Brod, J. (1971). The influence of higher nervous processes induced by psychosocial environment on the development of essential hypertension. In L. Levi (Ed.), *Society, Stress and Disease,* Oxford University Press, London. pp. 312–23.

Davis, R. C. (1957). Continuous recording of arterial pressure: an analysis of the problem. *J. Comp. Physiol. Psychol.,* **50**, 524–9.

Dobrin, P. B., and Rovick, A. A. (1969). Influence of vascular smooth muscle on contractile mechanisms and elasticity of arteries. *Am. J. Physiol.* **217**, 1644–51.

Dunne, J. F. (1969). Variation of blood pressure in untreated hypertensive out-patients. *Lancet*, **i**, 391–2.

Elder, S. T., Longacre, A., Welsh, D. M., and McAfee, R. D. (1977). Apparatus and procedure for training subjects to control their blood pressure. *Psychophysiology*, **14**, 68–72.

Flanagan, G. J., and Hull, C. J. (1968). A blood pressure recorder. *Br. J. Anaesthiol.*, **40**, 292–8.

Folkow, B., and Neil, E. (1971). *Circulation*, Oxford University Press, London.

Fukuda, Y. (1976). Measurement of blood pressure in the population. In S. Hatano, I. Shigematsu, and T. Strasser (Eds), *Hypertension and Stroke Control in the Community*. WHO, Geneva. pp. 175–83.

Gabe, I. T. (1972). Pressure measurement in experimental physiology. In D. H. Bergel (Ed.), *Cardiovascular Fluid Dynamics*, Vol. 2, Academic Press, London. pp. 11–41.

Geddes, L. A. (1970). *The Direct and Indirect Measurement of Blood Pressure.* Year Book Medical Publishers, Chicago.

Geddes, L. A., Hoff, H. E., and Badger, A. S. (1966). Introduction of the auscultatory method of measuring blood pressure—including a translation of Korotkoff's original paper. *Cardiovasc. Res. Center Bull.* **5**, 57–74.

Geddes, L. A., and Newberg, D. C. (1977). Cuff pressure oscillations in the measurement of relative blood pressure. *Psychophysiology*, **14**, 198–202.

Goldring, W., Chasis, H., Schreiner, G. E., and Smith, H. W. (1956). Reassurance in the management of benign hypertensive diseases. *Circulation*, **14**, 260–4.

Gow, B. S. (1972). Influence of vascular smooth muscle on the viscoelastic properties of blood vessels. In D. H. Bergel (Ed.) *Cardiovascular Fluid Dynamics*, Vol. 2, Academic Press, London. pp. 66–110.

Greatorex, C. A. (1971). Indirect methods of blood pressure measurement. In B. S. Watson (Ed.), *IEE Medical Electronics Monograph*, No. 1 Peter Peregrinus, London.

Gribbin, B. (1974). A study of baroreflex function and arterial distensibility in normal and hypertensive man. *MD Thesis*, University of Dundee, unpublished.

Gribbin, B., Steptoe, A., and Sleight, P. (1976). Pulse wave velocity as a measure of blood pressure change. *Psychophysiology*, **14**, 86–90.

Guyton, A. C., Coleman, T. G., and Granger, H. J. (1972). Circulation: overall regulation. *A. Rev. Physiol.* **34**, 13–46.

Henry, J. P., and Cassel, J. C. (1969). Psychosocial factors in essential hypertension: recent epidemiologic and animal experimental evidence. *J. Epidem.*, **96**, 171–200.

Herd, J. A., Kelleher, R. T., Morse, W. H., and Grose, S. A. (1974). Sympathetic and parasympathetic activity during behavioral hypertension in the squirrel monkey. In P. A. Obrist, A. H. Black, J. Brener, and L. V. DiCara (Eds), *Cardiovascular Psychophysiology: Current Issues in Response Mechanisms, Biofeedback and Methodology*, Aldine, Chicago, pp. 211–25.

Hochberg, H. M., and Salomon, H. (1971). Accuracy of an automated ultrasound blood pressure monitor. *Curr. Therapeutic Res.*, **13**, 129–38.

Holland, W. W., and Humerfelt, S. (1964). Measurement of blood pressure: comparison of intra-arterial and cuff valves. *Br. Med. J.*, **ii**, 1241–3.

Hoobler, S. W., Oesterle, B., and Early, H. (1976). Evaluation of a new automatic device for taking and recording blood pressures. *J. Lab. Clin. Med.*, **88**, 826–33.

Karlefors, T., Nilson, R., and Westling, H. (1966). On the accuracy of indirect auscultatory blood pressure measurement during exercise. *Acta Med. Scand., Suppl. 449*, 81–7.

Katona, Z., and Bolvary, E. (1975). Automatic indirect sphygmomanometry. *Biomed. Engng.*, **10**, 405–9.

Khosla, T., and Lowe, C. R. (1965). Arterial pressure and arm circumference. *Br. J. Preventive Socl. Med.*, **19**, 159–63.

Kirkendall, W., Burton, A., Epstein, F., and Freis, E. (1967). Recommendations for human blood pressure determination by sphygomanometry. *Circulation*, **36**, 980–7.

Korotkoff, N. S. (1905). On the subject of methods of measuring blood pressure. *Bull. Imp. Milit. Med. Acad., St. Petersburg*, **11**, 365–7.

Kortweg, D. J. (1875). Ueber die Fortpflanzungsgeschwindigkeit des Schalles in Elastischen Röhren. *Ann. Phys. Chem. Lpz.*, **5**, 585.

Krausman, D. T. (1975). Methods and procedures for monitoring and recording blood pressure. *Am. Psychol.*, 285–94.

Labarthe, D. R., Hawkins, C. M., and Remington, R. D. (1973). Evaluation of performance of selected devices for measuring blood pressure. *Am. J. Cardiol.*, **32**, 546–53.

Lategola, M. G., Harrison, H., and Barnard, C. (1966). Continuous measurement of human blood pressure transients without puncture. *Aerospace Med.*, **37**, 228–33.

Lenox, J. R., and Lange, A. F. (1969). Changes in systolic blood pressure. *J. Comp. Physiol. Psychol.*, **69**, 454–8.

Littler, W. A., Honour, A. J., Sleight, P., and Stott, F. D. (1972). Continuous recording of direct arterial pressure and electrocardiogram in unrestricted man. *Br. Med. J.*, **3**, 76–8.

London, S. B., and London, R. E. (1967). Critique of indirect diastolic end point. *Archs Intern. Med.*, **119**, 39–49.

McCutcheon, E. P., and Rushmer, R. F. (1967). Korotkoff sounds: an experimental critique. *Circulation Res.*, **20**, 149–61.

McCutcheon, E. P., Baker, P. W., and Wiederhielm, C. A. (1969). Frequency spectrum changes of Korotkoff sounds with muffling. *Med. Res. Engn.*, **8**, 30–33.

McDonald, D. A. (1974). *Blood Flow in Arteries*. Arnold, London.

Meldrum, S. J. (1976). Indirect blood pressure measurement. *Br. J. Clin. Equip.*, **1**, 257–65.

Miall, W. E., and Oldham, P. D. (1963). The hereditary factor in arterial blood pressure. *Br. Med. J.*, **i**, 75–7.

Moutsos, S. E., Sapira, J. D., Schein, E. G., and Shapiro, A. P. (1967). An analysis of the placebo effect in hospitalized hypertensive patients. *Clin. Pharmacol. Therapeutics*, **8**, 676–83.

Obrist, P. A. (1976). The cardiovascular–behavioral interaction – as it appears today. *Psychophysiology*, **13**, 95–107.

Obrist, P. A., Light, K. C., McCubbin, J. A., Hutcheson, J. S., and Hoffer, J. E. (1978). Pulse transit time: relationship to blood pressure. *Behaviour Research and Methods and Instrumentation*, **10**, 623–6.

Pickering, G. (1968). *High Blood Pressure*, 2nd ed, Churchill, London.

Ramsay, L. E., Nicholls, M. G., and Boyle, P. (1977). The Elag–Koln automatic blood pressure recorder—a clinical appraisal. *Br. Heart J.*, **39**, 795–8.

Raftery, E. B., and Ward, A. P. (1968). The indirect method of recording blood pressure. *Cardiovasc. Res.*, **2**, 210–18.

Rogge, J. D., Meyer, J. F. (1967). Estimation of diastolic aortic blood pressure by palpation of the brachial artery. *School of Aerospace Medicine. Technical Report* SAM — TR — 67 — 113. Brooks, AFB Texas.

Roman, J., Henry, J. P., and Meehan, J. P. (1965). Validity of flight blood pressure data. *Aerospace Med.*, **36**, 436–46.

Rose, G. A., Holland, W. W., and Crowley, E. A. (1964). A sphygmomanometer for epidemiologists. *Lancet*, **i**, 296–300.

Rushmer, R. F. (1976). *Structure and Function of the Cardiovascular System*, 2nd edn., Saunders, Philadelphia.

Schneider, R. A., and Cotisloe, J. P. (1975). Automatic monitoring of blood pressure and heart rate. *Am. Heart J.* **90**, 695–702.

Shapiro, D., Tursky, B., and Schwartz, G. E. (1970). Control of blood pressure in man by operant conditioning. *Circulation Res.*, **27**, *Suppl.* 1, 27–32.

Shapiro, D., Schwartz, G. E., and Tursky, B. (1972). Control of diastolic blood pressure in man by feedback and reinforcement. *Psychophysiology*, **9**, 296–306.

Short, D. (1975). A policy for hypertension. *Br. Heart J.*, **37**, 893.

Smirk, H. (1970). Discussion on haemodynamic aspects of hypertension. *Circulation Res.*, **27**, *Suppl.* 1, 66–68.

Steptoe, A. (1977a). Voluntary blood pressure reductions measured with pulse transit time: training conditions and reactions to mental work. *Psychophysiology*, **14**, 492–8.

Steptoe, A. (1977b). Blood pressure control with pulse wave velocity feedback; methods of analysis and training. In J. Beatty and H. Legewie (Eds), *Biofeedback and Behaviour*, Plenum, New York. pp. 365–68.

Steptoe, A. (1977c). Psychological methods in the treatment of hypertension: a review. *Br. Heart J.*, **39**, 587–93.

Steptoe, A., Smulyan, H., and Gribbin, B. (1976). Pulse wave velocity and blood pressure change: calibration and applications. *Psychophysiology*, **13**, 488–93.

Stott, F. D. (1977). Ambulatory monitoring. *Br. J. Clin. Equip.* **2**, 61–8.

Surwit, R., and Shapiro, D. (1977). Biofeedback and meditation in the treatment of borderline hypertension. In J. Beatty and H. Legewie (Eds). *Biofeedback and Behavior*. Plenum, New York, pp. 403–12.

Tursky, B. (1974). The indirect recording of human blood pressure. In P. A. Obrist, A. H. Black, J. Brener, and L. V. DiCara (Eds), *Cardiovascular Psychophysiology: Current Issues in Response Mechanisms, Biofeedback and Methodology*. Aldine, Chicago. pp. 93–105.

Tursky, B., Shapiro, D., and Schwartz, G. E. (1972). Automated constant-cuff pressure system to measure average systolic and diastolic pressure in man. *IEEE Trans. Biomed. Engng*, **BME-19**, 271–6.

Van der Hoeven, G. M. A., de Monchy, C., and Benekan, J. E. W. (1973). Systolic time intervals and pulse wave transit time in normal children. *Br. Heart J.*, **35**, 669–78.

Ware, R. W., and Kahn, A. R. (1963). Automatic indirect blood pressure determination in flight. *J. Appl. Physiol.*, **18**, 210–14.

Wolf, S., Pfeiffer, J. B., Ripley, H. S., Winter, O. S., and Wolff, H. G. (1948). Hypertension as a reaction pattern to stress. *Ann. Intern. Med.*, **58**, 1056–76.

Wright, B. M., and Dore, C. F. (1970). A random zero sphygomanometer. *Lancet*, **i**, 337.

Wyatt, R., Glares, J., and Cooper, D. J. (1974). Proximal skin necrosis after radial artery cannulation. *Lancet*, **i**, 1135–8.

Techniques in Psychophysiology
Edited by I. Martin and P. H. Venables
© 1980, John Wiley & Sons, Ltd.

CHAPTER 5

Measurement of Eye Movement

ELECTROOCULOGRAPHY*

PHYLLIS J. OSTER† AND JOHN A. STERN†

* This research supported in part by NSF Research Grant No. EPP-75-15388
† Research Associate.
‡ Professor of Psychology and Director of Research.

1.0 INTRODUCTION

1.1 The electrooculogram in the evaluation of subject-initiated changes in information processing

Records of eye movements can provide information not available from analyses of more traditional psychophysiological response variables. Because a stimulus may be perceived without eliciting any change in autonomic or motoric responses, records of these responses provide limited means for tracking perceptual and cognitive processes. One area of interest peculiarly susceptible to this limitation is subject-initiated changes in information processing strategy. Such changes can be systematically studied, however, with the use of continuous eye movement recordings which provide a protocol of visual information processing. For example, such protocols allow the isolation of regularities or patterns in eye fixation sequences. Analyses of such patterns obtained with the electrooculographic technique have been used to determine how good and poor readers differentially process the written word (Goltz, 1975) and how schizophrenics' performance in cognitive tasks differs from that of normals (Brockway, 1975). Further, the simultaneous recording of eye movements and other psychophysiological responses can enhance the study of complex behaviours. For example, synchronous recordings of eye movements and speech muscle activity have been used to obtain normative data on the changing relationship between quality of visual information processing and reliance on subvocalization during reading skill acquisition (Oster, 1979). The recording of eye movements is therefore a powerful tool for the psychophysiologist, making possible the use of more complex stimuli and tasks and the investigation of questions traditionally the province of cognition and perception.

1.2 Comparative advantages of the electrooculographic method

Electrooculography (EOG) is the method of recording voltage changes due to eye rotations. It is the only eye movement recording technique wherein signal energy is generated by a bioelectric event (Section 1.4); in most other methods signal energy is light reflected from ocular structures (cornea, iris, sclera, pupil) or surfaces attached to the eye. The advantages peculiar to the EOG method derive from its differing source of signal energy.

Because this source is located within the eye, head movements do not hinder accurate recording. No attachments, either to the eye or to spectacles, which may cause discomfort or interfere with normal vision, are required to record eye position with respect to the head. Devices for restraining or sensing head movement are necessary only when absolute eye position is desired. With the use of most methods requiring reflected light, slight movements of the head with respect to the light source produce disproportionately large calibration errors.

The physiological basis of electrooculography, while limiting calibration accuracies achievable with the method, enhances its effective range. Angular deviations of $\pm 30°$, and even $\pm 80°$, can be recorded along both horizontal and vertical planes of rotation, since visualization of the eye is not required. For the same reason, eye closure poses no obstacle for recording. Blinks, recorded on vertical EOG channels, do not produce discontinuities in horizontal recordings. Optical methods, immune to physiological noise, can provide superior accuracy, but their effective range is limited. The reflective properties of ocular structures are linear only for a restricted range, and, for large rotations, the cornea and iris tend to disappear behind the eyelids. Eye closure and blinking interrupt recording.

Standard equipment necessary to record and reproduce the small voltage deflections is relatively inexpensive and available in laboratories and hospitals where low level physiological responses are routinely recorded. Signal sensing devices are surface electrodes rather than more costly moving film or television cameras. Continuous polygraph records of the voltage changes are sufficient for data analysis in many applications. Alternatively, the voltage changes may be recorded on magnetic tape for off-line or on-line data reduction. The reduction of photographic records, which cannot be digitized directly, is comparatively arduous.

The voltage output obtained with the EOG method affords other advantages. The extent of angular deviations is more simply related to the amplitude of the EOG potential than to the output of optical systems involving the metrics of reflected light. The frequency response of the EOG system is superior to that of photographic systems limited by camera frames per second or the response time of television tubes. Unlike optical methods which measure angular displacement only, EOG enables one to obtain a measure of velocity from the primary record without differentiation. Synchronous recordings of eye movement and other parameters like electroencephalographic (EEG) or electromyographic (EMG) activity are easily obtained.

In summary, EOG is a versatile technique for the study of eye movements greater than ±1°. The necessary recording equipment is comparatively inexpensive, easily operated, and portable. The ease with which analogue records may be digitized allows rapid, economical reduction of data collected during extended recording sessions and from large numbers of subjects. (Reviews of eye movement recording methods appear in Alpern, 1972; Davson, 1969; Monty and Senders, 1976; Young and Sheena, 1975.)

1.3 Historical background

The existence of a standing potential across the eyeball has been known since du'Bois-Reymond (1849), but technique for the measurement of human eye movement based on this potential is a relatively recent development. In the late 1800s various workers observed that the standing potential in animal preparations increased with light stimulation and decreased with exposure to darkness (Kohlrausch, 1931). By 1874 Dewar and M'Kendrick had obtained a similar response from the human eye and had also noted that the amplitude of the measured potential was dependent on eye position. Nevertheless, tracings of human eye movements based on the standing potential were not produced until the 1920s (Meyers, 1929; Schott, 1922); and, then, steady-state information necessary to chart changing eye position was not considered critical to the work. Recording conditions were designed to elicit the jerky movements characteristic of nystagmus, and Meyers (1929) and Jacobson (1930a, 1930b, 1930c) attributed the recorded waveforms to the contraction of extraocular muscles. With d.c. amplification, Mowrer, Ruch, and Miller (1936) disproved this notion and established that the recorded responses could only reflect variations in a potential field emanating from the eyeball. Soon after this rediscovery of the standing potential, Miles (1939a, 1939b; 1940) introduced standardized electrode placements and recording procedures to facilitate comparison of potentials obtained from different individuals and from the same individuals under various experimental conditions.

Interest in the EOG waned, however, in part due to the popularity of other eye movement recording methods less subject to the caprices introduced by physiological variables and to the difficulties encountered with baseline drift in d.c. amplified recordings. Most EOG work until the 1950s concerned the recording of nystagmus (electronystagmography) for which a.c. amplification was adequate (see Marg, 1951 for review), but electrooculography was also employed to study reading and to evaluate the effects of stress and fatigue (Carmichael and Dearborn, 1947; Lion and Brockhurst, 1951). In the late 1950s relatively drift-free amplifiers became commercially available; and, following the work of François, Verriest, and de Rouck (1955, 1957) and Arden (Arden and Kelsey, 1962; Arden,

Barrada, and Kelsey, 1962), the light- and dark-induced EOG responses grew increasingly popular as clinical tools for the evaluation of retinal and choroidal integrity. These two advances, together with developments in sleep research and visual information processing, renewed interest in electrooculography. Histories of electrooculography are provided by Miles (1939a) and Marg (1951).

1.4 Principles of electrooculographic recording

The bioelectric event underlying the EOG is a d.c. potential measurable between the cornea and the fundus of the eyeball. The origin of the corneofundal potential (CFP) is still imperfectly understood, but its generation is dependent on the structural and functional integrity of several ocular structures including the retina, pigment epithelium, and choroid (Arden and Ikeda, 1966; Höhne, 1972; Roth, Alexandridis, and Pape, 1974).

Electrooculography concerns the indirect measurement of the corneofundal potential. Because the cornea is positive in vertebrates (Kikawada, 1968), with respect to the posterior of the eye, the eye

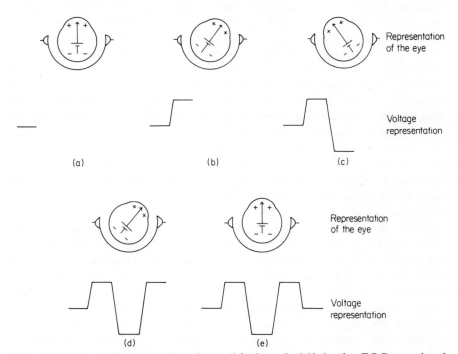

Figure 5.1   Successive alterations (parts (a) through (e)) in the EOG associated with changes in the potential field due to eye movements

resembles a battery situated in a variable conducting medium. The d.c. voltage, though originating within the eye, radiates into adjacent tissues, creating a potential field which rotates with the eye. Consequently, electrodes placed around the orbit, along the appropriate planes of rotation, transduce voltages which may be used to determine the direction and amplitude of the eye's movement with respect to the head.

The principle of EOG is illustrated for saccadic eye movement in Figure 5.1. When the eye is oriented straight ahead, the cornea and central fundus are assumed to be equidistant from the recording electrodes, and the EOG potential is, by definition, zero. Rotation of the eye from the midline, brings the positively charged cornea closer to one electrode and the negatively charged fundus closer to the other. The resultant voltage difference between a pair of recording electrodes is essentially linearly related to the angle of gaze for $\pm 30°$ and to the sine of the angle for $\pm 30°$ to $\pm 60°$. (Bicas, 1972; reviews: Geddes and Baker, 1975; Shackel, 1967).

1.5 Types of eye movements and their electrooculograms

The form of the recorded voltage deflection depends on the type of eye rotation (Figure 5.2). *Saccadic* movements are quick (20–700°/s) jumps of the eye to change the locus of fixation. *Smooth* movements are slow (1–30°/s), sweeping rotations of the eye which serve to maintain fixation on an object moving with respect to the head. They are called *pursuit* if elicited by movement of the object, and *compensatory* if elicited by head or body movement. Both saccadic and smooth movements involve *conjugate*, i.e. parallel, motion of the eyes. *Nystagmoid* movement, the general term for a large class of eye movements of an oscillatory or unstable nature, includes both smooth and saccadic components. This type of movement may be elicited by a stimulus moving with respect to the head (whether the observer is rotated or the object is moved) or by direct stimulation of the vestibular system. Nystagmus also occurs incident to oculomotor or vestibular disorder. *Vergence*, unlike smooth or saccadic movement, is disjunctive, involving slow (6–15°/s) rotation of the axes in opposite directions to maintain binocular fixation on an object approaching or moving away from the eyes. *Torsional* movements (not shown) are slow, compensatory rotations about the line of gaze. Large deflections associated with the eyeblink also appear in EOG recordings of vertical eye movement.

The scope of this paper precludes a description of eye movements adequate to prepare the reader for their recording or to familiarize the reader with important exceptions to general statements, like those regarding the symmetry of conjugate eye movements. Extensive reviews of

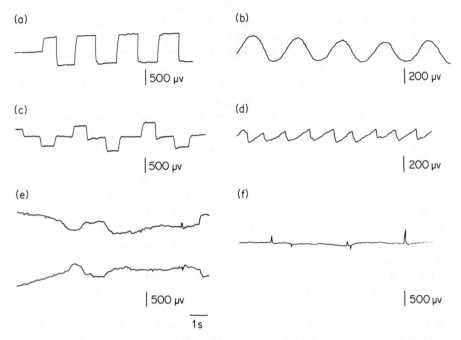

Figure 5.2 Electrooculograms: (a) saccadic movement; (b) pursuit movement to pendular motion; (c) compensatory movement elicited by head rotation to the left and right of a centre position; (d) nystagmus produced by tracking of horizontally moving, vertical stripes; (e) vergence, top trace right eye, lower trace left eye; (f) eyeblink. With the exception of the blink transient, all movements were recorded along the horizontal plane of rotation. In these horizontal recordings upward deflections are associated with right-going movement, and downward deflections with left-going movement

eye movements and their physiology are available elsewhere (Alpern, 1972; Bach-y-Rita, Collins, and Hyde, 1971; Collins, 1975; Davson, 1969; Ditchburn, 1973; Monty and Senders, 1976).

1.6 Properties of eye movements dictating instrumentation characteristics

Properties of the saccadic system dictate both the upper and lower limiting characteristics of the instrumentation (to be described in Sections 2.4 and 2.5), adequate to record all types of large eye movements. Intersaccadic pauses are essentially steady-state activity, requiring d.c. stability; saccades are the fastest eye movements, requiring the highest frequency components for their accurate reproduction, and therefore frequency response with the highest upper limit. Detailed signal description necessary for appreciation of the correspondence between signal characteristics and instrumentation will, therefore, be limited to saccadic eye movement.

Amplitude-dependent non-linearity characterizes the saccadic system. Both saccade duration and peak velocity are increasing non-linear functions of saccade amplitude. A 5° saccade takes approximately 20 to 30 ms, with each additional degree taking about 2 ms (Hyde, 1959; Robinson, 1964). Maximum velocity increases linearly with saccade amplitude up to about 20–30° and asymptotes between 600–700°/sec (Hyde, 1959; Westheimer, 1954; Zuber, Stark, and Cook, 1965). Velocity is not symmetric about the midpoint of the trajectory; deceleration begins before the midpoint is reached, the exact time varying with the amplitude of the saccade (Hyde, 1959). Saccadic bandwidth decreases non-linearly with increasing amplitude. Robinson (1964) suggested that bandwidth may decrease from about 19 Hz for a 5° movement to about 6 Hz for a 40° movement. Zuber, Semmlow, and Stark (1968) report average bandwidths of 16 Hz for 5° and 9 Hz for 20° horizontal saccades.

Information concerning the power spectra of naturally occurring saccades is fragmentary. Available data calculated on the basis of induced or forced saccades (Findlay, 1971, for microsaccades; Thomas, 1967, for saccades between 1.5 and 3°; Zuber, Semmlow, and Stark, 1968, for 5° saccades) suggest that above 40–50 Hz, energy drops sharply.

Average saccadic reaction time, about 200 ms (Westheimer, 1954), has been loosely equated with a saccadic refractory period (Young and Sheena, 1975; Zuber, Semmlow, and Stark, 1968). One should note, however, that reaction time (RT) experiments typically require the subject to shift his gaze from an initial fixation target upon the presentation of a second stimulus. Since angular distance between stimuli (Bartz, 1962), the predictability of stimulus onset (White, Eason, and Bartlett, 1962), and stimulus characteristics (Carlow and coworkers, 1975; Saslow, 1967) affect saccadic RT, findings from reaction time studies may bear little resemblance to intersaccadic intervals measured in visual tracking or subject-paced tasks. In such tasks, intersaccadic intervals as short as 80 ms (Johnson, 1963 in Fuchs, 1971, for tracking; Goltz, 1975, for reading) are commonly observed. The purported refractory period, then, appears to be a function of task demands rather than a characteristic of the saccadic system.

2.0 RECORDING TECHNIQUE AND INSTRUMENTATION

2.1 Skin and electrode preparation

Proper preparation of Ag–AgCl surface electrodes and skin is essential for adequate recording. (See Section 3.3.2 for further discussion of electrodes). To maximize conduction between skin and electrolyte, facial oils are removed by briskly rubbing with alcohol. Skin drilling (slight abrasion of the epidermis) may be used to minimize the confounding effects of skin conductance and skin potential changes (Shackel, 1959). When Beckman miniature biopotential electrodes are used, the electrode brim is fitted with a double-coated, pressure-sensitive tape ring and the recess is filled with conductive paste. The protective ring is then removed, taking with it excess paste and preventing paste from contaminating the adhesive surface. This procedure limits seepage of paste between adhesive surface and skin which could otherwise create slippage and lead to movement artifact (a fluctuation in voltage arising from mechanical disturbance of the skin/electrolyte/metal junctures). In addition, care should be taken to fill the electrode recess completely; air trapped between electrode and electrolyte or between skin and electrolyte results in increased series resistance and signal distortion.

2.2 Electrode placement

While there is no accepted convention for positioning electrodes with respect to the eye, there are general guidelines. To ensure that the electrode configuration does not contribute unequal voltages to common mode rejection, the common electrode is placed on the forehead equidistant from each of the two electrodes across which eye movement potentials are to be recorded. Since the size of the EOG potential decreases with increasing electrode distance from the eye (Cohn, 1957; MacKensen and Harder, 1954), the electrode should be placed as close to the eye as possible without producing discomfort to the wearer.

Horizontal conjugate eye movements are generally recorded binocularly with electrodes placed at the outer canthi. Electrodes are positioned at the outer and inner canthi of each eye when simultaneous recordings of left and right horizontal eye movements are required. Vertical eye movements are typically recorded from electrodes above and below the eye, but monopolar recordings may be preferable in some cases (see Section 3.2).

The planes of rotation described by orthogonal electrode pairs should intersect at right angles through the pupil as the participant looks straight ahead. Failure to properly align electrodes will exacerbate cross talk, i.e. deflection in the vertical EOG trace when only horizontal eye movement has occurred. Approaches to minimizing cross talk through vector electrooculography are given by Uenoyama, Uenoyama, and Iinuma (1964) for binocular recording and by Bles and Kapteyn (1973) for simultaneous recording from the two eyes. When these measures are insufficient to eliminate the effects of cross talk, mapping of the potential field as described by Kris (1960) and computer aided calibration may be used for refined eye movement analyses.

2.3 Calibration and accuracy

Calibration is carried out by asking the subject to shift his gaze between points of known visual angle and adjusting sensitivity until one achieves the desired relationship between voltage output and degree of eye rotation. The maximum calibration accuracy obtainable will vary with the signal to noise ratio which is in turn dependent on CFP amplitude and instrumentation. Shackel (1967) treats these issues in detail. Because illumination level affects CFP amplitude, calibration should be carried out after the subject has been allowed to adapt to the illumination level to be used throughout testing. With frequent recalibration or averaging of EOG responses, accuracies to $\pm$ 30' can be obtained for horizontal EOG (Weber and Daroff, 1971), but calibration accuracy is typically $^{\pm 1.0°}_{\pm 1.5°}$. Because vertical EOG amplitude is generally lower than horizontal amplitude, accuracies are correspondingly lower. When absolute eye position is calibrated on the basis of both vertical and horizontal movement, radial accuracy is about $\pm 2°$.

2.4 Amplification and recording

As previously discussed (Section 1.6), properties of saccadic movement dictate the upper and lower limits for instrumentation adequate to record all types of large (greater than $\pm 1°$) eye movements. The reproduction of all aspects of saccadic eye movement, including intersaccadic steady-state activity (0 Hz) and fast characteristics, requires an amplification-recording system with frequency response linear from d.c. (0 Hz) to better than 130 Hz. Stable d.c. recording and minimal interference from extraneous voltage sources, which may seriously distort the small unamplified signal, have been obtained with the d.c. system described below.

Shielded vertical and horizontal electrode leads are fed into separate high input (1 M Ω), low output impedance, differential preamplifiers with common mode rejection at 40 db. Incorporation of high common mode rejection at the preamplifier stage minimizes initial amplification of noise which is in phase and of the same amplitude at the two electrodes. The preamplifiers are sufficiently compact ($\frac{1}{2} \times 3 \times 8$ in) to allow their placement on the subject. This feature allows substantial reduction of the distance traversed by leads from the electrodes to the preamplifiers. Short preamplifier leads, together with amplification by 200 before transfer over the greater distance to the power amplifier, minimize the effect of interfering voltages which may develop across leads.

The preamplifier power source may be batteries or a regulated power supply. Battery powered preamplifiers may be preferable when, for example, data collection in the field requires frequent relocation of equipment, but their use does not provide an optimally stable system gain. Insidious decline in battery voltage can result in undetected differential gain across preamplifiers as well as a time-varying system gain. The use of regulated power supplies obviates these problems. If batteries must be used, they should be mercury batteries whose voltage loss is relatively abrupt.

Selectable power amplifier gain (in steps of 2, 5 or 10 × the preamplifier gain) provides a system gain of 400, 1000, or 2000 which is adequate for signals varying from 5–20 μV/deg. Gain is generally set lower on vertical channels to ensure that, when amplified, spontaneous blinks present voltages within the ±1.5 V range acceptable to IRIG standard instrumentation tape recorders. Automatic baseline control (correction for d.c. offset) is provided by continuously sampling the signal at the last stage of amplification where it is allowed to fluctuate between ±1 V. When the voltage exceeds this level for 100 ms, an equal but opposite d.c. voltage is imposed. Noise referred to shorted input with system gain at 1000 should be 2 μV or less to allow adequate reproduction of signals 4–5 μV in amplitude.

2.5 System frequency response

Modulation of signal frequency is effected at each stage of the recording–reproduction system. Frequency response is, therefore, determined by the narrowest bandwidth in the system regardless of the stage at which the restrictive filtering is introduced. The following remarks are, therefore, germane whether one is considering frequency response of tape recorders, auxiliary filters, or amplifiers.

Bandwidth need not extend from 0–130 Hz if only selected aspects of saccadic eye movement are of interest. To clarify the particular purposes for which a restricted bandwidth may be adequate, the effects of low and high frequency component rejection on the reproduction of saccadic eye movements and intersaccadic fixation pauses are shown in Figure 5.3. Attenuation of energy at low or high frequencies can introduce saccade amplitude loss and an associated phase distortion. These effects are, however, greater when filtering involves low frequencies at which considerable signal energy occurs. Since low frequency components contribute the basic shape of the saccadic waveform, their attenuation affects the maintenance of intersaccadic steady-state response. Higher frequencies at odd harmonics, though contributing progressively less energy to the saccadic waveform, account for the sharpness of the transition at the saccade–fixation juncture. The truncation of saccade amplitude and inflation of saccade duration which results from rejection of energy at high frequencies appears as a rounding of the saccade–fixation juncture.

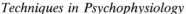

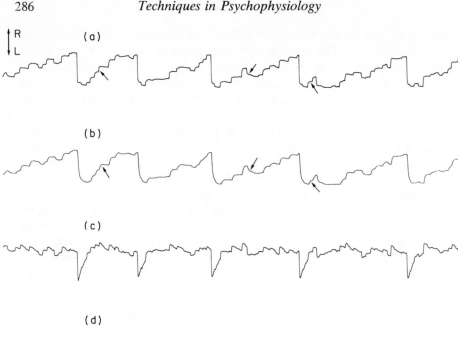

Figure 5.3   The effects of attenuating high and low frequency components of saccadic eye movements recorded during reading. High frequency components were attenuated by reproducing the record with: (a) no filtering other than that effected by the frequency response of the Beckman (Model R-611) Dynograph, linear to 70 Hz; and (b) low-pass filtering using a Krohn-Hite model 3322 set at 10 Hz. Low frequency components were attenuated by reproducing the signal with: (c) time constant (Beckman) of 0.3 s; and (d) time constant (Beckman) of 0.03 s. Note that while rounding of the saccade–fixation juncture (arrows) is severe when the signal is filtered at 10 Hz, rounding is also present in (a) due to the limited frequency response of the pen recorder

Since amplitude loss is suffered whether high or low frequency components are filtered, accurate reproduction of saccade amplitude requires a bandwidth of 0 to 130 Hz. If only number of saccades and the duration of intersaccadic intervals are required, a.c. amplification (see Figure 5.3(d)) will suffice provided high frequency response is adequate. To obtain only eye position, i.e. the difference in amplitude between steady-state positions preceding and succeeding a saccade, a bandwidth of 0–10 Hz, may be sufficient. If only saccade velocity and acceleration are of interest, frequency response linear to 130 Hz is necessary.

Since saccadic bandwidth varies non-linearly with amplitude, the degree of signal distortion will not be constant for saccades of different size. The varying degree of amplitude loss can be seen in Figure 5.3. Where, as in a.c. amplification, the relationship between the time constant of the amplifier and saccade duration determine the amount of signal distortion, the time constant should be chosen to accommodate saccade durations over the range produced by the experimental manipulation. Similar caution should be exercised in choosing a centre frequency with the use of auxiliary filters.

3.0 FACTORS AFFECTING THE EOG

Unwanted variability in the EOG arises from three sources: (1) fluctuation in the level of the corneofundal potential; (2) movement of the eyelid; and (3) bioelectric and electronic noise; factors which generally affect the recording of low frequency physiological responses.

3.1 Variation in the corneofundal potential

Change in the amplitude of the corneofundal potential has been assessed by means of an extended calibration procedure (Arden, Barrada, and Kelsey, 1962). The subject is repeatedly required to alternate his gaze between fixed targets. The resultant electrooculogram is a series of rectilinear pulses representing eye rotations of equal visual angle. Under controlled conditions, fluctuations in the height of these pulses should reflect only change in the amplitude of the corneofundal potential. Recent results (Skoog, 1975) indicate that variations in the CFP obtained with the indirect method do follow closely those obtained from direct recordings of the human CFP.

With this indirect method, intra- and interindividual variations in CFP amplitude of 10 μV/deg have been demonstrated (Müller and Haase, 1970). Such variations are associated with age, sex, metabolic factors like blood sugar (Henkes and coworkers, 1968; Kris, 1965) and diurnal variations (Kolder, 1959; Kris, 1957), globe protrusion, and myopia (Alexandridis, Ariely, and Gronau, 1975), and illumination transients. Moreover, CFP amplitude recorded from the two eyes may vary by as much as 19 μV for a rotation of 30° (Shackel and Davis, 1960). Bicas (1972) has demonstrated that interaction of contralateral potential fields could account for this variation.

Most of the variables influencing CFP amplitude are subject characteristics, and their effects can be controlled by appropriate subject selection. The effects of others, like diurnal variation, can be minimized by conducting recording sessions at the same time of day for the same individual (Shackel and Davis, 1960).

The indirect assessment of CFP amplitude may also be used to provide a control measure. For instance, if one wishes to determine how visual information processing is affected by variables, like psychoactive agents, which may alter CFP levels, CFP amplitude can be monitored during the course of testing. One can thus determine whether the agent affected information processing or merely appeared to affect oculomotor parameters through its action on CFP amplitude.

In the next two sections we discuss the effect of illumination transients because of its significance for all applications of the EOG method, and the effects of age and sex, because recent data, in contrast to previous results, suggest their importance.

3.1.1 Illumination transients

The sensitivity of the human corneofundal potential to abrupt changes in illumination is well documented. When the dark-adapted eye is suddenly illuminated, the corneofundal potential undergoes phasic changes within the first 60–80 s (Kris, 1958; Nikara and coworkers, 1976) and at about 1–5 min (ten Doesschate and ten Doesschate, 1956) rises steeply, reaching an apex within approximately 8–10 min (Arden and Kelsey, 1962; Krogh, 1975b). A damped oscillation ensues and stabilization is not complete for 30–90 min (Kolder, 1959; Kolder and Hochgesand, 1973; Kris, 1958), depending on the procedure and the individual. When the light-adapted eye is exposed to darkness, the potential undergoes changes which are analogous but opposite in direction.

The temporal course of the response may deviate widely from the pattern documented for the fully light- or dark-adapted eye, depending on the state of adaptation at which the illumination change is introduced (Arden and Kelsey, 1962; Thaler, Heilig, and Gordesch, 1976) and the periodicity of alternating light and dark intervals (Kolder and Brecher, 1966). The amplitude of the maximal light peak (Müller and coworkers, 1971), but not that of the minimal dark trough (Arden and Barrada, 1962; Kolder, 1959; Müller, Körber, and Körber, 1970), is dependent on the magnitude of the illumination change.

The latency and amplitude of the light- and dark-induced responses, as well as the light peak/dark trough ratio, are widely used measures of retinal and choroidal integrity (François and coworkers, 1974; Hochgesand and Schicketanz, 1976). The light response also provides the basis for electroretinography.

Where the light and dark responses are not of interest, transition from one level of illumination to another may introduce serious problems for calibration. The CFP response to transient illumination may occur so smoothly as to be mistaken for a response to ongoing stimulation. Most commonly, the light response would occur incident to calibration in normal room light before an experiment to be conducted in darkness as, for example, in sleep research or vestibular research requiring eye closure. In this situation, the amplitude of the EOG may decline by 30% within the first 10 minutes of data collection, creating a calibration error of similar magnitude. Errors of 60% may be encountered when the transition is from darkness to normal room light (Gonshor and Malcolm, 1971). A more complex light response may develop where the experimental protocol requires that the subject view stimuli through the darkened aperture of a tachistoscope and relax in normal room light. Successive test and rest intervals of 15 s duration produce continual slow oscillation of the CFP, intervals of 1 min produce continual fast oscillation (Kolder and Brecher, 1966). Whether the eye is exposed to a single change or repeated changes in illumination, calibration errors will not be constant over time and cannot be compensated for in *post hoc* calculations.

Fortunately calibration errors attendant to illumination transients may be averted. A light adaptation period of one and one-half hours is sufficient to preclude even substantial effect of the subject's recent light history and to ensure that all subjects have reached stable baseline responding prior to introduction of the experimental task. Individuals have been found to require from 29–52 min for stabilization of the CFP to within 10% of baseline, when transition is from darkness to room lighting, and from 17–51 min, when transition is from room lighting to darkness (Gonshor and Malcolm, 1971). Red light (Gonshor and Malcolm, 1971; Jacobs and coworkers, 1973) or very slight illumination, 1/10 lux (Krogh, 1975b), may be used to enable the experimenter to calibrate equipment in a darkened room without jeopardizing results.

3.1.2 Age and Sex

Recent studies have revealed a reliable covariation between age and sex and corneofundal potential levels. For a large sample of subjects, Höhne (1974) found the CFP to be significantly higher for women than for men throughout the entire course of dark–light adaptation. Minimum and maximum differences between potential values for men and women were 1.67 μV/deg and 3.33 μV/deg, respectively (authors' estimate). The absolute response range was also shown to be greater for women. Corroborative data are available from Krogh (1976a). Covariation of age and CFP level is also documented. Höhne found that potential levels tended to decline from age 11 to 32 years. Base and dark trough values decreased significantly between ages 18 and 26, for women, and between 17 and 26, for men. Krogh (1976a) found dark trough values declined between ages 10–19 and 30–39. Between ages 40–81 the dark trough values increased.

Table 5.1. Median light peak/dark trough ratios by sex and age group

		Under 50 years	Over 50 years
Females	Adams (1973)[a]	2.48 (40)[b]	2.08 (20)
	Krogh (1976b)	2.50 (18)	2.00 (18)
	Reeser and coworkers (1970)[a]	2.59 (31)	2.25 (9)
Males	Adams (1973)	2.10 (40)	2.10 (20)
	Krogh (1976b)	2.60 (20)	2.50 (16)
	Reeser and coworkers (1970)	2.24 (10)	— —

[a]Medians were calculated from individual values provided in publications.
[b]The number of subjects is in parentheses.

An interactive influence of age and sex on the magnitude of the light peak/dark trough ratio emerges from comparison of three studies utilizing large samples of subjects (Adams, 1973; Krogh, 1975a, 1976a, 1976b; Reeser and coworkers, 1970) (see Table 5.1). For males, the ratio remains relatively stable from age 10–60 years; for females, the ratio remains stable from 10–49 years, but declines sharply after 50. Adams (1973), whose sample was the only one in which males and females were equally represented at each age interval, found that up to age 50, values for women were higher than for men, but between ages 50 and 70 years, values for women linearly approached those for men. The effect is not an artifact of statistical averaging: women over 50 have been found to form a distinct group whether data compared are from the 10th, the 50th or the 90th percentile scores (Krogh, 1976b).

Generally, those who have found no effect of sex have used small samples (Davis and Shackel, 1960) or a distribution of age by sex which was unclear or unreported (Fenn and Hursh, 1937). Investigators reporting an insignificant, or only a slight, age effect have used a restricted age range (Shackel, 1960, and Shackel and Davis, 1960, taken as one longitudinal study), or have not separated out the effects of sex (Arden and Barrada, 1962; Reeser and coworkers, 1970).

3.2 Eyelid movement

The upper eyelid alters the contours of the potential field external to the eyeball by acting as a sliding resistance. Extension of the lid enhances conductivity between dipole and electrodes. In monopolar recording with the active electrode placed above the eye, downward movement of the lid over the positively charged cornea is associated with increasing positivity and retraction of the lid is associated with increasing negativity (Matsuo, Peters, and Reilly, 1975). Further, the magnitude of both horizontal and vertical recordings is greater with the eyes closed than with the eyes open (Cohn, 1957; Miles, 1939a; van Weerden, 1973). (This enhancement of the EOG level would be counteracted by a dark-induced fall in the CFP after an extended period of eyelid closure).

Cumulative evidence demonstrates that the movement of the upper eyelid relative to the eyeball is the source of the rider artifact. The rider artifact occurs when, with an upward shift of the gaze, the EOG potential continues to rise above the level established by the succeeding steady-state potential. The artifact resembles an overshoot with variable recovery time (Ford, 1959). The artifact appears only in vertical recordings, i.e. only when the distance of the upper eyelid from the electrode(s) is variable. When the eyelid is stationary, as when the eye is closed, no rider artifact is observed (Huddleston, 1970). Comparisons between synchronous EOG recordings and photographic recordings of eye and eyelid movements have shown that the rider artifact appears only when the upper lid is displaced relative to the eyeball. The lower lid follows quite closely the movement of the eyeball with little or no lag (Barry and Melvill Jones, 1965): thus, in monopolar recordings with the active electrode placed below the eye, the rider artifact observed in bipolar recordings is greatly diminished (Ford, 1959).

Matsuo, Peters, and Reilly (1975) have shown convincingly that eyelid closure during the blink contributes to the shape and to the exaggerated amplitude of the blink recorded electrooculographically. When the eyelid is immobile due to facial paralysis, the amplitude of the deflection recorded during the attempted blink is reduced by about 2/3 compared to that observed for the control eye. When the eyelid is free to move over a prosthetic eye, there is a slight upward and downward drift in the EOG trace, but no characteristic blink transient. Thus, the blink waveform is attributable to the moving eyelid's variable enhancement of the corneofundal potential.

3.3 Electrical noise

3.3.1 Bioelectric events

Muscle activity (EMG), skin potential responses, skin conductance changes, and cortical activity (EEG) can interfere with EOG recording because the frequencies at which they occur overlap signal frequencies. Since the amplitude and phase of these bioelectric events recorded at each of a pair of orthogonal electrodes is generally not the same, high common mode rejection aids little in their attenuation. EMG, EEG, and skin potential changes will be algebraically added to the EOG signal; the effects of skin conductance changes on the recorded EOG are complex and less

L

predictable. Fortunately, the effects of all these responses can be attenuated. Only intense EMG activity, for example, that arising from hard swallowing, teeth clenching, or pressure of the jaw on a chin rest, will contaminate EOG records if electrode loci are carefully chosen. Moreover, most of the recorded EMG activity occurs at frequencies which are high relative to those at which appreciable EOG activity occurs and can be effectively rejected by low-pass filtering. Skin conductance changes and the slow components of skin potential responses pose a more serious problem. As the effects of these events cannot be eliminated from EOG records, their attenuation through careful skin preparation is the more critical. The presence of EEG in horizontal eye movement recordings has been reported by Shackel (1967), and several earlier reports were reviewed by Armington and Chapman (1959). To date, noise clearly attributable to cortical rhythmic activity has not presented a serious problem for data analysis in this laboratory.

3.3.2 Instrumentation

High amplifier input impedance together with the ionic stability afforded by Ag–AgCl electrodes has largely eliminated polarization effects as serious obstacles to accurate d.c. recording. Large d.c. potentials up to 50 mV, can, however, develop across a pair of Ag–AgCl electrodes, in the absence of the bioelectric event or any imposition of current. The potential is due to differences in the properties of the two electrode surfaces with respect to the electrolyte. In d.c. recording this offset shifts the baseline, and the phasic signal 'rides on' the offset. If the potential is large and limited possibilities for compensation exist, difficulty in maintaining baseline within tape recorder (or pen) range and, therefore, difficulty in response recording are encountered.

Tests for bias potential should, therefore, be routinely carried out before and after recording sessions. In physical tests, electrode faces are filled with conductive paste and held firmly together while the potential difference is measured with a high impedance d.c. voltmeter. The measured differences should not exceed 2 mV. In physiological tests, electrodes are affixed to the subject and electrode leads fed into a differential preamplifier with high common mode rejection. The subject is requested to fix his gaze on a centrally located point. The measured voltage in this situation will reflect EOG and other biopotentials, in addition to d.c. offset, but with adequate electrode contact and appropriate electrode placement, it should not exceed a few millivolts.

In practice, some d.c. offset between a pair of electrodes must be tolerated, but its magnitude can be reduced by immersion of the electrode pair in physiological saline with leads shorted. Monotonic decrease in d.c.

potential has been observed for Beckman (9 mm diameter) type Ag–AgCl electrodes with a median stabilization value of 0.6 mV after 20 min in saline (Krogh, 1975a).

In d.c. recording, gradual drift of the baseline, whether attributable to changing amplitude of the CFP or to electrode contact potentials, confounds determination of response amplitude: increase (or decrease) in the baseline due to a response must be distinguished from that due to drift alone. During the execution of a saccade, some finite drift occurs altering the baseline level. The true amplitude of the saccade can be determined only if the angle of drift can be calculated, and, in practice, this is feasible only if the recording period is short or the drift rate is constant. Currently our programs do not calculate baseline drift. Measured intersaccadic drift amplitude reflects both baseline drift and drift arising from eye movements.

4.0 SIGNAL MANIPULATION AND DATA REDUCTION

4.1 Identification and elimination of noise

4.1.1 Discriminating wanted from unwanted signals

Since, as noted in the discussion above, higher frequencies contribute progressively less energy to the saccadic waveform, spectral analysis, yielding a plot of energy by frequency, is useful for identification of noise at these frequencies. For example, energy at 50 Hz has been found to represent approximately 10% of saccade amplitude (e.g. Zuber, Semmlow, and Stark, 1968). Therefore, if in the power spectrum energy at 50 Hz represents 33% of total energy, noise is present at that frequency. Before submission to spectral analysis, the analogue record should be devoid of d.c. offset. If the appropriate programming is not available, offset can be eliminated by high pass filtering at 1 Hz. In addition, the analogue record should not contain frequencies equal to or greater than 0.5 times the sampling rate to be used in analogue to digital (AD) conversion. The value 0.5 times the sampling rate is the Nyquist criterion (folding frequency), f_n = $1/(2\Delta t)$, where Δt is the sampling period. Failure to exclude frequencies at or above the folding frequency will result in aliasing energy at frequencies higher than f_n onto energy at frequencies lower than f_n (see Blackman and Tukey, 1959; Walter, 1963). For example, if a record containing activity up to 80 Hz is sampled at the rate of 100/s, activity at frequencies equidistant from 50 Hz would be confounded. For the same record, a sampling rate of 200/s would be adequate. If the sampling rate cannot be adjusted to a suitably high value, the record should be low-pass

294 *Techniques in Psychophysiology*

filtered before AD conversion to remove frequencies at or above 0.5 times the sampling rate. We generally use a conservative low-pass criterion of 0.4 times the sampling rate. Since noise present in one section of a data record is not necessarily predictive of noise present in a later section, power spectra should be obtained for data samples dispersed throughout the record.

This simple application of spectral analysis is not useful for identifying noise in the range 0–30 Hz, where noise and signal energies overlap; isolation of low frequency noise is best accomplished visually with an oscilloscope display of the data. Noise present during intersaccadic fixation pauses may be distinguished from signal on the basis of periodicity and amplitude. Periodic or nearly periodic noise of mechanical origin and bursts of EMG activity can be discerned amidst the irregular and much slower undulations characteristic of drift. Early components of complex skin potential responses are much faster and generally larger than drift, and their rounded waveform is not easily confused with the spike-like appearance of small saccades. Rough assessment of noise characteristics can be obtained by selecting sample points from a static oscilloscope display of the digitized signal and measuring the amplitude and frequency defined by these points. Assessment can be facilitated by selective bandpass filtering before digitization.

These procedures for the identification of low and high frequency components of noise in EOG recordings are adequate for most experimental purposes. Programming, superior to that described above, would enable one to submit selected segments of the EOG record, i.e. only intersaccadic activity or only saccades, to frequency analyses. Such capability would allow a more refined analysis of noise components and of the components contributing to saccade amplitude.

4.1.2 Filtering

Low-pass filtering is used to eliminate high frequency components of noise (unless the noise is band-limited in which case band-reject filtering is used). An example of the kind of saccadic waveform distortion which may result from the attenuation of high frequency components was given in Section 2.5. For that example we chose cut-off frequencies sufficiently low to render the rounding of the saccade–fixation juncture visible; at higher cut-off frequencies, rounding, though sufficient to alter results, is often barely perceptible. Similarly, phase shift may alter the temporal relationship between saccade initiation and extraneous events in the absence of exaggerated waveform distortion. As mentioned earlier the magnitude of these effects will vary with saccade amplitude.

For these reasons, and especially when computerized data reduction is undertaken, some measure of the distortion injected by filtering should enter into the determination of an appropriate low pass criterion. The measure of signal distortion chosen and the degree of distortion (and therefore the extent of high frequency attenuation) deemed acceptable will vary with the experimental purpose. If one is interested in the temporal characteristics of saccades, rounding constitutes a serious problem. Saccade duration and amplitude (as defined in Section 4.2.2.2) can provide simple and sufficiently sensitive indices of this aspect of high frequency attenuation. In other applications, appreciable rounding may be tolerated and a lower low-pass criterion may be advantageous. For example, if eye position only is desired, the removal of irregularities in the saccadic waveform will facilitate reliable measurement of the critical datum: the difference in amplitude between successive steady-state positions. If one is concerned, however, with measuring saccadic reaction time, evaluation of phase shift may be warranted. Whatever the measure of distortion, when data are to be computer analysed, its sensitivity is limited by the sampling rate. For example, when analogue data are sampled at the rate of 100/s, the smallest detectable reduction in saccade duration is 10 ms.

To determine the low-pass criterion which will achieve the desired signal to noise ratio without introducing unacceptable distortion, we use the following procedure. An unfiltered clean data sample is submitted to the program used to measure distortion. The output for this unfiltered run serves as the standard against which to compare output for the same data filtered at successively lower low-pass criteria. This step determines the lowest criterion which does not result in distortion. To determine the cut-off frequency at which a satisfactory signal to noise ratio is achieved, the same procedure is repeated for data from which noise is to be eliminated.

Noise at frequencies within the range 0–30 Hz cannot be eliminated with the use of auxiliary filters. More elaborate methods like digital subtractive filtering may be effective if the noise can be recorded independently of the signal. A replica of the noise is gain adjusted to match that found in the data channel and subtracted from the signal. Unless the low frequency noise constitutes a serious problem, the investment in processing time, however, may not be warranted. The extent to which low frequency noise complicates computer analysis of saccadic eye movement depends on how closely the rise time and amplitude of the noise approximates the corresponding criteria in the saccade identification routine. Visual monitoring during data reduction is used to determine whether 'noise' is erroneously recognized as saccadic movement and to exclude from data analysis sections of data contaminated by such noise.

We have limited discussion to filtering of saccadic eye movement. Similar considerations appropriate to bandpass filtering of the nystagmus waveform are treated by Ktonas, Black, and Smith (1975). They describe detailed methods for quantifying distortion introduced by bandpass filtering.

4.2 Computer analysis

It becomes evident that the recording of EOGs is a relatively simple and inexpensive procedure with currently available amplification and recording equipment. The reduction of such data in meaningful ways is very much dependent on the application of computer technology because of the vast quantity of data accumulated in a short time. For example, in the analysis of eye movements during reading there are often 250 saccades and associated fixation pauses for 1 minute of data collection. We have developed a system, utilizing a small general purpose computer (PDP-11/40) for taking some of the tedium out of the data reduction process.

4.2.1 Hardware

The basic system includes an amplifier–attenuator with d.c. offset manipulation, analogue to digital (AD) convertors, and a PDP-11/40 laboratory computer system.

The amplifier–attenuator enables gain and baseline adjustments preparatory to computerized data reduction. The adjustment of gain is necessary to compensate for the limited manipulability of the saccade amplitude criterion. Since the criterion can be adjusted only in discrete steps of 16 mV, there may be no criterion which, for a given record, ensures detection of the smallest saccade and also prevents identification of noise as saccades. This may be particularly true for records of vertical eye movement, since gain on the vertical channel must be reduced at the power amplifier stage to ensure blink amplitude compatible with instrumentation recorder requirements. An amplifier–attenuator with multipliers selectable in steps of 0.1 from 0.1 to 9.9 is therefore used to enable adjustment of gain over a nearly continuous set of values. Baseline adjustment is provided to compensate for d.c. offset which would otherwise restrict the extent to which the signal could be amplified without creating overflow, i.e. voltage exceeding the ± 2 V range acceptable to the AD convertor.

The extent to which gain can be manipulated in this manner is limited by the signal to noise (S/N) ratio. Not only noise arising from extraneous sources affects the S/N ratio. As is true of any psychophysiological variable, the amplitude of the CFP, and therefore the S/N ratio, varies over individuals. Therefore, the appropriate adjustments of gain must be determined for each record.

Oscilloscopic display of the digitized signal is an integral part of data reduction in this laboratory. Simultaneous display of data from two to four AD channels facilitates identification of synchronous events and makes possible the type of subtractive filtering alluded to in Section 4.1.2. Continuous monitoring of the visual display ensures quality control of the data submitted to computer analysis. The visual monitoring has its rewards; several noteworthy, recurrent eye fixation sequences have been discovered during the repetitive monitoring.

4.2.2 Software

4.2.2.1 Sampling rate

Sampling rate in saccade identification programs is dictated by the measurement error deemed acceptable for a given experimental purpose. For example, error of ±10 ms, and, therefore, a sampling rate of 100/s, is adequate for measuring fixation duration, the mean value of which generally varies between 190–300 ms. For most applications, including the study of reading and pattern discrimination, a sampling rate of 100/s is sufficient. Other applications, like comparing the latency of left and right eye movements, requires rounding error no greater than ±1 ms and hence a sampling rate of 1000/s. While sampling rates up to 1000/s are easily incorporated into software, their use does not necessarily indicate superior data handling. One may simply create more data than are necessary or than can be economically treated. When a program is to be used for many purposes, we incorporate into that program means for user selection of sampling rate.

4.2.2.2 Saccade identification program

Criteria. The saccade identification routine is comprised of three stages: the first identifies saccade initiation, the second saccade termination, and the third compares the voltage delimited by these points to a saccade amplitude criterion. The saccade identification criteria included in these three stages are values for the amplitude and duration of a saccade as well as requirements for its directional consistency. The saccade amplitude criterion can be selected in steps of 16 mV over the range 16 mV to 128 mV.

To identify saccade initiation the routine requires essentially 30 ms of monotonic function. For four consecutive 10 ms samples, the routine calculates the absolute difference in amplitude between successive samples and stores these values with their associated signs. If at least two of the three values are greater than 1/4 the saccade amplitude criterion and have the same sign (the third value must be zero or have the same sign), saccade initiation is tentatively identified. For example, given a saccade amplitude criterion of 32 mV, initiation of a left-going saccade would be identified if two values were −8.00 mV and the third was −1.0 mV.

To identify the termination of a left-going (negative sign) saccade, the program requires essentially 30 ms of no change in amplitude or 30 ms of monotonically increasing function within 200 ms of saccade initiation. The program simply continues to calculate the difference in amplitude between successive 10 ms samples until it finds, within a 30 ms period, two zero values or two values with positive sign. If the saccade termination criteria are not met within 200 ms, the program begins searching for saccade initiation.

If termination criteria are met, the routine compares the voltage delimited by the first data point contributing to saccade initiation and the first point contributing to saccade termination to the saccade amplitude criterion, 32 mV in our example. If the voltage is equal to or greater than 32 mV, saccade parameters are stored for printout. If the saccade amplitude criterion is not met, no saccade is identified and the program again searches for saccade initiation. The same procedure, with signs reversed, would identify a right-going saccade.

Output. The output of all saccade identification programs provides, in real time from onset of processing, a record of successive saccades and intersaccadic fixation pauses. This running account of saccadic eye motion includes the duration of each fixation, the amount of drift occurring during each fixation, and the duration, peak velocity, amplitude, and direction of each saccade. Fixation duration is the time between termination of one and initiation of the next saccade. Drift is calculated as the difference in amplitude between the first and last points contributing to fixation. Peak velocity is the largest millivolt change occurring in 10 ms during a saccadic movement.

Also appearing on the real time printout are symbols marking the occurrence of questionable saccades (voltage deflections greater than 3/4 but less than the saccade amplitude criterion), overflow (voltage levels exceeding the ±2 V limits of the AD convertor), and amplifier baseline resets (voltage deflections attributable to resets on the basis of their peak velocity). Change of the saccade amplitude criterion and interruption of data processing initiated by the operator are similarly denoted. The tag indicating the occurrence of small, questionable saccades facilitates selection of an appropriate saccade amplitude criterion; other tags provide a log of extraneous events and processing procedures and also identify data that will be excluded from the summary printout.

Frequency distributions of the primary data are provided in a summary printout. In addition, fixation pauses are classified according to the type of saccades which precede and succeed them. For example, fixation pauses occurring between two right-going saccades, R–R pauses, are distinguished from pauses preceded by a right-going and followed by a left-going (regressive) saccade, R–L pauses. Frequency distributions of fixation duration and saccade amplitude are printed for each pause type.

4.2.2.3 Derivative programs

The saccade identification program is the basis for a series of special purpose programs some of which will be described in this section.

Programs devoted to the analysis of eye movements recorded during reading identify line changes, i.e. the return of the eyes from the end of one line to the beginning of the next. A line change, as defined in these programs, is simply a left-going saccade which exceeds the line change amplitude criterion. This criterion, like the saccade amplitude criterion, may be adjusted by the user. The output of reading programs provides, in addition to the information available from the basic saccade routine, the time that was required to read each line and the parameters of line change saccades. Summary data include the number of right-going and regressive saccades per line. The several reading analysis programs provide options like: sampling at 1000/s, categorization of line change types, and keyboard input useful for identification of the temporal relationship between extraneous events and eye movements.

The nystagmus program searches for saccadic breaks in sinusoidal pursuit movements elicited by pendular motion. Two channels of data are processed concurrently: horizontal eye movements and a stimulus time marker, indicating in real time the period of pendular oscillation. Simultaneous oscilloscopic display of these data allows one to observe, as well as measure, alterations in eye movement with respect to the period of pendular motion.

In a program designed to analyse data collected during tachistoscopic viewing, saccade detection is initiated by a triggering signal time-locked to stimulus onset and is automatically terminated after a set period. Automated initiation and termination of data processing ensures that the saccade detection routine operates only for the brief period during which the stimulus was exposed. In other applications of the same program, the user may terminate the saccade search process.

In the version of this program used to evaluate saccade reaction time, the offset of a signal tone triggers search for saccade initiation. This version may be used to present visual stimuli in specified relationship to saccadic reaction time and is currently being used to investigate saccadic suppression, i.e. degradation of visual information processing before, during, and immediately after a saccade.

The eyeblink program computes temporal characteristics of the blink.

One such characteristic, closure duration, is defined as follows. The program calculates the amplitude of the blink (initiation to peak) and identifies the point of maximal closure. It generates a window around this point and identifies the times at which the blink enters and leaves the window. In our current program the amplitude of the window is proportional to blink amplitude.

5.0 APPLICATIONS

5.1 Reading

Since our purpose in collecting eye movement data is to learn how the reader processes information, our concern is with the 'processor' which determines where the eyes move rather than with eye movements *per se*. From analyses of sequential eye fixations we have been able to draw inferences concerning the kinds of strategies readers adopt and the circumstances which elicit changing strategy.

We have, for example, demonstrated that the strategies used by competent readers differ widely from those used by less competent readers. In Goltz (1975) the 20 best and poorest readers, identified from a sample of 100 students by their performance on the Nelson–Denny reading test, were asked to read a historical text under two instructional sets. The first required the reader to abstract general information and the second to abstract details.

For both groups, the shift from general to detailed information abstraction (regardless of order) was associated with a change in strategy. Contrasts between the right-going eye movements of good and poor readers, however, showed their strategies to be quite different. In addition to fixation pause duration, we analysed saccade amplitude to determine whether the size of the informational chunk, portion of a line abstracted per fixation pause, changed with task demands. We found that good readers were able to assimilate detailed information by increasing slightly the amount of time spent during each fixation pause; they did not reduce the size of the line segment abstracted during each pause. Poor readers, on the other hand, spent the same amount of time per fixation pause whether reading for general or for detailed information. Their changing strategy involved reducing the size of the informational chunk taken in during each fixation pause.

Another question asked in this research concerned the conditions associated with the making of regressive (left-going) eye movements. We were again interested in differences as a function of depth of information abstraction and reading ability. To evaluate the conditions which lead to abortion of information abstraction and the initiation of a regressive eye movement, we examined two types of fixation pauses. We looked at the pause preceding the regression (R–L), i.e. the pause during which the decision to abort information processing and return to an earlier portion of a line is made, as well as the R–R pause preceding this R–L pause. For the skilled reader this R–R pause is significantly longer than other within-line R–R pauses, while the amplitude of the first R saccade of the set does not discriminate it from other R saccades. For the less competent reader, the duration of the same R–R fixation does not differ from other within-line R–R pauses, but the amplitude of the first R is significantly greater than other right-going saccades (when reading for details).

These data suggest that the competent reader's regression is triggered by the need to compare information currently being processed with information appearing earlier in the text. The 'poor' reader is more likely to regress when he has attempted to process too large an informational chunk.

5.2 Psychopharmacology

Which aspects of eye movement are affected by psychotropic agents? Gentles and Llewellyn Thomas (1971) reported changes in the speed of saccadic eye movements attributable to the ingestion of benzodiazepines. We have evaluated the effect of both Valium (diazepam) and low doses of alcohol (blood level 35 mg%) on saccade velocity. The effect of Valium was studied in young men taking the drug for one week (Stern, Bremer, and McClure, 1974). Using a reading task and restricting the data analysis to saccades associated with line changes, we found that Valium significantly reduced the peak velocity and duration of such saccades while the placebo had no effect on these measures. Interestingly, self-report, psychiatric judgment, and psychological test measures considered sensitive to the effect of such medication, did not discriminate between subjects on active medication and those on placebo. Eye movement data not only provided a reliable measure of drug effects but also proved useful in discriminating between pre and post drug states.

Does Valium, in clinically effective dosage levels, produce decrements in reading performance? In general, the reader under the influence of Valium uses the same patterns and timing of saccades and fixations as he used before ingesting the drug. The drug, therefore, appears to produce no changes in information processing strategies. Valium does, however, slow down the reading process. A greater incidence of unusually long fixations (those exceeding 400 ms) accounts for most of the additional time to read a line. Though our Valium treated subjects did not report drowsiness as a side effect of medication more frequently than did placebo treated subjects, the increased incidence of long fixations suggests attentional decrements attributable to drug effects. Concomitant variation in a second index of drowsiness, blink closure duration (defined above, Section 4.2.2.3), provides support for this notion. We found that both average closure duration and the incidence of closure durations exceeding 70 ms were significantly increased with Valium use (Beideman and Stern, 1977).

We have found similar effects of alcohol on blink closure duration, with alcohol levels of 75 mg% (Beideman and Stern, 1977) and of 35 mg% (Sanders and coworkers, 1976). In the first study blinks were recorded during simulated driving and in the second during reading. The effect of alcohol on blink closure is thus probably not task specific.

5.3 Eye movement patterns in schizophrenia

As early as 1908, Diefendorf and Dodge reported impaired pursuit movement in chronically ill schizophrenic patients. These results have been sporadically re-investigated with much of the impetus for current research emanating from the laboratory of P. Holzman (Holzman and Levy, 1977; Holzman, Proctor, and Hughes, 1973). Patients are typically requested to track a pendulum oscillating at about 0.4 Hz, and the 'smoothness' of their tracking performance is evaluated. 'Velocity arrests', most of which involve saccadic eye movements, are found significantly more often in schizophrenic patients than those suffering from depression or other psychiatric disturbances. Shagass, Amadeo, and Overton (1974) and Shagass, Roemer, and Amadeo (1976) have reported that the phenomenon is not specific to schizophrenia but may be observed incidentally to any psychopathology. Holzman agrees that psychiatrically ill patients, in general, demonstrate more eye track abnormalities than normal subjects, but contends that the disturbance is most marked in patients suffering from thought disorders (schizophrenia) as diagnosed with the help of psychological tests.

Brockway (1975) used the EOG to investigate how schizophrenics' performance in a cognitive task differed from that of normals. The task involved searching a set of four pictures to identify the one which deviated from the general concept depicted by the other three. The fixation rate (number of fixations/unit time) of schizophrenics was found to be significantly greater than that of controls whether data were obtained during the primary picture search task or during attempted steady fixation of a point. Fixation rate, calculated for the period prior to response, discriminated between the performance of patient and control groups, whether subsequent response was correct or incorrect. Detailed analysis of the responses to one picture set (chosen because accuracy of judgment was comparable for schizophrenic and control groups), revealed that both schizophrenics and normals who solved the problem spent more time on the deviant (correct) picture. Normals, however, distributed their time roughly equally over the other three pictures, while the schizophrenic group spent a disproportionate amount of time viewing one picture of a graveyard scene, and very little time viewing a picture depicting the crowning of a beauty queen. These data are generally compatible with previous findings (Llewellyn Thomas, 1968; Moriya and coworkers, 1972; Stern, 1968).

5.4 Conjugate lateral eye movements

A number of researchers have been actively studying the phenomenon of conjugate, lateral eye movements associated with cognitive activity. Day (1964), Duke (1968), and Bakan (1969), have referred to such eye movements as CLEMs. Whether the eyes move in a truly conjugate fashion is unclear; that they move involuntarily during thinking is readily confirmed by observing the eye movements elicited when a person is asked to solve a mental arithmetic problem. Some persons show gaze deviation to the left, others to the right. The direction of such gaze deviation is purported to index which cerebral hemisphere is more strongly engaged in solving the problem. Left-movers (right-hemisphere processors) are more likely to use visualization techniques to solve the problem, while right-movers tend to solve the problem abstractly. Considerable debate has arisen over whether development of disproportionate activity in one hemisphere is task dependent (Kinsbourne, 1972) or subject dependent (Bakan, 1969). The issue is not yet settled, though one experiment by Gur, Gur and Harris (1975) suggests that the conditions of testing may determine the relative influence of task and subject. In face-to-face questioning, subjects respond in an idiosyncratic manner; regardless of question type, the person demonstrates CLEMs in a preferred direction. When observations are made more surreptitiously, the direction of CLEMs is determined by question type; questions which are best solved visually generate left-going, and those which are best solved conceptually, right-going eye movements. Using EOG procedures, which eliminate the need for the investigator to face the subject, we still find that data are more compatible with the notion of subject rather than task determined CLEM direction.

5.5 Blinks

Though eyeblinks appearing in the record of vertical eye movements are often treated as artifact, we have become increasingly impressed with their signal value. Earlier, we described eyeblink closure duration as an index of psychoactive drug effects. We have also observed that 'reflex' blinks do not occur at random, but rather at psychologically appropriate moments. For example, while reading an interesting novel, the intrigued reader may not blink at all for an entire page, generate a series of blinks as he turns a page, and then return to reading uninterrupted by blinks. Competent reading is associated with blinking at appropriate places, like the beginning or end of a line or end of a paragraph or sentence. Not only do we blink at appropriate moments, but other activity like swallowing also occurs at non-random moments and is generally coincident with the eyeblink.

6.0 SUMMARY

Use of electrooculography can enhance psychophysiological approaches to the study of perception and cognition. As we have demonstrated in the section on applications, a variety of theoretical and practical problems can be investigated with these procedures. The particular research areas reviewed do not constitute an exhaustive list but are rather illustrative of those currently being investigated in a number of laboratories.

REFERENCES

Adams, A. (1973). The normal electro-oculogram (EOG). *Acta Ophthal.*, **51**, 551–61.
Alexandridis, E., Ariely, E., and Gronau, G. (1975). Einfluss der Bulbuslage und der Bulbuslänge auf das EOG. *Albrecht von Graefes Arch. klin. und exp. Ophthal.*, **194**, 237–41.
Alpern, M. (1972). Eye movements. In D. Jameson and L. M. Hurvich (Eds), *Handbook of Sensory Physiology: Visual Psychophysics* (Vol. 7, Pt. 4) Springer-Verlag, Berlin. pp. 303–30.
Arden, G. B., and Barrada, A. (1962). Analysis of the electro-oculograms of a series of normal subjects. Role of the lens in the development of the standing potential. *Br. J. Ophthal.*, **46**, 468–82.
Arden, G. B., Barrada, A., and Kelsey, J. H. (1962). New clinical test of the retinal function based upon the standing potential of the eye. *Br. J. Ophthal.*, **46**, 449–67.
Arden, G. B., and Ikeda, H. (1966). Effects of hereditary degeneration of the retina on the early receptor potential and the corneo-fundal potential of the rat eye. *Vision Res.*, **6**, 171–84.
Arden, G. B., and Kelsey, J. H. (1962). Some observations on the relationship between the standing potential of the human eye and the bleaching and regeneration of visual purple. *J. Physiol.*, **161**, 205–26.
Armington, J. C., and Chapman, R. M. (1959). Temporal potentials and eye movements. *Electroenceph. Clin. Neurophysiol.*, **11**, 346–8.
Bach-y-Rita, P., Collins, C. C., and Hyde, J. E. (1971). *The Control of Eye Movements*. Academic Press, New York.
Bakan, P. (1969). Hypnotizability, laterality of eye-movements and functional brain asymmetry. *Percept. Mot. Skills*, **28**, 927–32.
Barry, W., and Melvill Jones, G. (1965). Influence of eyelid movement upon

electrooculographic recording of vertical eye movements. *Aerospace Med.*, **36**, 855–8.

Bartz, A. E. (1962). Eye movement latency, duration and response time as a function of angular displacement. *J. of Exp. Psychol.*, **64**, 318–24.

Beideman, L. R., and Stern, J. A. (1977). Aspects of the eyeblink during simulated driving as a function of alcohol. *Hum. Factors*, **19**, 73–7.

Bicas, H. E. A. (1972). Electro-oculography in the investigation of oculomotor imbalance. I. Basic aspects. *Vision Res.*, **12**, 993–1010.

Blackman, R. B., and Tukey, J. W. (1959). *The Measurement of Power Spectra*. Dover Publications, Inc., New York.

Bles, W., and Kapteyn, T. S. (1973). Separate recording of the movements of the human eyes during parallel swing tests. *Acta Oto-Laryng.*, **75**, 6–9.

Bois-Reymond, E. du (1849). *Untersuchungen über tierische Elektrizität.* (Vol. 2, Pt. 1). G. Reimer, Berlin. pp. 256–7.

Brockway, L. F. (1975). Attentional disturbance and thought disorder in schizophrenia as measured by eye movements and conceptual performance. *Doctoral dissertation*, Washington University, Saint Louis, Missouri.

Carlow, T., Dell'Osso, L. F., Troost, B. T., Daroff, R. B., and Birkett, J. E. (1975). Saccadic eye movement latencies to multimodal stimuli. Intersubject variability and temporal efficiency. *Vision Res.*, **15**, 1257–62.

Carmichael, L., and Dearborn, W. F. (1947). *Reading and Visual Fatigue*. Houghton Mifflin Co., Boston.

Cohn, R. (1957). Direct current recordings of eyeball movements in neurologic practice. *Neurology*, **7**, 684–8.

Collins, C. C. (1975). The human oculomotor control system. In G. Lennerstrand and P. Bach-y-Rita (Eds), *Basic Mechanisms of Ocular Motility and their Clinical Implications. Proceedings of the International Symposium, Wenner-Gren Center, Stockholm, 1974.* Pergamon Press, Oxford. pp. 145–80.

Davis, J. R., and Shackel, B. (1960). Changes in the electro-oculogram potential level. *Br. J. Ophthal.*, **44**, 606–18.

Davson, H. (1969). *The Eye; Muscular Mechanisms* (Vol. 3, 2nd edn.). Academic Press, New York.

Day, M. E. (1964). An eye movement phenomenon relating to attention, thought and anxiety. *Percept. Mot. Skills*, **19**, 443–6.

Dewar, J., and M'Kendrick, J. G. (1874). On the physiological action of light. *Trans. Roy. Soc. Edin.*, **27**, 141–66.

Diefendorf, A. R., and Dodge, R. (1908). An experimental study of the ocular reactions of the insane from photographic records. *Brain*, **31**, 451–89.

Ditchburn, R. W. (1973). *Eye Movements and Visual Perception.* Clarendon Press, Oxford.

Duke, J. D. (1968). Lateral eye movement behavior. *J. Gen. Psychol.*, **78**, 189–95.

Fenn, W. O., and Hursch, J. B. (1937). Movements of the eyes when the lids are closed. *Am. J. Physiol.*, **118**, 8–14.

Findlay, J. M. (1971). Frequency analysis of human involuntary eye movement. *Kybernetik*, **8**, 207–14.

Ford, A. (1959). Significance of terminal transients in electro-oculographic recordings. *Am. Med. Assoc. Arch. Ophthal.*, **61**, 899–906.

François, J., de Rouck, A., Verriest, G., de Laey, J. J., and Cambie, E. (1974). Progressive generalized cone dysfunction. *Ophthalmologica*, **169**, 255–84.

François, J., Verriest, G., and de Rouck, A. (1955). Modification of·the amplitude of the human electro-oculogram by light and dark adaptation. *Br. J. Ophthal.*, **39**, 398–408.

François, J., Verriest, G., and de Rouck, A. (1957). L'électro-oculographie en tant qu'examen fonctionnel de la rétine. *Fortschr. Augenheilk.*, **7**, 1–67.

Fuchs, A. F. (1971). The saccadic system. In P. Bach-y-Rita, C. C. Collins, and J. E. Hyde (Eds), *The Control of Eye Movements*. Academic Press, New York. pp. 343–62.

Geddes, L. A., and Baker, L. E. (1975). *Principles of Applied Biomedical Instrumentation*, 2nd edn., John Wiley & Sons, New York.

Gentles, W., and Llewellyn Thomas, E. (1971). Commentary: Effect of benzodiazepines upon saccadic eye movements in man. *Clin. Pharmacol. Therapeutics, St. Louis*, **12**, 563–74.

Goltz, T. H. (1975). Comparison of eye movements of skilled and less skilled readers. *Doctoral dissertation*, Washington University, Saint Louis, Missouri.

Gonshor, A., and Malcolm, R. (1971). Effect of changes in illumination level on electrooculography (EOG). *Aerospace Med.*, **42**, 138–40.

Gur, R. E., Gur, R. C., and Harris, L. J. (1975). Cerebral activation, as measured by subjects' lateral eye movements, is influenced by experimenter location. *Neuropsychologia*, **13**, 35–44.

Henkes, H. E., van Lith, G. H. M., Gaisiner, P. D., and de Haas, J. P. (1968). Electrodiagnostic procedures in diabetes. In J. François (Ed) *The Clinical Value of Electroretinography, International Society for Clinical Electroretinography (ISCERG) Symposium, Ghent, Belgium (1966).* S. Karger, Basel, Switzerland. pp. 393–402.

Hochgesand, P., and Schicketanz, H. K. (1976). The usefulness of the electro-oculogram as clinical test. *Bibliotheca Ophthal.*, **85**, 94–8.

Höhne, W. (1972). Zum Bestandpotential der pigmentepithelfreien Froschnetzhaut. Einfluss von Kalium und Natrium. *Acta Biol. Med. Germ.*, **28**, 813–21.

Höhne, W. (1974). Zur Auswertung des Elektrookulogramms. *Albrecht von Graefes Arch. klin. exp. Ophthal.*, **192**, 36–47.

Holzman, P. S., and Levy, D. L. (1977). Smooth pursuit eye movements and functional psychoses: A review. *Schizophrenia Bull.*, **3**, 15–27.

Holzman, P. S., Proctor, L. R., and Hughes, D. W. (1973). Eye-tracking patterns in schizophrenia. *Science*, **181**, 179–81.

Huddleston, H. F. (1970). Electronystagmographic studies of small vertical fixation movements. *Br. J. Ophthal.*, **54**, 37–40.

Hyde, J. E. (1959). Some characteristics of voluntary human ocular movements in the horizontal plane. *Am. J. Ophthal.*, **48**, 85–94.

Jacobs, L., Feldman, M., Rabinowitz, M., and Bender, M. B. (1973). Alterations of the corneofundal potential of the eye during sleep. *Electroenceph. Clin. Neurophysiol.*, **34**, 579–86.

Jacobson, E. (1930a). Electrical measurements of neuromuscular states during mental activities. I. Imagination of movement involving skeletal muscle. *Am. J. Physiol.*, **91**, 567–608.

Jacobson, E. (1930b). Electrical measurements of neuromuscular states during mental activities. III. Visual imagination and recollection. *Am. J. Physiol.*, **95**, 694–702.

Jacobson, E. (1930c). Electrical measurements of neuromuscular states during mental activities. IV. Evidence of contraction of specific muscles during imagination. *Am. J. Physiol.*, **95**, 703–12.

Johnson, L., Jr. (1963). Human eye tracking of aperiodic target functions. 37-B-63-8, Systems Research Center, Case Institute of Technology, Cleveland, Ohio.

Kikawada, B. (1968). Variations in the corneo-retinal standing potential of the vertebrate eye during light and dark adaptations. *Japan. J. Physiol.*, **18**, 687–702.

Kinsbourne, M. (1972). Eye and head turning indicates cerebral lateralization. *Science*, **176**, 539–41.

Kohlrausch, A. (1931). Elektrische Erscheinungen am Auge. In A. Bethe, G. von Bergmann, G. Embden, and A. Ellinger (Eds). *Handbuch der normalen und pathologischen Physiologie*, Vol. 12, Pt. 2, Julius Springer, Berlin. pp. 1393–496.

Kolder, H. (1959). Spontane und experimentelle Änderungen des Bestandpotentials des menschlichen Auges. *Pflügers Arch. ges. Physiol. Menschen Tiere*, **268**, 258–72.

Kolder, H., and Brecher, A. G. (1966). Fast oscillations of the corneoretinal potential in man. *Arch. Ophthal.*, **75**, 232–7.

Kolder, H. E., and Hochgesand, P. (1973). Empirical model of electro-oculogram. *Documenta Ophthal.*, **34**, 229–41.

Kris, C. (1957). Diurnal variation in periorbitally measured eye potential level. *Electroenceph. Clin. Neurophysiol.*, **9**, 382. (Abstract)

Kris, C. (1958). Corneo-fundal potential variations during light and dark adaptation. *Nature*, **182**, 1027–8.

Kris, C. (1960). Vision: Electro-oculography. In O. Glasser (Ed.), *Medical Physics* (Vol. 3), Yearbook Publishers, Chicago. pp. 692–700.

Kris, E. C. (1965). Cyclic corneo-fundal potential variations in diabetics. *Electroenceph. Clin. Neurophysiol.*, **18**, 203 (Abstract)

Krogh, E. (1975a). DC recording of the human corneofundal potential. *Albrecht von Graefes Arch. klin. exp. Ophthal.*, **193**, 205–15.

Krogh, E. (1975b). Normal values in clinical electrooculography. I. Material, method, methodological investigations and distribution of potential and time parameters. *Acta Ophthal.*, **53**, 563–75.

Krogh, E. (1976a). Normal values in clinical electrooculography. II. Analysis of potential and time parameters and their relation to other variables. *Acta Ophthal.*, **54**, 389–400.

Krogh, E. (1976b). Inter- and intraindividual variation of the EOG. An assessment and some possible contributing factors. *Bibliotheca Ophthal.*, **85**, 115–18.

Ktonas, P. Y., Black, F. O., and Smith, J. R. (1975). Effect of electronic filters on electronystagmographic recordings. *Arch. of Otolaryng.*, **101**, 413–17.

Lion, K. S., and Brockhurst, R. J. (1951). Study of ocular movements under stress. *Am. Med. Assoc. Arch. Ophthal.*, **46**, 315–18.

Llewellyn Thomas, E. (1968). Movements of the eye. *Science*, **219**(2), 88–95.

Mackensen, G., and Harder, S. (1954). Untersuchungen zur elektrischen Aufzeichnung von Augenbewegungen. *Albrecht von Graefes Arch. Ophthal.*, **155**, 397–412.

Marg, E. (1951). Development of electro-oculography. Standing potential of the eye in registration of eye movement. *Am. Med. Assoc. Arch. Ophthal.*, **45**, 169–85.

Matsuo, F., Peters, J. F., and Reilly, E. L. (1975). Electrical phenomena associated with movements of the eyelid. *Electroenceph. Clin. Neurophysiol.*, **38**, 507–11.

Meyers, I. L. (1929). Electronystagmography. A graphic study of the action currents in nystagmus. *Arch. Neurol. Psychiat.*, **21**, 901–18.

Miles, W. R. (1939a). Experimental modification of the polarity potential of the human eye. *Yale J. Biol. Med.*, **12**, 161–83.

Miles, W. R. (1939b). Reliability of measurements of the steady polarity potential of the eye. *Proc. Nat. Acad. Sci. U.S. Am.*, **25**, 128–37.

Miles, W. R. (1940). Modification of the human eye by dark and light adaptation. *Science*, **91**, 456. (Abstract)

Monty, R. A., and Senders, J. W. (1976). *Eye Movements and Psychological Processes*, Lawrence Erlbaum Associates, Hillsdale, New Jersey.

Moriya, H., Ando, K., Kojima, T., Shimazono, Y., Ogiwara, R., Jimbo, K., and Ushikubo, T. (1972). Eye movements during perception of pictures in chronic schizophrenia. *Folia Psychiat. Neurol. Japon.*, **26**, 189–99.

Mowrer, O. H., Ruch, T. C., and Miller, N. E. (1936). The corneo-retinal potential difference as the basis of the galvanometric method of recording eye movements. *Am. J. Physiol.*, **114**, 423–8.

Müller, W., and Haase, E.. (1970). Inter- und intraindividuelle Streuung im EOG. *Albrecht von Graefes Arch. klin. exp. Ophthal.*, **181**, 71–8.

Müller, W., Haase, E., Janzen, H., Pohl, W., Mirsch, E., and Thieme, G. (1971). Die Hellphase des Elektrooculogramms bei unterschiedlichen Beleuchtungsstärken. *Albrecht von Graefes Arch. klin. exp. Ophthal.*, **182**, 357–62.

Müller, W., Körber, H., and Körber, H. -J. (1970). Der Einfluss der Präadaptation auf den Potentialverlauf des EOG. *Albrecht von Graefes Arch. klin. exp. Ophthal.*, **180**, 317–24.

Nikara, T., Sato, S., Takamatsu, T., Sato, R., and Mita, T. (1976). A new wave (2nd c-wave) on corneoretinal potential. *Experientia*, **32**, 594–6.

Oster, P. J. (1979). Automatization and subvocal speech in reading. *Doctoral Dissertation*, Washington University, Saint Louis, Missouri.

Reeser, F., Weinstein, G. W., Feiock, K. B., and Oser, R. S. (1970). Electro-oculography as a test of retinal function. *Am. J. Ophthal.*, **70**, 505–14.

Robinson, D. A. (1964). The mechanics of human saccadic eye movement. *J. Physiol.*, **174**, 245–64.

Roth, H. J., Alexandridis, E., and Pape, R. (1974). The electro-oculogram in the early postoperative period following intracapsular cataract surgery. *Albrecht von Graefes Arch. klin. exp. Ophthal.*, **190**, 207–14.

Sanders, D. S., Burdette, L. J., Beideman, L. R., and Stern, J. A. (1976). Incidental learning and visual search activity under sober and alcohol conditions during reading. (Unpublished manuscript).

Saslow, M. G. (1967). Effects of components of displacement-step stimuli upon latency for saccadic eye movement. *J. Opt. Soc. Am.*, **57**, 1024–9.

Schott, E. (1922). Über die Registrierung des Nystagmus und anderer Augenbewegungen vermittels des Saitengalvanometers. *Dt. Arch. klin. Med.*, **140**, 79–90.

Shackel, B. (1959). Skin-drilling: A method of diminishing galvanic skin-potential. *Am. J. Psychol.*, **72**, 114–21.

Shackel, B. (1960). Pilot study in electro-oculography. *Br. J. Ophthal.*, **44**, 89–113.

Shackel, B. (1967). Eye-movement recording by electro-oculography. In P. H. Venables and I. Martin (Eds), *A Manual of Psychophysiological Methods*, N. Holland Publishing Co., Amsterdam. pp. 300–34.

Shackel, B., and Davis, J. R. (1960). A second survey with electro-oculography. *Br. J. Ophthal.*, **44**, 337–46.

Shagass, C., Amadeo, M., and Overton, D. A. (1974). Eye-tracking performance in psychiatric patients. *Biol. Psychiat.*, **9**, 245–60.

Shagass, C., Roemer, R. A., and Amadeo, M. (1976). Eye-tracking performance and engagement of attention. *Arch. of Gen. Psychiat.*, **33**, 121–5.

Skoog, K. -O. (1975). The directly recorded standing potential of the human eye. *Acta Ophthal.*, **53**, 120–32.

Stern, J. A. (1968). Toward a developmental psychophysiology: My look into the crystal ball. *Psychophysiology*, **4**, 403–20.

Stern, J. A., Bremer, D. A., and McClure, J. (1974). Analysis of eye movements and blinks during reading: Effects of Valium. *Psychopharmacologia*, **40**, 171–5.

Ten Doesschate, G., and ten Doesschate, J. (1956). The influence of the state of adaptation on the resting potential of the human eye. *Ophthalmologica*, **132**, 308–20.

Thaler, A., Heilig, P., and Gordesch, J. (1976). Light peak to dark trough ratio in clinical electro-oculography. Influence of dark oscillations on the following light peak. *Bibliotheca Ophthal.*, **85**, 110–14.

Thomas, J. G. (1967). The torque-angle transfer function of the human eye. *Kybernetik*, **3**, 254–63.

Uenoyama, K., Uenoyama, N., and Iinuma, I. (1964). Vector-electro-oculography and its clinical application. *Br. J. Ophthal.*, **48**, 318–29.

Van Weerden, T. W. (1973). Artefacts in electro-oculography. *Electroenceph. Clin. Neurophysiol.*, **35**, 105. (Abstract)

Walter, D. O. (1963). Spectral analysis for electroencephalograms: Mathematical determination of neurophysiological relationships from records of limited duration. *Exp. Neurol.*, **8**, 155–81.

Weber, R. B., and Daroff, R. B. (1971). The metrics of horizontal saccadic eye movements in normal humans. *Vision Res.*, **11**, 921–8.

Westheimer, G. (1954). Mechanism of saccadic eye movements. *Am. Med. Ass. Arch. Ophthal.*, **52**, 710–24.

White, C. T., Eason, R. G., and Bartlett, N. R. (1962). Latency and duration of eye movements in the horizontal plane. *J. Opt. Soc. Am.*, **52**, 210–13.

Young, L. R., and Sheena, D. (1975). Survey of eye movement recording methods. *Behav. Res. Meth. Instrum.*, **7**, 397–429.

Zuber, B. L., Semmlow, J. L., and Stark, L. (1968). Frequency characteristics of the saccadic eye movement. *Biophys. J.*, **8**, 1288–98.

Zuber, B. L., Stark, L., and Cook, G. (1965). Microsaccades and the velocity-amplitude relationship for saccadic eye movements. *Science*, **150**, 1459–60.

EYE MOVEMENT RECORDING USING OPTOELECTRONIC DEVICES

J. D. HAINES

1 INTRODUCTION

Techniques devised to detect the physical movement of the eye are of two types: contacting and non-contacting. Non-contacting measurement is achieved by radiating some form of energy toward the eye and detecting the reflected energy that returns. Contacting methods usually involve the use of a contact lens and often this incorporates a plane mirror surface to enable the same broad principle to be utilized. It is possible to radiate different forms of energy and to obtain reflections from various parts of the eye structure. Consideration of the eye as a reflector indicates the different techniques which are used. One of these is particularly suited for modification to use with recently developed semiconductor devices such as light emitting diodes (LEDs) and junction photodetectors. Details of these optoelectronic devices and the system which incorporates them will be described.

The applications of eye monitoring systems are numerous. Some recent uses have been for research into reading habits, advertisement viewing, ergonomic instrument displays, and the control of propelled vehicles. There is also considerable interest in how the various control loops of the six extra-ocular muscles normally exercise such very accurate highly damped control over eye movements.

2 THE EYE AS A REFLECTOR

The external surface of the eye is a regular but not a simple contoured surface. The predominant feature is the corneal bulge which has a radius of curvature less than that of the eye. Apart from the cornea the external layer of the eye forms the sclera which is white in colour. The cornea is transparent and the iris and its centre aperture (the pupil) may be seen through the space between it and the anterior lens surface.

Listed below are the different methods which record eye movement by use of reflected energy:

(1)   pupil–iris and iris–sclera boundary;
(2)   corneal reflection;

(3)   Purkinje images;
(4)   contact lens;
(5)   ultrasonic distance measuring.

Each of these techniques will be considered separately.

(1)   Pupil–iris and iris–sclera boundary

The sclera has greater reflectivity than the iris and the boundary between them is reasonably well defined. Fixed photodetectors will have an output which increases according to the area of sclera they 'see'.

The boundary between the pupil and the iris is also quite sharp, but the contrast is normally less than between the iris and the sclera. If collimated illumination is used, however, light is internally reflected within the eye and the pupil appears bright if viewed along the illumination axis.

Details of an eye recording system that uses the iris–sclera boundary appear later in this section.

(2)   Corneal reflection

If a light is placed in front of the eye an observer sees several images reflected therefrom. The brightest of these is the one reflected from the surface of the cornea. As the eye moves this image moves in the same direction, but because of the smaller radius of curvature of the cornea it also becomes displaced in the opposite direction to the optical axis. Mackworth and Mackworth (1958) used corneal reflection with their system of recording eye fixations on changing visual scenes.

(3)   Purkinje images

As mentioned above several images appear when a light is placed in front of the eye. The first Purkinje image is the corneal reflection; the second image is reflected from the rear surface of the cornea, the third from the anterior surface of the lens, and the fourth image from the posterior surface of the lens. Cornsweet and Crane (1973) tracked the first and fourth Purkinje reflections: these two images move together under eye translation but differentially under eye rotation. This method is named the double Purkinje image method.

(4)   Contact lens

Specially constructed lenses that fit accurately over the cornea and sclera enable movements of the eye to be recorded. These contact lenses usually have one or more plane mirror surfaces incorporated and light is reflected from these to be recorded using the optical lever principle. Ditchburn and Ginsborg (1953) recorded extremely small movements with this method.

(5) Ultrasonic distance measuring

Ultrasound air waves are reflected from most surfaces. Ultrasound reflected from the eye can interact with the source transducer to produce an electrical output proportional to the separation distance. The movement of eye surface contour relative to fixed transducers can therefore be recorded. O'Connor and Haines (1977) have used this method to record axial tremor.

Many of these foregoing methods have been used as a basis for commercial instruments.

3 THE ELEMENTS OF A DIFFERENTIAL REFLECTION SYSTEM

The optoelectronic components suitable for use in eye monitoring systems are semiconductor p–n junction devices. Light emitting diodes (LEDs) are available for the near infrared region of the electromagnetic spectrum and silicon photodiodes have a response which is also at a maximum at these frequencies. Figure 5.4. shows a section of the spectrum between the ultraviolet and infrared frequencies. The ultraviolet region is included as the silicon photodiode response is very wideband. The range of available visible LEDs is also shown, although unobtrusive near-infrared LEDs are preferable for eye monitoring systems. It should perhaps be mentioned at this point that it is a common practice in physics to use the word 'light' when referring to radiation outside the visible region. This convenient usage has continued into optoelectronics so light emitting diodes that

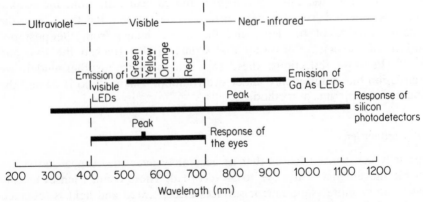

Figure 5.4 Spectral bands covered by optoelectronic junction devices

operate in both visible or infrared regions of the spectrum may be described without a change of nomenclature.

Unlike their thermionic counterparts semiconductor diodes can pass currents when the anode potential is negative with respect to the cathode. In this condition the diode is said to have a reverse voltage or reverse bias (V_R) and to pass a reverse current (I_R). Conversely when the anode potential is positive with respect to the cathode the diode has a forward voltage (V_F) and passes a forward current (I_F). Manufacturers of LEDs and photodiodes always quote forward and reverse direction ratings which should not be exceeded.

3.1 Light emitting diodes

LEDs are semiconductor p–n junction devices which emit radiation when passing current in the forward direction. The radiation is generated by electrons changing their energy levels within the atomic structure of the material composing the junction. The frequency of the radiation also depends upon the bandgap of this material. Gallium arsenide (GaAs) is the material used for the near-infrared radiation frequencies which are favoured for eye movement monitoring.

The relevant characteristics when selecting LEDs for eye monitoring purposes are: (a) the beamwidth; and (b) the power output.

(a) Beamwidth (θ_{HP}) is defined by the angle between the peak response and the half power points. Two narrow beamwidth LEDs $(\theta_{HP} = 10°)$ are used for one system under consideration, and the near-infrared radiation from each 'covers' slightly more than the area of sclera exposed when the eyes are horizontal and gazing directly ahead.

(b) The power output is a measure of the radiation emitted from a source. This is energy emitted per second and is termed radiant power or radiant flux in SI radiometric terms when the units are watts.

LEDs and photodetectors often have significant active areas and the fall-off of source to detector illumination is almost proportional to the cube of the separation between them. This contrasts with a point source in which the fall-off is proportional to the square of the distance. It is therefore an advantage to conserve a given amount of radiant power by containing it within the narrowest beamwidth necessary to cover a selected reflector area.

Further information on radiometry measurements, LED, and photodiode theory may be found in a textbook concerned with the subject (Hewlett-Packard and Company, Optoelectronics Applications Engineering Staff, 1977).

3.2 Photodiodes

Photodiodes are bipolar semiconductor devices in which irradiance of the p–n junction liberates electrons from the material of which it is composed and makes them available for conduction. The extended response of silicon photodetectors is shown in Figure 5.4 and it can be seen that the response extends through the visible region and into the ultraviolet part of the spectrum. For this reason precautions have to be taken to prevent strong ambient light from saturating the device.

This may be accomplished by reducing sensitivity with small load resistances or the use of optical filters such as the Kodak Wratten series. The characteristics of interest when selecting photodiodes are: (a) the active area; and, less importantly, (b) the dark current.

(a) The active area of a photodiode should be matched with the selected area of the eye from which it is wished to receive reflected energy. This may be achieved either by making the chosen area of the eye and the active area the same or by 'reducing' the chosen area with a lens. Penalties are incurred with both methods: a large active area photodetector has a lowered frequency response, while a small active area plus lens is less efficient and requires accurate and rigid setting-up adjustment. The chromatic aberration of a lens also exacerbates differences in eye reflectivity between subjects produced by different colourations of the iris.

(b) The dark current is the small current passed by a photodetector in the absence of irradiance. This internal current is due to diode and surface leakage and its value determines the maximum voltages and load resistors which may be used. The load resistors and junction capacitance have a time constant and it is this that controls the frequency response of the device.

A photodiode may be connected directly to the inverting input of an operational amplifier as shown in Figure 5.5. Reverse bias is provided by

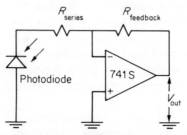

Figure 5.5   Photodiode   operational amplifier circuit

the feedback network of the amplifier. Such a circuit exhibits 'ringing' if the incoming light consists of low repetition frequency pulses generated by a LED. Increasing the frequency of the light pulses results in a progressive increase in gain until a maximum is reached at the ringing frequency. The photodiode reactance is responsible for these effects and it may also cause instability with some operational amplifiers. This may be eliminated by a resistor in series with the photodiode.

The amplifier circuit functioning in the mode described is frequency responsive due to the reactance of the photodiode capacitance. As the frequency is increased this reactance becomes smaller in comparison with the feedback resistance resulting in the gain rising to a maximum before it subsequently declines due to the 6 dB per octave roll-off characteristic of most operational amplifiers. The frequency sensitivity of the system also makes the response at 50 Hz at least 12 dB less than that at the ringing frequency and, providing the photodiode is shaded from direct fluorescent lighting, any interference from this source is minimal. The LED derived carrier frequency present at the output from the photodiode amplifier is coupled to the next stage via a capacitance. Providing the photodiode does not saturate, this capacitance ensures a low impedance path for the carrier frequency but blocks ambient lighting variations.

4 DEMODULATION

In a working system the output from the photodetector amplifier is an amplitude modulated carrier waveform. This signal has to be demodulated and filtered to obtain the low frequency component corresponding to eye movement. The choice of a pulse repetition rate for the system is related to the expected frequency components of eye movement. These would not normally extend beyond 200 Hz thus making the repetition rate (which should be at least one hundred times faster) a minimum of 20 kHz. An even higher rate is advantageous as this aids the choice of filtering time constant. This time constant has to be long enough to hold rectified carrier pulses at peak value, but short enough to permit the frequency components of eye movement to be followed. Figure 5.6 shows a simple detector with

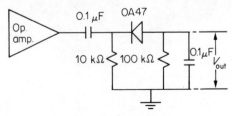

Figure 5.6   Demodulator circuit

component values suitable for a carrier frequency of 25–40 kHz with modulation to 100 Hz.

5 MOUNTING OPTOELECTRONIC DEVICES

Ideally both the light emitters and detectors should be attached to a platform which does not move with respect to the eye and which causes as little obstruction as possible to external vision. Both spectacle frames and goggles are used, the latter being more rigid and less easily displaced but they are susceptible to facial and forehead muscle movement. Minimal obstruction to vision is achieved by arranging the devices to lie along the line of the lower eyelid and then orienting them to face a horizontal line passing through the centre of the pupil.

Eyeblink detection is a special case in which the optoelectronic devices are best positioned to cover a central area. Movement of the eyelids is greatest at this point and with the eyes open both upper and lower eyelids should be presenting some reflective surface to the optical system.

Figure 5.7 shows goggles that can be used for recording eyeblinks. The circular metal piece below the left eye-piece rotates and also has a concentric locking screw to clamp the arm which holds the LED and photodiode. The length of the arm can be adjusted so that the optoelectronic devices may be positioned to accommodate individual differences.

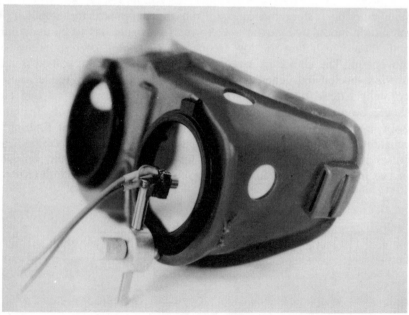

Figure 5.7   Goggles for recording eyeblinks

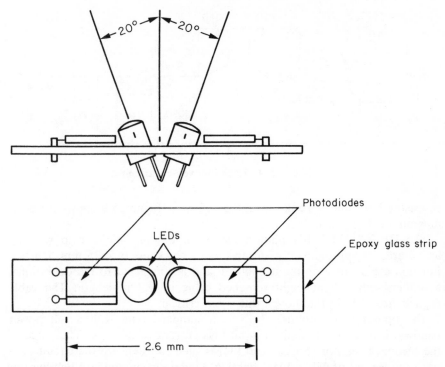

Figure 5.8 LED and photodiode layout for eye movement recording

The horizontal eye movement arrangement has two narrow beamwidth LEDS and two large area photodiodes mounted on a narrow strip of insulating material which slots into one side of a pair of spectacles. Figure 5.8 shows a drawing of this and a dimension is given as the distance between the outer edges of the photodiodes has to correspond with the width of an eye. The LEDs are mounted at an angle to direct their radiant power toward the sclera.

6 AN EYELID MOVEMENT SYSTEM

Eyelid movement is greatest over the central area of the eye and if the eyes are looking centrally ahead reflectivity differs between the eyelid surfaces and the iris. If the light radiation reaching the eye is a narrow vertical strip then some eye movement is possible before the relatively bright sclera changes the reflection contrast. This is achieved by the use of a wide beamwidth LED (Texas TIL 32, $\theta_{HP} = 35°$) fitted with a mask containing a 1.75 mm slot. The wavelength is 940 mm and it is operated in a series circuit with a 1.8 V peak-to-peak square wave input to the

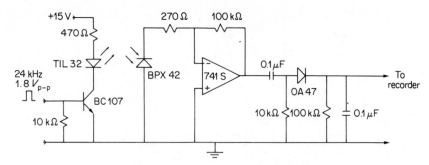

Figure 5.9   Eyelid movement circuit

transistor base and a peak current of 25 mA. Figure 5.9 shows a circuit diagram of the system.

The BPX42 (Mullard) photodiode is an oblong silicon chip with an active area of approximately 26 mm² and a thickness of 0.25 mm. It has a junction capacitance of about 1000 pF and is connected to the operational amplifier with a lightweight screened cable of 0.7 m length. The cable capacitance is 225 pF although this is not critical.

The operational amplifier 741S is a standard type with a full power bandwidth of 200 kHz and an input bias current of 200 nA. The value of the feedback resistor chosen (100 kΩ) is such as to ensure the circuit does not saturate in normal ambient lighting. Under strong ambient lighting this value could be reduced to 47 kΩ when the ringing frequency (maximum gain) will change from approximately 25 kHz to 35 kHz. The 270 Ω series resistor ensures stability of operation as the photodiode and the cable capacitance constitute a reactive input.

The operational amplifier output is capacitance coupled to a demodulator circuit consisting of a germanium diode and a filter circuit with a time constant of 0.01 s. The voltage output corresponding to a blink is of the order of 10 mV, but can vary between subjects due to such factors as iris colouration and skin pigmentation.

Output from the demodulator circuit forms one of the inputs to a balanced high input impedance recorder. The other balanced input is connected to a variable voltage source which cancels the standing d.c. from the demodulator (about 1.0 V) and zeros the recording trace. The output from the demodulator could be fed into a low input impedance recorder but then an operational amplifier connected as a voltage follower would have to be interposed.

6.1 An eyeblink record

Figure 5.10 shows a section of an eyeblink record taken using the apparatus described. Subjects were fitted with earphones and asked to

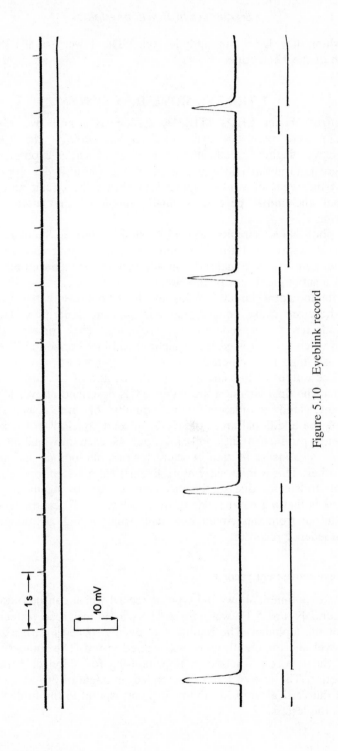

1 s

10 mV

Figure 5.10　Eyeblink record

blink when they heard an audible tone. The lower trace indicates the duration of the 1kHz tone.

7 THE EYE MOVEMENT SYSTEM

Two narrow beam LEDs (TIL31s, θ_{HP} = 10°) and two photodiodes (BPX42s) were used for eye movement recording. The LED beam coverage was slightly greater than the areas of sclera exposed when the eyes were centralized.The active area of the photodiodes approximately equalled the areas of sclera. Figure 5.11 shows the circuit and it can be seen that the initial part is a dual version of that used for eyelid monitoring.

The photodiode circuits are also similar but a feedback resistor adjustment is provided for one channel in order that the frequency of maximum gain can be equalised. An adjustment for balanced amplitudes is made in a subsequent part of the circuit.

The demodulator circuits differ in diode polarity connection. Equal inputs therefore cause equal value but opposite polarity voltages to be developed across the separate filter circuits. This corresponds to the situation when the eye is gazing straight ahead in a horizontal direction.

The last stage is an operational amplifier connected as a non-inverting adder. The output of this circuit is the direct sum of the two inputs and is zero when the dual channels are balanced as described above. Vertical eye movements tend to maintain the equality of both channel outputs providing the additional areas of sclera exposed are similar. Horizontal eye movements produce a differential output as each movement involves a reduction in exposure to area of sclera for one photodiode and an increase for the other. This is inherently more linear than a system operating from a single photodetector due to the push–pull circuit arrangement. A further advantage is that a greater range of movement (± 15°) can be recorded.

The output from this circuit may feed either a high or moderately low input impedance recorder.

7.1 An eye movement record

A simple experiment shows the type of record which can be obtained with this system. Figure 5.12 was produced as a subject read sixteen random letters of the alphabet. The letters were evenly spaced in a horizontal line at eye level and the eighth letter was circled in red. The subject was asked to scan the letters in their own time pausing for a longer period at the eighth letter. The row of letters subtended an angle of 30° to the subject's eye and the vertical 'steps' in the record correspond to the fifteen 2° spaces between the letters.

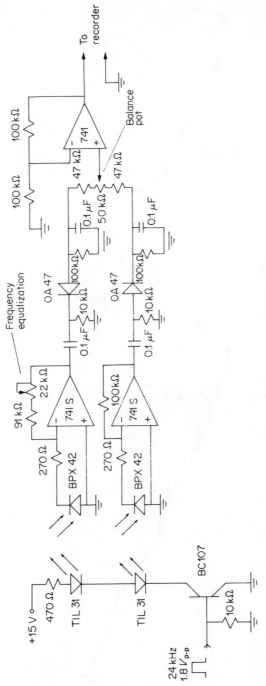

Figure 5.11 Eye movement circuit

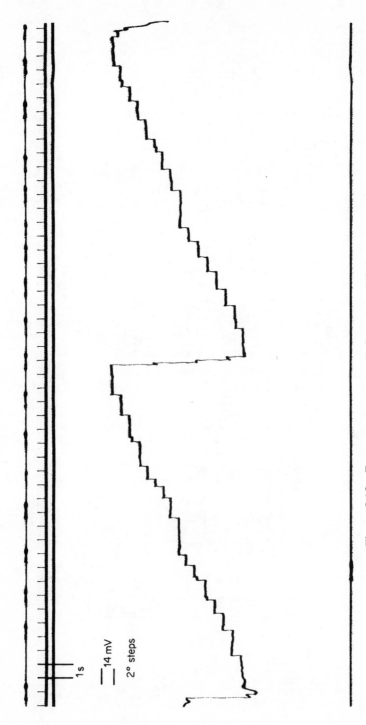

Figure 5.12   Eye movement record of random alphabet sequences

This record was made with a Mingograf 81 ink jet recorder which has a linear frequency response from d.c. to 500 Hz. Conventional pen recorders can produce clearer records at the slow (5mm/s) paper speeds used but the response of the pens is such that they are unable to follow the high frequency content of their electrical input.

8 SYSTEM PERFORMANCE

In an eye monitoring system using optoelectronic devices light is transported from the area of a source onto the sensitive area of the detector via the variable reflectivity of the convex contours of the eye. As mentioned in Section 3.1, a consequence of the light source and detector having significant areas is that optical path length is important. A dual channel system requires that the optical devices have equal spacing from the sclera and symmetrical beams. Radiation pattern and symmetry may be examined with a separate small area photodiode connected to an amplifier and demodulator circuit. Adjustment for equal spacing from the sclera is a mechanical feature of the device mounting arrangements, and is accomplished after electrical balance has been found with apparatus described below.

The ideal response from an optoelectronic devices system would be a high signal-to-noise ratio electrical output that is not only proportional to the type of eye movement to be measured but also has a frequency response from d.c. to a value sufficient for reproduction of the high frequency components of the movement. To measure some aspects of system performance an apparatus can be constructed which simulates the differential reflectivity between the iris and sclera. This comprises a drum 16.6 mm diameter (corresponding to the radius of curvature of the eye, but not of the cornea) whose periphery is divided into four equal alternate areas of matt light and dark grey coloured surface. The 45 mm long drum is driven concentrically by the shaft of a small variable speed electric motor and has a steady bearing remote from the driven end. When the devices are positioned the same distance from the drum as they normally are from the eyes (13 mm is a suitable value) the voltage steps appearing across a diode load when the drum is revolved should be equivalent to the difference in level measured when the eye is moved horizontally from a 15° left to a 15° right position. Signal-to-noise ratio may be measured with this apparatus when the noise voltage measured on a cathode ray oscilloscope with the drum in the most reflective position can be related with the voltage step from the adjacent coloured segment. The noise voltage is mostly residual carrier; it can be reduced by increasing the value of the filter capacitor, but at the expense of reducing the frequency

M

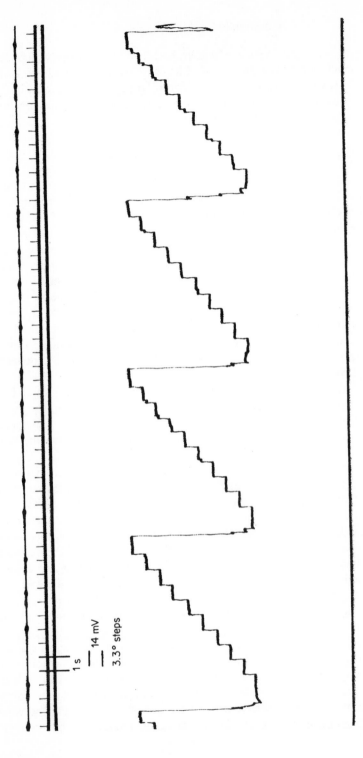

Figure 5.13 Eye movement record of illuminated lights sequences

response. Signal-to-noise ratios better than 350:1 are obtainable with this system.

The apparatus can be used to set the balance adjustment on a dual channel system. The devices should be positioned parallel to and 13 mm from the drum when the summed outputs from the channels are adjusted to be zero for both reflective conditions.

The frequency response may be examined by observing the voltages developed across the diode loads on a cathode ray oscilloscope whilst rotating the drum at various speeds. A typical frequency response is flat to 150 Hz, but with output waveform distortion discernable above 100 Hz. Frequency response can be improved by lowering the diode loads to 20 kΩ, but this lowers the signal-to-noise ratio.

Horizontal eye movement sensitivity and linearity cannot be easily simulated, but apparatus can be used as an aid to produce eye movement records which will show non-linearities. The apparatus consists of ten small lights each of which is sequentially illuminated for a one second period. The lights are evenly spaced and arranged to subtend an angle of 30° to the eye. A 'staircase' record obtained when using the apparatus is shown in Figure 5.13. Some of the steps show additional 'fixation' movements, but linearity estimates may be made by averaging several sequences. Correction of non-linearity can be made by mechanically altering the optical path length for one LED/photodiode combination.

9 SOME METHOD COMPARISONS

Differential reflection systems using optoelectronic devices have a horizontal eye movement resolution (1°–2°) that is similar to most other methods. The notable exceptions with a greater resolution are the contact lens (approximately 10 s of arc) and the double Purkinje image (approximately 3 min of arc) methods. The horizontal eye movement excursion obtainable with LED systems (±15°) is also the span of vision normally covered before a head movement is necessary. Electrooculography has a greater range of eye movement (approximately ± 70°), but linearity worsens beyond 30° of movement: the contact lens range is in the region of 5° of movement.

The frequency response of LED systems can be high (to above 300 Hz). However, in practice the recorder response often causes limitation to approximately 30 Hz. The preparation, calibration, and training times are minimal with these systems as electrode stabilization, light adaptation or contact lens familiarization are not needed. Subject discomfort and operating expenses are other factors involved when making a choice of eye movement systems. Expensive lenses needing the application of negative pressure are necessary with some contact lens systems; costly film or videotape and heavy attachments are needed with some versions of the head mounted corneal reflex camera system developed by Mackworth and Mackworth. The display in this latter method is a white spot that is superimposed on the visual field scene in a position that corresponds with the section being fixated. This complex system contrasts with the basic system described, but it is feasible to elaborate an eye position with respect to head measurement to an eye point-of-regard measurement by combining it with a head position monitoring system.

10 PAST AND PRESENT TECHNIQUES

The previously described system used a LED and a photodiode for each area of exposed sclera. Other differential reflection systems have used a single light source of wide beamwidth and either one or two photodiodes to detect reflection from selected areas of the eye. These detectors may view the appropriate parts of the eye either directly or indirectly via an image. All the systems require the head to be constrained and this is usually accomplished with the use of a biteboard or chin rest. These attachments are effective, but have the disadvantage that reading experiments requiring verbal communication with the subject are not practicable.

An early use of the differential reflection method was by Torok, Guillemin, and Barnothy (1951) who imaged one side of the eye on a horizontal slit aperture positioned in front of a photomultiplier. Another early system by Richter (1956) mounted the light source and photodetectors on goggles to use the direct light reflection from the sclera.

Overcoming interference from changes in ambient illumination by 'chopping' the light source was accomplished by Wheeless, Boynton, and Cohen (1966) who used a chopper wheel in the light path. Findlay (1974) used fibre optic light pipes both to transport light from its point of generation to the eye and to carry the reflected light to a photodetector. The separate fibre optic bundles are positioned together when quite close to the eye and enable small areas to be sensed.

Measurement of vertical eye position has been achieved by various techniques. Upper eyelid position varies with vertical eye movement, Young (1970) therefore tracked lid position with the output of two photodiodes arranged to have little response to horizontal eye movement. Jones (1973) used a broad beam light source with two photocells detecting light from two slightly angled oblong areas that covered both the iris and sclera. Vertical eye movement changed the light output in both photocells similarly, whereas horizontal movement changed it differentially. A vertical movement component was obtained by summing the two outputs and a horizontal one by subtracting them.

The many new applications currently being found for optoelectronic devices is giving impetus to their development. Among the increasing variety of products available are special operational amplifiers specifically for use with photodiodes, and infrared light emitting diodes with beamwidths that give an even narrower angle concentration of power. The measurement of eye movement by differential reflection is aided by these developments.

REFERENCES

Cornsweet, T. N., and Crane, H. D. (1973). Accurate two dimensional eye tracker using first and fourth Purkinje images. *J. Opt. Soc. Am.*, **63**, 921–8.

Ditchburn, R. W., and Ginsborg, B. L. (1953). Involuntary eye movements during fixation. *J. Physiol.*, **119**, 1–17.

Findlay, J. M. (1974). A simple apparatus for recording microsaccades during visual fixation. *Q. J. Exp. Psychol.*, **26**, 167–70.

Hewlett-Packard Company, Optoelectronics Applications Engineering Staff (1977). *Optoelectronics Applications Manual*, McGraw-Hill, New York.

Jones, R. (1973). Two dimensional eye movement recording using a photoelectric matrix method. *Vision Res.*, **13**, 425–9.

Mackworth, J. F., and Mackworth, N. H. (1958). Eye fixations recorded on changing visual scenes by television eye marker. *J. Opt. Soc. Am.*, **48**, 439–45.

O'Connor, K. P., and Haines, J. D. (1977). Ultrasonic measurement of axial movements of the eye. *Electroncenceph. Clin. Neurophysiol.*, **43**, 506.

Richter, H. R. (1956). Principes de la photo-electronystagmographic. *Rev. Neurologique*, **94**, 138–41.

Torok, N., Guillemin, V., and Barnothy, J. M. (1951). Photoelectric nystagmography. *Ann. Otol. Rhinol. Laryngol.*, **60,** 917–26.

Wheeless, L. L., Jr, Boynton, R. M., and Cohen, G. H. (1966). Eye movement responses to step and pulse-step stimuli. *J. Opt. Soc. Am.*, **56**, 956–60.

Young, L. R. (1970). *Biomedical Engineering Systems*, McGraw-Hill, New York. p. 16.

Techniques in Psychophysiology
Edited by I. Martin and P. H. Venables
©1980, John Wiley & Sons Ltd.

CHAPTER 6

Measurement, Quantification, and Analysis of Cortical Activity

RECORDINGS AND ANALYSIS OF BRAIN ACTIVITY[*]

LAVERNE C. JOHNSON

6.1 Spontaneous EEG

During the decade since the publication of *A Manual of Psychophysiological Methods* (Venables and Martin, 1967), there has been a marked increase in the recording of brain activity by psychophysiologists. This shift from autonomic to brain activity was noted by Johnson (1974) in

[*]Acknowledgement. This research was supported in part by Department of the Navy, Bureau of Medicine and Surgery, under Work Unit MR040.01.03-0153. The views presented in this paper are those of the author. No endorsement by the Department of the Navy has been given or should be inferred.

a survey of the types of articles published in *Psychophysiology*. When 1964 contents of *Psychophysiology* were compared to 1973 contents, studies of EEG activity rose from less than 5 to 25%. The number of studies of electrodermal activity dropped from 50 to 25%, and the number of heart rate studies declined only slightly during the decade. A check of the contents of *Psychophysiology*, **13**, 1976, revealed that 30% of the articles involved EEG activity and 15% electrodermal activity. Heart rate studies represented around 25% of the articles. The increase in EEG recording has been primarily due to the increased interest in the evoked potential, sleep, and use of biofeedback techniques to control EEG activity.

Psychophysiology has not been the only discipline to increase its study of brain activity. Künkel (1977), in a historical review of principal methods of EEG analysis, estimated that there were now over 2700 articles concerned with EEG analysis, of which about two-thirds were published in the last 10 years.

Several factors have played a role in this rapid expansion in EEG analysis. In the mathematical area, the development of efficient techniques for time-series analysis was an important contribution. The Cooley–Tukey fast Fourier transform (FFT) algorithm, for example, made spectral analysis a feasible and efficient method of EEG analysis that could be done on-line (i.e. simultaneously with data collection) in real time. In the data processing area, the rapid changes in hardware development have led to low-cost efficient computers that can serve as multipurpose laboratory instruments or be constructed to perform unique analytical functions. With the advent of the microprocessors, it is anticipated that the reduction in cost and size of recording and data processing equipment will continue. The convergence of mathematical algorithms with the rapid rise in computer technology suggests that those psychophysiologists who fail to come to terms with the computer and the probability textbook will be handicapped in the analysis of their data, especially that from the brain.

A striking example of the impact of computer technology has been in the area of the evoked potential, often referred to as the event-related potential (ERP). In addition to the cortical evoked response, the more recent demonstration that event-related responses can be detected and accurately measured from the brainstem auditory system by scalp electrodes has significantly increased both the research and clinical use of ERPs. Recent data have indicated that evoked brainstem activity in the somatosensory system may also be recorded (Wiederholt and Iragui-Madoz, 1977). Because of their current and probable increasing importance, the ERPs will be discussed separately by Terry Picton. This present section will be concerned only with the analysis of spontaneous EEG activity and, in particular, the use of computers in what has generally come to be known as automatic data processing.

6.1.1 Recording the EEG

While there have been dramatic technological advances in EEG data analysis, it perhaps would not be inappropriate to repeat the truism that the most sophisticated analytic tools will not overcome faulty research planning and poor recording procedures. The reader of this Handbook will not likely be concerned with chloriding silver–silver electrodes or, in most instances, drawing circuit designs for the fabrication of recorders. The various instrumentation companies now provide equipment that will meet recording standards for most research requirements. The reader, however, should be aware of the effects on data from faulty electrodes, electrode application, and the improper use of equipment. Sources of extracerebral potentials must be known and, if present, corrected unless the extracerebral physiological potentials are viewed as a signal of interest

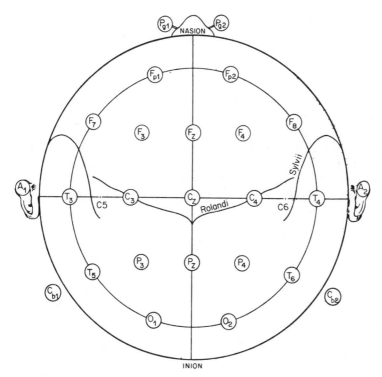

Figure 6.1 A single plane of the head showing all standard positions of the ten twenty electrode placement system. The location of the Rolandic and Sylvian fissures are also indicated. The outer circle was drawn at the level of the nasion and inion. The inner circle represents the temporal line of electrodes. (From Jasper, H. H. (1958). *Electroenceph. Clin. Neurophysiol.*, **10**, 371–5)

rather than as an unwanted signal or artifact. For example, body movements during sleep are excluded in most EEG spectral analyses, but the same muscle potentials may be an important signal in the study of the effects of drugs on good and poor sleepers. Eye movements, pulse rate, and respiration fall into this category. In contrast, artifacts that arise from external sources of electrical interference, and those due to faults in the recording procedure or apparatus, are an embarrassment. The electrode montage, number of electrodes, and electrode placement on the scalp will vary with the setting and reason for the recording. For recommendations concerning electrode requirements in sleep research, see Rechtschaffen and Kales (1968) and, for clinical runs, see references at the end of this section.

To establish more satisfactory communication of results in the literature, a committee was named at the First International Congress of the International Federation of EEG Societies in London in 1947 to standardize the placement of EEG electrodes on the scalp. The recommendation of this committee led to the general use of the 10–20 electrode system (Figure 6.1). If the 10–20 system is not used, care must be taken to describe how the electrode placements differ.

The 10–20 system uses standard landmarks as references for electrode placements. For example, the anterior-posterior measurements are based upon the distance between the nasion and the inion over the vertex in the midline. Five points are then marked along this line, designated frontal pole (F_p), frontal (F), central (C), parietal (P), and occipital (O). The first point, F_p, is 10% of nasion–inion distance above the nasion. The second point, F, is 20% of the nasion–inion distance back from F_p, and so on, in 20% steps back for C, P, and O, midline points. The name '10–20 system' thus refers to how the electrode points are determined.

In a similar manner, lateral measurements are based upon the central coronal plane. The anterior–posterior (AP) line of electrodes over the temporal lobe, frontal to occipital, is determined by measuring the distance between the F_p midline points, as determined above, through the T position of the central line and back to the mid-occipital point (see Figure 6.1). More discussion and illustrations are presented in the committee's report (Jasper, 1958).

Since the goal of this section is EEG analysis, no further efforts will be made to detail the problems in, and the importance of, good recording techniques. The reader is referred to the chapter by Margerison, St. John-Loe, and Binnie in the 1967 Venables and Martin manual, and to the several books on EEG technology. *Clinical Electroencephalography* by Kiloh, McComas, and Osselton (1972) and *Fundamentals of Electroencephalography* by Kooi (1971) are recommended, and in Vol. 3, Part C, of the *Handbook of Electroencephalography and Clinical*

Neurophysiology, MacGillivray (1974) presents a comprehensive review of traditional methods of examination in clinical EEG.

6.1.2 Why a computer?

The psychophysiologist who wishes to move beyond visual analysis to automatic quantitative analysis must turn his attention away from electrodes, amplifiers, and strip charts to even more complex instrumentation and recording problems. The psychophysiologist who would turn the analog EEG wiggles into numbers must be familiar with FM and digital recording equipment, computers, programming, and the various types of display systems. Should the data be stored on FM tape or digitized on-line and stored on digital magnetic tape? Should the data be processed and analysed on-line, or should they be only stored on-line and processed off-line? The answers to these questions may determine the type of computer necessary, or, more likely, the type of computer available will limit the options. The answers to each of the above will, of course, determine the software, computer programs, and software packages.

In the light of the complexity, expense, and the need to develop new areas of expertise to establish an automatic data processing capability, an appropriate question at this point might be, 'Should I join the computer crowd?' As the computer has become a part of our daily life, both in and out of the laboratory, perhaps the question is no longer 'should I?', but 'how do I join?'

The increasing tendency to 'let's see what the computer shows' has dulled many investigators' sensitivity to the basic rules of research, sometimes to the point that the definition of the problem is unclear. The speed and ease of statistical computation, even of complex multivariate analysis involving Ns of 1000 or more, have tempted many investigators to submit all possible comparisons for analysis with little concern over the subtleties of multiple testing and the risk of type I errors. The computer cannot substitute for thoughtful planning, or, as Medawar (1969, p. 29) put it, 'We cannot browse over the field of nature like cows at pasture'.

There are many goals achievable by computer in EEG research. Research questions most amenable to computer analysis in electroencephalography fall into two major categories: automation and analysis. In automation, the computer performs a precisely defined task which can be and usually is done by other, probably less efficient, means. An example would be the scoring of sleep records. The psychophysiologist seeking computer assistance in analysis of data, in contrast, hopes to find new and useful information from the data, information not necessarily known to be present, but which might be. The computer's manipulative and mathematical abilities are substituted for the limited human abilities in the attempt to correlate data with other factors. The determination of coherence, or degree of relationship, between several data channels within selected frequency bands is an example.

After establishing an overall goal, i.e. automation or analysis, the researcher must then evaluate alternative approaches. Walter (1972) raises these alternatives: (1) Does the problem really require a computer? (2) If yes, what type of computer; special purpose, general purpose, analog, digital, or one that includes both digital and analog capability? (3) If automation is the primary motivation, can the researcher precisely define what the computer is to do? (4) The time factors involved in computer analysis must be realistically considered. These time factors should include the planning stage, programming, debugging, and computer downtime. Use of computers is somewhat similar to air travel; once you are airborne, the travel is swift and usually pleasant. It is getting to the airport (computer) that takes time and frays nerves.

Of all the above, it is the first question (does the problem really require a computer) that is, of course, the most important. Whether to use a computer will involve the unique research tasks in each laboratory, but the generality of the problem, duration of need, and the expected difficulties in achieving the data-processing procedures are factors that should be considered.

In their discussion of why analyse, quantify, or process routine clinical EEG, Rémond and Storm Van Leeuwen (1977, p.2) emphasize that 'the aim of data processing in electroencephalography will remain doing with a machine things that were not conveniently done by hand'. For them, the computer adds speed, precision, and comprehension to EEG analysis. Comprehension is aided by the use of the computer for statistical manipulation of large data samples, and comparison not possible by visual inspection or manual analysis.

Perhaps the comment by Mary Brazier might be an appropriate summary statement on the value and use of computers. 'The computer is very useful in the sense that a housewife finds a vacuum cleaner useful—it keeps her from having to get on her hands and knees. It's useful but is it informative? When we use computers we need to ask what do we get out of it; does it suggest another experiment to us? If it does it is extremely valuable' (Brazier, 1972, p.312).

6.1.3 Processing the signal

EEG amplifiers can only produce gradually varying voltages. Analog signals have to be converted eventually into discrete digital values if the signal voltages are to be processed by digital computers. Further, there must be the ability to convert back again into language of voltages suitable

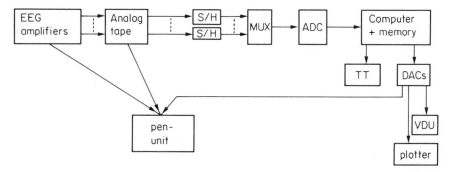

Figure 6.2   A schematic representation of the different elements in an EEG automatic data processing system. S/H = sample-and-hold; MUX = multiplexer; ADC = analog–digital   convertor;   TT = teletypewriter;   DAC = digital–analog convertor; VDU = visual display unit. (From Vos, J. E. (1977). In A. Rémond (Ed.), *EEG Informatics*, Elsevier/North-Holland Biomedical Press, Amsterdam, pp. 143–55. Reproduced with permission)

for plotters, visual display units, and perhaps EEG machines. Thus, equipment for analog-to-digital and then digital-to-analog conversion must be available. Processing by analog computer, of course, does not require digitization, but analog computers have generally been replaced by digital techniques. Vos (1977), in his lecture, presented a schematic representation of the different elements in an automatic EEG data processing system (see Figure 6.2). In the following brief overview of the major elements illustrated in Figure 6.2, only the highlights of some of their uses, advantages, and disadvantages will be discussed. The reader is referred to the article by Vos (1977) and that by Le Beux (1977) for an introduction to computers and their principle of operation.

6.1.4 FM recorders

Because of the complexity of the signal, EEG is usually recorded on FM tape. (See Harper (1976) for detailed information on recording on magnetic tape.) For compatibility, most laboratories use FM recorders that meet inter-Range Instrumentation Group (IRIG) Telemetry Standards Document 106-71. Usually, 14 channels are recorded on 1-inch tape or 7 channels on $\frac{1}{2}$-inch tape. The tape speed can vary from $^{15}/_{16}$ to 240 inches per second. The speed chosen determines the centre frequency and the deviations about this frequency. Up to 6 hours of recording can be obtained at $1^7/_8$ inch per second tape speed and takes 3375 feet of tape. Small portable cassette recorders are now available that handle up to 4 channels for 24 hours on ordinary C-120 cassettes (Ives and Woods, 1975; Wilkinson and Mullaney, 1976). The frequency range of the systems is limited usually from 0.5 to below 50 Hz, and special playback units are required.

Vos (1977) lists two main disadvantages of FM instrumentation systems: (1) the limited number of channels; and (2) the difficulties encountered when discrete data, like patient number, date of recording, etc., must be recorded together with the EEG. On most FM recorders, one channel is used for a time code because this information is critical to find discrete segments or synchronize the tape with other data. While multiplexing, a method of sampling from several variables, overcomes the channel limitations, recording on magnetic tape in digitized form avoids both FM disadvantages. Because of the increasing use of digital systems, few companies are continuing to make ½-inch FM tape systems and even fewer are offering 1-inch tape drives. Four-channel, ¼-inch recorders are more easily obtained. For reasons listed below, the researcher planning an automated data processing system should seriously consider the advantages of the digital system.

6.1.5 Digital recorders

To record on digital tape, the analog signal is digitized, or sampled, at certain well defined and usually equidistant instants in time. The word size of the analog-to-digital convertor (ADC) determines the digitization resolution. The smaller the resolution, the greater the number of points used to define the wave amplitude. The number of digitization values possible is 2^N, where N is the number of bits in the ADC word. In our laboratory, our ADC has a 12-bit word size, giving a 0 to 4095 point range, giving a total of 4096 points for our digital output. Since our ADC converts analog input voltages between $+5$ volts and -5 volts into the numbers between $+2047$ and -2048, we have a resolution of 0.0024 V.

6.1.6 Sampling rate

The frequency resolution of the ADC is determined by the computer hardware. The digitization rate (sampling rate) is determined (up to a limit) by the computer software. For appropriate sampling, a crystal controlled clock is needed to generate pulses at equidistant intervals. The rate at which this clock generates the interrupting pulse should be variable so that it can be set faster or slower, according to the maximum frequency rate to be sampled.

How is the sampling rate determined? Shannon's theorem states that even the smallest wavelength, fastest frequency, should be sampled at least twice. Thus, if we wish to analyse up to a frequency of 50 Hz, our sampling rate must be twice 50, or 100 samples per second. Care must be taken in the recording process before ADC that there are no frequencies higher than 50 Hz in the signal. For reasons explained by Blackman and Tukey (1959), frequency components higher than 50 Hz are misinterpreted as slower frequencies. The faster frequencies fold back over the slower frequencies; hence, a 55 Hz sine wave looks exactly like a 45 Hz sine wave. This problem is referred to as aliasing and the frequency equal to half the sampling rate is also known as the Nyquist frequency or folding frequency.

As there is no way to compensate for aliasing after sampling, frequencies higher than twice the sampling rate must be removed by analog low-pass filtering before digitizing or a Nyquist frequency must be chosen that is higher than the fastest frequency actually present. The most economical procedure is to remove the frequencies faster than the Nyquist frequency by filtering. Vos (1977) recommends that the anti-aliasing filters be set at 90% of the Nyquist frequency. In our laboratory, we digitize at 128 samples per second and filter out all frequencies above 50 Hz even though our Nyquist frequency is 64. Thus we also remove the ubiquitous 60 Hz noise.*

While most ADCs can only convert one signal at a time, several channels of data can be multiplexed so that each signal is connected to the ADC in turn. The samples from successive channels are separated in time, at least by the amount of time necessary for the ADC to perform one conversion. When the relationship in time, or in phase, between several traces is important, then the computer must be programmed to compensate for the discrepancy.

Vos (1977) lists the following advantages for recording information in digital form:

(1) Several signals can be recorded on one tape channel (and transmitted over one communication line); these signals may have different maximum frequencies, and therefore different sampling frequencies.

(2) The data on the tape are already in a form suitable for entry into a computer; they can, however, also be reproduced in analog form if that is required.

(3) The signal-to-noise ratio of the recording/reproducing system can be made arbitrarily high by choosing a sufficiently large word length in bits. The word bit length, however, for a particular computer is fixed.

(4) Noise inside the recorder electronics or in the tape material is relatively unimportant, since only 1's and 0's have to be recorded or reproduced; for either of these two symbols a wide range of possibly degraded voltage or magnetization values may be representative.

*60 Hz in the USA; 50 Hz in most parts of Europe.

(5) The recording/reproducing system is insensitive for tape speed variations within a relatively wide range; this allows the use of cheaper tape drives than are necessary for FM recording.

(6) A separate time code is not necessary. The position of a number on the list completely defines the instant of time to which it belongs, because the sampling interval is known. Time in this instance will, of course, refer to laboratory time which may not be tied to local time.

If the EEG activity is recorded in digital format, then the arrangement of Figure 6.2 is altered. Instead of an analog tape unit before the sample-and-hold, we would have a digital tape unit between the ADC and the computer.

6.1.7 Hybrid systems

When the researcher is faced with massive amounts of data (in all-night sleep studies, for example), hybrid systems which use both analog and digital processing systems have been used. Smith and his colleagues (1969, 1971) and Gaillard and Tissot (1973) have devised similar systems. A schematic of the Gaillard and Tissot system is presented in Figure 6.3. For comparative purpose, the system used by Smith and his colleagues is illustrated in Figure 6.4.

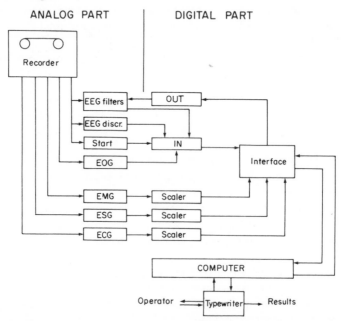

Figure 6.3 Schematic of the Gaillard and Tissot hybrid analysis system. (From Gaillard, J. M., and Tissor, R. (1973) *Comput. & Biomed. Res.*, **6**, 1–13, with permission)

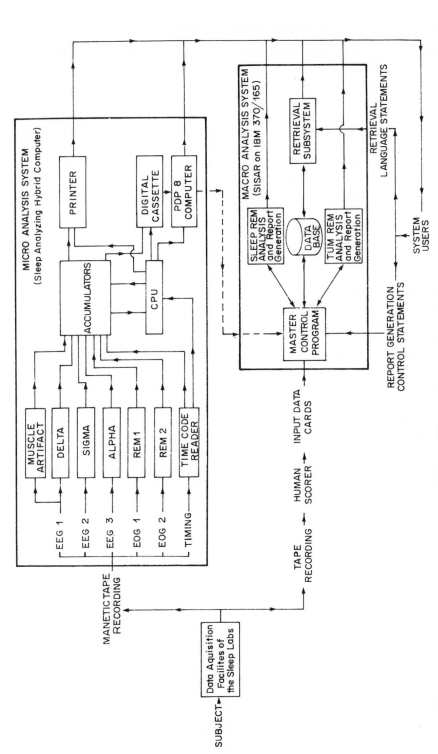

Figure 6.4 Schematic of the sleep analysing hybrid system. (From Su, S.Y.W., and Smith, J. R. (1974). *Comput. & Biomed. Res.*, 7, 432–48, with permission)

The Gaillard and Tissot and Smith systems are very similar in design and operation. The data first pass through analog detectors which, through the use of bandpass filters with sharp cut-off characteristics, pass only the desired EEG relevant frequency bands. There are also detectors which consist of several parallel processors scanning the multiple data channels. These detectors identify phasic events such as sleep spindles and rapid eye movements (REMs). A muscle-artifact detector plus a time-code reader are usually a part of the analog system, and one or more autonomic variables may be analysed. Summary information concerning the frequency and distribution characteristics throughout the night of each of these events is obtained through an interfaced computer. Such a system can be used to simultaneously analyse several channels of analog data, either on-line or 16 times as fast off-line.

In their system, Gaillard and Tissot record 7 channels consisting of 3 EEG leads, and one each for EOG, ECG, EMG, and ESG (respiratory rate). All activities are recorded only on magnetic tape and the next morning the tape is replayed 16 times faster and automatically analysed by the sleep analyser. Particularly appealing to sleep researchers is the statement by Gaillard and Tissot that their data are recorded 'without being watched over during the night.'

Another hybrid approach is pulse code modulation (PCM). Here one or more analog signals are sampled, i.e. converted into binary numbers, and the bits of these numbers are recorded on tape as the presence or absence of a pulse for 1 or 0, respectively. The time required to record such numbers can be much smaller than the interval between two signals from one analog signal. By the process of multiplexing, it is possible to sample several different signals and record the coded output on one tape channel.

The use of PCM modules to expand FM recording capacity is most useful when the signals vary widely in frequency range. Since all EEG channels have similar frequency ranges, PCM has limited application for EEG data processing.

6.1.8 To analyse on-line or off-line?

On-line processing means that the signal enters the computer immediately without prior storage. For on-line processing to be feasible, the time necessary for processing must be shorter than the duration of the signal, and the artifacts, if any, must be removed as they occur. The ever increasing efficiency of computers has overcome the processing time problem, and programs can be written to detect and remove unpredictable artifacts from the signal (Gevins and coworkers, 1977).

D. O. Walter (1977) focuses on this editing step as a source of bias. 'The methods by which a computer carries out editing and rejection of objectionable sections of a record are often not very clearly explained or justified by the person who wrote that part of the program; the criteria may concern unfamiliar measurements or be expressed in an unfamiliar language' (Walter, 1977, p.29). Walter goes on to point out that even when the language is familiar and about familiar measurements, the simplification necessary for rapidity of computation, or ease of programming, may lead to distortions. The researcher and the reader of research reports thus must be aware that peculiarities and prejudices may enter into the data-editing step, affecting what is subjected to analysis and what is not. Off-line editing by visual analysis can be influenced by subjective bias, plus the effects of fatigue and the shifting of standards from one editing session to another.

The increased speed of processing and the ability to detect artifacts and to delete irrelevant data have led to increased on-line data analysis. Most event-related data analysis is performed on-line. Immediate access to the subject's response is not only rewarding to the researcher; it also permits experimental interaction between stimulus and response which is lost when the data are stored for later analysis. On-line analysis not only involves the use of on-line computers, but also post-processing procedures. These procedures usually display the data visually, but numerical results are possible. Bostem (1977) describes several post-processing techniques. Off-line analysis, however, also has its advantages. In many instances, data can be processed at speeds faster than real time and there is the opportunity to subject the data to more than one method of analysis.

6.1.9 Methods of EEG analysis

Hans Berger's (1929) report that the majority of normal adult humans had a dominant rhythm at about 10 Hz might be considered the first example of EEG analysis. Visual inspection was, and still is for many clinical electroencephalographers, the primary method of EEG analysis. The basic EEG parameters of frequency (Hz) and amplitude (microvolts) are visually scanned. Frequency was, and still is, divided into bands: delta (0.5–4 Hz), theta (5–7 Hz), alpha (8–13 Hz), beta (18–24 Hz). Some electroencephalographers classify all waves above 13 Hz as beta waves. Others speak of slow beta as 13–20 Hz, and activity above 20 Hz as fast beta. During sleep stages 2, 3, and 4, 12–14 Hz spindling activity is present and these fusiform waves are called sigma waves or sleep spindles (Loomis, Harvey, and Hobart, 1935). Sleep spindles are the only EEG waves seen during sleep that are not present during waking and, conversely, these spindles are the only frequencies seen during sleep that are not present when awake. Most electroencephalographers are content to label EEG amplitude as low, moderate, or high. Clinical electroencephalographers also analyse the tracings for paroxysmal activity, synchrony, focal discharges, and the presence of spike activity.

In the few pages devoted to spontaneous EEG analysis, it will be impossible to detail all the advances and describe all the EEG analytic procedures now available. For more detailed discussions, the reader is referred to Volumes 4 and 5 of the *Handbook of Electroencephalography and Clinical Neurophysiology* (Rémond, 1972, 1973), 'Evaluation of bioelectrical data' in the proceedings edited by Dolce and Künkel (1975), and to the proceedings of a week-long course at which the methods and applications of EEG data processing were discussed (Rémond, 1977). In this section, I can only introduce the types of EEG activity and give an overview of the possible methods of analysis.

6.1.10 Categories of EEG activities

Dumermuth (1977, p.84) lists the following categories of EEG activities.

Spontaneous non-paroxysmal activity

Activities without significant temporal changes:

  normal spontaneous waking activity
  alpha variants
  beta activity
  continuous slow rhythm
  polymorphous slow activity.

Activities slowly changing with time:
  sleep activity
  postictal background activity
  fluctuating activity in coma
  hyperventilation activity
  seizure discharges.

Activities of intermittent type:

  sigma activity in form of sleep spindles
  mu-rhythm
  intermittent slow rhythms
  psychomotor variant pattern

Spontaneous paroxysmal activity

Spikes, sharp waves
Spike/wave-complexes

Rhythmic 3/s spike and wave formations
Paroxysmal slow waves
14+6/s positive spikes
SSLE complexes
K-complexes and vertex potentials in sleep.

Evoked activity

Evoked transient potentials
Photic driving (well suited for spectral analysis)
Arousal activity
Eye-closing effects
Lambda waves.

Reflecting both the primary interests and the technology available at the time, the first efforts at EEG analysis were directed toward frequency and amplitude analysis. The introduction of the frequency analyser (Baldock and Walter, 1946; Walter, 1943) is viewed by most as the first significant expansion of EEG analysis. In 1948, Drohocki introduced an electronic amplitude integrator (Drohocki, 1948; Goldstein, 1975). While the early workers were limited to frequency or amplitude analysis, the researcher of today can choose from among several methods of EEG analysis. In Table 6.1 is a list prepared by Matoušek (1973).

In his excellent overview of the various methods of automatic EEG analysis, Matoušek (1973) offers for each method: (1) brief characteristics; (2) technique and development; (3) application; and (4) evaluation of the method.

6.1.11 Analysis in the frequency versus time domain

In his choice of method of analysis, the researcher will find that each method will result in the sacrifice of some category of EEG activity. A simple example: if the choice is frequency analysis, the researcher has decided not to emphasize the amplitude data. Similarly, a decision to look at amplitude means that frequency is felt to be less important. If spectral analysis is chosen, then the unique contributions of both frequency and amplitude will be lost.

Those whose interests are in the single wave may prefer analysis in the time domain, while those with interests in trains of waves may opt for analysis in the frequency domain. The time domain treats single waves or half-waves as primary; the frequency domain treats trains of similar waves as primary (D. O. Walter, 1977). Harner (1977, p. 57) makes the following distinction between the time and frequency domains: 'the time

Table 6.1. Various methods of automatic EEG analysis.

Dominant quality	Source of observation	Names and various types of analyses	Remarks
Analysis of a single signal			
Amplitude	EEG in one derivation	*Amplitude analysis*: percentage time above a minimum level, integration, assessing amplitude distribution	Based on simple amplitude measurements Concerns all waves, neglecting wavelength
Wavelength	EEG in one derivation	*Periodometry* ('baseline crossing', 'interval analysis') and derived methods	Based on simple measurements of wavelength Most methods neglect amplitudes and prefer the dominant activity EEG processed like a pure aperiodic signal
Frequency and amplitudes	EEG in one derivation	*Frequency analysis*: broadband or narrowband frequency analysis, spectral analysis	More or less accurate approximation to frequency spectrum, measuring amplitudes of various frequency components
Waveshape	EEG in one derivation	*Pattern recognition* and some simplified methods	Detection and counting specific waves and/or wave complexes
Periodicity	EEG in one derivation	*Autocorrelation analysis* and related methods (reverse correlation, auto-averaging = auto-relation analysis)	Correlation between different parts of the same curve Extraction of periodic signal

Analysis of two simultaneously occurring signals

Phase relations	EEG in two derivations	*Phase analysis*	Simple time relations, all waves regardless of frequency and amplitude concerned
Phase relations	EEG and external stimuli	*Registration of evoked potentials:* superposition (summation), averaging and similar methods	Extraction of signal which is time-locked to stimulation, suppression of 'noisy' background activity
Correlation of two signals	EEG in two derivations or EEG and some other bioelectric phenomena	*Cross-correlation analysis* and related methods (cross-spectral analysis, coherence function, cross-averaging = cross-relation)	Extraction of periodic components which occur in common in both signals. Phase relationships of these components

Analysis of more than two simultaneously occurring signals

Phase relations	EEG in more than two derivations	*Toposcopy*	Topology and spreading of EEG potentials. All waves included
Clinical normality	EEG in more than two derivations	*Attempts at automatic evaluation* of the EEG	Searching for complex parameters which correlate in the best way with normality of the EEG curve

From Matoušek, M. (ed.) (1973). In A. Rémond (Ed.-in-Chief) *Handbook of Electroencephalography and Clinical Neurophysiology*, Vol. 5, Part A, Amsterdam, Elsevier, with permission.

domain will be taken to mean a description of EEG data which uses the temporal sequence of the data as an important element of the descriptive process. Thus, the untransformed EEG itself is a method of time domain analysis wherein no assumptions are made concerning the nature of the underlying process. This is in contradistinction to methods of frequency analysis which describe the EEG as a mixture of frequencies, each having a specified amplitude, centre frequency, and phase delay with reference to a specific epoch of time beginning at an arbitrary starting point.'

D. O. Walter (1977), after listing some methods and their domains or origin (see Table 6.2), observed that the hostility between those inhabitants of the time and frequency domains 'has recently become calmer, because practitioners in both domains have realized that underneath the superficial appearance of great differences in language and outputs, they are both describing the same 'elephant' and both approaches are needed for adequate analysis of EEGs' (p.31). After making this statement, Walter goes on to allay the concerns of those who still hold to two apparent requirements for analysis in the frequency domain; i.e. (1)

Table 6.2. Methods of EEG analysis, in rough chronological order within category. (Infrequently used methods bracketed.)

Methods mainly in the time domain	Methods mainly in the frequency domain
Amplitude analysis (Drohocki)	Frequency (later spectrum) analysis
Period analysis (Burch and coworkers)	(Grey Walter and coworkers)
Autocorrelation, cross-correlation	Cross-spectrum, coherence
(Brazier and coworkers)	(D. O. Walter and coworkers)
[Unstimulated summation	[Bispectrum, bicoherence
(Bernstein, Livanov)]	Johnson, Dumermuth)]
Normalized slope descriptors (Hjorth)	
[Reverse correlation (Kaiser, Petersen)]	
[Iterative interval analysis (Schenk,	
Matejcek)]	
[Mimetic analysis (Rémond and coworkers)]	

Methods primarily in time, but close to frequency	Methods primarily in frequency, but close to time
[Phase analysis (Darrow)]	Complex demodulation
[Toposcopy (Grey Walter)]	[Causality analysis (Granger, Gersch)]
Autoregression (Fenwick and coworkers)	[Inverse filtering (Lopes da Silva and
[Autocorrelation of filtered records	coworkers)]
(Grindel)]	[Cepstrum analysis (Childers,
[Alpha average (Rémond)]	Saltzberg)]
[Wiener input–output kernels]	[Kalman filtering (Isaksson)]
	[Adaptive segmentation (Creuzfeldt)]

From Walter, D. O. (1972). In A. Rémond (Ed.), *EEG Informatics*, Elsevier/North-Holland Biomedical Press, Amsterdam, p. 35, with permission.

the apparent need to divide data into epochs (non-overlapping segments with sharp beginnings and endings) for analysis; and (2) that the data were stationary (non-changing in their amplitude and frequency content during the epoch). The former ritual aspects of these two concepts now appear to be of historical interest only, and the concepts can now be treated rationally and, for the most part, in ways which are intuitively reasonable. In his review, Matoušek states that it may be difficult to classify all methods of EEG analysis according to the dichotomy of time versus frequency domain. The researcher thus no longer has to swear allegiance to either time or frequency domain, but only has to decide which method or combination of methods is most pertinent for a particular task and which provides the best discrimination of the different types of EEG activity under study. Perhaps we should no longer think in terms of time versus frequency, but refer instead to time and frequency domain analysis.

6.1.12 Some applications

The increasing efficiency and decreasing cost of all digital computer systems do not mean that the once popular frequency filters and special-purpose techniques such as the Drohocki amplitude integrator have no value or usefulness. Solid-state filters are now available which offer bandpass (ability to pass a specific frequency band), low-pass (low frequencies with high frequencies filtered out), high-pass (pass only high frequencies with low frequencies filtered out), and band reject (ability to reject any band of frequencies). Single frequencies can, of course, be passed and by cascading (placing in series) of filters the bandpass roll-off can be made sharper. The sensitivity and versatility of filters combined with counters can provide useful data when frequencies are the major interest. Even when digital computers are available, filters can be used effectively to screen out frequencies of little interest, frequencies above the Nyquist frequency, or activity that might be noise. The use of filters as part of a hybrid system was discussed earlier.

While filters are useful and, in some instances, essential to obtain an acceptable noise-to-signal ratio, they may also pose problems. Filters produce a phase shift. The narrower the frequency band passed, the more likely that sharp transients will produce a ringing effect. In this instance, frequencies not actually in the record are produced by the filters and passed as though recorded from the subject.

The purchase of any special-purpose device such as the Drohocki integrator is now only appropriate where there is no access to a computer and the only question involves amplitude. A digital computer can be programmed to compute the amplitude of any frequency or band of frequencies and write out the results at specified levels.

Special devices are attractive for their simple and straightforward approach to data analysis, and some devices such as that by Smith and his colleagues which detect delta, alpha, and sleep spindles, can be used to answer many questions. We found the spindle detector necessary to enable a stimulus to be presented during the spindle burst (Church, Johnson, and Seales, 1978). These special-purpose devices, however, cannot become general-purpose laboratory equipment and their output is often not easily amenable to statistical analysis. Any device that does not lead to easy quantification can be criticized for, as Knott (1953) noted, 'an instrument designed to complement visual analysis should not lead to further visual analysis'. For analysis, the Smith analyser output has to be connected to a counter or, preferably, recorded on FM tape for later computer analysis. One could reasonably argue that if the signals were recorded on digital tape, the computer could be used to obtain the same delta, alpha, and spindle counts without the intervening special-purpose detector.

6.1.13 Spectral analysis

With the introduction of the FFT and the small laboratory computer, spectral analysis soon became a popular method of EEG analysis. The EEG, as a set of continuous voltage/time graphs, can be considered as a time series and amenable to spectral analysis. Briefly, the spectrum (autospectrum, variance spectrum) of a stationary random signal gives an estimate of the mean square values or average intensity as a function of frequency. The term 'spectral intensity' is preferred by some to 'spectral power' and, further, the preferred units of intensity are squared microvolts per cycle per second (Walter, 1968). The intensity is based on the product of amplitude times frequency; thus, the unique contribution of frequency and amplitude is lost. From the spectral data, one can compute the cross-spectrum, the coherence spectrum, and the bispectrum. The cross-spectrum gives information on the statistical relationships between two simultaneous time series. The coherence spectrum is derived from the corresponding spectra and gives a measure of the squared correlation between two time series for each frequency component. The coherence values are always between 0 and 1. In Figures 6.5 and 6.6 are illustrations of the spectral profiles and coherence values found during the stages of sleep (Johnson and coworkers, 1972). The spectral profiles highlight the alpha peak during awake and REM sleep. Delta and sleep spindle activity are prominent during sleep stages 2, 3, and 4. The spectra clearly show the similarity of EEG activity during stages 1 and REM. The coherence profiles indicate that alpha and sleep spindles are the two rhythms with clearly defined coherence peaks.

In contrast to cross- and coherence spectra where the comparison is between two simultaneously recorded traces, bispectra present the degree

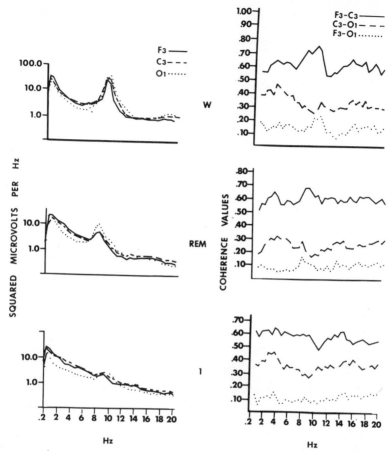

Figure 6.5 Spectral profiles and coherence values for 1-min samples of EEG activity during wake, stage 1, and sleep stage REM. (From Johnson, L. C. (1972). In M. H. Chase (Ed.), *The Sleeping Brain*, Brain Research Institute, Los Angeles, pp. 277–321, with permission)

of interaction of component waves making up an EEG trace, i.e. is there any coupling (interaction) between the various wave components? Dumermuth and coworkers (1971) have investigated the interrelations between frequency bands of the EEG by means of bispectrum, and Barnett and coworkers (1971) reported that component waves making up the EEG strongly correlated with alpha activity. About 50% of beta activity can be attributed to harmonic coupling with the alpha peak.

In addition to quantitative analysis of brief epochs, the spectra over long time periods can be compressed to highlight changes in spectral components over time. These compressed spectral arrays have been useful

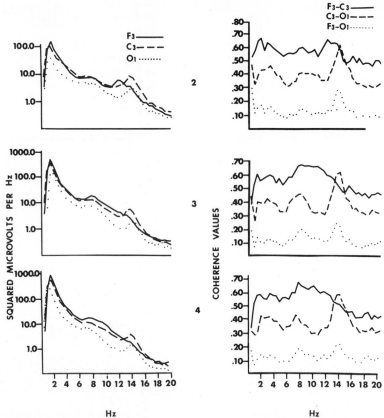

Figure 6.6 Spectral profiles and coherence values for 1-min samples of
EEG activity during sleep stages 2, 3 and 4. (From Johnson, L. C. (1972).
In M. H. Chase (Ed.), *The Sleeping Brain*, Brain Research Institute, Los
Angeles, pp. 277–321. Reproduced with permission)

to graphically illustrate changes during a night of sleep (Hanson and
coworkers, 1974; Dumermuth, 1973). Figure 6.7 illustrates the usefulness
of the somnogram to illustrate the increase in sleep spindle activity and
decrease in delta activity during administration of flurazepam (Johnson,
Hanson, and Bickford, 1976).

6.1.14 Clinical applications

While sensitive to trains of waves, spectral analysis is relatively insensitive
to brief phasic events such as spike waves, spike and slow wave complexes,
and brief paroxysmal discharges. The inability to detect these important
clinical measures has limited the acceptance of spectral analysis in clinical

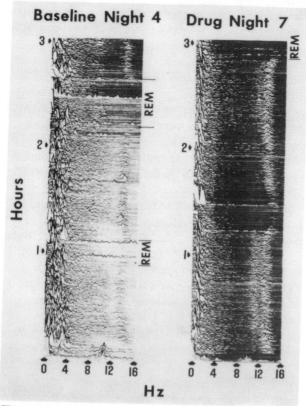

Figure 6.7   Somnogram of the first 3 hours of sleep on baseline night 4 and drug night 7, illustrating decrease in delta activity and increase in sleep spindles on drug (flurazepam 30 mg) night 7. (From Johnson, L. C., Hanson, K., and Bickford, R. G. (1976). *Electroenceph. Clin. Neurophysiol.*, **40**, 67–77, with permission)

laboratories. Bickford and his associates (Bickford, 1977; Bickford and coworkers, 1973; Chiappa and coworkers, 1976) have used the compressed spectral arrays to analyse background EEG activity in coma patients, during surgery, and in epileptic patients. Matoušek and Petersén (1973a, 1973b) as well as Dumermuth (1968) have used frequency and spectral analysis to quantify children's and adolescent EEG activity. Sterman and coworkers (1977) have used spectral analysis to record the EEG development during quiet sleep in infants. Matoušek (1977) also has shown how, by additional statistical analysis of the spectral data, parameters which summarize the clinical information of the EEG can be obtained. His analysis leads to automatic EEG assessment where both a verbal description and quantitative output are presented. In his 1977 paper, Matoušek reports 98% good agreement between automatic EEG assessment and the visual findings.

Spike detection, the crucial event for diagnosing of epilepsy, poses a challenging problem for automatic analysis. Though EEG spike detection for diagnosis of epilepsy may not be a primary interest for most psychophysiologists, the use of computers to recognize unique phasic EEG events may be. One general approach has been that subsumed under the heading of pattern recognition. This approach is sometimes referred to as feature extraction (see Demartini and Vincent-Carrefour, 1977). While pattern recognition refers to a general approach, MacGillivray (1977) details the application of automated EEG analysis for the detection of spikes and other epileptic phenomena. The procedure reported by MacGillivray (1977) and MacGillivray and Wadbrook (1975) relies on digital techniques to measure the sharpness of the wave for spike classification. For further information on automation of clinical electroencephalography, the reports of the symposia edited by Kellaway and Petersén (1973, 1976) would be useful.

For a detailed discussion of the mathematical determinants of spectral analysis, the reader is referred to Matoušek (1973), Dumermuth (1977), Blackman and Tukey (1959), and Jenkins and Watts (1968).

6.1.15 Period analysis

Period analysis (baseline crossing analysis, interval analysis) is a method similar to amplitude analysis but with wavelength (period) instead of amplitude as the measure of interest. Amplitude is not measured. It is also an alternative measure to frequency analysis (Burch, 1959; Burch and coworkers, 1964). The time occupied by each half wave and not the complete sine wave is measured and is called the major period. The intermediate period, based on the first derivative of the original series, is the time between successive zero slopes of the half waves. The major and intermediate periods usually encompass the dominant EEG rhythms. The minor period, based on the second derivative, is the time between successive points of inflection. The minor period includes the waves superimposed on, riding on top of, the dominant rhythms. Laboratory studies have found good correspondence between frequency, period, and visual analysis.

While equipment specific for period analysis can be built, digital computer programs for period analysis can be written. These period analysis programs can be faster than those for high-resolution spectral analysis even with the FFT, and they are also appealing because of their straightforward approach. Period analysis has been used very effectively for drug studies

(Fink, 1977; Fink, Itil, and Shapiro, 1967; Itil, 1968; Saltzberg, Lustick, and Heath, 1970; Schwartz and coworkers, 1971).

Period analysis is more sensitive to noise, both dc as well as fast waves, but the noise is particularly seen in the minor period. Period analysis does not detect bursts of EEG waves such as the sleep spindle. Also, there are many who believe that neglecting amplitude seriously limits the usefulness of the data, both clinically and with respect to electrophysiological meaning. In some instances, however, a separation of wave period and amplitude can be used to answer specific questions. Subjects who take flurazepam to induce sleep have less stage 4 in their EEG record. Data from Feinberg and coworkers (1977) and from our laboratory indicate that when period analysis is used to count delta waves, and a separate amplitude analysis of these waves is obtained, the results show that stage 4 is not scored primarily because of the decrease in delta wave amplitude. We found in our studies, however, that after five nights on the drug, there was also a significant decrease in the number of delta waves. Smith, Karacan, and Yang (1977) have found the decrease in stage 4 with advancing age is due to a decrease in delta amplitude and not to a decrease in percent time of delta.

These few examples illustrate that with the general-purpose digital computer, one has great flexibility in his approach to EEG analysis. With competent programming and technical assistance, the digitally recorded EEG waveforms can be subjected to either simple frequency or amplitude analysis or to the more complex techniques such as bispectra, *a posteriori* Wiener filtering, or to most of the techniques of either the time or frequency domain listed in Table 6.2. In conclusion, I would like to stress the concern raised earlier by D. O. Walter. The computer cannot replace scientific creativity and care must be taken to avoid the blunting of our scientific rigor. But perhaps, as Mary Brazier stated, most of us would, as the number of FM and digital tapes rapidly accumulate, appreciate the assistance of the computer to get us off our knees.

References

Baldock, G. R., and Walter, W. G. (1946). A new electronic analyzer. *Electron. Engng.*, **18**, 339–44.

Barnett, T. P., Johnson, L. C., Naitoh, P., Hicks, N., and Nute, C. (1971). Bispectrum analysis of electroencephalogram signals during waking and sleeping. *Science, 172*, 401–2.

Berger, H. (1929). Über das elektrenkephalogram des menschen. *Arch. Psychiat.* **87**, 527–70.

Bickford, R. G. (1977). Computer analysis of background activity. In A. Rémond (Ed.), *EEG Informatics. A Didactic Review of Methods and Applications of EEG Data Processing.* Elsevier/North-Holland Biomedical Press, Amsterdam, pp. 215–32.

354 *Techniques in Psychophysiology*

Bickford, R. G., Brimm, J., Berger, L., and Aung, M. (1973). Application of compressed spectral array in clinical EEG. In P. Kellaway and I. Petersén (Eds.), *Automation of Clinical Electroencephalography*, Raven Press, New York, pp. 55–64.

Blackman, R. B., and Tukey, J. W. (1959). *The Measurement of Power Spectra*, Dover, New York.

Bostem, F. (1977). Postprocessing techniques. In A. Rémond (Ed.), *EEG Informatics. A Didactic Review of Methods and Applications of EEG Data Processing*, Elsevier/North-Holland Biomedical Press, Amsterdam, pp. 171–92.

Brazier, M. A. B. (1972). Symposium on computers in sleep research. In M. H. Chase (Ed.), *The Sleeping Brain*, Brain Research Institute Publications Office, University of California, Los Angeles.

Burch, N. R. (1959). Automatic analysis of the electroencephalogram: A review and classification of systems. *Electroenceph. Clin. Neurophysiol.*, **11**, 827–34.

Burch, N. R., Nettleton, W. J., Jr, Sweeney, J., and Edwards, R. J., Jr. (1964). Period analysis of the electroencephalogram on a general-purpose computer. In W. E. Tolles (Ed.), *Computers in Medicine and Biology. Ann. NY Acad. Sci.*, **115**, 827–43.

Chiappa, K. H., Brimm, J. E., Allen, B. A., Leibig, B. E., Rossiter, V. S., Stockard, J. J., Burchiel, K. J., and Bickford, R. G. (1976). Computing in EEG and epilepsy—Evolution of a comprehensive EEG analysis and reporting system. In P. Kellaway and I. Petersén (Eds.), *Quantitative Analytic Studies in Epilepsy*, Raven Press, New York, pp. 329–42.

Church, M. W., Johnson, L. C., and Seales, D. M. (1978). Evoked K-complexes and cardiovascular responses to spindle-synchronous and spindle-asynchronous stimulus clicks during NREM sleep. *Electroenceph. Clin. Neurophysiol.*, **45**, 443–53.

Demartini, J., and Vincent-Carrefour, A. (1977). Topics on pattern recognition. In A. Rémond (Ed.), *EEG Informatics. A Didactic Review of Methods and Applications of EEG Data Processing*, Elsevier/North-Holland Biomedical Press, Amsterdam, pp. 107–26.

Dolce, G., and Künkel, H. (Eds.) (1975). *CEAN - Computerized EEG Analysis*, G. Fischer Verlag, Stuttgart.

Drohocki, Z. (1948). L'intégrateur de l'électroproduction cérébrale pour l'électroencéphalographie quantitative. *Revue Neurol.*, **80**, 619–24.

Dumermuth, G. (1968). Variance spectra of electroencephalograms in twins. A contribution to the problem of quantification of EEG background activity in childhood. In P. Kellaway and I. Petersén (Eds.), *Clinical electroencephalography of Children*, Almqvist and Wiksell, Stockholm, pp. 119–54.

Dumermuth, G. (1973). Numerical spectral analysis of the electroencephalogram. *Handbook of Electroencephalography and Clinical Neurophysiology*, Vol. 5, part A, Elsevier, Amsterdam, pp. 33–60.

Dumermuth, G. (1977). Fundamentals of spectral analysis in electroencephalography. In A. Rémond (Ed.), *EEG Informatics. A Didactic Review of Methods and Applications of EEG Data Processing*, Elsevier/North-Holland Biomedical Press, Amsterdam, pp. 83–105.

Dumermuth, G., Huber, P. J., Kleiner, B., and Gasser, T. (1971). Analysis of the interrelations between frequency bands of the EEG by means of the bispectrum. *Electroenceph. Clin. Neurophysiol.*, **31**, 137–48.

Feinberg, I., Fein, G., Walker, J. M., Price, L. J., Floyd, T. C., and March, J. D. (1977). Flurazepam effects on slow-wave sleep: Stage 4 suppressed but number of delta waves constant. *Science*, **198**, 847–8.

Fink, M. (1977). Quantitative EEG analysis and psychopharmacology. In A. Rémond (Ed.), *EEG Informatics. A Didactic Review of Methods and Applications of EEG Data Processing.* Elsevier/North-Holland Biomedical Press, Amsterdam, pp. 301–18.

Fink, M., Itil, T., and Shapiro, D. M. (1967). Digital computer analysis of the human EEG in psychiatric research. *Comprehensive Psychiat.,* **8**, 521–38.

Gaillard, J. M., and Tissot, R. (1973). Principles of automatic analysis of sleep records with a hybrid system. *Comput. Biomed. Res.,* **6**, 1–13.

Gevins, A. S., Yeager, C. L., Zeitlin, G. M., Ancoli, S., and Dedon, M. F. (1977). On-line computer rejection of EEG artifact. *Electroenceph. Clin. Neurophysiol.,* **42**, 267–74.

Goldstein, L. (1975). Time domain analysis of the EEG. The integrative method. In G. Dolce and H. Künkel (Eds), *CEAN - Computerized EEG Analysis,* G. Fischer Verlag, Stuttgart, pp. 251–70.

Hanson, K., Stockard, J. J., Kalichman, M., and Bickford, R. G. (1974). Compressed spectral somnogram—A multiparameter spectral sleep display. *Proc. San Diego Biomed. Symp.,* **13**, 545–8.

Harner, R. N. (1977). EEG analysis in the time domain. In A. Rémond (Ed.), *EEG Informatics. A Didactic Review of Methods and Applications of EEG Data Processing,* Elsevier/North-Holland Biomedical Press, Amsterdam, pp. 57–82.

Harper, R. M. (1976). Magnetic-tape recording. In A. Rémond (Ed.), *Handbook of electroencephalography and clinical neurophysiology.* Vol. 3, part B, Elsevier, Amsterdam, pp. 24–51.

Itil, T. M. (1968). Electroencephalography and pharmacopsychiatry. In F. A. Freyhan, N. Petrilowitsch, and P. Pichot (Eds.), *Clinical Psychopharmacology: Modern Problems of Pharmacopsychiatry,* Karger, Basel, pp. 163–94.

Ives, J. R., and Woods, J. F. (1975). 4-channel 24 hour cassette recorder for long-term EEG monitoring of ambulatory patients. *Electroenceph. Clin. Neurophysiol.,* **39**, 88–92.

Jasper, H. H. (1958). The ten twenty electrode system of the International Federation. *Electroenceph. Clin. Neurophysiol.,* **10**, 371–5.

Jenkins, G. M., and Watts, D. G. (1968). *Spectral Analysis and its Applications,* Holden Day, San Francisco.

Johnson, L. C. (1974). Psychophysiological research: Aims and Methods. *Int. J. Psychiat. Med.,* **5**, 565–73.

Johnson, L. C., Hanson, K., and Bickford, R. G. (1976). Effect of flurazepam on sleep spindles and K-complexes. *Electroenceph. Clin. Neurophysiol.,* **40**, 67–77.

Johnson, L., Naitoh, P., Lubin, A., and Moses, J. (1972). Sleep stages and performance. In W. P. Colquhoun (Ed.), *Aspects of Human Efficiency.* English Universities Press, London, pp. 81–100.

Kellaway, P., and Petersén, I. (Eds.) (1973). *Automation of Clinical Electroencephalography,* Raven Press, New York.

Kellaway, P., and Petersén, I. (Eds.) (1976). *Quantitative Analytic Studies in Epilepsy,* Raven Press, New York.

Kiloh, L. G., McComas, A. J., and Osselton, J. W. (1972). *Clinical Electroencephalography,* 3rd ed., Butterworth, London.

Knott, J. R. (1953). Automatic frequency analysis. *Electroenceph. Clin. Neurophysiol., Suppl.* **4**, 17–25.

Kooi, K. A. (1971). *Fundamentals of Electroencephalography,* Harper and Row, New York.

Künkel, H. (1977). Historical review of principal methods. In A. Rémond (Ed.), *EEG Informatics. A Didactic Review of Methods and Applications of EEG Data Processing,* Elsevier/North-Holland Biomedical Press, Amsterdam, pp. 9–25.

N

Le Beux, P. (1977). Computers – Principles of operation. In A. Rémond (Ed.), *EEG Informatics. A Didactic Review of Methods and Applications of EEG Data Processing,* Elsevier/North-Holland Biomedical Press, Amsterdam, pp. 127–42.

Loomis, A. L., Harvey, E. N., and Hobart, G. (1935). Potential rhythms of the cerebral cortex during sleep. *Science,* **81**, 597–8.

MacGillivray, B. B. (Ed.) (1974). Traditional methods of examination in clinical EEG. In A. Rémond (Ed.-in-Chief), *Handbook of Electroencephalography and Clinical Neurophysiology.* Vol. 5, part C, Elsevier, Amsterdam.

MacGillivray, B. B. (1977). The application of automated EEG analysis to the diagnosis of epilepsy. In A. Rémond (Ed.), *EEG Informatics. A Didactic Review of Methods and Applications of EEG Data Processing,* Elsevier/North-Holland Biomedical Press, Amsterdam, pp. 243–61.

MacGillivray, B. B., and Wadbrook, D. G. (1975). A system for extracting a diagnosis from the clinical EEG. In H. Künkel and G. Dolce (Eds.), *Computerized EEG Analysis,* Fischer Verlag, Stuttgart, pp. 344–64.

Margerison, J. H., St. John-Loe, P., and Binnie, C. D. (1967). Electroencephalography. In P. H. Venables and I. Martin (Eds.), *A Manual of Psychophysiological Methods,* North-Holland, Amsterdam, pp. 351–402.

Matoušek, M. (Ed.) (1973). Frequency and correlation analysis. In A. Rémond (Ed.-in-Chief), *Handbook of Electroencephalography and Clinical Neurophysiology,* Vol. 5, part A, Elsevier, Amsterdam.

Matoušek, M. (1977). Clinical application of EEG analysis: Presentation of EEG results and dialogue with the clinician. In A. Rémond (Ed.), *EEG Informatics. A Didactic Review of Methods and Applications of EEG Data Processing,* Elsevier/North-Holland Biomedical Press, Amsterdam, pp. 233–42.

Matoušek, M., and Petersén, I. (1973a). Frequency analysis of the EEG in normal children and adolescents. In P. Kellaway and I. Petersén (Eds.), *Automation of Clinical Electroencephalography,* Raven Press, New York, p. 318.

Matoušek, M., and Petersén, I. (1973b). Automatic evaluation of EEG background activity by means of age-dependent EEG quotients. *Electroenceph. Clin. Neurophysiol.,* **35**, 603–12.

Medawar, P. B. (1969). *Induction and Intuition in Scientific Thought.* American Philosophical Society, Philadelphia.

Rechtschaffen, A., and Kales, A. (Eds.) (1968), *A Manual of Standardized Terminology, Techniques and Scoring System for Sleep Stages of Human Subjects,* US Government Printing Office, Washington, DC.

Rémond, A. (Ed.-in-Chief) (1972). *Handbook of Electroencephalography and Clinical Neurophysiology,* Vol. 4, Elsevier, Amsterdam.

Rémond, A. (Ed.-in-Chief) (1973), *Handbook of Electroencephalography and Clinical Neurophysiology,* Vol. 5, Elsevier, Amsterdam.

Rémond, A. (Ed.) (1977). *EEG Informatics. A Didactic Review of Methods and Applications of EEG Data Processing,* Elsevier/North-Holland Biomedical Press, Amsterdam.

Rémond, A., and Storm Van Leeuwen, W. (1977). Why analyze, quantify or process routine clinical EEG. In A. Rémond (Ed.), *EEG Informatics. A Didactic Review of Methods and Applications of EEG Data Processing,* Elsevier/North-Holland Biomedical Press, Amsterdam, pp. 1–7.

Saltzberg, B., Lustick, L. S., and Heath, R. G. (1970). A non-parametric method of determining general EEG changes due to the administration of drugs. *Electroenceph. Clin. Neurophysiol.,* **28**, 102.

Schwartz, J., Feldstein, S., Fink, M. Shapiro, D. M., and Itil, T. M. (1971). Evidence for a characteristic EEG frequency response to thiopental. *Electroenceph. Clin. Neurophysiol.,* **31**, 149–53.

Smith, J. R., and Karacan, I. (1971). EEG sleep stage scoring by an automatic hybrid system. *Electroenceph. Clin. Neurophysiol.*, **31**, 231–7.

Smith, J. R., Karacan, I., and Yang, M. (1977). Ontogeny of delta activity during human sleep. *Electroenceph. Clin. Neurophysiol.*, **43**, 229–37.

Smith, J. R., Negrin, M., and Nevis, A. H. (1969). Automatic analysis of sleep electroencephalograms by hybrid computation. *IEEE Trans. Syst. Sci. Cyber.*, **SSC-5**, 278–83.

Sterman, M. B., Harper, R. M., Havens, B., Hoppenbrouwers, T., McGinty, D. J., and Hodgman, J. E. (1977). Quantitative analysis of infant EEG development during quiet sleep. *Electroenceph. Clin. Neurophysiol.*, **43**, 371–85.

Venables, P. H., and Martin, I. (Eds.) (1967). *A Manual of Psychophysiological Methods*, North-Holland, Amsterdam.

Vos, J. E. (1977). Between EEG-machine and computer: Data storage and data conversion. In A. Rémond (Ed.), *EEG Informatics. A Didactic Review of Methods and Applications of EEG Data Processing*, Elsevier/North-Holland Biomedical Press, Amsterdam, pp. 143–55.

Walter, D. O. (1968). On units and dimension for reporting spectral intensities. *Electroenceph. Clin. Neurophysiol.*, **24**, 486–7.

Walter, D. O. (Ed.) (1972). Digital processing of bioelectrical phenomena. In A. Rémond (Ed.-in-Chief), *Handbook of Electroencephalography and Clinical Neurophysiology*, Vol. 4, part B, Elsevier, Amsterdam.

Walter, D. O. (1977). The context of EEG analysis, and classification of some methods for such analysis. In A. Rémond (Ed.), *EEG Informatics. A Didactic Review of Methods and Applications of EEG Data Processing*, Elsevier/North-Holland Biomedical Press, Amsterdam, pp. 27–35.

Walter, W. G. (1943). An automatic low-frequency analyser. *Electron. Engng.*, **16**, 9–13.

Wiederholt, W. C., and Iragui-Madoz, V. J. (1977). Far field somatosensory potentials in the rat. *Electroenceph. Clin. Neurophysiol.*, **42**, 456–65.

Wilkinson, R. T., and Mullaney, D. (1976). Electroencephalogram recording of sleep in the home. *Postgrad. Med. J.*, **52**, *Suppl.* 7, 92–6.

THE USE OF HUMAN EVENT-RELATED POTENTIALS IN PSYCHOLOGY*

TERENCE W. PICTON

*Acknowledgements. The author gratefully appreciates the research assistance of Guy Proulx, Jacinthe Baribeau-Braun, and Donald Stuss; the secretarial help of Barbara Reynolds and Janice O'Farrell; and the financial support of the Medical Research Council of Canada and the Ontario Mental Health Foundation.

1 Event-related potentials (ERPs)

The event-related potentials (ERPs) are changes in the electrical activity of the nervous system recorded in response to physical stimuli, in association with psychological processes, or in preparation for motor activity. This chapter will consider the methodology of the recording and analysis of ERPs, and will review the principle of their use in human psychology. Reference will be made to the experimental ERP literature in an illustrative rather than an exhaustive manner.

2 Recording techniques

2.1 Principles of averaging

Occasionally, for example during sleep or in response to particularly intense or meaningful stimuli, it is possible to recognize ERPs in the conventional EEG recording. For the most part, however, human ERPs recorded from the scalp are too small to detect in the ongoing EEG. The recognition of these ERPs therefore requires the use of techniques to distinguish them from the obscuring background activity. The most common technique used is 'signal averaging' (Cooper, Osselton, and Shaw, 1974, pp. 159–77; Picton and Hink, 1974; Vaughan, 1974; Glaser and Ruchkin, 1976, pp. 177–219).

The averaging of ERPs requires that the physical stimulus, psychological activity, or behaviour be repeated. With each occurrence the electrical activity is recorded over a period of time related to the event. This electrical activity will consist of a combination of 'signal' potentials specifically related to the repeating event, and unrelated background electroencephalographic 'noise'. This recorded activity is converted into a series of numbers denoting the voltage values at particular times related to the event. This process is termed 'analog-to-digital' (AD) conversion, since the recorded waveform that varies continuously with the voltage at the scalp is changed into a series of discrete numbers. The sequences of numbers recorded at the same times in relation to the repeating events are then averaged together. The background activity, being random with respect to the event, will on averaging tend toward a similar mean value at each point in time, with less and less deviation from the mean as the averaging proceeds. Thus, with averaging the EEG will approach but never actually reach a straight line. If the background activity is a normally distributed random variable, its amplitude range decreases by a square root factor of the number of trials averaged. The ERP, however, being the same with every event, remains constant during the averaging process and becomes more and more recognizable in the decreasing EEG noise. The process of averaging is illustrated diagrammatically in the right portion of Figure 6.8.

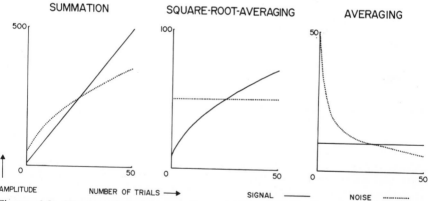

Figure 6.8 Theory of signal averaging. Averaging is based upon the fact that whereas the average of a constant waveform ('signal') remains constant, the average of a random variable (the 'noise') approaches a mean value (a straight line) and its range of deviation from that mean decreases as a function of the square root of the number of trials. This is illustrated in the right section of this figure. An ERP signal of 10 μV unrecognizable in a background EEG noise of 50 μV becomes visible through averaging. Most computers simply add the single-trial waveforms together as illustrated in the left section of the figure. The summed waveform can then be scaled prior to write-out. If the scaling is done by a factor equivalent to the reciprocal of the number of trials averaged, then true averaging occurs. If the summed waveform is divided by the square root of the number of trials, however, the general noise level remains constant, and any waveform that continues to grow represents a definite signal. This is illustrated in the middle section of the figure as 'square-root averaging'

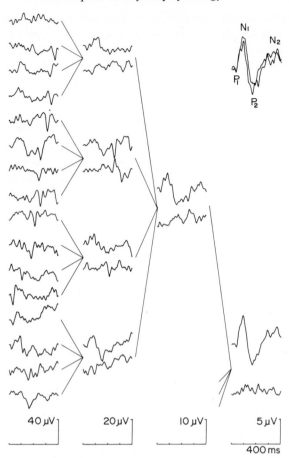

Figure 6.9   The process of ERP averaging. This figure illustrates the averaging of
the slow components of the auditory evoked potential. The first column shows
sixteen-trial responses to a 70 dBSL, 1 kHz, 50 ms toneburst with 5 ms rise and
fall times presented to the left ear. These responses were recorded between vertex
and right mastoid with relative negativity at the vertex showing as an upward
deflection. In the second column, groups of four responses have been averaged
together. In the upper tracings the responses have all been added together, and
in the lower tracings they have been alternately added and subtracted so as to
give   a   representation   of   the   level   of   residual   unaveraged   background
noise—the ($\pm$) average. The third column shows the average of all 16 responses,
again with a ($\pm$) average in the lower tracing. At the bottom of the fourth column is
the average of 64 responses to the toneburst. In the upper right corner of the figure
are superimposed two averages of 32 responses each. This superimposition
illustrates the replicability of the response. These tracings have been labelled using a
sequential nomenclature of P_1, N_1, P_2, N_2. The general scaling of the responses
(shown at the bottom of the figure) has been adjusted so that the range of the
averaged   noise   remains   approximately   constant—the   'square-root   averaging'
illustrated in Figure 6.8

Most special purpose averaging computers do not actually average, but rather just add the digitized waveforms together. The amplitude of the averaged activity is then appropriately scaled for monitor display or for write-out. When simple summation is used the ERP will continue to increase in size according to the number of trials averaged, whereas the background activity will increase only according to the square root of the number of trials. This is illustrated in the left portion of Figure 6.8. A process that perhaps allows optimal monitoring of the averaging process is one wherein the background noise levels are maintained relatively constant. To do this the summated activity is divided by the square root of the number of trials, in a process that may be termed 'square-root averaging'. Using this procedure any waveform that continues to increase in size will represent a real ERP as distinct from the background noise which remains relatively constant. This process is diagrammed in the middle section of Figure 6.8, and illustrated with actual ERP waveforms in Figure 6.9.

A major problem with the averaging process is that it may be difficult to determine that the final waveform represents an actual ERP and not just residual background activity that has not been completely eliminated by averaging. There are several approaches to this problem (Glaser and Ruchkin, 1976, pp. 180–8). If the computer can be programmed and there is sufficient memory, a standard deviation for the average waveform can be calculated, and one can then evaluate how significantly different the actual waveform is from the expected mean value of the background noise using a simple *t*-statistic. A second technique involves replicating the average tracing. The separation between the superimposed average waveforms gives visual demonstration of the variability of the recording since the standard error of the mean waveform is approximately equal to half the separation of the replicate waveform. This use of superimposed tracings is illustrated in the upper right of Figure 6.9.

Another way of estimating the amount of residual background activity is the '(±)average' (Schimmel, 1967). This procedure alternately adds and subtracts the recorded activity so as to cancel out any ERP effect. The background noise, however, remains similarly random regardless of its polarity and averages out in much the same way as during the simple additive averaging. The (±) average then gives an estimate of the level of remaining background activity in the absence of any ERP. In Figure 6.9 (±) averages are shown below the averaged ERP waveform at each of the averaging stages.

2.2 Assumptions and problems of averaging

The formal requirements of the averaging process are that the ERPs be identical with each event, and that the EEG noise be normally distributed about a mean and independent with each repetition. These requirements are not always met during the recording of average ERPs. It is therefore important to understand the distortion that may result if these requirements are not fulfilled, and the possible techniques available to evaluate and reduce such distortions (Glaser and Ruchkin, 1976, pp. 189–219).

The ERP may not be constant with repetition. If it changes in amplitude, the averaged ERP will represent the mean amplitude of all the individual ERPs and will give little indication of the changes in the ERP amplitude that occurred during the averaging process. This variability of the ERP over the time of the averaging can be assessed by using repeated subaverages, or by using cumulative summing procedures. The latencies of ERP components may also fluctuate during the averaging session, and this may distort the amplitude, latency and the morphology of the resultant waveform (Callaway, 1975, p. 64). This distortion can be reduced in certain cases by using special adaptive filtering techniques (Woody, 1967). Each individual recorded waveform is cross-correlated to a postulated template of what the ERP probably looks like (for example the conventional average waveform) in order to get an estimation of the latency of maximum correlation. The data are then aligned according to these latencies and re-averaged to form a second template. This procedure is repeated until the average correlation between the template and the individual recordings does not change significantly with further iteration. This technique requires a fair amount of computer manipulation and is only valid when the ERP waveform is large enough to be reasonably recognizable in the background activity by the correlation procedure.

The recorded EEG may not fulfil the 'noise' requirements of the averaging process. Occasionally amounts of electrical activity may be recorded, usually in relation to artifacts, that are far beyond the usual range of the background EEG. These aberrant recordings will distort the normal distribution of the background activity and may remain in the final waveform despite the averaging. One approach to this problem involves the calculation of the 'median' of the ERP, such an estimate of the central value being much less susceptible to aberrant data than the arithmetic mean. A second approach to this problem is to reject from averaging all trials wherein the normal range of values is exceeded. When the background noise is rhythmic, as is often the case with the EEG, averaging may not cancel out this activity since there will be some correlation between the noise samples among trials. In this case the averaged ERP waveform may effectively 'lock-on' to a rhythm in the EEG or the recording equipment. This problem can be diminished by making the event aperiodic and infrequent relative to the noise frequencies.

One major problem with averaging is that it requires repetition of the event and is therefore often unsuitable for the evaluation of processes that occur singly or in small numbers. Two approaches may be considered if it is necessary to have some evaluation of single trial ERPs. The recognition of a signal in background noise can be optimized prior to single-trial evaluation or to a small-number averaging by using special filtering procedures (Wiener, 1949). A 'Wiener filter' is a type of bandpass filter with a frequency transfer function that is proportional to the signal-to-noise ratio at each frequency (Doyle, 1975). For example, in order to optimize the recognition of a visual evoked potential (with major frequencies in the 1–5 Hz region) that is obscured in an alpha rhythm background (8–13 Hz), a Wiener filter would pass the lower frequency activity but reject the alpha-frequency activity (Hartwell and Erwin, 1976). Another approach to the evaluation of single-trial ERPs involves discriminant analysis. If the single trial recordings are known to belong to one of two separate classes (for example, 'ERP-present' versus 'ERP-absent', or one type of stimulus versus another), they can be identified as being more similar to one or the other class by using a simple discriminant function derived from the analysis of a training series of ERPs of known classification (Squires and Donchin, 1976; Glaser and Ruchkin, 1976, pp. 220–30).

As a technique for evaluating the human ERPs, therefore, averaging is not perfect. Nevertheless, provided one is aware of its limitations, averaging remains the most powerful and reliable of the techniques available for the recording of human ERPs.

2.3 Necessary equipment

The equipment necessary for recording average ERPs divides into four basic parts as shown in Figure 6.10.

The first section of the equipment allows the experimenter to organize the general experimental paradigm. This may be done by using logic and timing modules, or by using the interactive capabilities of a small laboratory computer. The purposes of this section of the equipment are to provide the general timing for the stimulus presentation, and to evaluate various behavioural responses. Different types of stimuli and/or responses are then classified and specific synchronization pulses are provided to time-lock the averaging process to these events.

The second section of the equipment involves the generation of the sensory stimuli and their presentation to the subject. This is synchronized by the timing process of the experimental logic. The general purpose of this section of the equipment is to control the physical characteristics of the sensory stimuli that are presented to the subject.

The third part of the experimental equipment is concerned with the recording of the EEG from scalp electrodes. This electrical activity is

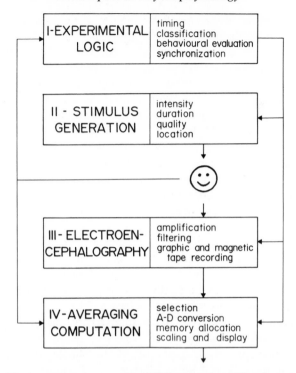

Figure 6.10   Equipment necessary for ERP averaging. The four sections of the equipment shown diagrammatically in this figure are not necessarily separate in reality. For example, both the stimulus presentation and the ERP averaging may be done using the same laboratory computer. The connecting lines to the right of the figure represent the synchronization processes whereby the stimuli are generated, the tape-recordings are coded, and the evoked potentials averaged. The lines to the left represent the monitoring of responses from the subject, for example, by a variety of button-press reactions

amplified so as to be of sufficient voltage to be evaluated by the AD convertor of the averaging system. The activity is also filtered to remove those frequencies in the recording which may unnecessarily increase the variability of the ERP waveform. In general the filter should just pass the frequencies necessary for the accurate delineation of the ERP waveform. If these frequencies are not known, two rules-of-thumb are that the highest frequency to be admitted for averaging should be approximately one quarter of the AD conversion rate, and the lowest frequency should have a wavelength of less than four times the period over which the average ERP is recorded (Picton and Hink, 1974). The amplified and filtered EEG may be input directly to the averaging computer, or may be stored along with the synchronization pulses on magnetic tape for later analysis. If possible, it is usually advantageous to record a graphic monitor of the EEG and the synchronization pulses, in order to obtain a permanent record of what occurred during the experiment.

The final stage of the equipment involves the computer that calculates and displays the average ERP. This computer acquires the EEG data over a selected period of time in relation to the synchronization pulses from the experimental logic. During this period of time the EEG is converted at a selected rate into a series of digital values and stored in the computer memory. The storage procedure may involve simple addition to previously stored data, or may also involve allocation of different ERPs to different memory locations according to different classifications provided by the experimental logic. The average waveforms present in the memory can then be manipulated and displayed. The final waveform is usually written out on paper, but can also be transferred to magnetic tape or disc for further analysis.

3 Non-cerebral potentials

3.1 General principles

There are a multitude of non-cerebral potentials that can be recorded as part of the average ERP (Picton and Hink, 1974). Unless these can be identified and their effect minimized, such artifacts can markedly distort the morphology of the recorded waveform and confuse its interpretation. Since the averaging technique makes visible what is not visible in the background EEG, the student of ERPs must have a much greater concern with possible non-cerebral artifacts than the electroencephalographer. If possible such artifacts must be eliminated, and if this is impossible they must be identified and monitored so as to prevent their misinterpretation as deriving from the brain. A general philosophy with which to approach ERP research is to consider all recordings to be artifact until there is reasonable proof that they are not. There are basically two kinds of artifact that one should consider in ERP research—those deriving from the subject in the form of non-cerebral physiological potentials, and those resulting from the electrical noise in the subject's surroundings.

3.2 Electrical artifacts

Electrical contaminants of the ERP recording can derive from many possible sources (Lindsley and Wicke, 1974, pp. 64–76). Simple electrostatic potentials induced in a subject by such things as friction with clothing can change with movement and cause large artifacts in the scalp-recorded activity. Potentials may also be induced in the subject or the recording electrodes by the electromagnetic fields surrounding power lines, electrical transformers and electrical motors. Such artifacts can be reduced by moving the subject as far as possible from the source of the artifact, adequately grounding the subject, and/or by shielding the recording area with a material of high electrical conductivity and magnetic permeability. Probably the most troublesome of such artifacts in ERP research are those related to the sensory stimuli that are presented to the subject. Such artifacts will occur repeatedly and consistently with each stimulus and cannot be removed by averaging. These potentials can be decreased by shielding the stimulator, and in some cases by using stimuli of alternating electrical polarity.

Voltages can also be picked up from electromagnetic radiation fields deriving from general radio transmissions and switching circuits in the experimental logic. These artifacts can be reduced by shielding. Since such artifacts are usually picked up fairly equally in all of the recording electrodes, they may also be reduced by using differential amplifiers with high common-mode-rejection.

The final source of electrical artifact occurs when electrical current is directly injected into the subject as a stimulus in the evaluation of the somatosensory evoked potentials. Artifacts from this source can be decreased by minimizing the current necessary for stimulation (for example, by having the electrodes as close as possible to the nerve being stimulated) and by using a large low-impedance ground electrode located between the stimulating and recording electrodes.

Once the pick-up of electrical noise has been minimized by the preceding techniques, its effect on the average ERP recording can if necessary be further reduced by several techniques. Notch-filtering can be used to remove such things as line noise from the recording, provided such filtering does not distort the ERP. If distortion of the ERP might result from this filtering, the stimuli can be presented at intervals equal to an odd number of half-periods of the line noise, such that with averaging the noise will continually cancel itself out.

3.3 Physiological artifacts

Electrical activity deriving from multiple physiological sources other than the brain can occur during the recording of ERPs. These artifacts can interfere with the interpretation of the ERP either by increasing the general noise level of the recording or by being temporally related to the event eliciting the cerebral ERP.

The human eyes provide major sources of non-cerebral activity that can contaminate human ERP recording. There is a standing potential of several millivolts between the cornea and the retina of the normal human eye, with the former being positive with respect to the latter. Eyeblinks cause a positive potential in the anterior scalp regions by connecting those areas to the positive potential at the cornea (Matsuo, Peters, and Reilly, 1975). Eye movements contribute a positive potential to those areas of the scalp toward which the eyes are moved (Hillyard and Galambos, 1970). Some ocular artifacts can be subtracted from the recorded EEG, for example by using as a reference electrode a potentiometer combination of forehead and mastoid electrodes (Cooper, Osselton, and Shaw, 1974, p. 176).

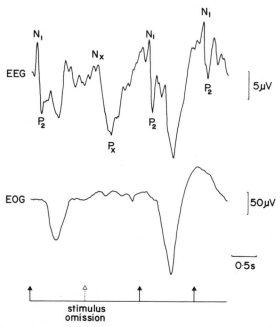

Figure 6.11 Electro-ocular artifacts in ERP research. Clicks of 55 dBSL intensity were presented regularly every 1.1 seconds to the right ear and occasionally one of the clicks was omitted. The subject was instructed to attend to this train of click stimuli and to count the number of omissions. The upper tracing in this figure represents the average ERPs over 32 trials recorded between the vertex and right mastoid with negativity at the vertex being represented by an upward deflection. The averaging sweep began at the click immediately preceding the omission and continued for 5.12 seconds. The lower tracing represents a simultaneously averaged electro-oculogram (EOG) recorded between the upper and lower orbital ridges of the right eye, at 1/13 the gain of the EEG. Each click evokes a clear N_1-P_2 complex in the averaged EEG tracing. As well, there are large late positive waves following the first click, the stimulus omission, and the subsequent click. As can be seen from the EOG monitor the late positive waves following the clicks represent eyeblinks recorded from the vertex at a distance from their generation. The late positive component following the stimulus omission, however, represents a definite cerebral event, being part of an N_x-P_x 'decision-complex' associated with the detection of the stimulus omission

However, since the scalp distribution of the potentials related to blinks and to eye movements are different, it is impossible to subtract both artifacts in this manner. In most cases it is preferable to monitor artifacts using peri-orbital electrodes, to reject contaminated trials from averaging and to average the electro-oculogram simultaneously to ensure that the rejection is effective. Figure 6.11 illustrates how ocular artifacts can cause great distortion in the ERPs recorded from the vertex.

The scalp musculature may show small reflex responses to stimuli that are being presented to the subject. Such 'microreflexes' (Bickford, 1972) are particularly evident when intense stimuli are used and when the muscles are under some degree of resting tension. The reflexes tend to occur mainly in the 8–80 ms region after a stimulus, and the recorded potentials in this latency range are often extremely difficult to interpret. The cerebral ERPs at this latency can be shown to have different scalp distributions from the muscle reflexes and to continue to be present with the muscle relaxation of moderate to deep sleep. It is impossible however, to determine at these latencies whether small changes in the recorded waveform are due to actual changes in the cerebral ERP or to the superimposition of muscle artifact.

Movement of the muscles of the face and tongue can also cause large electrical fields that will be picked up from scalp electrodes. These pose particular problems for the study of speech-related potentials (Szirtes and Vaughan, 1977). Such artifacts should be closely monitored during the experiment with facial and submental electrodes, and contaminated trials must be eliminated from averaging.

Stimulus-related potentials generated in the skin underneath the recording electrodes can markedly distort the measurement of cerebral slow potentials (Picton and Hillyard, 1972). The most efficient way of preventing such problems is to scratch the skin under the recording electrodes such that an interelectrode impedance measurement is less than 1 kΩ in the 0–50 Hz frequency range.

4 Human ERP components

4.1 Definition and nomenclature

The human ERP reflects a complex interactive process between an individual and the environment. Different parts of this waveform may specifically relate to different aspects of the environment, to different psychological integrations within the brain, or to different response systems.

The usual means of identifying ERP components involves the visual recognition of 'peaks' in the recorded waveform. Such peaks can then be named according to their sequence (in numerical or alphabetical order) and polarity, as is illustrated in Figure 6.12 which shows the various sensory-evoked potentials recorded from vertex to mastoid electrodes in response to an auditory stimulus (Picton and coworkers, 1974). The 'fast' components of the response are identified as a series of small positive waves recorded in the first 10 ms and numbered sequentially using Roman numerals. The 'middle' latency components occur in the 10–50 ms range and are identified using polarity and a combined numerical and alphabetical sequence (the relatively small N_O and P_O components having been recognized after the later components!). The 'slow' components occur between 50 and 500 ms and are identified as P_1, N_1, P_2, N_2.

Obviously a sequential nomenclature is open to criticisms of confusion and complexity, and a latency nomenclature has also been proposed wherein components are identified by their polarity and peak latency (Donchin and coworkers, 1977). In this nomenclature the wave V of the

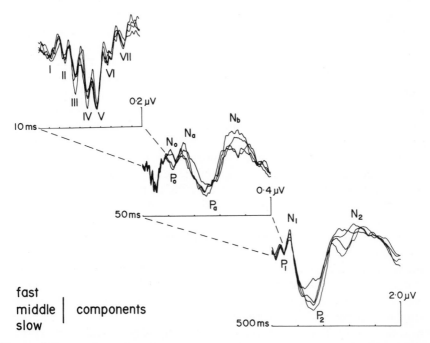

Figure 6.12   Auditory evoked potentials. This figure shows the evoked potentials to a 60 dBSL click stimulus presented to the right ear at a rate of once a second. Recordings were made between the vertex and right mastoid with relative negativity at the vertex being represented by an upward deflection. Averaging was done using three separate time bases to show the fast, middle and slow components of the evoked potential. Each tracing represents the average of 1024 individual responses. This figure is adapted from data of Picton and coworkers (1974)

fast auditory response would be called P6 and component N_1 would be identified as N90. This is more accurate than the sequential nomenclature but its very precision can at times cause problems. The latency of a component may vary with the intensity or rise time of the stimulus, or with the time required for perceptual processing. Wave V varies in latency from 5.5–8.5 ms as intensity decreases without obviously changing its identity, and the late positive component of the sensory evoked potential related to perceptual decisions may vary in peak latency from 300 to 900 ms depending upon the difficulty of the decision. To allow for such variance, theoretical components may be identified by their characteristic latency, and a superimposed line used to show that such an identification is theoretical rather than observational, for example 'P300'.

Another parameter that must be considered in the identification of ERP components is the location of the recording electrodes. Part of the primary cortical somatosensory response is generated in the posterior wall of the Rolandic fissure creating a dipole that is parallel to the scalp surface. The same ERP component can therefore be recorded from the anterior scalp regions as a positive wave with peak latency of 20 ms and more posteriorly as an N20 wave. Furthermore it is quite possible that components with the same polarity and general latency recorded from different scalp areas, such as the negative components at around 150 ms recorded in response to visual stimuli from the vertex and from the occiput, reflect separate and distinct underlying components.

The actual component structure of an ERP waveform may not correlate with visually recognizable peaks. It is impossible to determine whether these peaks represent discrete physiological events or whether they are actually a recording artifact resulting from several overlapping components of similar latency. Probably the most important factor in the definition of ERP components is the functional relationship of a part of the waveform to experimental variation (Donchin, Ritter, and McCallum, 1978). Any distinct component of the waveform must be affected by experimental manipulation in a manner unique from any other component. Such an approach to component identification lends itself to objective mathematical evaluation. An analysis of the principal components of a waveform yields a series of components contributing independently to the recorded variance during an experiment (Glaser and Ruchkin, 1976, pp. 233–90; Squires and coworkers, 1977). Such a technique can be extremely helpful provided that its limitations are recognized. Changes in the latency of a component and non-linear interactions among different components can reduce the effectiveness of the procedure. Furthermore, such an analysis will not identify components of the waveform that remain unaffected by the limited experimental manipulations that are studied. Nevertheless, such techniques, when applied with appropriate judgement and imagination, can greatly further our understanding of the structure of the scalp-recorded ERP and its relation to human information processing.

There is a large variety of different ERP components that can be recorded from the human scalp. Perhaps the most useful present classification depends upon the relationship of the component to external stimuli. 'Exogenous' or 'evoked' components of the ERP are largely determined by the physical characteristics of the external stimulus. 'Endogenous' (Sutton and coworkers, 1965) or 'emitted' (Weinberg and coworkers 1974) potentials occur independently of the external stimuli, being 'invoked' by the psychological demands of a situation (Donchin, Ritter, and McCallum, 1978). Certain components of the ERP, such as the N_1 component of the vertex potential which are determined both by physical and by psychological factors, may be considered 'mesogenous' (Hillyard, Picton, and Regan, 1978).

The exogenous components can be further divided into 'transient', 'sustained', and 'steady-state' responses (Hillyard, Picton, and Regan, 1978). Transient evoked potentials are elicited by a stimulus change whereas sustained potentials occur during the continuation of a stimulus (Picton, Woods, and Proulx, 1978). Steady-state evoked potentials are evoked by stimuli of sufficiently high repetition rate that there is an overlapping of responses to form a continuous waveform with constant amplitude and phase relationship to the repeating stimulus (Regan, 1972, p. 36).

The endogenous components of the human ERP can be further classified into 'preparatory' and 'integrative' potentials. The preparatory potentials are those related to specific motor activity such as the 'readiness' potential that occurs prior to self-paced motor actions (Deecke, Scheid, and Kornhuber, 1969). The integrative components are related to complex human perceptual activity, and include such waveforms as the 'late positive component' of the sensory-evoked potential (Sutton and coworkers, 1965) and the 'contingent negative variation' (Walter and coworkers, 1964).

4.2 Exogenous components

All parts of a sensory system from the receptor to the association areas of the cerebral cortex can contribute to the sensory-evoked potentials that are recorded from the human scalp. This is particularly true for the auditory system (Picton and coworkers, 1977). The cochlear microphonic potential generated by the hair cell receptors of the cochlea can be recorded from electrodes on the mastoid or auricle. A series of vertex-positive waves recorded in the first 10 ms after an abrupt auditory stimulus represents the activation of the cochlear nerve and brainstem auditory nuclei. Between 10 and 50 ms there is a complex response recorded from the scalp that reflects auditory activity in the thalamus and cortex as well as possible scalp muscle artifacts. The slow components of the transient auditory response probably derive from the activation of various areas of primary and association cortex. Auditory sustained potentials can be recorded from the human scalp in response to sounds of more than a few tenths of a second in duration (Picton, Woods, and Proulx, 1978).

The somatosensory evoked potentials are usually elicited by electrical stimulation of a peripheral nerve. Responses to mechanical stimulation have somewhat smaller amplitudes and longer latencies than those following electrical stimulation. In response to median nerve stimulation it is possible to record a series of early components deriving from the brachial plexus, spinal cord and brainstem (Cracco and Cracco, 1976; Jones, 1977). Following these early components there is a wave of

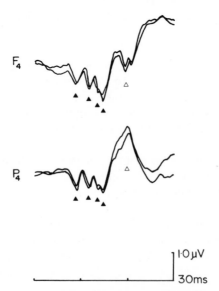

Figure 6.13 Near- and far-field components of the somatosensory evoked potential. ERPs were recorded from right frontal and parietal electrodes referred to the right shoulder with negativity of the scalp electrodes being represented by an upward deflection. Electrical pulses of 0.1 ms duration were delivered at a rate of 10 per second through subdermal needle electrodes to the left median nerve at the wrist. The intensity of these stimuli was 20% in excess of the threshold intensity necessary to elicit a twitch in the thenar muscles. Each tracing represents the average of 2048 responses. Four early positive waves, occurring at 9, 11.5, 13.5, and 15 ms, and identified in the figure by filled triangles, are very similar at both electrode sites. These are far-field responses generated from the brachial plexus, spinal cord, brainstem and thalamus. At 20 ms there is a component identified with open triangles that is recorded as a positive wave from the frontal electrode and as a negative wave from the parietal region. This is a near-field response generated in the primary somatosensory cortex on the posterior bank of the Rolandic fissure

probable thalamic origin at approximately 15 ms (Cracco, 1972) and then a series of complexly overlapping components reflecting the activation of the various somatosensory cortices (Allison and coworkers, 1979). These components of the somatosensory-evoked potential are illustrated in Figure 6.13. The slow components of the somatosensory response seem to reflect the overlapping fields of 'parallel' late waves generated in the primary sensory area and in association cortex (Donald, 1976).

Visual-evoked potentials from the neurons of the retina may be recorded as the electroretinogram using peri-orbital electrodes. In the occipital regions of the brain a flash stimulus elicits a complex series of waves beginning at around 25 ms (Broughton, Meier-Ewart, and Ebe, 1969). The morphology of this response in the 50–250 ms range is quite dependent upon the contrast and pattern of the visual stimulus (White, 1974; Spekreijse, Estevez, and Reits, 1977). When a stimulus involves mainly a change in pattern without any change in the intensity of the stimulus, the morphology of the occipital response becomes much simpler. In response

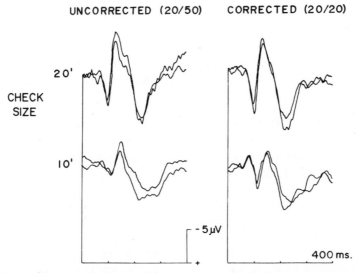

Figure 6.14   Visual evoked potentials to pattern stimuli. Responses were recorded between the right occipital region (0_2) and the right mastoid, with relative negativity of the occiput being shown as an upward deflection. Circular checkerboard stimuli subtending a visual field of 16° were presented to the right eye. The checkerboard pattern was reversed (over 10 ms) every second, and the evoked potentials were averaged in response to this pattern reversal. Each tracing represents the average of 64 individual responses. The pattern-evoked potentials were recorded using two different check sizes when the subject viewed the stimulus with and without refractive correction for myopia. The amplitude of the ERP components is dependent upon the size of the checks, and also upon the clarity with which such stimuli arrive at the retina

to a reversing checkerboard, for example, there is a simple bi- or triphasic response containing a distinct positive component in the 80–120 ms range (depending upon the speed of the pattern reversal) that is best recorded using a frontal reference electrode (Halliday, McDonald, and Mushin, 1973). This response is illustrated in Figure 6.14. In response to rapidly repeating visual stimuli a multitude of steady-state responses can be recorded from the occipital region (Regan, 1972).

4.3 Mesogenous components

In all sensory systems there is a large complex of waves recorded from the vertex region with latencies in the 50–250 ms range. This response to stimulus change has often been termed the 'vertex potential'. The morphologies and scalp distributions of these responses in the various sensory modalities are quite similar, suggesting that the vertex potential reflects similar though not necessarily identical underlying processes in each sensory system (Goff and coworkers, 1977; Allison, 1977). There are large interactions among the responses to stimuli in different sensory modalities (Davies and coworkers, 1972), suggesting that the vertex potentials derive from generators activated by all sensory modalities. It has therefore been suggested that the vertex potential might reflect the convergence of sensory information from different sensory modalities onto areas of association cortex particularly in the frontal lobe (Picton and Hink, 1974).

It is probable that several underlying sources contribute to the scalp-recorded waveform in the latency range of the vertex potential. In the somatosensory system, for example, specific late responses from the region of the primary somatosensory cortex have been distinguished from a more non-specific vertex potential deriving from frontal association cortex (Donald, 1976; Goff and coworkers, 1979). This concept of several underlying components raises the possibility that the so-called mesogenous components represent overlapping exogenous and endogenous components of the ERP. Whether there are distinct components in this latency range that are related on the one hand to stimulus parameters and on the other hand to psychological factors is, however, still unknown. If indeed there are such overlapping components, one can hypothesize that they might reflect a general comparative process whereby incoming exogenous information is related to relevant endogenous memories prior to its interpretation (Picton and coworkers, 1978a).

4.4 Endogenous components

After 200 ms there is a large number of waves related more to the psychological context than to the physical characteristics of a stimulus. This variety of electrical responsiveness probably reflects the general adaptability of the human brain in the processing of sensory information to behavioural response.

One of the most widely studied of these late endogenous components of the ERP is a parietocentral positive wave occurring with a latency of 300 ms or more and variously named the 'P_3', 'P300', 'late positive component', or 'association cortex potential'. This component follows a point in time when task-relevant information becomes available to a subject regardless of whether that point in time is indicated by a specific stimulus or not (Sutton and coworkers, 1967). This P_3 component is quite similar in morphology and scalp distribution regardless of the sensory modality of the information. Its amplitude increases with the improbability of a task-relevant stimulus (Tueting, Sutton, and Zubin, 1971) and decreases with the subjective uncertainty about the information presented by that stimulus (Johnson and Donchin, 1978; Ruchkin and Sutton, 1978). The peak latency of this component may vary with the perceptual difficulty of the task (Kutas, McCarthy, and Donchin, 1977).

The P_3 component is usually preceded in time by a smaller negative component 'N_2' or 'N200'. Unlike the P_3 wave this negativity is modality-specific in its scalp distribution and might therefore reflect the actual recognition of the informative target within a specific sensory channel (Simson, Vaughan, and Ritter, 1976, 1977a).

Several other late positive components of the human ERP have also been described. A small P_{3a} wave occurring somewhat earlier than the larger P_3 component has been associated with the occurrences of improbable stimuli independently of whether or not they were task-relevant (Squires, Squires, and Hillyard, 1975). A frontocentral late positive wave has been recorded in response to unexpected novel visual stimuli, differing markedly from the parietocentral positive wave recorded to expected signal stimuli (Courchesne, Hillyard, and Galambos, 1975). A long slow posterior positive wave, often associated with some frontal negativity, occurs in response to meaningful stimuli usually in combination with the more transient P_3 component (Squires, Squires, and Hillyard, 1975). A discrete P_4 wave with a longer latency and a more posterior scalp distribution than the P_3 has been recorded in response to disconfirming feedback during a trial-and-error learning task (Stuss and Picton, 1978).

Drowsiness and sleep cause very striking changes in the later components of the sensory ERP. The most prominent component of the sensory ERP during sleep is a large late negative component with peak latency of 300 ms or more depending upon the stage of sleep (reviewed by Picton and coworkers, 1978a).

If a stimulus serves as a warning for an upcoming 'imperative' stimulus requiring a response, a negative baseline shift develops between the two

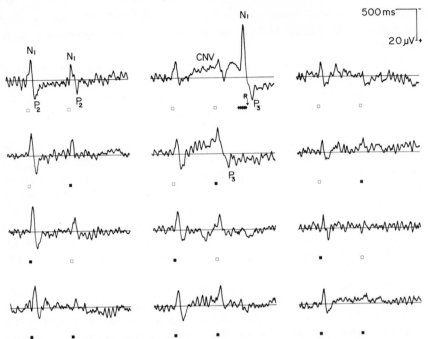

Figure 6.15 Contingent negative variation. In this experiment pairs of brief (50 ms) tones were presented to the right ear every 6–8 seconds. The tones were of either high (open squares—2kHz) or low (filled squares—1kHz) frequency, and the four different pairs of tones occurred in random sequence. Average evoked potentials were recorded from vertex to left mastoid, with negativity at the vertex being represented by an upward deflection. EOG activity was recorded between the upper and lower right orbital ridges, and this was partially subtracted from the vertex recording so as to remove any eye movement artifacts. During the experiment 90 dBSL buzzer sounds were presented to the left ear, and the subject was instructed to turn off these sounds as quickly as possible by pressing a button in his right hand. In the initial part of the experiment, shown in the right column, these buzzer sounds occurred randomly every 8–60 seconds. In the middle section of the experiment (centre column) the buzzer always occurred 600 ms after the second tone if the sequence was high–high. In the final section of the experiment (the right column) the buzzer again occurred randomly. In response to the auditory stimuli an N_1–P_2 complex is recognized, with the second complex of a pair being of less amplitude than the first because of refractory period effects. As the subject learned the association between the buzzer and the high–high tone sequence in the middle section of the experiment, a contingent negative variation (CNV) developed after the initial high tone. This was discharged either by the buzzer or by the low tone in the case of a high–low tone sequence. Together with the discharge of the CNV there also occurred a small late positive wave (P_3) with a latency of around 300 ms from the time of the relevant stimulus. The modal reaction times to the buzzer in the three sections of the experiment were 208, 164, and 240 ms. The recordings were made with a frequency band pass of 0.02–30 Hz and averaging was carried out over 36 trials. The data in this figure were obtained by Guy Proulx

stimuli. This 'contingent negative variation' (Walter and coworkers, 1964) reflects the understanding of a meaningful association between the two stimuli and usually terminates with the completion of the response to the second stimulus. This is illustrated in Figure 6.15. There have been several underlying components described in the CNV (for example, Rohrbaugh, Syndulko, and Lindsley, 1976). The early portion of the CNV probably represents the orientation to the meaning of the warning stimulus and is specific in its scalp distribution to the modality of that first stimulus (Simson, Vaughan, and Ritter, 1977b). The later portion of the CNV is more related to the actual areas of cortex necessary for the perceptual or motor response to the imperative stimulus. There is probably also a further sustained negativity recorded mainly from the frontal regions and associated not so much with the specific requirements of the task as with the conscious effort invested in task-performance (Picton and coworkers, 1978a). A persistence of the CNV after its usual resolution with the imperative stimulus—a 'post-imperative negativity' may be associated with continued uncertainty of the subject about his performance. This may occur in normal subjects when the task is difficult (Picton and Low, 1971), and in psychotic patients with even simple tasks (Timsit-Berthier and coworkers, 1973; Dongier, Dubrovsky, and Engelsmann, 1977).

The readiness potential is a slow negative shift occurring before a self-initiated movement in the absence of any external stimulus (Deecke, Scheid, and Kornhuber, 1969; Vaughan, Costa, and Ritter, 1968; Gerbrandt, Goff, and Smith, 1973; Kutas and Donchin, 1974). This negativity begins several hundred milliseconds before the movement and has a fairly widespread scalp distribution although there is some localization toward the area of cortex controlling the appropriate muscles. This slow negative shift is one of several possible movement-related potentials such as the 'pre-motion positivity' and a brief negative peak just before the movement, but these other potentials are small and inconsistent. Following the motor activation there is a large complex of waves that reflect the sensory feedback from the movement.

5 Origins within the brain

5.1 Electrical fields

Electrical fields are generated by the separation of charge in a conducting medium. In the brain such charge separation occurs mainly across the membranes of neuronal and glial cells. In neurons this electrical activity consists of either fast (milliseconds) 'all-or-none' action potentials, or relatively slow graded potentials resulting from synaptic activation. In glial cells slow potential changes occur usually in relation to changes in extracellular ionic concentrations. All of these potentials can be recorded at a distance from their origin, with an attenuation that depends upon the extent and nature of the intervening conducting medium. Some of the largest electrical fields generated within the brain result from the synchronous focal synaptic activation of a sheet of aligned neurons, as occurs with the primary sensory afferent volley from thalamus to cortex. The initial activation results in depolarization of the pyramidal cell bodies causing a local negative potential 'sink' and a corresponding positive 'source' in the apical dendrites. A 'dipole' is therefore set up such that a positive wave is recorded at the surface of the cortex and a negative wave from below the cortex. Within a few milliseconds the apical dendrites become depolarized, and the surface then becomes negative.

When a recording electrode is close to the source of an electrical field small changes in the position of the electrode can cause large alterations in the waveform of the recorded response. An electrode just above the cortex will record a positive–negative response to primary afferent input, whereas another electrode a few millimeters away just below the cortex will show potentials of exactly opposite polarity. When a recording electrode is at a relatively large distance from the source of an electrical field, changes in electrode position will have little effect on the recorded 'far-field' potentials (Jewett and Williston, 1971). Figure 6.13 shows an example of both far-field and near-field recordings. The early somatosensory potentials recorded from the brachial plexus, spinal cord, and brainstem show little change in waveform when recorded at frontal or parietal scalp electrodes. The component at 20 ms, however, shows a definite inversion of polarity between the two electrodes. This component represents the primary afferent response of the cortex located on the posterior wall of the Rolandic fissure.

One important limitation to consider in the evaluation of the brain's electrical fields is that recordings made from the scalp can never give more than a very incomplete picture of what is going on within the brain (Donald, 1978). Many brain electrical processes occur in such a way that they do not create large fields. Neuronal groups that react with a variable time relationship to stimuli, that interact with both excitatory and inhibitory effects, or that are geometrically amorphous, may not generate electrical fields that can be recognized in scalp recordings. Nevertheless, these recordings do provide us with a definite glimpse, albeit limited, into the electrical activity that underlies the functioning of the human brain.

5.2 Scalp distribution studies

To the psychologist working with normal human subjects, scalp distribution studies provide the only access to the underlying sources of the

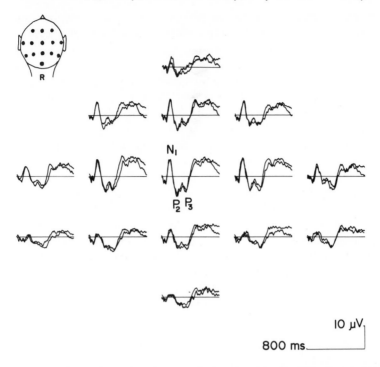

Figure 6.16 Evoked potentials to feedback stimuli. Tonebursts of 1 kHz frequency, 50 ms duration, and 50 dBSL intensity were used to provide confirming feedback about performance on a task involving a difficult discrimination between different visual flicker frequencies. Evoked potentials were recorded from 15 scalp locations (F_{pz}; F_3, F_z, F_4; T_3, C_3 C_z, C_4, T_4; T_5, P_3, P_z, P_4, T_6; O_z) using a non-cephalic reference. This reference was the centre tap of a 50 kΩ potentiometer, one end connected to the right sternoclavicular junction and the other to the seventh cervical vertebra, adjusted so as to minimize ECG artifacts. Relative negativity of the scalp electrodes is shown by upward deflection. All components of the evoked potential were maximally recorded at the vertex (C_z) where the N_1, P_2, and P_3 components have been labelled. The P_3 wave is distinctly more widespread and more posterior in its scalp distribution than the N_1 or P_2 components. This can be seen in the temporal, parietal, and occipital electrodes where the P_3 is greater in amplitude than the P_2 component, whereas in the more anterior locations the reverse is true. The data in this figure are unpublished recordings from Hillyard and coworkers (1976)

scalp-recorded ERPs. Knowing the characteristics of the electrical field at the scalp, and having some basic idea of the possible generator sources for the recorded activity, allow one to extrapolate back through the geometry of the brain and its coverings to the source of the scalp-recorded activity (Vaughan, 1974). Caution must be exercised, however, since any particular scalp distribution may derive from different possible generators (Picton and coworkers, 1978b). This is especially true when several underlying generators contribute simultaneously to the scalp-recorded activity.

One of the most important present uses of scalp distribution studies is the differentiation of the components of an ERP. Scalp-recorded events with different voltage distributions must derive, at least in part, from different sources. The evaluation of ERPs at multiple scalp locations therefore becomes a very powerful tool in the dissection out of distinct psychophysiological events. This is illustrated in Figure 6.16. The N_1, P_2 and P_3 components of the response to a toneburst giving feedback information about performance on a preceding task are all maximally recorded at the vertex. The N_1 and P_2 components, however, have a frontocentral scalp distribution, whereas the P_3 component is much more widespread and somewhat more posterior in its distribution. These results indicate that the process underlying the P_3 component is physiologically quite distinct from that underlying the vertex potential components. Scalp distribution studies like these have shown that the P_3 component is similar in a variety of tasks (Hillyard and coworkers, 1976), and, unlike the preceding N_2 component, is unaffected by the sensory modality of the stimulus (Simson, Vaughan, and Ritter, 1976, 1977a).

5.3 Identification of generator sources

In order to determine the underlying sources of scalp-recorded events, it is necessary to correlate these measurements to intracranial recordings in animal and human subjects, and to scalp recordings in patients or animals with known lesions of the nervous system. All of these sources of additional information have both limitations and advantages.

Human intracranial recordings are to be interpreted with caution because of two major difficulties. Firstly, they are performed in patients who are being investigated for brain dysfunction and whose recordings may therefore be distinctly different from those of normal subjects. Secondly, the intracranial electrodes placed for diagnostic and/or therapeutic reasons may not necessarily be properly located or sufficiently numerous to allow accurate assessment of cerebral evoked potential sources. These difficulties notwithstanding, there have been some extremely informative studies of human intracranial ERPs, particularly in the somatosensory system (Allison and coworkers, 1978).

Animal recordings are problematical because of the unknown physical and psychological homologies between animal and man. This is less important to the evaluation of those parts of the nervous systems, such as the primary sensory pathways, that are phylogenetically old and stable across species. The evaluation of the endogenous components of the ERPs may cause difficulties, however, because of the problems in relating the cerebral anatomy and the psychological behaviour of animals to man.

Nevertheless, the work of Arezzo, Pickoff, and Vaughan (1975) has demonstrated the complex overlapping patterns of activity that underly the late components of the auditory evoked potential, and has shown their far-field as well as near-field origins.

Studies of animals with experimentally induced lesions, or of human patients with pathological lesions, can provide a further source of convergent evidence relevant to our understanding of the sources of the human scalp-recorded events. In the interpretation of such data, one must, however, consider that any lesion will have complex physiological effects far beyond its own circumscribed location. For example, if one is no longer able to record an ERP component after a lesion, it is possible that, as well as possibly destroying the generator source, the lesion might have removed some necessary facilitation of the ERP generation, released some inhibitory process, or distorted the conductive medium. The absence of late somatosensory-evoked potential components after lesions of the primary somatosensory cortex does not mean that the late components are normally generated within the primary cortex, but only that the integrity of the primary sensory pathway is essential to their occurrence possibly because of its connections to the area of their generation (Williamson, Goff, and Allison, 1970).

6 Psychological ERP research

6.1 Physical, physiological, and psychological variables

Human ERP research always deals with a combination of physical, physiological and psychological variables. Any physiological measurement like the sensory evoked potential will be determined in part by the physical characteristics of the stimulus, and in part by the psychological processes related to the perception of and the behavioural response to that stimulus. The most difficult part of human ERP research in psychology is often not the recording of the physiological responses, but the definition and isolation of the behavioural variables affecting such responses—the evaluation and control of 'subject option' (Sutton, 1969).

The exact physical characteristics of the stimulus used must be known throughout the period while the evoked potentials are being recorded. This knowledge requires sufficient familiarity with the stimulation equipment and its calibration to ensure a reasonable trust in its operation. Furthermore, the delivery of the stimuli to the subject must be done in a manner that the subject cannot alter. Auditory stimuli should be presented through earphones rather than free-field speakers; electrical pulses to peripheral nerves should preferably be given with constant current stimulators; and visual stimuli should be presented when the subject's gaze and accommodation are controlled.

The evaluation of the psychological variables in an ERP experiment involves four essential procedures. Firstly, the paradigm must be designed to manipulate the required psychological variable without affecting other psychological processes. For example, if the physiological correlates of learning are to be studied, the experimental design must distinguish learning from other nonspecific processes such as arousal that are often associated with learning. Secondly, control sessions must be performed to isolate further those ERP changes specific to the manipulated psychological variable. For example, asymmetries of the ERP in relation to a task considered as characteristic of the perceptual mode of one hemisphere have little meaning unless they can be reduced or reversed when the task is changed to be characteristic of the opposite hemisphere (Donchin, Kutas, and McCarthy, 1977). Such control sessions do, however, have their own limitations, and one must always consider the possibility of 'carry-over' effects when the same subjects are used in experimental and control conditions. For example, it is often difficult for a subject to ignore a stimulus that he has previously learned to consider as highly significant (Stuss and Picton, 1978). Thirdly, the subject must be precisely and consistently instructed as to what he must do during an experiment. Finally the behaviour of the subject must be monitored throughout the recording session. Simply instructing the subject to perform a certain perceptual task is no evidence that he will actually do this while the ERPs are being recorded.

Prior to analysis, ERPs should be sorted as much as possible according to both the stimuli and the monitored behavioural responses. In this way the separate physical and psychological contributions to the experimentally recorded ERP variance can be distinguished. For example, if the evoked potentials to threshold-level sounds are separately analysed according to whether or not the sounds were detected, it can be seen that a detected sound is associated with a large late positive wave that is not present when a sound goes undetected (Hillyard and coworkers, 1971). It is important to emphasize that this sorting on the basis of detection must be done relative to the actual stimulus-response sequence that the ERP is measuring. If behavioural thresholds are determined in a separate session from the ERP recording, the correlation of psychological to physiological parameters can lead to confusion since the threshold need not necessarily remain constant between the two sessions (Donchin and Sutton, 1970).

6.2 Sensory processes

The human sensory evoked potential provides an objective indication of the processing of sensory information within the brain. As such it can be useful to the understanding of the general principles of human sensory analysis. Furthermore, the physiological ERP measurements can give a variety of latency and magnitude data that is not available to behavioural analysis.

The contribution of ERP research to the further understanding of human sensation derives mainly from the study of the exogenous components. This is particularly true for the evaluation of visual sensory processes in the occipital region using either the transient or the steady-state evoked potential (Regan, 1972, pp. 31–132; Desmedt, 1977; Hillyard, Picton, and Regan, 1978). Such ERP research has demonstrated that there are multiple parallel channels of information analysis in the human visual system. Such channels may be specific to the colour, spatial frequency, and the orientation of the visual stimulus. In general, channels of information processing can be demonstrated through ERP research by several techniques. Firstly, it can be shown that in response to various aspects of sensory information there are ERPs that are distinct in their scalp distribution or temporal responsiveness. Secondly a specific channel of information processing can be demonstrated by showing the selective adaptation of a particular ERP response by prior stimulation with other stimuli that are either processed within the same channel causing reduction in the response, or in different channels causing no change in the response (Campbell and Maffei, 1970). Finally, masking studies may be used to dissect out various parts of an ERP response, and to demonstrate their different origins (Musso and Harter, 1975; Harter, Towle and Musso, 1976; Harter and coworkers, 1977; Don and Eggermont, 1978).

Psychophysical correlation has been much less successful with the endogenous components of the ERP. These components are quite susceptible to changes in subjective attention, and it is probable that ERP changes at these latencies reflect as much the subject's cognitive approach to sensory information as any underlying physiological principle. It is perhaps impossible to rule out all subject options in the evaluation of such components and it is doubtful that ERPs will give any greater insight into such concepts as 'sensory magnitude'. The problems of relating sensory ERPs to estimations of sensory magnitude are extensive (Rosner and Goff, 1967; Pratt and Sohmer, 1977; Hillyard, Picton and Regan, 1978). At the present time it appears that the sensory-evoked potential has a far more complex structure than the simplicity required for a one-dimensional analysis of sensory information. If there is to be a correlation of physiological to behavioural measurements according to a postulated psychological law, the behavioural measurements must be taken concurrently with the physiological, both the physiological and behavioural variables measured must be accurately defined and isolated from other possible concurrent effects, and the correlation according to the postulated law must be shown to be significantly better than to other possible hypotheses that could explain the data.

6.3 Cognitive psychophysiology

Probably the most important area of present psychological ERP research involves the use of ERP measurements to further our understanding of human cognition (Donchin, Ritter, and McCallum, 1978). Behavioural approaches to human cognition are somewhat restricted because their only access to the cognitive response occurs after it has finished and appropriate behaviour has been initiated. ERP recording allows analysis of the physiological events occurring in the brain during cognition. At the present time, it is not possible to extrapolate back from the scalp-recorded ERP to the location and nature of cognitive activity within the brain. Nevertheless, it is possible to give some understanding of the timing and organization of cognitive processes through the analysis of the component structure of the ERP.

Recent experiments on the nature of human selective attention may be used to illustrate how a further understanding of human cognition can derive from sophisticated evaluation of scalp-recorded ERPs (Hillyard and coworkers, 1973; Näätänen, 1975; Picton, Hillyard, and Galambos, 1976; Hillyard and Picton, 1979; Picton and coworkers, 1978a). Behavioural analyses of selective attention have resulted in several theoretical models. Some workers have proposed that there are hierarchical levels of selection such that a subject attends to a particular sensory channel, detects an important target signal within that channel, and chooses an appropriate response to that target. Others have suggested that there is a single selective process that responds to those stimuli that after full evaluation are considered most important.

The ERP correlates of selective attention were examined in a binaural listening task. Different series of auditory stimuli were presented to each ear, and the subject was instructed to attend to the stimuli in one ear and ignore those present in the other. ERPs could then be recorded to attended and ignored stimuli within the same recording session rather than at different periods when changes in general arousal and motivation could affect the response. Attention was monitored by recording the subject's detection of occasional signal stimuli within the attended channel. The stimuli were presented at a sufficiently rapid rate, and the detection task was sufficiently difficult, that it was impossible for the subject to switch attention between the channels without severe decrement in his performance. Stimulus presentation times were randomized so that the subject could not predict (and prepare for) the occurrence of relevant stimuli. The analysis of the early components of the auditory evoked potential before 50 milliseconds showed no consistent change with attention. This suggests that there is an early registration and analysis of auditory information that proceeds in much the same manner regardless of the direction of attention. Because of the limitations of the recording techniques, small or variable changes in the ERP might not have been noted, and early changes in auditory analysis that do not contribute to the far-field recordings cannot be ruled out. Nevertheless, at least some part of the early auditory system responds quite independently of attention. Despite this stability of the early response, there are striking attention-related changes noted in the later components of the auditory ERP. When attention is directed toward one ear there is an increase in the amplitude of the N_1 component of the auditory-evoked potential to all stimuli presented to that ear. Furthermore, a large P_3 component appears in response to the detected signal within the attended channel, but not in response to the non-signal stimuli, nor in response to signal stimuli in the unattended ear. These results are illustrated in Figure 6.17. Such ERP studies demonstrate that there are

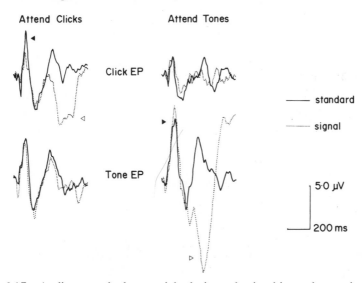

Figure 6.17 Auditory evoked potentials during selective binaural attention. Tone pips of 7.5 ms duration and 500 Hz were presented to the left ear at an intensity of 45 dBSL, and equally loud 100 μs clicks were presented to the right ear. These stimuli were presented according to a randomized time-schedule with overall interstimulus intervals between 150 and 800 ms. The subject was instructed to attend to one ear in order to detect and count a random infrequent 'signal' stimulus (580 Hz tone pips or 10 dB fainter clicks). Evoked potentials were recorded between vertex and right mastoid with negativity at the vertex being represented by an upward deflection. Each tracing represents the average of 2048 responses for the standard stimuli, and 200 responses for the signals. In the left column of the figure are shown the evoked potentials when the subject attended to the clicks in the right ear, and in the right column are the evoked potentials when the subject attended to the tones. There is an enhancement of the N_1 component to both standard and signal stimuli within the attended channel compared to when that channel is ignored. This is shown in the figure with the filled triangles. Furthermore, there is a large P_3 component in response to the attended signal stimuli, but not in response to the other stimuli within that channel, or in response to the signal stimuli in the attended channel. This is shown in the figure with the open triangles. The data for this figure were obtained by Jacinthe Baribeau-Braun

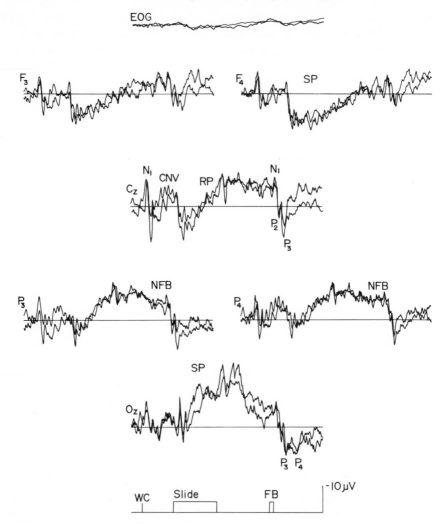

Figure 6.18 Evoked potential correlates of human concept formation. In this experiment the subject was required to learn the correct sorting criterion for a block of visual stimuli. An 80 dBSL click (WC) warned the subject of a 'slide' stimulus that followed 800 ms later and lasted 1.2 seconds. The slide could be classified according to 5 possible criteria. The subject hypothesized as to which might be the correct criterion, and responded appropriately in the one second following the slide offset. An 80 dBSL feedback toneburst (FB) lasting 100 ms occurred 1.5 seconds after slide offset, and informed the subject whether his response had been correct (a 1 kHz toneburst) or incorrect (a 4kHz toneburst). Using this feedback information the subject was able to learn through trial-and-error the correct response criterion. The ERPs shown in this figure were from those 'pre-insight' trials prior to the subject determining the correct criterion, when he was making errors and ruling out hypotheses. Each tracing represents the

two distinct processes that occur within the brain in association with selective attention. There is an N_1 change associated with all stimuli within an attended channel, and a P_3 component associated only with the detected signal stimuli within that attended channel. These processes seem to be sequential in time with the P_3 component occurring much later than the N_1 component. Furthermore they can be hierarchical in their organization, with the P_3 component only occurring in response to signals within an attended channel which have evoked an enlarged N_1 component. Such results provide powerful evidence against the hypothesis that attention is determined only by a single final response selection process.

ERP studies can thus bring a wealth of physiological information to the analysis of human cognition. This is further illustrated in an experimental evaluation of human concept formation (Stuss and Picton, 1978). In this study recordings were taken from multiple scalp locations, and the experiment demonstrates the importance of scalp distribution information in the definition of distinct psychophysiological events. During this task the subject was required to determine the sorting criterion for a block of visual stimuli, each of which could be classified according to five possible criteria (e.g. colour, shape, etc.). On each trial a warning click signalled the onset of the visual stimulus. The subject then indicated his classification of the stimulus according to a hypothesized criterion and received feedback as to whether his response had been correct or not. Using this feedback information, within a few trials the subject learned the correct sorting criterion and responded correctly until the block of stimuli was finished.

---

average of 12 responses. Recordings were made from left and right frontal (F_3, F_4), left and right parietal (P_3, P_4), vertex (C_z) and occiput (O_z) referred to a linked mastoid reference. The total averaging sweep was 5.12 seconds. An EOG monitor taken between upper and lower orbital ridges was simultaneously averaged at 1/5 of the EEG channel gains. A number of ERP components each with a particular scalp distribution can be recognized in the tracings. In response to the warning click there is a characteristic N_1–P_2 complex, the N_1 component of which has been labelled at the vertex location. Between the warning click and the slide a small contingent negative variation (CNV) develops. At the onset of the slide there is a complex series of visual evoked potentials recorded from the occiput and the more anterior electrodes. During the slide there is a sustained potential (SP) that is recorded as a negativity in the posterior regions and a positivity in the frontal electrodes. As the subject prepares to respond by pushing a button with his right hand, there is a slowly developing negative readiness potential (RP) superimposed on the visual SP maximally recorded from the vertex and left frontal area. Prior to the feedback stimulus there is a negative wave (NFB) that is maximally recorded in the parietal regions. In response to the feedback potential there is the usual N_1–P_2 complex followed by a large P_3 component maximally recorded in the centro-parietal regions and a later P_4 wave with a more posterior scalp distribution. Unpublished data from Stuss and Picton (1978)

o

The process was then repeated with further blocks of visual stimuli. The ERPs were separately evaluated for different stages of concept formation, such as 'pre-insight' trials wherein the subject was making errors prior to learning the correct criterion, and 'insight' trials wherein the subject received his first positive feedback. The ERPs recorded during 'pre-insight' trials for one individual are shown in Figure 6.18. These recordings show the multiple physiological processes that occur during concept formation. There is a response to the warning click stimulus that is followed by a contingent negative variation that probably reflects the subject's attentive expectancy for the upcoming visual stimulus. During the visual stimulus there are multiple distinct psychophysiological processes going on. There is a sustained occipital negative shift that probably reflects the processing of visual information in the posterior regions of the cerebral cortex. In the frontal areas there is a concurrent sustained positivity that might be correlated with processes of general perceptual strategy. Toward the end of the visual stimulus there is an increasing negativity, best recorded at the vertex and left frontal regions, that probably represents a readiness potential in preparation for the response with the right hand. After the response there is a negative potential prior to the feedback stimulus that is associated with expectancy for the feedback information. The feedback-evoked potential contains the usual N_1–P_2 components and then two later positive waves called P_3 and P_4. These positive waves are distinct in their scalp distribution with the P_4 component being more posterior. This scalp distribution difference might be caused by the P_3 being related to the evaluation of the feedback information, and the P_4 to the utilization of that information in the reorganization of perceptual hypotheses for the next trial.

6.4 Disorders of higher nervous function

The use of scalp-recorded ERPs in the evaluation of human brain disorders is an important and exciting area of research. The exogenous components of the ERP are presently used with great benefit in the objective evaluation of sensory thresholds and in the precise localization of functional disorders in the sensory pathways (Picton and coworkers, 1977; Coats and Martin, 1977; Stockard and Rossiter, 1977; Starr, 1978). It is possible that with further research human ERP studies can also provide us with a greater understanding of the disorders of higher nervous function seen in psychiatry and neurology.

Two distinct approaches to the disorders of higher nervous function have been described—the 'pathophysiological' and the 'psychophysiological' (Shagass, 1972, 1976; Shagass and coworkers, 1978). The pathophysiological approach aims to define ERP evidence of abnormal cerebral processes. These abnormalities would then be considered the physiological basis of the disordered psychological function, and the presence of such abnormalities would be of great objective diagnostic value in determining the presence and extent of disorder. For example, if all patients with a particular clinical disorder show an abnormal enlargement of a particular ERP component, one can hypothesize that the clinical disorder is related to some disinhibition of this component, and one can use its measurement to diagnose the disorder. More likely than not, the abnormalities might be very complex and the diagnosis based on a multivariate cluster analysis of many EEG and ERP measurements, as in the recent work with 'neurometrics' (John, 1977). The psychophysiological approach, on the other hand, uses the patient as a means of testing hypothesized relations between the ERP and psychological processes. For example, if a certain group of patients is characteristically unable to attend to particular stimuli, they should not show the attention-related ERP changes found in normal subjects. It is probable that a combination of these two approaches is the most efficient way of evaluating abnormal human cognitive function.

In the evaluation of patients with disorders of higher nervous function there are four dimensions of variables: physical, physiological, psychological, and pathological. Differences in physiological ERP measurements, when the physical stimulus conditions are held constant, may be caused by psychological changes, by pathological changes, or by an interaction between psychology and pathology. Abnormalities in the attention-related late ERP components may, for example, be caused by the patient not following instructions, by the patient not having the cerebral mechanisms necessary for ERP generation, or by the patient not being able to follow the instructions because of his brain dysfunction. Each dimension of possible variation can contribute to the overall understanding. In the physical dimension, for example, it may be found that a patient can perform an attention task when the stimulus presentation rate is slower. The physiological ERP measurements may demonstrate that the N_1 attention effect is present but the P_3 mechanisms are disordered. Behavioural evaluation may show lapses in task performance, during which the ERP measurements are different from when the subject is performing correctly. Pathological evaluations may show that, although their performance in the experimental task is the same, there are distinct subgroups of patients characterized clinically, chemically or anatomically, each of which may show a distinct pattern of ERP measurements. Such evaluations are complex, but the possible rewards in our further understanding of human mental health are large.

7 Conclusions

7.1 Principles and limitations

Good psychological ERP research is built upon several basic foundations. The first general principle upon which such research is based is the technique of signal averaging. With averaging a constant signal remains constant, whereas a random variable approaches a mean value with the range of its deviation decreasing by a factor of the square root of the number of trials averaged. Averaging has several limitations based upon the assumptions of the technique; in particular, averaging is limited to recording events that are constant in timing and morphology during the averaging process. Another important principle of psychological ERP research is that any recorded ERP change should be considered as artifactual in origin until there is reasonable evidence of its intracerebral generation. One must at all times be aware that the scalp-recorded ERP is a complex waveform consisting of many overlapping components each of which may have particular significance to various aspects of human information processing. Any scalp-recorded activity is, however, not exhaustive in its description of underlying brain activity and only reflects those cerebral processes that create electrical fields measurable at the scalp. In general, it is advantageous in psychological ERP research to use multiple recordings from different areas of the scalp to improve the delineation of the components of recorded waveforms and, together with knowledge from intracerebral recordings and pathological correlations, to suggest the sources of their generation. In the ERP evaluation of human psychological processes, it is as essential to record and define behavioural evidence of these processes as it is to measure the ERP correlates thereof. Finally, in the evaluation of patients with disorders of higher nervous function it is important also to consider their ERPs from the vantage of the different possible pathologies that might lead to their clinical disorder.

7.2 Signs and codes

The nature of the relationship of the scalp-recorded ERPs to the psychological processes of the human brain is at present unknown. ERP correlates of psychological activity may be either 'signs' or 'codes' of the psychological processes (Uttal, 1967). As signs, the ERP may reflect the processes necessary for the psychological activity but would themselves not be a necessary part of these processes. A fair number of recent reports have suggested that the scalp-recorded potentials reflect mechanisms that control the switching and handling of the information being processed but not the actual information processing itself (Schwartz, 1976; Donald, 1979). Others have proposed that the electrical fields of the brain, which are partially recorded in the scalp ERP, actually encode the processes of human mental experience (John, 1976). Neither the exact relationship of the scalp ERP to human information processing, nor the final limits to which such recordings can further our knowledge of normal and abnormal human psychology, are known. Such knowledge awaits your further experimental evaluation.

References

Allison, T., Goff, W. R., Williamson, P. D., and VanGilder, J. C. (1979). On the neural origin of early components of the human somatosensory evoked potential. In J. E. Desmedt (Ed.), *Progress in Clinical Neurophysiology*, Vol. 7, Karger, Basel.

Allison, T., Matsumiya, Y., Goff, G. D., and Goff, W. R. (1977). The scalp topography of human visual evoked potentials. *Electroenceph. Clin. Neurophysiol.*, **42**, 185–97.

Arezzo, J., Pickoff, A., and Vaughan, H. G. (1975). The sources and intracerebral distribution of auditory evoked potentials in the alert rhesus monkey. *Brain Res.*, **90**, 57–73.

Bickford, R. G. (1972). Physiological and clinical studies of micro-reflexes. *Electroenceph. Clin. Neurophysiol. Suppl.*, **31**, 93–108.

Broughton, R., Meier-Ewert, K., and Ebe, M. (1969). Evoked visual, somatosensory and retinal potentials in photosensitive epilepsy. *Electroenceph. Clin. Neurophysiol.*, **27**, 373–86.

Callaway, E. (1975). *Brain Electrical Potentials and Individual Psychological Differences*, Grune and Stratton, New York.

Campbell, F. W., and Maffei, L. (1970). Electrophysiological evidence for the existence of orientation and size detectors in the human visual system. *J. Physiol*, **207**, 635–52.

Coats, A., and Martin, J. L. (1977). Human auditory nerve action potentials and brainstem evoked responses. *Arch. Otolaryng.*, **103**, 605–22.

Cooper, R., Osselton, J. W., and Shaw, J. C. (1974). *EEG Technology*, 2nd edn, Butterworths, London.

Courchesne, E., Hillyard, S. A., and Galambos, R. (1975). Stimulus novelty, task relevance, and the visual evoked potential in man. *Electroenceph. Clin. Neurophysiol.*, **39**, 131–43.

Cracco, R. Q. (1972). The initial positive potential of the human scalp-recorded somatosensory evoked response. *Electroenceph. Clin. Neurophysiol.*, **32**, 623–30.

Cracco, R. Q., and Cracco, J. B. (1976). Somatosensory evoked potential in man: far field potentials. *Electroenceph. Clin. Neurophysiol.*, **41**, 460–6.

Davis, H., Osterhammel, P. A., Wier, C. C., and Gjerdingen, D. B. (1972). Slow vertex potentials: interactions among auditory, tactile, electric and visual stimuli. *Electroenceph. Clin. Neurophysiol.*, **33**, 537–45.

Deecke, L., Scheid, P., and Kornhuber, H. H. (1969). Distribution of readiness potential, pre-motion positivity and motor potential of the human cerebral cortex preceding voluntary finger movements. *Exp. Brain Res.*, **7**, 158–68.

Desmedt, J. E. (Ed.) (1977). *Visual Evoked Potentials in Man: New Developments*, Oxford University Press, Oxford.

Don, E., and Eggermont, J. J. (1978). Analysis of the click-evoked brainstem potentials in man using high pass noise masking. *J. Acous. Soc. Am.*, **63**, 1084–92.

Donald, M. W. (1976). Topography of evoked potential amplitude fluctuations. In W. C. McCallum and J. R. Knott (Eds), *The Responsive Brain*, John Wright, Bristol.

Donald, M. W. (1979). Limits on current theories of transient evoked potentials. In J. E. Desmedt (Ed.), *Progress in Clinical Neurophysiology*, Vol. 6, Karger, Basel.

Donchin, E., Callaway, E., Cooper, R., Desmedt, J. E., Goff, W. R., Hillyard, S. A., and Sutton, S. (1977). Publication criteria for studies of evoked potentials (EP) in man. In J. E. Desmedt (Ed.), *Progress in Clinical Neurophysiology*, Vol. 1, Karger, Basel.

Donchin, E., Kutas, M., and McCarthy, G. (1977). Electrocortical indices of hemispheric utilization. In S., Harnad, R. W. Doty, L. Goldstein, and G. Krauthames (Eds), *Lateralization in the Nervous System*, Academic Press, New York.

Donchin, E., Ritter, W., and McCallum, W. G. (1978). Cognitive psychophysiology: the endogenous components of the ERP. In E. Callaway, P. Tueting, and S. H. Koslow (Eds), *Event Related Brain Potentials in Man*, Academic Press, New York.

Donchin, E., and Sutton, S. (1970). The 'psychological significance' of evoked responses: a comment on Clark, Butler, and Rosner. *Commun. Beh. Biol.*, **5**, 111–4.

Dongier, M., Dubrovsky, B., and Engelsmann, F. (1977). Event related slow potentials in psychiatry. In C. Shagass, S. Gerston, and A. Friedhoff (Eds), *Psychopathology and Brain Dysfunction*, Raven, New York.

Doyle, D. J., (1975). Some comments on the use of Wiener filtering for the estimation of evoked potentials. *Electroenceph. Clin. Neurophysiol.*, **38**, 533–4.

Gerbrandt, L. K., Goff, W. R., and Smith, D. B. (1973). Distribution of the human average movement potential. *Electroenceph. Clin. Neurophysiol.*, **34**, 461–4.

Glaser, E. M., and Ruchkin, D. S. (1976). *Principles of Neurobiological Signal Analysis*, Academic Press, New York.

Goff, G. D., Matsumiya, Y., Allison, T., and Goff, W. R. (1977). The scalp topography of human somatosensory and auditory evoked potentials. *Electroenceph. Clin. Neurophysiol.*, **42**, 57–76.

Goff, W. R., Williamson, P. D., Van Gilder, J. C., Allison, T., and Fisher, T. C. (1979). Neural origins of long latency evoked potentials recorded from the depth and cortical surface of the brain in man. In J. E. Desmedt (Ed.), *Progress in Clinical Neurophysiology*, Vol. 7, Karger, Basel.

Halliday, A. M., McDonald, W. I., and Mushin, J. (1973). Visual evoked response in diagnosis of multiple sclerosis. *Br. Med. J.*, **4**, 661–4.

Harter, M. R., Towle, V. L., and Musso, M. F. (1976). Size specificity and interocular suppression: monocular evoked potentials and reaction times. *Vision Res.*, **16**, 1111–17.

Harter, M. R., Towle, V. L., Zakrzewski, M., and Moyer, S. M. (1977). An objective indicant of binocular vision in humans: size-specific interocular suppression of visual evoked potentials. *Electroenceph. Clin. Neurophysiol.*, **43**, 825–36.

Hartwell, J. W., and Erwin, C. W. (1976). Evoked potential analysis: on-line signal optimization using a mini-computer. *Electroenceph. Clin. Neurophysiol.*, **41**, 416–21.

Hillyard, S. A., Courchesne, E., Krausz, H. I., and Picton, T. W. (1976). Scalp topography of the P_3 wave in different auditory decision tasks. In W. C. McCallum and J. R. Knott (Eds), *The Responsive Brain*, John Wright, Bristol.

Hillyard, S. A., and Galambos, R. (1970). Eye movement artifact in the CNV. *Electroenceph. Clin. Neurophysiol.*, **28**, 173–82.

Hillyard, S. A., Hink, R. F., Schwent, V. L., and Picton, T. W. (1973). Electrical signs of selective attention in the human brain. *Science*, **182**, 177–80.

Hillyard, S. A., and Picton, T. W. (1979). Event-related brain potentials and selective information processing in man. In J. E. Desmedt (Ed.), *Progress in Clinical Neurophysiol.*, Vol. 6 Karger, Basel.

Hillyard, S. A., Picton, T. W., and Regan, D. M. (1978). Sensation, perception and attention: analysis using ERPs. In E. Callaway, P. Tueting, and S. H. Koslow (Eds), *Event Related Brain Potentials in Man*, Academic Press, New York.

Hillyard, S. A., Squires, K. C., Bauer, J. W., and Lindsay, P. H. (1971). Evoked potential correlates of auditory signal detection. *Science*, **172**, 1357–60.

Jewett, D. L., and Williston, J. S. (1971). Auditory-evoked far fields averaged from the scalp of humans. *Brain*, **94**, 681–96.

John, E. R. (1976). A model of consciousness. In G. E. Schwartz and O. Shapiro (Eds), *Consciousness and Self-regulation: Advances in Research*, Vol. 1, Plenum, New York.

John, E. R. (1977). *Neurometrics: Clinical Applications of Quantitative Electrophysiology*, Lawrence Erlbaum, Hillsdale, New Jersey.

Johnson, R., and Donchin, E. (1978). On how P300 amplitude varies with the utility of the eliciting stimuli. *Electroenceph. Clin. Neurophysiol.*, **44**, 424–437.

Jones, S. J. (1977). Short latency potentials recorded from the neck and scalp following median nerve stimulation in man. *Electroenceph. Clin. Neurophysiol.*, **43**, 853–63.

Kutas, M., and Donchin, E. (1974). Studies of squeezing: handedness, responding hand, response force and asymmetry of readiness potential. *Science*, **186**, 545–8.

Kutas, M., McCarthy, G., and Donchin, E. (1977). Augmenting mental chronometry: the P300 as a measure of stimulus evaluation time. *Science*, **197**, 792–5.

Lindsley, D. B., and Wicke, J. D. (1974). The electroencephalogram: autonomous electrical activity in man and animals. In R. F. Thompson and M. M. Patterson (Eds), *Bioelectric Recording Techniques: B-Electroencephalography and Human Brain Potentials*, Academic Press, New York.

Matsuo, F., Peters, J. F., and Reilly, E. L. (1975). Electrical phenomena associated with movements of the eyelid. *Electroenceph. Clin. Neurophysiol.*, **38**, 507–11.

Musso, M. F., and Harter, M. R. (1975). Visually evoked potentials and selective masking with patterned flashes of different spatial frequencies. *Vision Res.*, **15**, 231–8.

Näätänen, R. (1975). Selective attention and evoked potentials in humans—a critical review. *Biol. Psychol.*, **2**, 237–307.

Picton, T. W., Campbell, K. B., Baribeau-Braun, J., and Proulx, (1978a). The neurophysiology of human attention: a tutorial review. In R. Requin (Ed.), *Attention and Performance VII*. Lawrence Erlbaum, Hillsdale, New Jersey.

Picton, T. W., and Hillyard, S. A. (1972). Cephalic skin potentials in electroencephalography. *Electroenceph. Clin. Neurophysiol.*, **33**, 419–24.

Picton, T. W., Hillyard, S. A., and Galambos, R. (1976). Habituation and attention in the auditory system. In W. D. Keidel and W. D. Neff (Eds), *Handbook of Sensory Physiology*, Vol. V/3 Springer-Verlag, Berlin.

Picton, T. W., Hillyard, S. A., Krausz, H. I., and Galambos, R. (1974). Human auditory evoked potentials: 1 Evaluation of components. *Electroenceph. Clin. Neurophysiol.*, **36**, 179–90.

Picton, T. W., and Hink, R. F. (1974). Evoked potentials: how? what? and why? *Am. J. EEG Technol.*, **14**, 9–44.

Picton, T. W., and Low, M. D. (1971). The CNV and semantic content of stimuli in the experimental paradigm: effects of feedback. *Electroenceph. Clin. Neurophysiol.*, **31**, 451–6.

Picton, T. W., Woods, D. L., Baribeau-Braun, J., and Healey, T. M. G. (1977). Evoked potential audiometry. *J. Otolaryng.*, **6**, 90–119.

Picton, T. W., Woods, D. L., and Proulx, G. B. (1978). Human auditory sustained potentials: I The nature of the response and II Stimulus relationships. *Electroenceph. Clin. Neurophysiol.*, **45**, 186–210.

Picton, T. W., Woods, D. L., Stuss, D. T., and Campbell, K. B. (1978b). Methodology and meaning of human evoked potential scalp distribution studies. In D. Otto (Ed.), *Multidisciplinary Perspectives in Event-Related Brain Potential Research*, US Government, Washington.

Pratt, H., and Sohmer, H. (1977). Correlations between psychophysical magnitude estimates and simultaneously obtained auditory nerve, brain stem and cortical responses to click stimuli in man. *Electroenceph. Clin. Neurophysiol.*, **43**, 802–12.

Regan, D. (1972). *Evoked Potentials in Psychology, Sensory Physiology and Clinical Medicine*, Wiley, New York.

Rohrbaugh, J. W., Syndulko, K., and Lindsley, D. B. (1976). Brain wave components of the contingent negative variation in humans. *Science*, **191**, 1055–7.

Rosner, B. S., and Goff, W. R. (1967). Electrical responses of the nervous system and subjective scales of intensity. In W. D. Neff (Ed.), *Contributions to Sensory Physiology*, Vol. 2, Academic Press, New York.

Ruchkin, D. S., and Sutton, S. (1978). Equivocation and P300 amplitude. In D. Otto (Ed.), *Multidisciplinary Perspectives in Event-Related Brain Potential Research*, US Government, Washington.

Schimmel, H. (1967). The (±) average: accuracy of estimated mean components in average response studies. *Science*, **157**, 92–4.

Schwartz, M. (1976). Averaged evoked responses and the encoding of perception. *Psychophysiol.*, **13**, 546–53.

Shagass, C. (1972). *Evoked Brain Potentials in Psychiatry*, Plenum, New York.

Shagass, C. (1976). An electrophysiological view of schizophrenia. *Biol. Psychiat.*, **11**, 3–30.

Shagass, C., Ornitz, E. M., Sutton, S., and Teuting, P. (1978). Event related potentials and psychopathology. In E. Callaway and S. H. Koslow (Eds), *Event Related Brain Potentials in Man*, Academic Press, New York.

Simson, R., Vaughan, H. G., and Ritter, W. (1976). The scalp topography of potentials associated with missing visual or auditory stimuli. *Electroenceph. Clin. Neurophysiol.*, **40**, 33–42.

Simson, R., Vaughan, H. G., and Ritter, W. (1977a). The scalp topography of potentials in auditory and visual discrimination tasks. *Electroenceph. Clin. Neurophysiol.*, **42**, 528–35.

Simson, R., Vaughan, H. G., and Ritter, W. (1977b). The scalp topography of potentials in auditory and visual Go/No Go tasks. *Electroenceph. Clin. Neurophysiol.*, **43**, 864–75.

Spekreijse, H., Estevez, O., and Reits, D. (1977). Visual evoked potentials and the physiological analysis of visual processes in man. In J. E. Desmedt (Ed.), *Visual Evoked Potentials in Man: New Developments*, Oxford University Press, Oxford.

Squires, K. C., and Donchin, E. (1976). Beyond averaging: the use of discriminant functions to recognize event related potentials elicited by single auditory stimuli. *Electroenceph. Clin. Neurophysiol.*, **41**, 449–59.

Squires, K. C., Donchin, E., Herning, R. I., and McCarthy, G. (1977). On the influence of task relevance and stimulus probability on event-related-potential components. *Electroenceph. Clin. Neurophysiol.*, **42**, 1–14.

Squires, N. K., Squires, K. C., and Hillyard, S. A. (1975). Two varieties of long-latency positive waves evoked by unpredictable auditory stimuli in man. *Electroenceph. Clin. Neurophysiol.*, **38**, 387–401.

Starr, A. (1978). Sensory evoked potentials in clinical disorders of the nervous system. *Ann. Rev. Neurosci.*, **1**, 103–27.

Stockard, J. J., and Rossiter, V. S. (1977). Clinical and pathological correlates of brain stem auditory response abnormalities. *Neurology*, **27**, 316–25.

Stuss, D. T., and Picton, T. W. (1978). Neurophysiological correlates of human concept formation. *Beh. Biol.*, **23**, 135–62.

Sutton, S. (1969). The specification of psychological variables in an average evoked potential experiment. In E. Donchin and D. B. Lindsley (Eds), *Average Evoked Potentials: Methods, Results, and Evaluations*, NASA SP-191, Washington.

Sutton, S., Braren, M., Zubin, J., and John, E. R. (1965). Evoked potential correlates of stimulus uncertainty. *Science*, **150**, 1187–8.

Sutton, S., Tueting, P., Zubin, J., and John, E. R. (1967). Information delivery and the sensory evoked potential. *Science*, **155**, 1436–9.

Szirtes, J., and Vaughan, H. G. (1977). Characteristics of cranial and facial potentials associated with speech production. *Electroenceph. Clin Neurophysiol.*, **43**, 386–96.

Timsit-Berthier, M., Delaunoy, J., Koninckx, N., and Rousseau, J. C. (1973). Slow potential changes in psychiatry. I Contingent negative variation. *Electroenceph. Clin. Neurophysiol.*, **35**, 355–61.

Tueting, P., Sutton, S., and Zubin, J. (1971). Quantitative evoked potential correlates of the probability of events. *Psychophysiology*, **7**, 385–94.

Uttal, W. R. (1967). Evoked brain potentials: signs or codes? *Perspect. Biol. Med.*, **10**, 627–39.

Vaughan, H. G. (1974). The analysis of scalp-recorded brain potentials. In R. F. Thompson and M. M. Patterson (Eds), *Bioelectric Recording Techniques: B-Electroencephalography and Human Brain Potentials*, Academic Press, New York.

Vaughan, H. G., Costa, L. D., and Ritter, W. (1968). Topography of the human motor potential. *Electroenceph. Clin. Neurophysiol.*, **25**, 1–10.

Walter, W. G., Cooper, R., Aldridge, V. J., McCallum, W. C., and Winter, A. L. (1964). Contingent negative variation: an electric sign of sensori-motor association and expectancy in the human brain. *Nature*, **203**, 380–4.

Weinberg, H., Walter, W. G., Cooper, R., and Aldridge, V. J. (1974). Emitted cerebral events. *Electroenceph. Clin. Neurophysiol.*, **36**, 449–56.

White, C. T. (1974). The visual evoked response and patterned stimuli. In G. Newton and A. H. Riesen (Eds), *Advances in Psychobiology*, Vol. 2, Wiley, New York.

Wiener, N. (1949). *Extrapolation, Interpolation and Smoothing of Stationary Time Series*, Wiley, New York.

Williamson, P. D., Goff, W. R., and Allison, T. (1970). Somatosensory evoked responses in patients with unilateral cerebral lesions. *Electroenceph. Clin. Neurophysiol.*, **28**, 566–75.

Woody, C. D. (1967). Characterization of an adaptive filter for the analysis of variable latency neuroelectric signals. *Med. Biol. Engng.*, **5**, 539–53.

APPLICATION OF THE CONTINGENT NEGATIVE VARIATION IN PSYCHOPHYSIOLOGY

KIERON PHILIP O'CONNOR

1 INTRODUCTORY REMARKS

1.1 Introduction

The contingent negative variation is an EEG component of recent discovery whose event-related nature has enormous potential for psychophysiologists in providing new ways of studying decision making, reaction time, and affective behaviour. However, because of difficulties in recording and controversy as to its psychological and physiological origins, applications until recent years have largely been in the medical rather than psychological fields. It has several characteristics to recommend it to psychophysiologists. Firstly, it is event related, and is a direct measure of electrocortical processing, in preparation rather than after receipt of a signal, and so presents a direct link between cortical and cognitive processes. It lasts long enough to allow psychologically meaningful manipulation of behaviour in an experimental paradigm. It is sensitive to subject, state, and situation interactions, and shows reliable individual differences. Also, with the advent of small laboratory computers and stable amplifiers, its recording is now fairly straightforward.

1.2 Discovery

Walter and coworkers (1964), whilst examining habituation of evoked responses to stimuli that were separated but associated in time, noted that a slow negative shift occurred in the baseline potential of the EEG in the interval between stimuli. Walter considered this interstimulus variation in the negativity of the EEG signal to be event-related and contingent upon the subject entering into a constant foreperiod reaction time experiment. It was thus termed the contingent negative variation (CNV). Walter and his colleagues found it to be maximal over the frontal cortex, and to be enhanced when the subject was required to make an overt decision or take action in response to the second stimulus. Further, it did not habituate over hundreds of trials, though it reached maximal amplitude after only twenty.

1.3 General features

An example of the classic CNV paradigm is given in Figure 6.19. A warning stimulus (a click or a flash) precedes an imperative stimulus which instructs the subject to make some overt or covert response. The onset of the CNV commences after the last positive peak of the evoked potential elicited by the warning stimulus, and terminates after response to the second stimulus with a fairly rapid return to baseline. Three characteristics of the CNV waveform will be noted from this illustration which differentiate it from the faster evoked potentials. Firstly, it has a slow rise time, which remains negative (i.e. upward going on the polygraph write out). Secondly, its length can be extended as a function of interstimulus interval. In fact the CNV can be sustained as long as 20 seconds, though waveform and topographical differences have led some authors to argue that it is not the same CNV as that recorded during the 'classic' 1-second interstimulus interval. Thirdly, it is generally of larger magnitude than other evoked potentials, being usually in the region of 10–40 μV. These amplitude, frequency, and time-locked characteristics dictate the appropriate recording, measurement and analysis techniques to be used with the CNV.

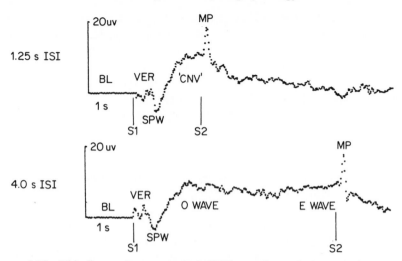

Figure 6.19 This figure shows a typical CNV paradigm where a contingency between a warning stimulus and an imperative stimulus is established within a foreperiod reaction time experiment. Vertex CNV was recorded between Cz and linked earlobes and averaged over 32 trials. The first stimulus was a flash and the second stimulus was a continuous tone terminated by a push button response. Note the separation of early and late components in the 4 second interstimulus interval. (From O'Connor, 1979.) BL = baseline; VER = visual evoked response to S1; SPW = slow positive wave preceding CNV; MP = motor potential elicited by response; O wave = orienting component of the CNV; E wave = expectancy component; ISI = interstimulus interval

2 RECORDING TECHNIQUES

The CNV is conventionally recorded as a potential difference between two electrodes on the scalp, one placed over the cortical generator of the signal and the other placed on an inactive site. In recording the CNV as with any bioelectric event the aim is to transfer the characteristics of the signal as faithfully as possible from the subject to the measuring instrument. This transfer operation depends solely on the characteristics of the electrodes, amplifiers, and the quality of the connections between them, as schematized in Figure 6.20.

2.1 Electrodes

Electrodes are artificial terminals placed on the subject to enable the bioelectric event of interest to be recorded. The potentials appearing across the electrode terminals will be the basis of the signal recorded on the polygraph. Thus electrodes are the first possible source of signal distortion. Electrode qualities to be controlled are: (1) the capacitance; (2) the resistance, which together form the effective impedance presented to the

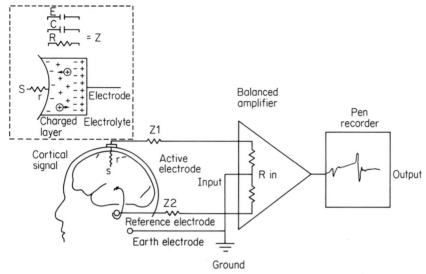

Figure 6.20   This figure shows the balanced amplifier circuit typical of most CNV recording. The inset is a representation of the electrical double layer that is created at the electrode-electrolyte scalp interface. Electrical properties present are a potential (E), a capacitance (C), and a resistance (R). The impedance (Z) of the electrode is determined by R and C. The total impedance accompanying the signal source (S) on input to the balanced amplifier is thus r (subject resistance)$+Z_1 + Z_2 + R_{in}$. The amplifier is balanced by a resistive network so that it discriminates against in-phase or common mode signals such as 50 Hz interference in favour of the anti-phase bioelectric events. To maintain a good discrimination ratio, and to measure as much of the bioelectric signal as possible, the input impedances should be at least 100 times greater than the electrode impedances. Most EEG amplifiers have small capacitors of equal value in series with each input lead. Larger values of R_{in} may then be required to maintain a long time constant

amplifier stage; and (3) the standing potential. These electrical properties are determined by the type of metal and size of the electrode, and the quality of the ionic layer and electrolytic interface with the subject.

Choice of Metal

When any metal comes into contact with an electrolyte junction such as body fluids or electrolytic paste, there is a local charge distribution known as an electrical double layer which creates a potential difference (E) between the electrode and the solution, a finite time constant (C) determining the rate of current flow through the medium, and a resistance (R) to the current flow. Different types of metals form different double layers, and for CNV recording, silver/silver chloride is the most appropriate metal. This is because it has a low standing potential (0.22 V), a long time constant (nearly infinite) and low resistance. On the other hand, gold, copper, and stainless steel are unsuitable as they have inappropriate characteristics. A low electrode potential is optimal since the very small voltage of the CNV must be superimposed upon this comparatively larger voltage. When capacitively coupled amplifiers are used, as is the case in ordinary EEG recording, this standing potential is blocked by the input capacitors and only the changing cortical potentials are recorded, but in the directly coupled (d.c.) type of amplifiers sometimes used for CNV recording this is not so.

The electrode potential difference is increased if active and reference electrodes are of different metals. For instance, if a silver electrode is paired with a copper electrode in an electrolytic medium, a potential of about $\frac{1}{2}$ V develops between the electrodes. This large voltage could easily block any CNV recording. Even electrodes of the same metal may still develop potentials in the order of millivolts, and this may change further during *in vivo* recording, due to small electrochemical changes. Chloriding electrodes simultaneously in the same solution helps achieve equipotentiality; a slow rate of current flow (0.1 mA passed in 5% saline solution for approximately 1 hour) and an excess of chloride favour stability. Electrodes should also be shorted together and immersed in saline when not in use to aid stabilization.

The large capacitance of silver/silver chlorided electrodes gives them a long time constant and means that their double layer will pass very slow frequency signals such as the CNV with a minimum of distortion, whereas gold and stainless steel electrodes distort the CNV considerably due to their short time constant. Capacitance is proportional to surface area, so that the time constant increases with electrode diameter, though in practice electrodes of 6mm diameter are adequate. One way to check the distortion that electrodes may have on a slow potential coming from the brain is to use them to record the EOG (as detailed later). A steady potential is generated by right and left eye movements, and with the use of chlorided silver electrodes and a d.c. amplifier these should take the form of a square wave.

Electrodes having a low resistance will pass current, i.e. record a change in potential, upon application of a very small electrical voltage above or below the electrode potential. These electrodes such as silver/silver chloride are said to be non-polarized or reversible, and are optimal for CNV recording. Polarized electrodes do not permit sensitive recording of steady or slowly changing potentials.

In summary, properly chlorided large area (≥ 6 mm) silver electrodes are the most stable electrodes for CNV recording, and gold, copper, and stainless steel the most unsuitable as these are noisy, unstable, and with the wrong electrical properties. Care of electrodes cannot be over-emphasized, since any slight damage of the coating with an impurity or uneven chloriding will dramatically reduce the quality of the recorded signal. Also silver/silver chlorided electrodes are photovoltaic, i.e. they convert light energy into a voltage, and if a strong visual source is to be used as a stimulus, it is recommended that the electrodes should be immersed in a bowl of saline and exposed to the light and a recording taken to determine the size, if any, of this photovoltaic artefact.

2.2 Electrolyte

The type of electrolyte medium used at the electrode skin interface is very important, since its saline properties will determine the current passing properties of the double layer (Figure 6.20). Both change in skin resistance and skin potential can alter electrode potential and cause a drift in the electrode potential by disturbing the ionic balance of the charged layer. Shackel (1958) suggests the use of isotonic electrode jelly, that is, jelly having a concentration of salt similar to skin and tissue. Such a jelly would have a concentration of around 1 g NaCl. On the other hand hypertonic jellies with high saline concentration are to be avoided. It is also wise to cleanse the scalp with methylated spirits to minimize resistance. Foreign particles can, of course, interfere with the low resistive properties necessary for recording, and the scalp and electrodes should be cleaned as a matter of hygiene to minimize the possibility ˌof transmission of skin ailments. In manufactured electrodes a cup-shaped cavity with aperture is allowed for the introduction of electrolytic jelly with a syringe and blunt needle. Since this needle often scratches the surface of the skin, it should be subjected to some sterile procedure, such as soaking in methylated spirits prior to application.

2.3 Electrode application

The best method of affixing electrodes is by use of collodion, since this glues the electrode firmly on the scalp.* Collodion is commercially available, and is preferable to other paste methods of application, since it affords good and lasting scalp contact and minimizes electrode movement artifact.

The usual procedure in putting on electrodes is to hold the electrode in position whilst placing the collodion around the circumference of the electrode. The hair should be parted around the electrode and not caught underneath it. The glue is then dried with an air blower and the electrolytic jelly inserted through a hole in the electrode cup with a blunt sterilized needle and syringe. The electrodes should then be left to settle down to form an equilibrium with the jelly and scalp interface for a few minutes. The impedance of the electrodes and tissue can then be measured, preferably by a sine-wave calibration as direct currents such as

*However, where one is putting electrodes on a hair-free area or a bald person, sticky adhesive disks can be safely used in place of glue, and these are commercially available.

applied by an avometer can change conditions at the electrode surface. A good method is to feed the electrode inputs into a skin impedance meter. The electrode impedance should ideally be below 5 kμ and thus small in comparison to the input impedance of the amplifier (Figure 6.20).

2.4 Electrode montage

Where electrodes are placed depends very much on the hypotheses under study. As will be discussed in the measurement section, the CNV has a varying topographical distribution over the cortex, and this is responsive to stimulus manipulations involving functional specialization in the brain. So, for instance, if one is interested in modality specific effects electrodes should be placed over the primary sensory projection areas. For the specific effects of language the left parietal lobe should be the site. For a maximal 'non-specific' CNV the vertex is considered the most suitable site for the active electrode, and this position can be located systematically for each subject using the standard 10–20 system placement. (see Figure 6.1). Whatever site is used the method of connecting the electrodes to the amplifier head box should be as follows: the lead to the amplifier which when made electronegative to the other lead produces an upward deflection on the recorder should be attached to the active electrode, the other lead to the reference electrode. These leads are usually labelled clearly (black and white respectively on conventional EEG machines) on the head box. Attention to this polarity is important since in electrophysiology negative by convention is up, probably because negative going action potentials were neurophysiologists' earliest preoccupation.

Electrodes on the head can be connected either in a bipolar or mono(uni)polar or common reference montage*. With a bipolar montage the potential difference between two electrodes over different active areas of cortex is recorded; however, a change in negativity may be present in some form over the whole surface of the cortex, and if the two signals are of equal amplitude and phase the difference between them will be zero, and little may be recorded. A unipolar technique is preferable for CNV recording with an active electrode over the generator site and a reference or indifferent electrode at a 'neutral site' with zero activity. The neutral site most frequently chosen is the mastoid or linked mastoid processes. Unfortunately there exists no point of exact zero activity on the head because the electrical generators are not surrounded by an insulator and therefore the activity is not restricted to the immediate environment of the electrical sources. In fact, activity recorded from the mastoid may be quite

---

*Electrodes can also be connected in the less commonly used average reference montage, where a single electrode is referred to the mean activity of all other active electrodes. This method has been used successfully with CNV recording (Pfurtscheller and Cooper, 1975b) but requires a large electrode array, and the appropriate resistive network to average the signals (see St John-Loe, 1973).

large and similar in frequency to vertex recordings (Pfurtscheller and Cooper, 1975a). Since the site cannot have zero potential it should at least be as electrically independent from the source electrode site as possible and not contaminated by other extracerebral potentials. A possible site is the chin, though resistance here is high in males and it tends to be contaminated with artifacts. The nose has also been used, but Curry and McCallum (1978) have found this site more active than the mastoid. The present author considers the ear lobes to be particularly suitable as disc electrodes can be easily applied, and EEG activity there, though still detectable, is minimal (Von Hasselt, 1972). For purposes of screening 50 Hz interference and subject electrostatic pick-up it is usually necessary to have an independent earth electrode. This can be placed anywhere on the scalp, but most conveniently on the forehead or ear lobe. If the ear lobe or mastoid is being used as a reference site, placing the earth on the ear or mastoid will have the effect of making the reference approximately equal to earth potential which should be zero relative to the system used. However, some authors (Cooper, Osselton, and Shaw, 1974) argue that linked ear lobes or mastoids should be used to minimize eye movement artifact since this will cancel out the effects of lateral eye movement (see section on artifacts) in which case an alternative site for earth should be found (although not off the head). The linked procedure consists of simply connecting the two lead terminals together to make a single input in the 'white' lead of the amplifier. The efficacy of this and other eye movement compensating procedures and their effect on the reference site is discussed in a later section under eye movement artifact.

2.5 Amplification

The amplifier boosts the CNV signal so that it appears across the moving coil of the recorder pens as a recognizable potential in the order of volts. The same electrical properties that affect the signal at the electrode stage apply to the amplification stage. If an a.c. amplifier is used both the input capacitance and impedance need to be as large as possible as this will give the system the long time constant needed to record the CNV. The large impedance ($\simeq 1$ MΩ) will also minimize the effect of electrode potential and impedance artifacts (see Figure 6.20). In addition, the amplifier will have a balanced noise rejection facility (see Artifact section) and a sensitivity or gain control, which should have been set to a standard setting in the calibration procedure (see Calibration section).

The slow build up of the CNV over a time course of seconds requires that either d.c. amplifiers or a.c. amplifiers with very long time constants (>5 s), be used in recording. A d.c. amplifier has constant sensitivity down to zero frequency, and thus allows recording of steady potentials and slow fluctuations in level of potential. It is only in the last two decades that d.c.

amplifiers stable enough and with low enough noise for recording purposes have been developed. Even so, total elimination of natural drift can only be accomplished with loss of sensitivity and on top of this d.c. amplifiers are sensitive to slow drifts from extracerebral sources.

The CNV, unlike the ongoing EEG, is a steady non-fluctuating voltage, or more accurately a potential that fluctuates at very low frequencies (<0.01 Hz). It is thus evident that extracerebral sources of drift such as electrodes and amplifiers must be kept to a minimum or detecting the CNV becomes impossible, and amplifiers with drift rates above 20 μV per minute should not be used. In addition, CNV amplifiers should have a high noise rejection ratio, a high linear gain and high input impedance.

The usual impedance of EEG amplifiers (10^7 Ω) reduces the potential difference between electrodes, and it is unusual to find less than 1 mV between electrode pairs. When a.c. amplifiers are used, these steady potentials are blocked by coupling capacitors. However, with no coupling capacitors in the input circuit, the steady potential may drive the first stage of amplification beyond its linear range. Unfortunately electrode potentials may vary considerably during the recording and give rise to baseline drift. Scalp movement is the most common cause of potential difference change between electrodes, since movement alters resistance, causing current to flow between electrodes.

Compensating for Drift

When a d.c. amplifier is used changes in steady potential can overload the input stage, and this can be overcome by generating a voltage in the recording polygraph to 'back off' the large steady potential in the input circuit. This d.c. balance or 'bucking' control may be calibrated to allow for the steady potential difference (p.d.) between electrodes. Since the steady potentials can be either positive or negative, this control must compensate for both polarities. It is used in a manner similar to the pen centering control to keep the written trace in the middle of its recording range. Where the changes of steady potential are much larger than the EEG signal, it is advisable to record the signal on two channels, one a.c. coupled with high sensitivity (50 μV/cm) the other directly coupled at very low sensitivity (200 μV/cm); this is acceptable practice amongst researchers.

Cooper, Osselton, and Shaw (1974) in fact suggest that as long as time constants are above 5 s, a.c. amplifiers can be used to record CNV, as these eliminate the problems of compensating for drift with d.c. recording. However, the length of the time constant needed depends on the length of interstimulus interval (ISI) during which the CNV is recorded. For long ISIs, long time constants are necessary and even with short ISIs though distortion is minimal with a 6 s time constant it is still present, as is demonstrated in Figure 6.21.

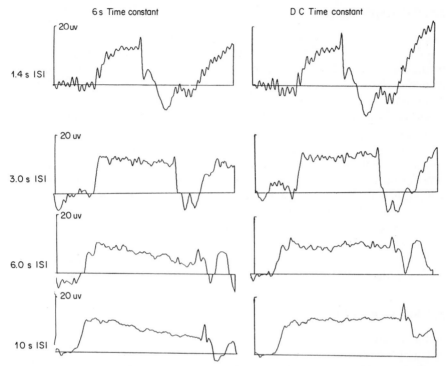

Figure 6.21   This figure shows the same CNV recorded through both a normal EEG amplifier with a 6 second time constant and an amplifier with infinite time constant. As the interstimulus interval lengthens the loss of signal due to the decay time of the a.c. amplifier becomes apparent. Note also the loss in signal resolution with the longer intervals due to digital sampling limitations. For the 10 second interval each data point represents 400 milliseconds of original EEG. (From O'Connor (1978b))

One might argue that where a study is concerned with within subject change-over conditions, the length of time constant is immaterial providing it is constant. However, it may well be the later CNV components that are lost through the use of a short time constant, that will vary most between conditions. A rule of thumb is that if one is using a.c. amplifiers the time constant should be at least twice the value of the ISI being used. To summarize: in choosing an amplifier for CNV recording it is essential to check that: (1) the input impedance is high (>1 MΩ); (2) if a.c. coupling is used that the time constant is long enough (>5 s); (3) the sensitivity or gain range is adequate for CNV (100 μV signal should come out as at least 1 V deflection); (4) the signal to noise ratio is adequate ($>30,000/1$); (5) it is free of thermal and other sources of drift.

Manufacturers are usually helpful in tailoring apparatus to meet requirements.

2.6 Polygraph writeout

The polygraph writeout of the CNV is the proof of a good recording and should never be omitted. Allowing for the fact that analogue tape recorders usually have a wider sensitivity range and better frequency response than pen recorders, it is evident that the quality of the record determines the quality of the signal to be analysed. If the CNV trace is obscured by noise, drift, artifact or general kerfuffle, it is no good hoping that the computer or averaging process will not be affected by this. Averaging will only extract a CNV if one was properly recorded. Paper speed is important for record inspection and normally should be kept to a slow speed of say 1.5 cm or 3.0 cm per second since this allows adequate separation of artifact from signal, but will also show up a furry record. The record can then be speeded up to see if there is any rhythmic superimposition on the trace. The chart record should carry the calibration signal on each channel, so that inequalities in sensitivity of recordings can be detected. Event markers should also be on the record, so that the EEG trace can be monitored with respect to progress of the experiment.

2.7 Recording artifacts

Artifacts are most easily detected and removed from examination of the polygraph write out.
There are two common sources of artifact:

(1) Those due to faults on the input circuit (i.e. electrodes and their connections to amplifiers (See Figure 6.20)).
(2) Those due to other irrelevant bioelectric events.

Electrode artifacts may be caused by loose contact or scalp movement disturbing the electrochemical balance of the double layer and will show up on the record as a fast transient or intermittent deflection on the channel corresponding to the faulty connection. One particularly nasty form of electrochemical artifact can be encountered when the junction of the wire that is soldered to the electrode metal becomes wetted with electrode paste. At this point there is an opportunity for currents to flow in the electrode paste due to the creation of potentials between the lead and the electrode. Thus the electrode lead should always be well insulated. Artifacts due to bad connectors will take the form of large sweeps off range, accompanied by bursts of large 50 Hz hum. When this hum is above 1 cm on the record, it usually indicates an open circuit with one electrode input to the balanced amplifier absent. It may require replacement of a faulty electrode. A small amplitude hum on the trace usually indicates high electrode impedance, of which the most common source is high resistance at the skin/electrolyte surface. This can sometimes be overcome by slight abrasion of the skin with the blunt needle. The earth electrode should be examined similarly. If this does not remove the hum then it is possibly 50 Hz pick-up from either the mains or the flux field of a powerful appliance. Strong electric light bulbs are often responsible. When choosing a recording room for the apparatus it is advisable to check on the type of mains wiring, the screening of the room, and that there is not a power generator next door (see Chapter 10).

Bioelectric artifacts include eye movement potentials, skin potentials, muscle activation, heart rate, and possibly respiration. The relationship between respiratory cycle and the CNV is unclear (Papakostopoulos and McCallum, 1973). It has been reported that inspiration facilitates CNV amplitude (Gullickson and Darrow, 1973). However, though there may be a metabolic association between CNV and respiratory activity, the only direct influence on CNV seems to be via scalp movements which can be produced by heavy breathing. Skin potential changes may be caused by a change in the state of arousal of the subject, or a temperature change, and will show up on the record as very slow cyclic drift in the trace. It may be rectified by attention to subject conditions, re-application of electrodes or as Karrer, Kohn, and Ivins (1973) suggest, skin drilling, hydration or injection of atropine under each electrode. The mastoid is particularly prone to cephalic skin artifacts, and adequate room ventilation is advisable for long experimental sessions in hot weather.

Occasionally electromyographic (EMG) activity from trapezoid, jaw or neck muscles will be superimposed on the EEG trace, particularly in occipital regions, and this can be overcome by relaxing the muscles, either by alteration of head or jaw position, or if this fails by use of some general relaxation schedule. EMG activity will show up as a spiky fuzz over the primary trace, and can be distinguished from 50 Hz hum by speeding up the chart and observing its irregular rhythm. Interference from EMG can be reduced by lowering the high frequency cut off response of the amplifier, but attempts at behavioural remedies should precede electrical ones. Electrocardiac activity shows up as the conventional QRS complex on the trace, and is caused by pick-up from the main cerebral arteries. It can often be reduced by altering electrode location by a few millimetres.

It should be remembered that the EEG has the smallest power of all the bioelectric potentials, and so can easily be swamped by the larger amplitude signals.

Eye movements have traditionally been considered a major contaminating source in recording CNVs. At one time a causal relationship was postulated (Lippold, 1973). However, recordings taken intracerebrally (Cooper, 1968) and in patients with no eyes (Low and coworkers, 1966) have established the CNV as an independent phenomenon. Nevertheless the generation of the corneoretinal dipole potential over the surface of the scalp can produce eye potential artifacts in scalp recordings, and the CNV recorded at the vertex may be very difficult to distinguish from the concurrent electrooculographic activity (Shagass, 1972). Straumanis, Shagass, and Overton (1969) showed that ocular potential shifts accompanying a voluntary response parallelled those of the CNV. The EOG changes seemed to be a concomitant of a voluntary downward eye movement. Whilst Von Becker and coworkers (1973) have shown that saccadic eye movements in any direction also enhance CNV amplitude, Hillyard and Galambos (1970) considered the effects of voluntary as well as involuntary eye movement upon CNV. These authors reported that eye movement artifact contributed a total of 23% of the total CNV amplitude, and detailed a method for partialling out eye movement components. Wasman and coworkers (1970) found similar results to Hillyard and Galambos, even with eyes closed.

All these authors agree that ocular fixation is a necessary minimal requirement for CNV recording, but even so, this will not eliminate involuntary saccadic and oscillatory eye movements, or blinks, and other strategies detailed below have been employed to reduce these effects.

Although blinks can be reduced by closing the eyes, augmentation of the alpha rhythm when the eyes are closed increases the 'noise' and makes averaging less effective. In a method proposed by Walter (1967), potentials due to blinks or residual eye movements are compensated by a suitable choice of reference electrode placement. If, for instance, the mastoid processes are linked together, the effect of lateral eye movements is much reduced, since rotation of the eyes to right or left will increase the potential at one electrode and decrease it at the other. Thus the voltage from the two reference electrodes will not change. However, this reference system will not take into account the effect of vertical eye movements, and the transverse potential distribution of these eye movements makes it necessary to place the reference electrode on the same equipotential line as the vertex. This placement can be simulated by means of a variable potentiometer connected between supra-orbital, vertex, and mastoid electrodes. However, this method is only suitable for a single channel recording, and will not compensate for rolling eye movements. Another problem with the linking and potentiometer operations is that one is not quite sure what is the true reference site. Unlesss, in the linking operation, the electrode resistances are balanced by a bridge, the reference will be the electrode site with least resistance. In the potentiometer method the voltage compensation applied between reference and frontal eye movements shifts the reference to an unknown equipotential point. Details of the patterns of potential distribution produced by different eye movements are given in Overton and Shagass (1969). These authors also suggest that adequate monitoring of eye movements at their source will allow prediction of propagated potentials at other scalp locations.

Hillyard and Galambos (1970) have actually suggested correcting CNV measurement by means of a factor derived from the EOG recording. They claim to have separated two additive and separable components of the CNV, one determined by response effort, the other by ocular displacement.

Rejection of contaminated trials seems a safer method than compensation by the techniques described, for two reasons: (a) compensation assumes a constant additive and linear relationship between CNV and eye movement artifact (whereas the artifact varies in influence over different areas); (b) it ignores, where electrooculograms are the criterion for eye artifact detection, the possibility that electrocortical potentials may contribute to electrical potentials recorded at the eye.

The most satisfactory method of rejection to date seems that proposed by Papakostopoulos, Winter, and Newton (1973) for multichannel CNV recordings. By this technique, eye movements are monitored mechanically, and any movement above 3° is cancelled from the trial average, though they found that visual feedback of eye movement to the subject, via introduction of a mirror for fixation, strikingly reduced the number of movements above 3°. If selected eye movement trials are then averaged with the CNVs, the averaged eye tracing is near to zero (Papakostopoulos, Winter, and Newton, 1973). This method, though the most satisfactory from a technical point of view, does raise statistical problems of sample selection. The most suitable EOG placement for this method is diagonally across the internal and external canthi of the right eye to detect both vertical and lateral movement.

2.8 Calibration

Calibration of eye movements can be best achieved by setting up two points 3° of visual angle apart in front of the subject, and asking him to move his eyes back and forth between them before the CNV recording commences; 3° of visual angle can be calculated by use of Pythagoras' theorem that the tangent of the angle between two lines is a function of the ratio of the opposite and the adjacent distance between them. Calibration of the recording system should also be carried out prior to actual biological recording.

Amplitude calibration is an essential part of any evoked potential study. The usual method (Cooper, Osselton, and Shaw, 1974) is to include in each trial a calibration waveform which occurs at a constant time with respect to the stimulus. This calibration pulse (square or triangular) is usually included in the EEG signal by means of a secondary transformer, and appears in the prestimulus part of the average. The disadvantage of this method is that the calibration waveform is now in the epoch with the evoked response, and is not easily eliminated before analysis. An alternative method is to average a set of trials in which only the calibration

pulse is present. The advantage of this method when using a general
purpose computer is that inequality of sensitivity in different channels can
be calculated and all subsequent data corrected to a standard value. Also
this method can allow calibration of the whole system, from head box
through to computer, rather than just a local calibration of the EEG
preamplifier stage. This calibration should be carried out with both a
square wave calibrator and a low frequency generator with low output
impedance applied to the amplifier inputs. This will allow accurate
computation of the frequency response and sensitivity of the whole system.

3 ANALYSIS

3.1 Detection of CNV by averaging

Once the EEG signals have been satisfactorily recorded, it is necessary to
transform the data for analysis and measurement. This is usually achieved
by feeding the signal into an analog to digital convertor on a small
laboratory computer and storing the signal in digital tape blocks. In digital
form the signal is represented by data points with numerical values,
sampled at specified intervals from the primary analogue waveform. The
resolution of the digital values will depend on how close in time the values
were sampled. Hence the length of primary signal represented by one
computer data point may vary between 1 ms and 100 ms, depending on the
length of the signal stored on one digital block. The degree of resolution
becomes important when considering latency components, and where the
CNV is recorded over many seconds resolution should always be specified
in scientific communications.

   Once in digital format the signal is easier to manipulate for averaging
and other statistical procedures. Computer programs designed for such
digital processing operations on the CNV are available in Great Britain
from the Burden Neurological Institute, Bristol, and the Institute of
Psychiatry, London (see Chapter 13).

   Averaging of the CNV is necessary since it is not easily seen in a single
trial as its mean amplitude ($\approx 10\ \mu V$) is small relative to the mean amplitude
of the background EEG ($\approx 40\ \mu V$). However, its event related nature gives
it a consistency over several trials, in contrast to the random nature of the
EEG, and allows common features to be extracted by a summing or
averaging process.

Procedures

Averaging is most conveniently done using digital techniques which have
largely replaced the earlier analog devices. The degree of improvement in
signal to noise ratio obtained by averaging depends on a number of factors.

With unlimited bandwidth the reduction of noise by averaging is proportional to $\sqrt{N}$ where N is the number of trials. Thus the biggest signal to noise improvement comes at the beginning of a series. For a series of nine trials the noise decreases by a factor of three, but another 72 trials are necessary for the next factor of three. The square root law is not accurate if transients such as sharp waves constitute part of the background activity. In a small series transients are less likely to recur at the same place. Also as Walter (1965) points out, the background EEG is rarely truly random, and if all of the background activity consisted of transients without coincidence the signal to noise gain would be proportional to N rather than $\sqrt{N}$. Thus overall a small number of trials is optimal for a CNV average. Becker (1972) has proposed that for evoked potentials of 5 μV, where both the signal and noise are a periodic function of relatively constant amplitude and frequency but with random phase, a sample size of approximately 200 is necessary for a satisfactory signal to noise ratio. For the CNV, however, most researchers use an average of from 4–30 trials.

Earlier analogue techniques tended to sum or superimpose responses rather than to average them, mainly because storage capacity was usually limited on these devices. Superimposition of one trace upon another has advantages over averaging to the extent that all responses are individually preserved and the only loss of information is their order. Also in some cases the event related response may simply be an attenuation of the ongoing EEG activity (e.g. alpha blocking) and this will not be detected by averaging, but will by superimposition. However, averaging is statistically more useful as loss of information can to an extent be retrieved through computation of inter-trial variance. Averaging also gives a representation of the CNV with a clearer resolution. With digital techniques resolution can also be improved by varying the sampling rate of the signal. Here the amplitude of the signal is sampled at a series of points in time, coded in binary form and stored in a set of memory addresses. If for instance the sampling epoch is 1 s, and the computer has 400 addresses available then 400 points in the epoch can be sampled with each sweep. If there are N trials, then there will be N sweeps, and some addresses will tend to zero while some will increase positively or negatively according to the consistency of the waveform. At the end of N trials, the averaged waveform will be computed and reconstituted.

The sum of the sampled points will increase with the number of trials, but the average should theoretically be independent of the number of presentations, providing the variance of CNV characteristics is minimal over trials.

3.2 Variance estimation

The concept of CNV variance is thus crucial to the discussion of the averaging process. As Shagass (1972) points out the investigator must decide, empirically, upon averaging that number of observations which will provide the most reasonable compromise between a reliable, noise-free measurement, minimal risk of recording from a subject in more than one state, and minimal expenditure of time. Both random and systematic changes can take place in the averaging sequence and the average may conceal much variation occurring during the course of the recording that may be of interest. If waveshape and timing remain constant as is usual in sensory evoked responses, and only amplitude varies, then the average may be representative. However, the cognitive aspects of the CNV paradigm can easily lead to change in subject expectation from trial to trial, which would more likely be reflected in variation of latency. In this case, the average would be quite unrepresentative of the course of events. The extreme case of latency variability or 'jitter' involves a random temporal dispersion of signal peaks, whose averaged response would be zero. Apparent reduction in amplitude may thus represent variation in latency without actual amplitude change, since the average of a number of variable amplitude responses is indistinguishable from the average of a similar number of variable latency responses (Callaway, 1975).

A related problem is the effect of extreme values or 'outliers', which may contain a lot of artifact and distort the average disproportionately. The larger the number of trials, the more likely are some to be contaminated by artifact which cannot be eliminated at source. One way of reducing the effect of outliers is to compute the median of the responses instead of their average (Borda and Frost, 1968). However, this requires storing each trial individually and multiplies the store capacity beyond that of most laboratory computers.

In practice the most satisfactory method is to compute the average over as few trials as are necessary to give a clear response and also to compute the variance. As Brazier (1964) has stressed, amplitude, latency, and variability are not independent, and variability rather than being something to eliminate, may be a more fundamental phenomenon than either latency or amplitude. Variability of responses from trial to trial can be obtained by calculating either the mean amplitude deviation, or the variance at points along the time axis. The mean amplitude deviation is the average value of amplitude deviations from the mean irrespective of sign.

If at a particular point in time following the presentation of each stimulus the evoked responses have the value V through V_N in a set of N trials the *average* value of the responses at that time is

$$V_A = \frac{1}{N}(V_1 + V_2 + \cdots + V_N)$$

the *mean deviation* is:

$$\frac{1}{N}(V_1 - V_A + V_2 - V_A + \cdots + V_N - V_A)$$

The *variance* is:

$$\frac{1}{N}[(V_1 - V_A)^2 + (V_2 - V_A)^2 + \cdots + (V_N - V_A)^2]$$

$$= \frac{1}{N}(V_1^2 + V_2^2 + \cdots + V_N^2 - V_A^2)$$

Thus to calculate the variance in real time only the sum of the data points and sum of their squares is required for all points in the epoch. This involves considerably less storage than for computing the median response. However, this analog measure of signal variance will not replace all lost information, for the following three reasons.

First, computationally the variance is a measure of amplitude deviation, but it is difficult from this measure to separate the contributions of amplitude variability, and variability in time. Second, there are two types of variation: random variation over trials, and systematic change of amplitude over a long series of trials, such as may occur in habituation. Finally, the evoked response is only a fraction of the total electrical activity recorded; thus it contributes only a small portion of the total variance, which will be dominated by the larger EEG variance. It is not possible to discriminate the variance contributed by the evoked response from that originating in 'spontaneous' activity. An estimate of the contribution of the EEG to the total variance can be obtained from EEG recordings taken in the absence of stimulation. However, this again depends on the stochastic nature of the EEG which may vary from time to time and from subject to subject.

The significance of CNV variability and individual differences and its complex interaction with state, stimulus, and situation, is important, since both Callaway and Halliday (1973) and Cappola, Tabor, and Buchsbaum (1978) have shown that there are systematic components to this variability, beyond what could be expected from random error contributions and which suggest subject-specific factors. It is possible though that large variability amongst CNV averages may simply represent a poorly controlled procedure, and caution is advised in proclaiming CNV variability as a positive finding, particularly within subjects.

To summarize: the most satisfactory method of averaging CNVs is to average a small number in signal form to acquire a reasonable signal to noise resolution (4–30), then extract numerical values of the waveform and compute mean and variance on these digitally, as this will allow a more selective and accurate estimation of the variance of different components. Pfurtscheller and Cooper (1975b) have reported considerable intertrial variation in both latency and amplitude of the CNV, which depending on magnitude of the CNV and stationarity of the background EEG, can make an average unrepresentative of its single trial constituents. A measure of single trial variance would thus be optimal. Occasionally a CNV of recognizable form is elicited on a single trial, and hopefully when psychophysiological determinants of CNV magnitude are better defined experimental methods to enhance single trial stability of the CNV will become routine. In the meantime some progress has been made towards single trial detection of the CNV by statistical techniques of signal recognition.

3.3 Single trial CNV detection

Detection techniques have included the use of Wiener filtering, by which method a filter is tuned to select signals on the basis of specified frequency, phase, and amplitude characteristics to the exclusion of others (Walter, 1969). Although theoretically Wiener filtering and another related adaptive filtering technique devised by Woody (1967) are of use in detecting signals with variable latency such as the CNV, in practice the transient (i.e. non-stationary) nature of the CNV, its fast and slow wave components, and its interaction with background EEG noise, make applications difficult (Ungan and Basar, 1976). A more suitable technique is the recognition index described by Weinberg and Cooper (1972), in which the product of two correlation coefficients is used to make decisions about the presence or absence of the CNV. The EEG sample is correlated in signal form with a prototype CNV and rejected if the coefficient is low. The criterion for selection of the initial template presents problems as there are many aspects of the signal to be considered. The template can be part or all of a single trial, an averaged CNV or an artificial waveform with one or more components. Pfurtscheller and Cooper (1975b) have recently combined this correlative detection technique with a selective averaging technique whereby a template matching process decides whether a trial has adequate amplitude and latency to be included in the average. Though this technique has the advantage of using a subject-specific empirically obtained template, inevitably there will be a statistical bias attached to a sample selected in this way, which may make later interpretation doubtful. A stepwise discriminant function technique of single CNV trial detection has been proposed by Donchin and Herning (1975) by which the ratio of event related potentials over trials to non-event related potentials within trials is maximized. However, this technique is probably more suitable in detecting components most influenced by changing conditions, as the between subject variability of the CNV is high, and the components of signal variance are not necessarily linear and additive. A further univariate procedure has been proposed by Wicke and coworkers (1978) in which a set of comparisons between two consecutive pre-stimulus EEG epochs, and an equal post-stimulus epoch are tested for significance by use of Sandler's 'A' test, the criterion for detection being the operating confidence level of significance. All these techniques aim towards minimizing noise contributions to single CNVs; an alternative would be to enhance stability of the signal experimentally, though this requires more research into the experimental sources of amplitude and latency variability.

3.4 Simultaneous analysis of background EEG and eye movements

If the background EEG and other components are to be examined with the CNV, the digital sampling rate by which the data points are constructed will need to be considered with respect to the Nyquist criterion which states that the rate should be at least twice the fastest frequency to be considered (see page 293). It is advisable to have some index of background EEG, since statistical and biological correlations have been porposed between dominant EEG frequency and CNV appearance. The relationship is by no means clear but there is evidence that the CNV is higher in subjects with desynchronized alpha (Pfurtscheller and Aranibar, 1977). The CNV is an electrocortically more diffuse phenomenon than the ongoing EEG and it is possible that the CNV may arise electrically from a phase synchronization of alpha generators (Sayers, Beagley, and Henshall, 1974).

Eye movement signals should be digitized and averaged in the same way as the CNVs, and this average compared and, if possible, correlated (in signal or numerical form) with the CNV average to determine degree of independence. If eye movements are properly controlled the correlation should be low.

3.5 Statistical signal analysis

The definition of event related slow potentials, and classification of their components is as a function of time. Statistical procedures on the CNV in signal form are thus usually limited to the time domain and include (1) waveform analysis such as cross/autocorrelations, (2) Hjorth's (1973) activity, mobility, and complexity parameters, and (3) spatiotemporal analysis (Cooper, Osselton, and Shaw, 1974). The CNV is statistically a transient and frequency domain analysis is thus of doubtful mathematical validity. The analysis of different frequencies comprising the CNV waveform is also likely to be of doubtful biological validity since the CNV is a steady potential, and faster frequencies are likely to be artifactual. Nevertheless functional relationships between frequency components of CNV and the background activity and also eye movements (Whitton, Lue, and Moldofsky, 1978) may be legitimately explored by frequency domain techniques such as power, coherence, and phase spectra, but there are strict data sampling and shaping criterion that need to be considered before these techniques can be of value, and frequency analysis cannot be applied willy-nilly to a single CNV (Bendat and Piersol, 1971; Beauchamp, 1973). A less complicated non-parametric measure of computing contingency between signal waveforms has been proposed by Callaway (1975), based on estimation of the probability of the polarity and derivative of a component at specific points in time. This method has the advantage of requiring no assumptions as to signal form and being computationally fairly straightforward.

4 MEASUREMENT

The value of the mean prestimulus EEG is not necessarily zero because of electrode potential drift. Averaging of trials that are biased in this way results in the CNV being superimposed on a steady level: consequently the measurement of the magnitude of the CNV above the true baseline is difficult.

4.1. Baseline measurement

The establishment of a prestimulus baseline is frequently accomplished by visual inspection. However, a more satisfactory method is to average a section of prestimulus EEG which will be unrelated to the CNV, and use this as the baseline. Alternatively the EEG can be continually sampled in the intertrial interval and the mean value of the d.c. level determined for a short period or as a running average before the CNV epoch starts. This value can then be subtracted from all data points sampled during the CNV epoch and the CNVs thus 'normalized' with respect to a common baseline. It has been suggested that the CNV is susceptible to initial values effects (Gaillard and Näätänen, 1978) and this is another reason for accurate estimation of the baseline.

It can be seen that directly related to the question of what constitutes a satisfactory 'baseline' is the problem of what constitutes an adequate measure of the CNV.

4.2 Standard CNV measures

Unfortunately the value of standardization of measures of the CNV is still in debate. For instance in a conference discussion on the issue (McCallum and Knott, 1973), Tecce and Donchin both proposed that agreement of standardized procedures could lead to a solid body of normative data, and facilitate inter laboratory comparison. Walter and Lacey strongly disagreed with this viewpoint and suggested it would lead to an overstandardization that would hamper discovery. Lacey suggested that rather than standardizing measures, an 'anchor' experiment should be conducted previous to all experiments, which would be a kind of biological calibration of 10–15 trials of the S_1–S_2–R paradigm. This could then be used to assess homogeneity across laboratories.

Current CNV measures can be divided into integrated and single point measures. The advantages of each depend specifically on the psychological variable being manipulated and the interstimulus intervals used. Thus whereas Irwin and coworkers (1966) measure peak amplitude anywhere in the S_1–S_2 period, McCallum and Walter (1968) prefer mean amplitude of the 150 ms period just prior to S_2. Low and McSherry (1968) measure area under the curve, which may or may not include the evoked response to S_1 and S_2. Van Veen and coworkers (1973) measure the mean amplitude in each of the 10 segments in the interval beginning 450 ms after S_1 up to S_2 onset. Kopell, Tinklenberg, and Hollister (1972) and Costell and coworkers (1972) have used a measure based on the maximum positivity after S_1 onset.

Tecce (1972) has advocated the use of multiple measures which include area under curve and amplitude. Since he felt that one of the important features to be quantified in the CNV is the shape of the ascending part of the curve, Tecce (1972) suggests that additional use of onset latency to peak or other 'rise time' measures could be helpful.

Fluctuations in the ongoing EEG which ride on top of the averaged CNV make accurate measurement of peak amplitude difficult, and as a result some authors visually fit a smooth curve onto the CNV, although smoothing is better achieved by proper mathematical or digital smoothing techniques. Coarse or 'bastard' type smoothing where adjacent data points are simply collapsed, is to be avoided as this reduces latency and component resolution. Area measures on the other hand average out irregularities due to the ongoing EEG, though Borda (1973) proposed that mean amplitude measures give the same results as area measures. Van Veen and coworkers (1973) countered this suggestion by showing that valuable information of the variable time course of the CNV in different populations is lost by taking mean measures. However, mean amplitude does have merit as a criterion for single trial selection (McCallum and Papakostopoulos, 1973).

Hamilton, Peters, and Knot (1973) presented data based on two CNV measures, baseline to peak negativity, and peak positivity to peak negativity. The two measures gave disparate results with the same data. Similarly, Peters, Knott, and Hamilton (1976) compared 6 different measures of the CNV. These were: (1) peak amplitude (anywhere in S_1–S_2 interval) from baseline as determined by a visual smoothing of the interval; (2) peak amplitude from EP peak positivity to S_2; (3) area from S_1 onset to S_2 onset; (4) area beginning 450 ms after S_1 to S_2 onset; (5) mean amplitude from baseline in the 200 ms epoch preceding S_2; (6) mean amplitude in each of 19 segments beginning 450 ms after S_1 to the end of the average. All measures were based on the same prestimulus baseline. The paradigm used was a discriminative reaction time and CNVs were collected under 20 response and 20 no-response conditions. Pearson product moment correlations obtained between measures, over conditions, showed that measures agreed well on the change in CNV. Only the measure based on the peak positivity to S_1 failed to show the expected response versus non-response difference. The large intrasubject variability in this measure seemed to indicate that changes in the evoked response component confounded change in the CNV.

Loveless and Sanford (1973) suggest that CNVs should be normalized to a point of inflection between the first evoked response and the slow potential change at approximately 400 ms after warning signal onset. This is also identified by Rebert and Knott (1970) as the origin of the CNV. This normalization enhances the resolution of the later component of the CNV. In view of recent emphasis on the contribution of different components from possibly distinct cortical generator sites to the composition of the CNV, a combination of two or more single point measures relating to both early and terminal amplitude (taken with reference to the baseline) together with an overall mean or area measure would seem advisable. Evoked potential components from N_1–P_3 elicited by warning and imperative stimuli can also usefully be measured for later comparison with CNV components.

4.3 Component measures

Weerts and Lang (1973) and Loveless and Sanford (1974) have identified two phases to the CNV: an orientation wave (0-wave) which reaches its peak within 500 ms after S_1; and an expectancy wave (E-wave) which rises in anticipation or preparation for S_2. Experimental evidence for the functional separation of these two components is now well validated. The initial component is more affected by sensory set and overt stimulus factors, such as modality and intensity (Gaillard, 1976), whilst the later component is more affected by manipulations in response preparation, such as change in intersignal interval (ISI) (Loveless and Sanford, 1975). Loveless and Sanford (1974) claim that only in ISIs above 4 s are these two components visibly separated (see Figure 6.19) and that in the classic one or two second ISI, there is a blending of the two components into a hybrid CNV. Donchin, Kutas, and McCarthy (1977) used principal components analysis to verify the overlapping of two components in a 1 s ISI. The distinction between phases shows promise of clearing much conceptual muddle in terms of psychological processes underlying the

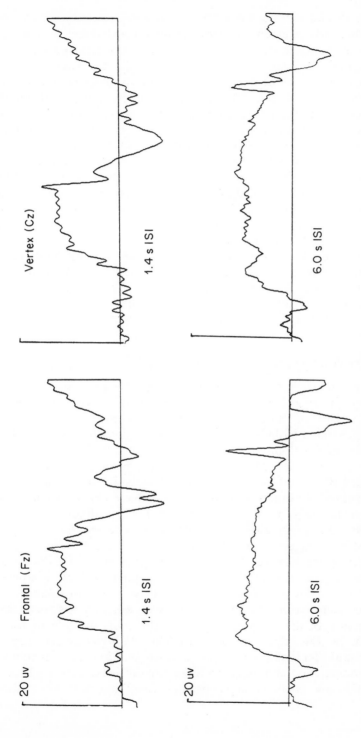

Figure 6.22 This figure shows topographical differences in CNV morphology between frontal and vertex placements averaged over 32 trials. The frontal focus of the early component and the central focus of the later components is more easily detected with the longer interstimulus interval. (From O'Connor (1978b))

P

CNV, in particular whether the CNV is principally related to attention or arousal. The early component seems more affected directly by level of activation, as evidenced by its change under different levels of stimulation and perceptual sensitivity (Loveless, 1975) whilst the later component changes with response demands such as task complexity and decision making criterion (Gaillard, 1978). Rohrbaugh, Syndulko, and Lindsley (1976) have proposed that the later component of the CNV is identical to the readiness potential (RP) which arises prior to non-signalled intentional motor acts. However, there are topographical differences between the CNV and the RP, with the RP showing greater lateralization effects. A third positive component of the CNV has been tentatively suggested both by Loveless (1979) and Gaillard (1978). Gaillard terms this the slow positive potential occurring 200–400 ms after the warning stimulus and relates its magnitude to the input process by which stimulus information is integrated and evaluated. Loveless considers this post warning stimulus positivity to indicate an effort to control irrelevant activity. Both authors agree that its cortical site of origin is probably parietal; O'Connor (1979) has reported individual differences in distribution of initial positivity.

The topographical distribution of CNV components is an important consideration in placement of electrodes and interpretation of measures (Figure 6.22).

4.4 Topographical measures

The 'classical' CNV is documented to have an anterior–posterior gradient in distribution (Papakostopoulos and Fenelon, 1975) with bilateral symmetry. There is some evidence that asymmetry can arise from potentials generated in the specific sensory projection areas associated with different modalities (Simson, Vaughan, and Ritter, 1977) and also from the effect of right or left hand responses on contralateral activation of the motor cortex (Otto and Leifer, 1973; Rohrbaugh, Syndulko and Lindsley, 1976). However, if we accept the proposal outlined above that the CNVs recorded under ISIs of 4 s are a summation of different functional components, the topographical considerations become more complex. Loveless (1979) suggests that the initial O-wave of the CNV is generated frontally, whilst the E-wave has a parietal origin. Gaillard (1978) suggests that the time course of the CNV takes the topographical form of a parietal positivity followed by a frontal negativity, followed by vertex negativity in the terminal phase of the ISI. Prolonged frontal negativity has been related to maintenance of the orienting response. However, the role of parietal mechanisms is less clear though Loveless (1979) suggests they are associated with inhibition of response intention, in such situations as cancelling preparation in a no-go response paradigm. Loveless suggests, for instance, that low apparent initial negative amplitude with visual stimuli may be due to the positive influence generated in attempts to inhibit eye blinks. Response resolution factors affecting post imperative positivity would support Loveless's interpretation but more research is needed to establish the functional interrelationships amongst positive and negative components. However, it is reasonable to conclude that caution is required in interpreting changes in form or amplitude of a single channel vertex CNV, especially if a short interval is used, since the interactive effects of specific components may confound any generalized interpretation. The concept of a unitary CNV may in the future have to be discarded, but meanwhile, where possible, it is worth adhering to Vaughan and Ritters' (1973) suggestion that each experiment should entail a detailed spatial mapping of the CNV potential changes.

Use of at least two channels located preferably on an anterior–posterior line is advised here.

4.5 Psychophysiological interpretation

The interpretation one places on the measures depends on what is known of the cortical and psychological origins of the different CNV components.

Cortical Origins

The origins of slow potential shifts in the cortex can be either vascular, glial, or neuronal. A neuronal generator model of the CNV seems best supported. The CNV has a time course too rapid for reported vascular changes, and the role of the glia in nervous function seems to be dependent on neuronal excitation, rather than active participation in the generation of the potential. The known properties of the neuronal membrane offer the simplest explanation of low potentials of less than 10 s duration (McSherry, 1973). Intracellular data have shown that evoked potentials in the sensorimotor cortex and certain slow potentials are correlated with interneuronal events.

On the basis of his research, Creutzfeldt (1966) has proposed a widely accepted neuronal model for both fast and slow evolving evoked potentials. His discovery that the CNV has a superficial negative component and an intracortical positive component (with respect to subadjacent white matter) suggests a simultaneous superficial depolarization and deep hyperpolarization. This suggests a balance of excitatory–inhibitory input at different levels. Clare and Bishop (1956) have reported that after cortical stimulation one sees both short latency exosomatic positive potentials and long latency dendritic negative potentials. Creutzfeldt thus explained the CNV as arising from a combination of prolonged superficial axodendritic excitatory volleys, and prolonged deep axosomatic inhibitory volleys.

As regards specific brain structures, Rebert (1973) has reported large, fast rise time negative waves over midline thalamus, midbrain reticular formation, and hypothalamus. Positive potentials were recorded from caudate nucleus, medial preoptic, and cingulate area. Several areas were silent.

There is evidence, as Loveless (1979) has pointed out, that surface positive going potentials may reflect inhibition of neuronal activity and surface negative potentials such as the CNV facilitation of activity and increased neuronal firing. Though the CNV may be generated subcortically it is undoubtedly modulated cortically by the involvement of numerous generators in psychological aspects of the task, and this has been shown by experimentally induced dissociation of frontal and central generators (Rebert, 1976). To arrive with such large amplitude at the scalp, the CNV must be synchronized neuronally over a large area (≈ 6 cm^2) and compared with EEG suffers a fairly small attenuation factor ($2:1$) in transfer from the cortex through the skull (Cooper and coworkers, 1965). Anatomically then the generation of the CNV is related to the neuronal excitation of selected cortical regions regulated subcortically possibly through thalamic relay nuclei.

4.6 Psychological interpretation

Walter's original interpretation of the CNV was in terms of the conditioning paradigm in which it was first elicited (S_1–S_2–MR). The initial stimulus (S_1) is considered the conditioned stimulus; the second stimulus (S_2) the unconditioned stimulus. The CNV is the conditioned response to S_2, conditional on S_2 arriving when expected and entailing a motor response (MR). Walter supported his interpretation with evidence of extinction of the CNV during a conditioning paradigm requiring no voluntary responses, and with omission of S_2.

In subjective terms the CNV is an anticipatory response, since decrease in the probability of signal association is a decrease in expectancy that S_2 will occur. When subjects' expectancy was varied by either verbal or experimental dictates, CNV amplitude was reduced (Walter, 1965). Walter thus also termed the CNV the expectancy or E-wave, by which it is still sometimes known.

Almost immediately Walter's interpretation of the CNV was challenged. Low and coworkers (1966) showed that the CNV was not confined to a response paradigm and suggested that 'conation' rather than contingent might be a more appropriate descriptor of the 'intention' to act which elicited the negative variation.

However, even though the CNV may be demonstrated independently of an overt motor response, as when a subject anticipates seeing a picture or simply thinks about a word after S_2 (Cohen, 1969), this cannot be taken as direct evidence that covert motor activity is not involved. Kornhuber and Deecke (1965) described a consistent 'readiness potential', or *Bereitschaft* potential, immediately preceding voluntary movement, that was enhanced by 'attentional engagement' of the subject. Thus Gilden, Vaughan, and Costa (1966) questioned whether the CNV might be an initial long negativity component of this pre-motor potential. Similarly both Rebert and coworkers (1967) and Vaughan, Costa, and Ritter (1968) considered the maximum amplitude of the CNV over the vertex, i.e. above the motor cortex, to indicate the CNV as a cortical priming mechanism causally related to motor facilitation.

Tecce (1971) claimed support for the expectancy hypothesis by eliciting two distinct CNV shapes, type A and type B, as a function of subjects' expectancy. Subjects who were uncertain of S_2 arrival showed a quick rise to peak (type A) and subjects who were certain showed a slow rise to peak resembling a negative ramp shape (type B).

The finding of Low and coworkers (1966) that in some subjects the CNV was maximal in the anterior frontal region led to much speculation on the possible higher decision making processes involved in CNV genesis. Otto and Leifer (1973) for instance rejected a correlation between CNV amplitude and simple frequency of events, and proposed predictive outcome and 'astuteness' of choice as important variables affecting the CNV. This has led to a concentration on the post imperative stimulus components of the CNV and CNV interaction with S_2 evoked responses (Donchin and Smith, 1970; Hartley, 1970; Donald and Goff, 1971; Näätänen, 1975). In particular, the relationship between CNV and P300 components of the evoked potential has been extensively investigated by Tueting and Sutton (1973), Tueting (1978), and Donchin, Kutas, and McCarthy (1977).

Most of these interpretations seem rather semantic functions of the authors' conceptual frameworks and paradigms rather than of the phenomenon itself. Operationally the separate influences of readiness, anticipation, expectancy, conation, and motivation on the CNV development, cannot be isolated. For instance, Irwin and coworkers (1966) reported an increase in CNV where S_1 signalled a strong shock which they interpreted in terms of motivation, whereas Knott and Peters (1972) saw the same result in terms of stress effect and raised anxiety level. Conversely, Donchin (1973) reported two identical experiments carried out under different conceptual paradigms, that yielded conflicting results. In Walter's terminology elimination of a proportion of S_2 occurrences leads to partial reinforcement, and should lead to an 'equivocation' of expectancy, so reducing CNV amplitude. Walter and coworkers (1964) have reported this. However, presentations of the 'warning signal' without an 'imperative' stimulus in preparatory reaction time terminology should eliminate anticipatory motor responses and so enhance CNV amplitude. Hillyard and Galambos (1970) have found this to be so. This pinpoints a most interesting peculiarity of the CNV that it is sensitive to subject/researcher interaction instructional set, situation, and other variables within the experimental procedure itself (Shagass, 1972). For instance, Cohen (1969) found that test–retest reliability of CNV amplitude was 0.8 in 34 subjects who were studied in the same setting on two occasions separated by 2 and 8 days. By contrast, Straumanis, Shagass, and Overton (1969) found very little consistency of CNV amplitude when measurements were made on the same day but in completely different settings. Janssen and coworkers (1978) reported that CNV reliability was a function of personality and that it might be a trait variable for introverts but a state variable for extraverts. Roth and coworkers (1975) reported that the CNV had a subject consistency of 0.68 in retests separated from 5 minutes to 7 days. They concluded that CNV reliability is higher than expected for a measurement of a purely state variable but lower than desired for measurement of a trait variable. It is most likely that state, trait, and situation factors interact in determining CNV amplitude.

The effect of sex, stress, anxiety, subject state, and situation (Knott and Peters, 1972, 1973; Peters and Knott, 1976) as well as signal factors on CNV variation has led researchers away from specific paradigms to postulate more general underlying mechanisms behind CNV variability. These generalized processes have most commonly included 'attention' or 'arousal' models of the CNV. As an example, Tecce (1972) proposed that the CNV is related non-monotically to 'arousal' in the familiar inverted U shape but linearly to 'attention', and he characterized arousal as reflecting a non-specific energizing force, and attention as giving a steering or directional property to behaviour. It is difficult operationally to distinguish these two processes, and more recently Tecce, Savignano-Bowman, and Meinbresse (1976) have proposed a revised arousal–distraction coupling theory to better explain the dual effects. By this theory under high arousal the subject is more distractible and so shows low CNV magnitude, whilst under low arousal the subject is more attentive and shows larger CNV magnitude. This link emphasizes the joint influences of the physiological and psychological factors in producing the CNV.

5 FUTURE CONSIDERATIONS

There is a tendency for investigators in theorizing about the CNV to jump to generalized intra-organismic explanations of what are essentially responses elicited by very specific behavioural procedures (O'Connor, 1978a). The effects of instructional set, and subjects' task engagement in particular have a major but little explored effect on CNV development.

Also in view of recent discoveries on the functional separation of CNV components, it seems advisable to recommend that future speculation should steer away from grand theories and be limited to examining the effects of detailed procedural manipulations on CNV form. In particular, assessment of individual differences responsible for variable latency and amplitude of the CNV is an important and neglected area. Tecce (1971) has reported distinct CNV shapes which he termed type A fast rise and type B ramp-shaped CNVs and which he related to excitable and cautious personality types respectively. Knott and Irwin (1967) have reported lower CNVs in anxiety-prone patients, and Van Veen and coworkers (1973) found field-dependent subjects had higher terminal CNV amplitude.

The best validated personality differences to date are between extraverts and introverts, with several authors showing the differential effect on the CNV of manipulation of internal and external conditions of stimulation (Ashton and coworkers, 1974; Janssen and coworkers, 1978; Eysenck and O'Connor, 1978; O'Connor, 1979a). Investigation of subject-state–situation interactions is important for both psychological and physiological reasons. Psychologically, individual differences may determine the effect of such variables as distraction, motivation, and even stimulus intensity on the subject's attitude and strategy employed in CNV development, and consequently affect the reliability of the CNV. Physiologically, individual differences may determine the pre-stimulus level of EEG on which the CNV is superimposed (Werre, Faverey, and Janssen, 1975; O'Connor, 1979a).

Personality differences extend into the clinical field, and Tismit-Berthier and coworkers (1976) have identified small CNVs and prolonged post imperative negative variations (PINVs) characteristic of psychotics and neurotics. O'Connor (1977, 1978b) has reported similar findings in senile psychosis. The plateau or dome-shaped PINV is reported by Dongier, Dubrovsky, and Engelsmann (1977) to be highly characteristic of acute schizophrenia. Whether the PINV is an extension of the CNV or a separately generated potential is as yet unclear (Roth, 1977). The state or trait nature of CNV differences has been raised by Abrahams and McCallum (1977) who found long term changes in the CNV of schizophrenics even during remission of symptoms. The clinical and diagnostic power of such CNV features as the PINV or CNV amplitude itself is reduced by inadequate knowledge both of their interaction with personality characteristics, and of the different physiological components responsible for their genesis. It is important, therefore, to discover more of the morphological and topographical relationships between both positive and negative event related cortical components elicited under different information processing demands before the CNV can become an independent variable in psychophysiological research.

References

Abrahams, P., and McCallum, W. (1977). A permanent change in the EEG (CNV) of schizophrenics. *Electroenceph. Clin. Neurophysiol.*, **43**, 533.

Ashton, M., Millman, J. E., Telford, R., and Thompson, J. W. (1974). The effect of caffeine, nitrazepam, and cigarette smoking on the contingent negative variation in man. *Electroenceph. Clin. Neurophysiol.*, **37**, 59–71.

Beauchamp, K. (1973). *Signal Processing*. George Allen and Unwin, London.

Becker, R. O. (1969). The phylogenetic and functional significance of d.c. potentials in living organisms. *Psychophysiology*, **5**, 573.

Becker, R. O. (1972). Readiness potential, premotor positivity and other brain potentials during saccadic eye movements. *Vision Res.*, **12**, 421–36.

Bendat, J., and Peirsol, A. (1971). *Random Data*. Wiley, New York.

Borda, R. P. (1973). Relationship of CNV to behaviour in animals. *Electroenceph. Clin. Neurophysiol. Suppl.*, **33**, 249–56.

Borda, R. P., and Frost, J. D. (1968). Error reduction in small sample averaging through the use of the median rather than the mean. *Electroenceph. Clin. Neurophysiol.*, **25**, 391–2.

Brazier, M. A. B. (1964). Evoked responses recorded from the depths of the human brain. *Ann. N.Y. Acad. Sci.*, **112**, 33–59.

Callaway, E. (1975). *Brain Electrical Potentials and Individual Psychological Differences*. Grune and Stratton, New York.

Callaway, E., and Halliday, R. (1973). Evoked potential variability: effects of age, amplitude and methods of measurement. *Electroenceph. Clin. Neurophysiol*, **34**, 125–33.

Cappola, R., Tabor, R., and Buchsbaum, M. (1978). Signal to noise ratio and response variability measurements in single trial evoked potentials. *Electroenceph. Clin. Neurophysiol.*, **44**, 214–23.

Clare, M., and Bishop, G. (1956). Potential wave mechanisms in the cortex. *Electroenceph. Clin. Neurophysiol.*, **8**, 583–602.

Cohen, J. (1969). Very slow brain potentials relating to expectancy: the CNV. In E. Donchin and D. Lindsley (Eds), *Average evoked potentials*, NASA SP-191, Washington.

Cooper, R. (1968). Physiological data from electrodes implanted for investigation and treatment of psychiatric and other disorders. In N. S. Kline and E. Laska (Eds), *Computers and Electronic Devices in Psychiatry*. Grune and Stratton, New York.

Cooper, R., Winter, A., Crow, H., and Walter, W. (1965). Comparison of subcortical, cortical and scalp activity using chronically indwelling electrodes in man. *Electroenceph. Clin. Neurophysiol.*, **18**, 217.

Cooper, R., Osselton, J., and Shaw, J. C. (1974). *EEG Technology*, 2nd edn., Butterworths, London.

Costell, R., Lunde, D., Kopell, B., and Wittner, W. (1972). CNV as an indicator of sexual object preference. *Science*, **177**, 718–20.

Creutzfeldt, O., Watanabe, S., and Lux, M. (1966). Relation between EEG phenomena and potentials of single cells. *Electroenceph. Clin. Neurophysiol.*, **20**, 1–18.

Curry, S. M., and McCallum, W. C. (1978). Some observations of the late components of the human auditory response. *Psychophysiol. Gp. Newslett.*, **5**, 19.

Donald, M., and Goff, W. (1971). Interactions between the contingent negative variation, sensory evoked potentials and attention. *Electroenceph. Clin. Neurophysiol.*, **31**, 299.

Donchin, E. (1973). Methodological issues in CNV research. *Electroenceph. Clin. Neurophysiol. Suppl.*, **33**, 3–19.
Donchin, E., and Smith, D. (1970). Contingent negative variation and the late positive wave of the averaged evoked potential. *Electroenceph. Clin. Neurophysiol.*, **299**, 201–3.
Donchin, E., and Herning, R. (1975). A simulation study of the efficacy of stepwise discriminant analysis in the detection and comparison of event related potentials. *Electroenceph. Clin. Neurophysiol.*, **38**, 51–68.
Donchin, E., Kutas, M., and McCarthy, G. (1977). Electrocortical indices of hemisphere utilization. In S. Harnad and coworkers (Eds), *Lateralization in the Nervous System*, Academic Press, New York.
Dongier, M., Dubrovsky, B., and Engelsmann, F. (1977). Event related slow potentials in psychiatry. In *Psychopathology and Brain Dysfunction*. Raven, New York.
Eysenck, H. J. and O'Connor, K. (1978). Smoking, arousal and personality. *Proc. Int. Symp. on the Effects of Nicotine*, Salpetière, Paris, in press.
Gaillard, A. (1976). Effects of warning signal modality on the contingent negative variation. *Biol. Psychol.*, **4**, 139–54.
Gaillard, A. (1978). *Slow Potentials Preceding Task Performance*, Academische Pers. BV, Amsterdam.
Gaillard, A., and Näätänen, R. (1978). CNV and the law of initial values. *Institute for Perception, Saesterberg, Nederlands*, unpublished study.
Gilden, L., Vaughan, M., and Costa, L. (1966). Summated human EEG. *Electroenceph. Clin. Neurophysiol.*, **20**, 433–8.
Gullickson, G. R., and Darrow, C. W. (1973). Contingent Negative Variation modified by respiratory phase. *Electroenceph. Clin. Neurophysiol. Suppl.*, **33**, 295–7.
Hamilton, C., Peters, J., and Knott, J. (1973). Task initiation and amplitude of the CNV. *Electroenceph. Clin. Neurophysiol*, **34**, 587–92.
Hartley, L. (1970). The effect of stimulus relevance on the cortical evoked potentials. *Quart. J. Exp. Psychol.*, **22**, 531–46.
Hillyard, S., and Galambos, R. (1970). Eye movement artefact in the CNV. *Electroenceph. Clin. Neurophysiol.*, **28**, 173–82.
Hjorth, B. (1973). The physical significance of time domain descriptors in EEG analysis. *Electroenceph. Clin. Neurophysiol.*, **34**, 321–25.
Irwin, D., Knott, J., McAdam, D., and Robert, C. (1966). Motivational determinants of the contingent negative variation. *Electroenceph. Clin. Neurophysiol.*, **21**, 241–5.
Janssen, R., Mattie, P., Plooij-Van Gorsel, P., and Werre, P. (1978). The effects of a depressant and a stimulant drug on the contingent negative variation. *Biol. Psychol.*, **6**, 209–18.
Karrer, R., Kohn, H., and Ivins, J. (1973). Large steady potential shifts accompanying phasic arousal during CNV recording in man. *Electroenceph. Clin. Neurophysiol. Suppl.*, **33**, 119–24.
Knott, J. R., Irwin, D. A. (1967). Anxiety, stress and the CNV. *Electroenceph. Clin. Neurophysiol.*, **22**, 188.
Knott, J., and Peters, J. (1973). Sex, stress, interstimulus interval, and CNV. *Electroenceph. Clin. Neurophysiol.*, **33**, 238–9.
Knott, J., and Peters, J. (1973). Sex, stress and interstimulus interval. *Electroenceph. Clin. Neurophysiol. Suppl.*, **33**, 191–3.
Kopell, B., Tinklenberg, J., and Holister, L. (1972). CNV amplitudes. *Arch. Gen. Psychiat.*, **27**, 809–11.

Kornhuber, H., and Deecke, L. (1965). Changes in the human brain potential in voluntary movements and passive movements in man. *Pflügers Arch. Ges. Physiol.*, **281**, 51.

Lippold, O. (1973). *Origin of the Alpha Rhythm.* Churchill-Livingstone, London.

Loveless, N. (1975). The effect of warning interval on signal detection and event-related slow potentials of the brain. *Percept. Psychophys.*, **17**, 565–70.

Loveless, N. (1979). Event-related slow potentials of the brain and expressions of orienting function. In Kimmel, H. D., van Olst, E. H., and Orlebecke, J. F. (Eds), The *Orienting Reflex in Humans*, in press.

Loveless, N., and Sanford, A. (1973). The CNV baseline: considerations of internal consistency of data. *Electroenceph. Clin. Neurophysiol. Suppl.*, **33**, 19–23.

Loveless, N., and Sanford, A. (1974). Slow potential correlates of preparatory set. *Biol. Psychol.*, **1**, 303–4.

Loveless, N., and Sanford, A. (1975). The impact of warning signal intensity on reaction time and components of the contingent negative variation. *Biol. Psychol.*, **2**, 217–26.

Low, M., Borda, R., Frost, J., and Kellaway, P. (1966). Surface negative slow potential shift associated with conditioning in man. *Neurology (Minneapolis)*, **16**, 771–82.

Low, M., and McSherry, J. (1968). Further observations of psychological factors involved in CNV genesis. *Electroenceph. Clin. Neurophysiol.*, **25**, 203–7.

McCallum, W., and Knott, J. (1973). *Event-Related Slow Potentials of the Brain.* Elsevier, Amsterdam.

McCallum, W., and Papakostopoulos, D. (1973). The CNV and reaction time in situations of increasing complexity. *Electroenceph. Clin. Neurophysiol. Suppl.*, **33**, 179–85.

McCallum, W., and Walter, W. G. (1968). The effects of attention and distraction on the CNV in normal and neurotic subjects. *Electroenceph. Clin. Neurophysiol.*, **25**, 319–29.

McSherry, J. (1973). Physiological origins: a review. *Electroenceph. Clin. Neurophysiol. Suppl.*, **33**, 53–61.

Näätänen, R. (1975). Selective attention and evoked potentials in humans–a critical review. *Biol. Psychol.*, **2**, 237–307.

O'Connor, K. (1977). Contingent negative variation differences between elderly normal and demented subjects. *Electroenceph. Clin. Neurophysiol.*, **43**, 471–2.

O'Connor, K. (1978a). The CNV as a measure of effort. *Psychophysiol. Gp. Newslett.*, **5**, 27.

O'Connor, K. (1978b). The contingent negative variation and attention dysfunction in senile dementia. M.Phil. thesis, University of Sussex.

O'Connor, K., (1979a). The contingent negative variation and individual differences in smoking behaviour. *J. of Individual Differences.* (in press).

O'Connor, K. (1979b). Post-stimulus positivity and personality (in preparation).

Otto, D. A., and Leifer, L. J. (1973). Effects of varying the magnitude, duration and speed of motor response on the contingent negative variation. *Electroenceph. Clin. Neurophysiol.*, **34**, 695.

Overton, P., and Shagass, C. (1969). Distribution of eye movement and eye blink potentials over the scalp. *Electroenceph. Clin. Neurophysiol.*, **27**, 546.

Papakostopoulos, D., and McCallum, W. C. (1973). The CNV and autonomic change in situations of increasing complexity. *Electroenceph. Clin. Neurophys. Suppl.*, **33**, 287–93.

Papakostopoulos, D., Winter, A., and Newton, P. (1973). New techniques for the control of eye potential artefacts in multichannel CNV recordings. *Electroenceph. Clin. Neurophysiol.*, **34**, 651–3.

Papakostopoulos, D., and Fenelon, B. (1975). Spatial distribution of the contingent negative variation and the relationship between the CNV and reaction time. *Psychophysiology*, **12**, 74–8.

Peters, J., and Knott, J. (1976). CNV and post-response negativity with stressful auditory feedback. In W. McCallum and J. Knott (Eds), *The Responsive Brain*. Bristol, Wright.

Peters, J., Knott, J., and Hamilton, C. (1976). Further thoughts on measurement of the CNV. In W. McCallum and J. Knott (Eds), *The Responsive Brain*. Bristol, Wright.

Pfurtscheller, G., and Aranibar, A. (1977). Event-related cortical desynchronization detecte ! by power measurements of the scalp EEG. *Electroenceph. Clin. Neurophysiol.*, **42**, 817–26.

Pfurtscheller, G., and Cooper, R. (1975a). Frequency dependence of the transmission of the EEG from cortex to scalp. *Electroenceph. Clin. Neurophysiol.*, **38**, 93–6.

Pfurtscheller, G., and Cooper, R. (1975b). Selective averaging of the intracerebral click evoked responses in man: an improved method of measuring latencies and amplitudes. *Electroenceph. Clin. Neurophysiol.*, **38**, 187–90.

Rebert, C. (1973). The effect of reaction time feedback on reaction time and the CNV. *Psychophysiology*, **9**, 334–9.

Rebert, C. (1976). Slow potential changes during a reaction time foreperiod. In W. McCallum and J. Knott (Eds), *The Responsive Brain*. Bristol, Wright.

Rebert, C., McAdam, D., Knott, J., and Irwin, D (1967). Slow potential changes in human brain related to level of motivation. *J. Comp. Physiol. Psychol.*, **63**. 20–3.

Rebert, C., and Knott, J. (1970). The vertex non-specific evoked potential and latency of the CNV. *Electroenceph. Clin. Neurophysiol.*, **28**, 561–5.

Rohrbaugh, J., Syndulko, K., and Lindsley, D. (1976). Brain wave components of the contingent negative variation in humans. *Science*, **191**, 1055–7.

Rohrbaugh, J. W., Syndulko, K., and Lindsley, D. B. (1979). Cortical slow waves following non-paired stimuli: effects of modality, intensity and rate of stimulation. *Electroenceph. Clin. Neurophysiol.*, **46**, 416–27.

Roth, W. (1977). Late event-related potentials and psychopathology. *Schizophrenia Bull.*, **3**, 105–20.

Roth, W., Kopell, B., Tinklenberg, J., Huntsberger, G., and Kraemer, H. (1975). Reliability of the contingent negative variation and the auditory evoked potential. *Electroenceph. Clin. Neurophysiol.*, **38**, 45–50.

Sayers, B., Beagley, H., and Henshall, W. (1974). The mechanism of auditory evoked EEG response. *Nature*, **247**, 181.

Shackel, B. (1958). A rubber suction cup surface electrode with high electrical stability. *J. Appl. Physiol.*, **13**, 153.

Shagass, C. (1972). *Evoked Brain Potentials in Psychiatry*, Plenum, New York.

Simson, R., Vaughan, H., and Ritter, W. (1977). The scalp topography of potentials in auditory and visual go/nogo tasks. *Electroenceph. Clin. Neurophysiol.*, **43**, 864–75.

St. John-Loe, P. (1973). On connecting amplifiers to electrodes, Part III. *J. Electrophysiol. Technol. Assoc.*, **20**, 115–29.

Straumanis, J., Shagass, C., and Overton, D. (1969). Problems associated with application of the CNV to psychiatric research. *J. Nerv. Ment. Dis.*, **148**, 170–9.

Tecce, J. (1971). Contingent negative variation and individual differences. *Archs Gen. Psychiat.*, **24**, 1–16.

Tecce, J. (1972). CNV and psychological processes in man. *Psychol. Bull.*, **77**, 73–108.

430 *Techniques in Psychophysiology*

430 *Techniques in Psychophysiology*

Tecce, J., Savignano-Dowmany, J., and Meinbresse, D. (1976). CNV and the distraction-arousal hypothesis. *Electroenceph. Clin. Neurophysiol.*, **41**, 277–86.
Tismit-Berthier, M., Delaunoy, J., and Rousseau, J. C. (1976). Some problems and tentative solutions to questions raised by slow potential changes in psychiatry. In: W. C. McCallum, and J. R. Knott (Eds), *The Responsive Brain*. Bristol, Wright.
Tueting, P. (1978). Event related potentials, cognitive events and information processing. In D. Otto (Ed.), *Multidisciplinary Perspectives in Event Related Brain Potential Research*, US Government Printing Office, Washington, DC.
Tueting, P., and Sutton, S. (1973). The relationship between pre-stimulus negative shifts and post-stimulus components of the averaged evoked potential. In S. Kornblum (Ed.), *Attention and Performance IV*, Academic Press, New York.
Ungan, P., and Basar, E. (1976). Comparison of Wiener filtering and selective averaging of evoked potentials. *Electroenceph. Clin. Neurophysiol.*, **40**, 516–20.
Van Hasselt, P. (1972). A short latency visual evoked potential recorded from the human mastoid process and auricle. *Electroenceph. Clin. Neurophysiol.*, **33**, 517–9.
Van Veen, W., Knott, J., Peters, J., Miller, L., and Cohen, S. (1973). CNV shape differences and perceptual mode. *Electroenceph. Clin. Neurophysiol.*, **33**, 327–8.
Vaughan, H., Costa, L., and Ritter, W. (1968). Topography of the human motor potential. *Electroenceph. Clin. Neurophysiol.*, **25**, 1–10.
Von Becker, W., Hoehne, O., Iwase, K., and Kornhuber, H. (1973). Cerebral and ocular muscle potentials preceding voluntary eye movements in man. *Electroenceph. Clin. Neurophysiol. Suppl.*, **33**, 99–104.
Vaughan, H., and Ritter, W. (1973). Physiological approaches to the analysis of attention and performance. In S. Kornblum (Ed.), *Attention and Performance*, Academic Press, New York.
Walter, D. (1969). A posteriori 'Wiener filtering' of average evoked responses. *Electroenceph. Clin. Neurophysiol. Suppl.*, **217**, 61–70.
Walter, W. G. (1965). Brain responses to semantic stimuli. *J. Psychosom. Res.*, **9**, 51–91.
Walter, W. G. (1967). The analysis, synthesis and identification of evoked responses and the CNV. *Electroenceph. Clin. Neurophysiol.*, **23**, 489.
Walter, W. G., Cooper, R., Aldridge, V., McCallum, W., and Winter, A. (1964). Contingent negative variation: an electrical sign of sensori-motor association and expectancy in the human brain. *Nature*, **203**, 380–4.
Wasman, M., Morehead, S., Lee, H., and Rowlands, V. (1970). Interaction of electro-ocular potentials with the CNV. *Psychophysiology*, **7**, 103–11.
Weerts, T., and Lang, P. (1973). The effects of eye fixation and stimulus and response location on the CNV. *Biol. Psychol.*, **1**, 1–19.
Weinberg, H., and Cooper, R. (1972). The recognition index: a pattern recognition technique for noisy signals. *Electroenceph. Clin. Neurophysiol.*, **33**, 608–13.
Werne, P., Faverey, H., and Janssen, R. (1975). Contingent negative variation and personality. *Ned. J. Psychol.*, **30**, 277–99.
Whitton, J., Lue, F., and Moldofsky, (1978). A spectral method for removing eye movement artefacts from the EEG. *Electroenceph. Clin. Neurophysiol.*, **44**, 735–42.
Wicke, J., Goff, W., Wallace, J., and Allison, T. (1978). On line statistical detection of averaged evoked potentials. *Electroenceph. Clin. Neurophysiol.*, **44**, 328–44.
Woody, C. (1967). Characterization of an adaptive filter for the analysis of variable latency neuroelectric signals. *Med. Biol. Engng.*, **5**, 539–53.

Techniques in Psychophysiology
Edited by I. Martin and P. H. Venables
© 1980, John Wiley & Sons Ltd.

CHAPTER 7

Measurement of Genital Arousal in Human Males and Females

JAMES H. GEER*

1. INTRODUCTION

Most research areas in psychophysiology are not steeped in controversy stemming from the nature of the response under study. Unfortunately, such is not the case for the study of sexual behaviour. In western society sex has been a topic of concern for many years, and those concerns have been reflected in restraints and problems in sex research. There are few, if

*Acknowledgement. The author wishes to acknowledge the assistance of Ms Jeanne Devine who helped in the formulation of this chapter.

any, other fields of inquiry faced with such anti-research biases. The repressive attitudes have important negative consequences. First, governmental funding agencies, being sensitive to adverse publicity, are often concerned about awarding grants or contracts that may be questioned by politicians or others who view themselves as guardians of the public's morals. Second, institutions that have research missions, such as universities, also are often sensitive to the same pressures as funding agencies and may restrict sex research for fear of adverse reactions. Hopefully, we are seeing a reduction in these restrictive practices, but the end is not in sight.

Another major problem in sex research is methodological. These problems are the principal focus of this chapter. The development of reliable and valid quantitative psychophysiological measures of genital responses is very recent. Prior to the 1960s sex research was conducted via questionnaires, interviews, or using indirect psychophysiological measures such as GSR or cardiac responses. The development of a technique for identifying and quantifying volume changes in the penis (Freund, 1963) opened the door to studying genital changes. There was a delay in the development of genital measurement devices in women; however, the measurement of vaginal responses is now possible. This chapter will describe those techniques now available for both sexes and will describe some of the uses to which they have been employed.

Before beginning a discussion of the methodologies of measuring sexual responses, some background material may be of value. We shall begin with a brief discussion of some aspects of genital anatomy and responding, and we shall limit our discussion to those aspects that are relevant to the topic of this chapter.

In males, the external sex organs consist of the penis and the scrotum which contains the sperm producing testes. Figure 7.1 contains drawings of the male external genitals in cross section and a cross section of the penis. Of interest to this chapter is the internal structure of the penis. There are three cylindrical sponge-like bodies of erectile tissue in the penis; the two lying dorsally are called the corpora cavernosa and the one lying ventrally is called the corpus spongiosum. These structures contain small irregular compartments (vascular spaces) separated by bonds of smooth muscle tissue. These bodies become engorged with blood during erection.

Erection is a vascular response. There is some controversy concerning the mechanism of erection; however, the following is a summary of current thoughts on the process (Weiss, 1972). The erectile tissues of the penis receive blood from the left and right terminal branches of the internal pudendal arteries. Between the arterioles and the vascular spaces are anastomoses (Openings) containing valve-like structures made of smooth muscles called polsters. In the flaccid state the polsters are relatively

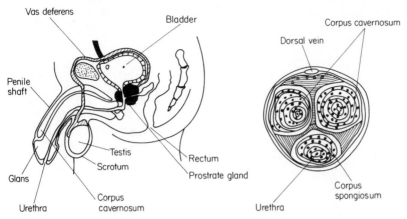

Figure 7.1   The male genitals in cross section and a cross section of the penis

closed, very little blood enters the vascular spaces, and they are collapsed. Parasympathetic stimulation of the polsters via the nervi erigentes from the sacral plexus during sexual arousal results in the opening of the anastomoses permitting the vascular spaces to be filled with blood under high pressure. The erectile bodies are encased in strong coats of fibrous material that balloon outward when the vascular spaces are filled with blood under high pressure. Since venous outflow is less than arterial inflow, the erectile bodies engorge with blood. The penis thus shows the characteristic increase in volume and rigidity during erection. It also has been suggested that the tumescence change results in a displacement of the venous system so that partial occlusion results in further increasing tumescence. It is felt that the loss of erection requires a neural response to reduce blood inflow.

We present in Figure 7.2 a view of the external female genitals and a cross sectional view. The organ which has been the principal focus of psychophysiological measurement in women has been the vaginal barrel. The vaginal barrel is a collapsed canal which is more of a potential rather than a permanent space. The tissues of the barrel are heavily vascularized. During sexual arousal vasocongestion occurs, and it appears that vaginal lubrication occurs as a result of changes occurring with the vasocongestion. The tissue around the introitus and extending to the clitoris is erectile much like the penis (Guyton, 1971). Vascular responding of these tissues is, as with the penis, controlled by the parasympathetic nerves that pass through the nervi erigentes from the sacral plexus.

Masters and Johnson (1966) have presented a model to describe the human sexual response cycle. The model describes the course of sexual arousal throughout a complete sequence of sexual behaviours. The model

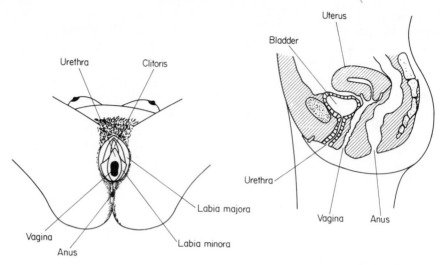

Figure 7.2   The female genitals in an external and a cross sectional view

is described in terms of four sequential stages or phases. These phases, in sequence, are: (1) the excitement phase; (2) the plateau phase: (3) the orgasmic phase; and (4) the resolution phase. Masters and Johnson have described the genital and extragenital responses that are typically associated with each phase. Shortly, we shall describe how these responses provide cues as to psychophysiological measures that might provide helpful indices of sexual arousal as it varies throughout the cycle. Masters and Johnson note that two physiological responses characterize the response to sexual stimulation. These are widespread vasocongestion and a generalized increase in muscle tension.

To return to the model, the first phase (excitement) describes the initial response to 'effective' sexual stimulation. During the excitement phase there is a continuous increase in the level or intensity of arousal. If effective stimulation is continued the individual will enter the plateau phase. During this phase of high level of response, continued stimulation will ultimately result in orgasm. However, cessation of stimulation during the plateau phase results in eventual return to prestimulation levels. The orgasmic phase is of brief duration and represents the involuntary reaching of maximal sexual tension. The resolution phase is an involuntary loss of tension that reverses the sequence of tension increments and results in eventual return to prestimulation levels. Masters and Johnson note that there are substantial individual differences in sexual response cycles. Their model is presented here as a heuristic for further discussion not as an absolute.

Masters and Johnson provide an enumeration of physiological changes that are described as occurring during each of the four phases in their model. In describing the changes they separately discuss genital and extra genital responses. We follow that scheme in Table 7.1, which outlines the responses that Masters and Johnson report during the four phases in the sexual response cycle. We have not described all of the internal genital responses (e.g. prostate) as they are not presently amenable to psycho-physiological assessment. Of importance to this chapter is the recognition that the responses reported by Masters and Johnson hold out promise for the development of reliable and valid measurement of sexual arousal. Their description of sexual responses emphasize two generalized responses to sexual stimulation: vasocongestion and myotonia. As we shall see, up to this time the former has proven more useful in research. We shall learn of some problems with the Masters and Johnson description; however, as a general guide to understanding the physiological responses that occur during sexual arousal, the formulation remains quite useful.

Table 7.1. A summary of the Masters and Johnson report of changes during the the sexual response cycle

	Male responses.
Genital changes	
Penis	
excitement phase	erection begins rapidly and may become maximal.
plateau phase	some small diameter increases may occur; glans penis may become deeper reddish-purple.
orgasmic phase	Contractions of urethra and pelvic muscles cause penis to show contractions and ejaculation of seminal fluid. Contractions occur at 0.8 s for 3–4 then reduce in strength and frequency for the 2–4 terminal contractions.
resolution phase	detumescence—a two phase process. Primary phase reduces tumescence 50% rapidly. Secondary phase reduces tumescence to prestimulation level over much longer period.
Scrotum	
excitement phase	thickening of walls and a constriction due to both vaso-congestion and smooth muscle contraction. This tension may relax if excitement phase lasts a long time.
plateau phase	no further change.
orgasmic phase	no further change.
resolution phase	two patterns: the most frequent (75%) is a rapid change back to prestimulation levels, the second pattern is a slow loss of the response (1–2 hours).
Testes	
excitement phase	elevate towards the body and rotate during elevation
plateau phase	attain maximum elevation to a position next to the body.
orgasmic phase	no specific additional response.
resolution phase	return to prestimulation levels in same two patterns described for scrotum.

Table 7.1. Continued

Male responses

Extragenital changes
Sex flush
  excitement phase   appears late in the phase and occurs much less frequently and regularly in men than in women.
  plateau phase   full development of the sex flush.
  orgasmic phase   no specific changes.
  resolution phase   disappears rapidly and in reverse order of appearance.

Breasts
  excitement phase   nipple erection on occasion in about 60%.
  plateau phase   nipple tumescence, if it occurs, will be in this phase.
  orgasmic phase   no specific changes.
  resolution phase   detumescence and retraction relatively slow.

Myotonia (specific muscle involvement depends upon body's position)
  excitement phase   becomes obvious during later part of phase.
  plateau phase   spasmodic contraction of both voluntary and involuntary muscles. Carpopedal spasm may be seen.
  orgasmic phase   involuntary spasms of many facial, pelvic, and abdominal muscle groups.
  resolution phase   rapid loss of tension.

Rectum
  excitement phase   irregular contractions.
  plateau phase   irregular contractions.
  orgasmic phase   2–4 contractions at 0.8 s.
  resolution phase   no change.
Respiration
  excitement phase   little change reported.
  plateau phase   rapid breathing.
  orgasmic phase   rapid breathing—up to 40/min.
  resolution phase   return to prestimulation.

Heart rate
  excitement phase   increases directly with level of arousal.
  plateau phase   continued increase: up to 175 bpm.
  orgasmic phase   peak in heart rate: up to 180 bpm.
  resolution phase   return to prestimulation levels.

Blood pressure
  excitement phase   increases directly with level of arousal.
  plateau phase   elevation up to 40 mm Hg diastolic or 80 mm Hg systolic.
  orgasmic phase   peak elevation up to 50 mm Hg diastolic and 100 mm Hg systolic.
  resolution phase   return to prestimulation levels.

Sweat glands
  excitement phase   no observed change.
  plateau phase   no observed reaction.
  orgasmic phase   no observed reaction.
  resolution phase   sweating, usually confined to palms and soles of feet.

Female responses

Genital responses
Clitoris

excitement phase	clitoral shaft increases in diameter and length due to vasocongestion.
plateau phase	withdraws under clitoral hood.
orgasmic phase	no observed reaction.
resolution phase	returns rapidly to original position and detumesces slowly.

Vagina

excitement phase	lubrication begins 10–30 s after stimulation; vaginal barrel lengthens and widens; vaginal walls become darker purple due to vasocongestion.
plateau phase	development of orgasmic platform in outer 1/3 of vagina and continued lengthening and widening of vaginal barrel.
orgasmic phase	orgasmic platform contracts at 0.8 s intervals 5–12 times with frequency and strength lessening after first 3–6.
resolution phase	rapid loss of orgasmic platform and slower loss of tumescence of vaginal walls.

Labia Majora (women who have given birth respond differently than women who have not)
excitement phase

given birth	increase in diameter and slight movement away from vaginal opening.
no children	flattening and movement away from vaginal opening.

plateau phase

given birth	continued size increase due to vasocongestion.
no children	extensive swelling due to vasocongestion.
orgasmic phase	no observed responses.
resolution phase	detumescences to prestimulation condition.

Labia Minora

excitement phase	thickens due to vasocongestion.
plateau phase	colour change from bright red to deep purple indicates orgasm imminent.
orgasmic phase	no observed response.
resolution phase	colour change back to original very rapidly with slower loss of tumescence.

Extragenital responses
Sex flush

excitement phase	appears late in phase but spreads rapidly (occurs in 75% of women).
plateau phase	increases and may be widespread over the body.
orgasmic phase	extent and intensity of flush parallels intensity of orgasm experience.
resolution phase	quickly disappears in reverse order of appearance.

Breasts

excitement phase	nipple erection; areola tumescence; breast increases in size due to vasocongestion.

Table 7.1. Continued

	Female responses
plateau phase	nipples harden; areola tumescence increases; continued breast size increase.
orgasmic phase	no observed responses.
resolution phase	rapid loss of nipple and areola tumescence; slower loss of increased breast size.
Myotonia	
excitement phase	increases in voluntary muscle tension.
plateau phase	continued increase with non-voluntary muscles becoming increasingly involved.
orgasmic phase	many involuntary spastic contractions.
resolution phase	rapid loss of muscle tension.
Rectum	
excitement phase	no observed responses.
plateau phase	voluntary contractions.
orgasmic phase	involuntary contractions coinciding with vaginal contractions.
resolution phase	no observed responses.
Respiration phase	
excitement phase	no observed change.
plateau phase	rapid breathing occurs late in phase.
orgasmic phase	rapid breathing up to 40/min with intensity paralleling strength of orgasm.
resolution phase	quickly returns to prestimulation levels.
Heart rate	
excitement phase	increases directly with level of arousal.
plateau phase	continued increase: up to 175 bpm.
orgasmic phase	peak in heart rate: up to 180 bpm.
resolution phase	return to prestimulation levels.
Blood pressure	
excitement phase	increases directly with level of arousal.
plateau phase	elevations up to 20 mm Hg diastolic and 60 mm Hg systolic.
orgasmic phase	peak elevation up to 40 mm Hg diastolic and 80 mm Hg systolic.
resolution phase	return to prestimulation levels.
Sweat glands	
excitement phase	no observed response.
plateau phase	no observed response.
orgasmic phase	no observed response.
resolution phase	widespread sweating not related to amount of effort.

Several features of the outline of the sexual response cycle as abstracted in Table 7.1 should be noted. First, we have accepted the Masters and Johnson reports uncritically for the purposes of exposition. There are many questions that can be raised; however, we shall delay these until later in the chapter. For example, there are questions concerning the nature of the heart rate response, there are problems with the concept of the plateau phase, and there are difficulties in the methodologies used by Masters and Johnson for data collection. Secondly, as we noted, our table omits several items. Finally, as will be discussed in detail below, there are responses that other investigators have reported as being associated with the sexual response cycle. These have not been included in the table which is limited to those reported by Masters and Johnson.

1.1 Extragenital measures

The extragenital measures of heart rate, respiration, blood pressure, and sweat gland activity have been used by investigators other than Masters and Johnson. Zuckerman (1971) reviewed the literature and concluded that only genital measures were specific to sexual arousal and that the nongenital measures were not only responsive to non-sexual stimuli, but were only weakly associated with sexual arousal. For example, while Masters and Johnson report that heart rate increases directly with sexual arousal, Wenger, Averill, and Smith (1968) reported a decrease in heart rate during the early stages of arousal, a finding consistent with a model that proposes that parasympathetic effects dominate early in sexual arousal. Hoon, Wincze, and Hoon (1976) reported that heart rate failed to discriminate between dysphoric and erotic videotapes, but noted that systolic blood pressure did increase during the erotic stimulus. In respect to respiration, the Masters and Johnson report was not confirmed by Wenger, Averill, and Smith (1968); however, Bartlett (1956) noted respiratory changes at orgasm. The point is that neither heart rate nor respiration is a sensitive measure of sexual arousal, particularly at low levels. On the other hand, blood pressure may hold promise as an index of sexual arousal.

In the past, measures of sweat gland activity were commonly used to index sexual arousal. Wilhelm Reich in 1937 attempted to measure the galvanic skin response (GSR) in the genitals in perhaps the earliest investigation of this type. GSR and skin conductance (SC) have proven successful in detecting responding to the sexual stimuli; however, they have not been successful in discriminating between sexual arousal and emotional arousal of other varieties (Zuckerman, 1971). Skin temperature has been used in attempts to measure sexual arousal. Hoon, Wincze, and Hoon (1976) reported that forehead temperature increased in the presence of erotic stimuli while Wenger, Averill, and Smith (1968) reported that finger temperature decreased to erotic stimuli and that facial temperature did not discriminate between erotic and control stimulation. Zuckerman (1971) reviewed studies conducted up to the time of his paper and concluded that skin temperature does not reliably measure sexual arousal. At this time no one has reported any attempts to measure the 'sex flush'* in an objective or systematic manner. In fact, we do not know how it was measured in the Masters and Johnson report.

There have been several extragenital measures of sexual arousal attempted that were not reported upon by Masters and Johnson. Several investigators have examined EEG activity during sexual arousal. Lifschitz (1966) reported that evoked responses did not discriminate erotic from non-erotic stimuli. However, Cohen, Rosen, and Goldstein (1976) examined laterality changes during masturbation. They reported significant shifts in laterality during orgasm; potential artifacts in that study urge replication before the results can be accepted as reliable. Most readers will recall that pupil dilation has been reported to reflect sexual interest (Hess, 1968; Hess and Polt, 1960). The many methodological problems associated with pupillography have restricted its application to detection of sexual arousal. Thus far, very little is known beyond the original reports suggesting that pupillography has potential in detection of sexual arousal.

Finally, biochemical measures of either hormone production or physiological activity in genitals have been used to assess sexual arousal or interest. Urinary acid phosphatase, apparently produced by prostate activity, has been used in males as an index of sexual arousal (e.g. Barclay, 1970; Gustafson, Winokur, and Reichlin, 1963). These studies reported an increase in urinary acid phosphate in response to sexual stimulation; however, Barclay's work also noted that levels were affected by anger and previous sexual experience. Thus that biochemical measure has specificity problems as well as the problems associated with its reflecting relatively long time periods. Blood hormone levels represent a technology not readily available to most psychophysiologists and thus will not be included in this chapter. Hormone assays have not as of this time proven useful in measuring sexual arousal.

The cursory review of extragenital measures has illustrated the point that there are serious problems with their use as an index of sexual arousal. First, the measures seem only weakly correlated with subjective estimates of sexual arousal. Second, the measures are often not specific to sexual arousal and therefore are open to potential confounding with other emotional states. These problems are not unique to psychophysiological indices of emotions; however, sexual arousal is different in that there appears to be a straightforward solution to the problems. Genital responses

*The sex flush is a measles-like rash that appears first over the epigastrium and may spread to the breasts, chest wall, lower abdomen, shoulders, thighs, buttocks, and back.

appear to circumvent the problems to a large extent. They have correlations with subjective judgements that are higher than those associated with nongenital measures (Geer, 1976), and genital responses have thus far shown a high level of specificity. At this time, genital measures are the best physiological indices available to study sexual behaviour and arousal. When used in concert with subjective and behavioural measures, they provide a powerful set of research strategies for expanding our knowledge concerning sex in specific and perhaps emotion in general. With these points in view, we now turn to a detailed description of the currently available techniques for measuring genital responses.

2 GENITAL MEASUREMENT DEVICES—MALES

2.1 Volumetric plethysmographs

While Masters and Johnson have noted responses in the scrotum and testes, clearly the most obvious and dramatic change that occurs in the male genitalia is erection of the penis. There have been two principal approaches to quantifying erections: volumetric and circumferential. Freund (1963) developed a volumetric device that was designed to detect changes in penile volume. The device has as its basic components a glass cylinder with a funnel at one end. The penis is prepared by the experimenter by first placing a sponge-rubber ring over the penis then a plastic ring with an inflatable cuff made from a condom is placed over the sponge-rubber ring. With the glass cylinder in place, the cuff is inflated to make an air-tight seal encasing the penis within the cylinder. When the penis changes volume a pressure transducer records the changes in air displacement. Figure 7.3 is a drawing of the device adapted from the Freund, Sedlacek, and Knob (1965) report.

McConaghy (1967) devised an air-filled volumetric penile plethysmograph made of materials more readily accessible than was Freund's. His device is made from a tin cylinder $2\frac{1}{4}''$ in diameter by $3\frac{1}{2}''$ in length with a finger stall fitted on one end of the cylinder and a nipple with an air tube at the other end. McConaghy reported little information on the methods of attachment and noted that absolute blood volume changes could not be measured.

Fisher, Gross, and Zuch (1965) developed a penile plethysmograph that displaced water rather than air. It was reported to be both awkward and bulky, and they comment that one subject asked if it was an 'artificial vagina'. It is fair to conclude that volumetric penile plethysmographs have not proven popular in large part due to their bulk and awkwardness in use. They do provide, however, rather precise information concerning overall

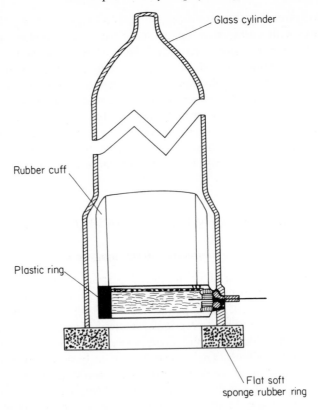

Glass cylinder

Rubber cuff

Plastic ring

Flat soft
sponge rubber ring

Figure 7.3 Freund's volumetric penis plethysmograph. (Adapted from Freund, Sedlacek, and Knob,
1965)

changes in the penis as contrasted with the data supplied by strain gauge
devices that are described next.

2.2   Strain gauge plethysmographs

Fisher, Gross, and Zuch (1965) described the use of a mercury strain
gauge developed by Shapiro and Cohen. This device consists of a hollow
rubber tube filled with mercury and sealed at the ends. Electrodes are
placed in the sealed ends and they lead to a bridge circuit for connection
to a polygraph. Parks Electronics in Beaverton, Oregon market several
sizes of this gauge at a relatively low cost. Figure 7.4 illustrates the design
of the mercury strain gauge. The operation of the gauge is quite simple. As
the penis changes its circumference the tube stretches or shortens The
mercury column inside the hollow tube increases or decreases its diameter

with the changes. Since the resistance of the mercury varies directly with the diameter of the column, a display of resistance changes in the mercury reflects changes in the circumference of the penis. The device can be readily put in place by the subject, a major advantage of all strain gauges. Placement has varied across studies with directly behind the coronal ridge and flush against the body wall being the two most commonly reported sites. Two disadvantages have been noted with the mercury filled gauge. One is that there is a restricted shelf life (about 3 months) and second, subjects have broken the gauge by stretching it too much during placement or removal. The advantages of light weight and unobtrusiveness are significant factors in favour of the mercury gauge. Karacan (1969) has reported the modification of a Parks-like gauge where the electrode attachment section is reduced in size. A detailed description of that device is available in Karacan's report.

Another type of mercury strain gauge was developed by Bancroft, Jones, and Pullan (1966). It employs the rubber tube filled with mercury, but in addition has a plastic supporting structure that allows the device to be fitted to the individual penis. The device may be fitted by the subject; and while slightly bulkier than the Parks gauge, it can also be worn under clothing. The Bancroft gauge is quite sensitive and is readily calibrated. Bancroft (1974) provides complete details on construction and use.

Jovanovic (1967) reported the development of a rubber tube strain

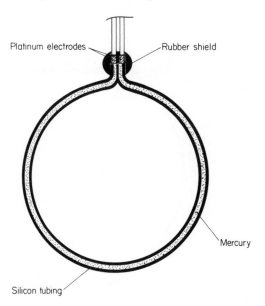

Figure 7.4   A schematic view of a mercury strain gauge

gauge where the conducting material was graphite rather than mercury. The device is quite sensitive to small changes and can be used in either the a.c. or d.c. mode. The graphite column may become discontinuous when large changes occur, and Jovanovic's device has a plastic component that reportedly may be uncomfortable under some conditions.

A widely used penile strain gauge was developed by Barlow and coworkers (1970). It is a variant of a gauge described by Johnson and Kitching (1968). The device is made of two arcs of surgical spring material joined with two mechanical strain gauges. These gauges are flexed when the penis changes in circumference producing changes in their resistance which is then displayed on a polygraph. Figure 7.5 illustrates the design of the Barlow gauge. There have been modifications of the gauge (e.g. Laws and Pawlowski, 1973) that have improved the original. The mechanical strain gauges are quite sensitive and more rugged than the rubber tube devices. However, if incorrectly designed or fitted they can yield many artifacts if they move or if the ends of the arcs touch.

As noted, some investigators record two channels of information. In that arrangement researchers (e.g. Rosen 1973) have incorporated a second parallel channel in which the strain gauge response is coupled to a time

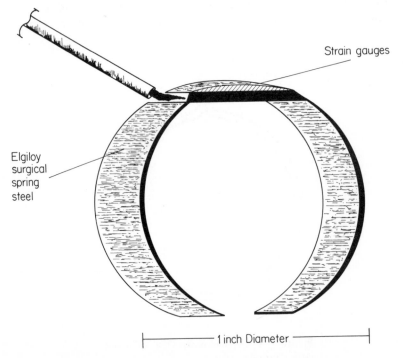

Figure 7.5 A schematic view of the Barlow strain gauge

constant (typically 1 s) so that small rapid changes in tumescence, including pressure pulse, are not masked by larger slower changes. In the two-channel system, one channel provides unmodified information concerning changes in the diameter of the penis. On the unmodified channel, amplification must be relatively low, since large increases in tumescence occur. This low amplification means small changes are not detected. The two-channel system allows measurement in a manner similar to tonic versus phasic changes in electrodermal activity (EDA). Figure 7.6 shows a typical tracing from a penile strain gauge, Barlow-type.

There are no data at the present time to suggest that these two classes of changes (large slow versus small fast) are either independent or are reflecting different psychological phenomena as may be the case in electrodermal activity. However, to the extent that researchers are interested in small rapid tumescence changes, the two-channel system is necessary to permit their detection. When interest is focused exclusively on large changes, the two-channel system is unnecessary.

The literature reveals a few comparative studies on penile plethysmographs. Freund, Langevin, and Barlow (1974) compared Freund's volumetric plethysmograph with Barlow's mechanical strain gauge. Equipment problems required elimination of over half of the subjects. They reported that the volumetric device was more sensitive.

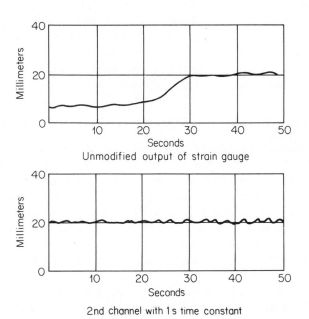

Figure 7.6   Tracing from a record of a Barlow strain gauge showing a rapid response

McConaghy (1974) compared his volumetric device with a Bancroft mercury strain gauge. The results, while difficult to interpret due to methodological problems, suggest that the volumetric device was more sensitive and that upon occasion the two devices yielded different findings. Finally, Laws and Pawlowski (1973) compared the Barlow with the Parks mercury strain gauge. They also used a Farrall photoelectric gauge (not described in this chapter). The Farrall gauge had serious problems and the Barlow gauge slipped when the penis' circumference became smaller than the gauge. A lack of statistical comparisons prevent any statement other than that the gauges differed at times.

There can be no definitive statement concerning which of the various penile devices should be employed in a given study. This reviewer prefers the Barlow-type gauge because of its sensitivity and ruggedness. All circumferential devices have the disadvantage of having to face the fact that the penis is non-isotropic (McConaghy, 1974), that is, that changes in volume are not uniformly reflected in circumference changes at different sites on the penis. On the other hand, the bulkiness of the volumetric devices preclude their use in many situations.

At the present time, simple and reliable alternatives to the measurement of penile changes have not been widely explored. Fisher, Gross, and Zuch (1965) attempted to use a thermistor to detect changes. The fact that of 17 subjects only two yielded usable results biases the findings to the point of their being unacceptable. Fisher, Gross, and Zuch suggested that circumference and temperature changes were correlated as measured by visual inspection of the records. Attempts to measure scrotal or testicular responding have not proven useful as the response is not specific to sexual arousal (see Zuckerman, 1971).

3 GENITAL MEASUREMENT DEVICES—WOMEN

The measurement of genital responding in women has a more recent history than that for men. Zuckerman (1971) noted that the lack of genital measurement in women was an obstacle to research on sexuality. Masters and Johnson's report of vaginal vasocongestion gave researchers the impetus to develop a vaginally based genital measure of sexual arousal. Two techniques have proven useful in the detection and measurement of vaginal vasocongestion. They are a vaginal flow meter developed by Cohen and Shapiro (1970), and vaginal photoplethysmography developed by Sintchak and Geer (1975).

The Cohen and Shapiro device has not been widely used, but reportedly works quite well in detection of changes in vaginal blood flow. They constructed a vaginal thermal flow meter by mounting two thermistors on the rim of a vaginal diaphragm. When the device is in place, one thermistor is in contact with the vaginal wall and is heated slightly above core temperature (4 °C) and the second thermistor, which is placed so as to avoid contact with vaginal tissue, records intravaginal or core temperature. Through its circuitry, the amount of current necessary to keep the first thermistor a constant temperature above the second is reflected in changes that are recorded on a polygraph. The current necessary to maintain the constant temperature difference reflects dissipation of heat into the vaginal tissues, and, since change in heat dissipation is primarily a function of the blood flow in the surrounding tissues, this device measures blood flow, not vaginal temperature. Cohen and Shapiro used this device to measure arousal during sleep, and it would seem that this device might have some advantages over a vaginal probe, since the diaphragm would be less likely to be accidentally dislocated. The main disadvantages of this device are that it is a relatively delicate instrument, and it requires custom fitting of the diaphram by medically trained staff. This can be both time-consuming and expensive as well as more disruptive than self-placed devices. Details on construction of the blood flow device are not available from the published report.

The first researchers to adapt the principles of photoplethysmography to the study of vaginal blood flow were Palti and Bercovici (1967). They modified an ordinary vaginal speculum by equipping it with a photoelectric cell sensitive to red light and a miniature light bulb. The objectives of their study were not related to the investigation of sexual responding. Although their method does measure vaginal blood flow and vaginal pulse it has not been adapted for use in sex research. Sintchak and Geer (1975) report the development of a vaginal probe that uses the principles of photoplethysmography to assess sexual arousal in the human female.

The Sintchak and Geer vaginal photoplethysmograph is $\frac{1}{2}''$ in diameter and $1\frac{3}{4}''$ in length, shaped and sized like a menstrual tampon and made of clear acrylic plastic (see Figure 7.7). Imbedded in the front end of the

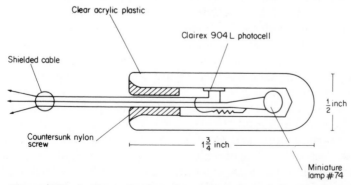

Figure 7.7 A schematic view of a vaginal photoplethysmograph

body of the probe is a light source which illuminates the vaginal walls via the clear plastic that helps diffuse the light. Direct light from this light source is not recorded; rather, indirect light is reflected and diffused through the vaginal wall tissue and reaches a photoreceptive cell surface. When the probe is placed approximately $1\frac{1}{2}''$ into the vaginal barrel, the photocell is in direct contact with the vaginal wall. Changes in the resistance of the cell correspond to the amount of light reaching the light sensitive surface. The amount of blood in the tissues affects the amount of light reaching the photocell. The areas around the photocell and the cable exit are sealed with dental cement and smoothed so that there are no rough edges. This also serves to waterproof the probe and helps facilitate easy cleaning and sterilization.

A clairex model 904L cadmium selenide (CdSe) photocell was selected for use in the probe because of its small size, high sensitivity, and spectral response to light in the red region. Since the photocell is operated at low light levels, its response is very linear and its speed of response is sufficient to follow pulse wave variations.

The light source used was a 1705 miniature lamp with its normal voltage reduced to 4.3 V. The spectral output was shifted into red, which stabilized the light output level and increased its lifetime. The current of the lamp was reduced to 14 mA and the power dissipated is 60 mW to reduce local heating effects.

A standard transducer bridge circuit was built into a Beckman 980 input coupler. A common ground return for the photocell lamp was utilized so that only three wires would connect to the probe. This minimized the cable weight pulling on the probe when it was in operation. A 3 circuit phone plug was put on the end of about six feet of this flexible cable so that the subject could insert the probe herself and walk from place of insertion to experimental apparatus and plug the cable into the appropriate jack. If four wires are used to connect the probe, the photocell and lamp circuits can be separated and any standard bridge circuit capable of balancing 100 kΩ can be used. The recording system is operated with two channels. The main channel with the modified 9801 coupler is used at low sensitivity and a second channel is a.c. coupled (time constant = 1 s) using a 9086A coupler to the main channel. The second channel is operated at a greater sensitivity than the main channel. Figure 7.8 shows a typical tracing from a vaginal photoplethysmograph.

This system has been validated and found to be reliable by Geer, Morokoff, and Greenwood (1974), and is widely used by other researchers as well. Hoon, Wincze, and Hoon (1976) have reported an improvement. They used an infrared light-emitting diode (LED), and phototransistors were used in place of an incandescent light source and selenium photocell respectively. The use of an LED and phototransistor eliminated potential

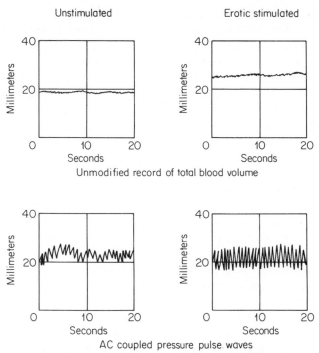

Figure 7.8   Tracing from a record of a vaginal photo-plethysmograph. One subject and sensitivity setting, two levels of erotic stimulation

artifacts associated with blood oxygenation levels. This change also reduces problems of hysteresis and light history effects discussed by Novelly, Perone, and Ax (1973) and Tahmoush and coworkers (1976) which are intrinsically connected with photoplethysmography. Van Dam and coworkers (1976) also reported the development of a vaginal photoplethysmograph similar to the Sintchak and Geer model.

The vaginal probe has several advantages over the blood flow device. The ease of use and subject comfort and acceptability are major advantages. Also the a.c. coupled channel provides information on vaginal pressure pulse not available from the blood flow system. Research (Heiman, 1977) suggests that vaginal pressure pulse may be particularly sensitive as an indicant of sexual arousal. Disadvantages include the fact that certain sexual behaviours (e.g. coitus) cannot be studied while the device is in operation. In our laboratory we experienced difficulty with the LED modification to the vaginal probe. Apparently the amount of vaginal tissue between the light source and the photosensitive surface is critical. LEDs that have their focus close to the photosensitive surface may result in unreliable readings due to artifacts of placement. Since Hoon, Wincze, and Hoon (1976) did not describe such problems, their system must have circumvented that difficulty. We also note that Gillan (1976) reports that the vaginal probe when placed in the rectum detected vascular responses but they did not appear correlated with sexual arousal.

Other genital measures which have been attempted are reviewed by Zuckerman (1971) and Geer (1975). They have not proven useful for a variety of reasons. Shapiro and coworkers (1968) attempted to measure secretions from the vaginal wall. By using a platinum electrode held in place by a tampon saturated with hypotonic saline, they attempted to measure production of lactic acid in the vagina by measuring pH. These measures have failed to yield reliable data. Uterine contractions have also been measured by a balloon-like device called the Kolograph which was developed and tested by Jovanovic (1971). This method too has not been very successful in assessing sexual arousal in women especially since uterine contractions occur mainly during orgasm and even then not reliably so.

Groin temperature was used by Hoon, Wincze, and Hoon (1976) with limited success. Vaginal temperature has not proven successful. A major problem is that the vagina is within the body core so that changes in blood supply have minimal effects upon vaginal temperature. At this time vaginal photoplethysmography appears to be the best choice for genital measurement of sexual arousal in women. Certainly there will be improvements in the technology and entirely new systems may emerge. For example, techniques to detect labial changes may prove useful. Recent reports have described the use of a thermistor clipped on the labia minor as a device to measure sexual arousal (Henson, Rubin, and Henson, 1978). These authors have obtained high correlations with subjective report in a sample of six subjects and high correlations across a four week period. The device holds promise as a measure of genital arousal in women. However, at the present time, vaginal photoplethysmography appears to be the most appropriate choice.

4 MEASUREMENT OF GENITAL RESPONSES

4.1 Males

Two principal approaches have been followed towards the development of measurement conventions for assessing penile changes. The first is the direct measure of changes on the polygraph record. In this approach, changes in the polygraph tracing are translated into either circumference or volume changes. This can readily be done by calibrating the measuring devices with known standards. These absolute volume or circumference changes can be transformed if necessary or analysed directly. These measures have the problems inherent in many psychophysiological measures. Individual differences in reactivity are ignored and no correction, if necessary, for the law of initial values or penis size is made.

The second approach that has been widely used (e.g. Barlow and coworkers, 1970; Laws and Rubin, 1969) is to convert the polygraph records to a percentage of erection measure. This is accomplished by having the subject, either through self-stimulation or the presentation of powerfully erotic stimuli, produce a full erection. The recording at that point is defined as 100% and the 0% is the recording during baseline period of non-erotic stimulation or rest. The percentage scale can then be computed for any response. There is a sense in which this measure has face validity and has a certain appeal. However, there are some very serious problems associated with it. First of all, the measure depends upon the subjects' report of '100%'. That can vary day to day and is likely subject to experimental and experimenter influence. Visual observation (e.g. Fisher, Gross, and Zuch, 1965) of the extent of erection beside raising ethical problems does not eliminate the subjective nature of the scale. Another problem lies in the assumption of a linear relationship between the scale and subjective arousal. While this problem also can be found in the absolute change measures, the percentage scale may mislead investigators into assuming that the linearity assumption is fulfilled. There is a need for systematic evaluation of measurement issues for penile responding. At this time, there is no measurement convention that is demonstrably superior and the choice resides with the investigator.

4.2 Females

The vaginal photoplethysmograph yields two channels of information. One is the unmodified d.c. component that can be used to detect changes in the total blood volume of the vaginal walls. To measure that response, investigators have employed change scores in a manner analogous to those used for penile changes. There is, however, no absolute calibration possible and thus there is no information available on absolute blood volume changes. The second channel available is a.c. coupled and displays vaginal pressure pulse. Vaginal pressure pulse amplitude has been used with success in detecting sexual arousal, and Heiman (1977) reported that it was more sensitive than total volume measures. Individual researchers must decide such issues as how many pulses to sample and the specification of when to sample. Care must be taken to be certain that amplifier settings are constant across subjects, so as to make certain that differences in pulse amplitude are not affected by that factor. The total blood volume was noted by Geer and Quartararo (1976) to detect a vaginal component of the orgasmic response.

Q

Thus far, there has been no solution to the problem of developing measures that are comparable between the sexes. Penile volume and vaginal blood volume, let alone pressure pulse, are not directly comparable. The method of determination differs, the nature of the response differs, and the physiological mechanisms underlying the responses differ. These problems mean that at the present time one cannot make comparative statements between the sexes on questions such as, 'Are men or women more aroused by *x*?' What is needed is some conversion formula such as was attempted in Lacey's (1956) work on autonomic lability scores. At the present, it is only possible to speak of differences in slopes of curves between the sexes. Another possibly useful comparison measure might be latency. At present, latencies of genital measures have not been widely reported but may be of value in between sex comparisons.

4.3 Artifacts

There are artifacts in genital measures that merit comment. As is true in virtually all psychophysiological research, movement based artifacts are the major problem in genital measures. They are readily distinguished from the normal record because of their irregularity and amplitude. Movement artifacts may obscure important data, but it is highly unlikely that they will be mistaken for 'true' responses. Care in construction and placement of the devices will eliminate many movement problems.

In vaginal measurement we have noted slow cyclical baseline shifts on the a.c. coupled channel. They resemble respiration artifacts, but as yet we do not know for certain their source. There also appear to be problems of possible artifacts due to placement of vaginal probes. It is strongly recommended that researchers make certain that subject placement is constant. While there is no systematic evidence on the issue, there appears to be variation in response amplitude at various sites within individual subjects. Masters and Johnson's report of the formation of an orgasmic platform in the outer one-third of the vaginal barrel has led to our use of relatively shallow (inserted $1\frac{1}{2}''$) placement. Probes with multiple photosensitive surfaces can readily be constructed and would provide data relevant to defining optimal placement sites. As an example of a placement problem, if a vaginal probe with a LED sampling a small area were placed over a major blood vessel, there would be no recordable pressure pulse.

5   APPLICATION REVIEW

The focus of this chapter is not to review work in the field, but to speak to methodological issues. However, it would be remiss not to note some of the problems that have been studied using genital responses as dependent variables. For a more detailed discussion, the reader should consult some of the available reviews such as Zuckerman (1971) and Geer (1976).

Perhaps the best known research involving genital measures has been generated in clinical settings with males. This work commenced with the report of Kurt Freund (1963) in which he reported that he could, on the basis of penile volume changes, discriminate between hetero- or homosexual subjects' responses to photos of males and females. That work was replicated and expanded to other atypical populations by numerous investigators. A recent review of that research can be found in Geer (1977). As yet, there are no published reports of similar work using vaginal measures, although clearly such research is warranted.

Another relatively common application of genital measures has been their use in assessing treatment outcome and/or progress in treatment. In that work, again reviewed in Bancroft (1974) and Geer (1977), genital responses are measured to stimuli designed to evoke responding of interest to the therapist. While some success has been found with the clinical applications, there are many unresolved problems and issues. One clinical application of considerable interest is the possible use of genital biofeedback as a treatment procedure. As yet, we do not know whether or not such an application will prove of value.

The second application area is basic research on sexuality and emotions in general. This general area is in its infancy, but the promise for the future is great. The relatively high correlation between genital responses and subjective judgements (e.g. Spiess, 1977) makes the study of issues in the relationship between cognitive and physiological events a field where genital measures may make a significant contribution. I have argued elsewhere (Geer, 1976) that cognitive events play a major role in sexuality. It then follows that sexuality may well be an area in which cognitive events can be effectively studied. There have already been investigations of imagery, fantasy, and distraction that fit the use proposed above. If it is reasonable to assume that the emotions associated with sexuality follow the same 'rules' as other emotions, then sexuality would become a field where strides could be made by focusing on solving problems more general than issues limited to sexuality.

6 ETHICAL AND SUBJECT ISSUES

All researchers need to be concerned about ethical issues and subject rights. In sex research these problems are emphasized because of long-standing societal and cultural attitudes towards things sexual. In that context a discussion of some of the specific ethical issues is merited.

Confidentiality guarantees to all subjects are extremely important. Any participant in sex research should be assured that his or her data will not be identified or identifiable. Assurances should be clear and unequivocal on this issue so that no subject need fear being exposed to any unpleasant or unwanted experiences following participation. Related to confidentiality is the need for privacy. Subjects should know if any direct visual observation is to be undertaken and there should be full agreement if such is the case. As noted earlier, genital transducers can readily be placed in privacy by the subject and thus there need be no direct observation for placement purposes. It also would be ideal if when the subject comes to the experimental rooms conditions be such that they are not readily identifiable as those of sex research.

Subject comfort is a concern in sex research. Two separate components of subject comfort can be identified. First, physical comfort must be assured. Not only is there the concern for subjects' welfare, but also any distraction caused by discomfort will interfere with obtaining meaningful results. The second aspect of comfort is the 'emotional' comfort of the subject. Since sex is subject to many moral and ethical constraints, subjects should be treated with the utmost professional concern. The major factor assuring responsible treatment of subjects is the experimenter. Researchers using others as experimenters should exercise particular care in selecting assistants. Clear and unequivocal instructions about these issues should be a routine part of the training of all experimenters. Any experimenter who does not impart an attitude of confidence and a professional concern for his/her subjects should not be permitted to work with subjects. In particular, silliness or lack of appropriately motivated interest in sex research should be avoided. Experimenters who are competent and well trained will go a long way towards assuring the 'emotional comfort' of subjects.

A topic of concern to all involved in sex research using genital measurement is sterilization of the devices. This is of particular concern since lack of adequate sterilization procedures may result in the inadvertent spread of venereal disease. Of particular current concern is the rapid spread of a viral disease Herpes. There are two accepted sterilization procedures for killing viruses: autoclaving and certain sterilizing chemicals. Autoclaving may be impossible in those situations where heat will damage the genital device. Care must be taken in chemical sterilization to ensure that an appropriate agent is used. Viruses are highly resistant to many common chemical sterilizing agents. One agent that is effective against all organisms except bacteriological spores, tetanus, and botulism, which are not of concern in sex research, is a 10 minute bath in activated gluteraldehyde. Care in using activated gluteraldehyde, available commercially as Cidex or Cidex 7, should be observed. First, it must be replaced periodically and transducers must be rinsed after sterilization.

Rinsing avoids chemical sensitivities and the possibility of killing beneficial naturally occurring vaginal organisms. Regardless of the procedure investigators need assure themselves that sterilization is a certainty.

The final subject issue holds in all areas of human research—informed consent. The issues are not fundamentally different from those facing researchers in any area of inquiry. It is worth mentioning that subjects should be aware of any exposure to explicit sexual material to prevent an adverse reaction. In our laboratory we employ a procedure that is especially designed to insure voluntary participation. Subjects visit the laboratory prior to the actual experimental session for a briefing session. Full details of the experience are explained, and subjects are given the opportunity to decline to participate further. To insure non-coercive voluntary participation, subjects are not permitted to volunteer at that time but are dismissed from the laboratory. After a lapse of approximately three days they are contacted by phone and an appointment is made for the experimental session. There are many procedures that could be followed to insure informed voluntary consent. The one we follow is presented not as an absolute, but as one that clearly fits ethical considerations.

7 SOME GENERAL ISSUES

It has been noted that genital measures seem more closely tied to subjective judgements of sexual arousal than is the typical case in psychophysiology. A likely reason has to do with the nature of the genital response when compared with many other autonomic responses. The crucial difference may be that the genital response directly interacts with the environment. An erect penis is necessary for certain sexual behaviours to occur and a lubricated vagina, likely resulting from vasocongestion, facilitates certain sexual activities. Given that situation, it is not surprising that environmental events are directly associated with genital changes and also that genital changes are observable and detectable by the individual. A second point related to the above is that sexual behaviour has reinforcing properties. That fact also suggests that genital responses may be more readily detected and observed. In a previous discussion (Geer, 1977) it has been suggested that these features of genital responses have implications for potential application of biofeedback as well as helping explain the close cognitive–physiological link.

Sex research may provide the setting in which questions concerning issues broader than sexuality *per se* may be settled. Making the reasonable assumption that sexual behaviour is subject to the same constraints and controlling variables as other emotional states, sexuality may prove of very general interest as a research base. For example, since the cognitive–physiological ties are so close sexuality may prove a solid experimental field in which to do basic research on cognitive factors. The Geer and Fuhr (1976) study is an example of how this may be accomplished. Hopefully, the present chapter will encourage investigators to do both applied and basic research using genital measurements to index responses of interest.

REFERENCES

Bancroft, J. (1974). *Deviant Sexual Behavior: Modification and Assessment*, Clarendon, Oxford.
Bancroft, J., Jones, H. G., and Pullan, B. R. (1966). A simple transducer for measuring penile erection, with comments on its use in the treatment of sexual disorders. *Beh. Res. Therapy*, **9**, 239–41.
Barclay, A. M. (1970). Urinary acid phosphatase secretion in sexually aroused males. *J. Exp. Res. Personality*, **4**, 233–8.
Barlow, D. H., Becker, R., Leitenberg, H., and Agras, W. S. (1970). A mechanical strain gauge for recording penile circumference change. *J. Appl. Beh. Anal.*, **3**, 73–6.
Bartlett, R. G., Jr (1956). Physiologic responses during coitus. *J. Appl. Physiol.*, **9**, 469–72.
Cohen, H. D., Rosen, R. C., and Goldstein, L. (1976). Electroencephalographic laterality changes during human sexual orgasm. *Archs Sex. Beh.*, **5**, 189–99.
Cohen, H. D. and Shapiro, A. (1971). A method for measuring sexual arousal in the female. *Psychophysiology*, **8**, 251.
Fisher, C., Gross, J., and Zuch, J. (1965). Cycle of penile erection synchronous with dreaming (REM) sleep. *Archs. Gen. Psychiat.*, **12**, 29–45.
Freund, K. (1963). A laboratory method for diagnosing predominance of homo- or hetero-erotic interest in the male. *Beh. Res. Therapy*, **1**, 85–93.
Freund, K. (1971). A note on the use of the phallometric method of measuring mild sexual arousal in the male. *Beh. Res. Therapy*, **2**, 223–8.
Freund, K., Langevin, R., and Barlow, D. (1974). Comparison of two penile measures of erotic arousal. *Beh. Res. Therapy*, **12**, 335–40.
Freund, K., Sedlacek, F., and Knob, K. (1965). A simple transducer for mechanical plethysmography of the male genital. *J. Exp. Anal. Beh.*, **8**, 169–70.
Geer, J. H. (1975). Direct measurement of genital responding. *Am. Psychol.*, **30**, 415–18.
Geer, J. H. (1976). Genital measures: Comments on their role in understanding human sexuality. *J. Sex Marital Therapy*, **3**, 165–72.
Geer, J. H. (1977). Sexual functioning: some data and speculations on psychophysiological assessment. In J. D. Cone and R. P. Hawkins (Eds), *Behavioral Assessment: New Directions in Clinical Psychology*, Chap. 7, Brunner/Mazel, New York, pp. 196–209.
Geer, J. H., and Fuhr, R. (1976). Cognitive factors in sexual arousal: the role of distraction. *J. Consult. Clin. Psychol.*, **44**, 238–43.
Geer, J. H., Morokoff, P., and Greenwood, P. (1974). Sexual arousal in women: the development of a measurement device for vaginal blood volume. *Archs Sex. Beh.*, **3**, 559–64.
Geer, J. H., and Quartararo, J. D. (1976). Vaginal blood volume responses during masturbation and resultant orgasm. *Archs Sex. Beh.*, **5**, 403–13.
Gillan, P. (1976). Objective measures of female sexual arousal. *Proc. Physiol. Soc.*, 64P.

Gustafson, J. E., Winokur, G., and Reichlin, S. (1963). The effect of psychic and sexual stimulation on urinary and serum acid phosphatase and plasma non-esterified fatty acids. *Psychosom. Med.,* **25**, 101–5.

Guyton, A. C. (1971). *Textbook of Medical Physiology,* Saunders, Philadelphia.

Heiman, J. R. (1977). A psychophysiological exploration of sexual arousal patterns in females and males. *Psychophysiology,* **14**, 266–73.

Henson, D. E., Rubin, H. B., and Henson, C. (1978). Consistency of the labial temperature change measure of human female eroticism. *Beh. Res. Therapy,* **16**, 125–9.

Hess, E. H. (1968). Pupillometric assessment. *Res. Psychotherapy,* **3**, 573–83.

Hess, E. H., and Polt, J. M. (1960). Pupil size as related to interest value of visual stimuli, *Science,* **132**, 349–50.

Hoon, P. W., Wincze, J. P., and Hoon, E. F. (1976). Physiological assessment of sexual arousal in women. *Psychophysiology,* **13**, 196–204.

Johnson, J., and Kitching, R. (1968). A mechanical transducer for phallography. *Biomed. Engng,* 416–18.

Jovanovic, U. J. (1967). Some characteristics of the beginning of dreams. *Psychol. Fortsch.,* **30**, 281–306.

Jovanovic, U. J. (1971). The recording of physiological evidence of genital arousal in human males and females. *Archs Sex. Beh.,* **1**, 309–20.

Karacan, I. (1969). A simple and inexpensive transducer for quantitative measurements of penile erection during sleep. *Beh. Res. Meth. Instrum.,* **1**, 251–2.

Lacey, J. I. (1956). The evaluation of autonomic responses: Toward a general solution. *Ann. N.Y. Acad. Sci.,* **67**, 123–65.

Laws, D. R., and Pawlowski, A. V. (1973). A multi-purpose biofeedback device for penile plethysmography. *J. Beh. Therapy Exp. Psychiat.,* **4**, 339–41.

Laws, D. R., and Rubin, H. B. (1969). Instructional control of an automatic sexual response. *J. Appl. Beh. Anal.,* **2**, 93–9.

Lifschitz, K. (1966). The averaged evoked cortical response to complex visual stimuli. *Psychophysiology,* **3**, 55–68.

Masters, W. H., and Johnson, J. E. (1966). *Human Sexual Response,* Little, Brown and Company, Boston.

McConaghy, N. (1968). Penile volume changes to moving pictures of male and females nudes in heterosexual and homosexual males. *Beh. Res. Therapy,* **5**, 43–8.

McConaghy, N. (1974). Measurements of change in penile dimensions. *Archs Sex. Beh.,* **3**, 381–8.

Novelly, R. A., Perone, P. J., and Ax, A. F. (1973). Photoplethysmography: system calibration and light history effects. *Psychophysiology,* **10**, 67–73.

Palti, Y., and Bercovici, B. (1967). Photoplethysmographic study of the vaginal blood pulse. *Am. J. Obstet. Gynec.,* **97**, 143–53.

Rosen, R. C. (1973). Suppression of penile tumescence by instrumental conditioning. *Psychosom. Med.,* **35**, 509–14.

Shapiro, A., Cohen, H., DiBianco, P., and Rosen, G. (1968). Vaginal blood flow changes during sleep and sexual arousal. *Psychophysiology,* **4**, 349.

Sintchak, G., and Geer, J. H. (1975). A vaginal plethysmograph system. *Psychophysiology,* **12**, 113–15.

Spiess, W. (1977). The psychophysiology of premature ejaculation: Some factors related to ejaculatory latency. *Dissertation,* SUNY at Stony Brook, unpublished.

Tahmoush, A. J., Jennings, R., Lee, A. L., Camp, S., and Weber, F. (1976). Characteristics of a light emitting diode-transistor photoplethysmograph. *Psychophysiology,* **13**, 357–62.

van Dam, F. S. A. M., Heonebier, W. J., van Zalinge, E. A., and Barendregt, J. T. (1976). Sexual arousal measured by photoplethysmography, *Behav. Engng*, **3**, 97–101.

Weiss, H. D. (1972). The physiology of human penile erection. *Ann. Intern. Med.*, **76**, 793–9.

Wenger, M. A., Averill, J. R., and Smith, D. D. B. (1968). Autonomic activity during sexual arousal. *Psychophysiology*, **4**, 468–78.

Zuckerman, M. (1971). Physiological measures of sexual arousal in the human. *Psychol. Bull.*, **75**, 297–329.

Techniques in Psychophysiology
Edited by I. Martin and P. H. Venables
© 1980, John Wiley & Sons Ltd.

CHAPTER 8

Biochemical Methods*

MARGARET J. CHRISTIE and DAVID D. WOODMAN

*Acknowledgement. MJC acknowledges with thanks the support of the Social Science Research Council.

459

1 INTRODUCTION—BIOCHEMICAL AND PHYSIOLOGICAL INTERRELATIONSHIPS

After some fifteen years of *Psychophysiology's* publication, after the appearance of a couple of dozen books devoted to the discipline, after eighteen American and five British annual scientific meetings . . . does one *still* need to begin a chapter for *Techniques in Psychophysiology* with prolegomena? Does one still need to define psychophysiology and describe its basic methods? Perhaps so, hence our 'introduction' to and arguments for biochemical techniques. The origins of psychophysiology lie in the polygraph and its precursors. So, if one examines the psychophysiology of Darrow (Gullickson, 1973), the *Newsletter* which preceded the *SPR* journal, or the contents of this book's forerunner (Venables and Martin, 1967) the scene is dominated by *electro*physiological technology. Yet, if psychophysiological techniques *are* aimed at examining physiological correlates of psychological states, and the translation of psyche into soma, accomplished largely by the hypothalamus, results in neural *and* endocrine changes as we have indicated in the flow diagram below, this argues for extension of interest beyond the electrophysiological to the biochemical. To expand briefly on Figure 8.1, at the base of the hypothalamus, situated immediately below the median eminence, is the pituitary gland. The secretions of this gland act as an interface converting neural signals to the appropriate humoral messenger. The pituitary gland is composed of two distinct lobes derived embryologically from different tissues. The anterior lobe secretes a number of trophic hormones, responsible for controlling the endocrine activities of other organs, together with a number of functional hormones of its own.

The release of these pituitary hormones is regulated by the hypothalamus via the secretion of specific releasing and inhibitory factors (Buckingham, 1977). The trophic hormones include thyroid stimulating hormone (TSH), adrenocorticotrophic hormone (ACTH) and the gonadotropins. Hormones secreted directly by the anterior lobe include growth hormone and prolactin.

The posterior lobe secretes anti diuretic hormone (ADH, vasopressin) under the influence of direct neural stimulation from the hypothalamus.

Detailed descriptions of the metabolic actions of these hormones are

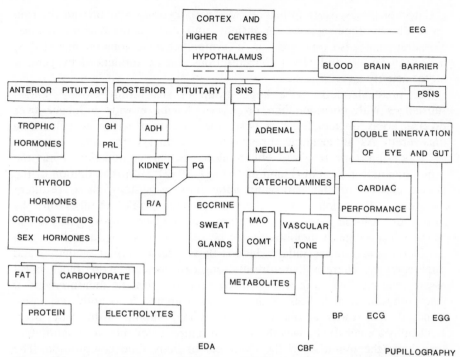

Figure 8.1 Areas of interest. SNS, Sympathetic nervous system; PSNS, parasympathetic nervous system; GH, growth hormone; PRL, prolactin; ADH, antidiuretic hormone; PG, prostaglandins; R/A, renin–angiotension; MAO, monoamine oxidase; COMT, catecholamine-0-methyl transferase; EDA, electrodermal activity; CBF, capillary blood flow; BP, blood pressure; EEG, electroencephalogram; ECG, electrocardiogram; EGG, electrogastrogram

well documented, but it is perhaps pertinent to point out that most have primary effects on protein, carbohydrate, fat, and electrolyte metabolism; and even the more selective may have secondary effects which impinge on additional areas of metabolism. The hormones secreted by the pituitary gland alone therefore have controlling influences over all major areas of metabolism.

Although the hypothalamus is the prime mover in the stimulation of pituitary endocrine secretions, its actions can be moderated by negative feedback effects from released hormone, or altered metabolic balance resulting from its action, allowing the delicate balance between the stimulatory signal and its effect to be attained.

The sympathetic outflow from the brain is also responsible for stimulating the production of a number of metabolically active compounds such as catecholamines and some prostaglandins, as well as acting directly through its innervation of organs.

Catecholamines exert influence over carbohydrate and fat metabolism, especially by their actions on insulin, and on general haemodynamics. Noradrenaline also operates as a sympathetic nervous system (SNS) neurotransmitter, and blood concentrations can be influenced by general motor activity levels.

The prostaglandins are a large group of structurally closely related substances with hormone like properties, having a wide influence over diverse areas of metabolic activity, the extent of which is still being uncovered. As an example, prostaglandins influence the renal excretion of water and electrolytes, either alone or in conjunction with the renin angiotensin system (Dunn and Hood, 1977); with the addition of the neural activity of the parasympathetic nervous system, these resultant metabolic interactions are reflected in measurable changes in the functioning of the systemic circulation, sweat glands, eyes, gut, etc. So changes in peripheral metabolism can be seen in physiological indices such as blood pressure, capillary blood flow, electrodermal activity, and pupillography. There is therefore a strong case for conducting biochemical assays of body fluid constituents in conjunction with the measurement of electrophysiological indices as an integrated approach to body responses, rather than considering one or the other in isolation. Historically, overt electrophysiological changes have been more amenable to quantitation than have the minutiae of the dynamics of body fluid composition. The exact correlation between biochemical changes and specific physiological changes mediating behavioural responses has not surprisingly posed great and often insuperable problems.

However, in recent years, analytical biochemistry has evolved rapidly to such a level that many substances which were not previously even detectable can now be quantitated accurately, allowing minute changes to be followed. Much of the equipment involved is necessarily highly sophisticated and expensive, and the level of expertise required in its use is often high, but the synergy which can be generated by adopting both approaches, the electrophysiological and the biochemical, is such that the potential rewards to be gained from a multidisciplinary strategy to research may often outweigh the difficulties encountered in its organization.

All of the hormones and related metabolic areas shown in Figure 8.1 have been implicated in behavioural functions and responses, so this area of biological interest forms a complex interactive system which must be considered when the significance of any component variation is assessed. When contemplating the systems involved, it should be appreciated that there is a roughly pyramidal structure common to both the specificity of the response and the degree of difficulty of analysis. The nearer the apex the more selective the parameter, and the more sophisticated the analytical procedure required.

While this in no way invalidates the measurement of basic body fluid constituents which form the lower reaches of the pyramid, such as glucose, sodium, potassium, and so on, it is obvious that a deviation from the expected value for glucose for example could occur via a number of effector pathways.

There are of course areas where this finding alone is of interest (see Section 3.2) but equally there are others where the data merely generate the need to carry out work in greater depth to investigate the preceding sequences of events leading up to the increased values recorded. An understanding of the systems involved right through to the final measured effect is essential, both in interpretation and more fundamentally in the design of the experiment which generates the data.

It follows that in translating theories into investigative experiments, the first aim should be a thorough appraisal of which substances should be studied, together with a realistic assessment of the level of analytical expertise required in their measurement. So it is quite possible that in some cases the parameters of interest may be assayed on equipment which can be operated successfully after a minimum of training and practice. However, the instrumentation forms only the most obvious part of the picture, and a number of more basic considerations must also be taken into account if the venture is to be a success.

In conclusion we might usefully emphasize the fact that we are, as Figure 8.1 indicates, concerned principally with the biochemistry of the *periphery*, not of the CNS or its transmitter functions. We are, therefore, concerned with analysis of body fluids such as blood, urine, saliva, and sweat, and with the methodology of clinical biochemistry, or chemical pathology, such as one finds in basic handbooks like Varley, Gowenlock, and Bell (1976, 1979) in the UK, and Henry, Cannon, and Winkleman (1974) in the USA. As psychophysiologists, however, we may well find that the basic handbooks of *chemical pathology* have aims and interests slightly different from our own. A parallel situation arises when psychophysiology adopts methodology from clinical electroencephalography: the aim of the latter may be primarily that of discriminating between normal and abnormal function, whereas the former may wish to examine the relatively small variation existing within the normal range. Similarly, psychophysiologists adopting the methodology of clinical chemistry may find that the technological handbooks do not always answer their needs.

We hope that this chapter will be a modest *vade mecum*, a guide around the field. We have focused rather superficially on method rather than theory, but the literature suggested should enable any enquiring reader to dig more deeply. Lastly, we have written for target populations with minimal expertise but varying levels of available facilities: our discussions range from consideration of simple methods for blood glucose analysis to the complexities of catecholamine estimation. We should reiterate, however, that we aim at little more than a brief excursion, with the following customers in mind. In clinical settings such as psychiatric departments we envisage there being psychologists who may have some access to the sophisticated facilities of hospital laboratories. Here there will be automated techniques, computer analysis . . . and no doubt a *very busy* biochemist!

Hence we see the needs of our hypothetical clinical psychologist in terms of knowing what may be feasible, what questions to ask, how to avoid toes and brick-dropping rather than how-to-actually-do. Obviously, the simplest means of obtaining biochemical analytical data is to make arrangements for the analyses to be carried out in a clinical biochemistry laboratory. If the samples and assays are ones normally dealt with by the laboratory, this solution is eminently practicable. However, circumstances may militate against this approach. Many hospital laboratories may find it difficult to fit any substantial commitment into an existing busy schedule, but this may be circumvented by careful organization of sampling times.

More fundamental are the problems incurred by the use of 'non-standard' body fluids. Most clinical biochemistry laboratories are highly automated and designed to produce the greatest analytical capacity in terms of numbers rather than variety. This imposes a certain rigidity which is quite acceptable to the laboratory dealing almost exclusively with blood samples, but to obtain the most effective operational range the equipment is calibrated to cover the spectrum of values encountered in blood, and this, for example, would mean that the system would not be easily adapted to *sweat* or *salivary* electrolytes as the sodium and potassium levels in these fluids are fundamentally different from those in *blood*. It is of great importance in this respect to realize the limitations of the service that a routine clinical biochemistry laboratory is usually able to offer, and a great deal of time and trouble can be saved by seeking the advice of those operating the laboratory.

A second level of need we envisage is that of psychophysiologists who require a relatively sophisticated analysis, say of plasma cortisol or urinary adrenaline. For those who have some expertise and facilities available we offer a few guidelines, and for those who need to use commercial laboratories we have included some information about sample collection, preservation, etc.

If it proves impossible to have the analyses performed in the laboratories available through the health services, it may be worth considering the possibility of having assays performed commercially: the number of laboratories offerring such services may be limited and problems of sample transport may make such an approach untenable, but if no viable alternative is available, it certainly bears consideration.

If it proves impossible to arrange facilities for assays in specialist laboratories, it may be worth considering carrying out the work yourself, so thirdly we envisage the need for relatively simple procedures for an academic department of psychology. For example, a postgraduate student may yearn to look at fatty acids and 'social stress', or to follow Bradley and Cox (1978) in examining blood glucose and diabetics' life-events: here we write in terms of guidance for the supervisor or technical staff toward decisions about feasibility, about essential basic skills, and so on. And at this point the question to be asked is always *can* the established electrophysiological techniques provide equivalent information, is the biochemical journey *really* necessary? While clinical biochemistry is an intricate subject, and such an approach is not to be undertaken lightly, there are areas where techniques have been simplified to cope with such hospital situations as emergency out-of-hours work, or low technology environments where certain analyses can be undertaken with a minimum of expertise. It is therefore possible that the parameters of interest may be ones which can be measured with acceptable accuracy and precision by relatively inexperienced personnel. Care, commonsense, and a little practice may make such a solution practicable. But it must be constantly remembered that the data generated are only as good as the system which generates them, and that there are many pitfalls for the unwary which may invalidate the fruits of a great deal of diligent but underinformed effort.

Obviously there *are* cases like the examination of diabetics' blood glucose response to stress where a *biochemical* method is essential, and we hope, through the chapter, to describe some work and findings in such areas, together with our quick tour round the technology, beginning with the choice of a body fluid and collection procedures.

2 BODY FLUIDS—COLLECTION AND PRESERVATION

2.1 The body fluids

The psychophysiologist will almost certainly limit his attention to a small number of body fluids — blood, urine, sweat, and saliva being the most likely ones. However, a short *general* account of the physiology of body fluids is appropriate at this point: more comprehensive coverage is available in Woodbury (1966), or White, Handler, and Smith (1978).

Body fluids may be divided into two main compartments: the *extracellular* and the *intracellular*, with the cell membrane being the boundary between. The extracellular phase provides, somewhat paradoxically, the 'internal environment' of Claud Bernard. Digressing slightly, it is intriguing to note that the ionic composition of mammalian extracellular fluid (ECF) reflects the composition of seas in the Cambrian

period, when organisms were developing from their previously unicellular
to a multicellular state. Thus the supportive 'sea' of ECF which surrounds
our cells, providing appropriate temperature and nutrient conditions, and
carrying away the waste products of cellular metabolism is appropriately
designated! Strictly, though, it is a subcompartment of the extracellular
space which services the cells: it is the *interstitial fluid*, interposed between
them and the circulating blood, which flows through the tissue interstices.
Lymph is a small part of the interstitial space, and transcapillary fluid
movements provide easy access for most plasma constituents to and from
these two components of ECF. The other major subcompartment of the
ECF is, of course blood plasma — the intravascular compartment. Other
fluids, similar in composition to ECF, are secreted into portions of the
body separated from the main extracellular space by a continuous layer of
epithelial cells, which then modifies the fluid passing through them. These
modified ECFs are called *transcellular* fluids (TCF), and they include
cerebrospinal fluid (CSF) and secretions of sweat and salivary glands. This
modification of TCF assumes interest for us in the context of interpreting
salivary electrolyte values, as discussed in Section 3.3.

The intracellular compartment has a different composition from its
interstitial sea, active transport processes maintaining, for example, a K^+
concentration gradient of some $4/150$ mM between ECF/ICF.

This fact, of course, explains the need to avoid contamination of plasma
or serum samples with ICF when K^+ analyses are undertaken (see Section
3.3).

2.2 Choice of fluid

Given the choice for psychophysiologists of blood, urine, saliva or sweat,
decisions need to be made which take account of individual circumstances:
the following may help to provide some guidelines.

2.2.1 Blood

Blood is probably the first choice, in that values in this fluid most closely
reflect the ongoing metabolic status at the time of collection: see, for
example, the contrast with urine analyses (Section 2.2.2). Blood can be
collected as a venous or capillary sample: the composition of the latter is
similar to that of arterial blood. If a venous sample is collected, this
demands medical facilities, the availability of sterilized syringe and needle,
or commercially available disposable aspirating syringes such as Venules
(Bayer Products) or Vacutainers (Becton, Dickinson and Co.). The most
usual point for collection is from a superficial arm or antecubital vein: after
cleansing of the surface with alcohol, drying of the area, and application of

a tourniquet above the selected site, samples can usually be collected with relative ease. These are then *gently* (to avoid damage of cells and hence dispersal of ICF into ECF) transferred from syringe to suitably prepared container, or retained in the disposable aspirating syringe suitably closed to prevent loss or contamination of contents. Containers or disposable syringes contain *anticoagulant* if *plasma* samples are needed: after *gentle* mixing with anticoagulant the sample will not clot, but can be spun in a centrifuge to precipitate the cells and allow removal of the supernatant fluid. The choice of anticoagulant depends to some extent on the analysis being undertaken. In some cases, however, it is preferable to have *serum* samples: in this case no anticoagulant is added, the blood is allowed to clot, and after centrifuge treatment the supernatant serum is removed. The clotting process takes some 15 minutes, but for plasma or serum it is preferable to remove ECF from the cells, or the clot, at the earliest convenient moment.

The choice between plasma, serum, and whole blood, must be made with reference to the specific analyses required, but general guidelines are possible. If the substance is evenly distributed between cells and plasma then any of the fluids can be used, and whole blood may be the most convenient, particularly if samples are small: glucose can be estimated in whole blood samples. Since it is sometimes important to avoid haemolysis (e.g. for K^+ analyses), and the use of anticoagulant may increase the risk of this, serum should be chosen in such cases. If, however, immediate separation of fluid from blood cells is essential (e.g. for catecholamines) then plasma must be used.

Plasma and serum may then normally be stored in refrigerator or freezer until analysed: the length of storage time depends on the constituent being analysed, as does the container being used (Wilding, Zilva, and Wilde, 1977). One would, for example, beware of certain grades of soft glass containers particularly for the study of inorganic ions, lest these ions be leached from glass containers and contaminate the sample. Blood samples, however, may present problems for the psychophysiologist beyond that of needing medical facilities for collection. The process itself, the appearance of the syringe and needle, even anticipation of the effect, may be a potent psychological stressor for subjects, and if the neuroendocrine response to the perception of threat, which might involve a range of indices seen in Figure 8.1, affects the blood constituent to be analysed, unwanted variance is added to the data. An alternative is the use of an intravenous catheter which, if coagulation in its sampling apparatus can be prevented, allows the drawing off of a sample at a point in time relatively remote from the insertion of the needle and catheter, without the subject's conscious knowledge.

An alternative is to choose *capillary* rather than venous blood, and this has the advantage of being easily collected by the psychophysiologist in any setting. This can be obtained from thumb or finger, from the ball or the nail bed, using a disposable sterile needle or 'lancet'. Again, a small tourniquet of narrow rubber tubing or some similar material, can be briefly wound round the base of the digit. Prior to this, gentle arm swinging, shaking of the hand, or immersion of the digit in warm water, especially in cold weather, often facilitates flow, and after a little practice as much as 1.0 ml may be collected. Any squeezing of the digit to 'milk out' more blood must be avoided, though, as this may alter the concentrations of some constituents, due to contamination with ECF. Samples may then be used as whole blood, for example in analysis of blood glucose values (Section 3.2), or if large enough, collected into a suitable tube, to allow clotting, or to be added to anticoagulant for the preparation of plasma. There is increasing use of *small* samples for analysis, and sources such as Wootton (1974) give details: an alternative source of information may be the literature of paediatric medicine, where capillary samples, collected from the heel, are the rule rather than the exception; though many current methods used routinely require relatively small amounts of blood. Much of the newer types of sophisticated biochemical equipment such as centrifugal analysers require as little as 5–10 μl of plasma.

There are, however, some disadvantages to blood for the study of certain parameters when extra precautions required may render the procedure impractical. For example, many hormones have a half-life which can be measured in seconds, and fluctuations can be so fast that the picture supplied by a single sample, or samples taken at intervals of several hours, could be highly variable depending upon the point(s) in the sequence of secretion–action–catabolism (Granström, 1978) at which the sample was taken.

Furthermore, blood itself is not a homogeneous medium and consists of distinct components which are metabolically quite clearly defined. The level of a substance or even its presence may differ between the plasma, erythrocytes, white cells, and platelets, all of which may have particular applications as specific entities. While plasma remains the most widely useful of the blood fractions, some substances are better studied in the cellular elements of blood, e.g. catecholamine 0-methyltransferase is present in erythrocytes but not in plasma (Guldberg and Marsden, 1975), while 5-hydroxytryptamine tends to be concentrated in platelets (Coppen and coworkers, 1976).

An alternative approach is to examine either the substance or its appropriate metabolites in the urine. As urine is essentially a selective ultrafiltrate of plasma it bears a relationship to plasma which will in many instances reflect changes occurring in the peripheral circulation.

2.2.2 Urine

An initial response to this alternative body fluid may well be that of qualified enthusiasm: relatively large volumes are apparently made available with little effort, there is no need for medical aid in sample collection, and no risk of hypodermic phobia and its autonomic correlates! However, there *are* problems associated with urine chemistry, both psychological and technological. There is, indeed no risk of anxiety about the hypodermic and venipuncture, but there may be much more subtle psychological stress associated with requests to produce urine samples, within the non-medical, non-clinical environment of academic psychology, and especially so when the departments' toilet facilities are less than adequate! Indeed, some subjects with normally functioning urinary systems and normal urine *production* may be physically unable to *void* a sample if the experimental environment does appear to be stressful. One must also give some thought to the timing of sample collection, and one's analytical requirements. For some analyses a 24-hour sample is necessary; but anyone who has (as for example a student living in college accommodation) attempted to collect and store *all* samples passed through one circadian cycle knows how difficult *that* can be. A single early morning sample may sometimes suffice, or samples collected at specified points throughout a testing session. The Scandinavian work with urinary catecholamines uses this last named technique, and apparently with considerable success—given suitably timed glasses of water, and periods between samples of around an hour. Naturally organic dysfunction of the filtration system will invalidate the normal relationship, and where urine is used as the medium of choice, the functional integrity of the kidneys may first need to be ensured. Questioning about any atypically frequent micturition may be sufficient, but if these should be required, descriptions of the standard tests of renal function are available in sources such as Varley, Gowenlock, and Bell (1979). Having collected one's sample, though, there is still a need for preservation and for storage. It may be that a proportion can be taken for chilling or freezing, but as in the case of blood, the preservation and storage must be selected with reference to the analysis subsequently to be undertaken. The analysis may be that of a constituent circulating in blood, varying quantities of which are excreted in the urine. Or again a metabolite or degradation product may be estimated, the value of which gives some insight into the original blood value, but interpretation of this is not always straightforward. In many cases the urinary levels are higher than those in blood and many of the urinary metabolites are more stable than the original substance in blood.

Some knowledge of the metabolic derivation of urinary metabolites is essential, because more than one substance in blood may be metabolized to the same end product, e.g. adrenaline and noradrenaline to vanillylmandelic acid, and urine will contain metabolites derived from the brain as well as the periphery.

Interpretation of results from the next body fluid to be considered, namely saliva, is also far from simple, largely because of its transcellular nature, with active secretion being followed by selective reabsorption during subsequent passage along a ductal area, where there is a rate-limited process, and hence some relations between flow rate and subsequent concentrations.

2.2.3 Saliva

Saliva can prove a useful medium for certain applications. Inorganic constituents such as sodium, potassium, calcium, and chloride are readily measurable in saliva as are a variety of proteins, aminoacids and carbohydrates (see Documenta Geigy). It would also appear that the hormonal content of saliva may make it a suitable medium for the study of hormones such as cortisol and sex hormones (Landman, Sandford, and Howland, 1976; Gombe, 1977; Rybakona, 1978).

Bovard, in 1959, suggested that saliva might be a useful body fluid for psychologists interested in stress, and particularly in its neuroendocrine correlates, and associated electrolyte shifts. Since then, however, the literature has reported problems of interpretation (Mason, Harden, and Alexander, 1966; Morris, 1963), and one foremost worker in the field argues for abandoning saliva as a medium for electrolyte investigations (Shannon, Katz, and Beering, 1967). These interpretive problems, however, must be viewed in the context of the relevant experimental setting: if this is a clinical one where alternative body fluids are easily obtained and analysed, then there is perhaps, a weaker case for using saliva. The fluid has, however, proved its usefulness in less sophisticated surroundings: it was adopted by Williams (1961, 1966) for his studies of climbers at altitude, Brown (1966) commented on space medicine's rediscovery of salivary chemistry, Fowles and Venables (1970) used it within psychophysiology, De Marchi (1976) used salivary analysis as part of his extensive investigation of menstrual cycle phenomena; Venables and Christie (1974) examined it in a study of working day state, and ongoing studies by T. Cox (1978, private communication) and coworkers are investigating saliva within the context of industrial and laboratory stressors. Thus Bovard's claim that '. . . (it) can be conveniently obtained and the chemical analysis required is not too complicated for the psychologist . . .' deserves support. Even here, however, there are warnings that collection procedures are potentially stressful (Wenger, 1966): Wenger's 'spitting procedure' however can be replaced by the Lashley disk, which Terry and Shannon (1964) claim is a wholly stress-free method. This was used by Fowles and Venables (1968, 1970) in their examination of salivary electrolytes and relations between these, neuroticism, and electrodermal phenomena. A third method used by Venables and Christie (1974) is that of absorption on to weighed dental rolls, during a timed collection period, followed by reweighing and calculation of flow rate. (Salivary flow rate and electrolyte data relating to this method are available in Christie (1970).) Placement of such dental rolls should be determined by considerations of salivary physiology, as, for example, detailed in the American Physiological Society handbook (Code, 1967). Saliva is produced by several minor sources and the three major pairs of parotid, submaxillary, and submandibular glands. The first two pairs of glands come into Thayssen's (1960) category of 'group 1' exocrine glands: in these, which include eccrine sweat as well as submaxillary and parotid glands, the concentration of Na^+ varies with the secretion rate, and is always less than the concentration in plasma. K^+ concentration is apparently independent of wide ranges in variation of secretion rate, but shows a definite rise at very low rates of secretion. The extent to which concentration/flow relations exist varies with the constituent being examined, and this factor must be taken into account when studies are planned.

In general it can be said that secretions from the salivary glands vary in composition, the relative contribution to a 'mixed saliva' varies with experimental conditions (position of subject, etc.), the composition varies with flow, and this varies with the intensity of stimulation.

Jenkins (1978) comments that it is '. . . difficult to collect under physiological conditions . . .' that is, the method of collection is a form of stimulation which may determine the nature of the sample acquired — a phenomenon not unknown within psychology! Samples can be designated as 'resting' or 'stimulated': examples of the latter include Williams (1966, 1961) using paraffin wax, Shannon (1958) opting for rubber bands and Fowles and Venables (1968) choosing gustatory stimulation. 'Resting' saliva is, however, not strictly a 'non-stimulated' sample: secretion is apparently continuous in the waking state and is stimulated by movements of the jaw, psychic stimuli, etc. Thus while all secretion is 'stimulated' it is useful to consider the continuous flow taking place in the absence of any obvious stimulation as a 'resting' secretion, as defined by Burgen (1967).

'The subject is . . . awake and comfortably seated in a temperate environment, without talking, smoking, or undue movement. The stomach is essentially empty, but before there are sensations of hunger. The saliva is collected by a method which is not particularly stimulating.'

Burgen (1967) also notes that while there is enormous between-subject variability in the volume of resting flow there is, given standardized conditions, very little within-subject variability. He cites earlier interest in 'fast' and 'slow' secretors and adds the fact that these intersubject differences tend to disappear when glands are stimulated. His tentative explanation is that there may be differences in excitability in some link of the salivary reflex chain, or in the level of continuous stimulation to the receptors. Wenger (1966, 1972) of course, used salivary flow as one of his indices of autonomic balance, hence his comment on the putative stress of his 'spitting procedure', and the relevance of salivary innervation: sympathetic stimulation is associated with lower flow rates and parasympathetic influences with faster flow, especially in the parotid glands.

Lastly, as for any psychophysiological index one endeavours to control the variability of subjects' activities *before* they appear on the laboratory horizon for a testing session, so one must attempt to control conditions in the mouth. Food particles may be removed by having subjects rinse thoroughly with the jet from a polythene wash bottle; alternatively subjects may be asked to chew gum for some 30 minutes prior to their test session.

A dental roll can then be placed in the mouth at the chosen collection point, e.g. over Stenson's duct for a fluid of largely parotid origin, or below the tongue for a mixed sample. Unused dental rolls, taken from the supplier's package, should be processed through the elution procedure before any are used for sample collection. If the solution resulting from this procedure, when assessed with the flame photometer, has measurable amounts of Na^+ or K^+, all dental rolls from that package should be carefully washed with deionized water and dried in air (see Christie, 1970). Bilateral collection (De Marchi, 1976) may be chosen for some specific needs, but care should be taken that subjects are not then distressed by too much reduction of salivary flow and of its lubrication.

The collection procedure for saliva has been *briefly* outlined in Venables and Christie (1974): *detailed* description of a similar procedure is available in Bell, Christie, and Venables (1975). In the latter case the material is palmar surface film collected on to a suitable filter paper, but the principle is identical with the dental roll method for saliva.

As for blood samples, the final stage of collection/extraction is the centrifuge, or filtration. After this the supernatant can be removed and stored by chilling or freezing.

As has become apparent, much of the description offered has been related to salivary *electrolytes*, but there are various other constituents of saliva which have been analysed in this fluid, as an alternative to blood examination. Much of this work was published in the 1960s, during the expansion of space medicine and the interest in salivary analysis which Brown (1966) described. Some further discussion of electrolytes is included in the brief accounts of psychophysiological work with simple analytical methods, offered in Section 3: the present section concludes with a brief look at sweat as a body fluid for possible analysis.

2.2.4. Sweat

The eccrine sweat gland is, as we have noted, another type 1 gland (Thayssen, 1960) and therefore a focus of interest for electrodermatologists. In this context Fowles and Venables (1968, 1970) use salivary analysis in order to give some insights into sweat gland status, and in this context also Christie (1970), for palmar fluid collection, devised the method reported in Bell, Christie, and Venables (1975). In the latter case, however, the emphasis was on the electrolyte content of palmar surface film collected when sweat glands are inactive, in order to get some insight into epidermal Na^+ and K^+ concentrations (Christie and Venables, 1971a). In the clinical context, sweat electrolytes have been examined as a screening procedure for cystic fibrosis (Toivonen, 1967; Tarnoky, 1958); again samples are collected onto and eluted from suitable materials such as gauze or filter paper. Little use is made of sweat analysis, though it offers possibilities for examining drug excretion etc., and the general procedure for collection, described in Bell, Christie, and Venables (1975) is simple and non-invasive. Variables such as age, season, site of collection, and diet can all affect sodium and potassium levels, so again it is essential to have a detailed background knowledge of the physiological and environmental variables (see Christie and Venables, 1971a, 1971b) which can affect concentrations when considering the applicability of sweat as a medium for study.

3 SIMPLE METHODS

Compared to other branches of chemical analysis photometric measurement has the advantages of providing sensitivity, specificity, precision, and speed without the need for expensive sophisticated equipment.

Two simple techniques described below are *absorptiometry* and *emission flame photometry*: the range of complex methodology available is described in Section 4, but the present section is aimed at the psychophysiologist who may wish, with the most simple methods available, to do his own analysis in a relatively sparsely equipped situation.

3.1 Photoelectric absorptiometry

Substances for analysis may themselves be coloured, may form coloured derivatives, or be made to yield coloured material after a chemical reaction. The measurement of concentrations of such coloured materials forms the basis of *colorimetric analysis*.

Photoelectric absorptiometry involves the use of photoelectric equipment by means of which the concentration of a coloured solution is estimated by measurement of its *optical density* or *absorbance*, that is the amount of given light of a specific wavelength that it will absorb. This process involves the passage of relatively monochromatic light of appropriate wavelength through the coloured solution and subsequent measurement of transmitted light falling on a photocell. Comparison with a standard solution of known concentration allows calculation of the concentration in the test solution, after subtraction of the absorbance associated with the reagent blank. This reagent blank contains all the reagents but none of the substance under analysis, and allows compensation for background colour which may be introduced by, for example, the colour of the reagent.

The appropriate wavelength is usually that of the light most strongly absorbed by the coloured solution. This light may be provided by inserting a filter, usually of a colour complementary to the solution, between a white light source and the cuvette which contains the test, standard or blank solutions. Alternatively, in the more sophisticated instruments known as spectrophotometers, which isolate much narrower wavelength bands, the wavelength at which maximum absorption takes place is experimentally determined to provide greater specificity and sensitivity. These more sophisticated instruments such as grating spectrophotometers, glass or quartz prism spectrophotometers are not considered further: reference to relevant chapters in Varley, Gowenlock, and Bell (1979), Henry, Cannon, and Winkelman (1974) will provide detail and description, if this is required. A simple single-cell photoelectric colorimeter will be described in more detail here: equipment such as this is suitable for a range of analyses, and while extra precision is offered by the more complex apparatus, human error often controls the limits of accuracy. And it is here that the psychophysiologist can reduce the human error factor: there is probably a single operator analysing all samples, there will be fewer of these than are handled in a routine pathology laboratory, and there may well be considerably more time available for the processes of analysis. For these reasons, then, the psychophysiologist, working with relatively simple equipment, may well be able to produce a degree of precision approaching that of the laboratory working with much more sophisticated instruments.

3.1.1. The single-cell photoelectric colorimeter

Several good commercial models are available, such as those marketed by Corning, Perkin Elmer, Gallenkamp and Co., Fisons, or Pye Unican.

They all have the basic components of:

1 Light source → 2 Wavelength selector → 3 Cuvette →
4 Photoelectric detection system

(1.) The light source is usually a tungsten filament or quartz halogen lamp supplied by a battery or constant-voltage transformer, to maintain a steady light output.

(2.) Filters may be of dyed gelatine or glass: examples of the latter are the Chance red, green or blue filters, and the former include Ilford gelatine filters, which offer a greater range of wavelengths.

(3.) Cuvettes may be square optical cells or round test tubes. Care should be taken in the selection of tubes: they should be matched for equal light transmission, be free from blemishes, and marked to indicate the positioning in the instrument.

(4.) A selenium photocell generates current proportional to the light intensity reaching it; the cell activates a galvanometer, the scale of which is graduated in units of transmission or of optical density, and which can be adjusted to read zero with the blank cuvette in place.

While there are many basic spectrophotometers available, there is now a number of spectrophotometric systems available from manufacturers such as Vitatron and Beckman, which used in conjunction with manufacturers' kits of reagents provide standardized and automated means of assaying a wide variety of substances which would otherwise be beyond the technical capabilities of personnel not trained in clinical biochemistry. Operational training in the use of the equipment is obviously required, but high order analytical skills are not. Such instrumentation is necessarily expensive, but financial considerations aside its availability brings assays which would be otherwise out of the question within the realms of possibility.

3.1.2 Fluorimetry

(The following section has relevance for the material of Section 4, but is more appropriately included at this point.) Where colorimetric analysis relies on the ability of molecules to absorb light of a certain wavelength, fluorimetry uses the ability of some molecules to absorb light of one wavelength and re-emit light of a different wavelength. In effect colorimetry measures the decrease in incident light impinging upon a coloured solution whereas fluorimetry uses the incident light only as a source of excitation, and measures the light emitted, usually at right angles to the incident beam, by excited electrons returning to the unexcited ground state.

Since the incident beam is a source of excitation, increase in its intensity increases the light intensity emitted, so fluorescence techniques can be many times more sensitive than spectrophotometric or colorimetric techniques. Measurement of substances which can be made to fluoresce—such as catecholamines—can therefore be accomplished at the levels found in body fluids which may be much lower than that required for colorimetric determination.

With the advantages of high sensitivity come certain limitations. When measuring very low concentrations proportionately greater care needs to be taken to avoid contamination. Additionally fluorescence is sensitive to changes in solvent, pH, temperature, and the presence of ions, which can in certain cases 'quench' the fluorescence—that is reduce the light emitted from the solution. Details of the theory and technique of fluorescence measurement can be found in Udenfriend (1969) and White and Argauer (1970).

Basic layout for a simple fluorimeter consists of a source (usually a mercury or zinc lamp capable of emitting short wavelengths), a primary filter to separate the excitation wavelength, the sample cuvette, then at right angles to the incident beam a secondary filter to select the emitted wavelength (which is always longer than the excitation wavelength), a photosensor, and a display meter.

There are many models on the market of varying levels of sophistication from companies such as Aminco, Perkin-Elmer, etc.

3.2 Emission flame photometry

Earlier methods for estimation of materials such as Na^+, K^+, calcium, etc., involved complex and time-consuming precipitation procedures and colorimetry, but the 1950s saw development of emission flame photometry, which greatly simplified the analytical process. By the 1970s there was gathered together the array of sophisticated instrumentation for atomic emission, atomic absorption, and atomic fluorescence flame photometry described in sources such as Henry, Cannon, and Winkelman, (1974). These, however, need not concern us here: as in the case of the photoelectric absorptiometry, described in the preceding section, psychophysiologists may well find the simple limited-purpose flame photometer such as models produced by Corning and Instrumentation Laboratory, designed specifically for determining Na^+ and K^+ in body fluids, perfectly adequate, given time and care in processing. Additional care is indeed needed for Na^+ and K^+ processing, and especially so if relatively small or *semi-micro* amounts are present in the test sample: an outline of necessary precautions is therefore added, as Section 3.2.1. Returning to our simple instrument, the basic components are:

1 Solution → 2 Nebulizer → 3 Flame →
4 Wavelength selector → 5 Photoelectric sensor

(1) The solution *must* be wholly free of small particles as these are perhaps the commonest source of error in that they block the source of supply to (2), and so lead to abnormally low readings. The solution is drawn into the nebulizer and converted into a fine spray by passing bottled or compressor-produced air through an atomizer, then passed into a steady flame in which the solvent evaporates and the Na^+ or K^+ form neutral atoms. Atoms introduced into a flame become excited and energized by the heat resulting in electron transfer from the normal ground state to a higher unstable energy level. As this reaction decays and the electron returns to its stable ground state, it emits the excess energy as a photon, thus converting that heat energy to light energy. As the spectral patterns of the light energy emitted are highly characteristic of the ion involved, the most selective wavelengths emitted can be isolated, and their intensity, which is proportional to the concentration of that atomic species in the flame, measured as with the spectrophotometer by a photoelectric sensor whose output is displayed on a suitable meter. Again, suitable standard and blank solutions are prepared, and either a direct readout or a simple calculation then provides details of the sample's Na^+ or K^+ content. With simple instruments such as the Corning, it is possible to obtain perfectly acceptable levels of precision; indeed the recent work of Christie and Venables (1971a), of Bell, Christie, and Venables (1975), of De Marchi (1976) and of Cox and coworkers (1978) has all been undertaken with simple instruments such as this. There is, however, as we noted earlier, a need for care during analysis of Na^+ or K^+ in order to avoid random contamination, as detailed below, and for a background knowledge of the basic construction and operation of the instrument, otherwise unnoticed errors can occur to invalidate the results. Electrical equipment can suffer from drift, i.e. the recorded output can gradually increase or decrease despite a constant signal emanating from the sample source. Mechanical pumps can vary in their output and nebulizer orifices can suffer partial occlusion, especially from proteinaceous fluids. These types of possible fault make it essential to adopt adequate quality control procedures, that is the frequent aspiration of a precalibrated control serum as a secondary standard to ensure consistency of operation during an analytical run. Even with a perfect analytical system, the data generated will only reflect the level in the plasma sample, which is not necessarily the same as that of the subject's plasma levels *in vivo*.

3.2.1 Necessary precautions

These have been reviewed by Thiers (1957), and may be of increased importance in the psychophysiological setting where, as we have noted, the aim is to distinguish between variation within the normal range, in contrast to the clinician's interest in detection of frank abnormality.

First, we can again repeat the warning that ICF K^+ concentrations are considerably greater than those of ECF, hence any cell contents (e.g. from haemolysis of red blood cells) will markedly increase recorded ECF values, whether in plasma or saliva.

Next, unsuitable glassware should be avoided whenever possible, and only high quality borosilicate glass or synthetic material such as polythene used.

All water used for preparation of solutions or rinsing of containers, pipettes, etc. must be deionized or glass distilled: tap water introduces disaster!

Airborne contamination, e.g. from smokers, is another hazard, and a 'low level analysis area', quite separate from the general laboratory area, is a real investment. Furthermore, here one can ensure that procedures such as the preparation of electrode electrolyte are totally divorced from the operations of cation analysis: the former is quite incompatible with the latter!

Plastic forceps rather than (sweaty) fingers should be used for handling material and in general one needs to think ahead and remain aware of the many sources there are which can contaminate one's precious samples. Finally the *in vivo* effects of any drugs, and their in vitro effects on analytical procedures should always be ascertained and borne in mind if their administration is unavoidable (Young, Pestanen, and Gibberman, 1975).

3.3 Blood glucose in psychophysiology

Contemporary work in psychophysiology largely ignores blood glucose as a significant parameter, and yet the fact that neurones are unable to store carbohydrate, and are crucially dependent on an adequate supply of glucose in the blood, argues for some interest to be focused in this direction. Gellhorn and Loofbourrow (1963) did, of course, examine blood glucose in neurotic and psychotic patients, invoking in explanation of their findings their notions of sympathetico-adrenal and vago-insulin balance. Phaeler and Roessler (1965) examined glucose tolerance in subjects having high and low ego-strength (Es) scores, as measured by the Minnesota Multiphasic Personality Inventory (MMPI), and more recently Cox and coworkers (1978) have investigated human performance efficiency in relation to blood glucose level and ambient noise, while Bradley and Cox (1978) have explored relations, in diabetic subjects, between their life-events and blood glucose control.

Lastly, Christie and McBrearty (1979) have measured blood glucose changes after lunch, in relation to post prandial mood and efficiency, but these all represent a mere handful of studies. Perhaps one barrier to further work appears to be that of blood sample collection: yet adequate analyses are possible with capillary samples as small as 0.05 ml: Bradley and Cox (1978) and Cox and coworkers (1978) used these volumes, together with a Boehringer kit for blood glucose analysis (see Section 4.11).

The method involves adding a drop of capillary blood to a commercially prepared test strip, containing an enzyme capable of converting glucose to a blue coloured deviate. The intensity of the blue is determined by means of a simple instrument, and comparison made with the blue colour produced by a standard glucose solution.

The normal homeostatic processes serving to maintain acceptable values of blood glucose (Bloom, 1978) may be overridden by the neuroendocrine response in stress, as will be noted from Figure 8.1. This phenomenon provides the basis of the work of Cox (1978) and of Bradley and Cox (1978). In contrast the work of Christie and McBrearty (1979) aims to examine the effects of processes taking place in the absorptive and the post absorptive phases of digestion and metabolism.

3.4 Na^+ and K^+ in psychophysiology

Turning now to psychophysiological work on electrolytes, and specifically to that associated with analysis of body fluid Na^+ and K^+; some of this originated from interest in mechanisms underlying electrodermal activity, in the non-sudorific generation of palmar skin potentials, and particularly in the 'basal' value of skin potential level recorded when palmar eccrine sweat glands are quiescent (Christie and Venables, 1971a, 1971b, 1971c, 1971d; Christie, 1976). In order to assess the value of epidermal Na^+ and K^+ concentrations the method reported in Bell, Christie, and Venables (1975) was devised for collection and analysis of palmar epidermal surface film. This method was used by Bell (1973) for examination of menstrual cycle variation in epidermal K^+, and his mean values were remarkably close to those reported from a different laboratory by Christie and Venables (1971a) (see Table 8.1).

Salivary electrolytes were also examined by Christie (1970) and by Fowles and Venables (1968, 1970) in order to throw some light on electrolyte factors in SPL (see Chapter 1). Fowles and Venables (1968, 1970) have argued that in activated conditions of the palmar eccrine sweat gland the active transport of sodium across the sweat duct wall is associated with an increase in the negativity of recorded SPL. As this was thought to be under the control of aldosterone, a reflection of its activity would be seen in *salivary* Na/K ratios, as was reported by Fowles and Venables (1968, 1970). These workers incidentally used a Lashley disk collection method, with gustatory stimulation of parotid flow, and an

Table 8.1. Palmar surface film: normative data

No. of subjects	Time of day	Season	Mean palmar surface film (mg/h)	Mean (K⁺) (mEq/l)	Mean Na/K	No. of subjects	Phase of cycle	Mean (K⁺) (mEq/l)	Mean palmar surface film (mg/h)	Mean NA/K
			Male subjects					Female subjects		
14	noon	summer (hot)	42.3	16.20	2.43		follicular	15.28		
	evening	summer (cool)	43.5	16.70	2.42	8	luteal	22.31		
20	noon	summer (cool)	53.9	18.97	1.96					
20	noon	winter (cool)	50.35	20.80	1.76		menstrual	18.98		
Grand means:			47.51	18.17	2.14			18.83	47.32	2.15

The figures given in this table were compiled from data given in Bell (1973), Bell, Christie, and Venables (1975), Christie (1970) and Christie and Venables (1971a).

alternative to flame photometry for analysis: they worked with cation-sensitive electrodes, which are not considered here.

De Marchi used salivary analysis in his examination of menstrual cycle phenomena: his work, apart from one paper (De Marchi, 1976), included a comprehensive examination of EEG, EDA, cardiovascular phenomena, temperature, blood glucose, mood, and personality; it is still being prepared for publication and unfortunately not available for inclusion in this chapter. The salivary data show a marked increase in K^+ values at ovulation, Bell, Christie, and Venables (1975) report evidence of increases in palmar K^+ values at ovulation, and Bell, Christie, and Venables (1975) report evidence of increases in palmar K^+ during the luteal phase. Bell also reported an increase in euphoric mood at this stage of the cycle, which matches rather nicely some data of Venables and Christie (1974). These workers examined psychophysiological state, mood, and personality on Fridays and Mondays. One significant finding was that in the subject group whose neuroticism scores were significantly reduced on Mondays there was evidence from indices of K^+ status of increases in ECF K^+. One might then suggest that the above work, the Bell studies and the De Marchi findings indicate a need for further examination of relations between ECF K^+ and mood: the need for further examination by psychologists of the potassium ion, and its control has been argued by Christie (1975). Given its role in determining *tissue* excitability, it *may* be that behavioural excitability is in some way determined by cation status. There is of course, the additional argument from 'psychocardiology' and Raab (1971) for further study of K^+, given its role in cardiac function and the apparently therapeutic effects of K^+ salt administration.

One final observation is that while Na^+ and its associated water movements are now increasingly well documented (e.g. Fitzsimons 1972) there does seem to be a relative dearth of information about K^+ metabolism. Yet in much of the work described above, and in preliminary reports from the Cox group (1978) there is apparently more useful information for behavioural science in salivary than in the Na^+ ion, although urinary Na^+ analyses seem to provide useful data.

4 COMPLEX METHODS

From Figure 8.1 it is apparent that a range of biochemical indices may have relevance for the psychophysiologist. There is, however, need to limit the discussion, for the purposes of the present chapter, and this we have done by focusing on what appears to be a growing point of contemporary psychophysiology. This growth is associated with examination of 'stress' and of individual differences in response to stressors: it is in relation to these topics that psychophysiologists are asking about the feasibility of biochemical methods, and particularly about analysis of catecholamines and adrenal cortical steroids. Catecholamine analysis is, for example, relevant for the 'classic' psychophysiological question of stimulus-response-specificity and the anger/noradrenaline hypothesis (Ax, 1953); Funkenstein and Meade, 1954). This suggestion that 'anger-out', aggressive states are accompanied by a relative increase in concentrations of circulating noradrenaline has obvious relevance for psychophysiologists concerned with the behavioural aspects of cardiovascular disorder (Raab, 1971; Jenkins, 1978; Krantz, 1978) and the significance of aggressive state in the type A behaviour of coronary disease prone individuals.

The analysis of catecholamines is, however, not a simple procedure, and we have attempted in the following pages, to introduce the reader to some of the difficulties, problems, and pitfalls associated with this procedure.

4.1 Adrenaline and noradrenaline

Adrenaline and noradrenaline (or epinephrine and norepinephrine) are two catecholamines: a third is dopamine, but while this may have relevance for central nervous system transmission, and may have an active function in the lungs, intestine, and liver, it is not considered further in the present chapter. A catecholamine is an organic compound which has a *catechol* nucleus and an *amine* group—hence its name.

Most of the adrenaline in circulation originates from the adrenal medulla, while the main source of noradrenaline is sympathetic nerve endings. Circulating catecholamines are taken up by tissues to be stored or degraded, or are excreted in the urine. They disappear rapidly after an injection, with less than 5 per cent of the amount administered being excreted in the urine during the 24 hours following administration. Most of the injected material is excreted as inactive metabolites: the major one is vanillylmandelic acid (VMA), which is normally excreted in amounts up to some 8 mg per 24 hours.

4.1.1 General methodology

General accounts of the methods for catecholamine analysis are available in sources such as Cooper, Bloom, and Roth (1973) and Varley, Gowenlock, and Bell (1976). These sources, however, meet the needs of two different groups: the former write for neuropharmacologists, who are concerned with analysis of minute quantities of transmitter substance, while the latter are relevant to clinical biochemistry and its emphasis on investigation of abnormalities in body fluids. Neither source is wholly appropriate for the *psychophysiology* of body fluids: the methods of the neuropharmacologist may meet a need for even greater sensitivity and precision than our readers require, while the clinical biochemist may be able to tolerate less than is needed for investigation of quantities varying *within* the normal range of values.

Cooper, Bloom, and Roth (1973), however, provide a useful overview of sophisticated techniques, some of which may be available to psychophysiologists working in specialized situations such as national research establishments: these readers may wish to explore the possibilities inherent in bioassay techniques (Vane, 1966; Bell, 1971), gas chromatography (Clarke and coworkers, 1967; Goodwin and coworkers, 1973), radioisotope methods (Engelman and coworkers, 1968; Skelley, Brown, and Besch, 1973), or enzyme multiplied bioassay. It should, however, be emphasized that such techniques are highly specialized and require expert skills, though they do offer greater precision than the fluorimetric procedures described below. These latter procedures *may* be feasible for use by a psychophysiologist who has some basic biochemical skills and access to appropriate equipment and reagents. Such a psychophysiologist may also wish to explore the range of commercially produced kits, available for various analyses including catecholamines. There is a brief description of commercial kits and reagent sets in Henry, Cannon, and Winkelman (1974, pp. 282–286), and the US Department of Health, Education and Welfare (1971) has published a *List of Test Kits for Clinical Laboratories*. In the UK a trade journal *Medical Laboratory World* gives a comprehensive list of equipment which is currently available, and this includes details of kit and reagent sets. The biggest supplier of these is the Boehringer Corporation who market on a world-wide basis: further details are given in the Appendix to this chapter.

Turning to fluorimetric procedures for adrenaline and noradrenaline, Varley, Gowenlock, and Bell (1976) detail three methods which use two basic fluorimetric procedures for *urine* analysis: these are an ethylendiamine method for total urinary catecholamines and a trihydroxyindole method for urinary adrenaline and noradrenaline. Carruthers and coworkers (1970) used a variant of the trihydroxyindole method for *plasma* analysis, and examined potential sources of error in plasma catecholamine analyses. While the choice of plasma rather than urine may well increase the scope of a psychophysiologist's investigations in ways noted in Section 2.2.1 it does increase possible sources of error, ranging from the problems associated with venepuncture to methods of preservation and storage. A brief guide round urine and plasma procedures for catecholamines is therefore offered below.

4.1.2 Urine or plasma?

The choice between these two fluids will ultimately depend on the medical and technical facilities available 'on site', or on the availability of

R

commercial laboratory analyses, and *their* requirements. Any *general* statements made here should, therefore, be checked against any *specific* directions issued by relevant operators.

In general, urine samples contain only a small fraction of unchanged catecholamines released from chromaffine tissue and adrenergic transmission, but do provide the possibility of estimating sympathetic-adrenomedullary activity integrated over the temporal intervals of the 1 to 3 hours required between voiding of samples. Urine samples for catecholamine analysis should be preserved with hydrochloric acid as described by Varley, Gowenlock, and Bell (1976) and processed as soon as possible after being voided. After measurement of the total volume a sample of some 5–20 ml (the size depending on the method being used) is used for testing, with the remaining volume, or another sample of this, being frozen for storage. Transport of frozen samples can be carried out with vacuum containers and frozen carbon dioxide.

Analysis of samples begins with a separation of catecholamines by adsorption (i) on to alumina at pH 8.4 with protection from oxidation using EDTA (see Henry, Cannon, and Winkelman, 1974, p. 380) or (ii) with ion-exchange resins (Udenfriend, 1969; White and Argauer, 1970).

The trihydroxyindole reaction can be used after either of the separation processes, while the ethybenediamine method is suitable only for use after an ion-exchange procedure. After absorption and elution the resulting fluid can be frozen for transfer to an analytical laboratory, or else analysed on the spot. Normal values for urine catecholamines vary to some extent with the method used, and with the time of day for other than 24 hour samples. Data are available from Cox and coworkers (1978) which are in line with those of Campuzano, Wilkerson, and Horvath (1978) and Jenner, Reynolds, and Harrison (1978).

The selection of *plasma* rather than urine does allow detection of *transient* changes in secretion, though there is an increase in the range of one's methodological problems. The fluorimetric methods may be operating at their limits of sensitivity for the relatively small concentrations of catecholamines present in plasma, and for this reason radiochemical procedures such as those introduced by Engelman and coworkers (1968) and Passon and Peuler (1973) may be preferred by analysts. However, with careful attention to detail the fluorimetric methods can produce adequate results, and the review of Carruthers and coworkers (1970) has value at this point. Their examination of sources of error in plasma catecholamine analyses includes consideration of an indwelling venous catheter, and the need for this in relation to their report of significant increases in plasma adrenaline after venepuncture. Carruthers and coworkers (1970) emphasize the need for the shortest possible time to elapse between blood sample collection into a plastic tube containing calcium heparin anticoagulant and freezing, with solid carbon dioxide, of the resultant plasma. In addition to the anticoagulant the sample tube contains an antioxidant such as sodium metabisulphite and plastic separating granules. (An alternative to sodium metabisulphite is an EDTA/glutathione mixture.) Carruthers and coworkers (1970) describe an optimal procedure in which the blood sample is carefully but rapidly mixed, centrifuged for 2 minutes at 5000 rpm, decanted into 6 ml labelled plastic tubes which are frozen by contact with solid carbon dioxide in a vacuum container, then kept in the dark at $-20\,°C$ until analysed. The shortest achievable time between the collection and freezing stages was found to be 3 minutes, and Carruthers and coworkers (1970) examined the effects on plasma catecholamine values of delayed freezing. Ten subjects were examined, and variable lengths of time spent on a bicycle ergometer, before blood collections ensured the production of a range of plasma catecholamine levels. From each subject 60 ml of blood were drawn, and divided between 6 prepared sample tubes. These were immediately centrifuged and the first 10 plasma samples were frozen at 3 minutes after collection: the remaining 5 sets were separated, then samples were stored at 18 °C for 6, 12, 30, 24 or 48 hours after collection, and before being frozen. Plasma catecholamine values dropped rapidly over the first 30 minutes, and decreased further over the next two days. Other sources of error in plasma catecholamine measurements were examined, and the paper provides a useful guide to the area. It can be put alongside Sapira, Klaniecki, and Rizk (1971) who surveyed the range of mean 'normal' values ($0.2 - 2.1$ μ/ι for adrenaline and $0.2 - 6.6$ $\mu g/\iota$ for noradrenaline) which has been reported by various authors, and also alongside McDonald (1972) who pessimistically asks 'Are the data worth owning?' Our own answer would be that with adequate care and attention to detail it *is* possible to measure catecholamines with reasonable precision. Provided that collection and preservation of samples are given adequate consideration it is possible to control or eliminate many variables which might obscure those secretory changes which interest the psychophysiologist, and which are the result of experimentally administered stimuli. One might possibly express this in terms of catecholamine analysis being 50% art as well as 50% science: there are many minor details requiring attention, but a period spent at the side of someone working effectively in this field of analysis will undoubtedly pay dividends! Further, the particular interests of psychophysiologists need to be considered alongside those of the analytical chemist, together with the necessary controls which have to be borne in mind when working with active human subjects.

4.1.3. Necessary controls

A wide range of both external and internal stimuli can cause changes in catecholamine secretion and excretion: the *circadian variation* in release is reflected in blood values at 24.00 hours having the lowest (Cession-Fossion and coworkers, 1967) while mid morning to early afternoon samples have the highest concentrations of catecholamine (Turton and Deegan, 1974). Elmadjian, Hope, and Lamson (1957) reported that *urine* values of noradrenaline were 50% lower at night, while adrenaline concentrations were reduced by 10%. This rhythm appears to be independent of whether nights are spent in sleeping or in activity: Fröberg and coworkers (1970) studied soldiers who underwent a 75 hour period of duty which involved alternating 3 hour shifts and found a significant increase of urinary adrenaline, but this was superimposed on the normal cyclic rhythm.

Catecholamine values are increased by physical exertion: plasma values increased on changing from supine rest to a standing position (Christensen, 1972; Cryer, Santiago, and Shah, 1974). But when physical exertion is an aspect of aggressive sport there appears to be a greater increase in urinary *noradrenaline* (Elmadjian, Hope and Lamson, 1957). Driving in heavy traffic (Taggart, Gibbons, and Somerville, 1969; Taggart and Carruthers, 1971) as well as racing driving produces increases in noradrenaline, while parachute jumps and climbs over wet, slippery rocks result in adrenaline values being raised (Carruthers, 1975). While one's subjects may not necessarily undertake such heroic activities to reach the laboratory, driving through heavy traffic is worth noting as a potential source of increase in noradrenaline values! As is the evidence that tea, coffee, cocoa, cigarette smoking, etc. may result in the production of materials which interfere with the biochemical analysis of catecholamines.

Despite all these problems, however, there is a range of published reports relating to examination of catecholamine variation and psychological state. Sources such as the literature of psychosomatics and ergonomics as well as that of psychophysiology are worth consulting: in the United States the work of Mason and his colleagues (1968, 1972, 1975), together with that of Axelrod (e.g. (1964), and Schildkraut and Kety (1967), is probably familiar to readers. In Scandinavia, Levi and his co-workers (1971, 1972) and Frankenhaeuser and others (1975) are familiar to psychophysiologists, but perhaps less well known to them is the research of Rodahl and his colleagues in Norway (1974, 1977). In England Carruthers, Taggart and coworkers have examined catecholamine correlates of emotional states, while Woodman, Hinton and O'Neill (1977, 1978a, 1978b, 1978c) undertook a series of studies in which catecholamine values were examined in the aggressive offenders of a maximum security hospital. Aggressive personality was also examined by Ekkers (1975) in association with analysis of catecholamine metabolites. Stress studies include those of Cox and his coworkers (1978) and of Jenner and his colleagues (1978).

Studies such as these serve to emphasize the point that the measurement of catecholamines has value for psychophysiology, and that the data may indeed be 'worth owning'!

4.2 The Adrenal Cortex

We have considered in Section 4.1 the adrenal medulla and turn now to the adrenal *cortex*. These two structures arise from embryologically different sources and are anatomically distinct: facts which led to the belief that they were also functionally unrelated. Coupland (1953) however, noted during a comparison of species differences in adrenal gland configuration that in some animals the portion of the medulla adjoining the cortex contained mainly adrenaline, while remoter portions contained only noradrenaline. He concluded that the adrenal cortex had some influence on the synthesis of adrenaline from noradrenaline. This was confirmed by Wurtman and Axelrod (1966) who demonstrated that in hypophysectomized rats, deprived of pituitary gland function, there was reduced activity of the adrenomedullary enzyme phenylethanolamine-N-methyl-transferase (PENMT), which is responsible for catalysing the conversion of noradrenaline to adrenaline. Normal activity of PENMT could be restored by injections of ACTH or a synthetic glucocorticoid: the action of ACTH appeared to be indirect and the controlling factor to be glucocorticoids produced by the cortex.

Evidence of influences on the cortex from the medulla comes from Bernauer and Liebig (1973) who demonstrated that α-adrenergic receptor blockade in guinea pigs resulted in an inhibitory influence on corticosteroid production. Thus there appears to be catecholamine control over adrenal corticosteroid synthesis. In an animal subjected to stress the initial response is in the adrenal medulla: if the intensity of stimulation is low or its duration short there is little cortical involvement. With increased stress, however, increased levels of circulating catecholamines trigger the hypothalamo–pituitary–adrenal axis, resulting in increased release of corticosteroids from the adrenal cortex (Freeman, 1975). Psychophysiologists may, therefore, need to estimate adrenocorticosteroid values as well as catecholamines, and some general pointers are given, to indicate the problems and pitfalls associated with possible techniques. As a preliminary statement it could be said that less expertise is required for analysis in this area, compared with the higher level of skill needed for catecholamine assays. Some basic skills are, however, necessary, and the procedures require attention to details such as precision in timing and absolute cleanliness of equipment. We view the methods to be outlined in Section 4.2 as falling within the category of procedures which need the provision of established facilities, but which could be carried out by a psychophysiologist who has some basic biochemical skills and access to advice.

4.2.1. Adrenocorticosteroids

The adrenal cortex synthesizes a range of steroid hormones, and releases them into the adrenal gland. A steroid has a cyclopentenophenanthrene structure with a carbon atom at every junction point in the ring system, and a standard system for numbering these, as shown below:

Side chains are added at specific locations; the nature of the former and the position of the latter determine the properties of the resultant 'substituted' structure. Corticosterone, for example carries a side chain at

$$-c=o$$
$$|$$
$$CH_2OH$$

the 17 position and is an example of a 17-hydroxy(-OH) corticosteroid, i.e. 17-OHCS. Adrenal corticosteroids can be subdivided into glucocorticoids (the principal one of which is cortisol), mineralocorticoids (principally aldosterone), and androgens. The glucocorticoids and mineralocorticoids both have a total of 21 carbon atoms in the molecule: hence they are classified as C_{21} compounds, while androgens have 19 carbon atoms and are, therefore C_{19} compounds. This classification may be used in relation to discussion of the precision of analytical methods, and for this reason is mentioned briefly here. Nomenclature has, however, greater complexity, and sources such as Cantarow and Trumper (1975) or Harper and coworkers (1977) provide a more comprehensive coverage. The latter provides also in its appendix a general review of basic organic, physical, and general chemistry which may offer useful introduction/revision reading.

4.2.2. Cortisol

The major adrenocorticosteroid circulating in the human blood stream is cortisol, which is a 17-OHCS compound. Around 90% of the cortisol in circulation is bound to a protein, especially to one termed transcortin, but as blood levels of cortisol rise the protein's binding capacity is exceeded and free cortisol may exceed some 25% of the total amount. Only the free hormone can pass through the kidney and into the urine, so amounts of cortisol in this fluid are, in normal unstressed subjects, usually small: but there are some metabolites of C_{21} compounds excreted in urine.

4.2.3. Regulation of cortisol secretion

Factors regulating cortisol secretion, via pituitary ACTH, are the circadian rhythm, the negative feedback system, and the stress mechanisms: the first and last are of   significance for psychophysiologists.

4.2.4. Circadian variation

The circadian rhythm is apparently controlled by an intrinsic biological clock mechanism in the midbrain; this is maintained by pituitary ACTH secretion and mediated by corticotrophin releasing hormone (CRH) from the hypothalamus: circulating levels, in resting subjects, may be between 8–25 μg/100 ml at the beginning of the working day: these values represent the zenith of the circadian rhythm, the nadir being around midnight.

4.2.5. Cortisol in stress

Selye highlighted the role of the hypothalamic–pituitary–adrenocortical 'axis' and adrenal cortical hormones in the survival of animals when exposed to extreme stimuli or 'stressors'. There is a great increase in the secretion of cortisol, regardless of the time of day or operation of the normal feedback control. Thus, estimation of cortisol has become a popular choice in studies of 'stress', even when the stimuli bear little resemblance to the intense challenges of Selye's studies, and may, for example, be the everyday events of life with which one is only too familiar, such as coping with arithmetical computations against a background of distraction (Raab, 1968). Mason (1972) notes that in studies with human subjects there is almost unanimous support for the conclusion that 17-OHCS levels sensitively reflect psychophysiological influences, which argues for our inclusion of cortisol estimation within our brief appraisal of more complex methods.

4.2.6. Blood or urine?

As we have observed in Section 4.2.2 there is only a small proportion of circulating cortisol available unbound, for renal filtration, in normal unstimulated subjects. In stress studies there may well be increases in free cortisol, and hence the possibility of urine analysis if conditions require this. So, for example, a psychophysiologist who lacks the medical facilities for simple venepuncture or intravenous catheter collection of blood samples may consider the possibilities inherent in urine analysis, but in general it could be said that blood analysis is the method of choice in normally equipped analytical laboratories. This will be considered again in subsequent sections, but a brief treatment of urinary techniques is offered here. The 17-OHCS compounds will react with the Porter–Silber reagent to give a yellow colour which can be estimated by a colorimetric procedure. Such compounds include cortisol, cortisone, and their metabolites, so it is not specific for cortisol but would give an index of adrenal cortical activity. The method may still have some popularity in the United States, but in Britain has been largely replaced by the technique of De Moor and coworkers (1960) or of Mattingly and coworkers (1964), which is suitable for either urine or blood estimations and is therefore described briefly below.

The determination is one involving analysis of 11-hydroxycorticosteroids (11-OHCS): cortisol and corticosterone both have a hydroxy (-OH) group at the C-11 position, and there is acceptable specificity of the method. The urine specimen must be cooled immediately after voiding into a chemically clean container, e.g. one treated with nitric acid or cleaning fluid, then well rinsed with tap then with distilled water. If the analysis is not being undertaken immediately after the specimen has been voided, the volume should be measured, and a generous sample frozen. Some 2 ml of the sample will be needed for analysis, so 10–20 ml would be adequate for freezing. Analysis involves extraction of the 11-OHCS compounds with suitable solvents, then treatment with a reagent which produces a fluorescence, which is then estimated at an excitation wavelength of 470 nm and an emission setting between 520–530 nm. All glassware used in analysis must be kept scrupulously clean: contaminants may augment or quench the flurometric reading. Some drugs lead to spuriously high results, as may haemolysis. Oral contraceptive use can increase the concentration of transcortin and hence of cortisol binding capacity.

Normal ranges for healthy subjects are given by Mattingly and coworkers (1964) as 215–1030 nmol/24 h (or 78–372 μg/24 h) for males, with a mean of 630 nmol/24 h (229 μg/24 h). Female values in non-pregnant subjects are 490 nmol/24 h (or 178 μg/24 h).

Similar procedures are required for blood analysis: the sample must be separated as soon as possible after collection, hence plasma must be prepared, with heparin as an anticoagulant, and a careful avoidance of haemolysis. A 10 ml volume is advocated by Varley, Gowenlock, and Bell

(1976) with storage of plasma at 0–4 °C (not in a frozen state) for not more than 72 h. 2 ml of plasma are used for the analytical method described by Varley, Gowenlock, and Bell (1976), but smaller quantities may be suitable for alternative techniques. Careful timing reduces interference fluorescence, and the general procedure is similar to that for urine. Normal values for plasma are from 220–750 nmol/l with a mean of 470 nmol/l (80–270 μg/l, mean 170). While the values are expressed as 'cortisol' this includes a small proportion of corticosterone.

If exploration of commercial facilities is being undertaken it should be remembered that transport of samples to the laboratory will have to be accomplished within a temperature range of 0–4 °C which may preclude postal services. Individual laboratories should be consulted regarding their needs and facilities.

4.2.7. Alternative procedures

Alternative procedures, which some psychophysiologists may possibly have access to, are those of saturation analysis (Murphy, 1967; Baum, Tudor, and Landon, 1974). Here the ability of free cortisol to displace radioactively labelled cortisol from its bound form (to transcortin) is used. The amount of liberated labelled material can then be measured in a gamma counter. If radiochemical facilities *are* available then saturation analysis is the method of choice in that fluorimetry is technically more demanding and more time consuming. However, if such facilities are not available, it is not merely a matter of buying a counter, as special precautions must be taken, even with low energy sources, which require the provision of a separate laboratory area and frequent health screening of staff handling radiochemicals.

4.3. Concluding thoughts

In an attempt at conclusion we return, somewhat paradoxically, to our introduction, where we argued the case for extension of psychophysiologists' interests beyond the polygraph to the biochemical bench. We hope that our heavy emphasis on the problems and pitfalls of more complex methodology has not been too discouraging: we aimed to provide a preliminary guide to a fascinating area, not a series of prohibiting warnings on the threshold of a minefield. The 'simple methods' section will, we trust, encourage any whose journey into those biochemical regions does indeed appear to be a useful and necessary one. We look forward to following the progress of our readers in subsequent issues of 'Psychophysiology'!

492   *Techniques in Psychophysiology*

REFERENCES

Ax, A. (1953). The physiological differentiation between fear and anger in humans. *Psychosom. Med., 5,* 433–42.

Axelrod, J. (1964). In S. Eiduson, E. Geller, A. Yuwiler, and B.T. Eiduson (Eds), *Biochemistry and Behaviour,* Van Nostrand, Princeton NJ.

Baum, C.K., Tudor, R., and Landon, J. (1974). A simple competitive protein binding assay for plasma cortisol. *Clin. Chim. Acta, 55,* 147–54.

Bell, B. (1973). Psychophysiology and the menstrual cycle. *Ph.D. Thesis,* University of Birmingham, unpublished.

Bell, C. (1971). Rat supafused aortic strip for the bioassay of noradrenaline and adrenaline. *Br. J. Pharmacol., 41,* 711–12.

Bell, B., Christie, M.J., and Venables, P.H. (1975). Menstrual cycle variation in body fluid potassium. *J. Interdisciplin. Cycle Res., 6,* 113–20.

Bernauer, W., and Liebig, R. (1973). Plasma corticosteroid levels in anaphylactic shock of guinea pigs. *Res. Exp. Med., 161,* 233–42.

Bloom, A. (1978). The nature of diabetes. *J. R. Soc. Med., 71,* 170–9.

Bovard, E. W. (1959). The effects of social stimuli on the response to stress. *Psychol. Rev., 66,* 267–77.

Bradley, C., and Cox, T. (1978). Stress and health. In T. Cox (Ed.), *Stress,* Macmillan, London.

Brown, C. C. (1966). Psychophysiology at an interface. *Psychophysiology, 3,* 1–7.

Buckingham, J. C. (1977). The endocrine function of the hypothalamus. *J. Pharm. Pharmacol., 29,* 649–56.

Burgen, A. S. V. (1967). Secretory processes in salivary glands. In C. F. Code (Ed.), *Handbook of Physiology: Alimentry Canal,* Williams and Wilkins, Baltimore.

Cantarow, A. and Trumper, M. (1975). *Clinical Biochemistry* (Edited by A.L. Latner), Saunders, Philadelphia.

Carruthers, M. (1975). Biochemical responses to stress in the environment. *Proc. R. Soc. Med., 68,* 429–30.

Carruthers, M., Taggart, P., Conway, N., Bates, D., and Somerville, W. (1970). Validity of plasma catecholamine estimations. *Lancet,* ii, 62–7.

Cession-Fossion, A., Vandermeulen, R., Lefebvre, P., and Legros, J. J. (1967). Variations nycthémérales de la catécholaminémie chez l'homme normal au repos. *Revue Med. Liege, 22,* 285–6.

Christie, M. J. (1970). Temporal aspects of palmar skin potential and related cardiovascular and electrolyte measures. *Ph.D. Thesis,* University of London, unpublished.

Campuzano, H. C., Wilkerson, J. E., and Horvath, S. M. (1978). Fluorometric analysis of epinephrine and norepinephrine. *Analyt. Biochem., 64,* 578–87.

Christensen, N. J. (1972). Plasma catecholamines in long term diabetics with and without neuropathy and in hypophysectomized subjects. *J. Clin. Invest., 51,* 779–87.

Christie, M. J. (1975). The psychosocial environment and precursors of disease. In P. H. Venables and M .J. Christie (Eds), *Research in Psychophysiology,* Wiley, London.

Christie, M. J. (1976). Basal palmar skin potentials and body fluid potassium. *Med. Hypoth., 2,* 227–9.

Christie, M. J., and McBrearty, E. (1979). Psychophysiological investigations of post-lunch state in male and female subjects. *Ergonomics. 22,* 307–23.

Christie, M. J., and Venables, P. H. (1971a). Sodium and potassium electrolytes and 'basal' skin potential levels in male and female subjects. *Japan. J. Physiol.*, **21**, 659–68.

Christie, M. J., and Venables, P. H. (1971b). Basal palmar skin potential and the electrocardiogram T-wave. *Psychophysiology*, **8**, 779–86.

Christie, M. J., and Venables, P. H. (1971c). Effects on 'basal' skin potential level of varying the concentration of an external electrolyte. *J. Psychosom. Res.*, **15**, 343–8.

Christie, M. J., and Venables, P. H. (1971d). Characteristics of palmar skin potential and conductance in relaxed human subjects. *Psychophysiology*, **8**, 525–32.

Clarke, D. D., Wilk, S., Gitlow, S. E., and Franklin, M. J. (1967). Gas chromatographic determination of dopamine at the nanogram level. *J. Gas Chromat.*, **5**, 307–15.

Code, C. F. (Ed.) (1967). *Handbook of Physiology: Alimentary Canal*, Williams and Wilkins, Baltimore.

Cooper, J. R., Bloom, F. E., and Roth, R. H. (1974). *The Biochemical Basis of Neuropharmacology*, Oxford University Press, New York.

Coppen, A., Turner, R., Rowsell, A. R., and Padgham, C. (1976). 5HT in the whole blood of patients with depressive illness. *Postgrad. Med. J.*, **52**, 156–8.

Coupland, R. E. (1953). On the morphology and adrenaline-noradrenaline content of chromaffin tissue. *J. Endocr.*, **9**, 194–203.

Cox, T. (1978). *Stress*, Macmillan, London.

Cryer, P. E., Santiago, J. V., and Shah, S. (1974). Measurement of norepinephrine and epinephrine in small volumes of human plasma by a single isotope derivative method: response to the upright posture. *J. Clin. Endocr. Metab.*, **39**, 1025–29.

De Marchi, G. W. (1976). Psychophysiological aspects of the menstrual cycle. *J. Psychosom. Res.*, **20**, 279–87.

De Moor, P., Steeno, O., Raskin, M., and Hendrikx, A. (1960). Fluorimetric determination of free plasma 11-hydroxycorticosteroids in man. *Acta Endocr.*, **33**, 297–307.

Documenta Geigy Scientific Tables (1975). By K. Diem and C. Lenter (Eds), Geigy Pharmaceuticals.

Dunn, M. J., and Hood, V. L. (1977). Prostaglandins and the kidney. *Am. J. Physiol.*, **2**, 169–84.

Ekkers, C. L. (1975). Catecholamine excretion, conscience function and aggressive behaviour. *Biol. Psychol.*, **3**, 15–30.

Elmadjian, F., Hope, J. M., and Lamson, E. T. (1957). Excretion of epinephrine and norepinephrine in various emotional states. *J. Clin. Endocr.*, **17**, 608–20.

Engelman, K., and Portnoy, B. (1970). A sensitive double isotope derivative assay for norepinephrine and epinephrine. *Circulation Res.*, **26**, 53–7.

Engelman, K., Portnoy, B., and Lovenberg, W. (1968). A sensitive and specific double-isotope derivative method for the determination of catecholamines in biological specimens. *Amer. J. Med. Sci.*, **225**, 259–68.

Fitzsimons, J. T. (1972). Thirst. *Physiol. Rev.*, **52**, 468–561.

Fowles, D. C., and Venables, P. H. (1968). Endocrine factors in palmar skin potential. *Psychonom. Sci.*, **10**, 387–8.

Fowles, D. C., and Venables, P. H. (1970). The effects of epidermal hydration and sodium reabsorption on palmar skin potential level. *Psychol. Bull.*, **73**, 363–78.

Frankenhaeuser, M. (1975). Sympathetic-adrenomedullary activity, behaviour and the psychosocial environment. In P. H. Venables and M .J. Christie (Eds.), *Research in Psychophysiology*, Wiley, London.

494   *Techniques in Psychophysiology*

Freeman, B. M. (1975). Physiological basis of stress. *Proc. R. Soc. Med.,* **68**, 427–9.
Fröberg, J., Karlsson, C. G., Levi, L., Lindberg, L., and Seeman, K. (1970). Conditions of work: psychological and endocrine stress reactions. *Arch. Envtl. Health,* **21**, 789–96.
Funkenstein, D. H., and Meade, L. W. (1954). Norepinephrine and epinephrine like substances and the elevation of blood pressure during acute stress. *J. Nerv. Ment. Dis.,* **119**, 380–397.
Gellhorn, E., and Loofbourrow, G. N. (1963). *Emotions and the Emotional Disorders,* Harper and Row, New York.
Gombe, S. (1977). Salivary and plasma progesterone and oestrogen during the menstrual cycle and pregnancy. *E. Afri. Med. J.,* **54**, 476–9.
Goodwin, B. L., Ruthven, G. R. J., Sandler, M., and Hine, B. (1973). Loss of catecholamine derivatives during gas liquid chromatography. *Clin. Chim. Acta,* **44**, 271–2.
Granström, E. (1978). Radioimmunoassay of prostaglandins. *Prostaglandins,* **15**, 3–17.
Guldberg, H. C., and Marsden, C. A. (1975). Catechol-o-methyl transferase: Pharmacological aspects and physiological role. *Pharmacol. Rev.,* **27**, 135–206.
Gullickson, G. R. (1973). *The Psychophysiology of Darrow,* Academic Press, New York.
Harper, H. A., Rodwell, V. W., and Mayes, P. A. (1977). *Review of Physiological Chemistry,* Lange, Los Altos.
Henry, R. J., Cannon, D. C., and Winkelman, J. W. (Eds.) (1974). *Clinical Chemistry Principles and Techniques,* Harper and Row, New York.
Jenkins, D. C. (1978). Behavioural risk factors in coronary artery disease. *Ann. Rev. Med.,* **29**, 543–62.
Jenkins, G. N. (1978). *The Physiology of the Mouth,* Blackwell, Oxford.
Krantz, D. (1978). Coronary prone behavior pattern, current research and theory. *Paper given at the 1978 meeting of the Society for Psychophysiological Research, Madison, September.*
Jenner, D. A., Reynolds, V., and Harrison, G. A. (1978). Population field studies of catecholamines. *Paper presented at Ergonomics Society Conference: Psychophysiological Response to Occupational Stress, Nottingham, September.*
Landman, A. D., Sanford, L. M., and Howland, B. E. (1976). Testosterone in human saliva. *Experientia,* **32**, 940–1.
Levi, L. (Ed.) (1971). *Society, Stress and Disease,* Vol. 1, Oxford University Press, London.
Levi, L. (1972). *Stress and Distress in Response to Psychosocial Stimuli,* Pergamon, Oxford.
McDonald, J. R. (1972). Are the data worth owning? *Science,* **176**, 1377.
Mason, D. H., Harden, R. McG., and Alexander, W. D. (1966). Problems of interpretation in studies of salivary constituents. *J. Oral Med.,* **21**, 66–71.
Mason, J. W. (1968). Organization of psychoendocrine mechanisms. *Psychosom. Med.,* **30**, No. 5, Part II.
Mason, J. W. (1972). Organization of psychoendocrine mechanisms: a review and reconsideration of research. In N. S. Greenfield and R. A. Sternbach (Eds.), *Handbook of Psychophysiology,* Holt, Rinehart and Winston, New York.
Mason, J. W. (1975). Emotion as reflected in patterns of endocrine integration. In L. Levi (ed.), *Emotions—their Parameters and Measurement,* Raven, New York.
Mattingly, D. (1963). Plasma steroid levels as a measure of adrenocortical activity. *Proc. R. Soc. Med.,* **56**, 717–20.
Mattingly, D., Dennis, P. M., Pearson, J., and Cope, C. L. (1964). Rapid screening test for adrenal cortical function. *Lancet,* **2**, 1046–9.

Morris, G. C. R. (1963). Factors determining sodium and potassium concentrations of saliva with special reference to aldosterone. *MD. Thesis*, University of Oxford, unpublished.

Murphy, B. E. P. (1967). Some studies of the protein binding of steroids. *J. Clin. Endocri.*, **27**, 973–90.

Passon, P. A., and Peuler, J. D. (1973). A simplified radiometric assay for plasma norepinephrine and epinephrine. *Analyt. Biochem.*, **51**, 618–31.

Phaeler, G. T., and Roessler, R. (1965). Ego strength and intravenous glucose tolerance. *J. Psychosom. Res.*, **8**, 431–9.

Raab, W. (1968). Correlated cardiovascular, adrenergic and adrenocortical responses to sensory and mental annoyances in man. *Psychosom. Med.*, **30**, 809–18.

Raab, W. (1971). Cardiotoxic biochemical effects of emotional environmental stressors—fundamentals of psychocardiology. In L. Levi (Ed.), *Society, Stress and Disease*, Vol. 1, Oxford University Press, London.

Rodahl, K., Vokac, Z., Fugelli, P., Vaage, O., and Meehlum, S. (1974). Circulatory strain, estimated energy output and catecholamine excretion in Norwegian coast fishermen. *Ergonomics*, **17**, 585–602.

Rodahl, K., and Vokac, Z. (1977). Work stress in Norwegian trawler fishermen. *Ergonomics*, **20**, 633–42.

Rybakova, M. G. (1978). Endocrine function of the salivary glands. *Ark. Patol.*, **40**, 85–91.

Sapira, J. D., Klaniecki, T., and Rizk, M. (1971). Modified fluorimetric method for determining plasma catecholamines. *Clin. Chem.*, **17**, 486–91.

Schildkraut, J. J., and Kety, S. S. (1967). Biogenic amines and emotion. *Science*, **156**, 21–30.

Shannon, I. L. (1958). Sodium and potassium levels of human whole stimulated saliva collected under two forms of stimulation from subjects in a select age grouping. *J. Dent. Res.*, **37**, 391–9.

Shannon, I. L., Katz, F. H., and Beering, S. C. (1967). Steroids in parotid saliva, serum and urine of normal and diseased human subjects. In L. H. Schneyer and C. A. Schneyer (Eds), *Secretory Mechanisms of Salivary Glands*, Academic Press, New York.

Simpson, G. C., Cox, T., and Rothschild, D. R. (1974). The effects of noise stress on blood glucose level and skilled performance. *Ergonomics*, **17**, 481–7.

Skelley, D. S., Brown, L. P., and Besch, P. C. (1973). Radioimmunoassay. *Clin. Chem.*, **19**, 146–86.

Taggart, P., and Carruthers, M. (1971). Endogenous hyperlipidaemia induced by emotional stress of racing driving. *Lancet*, **i**, 363–6.

Taggart, P., Gibbons, D., and Somerville, W. (1969). Some effects of motor car driving on the normal and abnormal heart. *Br. Med. J.*, **4**, 130–4.

Tarnoky, A. (1958). *Clinical Biochemical Methods*, Hilger Watts, London.

Terry, J. M., and Shannon, I. L. (1964). Modification of a self-positioning device for the collection of parotid fluid. *Tech. Doc. Rep. No.* SAM-TDB-64-71.

Thayssen, J. H. (1960). Handling of alkali metals by exocrine glands other than the kidney. In O. Eichler and A. Farah (Eds), *Handbuch det experimentallen pharmakologie*, Springer, Berlin.

Thiers, R. E. (1957). Contamination in trace elements analysis and its control. In D. Glick (Ed.), *Methods of Biochemical Analysis*, Vol. 5, Interscience, New York.

Toivonen, S. (1967). Studies of the function of the pancreas in chronic bronchitis and heterozygous mucoviscidosis or cystic fibrosis. Vannala, Helsinki.

Turton, M. B., and Deegan, T. (1964). Circadian variations of plasma catecholamine, cortisol and immunoreactive insulin concentrations in supine subjects. *Clin. Chim. Acta*, **55**, 389–98.

Udenfriend, S. (1969). *Fluorescence Assay in Biology and Medicine*, Vol. 2, Academic New York.

US Department of Health, Education and Welfare, (1971). *List of Test Kits for Clinical Laboratories*, July.

Vane, J. R. (1966). The estimation of catecholamines for biological assay. *Pharmacol. Rev.*, **18**, 317–24.

Varley, H., Gowenlock, A. H., and Bell, M. (1979). *Practical Clinical Biochemistry*, Vol. 1, Heinemann, London.

Varley, H., Gowenlock, A. H., and Bell, M. (1976). *Practical Clinical Biochemistry*, Vol. 2, Heinemann, London.

Venables, P. H., and Christie, M. J. (1974). Neuroticism, physiological state and mood: an exploratory study of Friday/Monday changes. *Biol. Psychol.*, **1**, 201–11.

Venables, P. H. and Martin, I. (1967). *A Manual of Psychophysiological Methods*, North-Holland, Amsterdam.

Wenger, M. A. (1966). Studies of autonomic balance: a summary. *Psychophysiology*, **2**, 173–86.

Wenger, M. A., and Cullen, D. (1972). Studies of autonomic balance in children and adults. In N. S. Greenfield and R. A. Sternbach (Eds.), *Handbook of Psychophysiology*, Holt, Rinehart and Winston, New York.

White, C. E., and Argauer, R. J. (1970). *Fluorescence Analysis, A Practical Approach*, Marcel Dekker, New York.

White, A., Handler, P., and Smith, E. L. (1978). *Principles of Biochemistry*, 6th edn, McGraw-Hill, New York.

Wilding, P., Zilva, J. F., and Wilde, C. E. (1977). Transport of specimens for clinical chemistry analysis. *Ann. Clin. Biochem.*, **14**, 301–6.

Williams, E. S. (1961). Salivary electrolyte composition at high altitude. *Clin. Sci.*, **21**, 37–42.

Williams, E. S. (1966). Electrolyte regulation during the adaptation of humans to life at high altitude. *Proc. R. Soc. B*, **165**, 266–80.

Woodbury, D. M. (1966). Physiology of body fluids. In T. C. Ruch and H. D. Patton (Eds), *Physiology and Biophysics*, Saunders, Philadelphia.

Woodman, D. D., Hinton, J. W., and O'Neill, M. T. (1977). Abnormality of catecholamine balance relating to social deviance. *Percept. Mot. Skills*, **45**, 593–4.

Woodman, D. D., Hinton, J. W., and O'Neill, M. T. (1978a). Plasma catecholamines, stress and aggression in maximum security patients. *Biol. Psychol.*, **6**, 147–54.

Woodman, D. D., Hinton, J. W., and O'Neill, M. T. (1978b). Cortisol secretion and stress in maximum security hospital patients. *J. Psychosom. Res.*, **22**, 133–6.

Woodman, D. D., and Hinton, J. W. (1978c). Catecholamine balance during stress anticipation. *J. Psychosom. Res.*, **22**, 477–83.

Wootton, I. D. P. (1974). *Microanalysis in Medical Biochemistry*. Churchill Livingstone, Edinburgh.

Wurtman, R. J., and Axelrod, J. (1966). Control of enzymatic synthesis of adrenaline in the adrenal medulla by adrenal cortical steroids. *J. Biol. Chem.*, **241**, 2301–5.

Wurtman, R. J., Pohorecky, L. A., and Baliga, B. S. (1972). Adrenocortical control of the biosynthesis of epinephrine and proteins of the adrenal medulla. *Pharmacol. Rev.*, **24**, 411–26.

Young, D. S., Pestanen, L. C., and Gibberman, V. (1975). Effects of drugs on clinical laboratory tests. *Clin. Chem.*, **21**, *Suppl.* 1–432.

APPENDIX: BOEHRINGER ADDRESSES

Argentine

Boehringer Argentina S. A. C. I. el., Viamonte 2213/15, **1056-Buenos Aires**. Tel.: 47-0023 – 47-0026. 48-6081 – 48-6083. Dir. Telegr. alcaloid baries.

Australia

Bohringer Mannheim Australia Pty. Ltd., 2–6 Hardner Road, **Mount Waverley, 3149**. P.O. Box 331. Tel.: 5431055. Telex: AA 34526. Cable: 'alcaloid' melbourne.

Austria

Boehringer Mannheim GmbH Wien, Pasettistraβe 64, **A-1201 Wien XX**. Tel.: (0222) 336144. Telex: 75 675.

Belgium

Boehringer Pharma S.A., Avenue des Croix de Guerre 90, **B-1120 Bruxelles**. Tel.: 242.18.00. Telex: 25 259 bru b.

Brazil

Boehringer do Brasil Produtes Quimicos e Farmaceuticos, Avenida Brasil Tire a ZC-24, Caixa Postal 1912-ZC-00, **20000 Rio de Janeiro-RJ**. Tel.: 260-1552. Telex: 2122677 brgr br. Cable: cekace.

Bulgaria

Bulpharma, P.O. Box 1132, **Sofia**.

Canada

Boehringer Mannheim Canada Ltd./Ltée., 1475 Bégin, **Ville St. Laurent Quebec**, H4R 1 V8. Tel.: (514) 331-7440. Telex: 05-826599.

Colombia

Boehringer Mannheaim S.A., Apartado Aéreo 21445, **Bogota 2, D. E.**

Denmark

Boehringer Mannheim GmbH Biochemical Department c/o Ercopharm A/S, 13–15 Skelstedet, **DK-2950 Trørød-Vedbaek**. Tel.: (01) 890889. Telex: 37155 ercodk dk.

Ecuador

Boehringer Mannheim del Ecuador Cia. Ltda., Avenida 12 de Octubre 1830 y Luis Cordero, Casilla 4929 CCI, **Quito**, Tel.: 541-446 – 238-242. Telex: 02-2347 bmecula ed.
Avenida del Ejercito 603 y Quisquis, Casilla 6294, **Guayaquil**. Tel.: 390-437 – 394-591.

Federal Republic of Germany

Boehringer Mannheim GmbH Biochemica, P.O. Box 310120, **D-6800 Mannheim 31**, West Germany, Tel.: 0621/7591. Telex: 04 63 193 bmd. 04 62 420 bmd. Cable: alcaloid.

Finland

Orion-yhtymä Oy, Orion Pharamaceutical Co. Biochemical Department, P.O. Box 8, **02101 Espoo 10**. Tel.: 90-427011.

France

Boehringer Mannheim France S. A. R. L., 7, Boulevard de la Madeleine, **F-75 Paris (1er)**. Tel.: 2611438.

Great Britain

BCL · The Boehringer Corporation (London) Ltd., Bell Lane. **Lewes, East Sussex BN71LG**. Tel.: 07916-71611. Telex: 877487. Cable: enzymes lewis.

Greece

Boehringer Mannheim Hellas GmbH, Marni-Kumunduru 37, **Athen 107**. Tel.: 525201, 541505.

Hongkong

Dychem Trading Company (H.K.) Ltd., 1. Hysan Avenue 19th Floor, G. P. O. Box 610, **Hongkong**. Tel.: 5-760557. Telex: 74578 dtco hx. Cable: dyesimport hongkong.

Hungary

Medimpex, Postfach 126, **H-1808 Budapest-V**.

India

Boehringer-Knoll Ltd. United India Bldg., Sir Pheozeshah Mehta Road, **Bombay 4001**. Tel.: 267951. Cable: alcaloid.

Iran

Tehran Pharma AG/ Tehran Chemie AG, P.B. 1086, Ave. Tahkte Djamshid, West 126–128 . **Tehran.**

Ireland

The Boehringer Corporation Ltd. Valentine House, Blackrock, **CO. Dublin.**

Israel

Agentex Ltd., 13 Hanking St., P.O. Box 22184, **Tel Aviv.**

Italy

Boehringer Biochemia s.r.l., Via S. Uguzzone, 5, **1-20126 Milano.** Casella Postale 3772. Tel.: 02/2528. Telex: 35339 bmm.

Japan

Boehringer Mannheim Yamanouchi K.K., Kanda P.O. Box 168, **Tokyo.** Tel.: (03) 252-6521. Telex: 22-62 44 alcaloj.

Luxembourg

Prophac G.m.b.H., Postfach 2063, **Luxembourg.** Tel.: 482483. Telex: 2265 propha lu..

Mexico

Farmaceuticos Lakeside, S. A., Diagonal 20 de Noviembre 294 Col. Obrera, **Mexico 8, D.F..**
Apartado Postal 65–183, **Mexico 8, D.F.** Tel.: 578-20-11. Telex: 017-75-779 laksime. Cable: 'lakemex'.

Netherlands

Boehringer Mannheim b.v., Donker Curtiussraat 7–9, **Amsterdam.** Tel.: (020) 827575. Telex: 16 654.

New Zealand

Medical Supplies n.z. Limited, 147–161 Tory Street, (P.O. Box 1994). **Wellington.**

Norway

Boehringer Mannheim GmbH Biochemical Department, c/o Einar d. Fineide A/S. Karlstadgt. 8, **Oslo 5.** Tel.: (02) 35.14.00. Telex: 18 930 edfas.

Poland

Transactor. s.a., Ul. Stawki 2, P.O. Box 276, **00-950 Warszawa**. Tel.: 39-52-79.
Telex: 813 288 trwa pl.

Portugal

Ferraz, Lynce L.D.A., Rua Rosa Araujo 27–31. **Lisboa.** Tel.: 53 6805.

South Africa

Boehringer Mannheim (S.A.) (Pty.) Ltd., P.O. Box 68686. **Bryanston 2021.** Tel.:
48-96 80/4. Cable: alcaloid, Johannesburg.

Spain

Boehringer Mannheim S.A., Copérnico 61 y 63, **Barcelona 6.** Tel.:
211-01-50/54/58/62. Telex: 52 589 bme e.

Sweden

Boehringer Mannheim Scandinavia AB, Asögatan 180, **S-11632 Stockholm.** Tel.:
08-23 69 35.
Distribution: Erco-Läkemedel AB, Grevgatan 34, **S-11453 Stockholm.** Tel.:
042/38 11 66.

Switzerland

Boehringer Mannheim (Schweiz) AG, Riedstrasse, **CH-6330 Cham.** Tel.:
042/381166

Turkey

Sevgen Laboratuar Sanayii Ve Tic. A.S., Cumhuriyet Caddesi 101/7,
Elmadag-Istanbul. Tel.: 48 60 08. 48 60 09. Telex: 23 429 slsa tr. Cable: sevgen,
Istanbul.

USA

Boehringer Mannheim Biochemicals, 7941 Castleway Drive, P.O. Box 50816,
Indianapolis. Indiana 46250. Tel.: (317) 849-9350. Telex: 27-2330 bmb. ind.

Yugoslavia

Pliva, I. Lole Ribara 89, P.O. Box 384, **Zagreb.**

Techniques in Psychophysiology
Edited by I. Martin and P. H. Venables
©1980, John Wiley & Sons Ltd.

CHAPTER 9

The Measurement of Mood and Psychophysiological Activity Using Self-Report Techniques*

COLIN J. MACKAY

1. INTRODUCTION

Self-reports of mood and psychophysiological activity are becoming increasingly popular techniques in psychophysiology. The trend towards the investigation of 'states', and toward more longitudinal studies has involved

*Acknowledgements. The author would like to gratefully acknowledge support from the Science Research Council and the Medical Research Council during the preparation of this chapter.

the collection of self-reports of mood as an adjunct to the main physiological variables of interest. Often the covariation between these two types of measure is of primary concern (e.g. Roth and coworkers, 1976). Research in biofeedback and self-regulation has also made considerable use of self-report techniques. Here, the investigator may be interested in the subjective state associated with, for example, enhanced 'alpha' activity (e.g. Brown, 1970, 1971); or with the extent to which the perception and discrimination of bodily functioning is related to its subsequent self-control during feedback (e.g. Blanchard, Young, and McLeod, 1972). Alteration of somatic activity and disturbances in mood as experienced and reported by the patient also play an integral part in the clinician's basis of diagnosis (Wing, Cooper, and Sartorius, 1974).

Studies relevant to a discussion of mood, emotion, and psycho-physiological activity are diverse. For many centuries speculation on the interaction of bodily and subjective feelings had been a philosophical rather than scientific activity. Wright (1604) believed that the passions reside principally in the heart, but had to confess that certain passions may inhabit other parts of the body which then become 'stirred-up'. Hutcheson (1728) discussed in great detail the diversions of the various passions and affections and how the basic varieties combine to produce more subtle feelings. He was, however, able to dismiss the relationship between bodily events and emotional experiences as follows:

'Let Physicians or Anatomists explain the several motions in the *Fluids* or *Solids* of the Body, which accompany any Passion; or the *Temperaments* of Body which either make men prone to any Passion or are brought upon us by the long continuance or frequent returns of it. 'Tis only our purpose in general to observe, "that probably certain *Motions* in the Body to accompany every Passion by a fixed Law of Nature; or alternately, *that Temperament* which is apt to receive or prolong these Motions in the Body, does influence our *Passions* to heighten or prolong them".'

Later, the two aspects of mood and emotion noted by Hutcheson, their structure and dimensionality, and the role of bodily activity in the genesis of subjective feelings, came increasingly under scientific scrutiny. They were, however, pursued almost independently, the former by experimental psychologists and the latter by physiologists, until comparatively recently. James (1884) and concurrently Lange (1885), proposed that bodily changes were the precursors of emotional experience. At about the same time Willhelm Wundt (1905) proposed a three-dimensional theory of emotion, based upon introspective procedures. Apart from the universally agreed 'pleasant–unpleasant' dimension Wundt proposed two others; an 'aroused-subdued' and a 'tense-relaxed' dimension. Work in the early part of this century notably by Sherrington (1900) highlighted the inadequacies of the James–Lange theory. He was a firm believer, incidentally, that 'mental events are not examinable as forms of energy and therefore lie outside Natural Science'. Dana (1921) showed that patients with almost complete loss of afferent and efferent pathways were still able to report subjective feelings. He explained this by suggesting that impulses are projected downwards from the brainstem which activate the muscles, viscera, and glands. Impulses are also projected upwards to the cortex, via the thalamus. Here, the appropriate emotional experiences are aroused. Cannon (1929, 1931) emphasized the adaptive nature of the physiological response. The subjective component of emotion was, however, relegated to a secondary position. During this period, empirical studies of the relationship between electrophysiological indicants of emotion and subjective reports were being undertaken. A discrepancy between these two measures was often found. This led many investigators to question the accuracy and validity of verbal reports; many condemned them as unsatisfactory and unreliable (e.g. Syz, 1926).

Interest in the dimensions of mood continued in a sporadic fashion. Several schema were proposed based upon Wundt's pioneering work. Harlow and Stagner (1933), for example, mention four innate dimensions: 'pleasure', 'unpleasantness', 'excitement', and 'depression'. Stagner (1948) subsequently collapsed these dimensions into 'excitement–depression' and 'pleasantness–unpleasantness'. More recent factor-analytic studies have provided partial support for some of these hypotheses (Burt, 1950; Nowlis and Green, 1957; Davitz, 1969).

In recent years many writers have emphasized the role of cognitive factors in generating an emotional response (Schachter and Singer, 1962; Lazarus, 1966). The experimental manipulations of Schachter and Singer are well known. Their results show that the choice of an emotional descriptor is determined primarily by cognitive factors that reflect the individual's perception of the situation. Changes in bodily activity are reflected in the intensity of the feeling. Valins (1970), however, was able to show that individuals are aware of a qualitative relationship between visceral activity and emotions. Here, the emotional response of subjects to different types of slides was manipulated by providing false heart rate feedback. Different moods could be induced by altering the rate at which the false heart beat was presented to the subject.

Of the remaining four sections of this chapter, three will deal respectively with self-reported mood, self-reported activation and a selection of questionnaires dealing with specific bodily states. The fifth section will discuss tests involving the discrimination and identification of somatic and visceral activity. There are many clinical rating scales which also deal with aspects of mood and changes in bodily activity and functioning. The aim of this chapter is to discuss techniques of measurement in the general population and for this reason and because of space limitations these will not be mentioned. The interested reader is referred to the following: Beck and coworkers (1961); Goldberg (1972); Aitken and Zealley (1970); Aitken (1970); and Sarason (1960).

2. MOOD

2.1. The concept of mood

The term 'mood' has a long history. However, as Arnold (1970) notes, 'mood is a topic that has aroused sporadic interest but has been investigated haphazardly, without an overall theory to give direction to experimental research'. Other key words with which it seems to be related, such as stress, arousal, anxiety and depression have enjoyed considerable popularity. Colloquial, non-technical use of the term implies a weak emotion. Common language usage also implies a pervasive rather than transient state. The two appear to be related since emotional upheavals can affect mood. Emotions, however, are invariably related to objects or specific stimulus characteristics in the environment. This in turn would appear to determine a similarly narrow range of behaviour patterns. Moods provide an integrative, longer-lasting function and seem to have a general rather than specific effect on behaviour. They are slowly changing states which are not easily specifiable in terms of specific stimuli or behaviour patterns. Similarly, Ewart (1970) states that 'moods are background experiences of a diffuse nature. There is no differentation of experienced self and experienced world. Thus moods do not refer to persons, things or events. They possess no object reference.' There do appear, however, to be a number of determinants of mood; McNair and Lorr (1964) have mentioned in particular withholding reinforcement, environmental deprivation, emotional stimulation, and intra-organic events such as illness or disease. These suggest negative rather than positive appraisals but mood can be influenced by favourable as well as unfavourable conditions. Moods, then, are sensitive to, and reflect the general well-being of the organism. A 'good' mood is one in which the person can be satisfied with the achievement of current goals and desires to achieve new ones. Conversely, a bad mood is one in which the person has failed to meet set targets or has been subjected to conditions which may auger badly for the attainment of future goals. Nowlis (1963) uses a similar approach; he suggests that 'mood is a multidimensional set of temporary, reversible dispositions'. Elsewhere he has suggested that mood acts as an intervening variable or predispositional factor which provides a source of information to the organism about its 'current functioning characteristics' (Nowlis and Nowlis, 1956). It is clear from this that, apart from integrating information about recent experience and predictions about the achievement of current goals, mood also takes into account information relating to the physiological status of the individuals. This has a number of implications for the measurement of mood, which will be discussed in the following section (Section 2.2). These formulations provide a clue to the function of mood, a topic that is often cursorily dealt with in the literature.

Ruckmick (1936) wrote 'There is generally no conative impulse about it. It does not lead itself to any definite action. Biologically its function is very hard to determine . . it is probably more allied to physiological conditions than direct experience.' By 'direct experience' Ruckmick is presumably referring to the perception of events in the external, rather than internal, environment. Other writers have also emphasized the biological nature of mood. Meddis (1969) has suggested that mood acts as an economic regulator of behaviour, and that current mood state is determined primarily by the physiological well-being of the individual, the degree of success recently experienced and the perception of the external environment. Such a formulation suggests a straightforward mechanism bestowing a marked evolutionary advantage on the organism. However, because of its multidimensional basis, and non-specific nature the manifestations of mood may also be complex and varied. This simple non-specific mechanism may, of course, be maladaptive as well as adaptive. Moods associated with anxiety and depression have an overriding influence upon those unfortunate enough to suffer constantly from them. They have such a powerful influence on the person that any cognitive manoeuvres attempted, in order to reorientate, are often swamped. These various formulations do seem to suggest that mood is intimately linked to a variety of ongoing activities, in particular the physiological and psychological preparedness of the individuals. For discussions of alternative approaches to mood the reader is referred to Wessman and Ricks (1966), Nowlis (1965) and Cattell (1963). The relationship between the structure and function of mood will be discussed further in Section 2.2.1.1.

2.2 The measurement of mood

Mood may be inferred from the observation of overt bevhavioural acts, such as expressive movements, gestures, and posture, from facial expressions and from the person's verbal response. These verbal responses may be various aspects of spoken language, such as variations in tone, pitch, intonation, speech disturbance (see Mahl, 1959) or they may be direct reports from the subject of his current mood status. The remainder of this section is concerned wholly with a discussion of the most commonly used self-report measures of mood. There are, of course, a number of very powerful objections to the use of self-report techniques. Lazarus (1966) has noted three main objections to the use of introspective verbal report. First, individuals may use different verbal labels for describing the same mood, or the same person may describe a particular mood differently on separate occasions. These may be due to different linguistic habits, to vocabulary or to some aspect of memory. This 'individual response stereotypy' is not, however, unique to self-report measures. Typically the experimental psychologist uses grouped data to reduce distortions contributed by individual subjects. The opposite technique may also be of use; that is, to investigate mood changes over extensive periods in a single individual. The second objection concerns the willingness of the subject to provide a genuine and accurate reflection of his mood. An individual is easily able, for a variety of reasons, to distort the reporting process. Distortions may be due to factors such as 'social desirability set', the urge to present oneself in a way which appears favourable to the experimenter, or to the subject trying to influence the outcome of the experiment for similar reasons. These in turn may be determined by the situation in which the reports are obtained, the techniques used in gathering data and the instructions given to the subject. Such effects are likely to be more pronounced in the reporting of some moods, e.g. those related to anxiety, than others. The third and related objection is concerned with the unconscious (rather than conscious) efforts to see oneself in a particular light, i.e. forms of self-deception. A variety of solutions to these last two criticisms of self-report have been proposed. Many investigators have used questionnaires measuring social desirability simultaneously with their mood measure; others have incorporated 'lie scales'. Others have attempted to facilitate candid reports by the careful phrasing of instructions and by paying attention to the format and presentation of material. In a clinical situation, a gradual increase in rapport between the clinician and the patient may eventually unmask true feelings and moods by generating an atmosphere of mutual acceptance. This is often not possible (or desirable) in psychophysiological experimentation. Early workers distrusted verbal report because of the frequent discrepancy between it, and physiological measures. It is now thought that many of these discrepant findings are due to genuine differences (caused primarily by personality differences in methods of responding and the appraisal processes used by the individual) rather than unreliable aspects of the measurement technique *per se*.

Mandler (1962) has indirectly criticized the use of self-reports as a means of gathering information about inner experiences. Essentially, Mandler rejects the use of language for communicating private experiences as too insensitive a medium. Whilst it is accepted that many experiences are essentially incommunicable, due to the difficulty of translation and subsequent expression in terms of ordinary language, for most purposes language is sufficiently rich to allow the variety and complexity of moods to be expressed. For the most part the problems raised are empirical ones. How much resolution and detail does the experimenter require and how much error is he willing to tolerate? In conclusion it is worth stating that self-report techniques have a number of problems associated with them, some of which are unique, some of which are common to other measurement systems. Many of these problems can be removed, minimized, or used as sources of information in their own right. Apart from yielding information which is otherwise inaccessible, they have many advantages over other techniques, not the least being cost and ease of use. A number of approaches to the study of mood and subjective states have been taken: the adjective checklist approach, the questionnaire approach, and the rating scale approach. These are discussed below.

2.2.1. The adjective checklist

The adjective checklist approach is not a new one. Allport and Odbert (1936) used adjectives to compile a comprehensive list of trait names. A similar list was used by Cattell (1943) in some early research on personality. Indeed, the study of personality is the main area in which this approach has been used with the best known and most exhaustively developed checklist being the Gough–Heilbrun adjective checklist (ACL), (Gough and Heilbrun, 1965). The most extensively researched and widely used adjective checklists in the study of mood are the mood–adjective checklist of Nowlis and collaborators (Green and Nowlis, 1957; Nowlis and Green, 1957; Nowlis and Green, 1964; Nowlis and Nowlis, 1956; Nowlis, 1965) and the multiple affect adjective checklist (MAACL) of Zuckerman and Lubin (1965). Others include those of Zuckerman (1960) (subsequently incorporated into the MAACL); Jacobs, Kapek, and Meehan (1959); Knapp and Bahnson (1963); the Brentwood mood scale (Crumpton, Grayson, and Keith-Lee, 1967); McNair and Lorr (1964); McNair, Lorr, and Dropplemen (1971); Lorr, Daston, and Smith (1967); the Clyde mood scale (Clyde, 1963); Borgatta (1961); and those designed specifically for drug research (Cameron, Specht, and Wendt, 1967; Wendt, Cameron, and Specht, 1962).

The bases for the MACL constructed by Nowlis and Green (1957) were four intuitively derived dimensions of mood. These four dimensions (subsequently known as the 'Rochester hypothesis') were derived primarily from observation of drug effects. The four dimensions were as follows: (1) 'activation–deactivation'; (2) 'positive and negative social orientation'; (3) 'control and lack or loss of control'; and (4) 'positive and negative appraisal' (pleasantness and unpleasantness). Two features, crucial to a discussion of mood, are also incorporated in this hypothesis. These are the notions of *dimensionality* and of *polarity*. Investigation of these two characteristics have preoccupied mood researchers for the last two decades. According to Nowlis (1965), 'The MACL is based on one limited but easily accessible type of behaviour, namely, the tendency of persons in our* culture to apply to mood certain adjectives which complete the sentence, "I feel . . . " . ' The mechanism by which we become aware of our mood is unclear. The existentialist philosophers, for whom the phenomenological aspects of mood are of utmost concern, suggest that we are immediately aware of any change in mood. For Ryle (1949), however, the perception of mood is an indirect process. Awareness of mood only occurs after the utterance, either privately or publicly, of phrases such as 'I feel sad' or 'How sad I feel'. Typically, an individual uses at the most two or three phrases as a spontaneous description of his current mood state. Moreover, a covert response is only usually offered during heightened mood states. Whatever the mechanism, the aim of the MACL is to facilitate the process of accurately recording current mood states. Nowlis (1965) suggests that simplicity of instructions and test format are essential if the facilitation process is to be successful. Complex instructions, or long and complicated items, may delay the spontaneous response that is required and may ultimately 'destroy' the ongoing mood the experimenter wishes to elicit. Thus checklist adjectives act as prompts. These, Nowlis (1970) states 'even though superficial, trivial and often thoughtlessly and rapidly emitted, . . hopefully are also sincere, dependable and, indeed, susceptible to change in mood!'

From the literally thousands of words in the English language describing moods, Nowlis and Green selected 120 adjectives representative of the four hypothesized bipolar dimensions. A checklist containing these words was administered to 450 male college students in a variety of mood inducing situations. These included films, an 'aggressive hoax', and a contest for cash prizes. After elimination of some variables, factor analysis of these, and subsequent studies, revealed the presence of twelve factors. They have been consistently identified by Nowlis and by other mood researchers in further studies. The twelve interpreted factors with the corresponding variables are shown in Table 9.1.

Thus Nowlis obtained eight monopolar rather than four bipolar factors, together with a further four factors not originally anticipated. As Nowlis states, the result was of considerable interest because of the widespread assumption of bipolarity of affective phenomena An extended discussion of the status of these factors can be found in Nowlis (1965). Many studies have essentially replicated the work of Nowlis and collaborators. Borgatta

---

*Here, presumably, Nowlis is referring to Western rather than just American culture.

Table 9.1. The twelve monopolar factors extracted from the series of studies carried out by Nowlis and collaborators. Their relationship to the original Rochester hypothesis is as follows: activation–deactivation appears as vigour (K) and fatigue (F). Positive and negative social orientation appears as social affection (G) and aggression (A). Control and lack (or loss) of control appears as egotism (J) and anxiety (B). Positive and negative appraisal (pleasantness and unpleasantness) appears as elation (D) and sadness (H). Four further factors, not included in the original hypothesis, also appeared: urgency (C), concentration (E), scepticism (I), and nonchalance (N)

A AGGRESSION
   Defiant, rebellious, angry, grouchy, amazed, fed up
B ANXIETY
   Clutched up, fearful, jittery
C SURGENCY
   Carefree, playful, witty, lively talkative
D ELATION
   Elated, overjoyed, pleased, refreshed
E CONCENTRATION
   Attentive, earnest, serious, contemplative, concentrating, engaged in thought, intense, introspective
F FATIGUE
   Drowsy, dull, sluggish, tired
G SOCIAL AFFECTION
   Affectionate, forgiving, kindly, warm-hearted
H SADNESS
   Regretful, sad, sorry
I SCEPTICISM[a]
   Dubious, sceptical, suspicious
J EGOTISM
   Egotistic, self-centred, aloof, boastful
K VIGOUR[b]
   Active, energetic, vigorous
N NONCHALANCE
   Leisurely, nonchalant

[a]US spelling: skepticism.
[b]US spelling: vigor.

(1961) using forty words taken from the Nowlis–Green list obtained six factors sharply defined by between two and four adjectives. Lorr and coworkers (1961) carried out a number of analyses on 55 adjectives taken from the psychiatric outpatient mood scale (POMS). Five major mood dimensions were extracted ('tension', 'anger', 'depression', 'vigour' and 'fatigue') with two further, less well defined dimensions ('friendliness' and 'confusion'). Clyde (1963) obtained similar mood dimensions. Other mood checklists include those constructed by Jacobs, Kapek, and Meehan (1959). This instrument consists of 173 adjectives, measuring four dimensions:

'fear', 'anger', 'depression', and 'happiness'. Knapp and Bahnson (1963) have constructed a 117-word checklist for measuring six bipolar dimensions of emotion. Other self-report measures include those of Radloff and Helmreich (1968) and Crumpton, Grayson, and Keith-Lee (1967).

More recent studies have indicated a radically different picture of the structure of mood. A number of these (Meddis, 1972; Svensson, 1977; Sjöberg and Svensson, 1976) have tackled methodological problems. They have tended to contradict many of the hypotheses and findings of earlier studies, particularly those relating to the dimensionality and polarity of mood.

2.2.1.1. Polarity and dimensionality—rating scale artifacts

The original 'Rochester hypothesis' predicted four bipolar factors. In the obtained factor structure, bipolarity was almost negligible. Many subsequent studies also found predominantly monopolar factors. In discussing this finding, Nowlis has suggested that the commonly held view (by both scientists and laymen) of bipolarity in mood is unjustified. Thus, those moods typically thought to be interdependent upon one another may be functionally independent. One may be, at the same time, both elated and saddened, or vigorous and fatigued, since these variables lie on orthogonal (or nearly orthogonal) axes. Meddis (1969, 1972) has drawn attention to the surprising nature of this finding and has attributed its occurrence to the rating scales used by Nowlis and subsequently copied by most others. The original scale contained two categories of acceptance ('definitely; and 'slightly'), a category of confusion ('cannot decide') and one of rejection ('definitely not'). In particular, Meddis noted two difficulties with this scale, one of ordinality and the other of symmetry. The position of the 'cannot decide' category is, he suggests, unjustified because it violates the principle of ordinality. It also presents scoring difficulties. If one point is assigned to the 'definitely not' category (DN), two points to 'cannot decide' (CD), three to 'feel slightly' (FS) and four to 'definitely feel' (DF), the scoring is not ordinal since we cannot say with certainty that DC lies between DN and FS. If the word is irrelevant or its meaning unclear to the subject, the result should be treated as a missing datum. Also, the presence of two acceptance categories opposed to one of rejection produces an asymmetric scale. An *increase* in the scale for, say, HAPPY from 'slightly' to 'definitely' cannot be matched by a similar *decrease* in the score for SAD from 'no to 'definitely no'. An early study carried out by Meddis (1969) used a symmetric scale, i.e. 'definitely feel', 'feel slightly', 'do not feel' and 'definitely do not feel', but without a 'cannot decide' category. This version of the scale produced clearly bipolar factors, a finding subsequently replicated (Meddis, 1972). In this later study

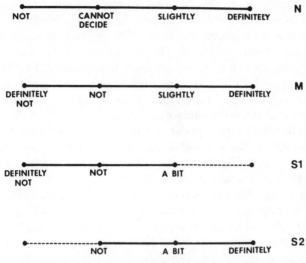

Figure 9.1 The four response scales used by Svensson (1977). N = Nowlis asymmetric scale, M = Meddis symmetric scale, S1 = Svensson asymmetric scale 1, S2 = Svensson asymmetric scale 2

Meddis was able to test the original 'Rochester hypothesis' by selecting 38 of the adjectives hypothesized to form the four bipolar factors. The new rating scale generated two bipolar and two monopolar factors, suggesting that at least in part the failure to find bipolarity was due to deficiencies in the rating scale used. This work has been further explored by Svensson (1977). Here, four response scales were used; the original Nowlis scale (N), the Meddis scale (M) and two, three category asymmetric scales (S1, S2). These are shown in Figure 9.1.

These scales used 32 pairs (of 64) adjectives, for example, glad–sorry. The adjectives were arranged singly, in random order, throughout the list. The respondent was asked to describe, 'how you feel, just now'. Svensson found that the proportion of positive and negative responses were equivalent in the symmetric (M) and the original asymmetric format (N). However, the type N scale led to an overall decrease in both negative and positive correlations, i.e. more correlations distributed around zero. The type M scale caused marked bipolar factors which accounted for more of the common variance than the other scales. The proportions of affirmative and negative responses were not, however, equally balanced in the two new asymmetric scales, S1 and S2. The results indicated a decrease in the proportion of responses at the truncated ends.

Some investigators have been able to achieve bipolar factors using the original asymmetric scale. In the development of an inventory for the measurement of self-reported arousal (see Section 3), Bohlin and Kjellberg (1973) obtained a mixture of both bipolar and monopolar factors. Moreover, they have criticized the symmetric (M) scale on more fundamental grounds. They state, 'Phenomenologically, the strength of a feeling as described by one adjective runs from its absence to a maximum experience of it, i.e. the experience is in a sense 'asymmetric'. The inclusion of several rejection categories implies a grading of the absence of a feeling, a task which must appear unnatural to the S.' Thus the question is, can the subject make a sensible distinction between 'do not feel' and 'definitely do not feel'. Unfortunately, it is impossible to provide an answer to this from presently available data. Perhaps respondents use one of the two rejection categories exclusively. However, the approximately normal distribution of responses in Svensson's asymmetric scale (M) suggests indirectly that subjects use both rejection categories and that they may be using scales of this type in two ways. First, they may be using the scale to provide an assessment of the *certainty* of a feeling being present, and secondly to provide an assessment of the *strength* of that feeling. Hendrick and Lilly (1970) have also investigated the effect of changes in rating scale upon mood dimensions. Two asymmetric scales were used, the original Nowlis scale and one with nine categories running from 'not at all' (1) 'to very much' (9). The authors report a high degree of congruence between the factors obtained from the two scales (Tucker and Lewis, 1973).

Sjöberg and Svensson (1976) have criticized previous work using mood adjective checklists along other grounds. As well as the use of inappropriate response scales, they suggest that the psychometric model, implicit in common factor analysis as used by most researchers, is invalid. They propose a radex model (Guttman, 1954) as more appropriate to the type of scaling procedure adopted. Initial factor analysis of their data (obtained from 440 subjects responding to a list of 89 mood descriptive words) revealed four bipolar factors corresponding to the 'Rochester hypothesis' together with a number of less well defined monopolar factors. In spite of its overall good fit and 'psychological meaningfulness', this factor analytic solution was rejected on statistical grounds. Analysis of the same data according to radex theory and employing multidimensional scaling showed that it is possible to descibe mood within a two-dimensional framework, the two dimensions being activation and pleasantness. All other moods, feelings, and emotions, can, they suggest, be defined in terms of their location within this two dimensional space, together with specific situational characteristics. Bush (1973) has suggested a multidimensional approach to the scaling of feelings. A paired-comparison technique was used to rate, on a ten-point scale, the similarity (or dissimilarity) of 264 adjectives partitioned across subjects. Three dimensions were found and

Table 9.2. A comparison of a representative sample of factor-analysis studies of mood using the original work of Nowlis as a reference (see also Table 9.1). Factor names in upper case indicate bipolar factors and are thus shown twice. In some cases (Meddis factors A and B for example), three of the original Nowlis factors are incorporated into one new bipolar factor. Some investigators used fewer adjectives than Nowlis, e.g. Clyde used only 48, and this may account for some of the differences observed

Nowlis	McNair and Lorr	Hendrick and Lilly	Clyde[7]	Meddis[8,9]	Sjöberg and Svensson[10]
Aggression (A)	Anger–hostility	[3]	Aggressive	FACTOR A	FACTOR III
Anxiety (B)	Tension–anxiety	Anxiety	—	—	FACTOR VI
Surgency (C)	—	Surgency[4]	—	(FACTOR A)	Surgency
Elation (D)	—	Elation	—	Elation	FACTOR I
Concentration (E)	(Confusion)[1]	Concentration–involvement[5]	Clear thinking	—	—
Fatigue (F)	Fatigue–inertia	FATIGUE–ACTIVATION	Sleepy	FACTOR B	FACTOR II
Social Affection (G)	Friendliness[2]	Social affection	Friendly	Social affection	FACTOR III
Sadness (H)	Depression–dejection	Sadness	Unhappy	FACTOR A	FACTOR I
Scepticism (I)	—	[6]	—	—	—
Egotism (J)	—	Egotism	—	—	FACTOR VI
Vigour (K)	Vigour–activity	FATIGUE–ACTIVATION	—	—	FACTOR II
Nonchalance (L)	—	—	—	(FACTOR B)	Nonchalance

[1] Opposite of concentration. [2] Occurred in only one of three analyses. [3] Aggression factor did not emerge, Nowlis variables appeared in anxiety factor with low loadings. [4] Also contained some variables of the Nowlis social affection (G) factor. [5] Only two variables with loadings over 0.35. [6] Did not emerge. [7] The 'dizzy' factor found by Clyde cannot easily be fitted into the Nowlis framework. [8] Used a symmetric scale. [9] Did not interpret any of the factors obtained. [10] Used a symmetric scale with oblique rotation to obtain four bipolar (corresponding to the original Rochester hypothesis) and two monopolar factors. Multidimensional scaling of the same data revealed a basic two-dimensional framework.

interpreted as pleasantness–unpleasantness, level of activation and level of aggression. A comparison of the various factor analytic and multi-dimensional scaling studies of mood is shown in Table 9.2.

2.2.1.2. Reliability

Of obvious concern to those contemplating the use of mood adjective checklists is the issue of reliability. This leads to something of a paradox since MACLs are supposed to be sensitive to changes in mood (i.e. they are state rather than trait measures)*, so one would expect and indeed hope for low test–retest reliability scores. Available data indicate very variable estimates of test–retest reliability. Borgatta (1961) found test–retest reliability coefficients ranging from 0.46 (fatigue) to 0.71 (social affection) in men, and 0.07 (fatigue) to 0.78 (social affection) in women. Thus the fatigue factor here may be measuring a true state whilst social affection is measuring a personality related dimension. Conversely, the coefficients may represent the degree of instability, and hence reliability in the factors. Nowlis and Green (1964) included ten words a second time amongst the last 30 words in the long (140 adjectives) form of the MACL. Coefficients of reliability of the checking of individual words ranged from 0.52 to 0.80. In another study (Green, 1965), 51 men reported their mood at the same time of day for up to 60 days. Correlations between factor scores at the beginning and end of this period ranged from 0.50 (aggression) to 0.75 (depression). This study also showed a tendency towards increasing response set as the study progressed, i.e. an increasingly stereotyped pattern of response. It is possible that test–retest reliabilities are dependent upon the time-referents inherent in the instructions presented to the subjects. On this basis, checklists which ask for mood states 'now', 'over the past few hours' or 'today' would show less test–retest reliability than those which asked about moods 'over the past week'; the latter may tap more enduring mood conditions related to personality variables. Zuckerman and Lubin (1965) found test–retest reliabilities from 0.54 (hostility) to 0.70 (anxiety) when subjects were asked 'generally' how they felt as compared with approximately 0.30 when asked 'how do you feel today'. Pankratz, Glaudin, and Goodmonson (1972) correlated scores on parallel forms of the MAACL ('today' form) administered over a one hour period. They report a high level of consistency between the two forms over this time period.

Typically, respondents are told to work quickly through the list of

*Cattell (1973, p. 196) has drawn attention to the fact that most MACL researchers have used 'R-technique' factor analysis, rather than the more appropriate 'chain-P' or 'dR-techniques' which suggest MACLs are measuring traits rather than states. This will be raised in Section 2.3.

adjectives, that first reactions are usually the most reliable, and therefore not to spend a long time considering each word. Subjects are not explicitly asked to respond consistently to synonyms or antonyms. Such responses, therefore, could be used as measures of internal consistency. Yagi and Berkun (1961) examined this possibility in a study of 147 enlisted military personnel on the original 140 word MACL. Ten words were included twice. The investigators concluded that a considerable number (62%) of the MACLs would need to be discarded because of inconsistencies in checking antonyms, low internal reliability based upon the ten words repeated twice and inconsistencies in checking words on the activation–deactivation factor. Internal consistency and stability has also been investigated by McNair and Lorr (1964). Kuder–Richardson (KR-20) coefficients were computed for five of their six factors. Only two of the factors, vigour (0.80) and fatigue (0.83), had KR-20 coefficients less than 0.90 indicating a high degree of stability. Test–retest reliabilities were compiled for 150 patients prior to, and following, four weeks of treatment. The authors note than the coefficients obtained (0.61 to 0.69) are 'considerably lower' than the 0.80 to 0.90 range usually expected of objective tests, but that this may be expected due to intraindividual fluctuation in mood. It is suggested that users of MACLs pay attention to internal measures of consistency by including adjectives twice in the list and by investigating inconsistencies in checking antonyms and synonyms. This could be achieved simply and easily by the use of computer scoring systems or manually by the use of overlays and scoring keys.

2.2.1.3 Response sets

Due to their construction and use it has been suggested that adjective checklists may be particularly prone to response factors which may invalidate scores. Three types of response sets have been particularly investigated; social desirability, acquiescence, and extreme responding. These factors are particularly important when repeated use of checklists is envisaged.

Different aspects of mood have different degrees of attractiveness (Nowlis, 1965). Subjects may be reluctant to rate themselves as in a bad mood, or angry or tired. Green (1965) found that the ten factors from a 39 word MACL were widely and bimodally distributed with respect to social desirability. As one might expect, social affection, concentration, pleasantness, and elation were rated as desirable, whilst depression, anxiety, fatigue, scepticism, aggression, and egotism were rated as undesirable. However, when the same subjects were asked to complete a MACL with the usual instructions ('how you feel right now') the ratings of desirability were more or less independent of the MACL scores. It is likely that this independence is based, in part, on the fact that when asked to rate their *momentary* mood subjects are less likely to be influenced by social desirability effects than inventories measuring more enduring aspects of mood. Bates (1970) found that endorsement of individual adjectives correlated with rated social desirability. McNair and Lorr (1964) investigated social desirability effects using the Crowne and Marlowe (1964) system. Most mood factors had low to moderate correlations: tension (-0.21), anger (-0.52), depression (-0.36), vigour (0.33) and fatigue (-0.18); although some of these are quite high. It might be worthwhile, therefore, to include a measure of social desirability in investigations of mood as a matter of course. A shortened version has been produced by Strahan and Gerbasi (1972).

The problem of acquiscence (the propensity to always answer 'yes') in mood questionnaires has been examined by Johnston and Hackman (1977). Acquiescence in responding to the MACL (Zuckerman and Lubin, 1965), the Lorr, Daston, and Smith (1967) mood scales and the Spielberger, Gorsuch, and Lushene (1970) state–trait anxiety inventory (STAI), was investigated by assigning 1 to the 'not at all' category up to 4 for the 'very much' category. Little evidence of acquiescence was found, nor a relationship between acquiescence and mood scores on the STAI and MAACL. However, with the Lorr, Daston, and Smith scales, asquiescence correlated with scores on four of the eight factors on two separate occasions, the highest correlation (0.71) being with the thoughtful factor. No relationship between acquiescence and total number of items checked* was found. Others (Johnson, 1970; Herron, Bernstein, and Rosen, 1968) have shown significant negative correlations between the number of items checked and positive scores on this instrument. Herron (1969) has shown that with this type of free checking system, gross errors in interpretation can easily be made. There is also uncertainty about the meaning of an unchecked item. Herron found that an anxiety provoking situation produced an increase in the anxiety factor of the MAACL. However, the total number of items checked also increased, suggesting that the experimental variables may differentially alter checking behaviour.

Johnston and Hackman (1977) also investigated extreme responding, i.e. the extent to which subjects check the extreme, rather than central, parts of the scale. Extreme response set was not apparent with the STAI but was negatively correlated with some of the mood factors on the Lorr, Daston, and Smith scale. The authors suggest that response set effects with the MACL are probably due to an artifact in the scoring system used, but

---

*Respondents on the MAACL are not required to respond to all adjectives. They are asked to check only those adjectives that do or do not apply to their mood.

that the use of within-subjects designs will minimize these unwanted effects. A new method for scoring mood questionnaires, in order to remove response set effects, which involves the use of signal detection theory is discussed in Section 2.2.1.4. Warr and Knapper (1967) have drawn attention to the possibility that systematic changes in response tendencies occur as subjects work through the list of adjectives, particularly serial position effects. Indeed, they showed a primacy effect for items in extreme positions. However, this was not large and did not occur in central positions. They suggest using a variety of lists with adjectives in different positions in order to compensate for this effect. They also found a gradual decline in the number of adjectives checked from the beginning to the end of the list. Here again the argument seems to point towards the use of short lists, which require the subject to respond to every adjective.

2.2.1.4. Administration and scoring

Many of the commonly used checklists employ a variety of different methods of administration and scoring. Some of these procedures can lead to considerable difficulties in interpretation. Some checklists such as the Zuckerman and Lubin MAACL use a free response format to allow the subject to check as many or as few adjectives as he thinks necessary to describe his mood. The Nowlis MACL, however, requires that subjects respond to all adjectives on the list. Problems with the forced choice versions have been raised in the previous section. Uncertainty regarding checking behaviour also occurs with free-response formats; unless the experimenter makes detailed enquiries after the subject has completed the list it is difficult to determine whether an unchecked item was genuinely inappropriate or was merely overlooked. As noted earlier, serial position effects may also occur. There are also vast individual differences in the number of adjectives checked. Modifications of scales to true–false format (Siller and Chipman, 1963) or 'yes', 'no' and 'irrelevant' (Warr and Knapper, 1967) may give different results than the original scale. Little is known about the effect of such changes. Because of the nature of mood checklists, Nowlis has emphasized the need for extreme simplicity of instruction and format in order not to disrupt what may be a transient mood state. For university or college level subjects, the method of completion is self-evident, and thus the requirement for minimal instructions is possible. For the general population, particularly those not used to completing forms, who may have a lower level of comprehension or a restricted vocabulary, more explicit instructions need to be given; these may either be written or verbal. If testing is carried out in the field, such as a factory, it is usually easier to test people in ones and twos rather than more so than the investigator can be on hand to answer queries. Also, some of the fairly uncommon words used in checklists (e.g. introspective, aloof, nonchalant) may present difficulties to some of the population. It may be possible to substitute alternative adjectives but this should be attempted with caution. Allowance must also be made for the time needed to complete the checklist. There are considerable individual differences. Many can complete a fifty item checklist in approximately two minutes; others, however, can take up to ten minutes. Attempts to hurry these slower subjects may lead to feelings of inferiority or anxiety; this should be avoided if at all possible.

Another crucial aspect of administration concerns the timebase over which the subject is asked to provide his checklist response. Following Nowlis, most investigators ask the subject to report his mood at the moment of completing the checklist. Others, notably Zuckerman and Lubin (1965), have used longer timebases such as 'over the past few hours', 'today' and 'over the past week'. It is likely that with the longer timebases the checklists will be estimating more enduring factors probably related to personality. As we have seen, responses to these forms are more influenced by response set effects. Moreover, it may be difficult to determine the response strategy adopted by the subject. Some may provide an estimate of all the moods experienced during the previous week, others may respond in terms of their most heightened or enduring mood state and others may give an 'on average' estimate. It is likely that 'recency' effects also occur.

These timespan effects may be particularly important in psychophysiological research. Often investigators wish to examine the relationship between changes in physiological systems and changes in mood and feelings. It may be likely that slowly changing systems such as metabolic rate, and cumulative measures such as urine catecholamines will be related to mood changes taken during corresponding periods. Similarly instantaneous mood states may be more accurately reflected by rapidly changing physiological systems (heart rate, skin conductance, respiration, etc.). The use of checklists may be constrained in other ways. If the subject is performing a task which requires continuous attention, checklists cannot be completed unless the task is stopped temporarily. One solution is to give a checklist at the start of the task and one at the end, a difference score can then be taken. Unless fluctuations in mood during the task period are required (in which case the task must be stopped and a checklist administered), as an alternative method the final checklist can be completed for the 'average mood or feelings during the task'. Subjects appear quite able to provide a sensible rating on this basis. It will of course depend upon the length of the task. More importantly, any movements needed for writing or checking adjectives may produce 'noise' or artifacts in the recording of physiological parameters. The experiment may require the subject to have his eyes closed. In this case it may be possible to present the list of adjectives verbally to the subject who could then respond to each adjective with the appropriate scale response (e.g. definitely, slightly, cannot decide, definitely not). The subject could be trained to code his response to the list of adjectives presented verbally by the experimenter. The coded response could then be recorded directly on the polygraph (or other recording device) by the subject activating the appropriate touch sensitive key. The circuitry for such a device has been described by Strahan (1970).

Considerable variations in scoring procedures exist. The Zuckerman and Lubin MAACL is scored for three scales: anxiety, hostility, and depression. Each scale is scored by counting the number of plus items checked and the number of minus adjectives that are not checked. The Nowlis MACL is based upon a four point score, definitely feel (4 points), feel slightly (3 points), cannot decide (2 points), and definitely do not feel (1 point). Each factor is scored by adding the total rating for all adjectives. A variant of this has been used by Herbert, Johns, and Dore (1976), who asked people to respond yes or no to adjectives. If a yes response was appropriate, they were asked to rate the strength of the feeling on a three point scale. The problem of violating ordinality with this scale, however, would still remain. With suitable statistical analysis and data processing facilities it may be possible to treat the 'cannot decide' category as a missing datum. Some suggestions for the scoring of different scales, and for scoring bipolar as well as monopolar factors are shown in Table 9.3.

Table 9.3. Some suggestions for scoring and analysis of adjective checklists

---

A   SCORING

---

1. Monopolar factors (Nowlis)
    Four point asymmetric scale: definitely do not feel (DN) = 1, cannot decide (CD) = 2, feel slightly (FS) = 3, and definitely feel (DF) = 4.

    Example: Nowlis factor D, ELATION

	DF	FS	CD	DN
ELATED	(+ +)	+	?	−
OVERJOYED	+ +	(+)	?	−
PLEASED	(+ +)	+	?	−
REFRESHED	+ +	+	(?)	−

    Score = 4 + 4 + 3 + 2 = 13

---

2. Bipolar factors (Meddis)
    Several methods of scoring bipolar factors can be found in the literature. Clements, Hafer, and Vermillion (1976) (see page 536 for discussion) assigned values of +1 to positively loaded, and −1 to negatively loaded adjectives.

Table 9.3. Continued

A constant is then added to the obtained score in order to remove negative values.

Kjellberg and Bohlin (1974) (see page 536 for discussion) used a reversed scoring procedure so that for negatively loaded adjectives DF = 1, FS = 2, CD = 3, and DN = 4. In scoring the SACL (see page 536) the author has used a system similar to that used by Goldberg (1972) in scoring the General Health Questionnaire.

Example: Arousal factor from SACL

For POSITIVE adjectives $(a_1 - a_8)$, FS(+) and DF(+ +) both score 1
             CD(?) and DN(+) score 0.

For NEGATIVE adjectives $(a_9^+ - a_{15}^-)$, CD(?) and DN(–) both score 1
             FS(+) and DF(+ +) score 0.

This system would also be suitable for a symmetric scale, i.e. definitely feel (+ +), feel slightly (+), do not feel (−) and definitely do not feel (− −)

POSITIVE						Score	NEGATIVE						Score
LIVELY	a_1^+	⊕+	+	?	−	1	DROWSY	a_9^+	++	+	?	⊖	1
ALERT	a_2^+	++	⊕	?	−	1	DULL	a_{10}^+	++	+	⊘	−	1
STIMULATED	a_3^+	++	+	?	⊖	0	SLUGGISH	a_{11}^-	++	+	?	⊖	1
ACTIVE	a_4^+	⊕+	+	?	−	1	TIRED	a_{12}^-	++	+	?	⊖	1
ENERGETIC	a_5^+	++	⊕	?	−	1	SLEEPY	a_{13}^-	++	+	⊘	−	1
VIGOROUS	a_6^+	++	⊕	?	−	1	SOMNOLENT	a_{14}^-	++	+	?	⊖	1
ACTIVATED	a_7^+	⊕+	+	?	−	1	PASSIVE	a_{15}^-	++	⊕	?	−	0
AROUSED	a_8^+	++	⊕	?	−	1							

Total (+) = 7   Total (−) = 6

Arousal factor score = 7 + 6 = 13

B   ANALYSIS

Often the experimenter is interested in the levels of various mood factors in an experimental as compared with a control condition. Analysis is comparatively straightforward although transformation of the data may be desirable if ANOVA is being used. In other circumstances the experimenter may wish to investigate the *change* in mood brought about by an experimental manipulation. The change score (D) is usually calculated by subtracting the response level (Y) from the prestimulus level (X). The change score as computed in this way may not always be a valid estimate since it may depend on prestimulus levels, i.e. D is related to X. Work with the SACL for example has indicated a strong negative relationship between D and X indicative of the law of initial values. Statistical treatment of the raw scores using the ALS of Lacey (1956) or analysis of covariance may be appropriate in this case; however, the reader's attention is drawn to the work of Cronbach and Furby (1970) for a discussion of the problems of using such techniques. Further discussion of these issues from a psychophysiological standpoint can be found in Lykken (1976), Mefferd (1976) and Edgren (1971). See also Chapter 12.

An alternative form of scoring relies upon the use of the signal detection approach. Clark and coworkers (1976) suggest that the virtue of this system is that it eliminates the problem of response sets, such as acquiescence and extreme responding (see Section 2.2.1.3). Two numerical parameters are calculated which can be used to determine fluctuations in mood. The first is a measure of discriminability, d' (d-prime), indicating the person's ability to distinguish which of two possible classes of events is present; it is unconfounded by response bias. The second parameter is the report criterion, expressed as a likelihood ratio L_x. It measures a subject's tendency (bias) to report a signal as present irrespective of whether or not it is actually present. Thus on a mood adjective checklist items representing the 'happy' pole of a factor would be designated as signal and noise $(S + N)$, and those representing 'sad' items as noise (N) only. Thus a high positive value of d' represents a happy mood, $d = 0$ represents an intermediate state and a negative d', a sad state. Changes in L_x represent changes in response bias. High values of L_x indicate that the subject seldom says yes (or 'extremely') to either class of checklist items, conversely a positive value of L_x indicates that extreme responses occur frequently. Multi-items, as well as simple yes/no (dichotomous) scales can both be treated in this way. A major advantage of this technique is that the two parameters, d' and L_x are independent.

2.2.2 Rating scales

An alternative approach to the rating of mood and subjective feelings relies upon the use of rating scales. Two approaches have been developed. First are the visual analogue scales (VAS) and secondly, the graphic rating scales which rely upon a *direct* estimation of the magnitude of a feeling. The basis for the use of such scores is as follows; although a person may appreciate precisely his state on a selected dimension, words may fail (or he cannot find, or does not know the correct word) to describe the *exactness* of the subjective experience. The choice of suitable terms with which to describe and convey quantitative estimates of feeling makes communication of those feelings difficult. The use of categories to describe the presence of a feeling is, in fact, attempting to grade *continuous* phenomena artificially. A *digital* (discontinuous) system is imposed upon the subject where, in fact, an *analogue* (continuous) system would be more appropriate (Aitken, 1969a, 1969b).

2.2.2.1 *Visual analogue scales*

With a visual analogue scale, the subject is required to place a mark across a horizontal line equivalent to the strength of a particular feeling at that time. At each end of the line is a word (these are usually opposites) such as 'calm' and 'excited'. According to the advocates of this rating system the problem of unequal category widths and failure to account for nuances of feeling are, more or less, overcome (Aitken, 1969b; Zeally and Aitken, 1969). Scaling procedures of this type are not new. They were first advocated by Hayes and Patterson (1921) and later by Freyd (1923). Amongst the list of advantages, noted by Freyd, of such scales were: easy for the subject to grasp, quick to fill out and score, small amount of subject motivation needed and, perhaps most important, the subject can make as fine a discrimination as is needed. Joyce (1968) claims that such a method reduces the problem of response set. The style of VASs has some similarities to the semantic differential technique of Osgood, Suci, and Tannenbaum (1957).

Bond and Lader (1974) based their series of VASs on those of Malpas (1971) and Norris (1971). These were administered to members of the general population. After transforming the raw scores, using $\log_e$ to remove skewness, factor analysis revealed the presence of three factors subse-

Table 9.4. The visual analogue scales used in the Bond and Lader (BL) and Herbert, Johns, and Dore (HJD) studies. Bond and Lader found three factors: Alertness (A), Contentedness (CO), and Calmness (C). Herbert, Johns, and Dore found two factors: Alertness (A) and Tranquillity (T). Subscripts refer to the ranks of the loadings on each factor, i.e. 1 = highest loading

			BL	HJD
ALERT	————	DROWSY	A_1	A_2
CALM	————	EXCITED	C_1	T_2
STRONG	————	FEEBLE	A_7	A_6
MUZZY	————	CLEAR-HEADED	A_4	A_7
WELL CO-ORDINATED	————	CLUMSY	A_5	A_8
LETHARGIC	————	ENERGETIC	A_3	A_4
CONTENTED	————	DISCONTENTED	CO_4	T_3
TROUBLED	————	TRANQUIL	CO_3	T_1
MENTALLY SLOW	————	QUICK-WITTED	A_6	A_1
TENSE	————	RELAXED	C_2	T_4
ATTENTIVE	————	DREAMY	A_2	A_3
INCOMPETENT	————	PROFICIENT	A_9	A_5
HAPPY	————	SAD	CO_1	T_5
ANTAGONISTIC	————	AMIABLE[1]	CO_2	T_6
INTERESTED	————	BORED	A_8	A_{11}
WITHDRAWN	————	GREGARIOUS[2]	CO_5	T_7
DEPRESSED	————	ELATED[3]	—	A_9
SELF-CENTRED	————	OUTWARD-GOING[3]	—	A_{10}

[1]'Friendly' used in the HJD study. [2]'Sociable' used in the HJD study. [3]These scales were not used in the BL analysis.

quently labelled 'alertness', 'contentedness' and 'calmness'. These scales together with the three factors are shown in Table 9.4.

A study was conducted by Herbert, Johns, and Dore (1976) using a similar scale to that of Bond and Lader. Thirty-eight subjects completed the VASs on a number of occasions. Two factors were extracted from the transformed data. The first factor is, according to the authors, related to psychomotor performance. The second factor is a combination of Bond and Lader's second and third factors. A comparison of the two studies is made in Table 9.4. The alertness factor is identical in both studies, apart from the two extra scales in the Herbert, Johns, and Dore analysis. The factors in both studies appear to be rather heterogeneous in terms of their item content and for this reason, it is suggested that analysis is carried out at the item level (i.e. for each scale) as well as overall factor scores when assessing the effects of experimental manipulations. The scales were originally designed to assess the effects of drugs on subjective experiences; this is evident from scales such as 'clear-headed–muzzy'. Factor one for example, seems to be a combination of activation describing adjectives (see Section 3), Nowlis-like 'moods' such as 'elation–depression' and behaviourally determined items such as 'proficient' and 'well-coordinated'. Both scales, however, do appear to be valid, in that they are sensitive to pharmacological manipulations (Bond and Lader, 1974) and effects of sleep loss (Herbert, Johns, and Dore, 1976).

An extended study using the Bond and Lader scales can be found in Tyrer (1976). Tyrer carried out analyses at both the factor and item level and was able to demonstrate the effect of a number of drugs in reducing anxiety. A number of correlations between self-reported subjective state and physiological measures were also found.

A similar series of rating scales has been developed by Meddis (1969). Here, 19 bipolar scales were used. A control group of 70 subjects completed the scales at a specified time of day. Three stable factors were extracted. An experimental group of 7 subjects also completed the form every waking hour for three consecutive days. Using a 'P-technique' analysis model (see Section 2.4), three factors were found which were consistent over all subjects. The scales and factors for the control group are shown in Table 9.5.

Meddis reports that all subjects found the procedure of completing the form quite natural and no difficulties of administration were encountered. There were, however, some objections to a number of the pairings such as 'joyful–sickly'. Investigators planning to use such techniques must be careful to ensure that the scales have, as far as possible, semantic opposites, otherwise the task of completing the form may become difficult or annoying for the subject.

Table 9.5. The visual analogue scales used by Meddis (1969). Three factors were
extracted: vigour (V), well-being (W), and tension (T). Subscripts refer to the rank
of the loadings on each factor. Minus signs indicate negative loadings. Asterisks
refer to a factor relating to physical state which was not elaborated upon by
Meddis

UNFIT	————	FIT	V_3
COMFORTABLE	————	UNCOMFORTABLE	$*W_7$
THIRSTY	————	NOT THIRSTY*	
BRIGHT	————	DULL	V_4
UNCONFIDENT	————	CONFIDENT	
IRRITABLE	————	PLACID	T_3 W_5
LOOSE	————	TIGHT	T_1
ENERGETIC	————	EXHAUSTED	$-V_1$
BORED	————	INTERESTED	W_2
DISSATISFIED	————	SATISFIED	W_1
TENSE	————	RELAXED	T_2
JOYFUL	————	SICKLY	
HOSTILE	————	FRIENDLY	W_6
HAPPY	————	SAD	
ILL	————	WELL*	
COLD	————	WARM*	
HUNGRY	————	SATED*	
TIRED	————	AWAKE	
CONTENTED	————	DISCONTENTED	W_3

2.2.2.2 Scoring

Raw scores are obtained simply by measuring from the left hand end of
the scale to the subject's vertical mark. Typically, 100 mm lines have been
used with words of opposite meaning at each end. Transformations, such as
$\log_e$ or arcsin (see Winer, 1962) can be made on the raw scores if the frequency distributions do not appear to be normal, or if scores of zero are
found. If repeated administration of the form is intended, a weighting procedure can be adopted by the use of factor scores (if these are available).
A factor score would be the raw score for all the scales each multiplied by
the loading of that scale on the factor under consideration. In mathematical notation (Meddis, 1969);

$$f_{ij} = \sum^k l_{ik}z_{jk},$$

where f_{ij} is the factor score for the ith factor on the jth administration
of the form; l_{jk} is the loading of the kth scale on the ith factor, and z_{jk} is
the raw score on the kth scale for the jth administration. $\log_e z_{jk}$ may be
substituted for the raw score for the reasons outlined above. Meddis also
noted idiosyncratic use of the scale by some individuals. To compensate for
this he suggests the use of standardized scores for f_{ij}'s.

2.2.3 Direct scaling methods

Several Scandinavian investigators (Fröberg and coworkers, 1975; Singer, Lundberg, and Frankenhaeuser, 1974) have adapted the direct magnitude estimation method of Stevens (1972) for use in psychophysiological studies. Self-ratings of mood and subjective experiences have been gathered using this scaling technique. It relies upon the fundamental assumption that the subject is capable of reporting a *quantitative* estimate of a subjective experience or of reporting *quantitative* relations between subjective experiences. Subjects are more able than most people think (including the subjects themselves) to produce meaningful quantitative estimates of their experiences (Lundberg, personal communication). Psychophysical studies using this technique suggest that estimates are not always accurate but they are without any serious systematic error. Unfortunately in studies of mood we have no external standard by which we can assess accuracy of reporting. The method used is a very simple one although several slight variations exist. Johansson (1976) used a 120 mm graphic scale. Subjects were asked to let the endpoints of the score represent recollections of their maximum and minimum experience of the eight mood variables under investigation. The subjects were instructed, for each occasion of testing and for each scale, to first indicate by a vertical *line* the position of their 'ordinary' state of mind, and secondly to indicate by means of a vertical *arrow* their state of mind during the preceding experimental session. An example is shown in Figure 9.2.

After several administrations an estimate of the mean value of *A* could be made. This could then be used in subsequent analyses for determining the values of *S* under different experimental manipulations. However, it is not clear on what basis the subjects make estimates of *A* and it is possible that because of the nature of the scale (maximum–minimum ever experienced) they will make estimates of *A* towards the centre of the line. These scales may also be prone to response set effects. Some of the methods described already may be useful in minimizing these effects. The use of

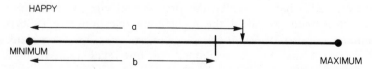

Figure 9.2 Direct magnitude estimation scaling technique used by Johansson (1976). The vertical line is an estimate by the person of his 'usual' state. The arrow indicates the persons response to the preceding experimental situation. The relative response (R) is given by the value of b−a

geometric, rather than arithmetic, means is recommended for manipulating raw data from these scales (Stevens, 1972). An indication of the validity of such scales is provided by Eckman and coworkers (1964). These workers investigated the effect of alcohol consumption upon blood alcohol levels (BALs) and subjective intoxication. The BALs and the subjective estimates of intoxication showed remarkably similar changes as a function of time after drinking.

2.2.4 Questionnaire techniques

Some investigators, notably Cattell and colleagues (Cattell, 1973) have taken a more orthodox approach to the study of mood. The basis of their approach is that moods are *states*. In order to determine their structure adequately, it is critical to separate them from *traits*, and thus analysis must proceed on a different basis. Since, in the case of states, we are interested in fluctuations, measurements on the hypothesized mood variables must be made on at least two occasions. Two factor analytic techniques have been used for this purpose. The first technique is called (longitudinal) P-technique (P refers to person). Here, analysis is performed on raw data obtained from a single person over many occasions (typically 100 days). It was first reported by Cattell, Cattell, and Rhymer (1947). P-technique factor analysis reveals state-response dimensions. The second approach, differential R-technique (dR for short) measures N people on m variables on two separate occasions sufficiently spaced in time to allow changes in mood to have occurred. The raw data for analysis are made up of the *difference* scores on the variables between the two occasions. Cattell criticizes much of the adjective checklist work because investigators have invariably used R-technique (i.e. analysis of N people on the variables on a *single* occasion). This Cattell argues only reveals information about the presence of traits. The conceptual and methodological arguments cannot be dealt with here. A detailed discussion is presented in Cattell (1973, Chap. 6). For our present purposes, it is only worth noting that both P and dR analysis techniques produce essentially similar 'state' factors. Various analyses (Cattell, 1973; Barton, Cattell, and Connor, 1972; Barton, Cattell, and Curran, 1973) have revealed the presence of eight state factors. The published instrument is called the eight state questionnaire (8SQ)* The questionnaire consists of 96 items, 12 of which measure each state. Two parallel forms, A and B, are available, The test takes approximately half an hour to complete.

*Available from Institute of Personality and Ability Testing, 1602 Coronado Drive, Champaign, Illinois 61820 USA, or in the UK from National Foundation for Educational Research, Darville House, 2 Oxford Road East, Windsor SL4 1DF.

The form of the questions is shown in the two examples below:

Example 1: 'I am doing as well as I really can today',
        (a) very true
        (b) fairly true
        (c) fairly false
        (d) very false

Example 2: 'At this moment I'd rather',
        (a) lie down and rest
        (b) just take it easy
        (c) do something, but nothing too active
        (d) do something active and exciting

Details of administration, scoring, and calculation of standard scores are given in the test manual. The eight scales measured by the 8SQ are ANXIETY (worried, emotionally upset); STRESS (feeling a lot of pressure, hectic, unhappy with own performance); DEPRESSION (unhappy, disagreeable); REGRESSION (confused, difficulty in coping); FATIGUE (exhausted, no energy); GUILT (regretful, unkind, dissatisfied with self); EXTRAVERSION (sociable, outgoing); and AROUSAL (alert, keyed up).

Reliability coefficients from a test–(immediate) retest analysis are in the region of 0.90. After one week, the stability coefficients, as one would expect, have become considerably less, 0.53–0.62 (forms A + B). The length of time needed for completion, stability over short durations, and wording of some questions suggest that the 8SQ is most appropriate for the measurement of mood changes over periods of days and weeks. The intercorrelations between factors are surprisingly high. For example, on a population of 1266 men and women, the correlation between arousal and extraversion was 0.71, and between anxiety and depression 0.77. Cattell (1973) suggests that these high intercorrelations are due to the sensitivity of state measures to time sequence effects which tend to inflate relationships between scales, e.g. 'a frustrating situation arouses anger, which is likely to produce attack, which is likely to produce anxiety, which in most cases without solution is likely to end in depression' (Cattell 1973, p. 221). The instrument does seem to be sensitive to fluctuations in mood throughout the day and it has been suggested that separate 'norms' which reflect these differences be used when assessing changes in mood (Barton and Cattell, 1974). However, until more empirical studies are reported in the literature using the 8SQ, the exact nature of these intercorrelations and other aspects of the test remain unclear.

2.3 Mood and psychophysiological studies

In a number of studies mood adjective checklists have been used in conjunction with psychophysiological variables. What follows is a fairly representative list of studies. Meddis (1969) found low but significant correlations between sublingual body temperature and mood clusters obtained from longitudinal P-technique. High body temperature was related to wakefulness and low temperature to drowsiness. In one individual, however, this pattern of correlation was reversed. Zuckerman, Persky, and Link (1969) found that anxiety scores on the MAACL were correlated with skin conductance changes. Roessler, Burchard, and Childers (1966) found some correlation between scores on the Clyde mood scale and skin resistance. Malmstrom (1968) found a correlation between various mood scales and heart rate. Similarly, Roth and coworkers (1976) found correlations between heart rate and factors on the Lorr, Daston, and Smith POMS. The factor with the highest correlations was that of vigour. The authors note that this may reflect physical rather than mental activity. This difficulty in separating effects from physical and emotional components may be crucial in longitudinal studies (e.g. occupational settings) where there are likely to be equal amounts from each source. Handlon (1962) used the Nowlis MACL with a modified scoring system to investigate the effects of hospitalisation. Increases in three of the scales (anxiety, depression and aggression) were related to increases in urinary 17-hydroxycorticosteroid levels, whilst increases in scores on pleasantness, social affection and activation were related to decreases in output. Christie and Venables (1973) investigated changes in mood in relation to age, Maudsley Personality Inventory (MPI) score, day, and time of day. Although no physiological data were reported, a number of interesting findings emerged. Several of the original MACL factors were merged (as with the Handlon study) to provide three new dimensions: concentration, activation, and deactivation were summed to produce a dimension called efficiency; anxiety and depression were summed to produce a 'dysphoria' dimension; and social affection and pleasantness were used to form a euphoria dimension. The efficiency dimension showed the most significant changes. In general, the largest factor score changes were found in high neuroticism (N)/low extraversion (E) subjects, and were lowest in low N/high E subjects. A further study (Venables and Christie, 1974) investigated personality changes, mood, and salivary flow and concentration at the beginning and end of the week. Here, however, no clear relationships between mood and the other variables of interest were found. Seligman (1975) investigated mood shifts and skin potential changes in students during a series of counselling sessions. The short form of the Nowlis MACL was used. In addition, subjects were asked to select and rank only their three strongest feelings rather than all 33 adjectives on the list. The list was administered to each subject five times during the interview at points where 'distinctive' patterns of change in skin potential occurred. Feelings characterized as 'pleasant' (carefree, elated, overjoyed, playful, pleased, witty) were frequently accompanied by negative skin potential deflections, whereas feelings described as 'unpleasant' (sad, sorry, etc.) were associated with positive and, less often, neutral skin potential waves. Katkin (1966) investigated the effect of threat of shock on two experimental groups; those who scored high on the AACL (Zuckerman, 1960) and those who had a low score. There was no difference in the mean number of spontaneous GSRs between the two groups in response to the threat of electric shock. However, the high scoring group took significantly longer for their GSRs to recover to baseline levels.

In a number of studies, Lazarus and collaborators (1962) have used a motion picture of gruesome surgical operations to induce stress in subjects. Measures of skin resistance, heart rate, and mood changes on the MACL were monitored simultaneously. Whilst the mood and physiological parameters both changed significantly during the film, no correlations were observed between them. Lazarus suggests that the dependability of the subjects would argue against a social desirability effect, rather the lack of correlation indicates a true independence between physiological and self report systems. Lack of correlations should not therefore be automatically interpreted in terms of unreliable measurement systems.

2.4 EEG measures and subjective reports

A major area in which reports of subjective state have been used as the primary dependent variable of interest is that of alpha and other rhythms. Many of the early experiments in this area reported that subjects experienced altered or heightened mood during the alpha feedback sessions reminiscent of those known to accompany meditational states associated with zen and yoga. Typically, subjects reported feelings of peacefulness, tranquillity, distorted time perception and loss of bodily sensation (Brown, 1970; Kamiya, 1969; Nowlis and Kamiya, 1970). More recent studies, however, have failed to find a relationship between subjective experiences and alpha activity, or have found inconclusive evidence (Plotkin, 1976; Sacks and coworkers, 1972). A number of related reasons for these discrepant findings have been proposed. Walsh (1974) has shown that for an 'alpha experience' to occur not only do alpha waves need to be present but, prior to the feedback session, the subject needs to be given an appropriate instructional set, i.e. the subject needs to be prepared for the situation by being told what he is likely to experience. Lynch and Paskewitz (1971) have suggested that some of the reports of feelings of well-being and general positive mood may stem from the satisfaction the subjects feels from succeeding at the alpha feedback task. Another major determinant of the occurrence of alpha related subjective reports is that of the state of relaxation of the subject. Marshall and Bentler (1976) have shown that deeply relaxed subjects report significantly more alpha states than less relaxed subjects. The same authors also found some evidence for the hypothesis that subjective reports are related to the precise frequency of alpha brainwaves used for feedback. Other possible related factors are the occurrence of mild sensory deprivation leading to lack of awareness of bodily boundaries (Peper, 1971) and similarly perceptual deprivation effects due to unfocusing of externally directed attention (Lynch and Paskewitz, 1971).

The gathering of subjective reports in biofeedback experiments has followed traditional lines. Most studies have relied upon some form of post session interview or questionnaire; typically copies of the written protocols are circulated 'blind' to a number of judges for the purpose of coding using criteria usually derived from previous literature. Walsh (1974) used five such criteria: state of arousal, body awareness, emotional state, state of consciousness, and visual attentiveness. Each item in the protocol was scored on a five point scale from -2 denoting non-alpha experience to $+2$ denoting definite alpha experience. These were then summed to produce an overall subjective report score. A similar scoring procedure was used by Marshall and Bentler (1976). In addition these authors used a 57 item adjective checklist composed of alpha and non-alpha related experiences. This was scored using the same criteria as the written descriptions of the subjects of their experiences during the feedback session. Although the experimenter wishes to collect as full a picture as possible of the subjects' experiences, very complex or lengthy post experimental sessions may place an excessive demand upon the person and may lead to frustration and impaired recall of what may be quite transient and unfamiliar mood states. This may be particularly the case when the subject is naive. An alternative approach used by some investigators is to employ spontaneous reports of mood during the feedback session. Rather than verbal reports subjects could be trained to touch sensitive keys which with an appropriate coding system would allow the recording of quite complex mood changes in synchrony with shifts in brainwave activity. Highly practiced subjects may be required here if the coding task demands levels of mental activity that disrupt or mask the brainwave activity under investigation (e.g. alpha blocking taking place).

2.5 Self-reported mood: summary and recommendations

Studies investigating the structure and measurement of self-reported mood have produced inconsistent findings. Early work by Nowlis and his collaborators found, using factor analytic studies, a large number of mood dimensions, each composed of a few adjectives. Changes in these mood factors have been reported in many studies and some have varied in a similar fashion to physiological variables. However, more often than not, factors have altered in a similar fashion or not at all; a finding one would not often expect if they were independent. Moreover, where factors have altered in a complex fashion the investigator has been hindered by the lack of a conceptual schema in which to fit his data. Often investigators have collapsed three or more factors into a larger one, supposedly tapping 'unpleasant moods' or 'positive (euphoric) moods'. More recent work has been critical of the Nowlis type studies on methodological grounds. Deficiencies in the type of rating score used (Meddis, 1969, 1972; Svensson, 1977) and inappropriate psychometric models (Sjöberg and Svensson, 1976) have been shown to be primarily responsible for the unwieldy multifactor solutions previously found. With these deficiencies removed a much simpler picture of the structure of mood emerges. Whilst the evidence is by no means overwhelming, it is tempting to suggest that mood is essentially two dimensional. One dimension has been labelled activation (Sjöberg and Svensson, 1976) and vigour (Meddis, 1969). A similar factor has also been found by Bush (1973) and Davitz (1969). Because of its obvious significance as a psychophysiological concept the measurement of self-reported arousal is discussed at length in Section 3. The second dimension has been variously labelled pleasantness–unpleasantness (Sjöberg and Svensson, 1976; Bush, 1973) and hedonic tone (Meddis, 1969). This dimension would also appear to have a biological basis. An organism is in a continual transaction with both its internal and external environments, which involves problem solving activities aimed at meeting both internal and external demands. This pleasantness/hedonic tone dimension reflects the appraisal of the likelihood of these demands being met which will in turn depend upon the current preparedness of the organism (both physical and psychological well being) and the probability of success against failure and its consequences. All other moods, emotions and feelings can thus be interpreted within this two-dimensional non-specific framework. These reflect or are induced by situational determinants: factors associated with the immediate environment (internal and external) of the person. It is possible, however, that these two levels, the non-specific and the situational level, are continually interacting. It is also likely (Meddis, 1969) that over the middle ranges these two dimensions are truly orthogonal. Under extreme circumstances, however, one would expect large correlations.

This two factor formulation has a number of implications for the routine measurement of mood. Although a two-dimensional approach removes many of the difficulties and complexities of analysis and interpretation inherent in multifactor checklists, such a checklist does not exist at the time of writing (the reader's attention is drawn, however, to the stress–arousal checklist (SACL) discussed on p. 536) Several options exist. Investigators may continue to use the original lists of adjectives as presented by Nowlis and others but should bear in mind first, that the asymmetrical scale has a number of drawbacks and a symmetric scale may be more appropriate; and secondly that a two factor framework would seem to be the most satisfactory way of conceptualizing mood data. Those wishing to use self-reported mood as a principal variable of investigation are urged to experiment with a selection or combination of factors, adjectives, and scales, and to examine alternative scoring methods. It is recommended that possible occurrence of response set effects, inconsistent checking of opposites and possible social desirability effects be monitored. This can be achieved fairly straightforwardly by the methods outlined above.

3. SELF-REPORTED AROUSAL

3.1 Checklists measuring self-reported arousal

The original work of Nowlis and Green (1957), described earlier, had as several of the extracted factors some which described feelings and moods related to the hypothetical continuum variously called 'arousal; or 'activation'. These three factors Nowlis labelled anxiety (factor B), fatigue (factor F) and vigour (factor K). (The reader may wish to refer back to Table 9.1.) Some or all of these factors have emerged, or have been hypothesized, in many of the other checklist studies (Zuckerman, 1960; McNair and Lorr, 1964; Hendrick and Lilly, 1970; Clyde, 1960).

In several studies, Thayer (1963, 1967) has refined the activation descriptive factors originally found by Nowlis. The bases for Thayer's work were as follows:

(1) Imprecise and poorly defined activation descriptive factors found by Nowlis and others.

(2) The advantage of having a self-report measure of arousal which would eliminate the need for apparatus.

(3) The fact that some bodily systems may be more representative of total organismic activity than others (based upon the Lacey (1967) hypothesis). A system with comparable measurement properties across individuals would remove the problem of 'individual response stereotypy'. The phenomenological awareness of all bodily systems contributing to the level of arousal may provide such a system and would therefore be a better indicant than a single peripheral physiological measure.

(4) Such a self-report system would have the added benefits of low cost and ease of administration and scoring.

In particular, Thayer investigated the merits of self-reported arousal as against one, or a combination of, the usual physiological indices. As a starting point Thayer used the theoretical position of Duffy (1962) together with the methodological approach and empirical evidence of Nowlis and Green (1957). Thus activation descriptive adjectives were selected on the basis that they described 'all aspects of a non-directional intensity continuum ranging from extreme excitement to deep sleep' (Thayer, 1967). 49 adjectives were used in all, 29 of which had clear activational content. The remainder were a variety of mood adjectives (i.e. they implied *direction* as well as *intensity*), some of which were used by Nowlis. The purpose of the 'true' mood adjectives was to disguise the purpose of the checklist. These adjectives together with the same four point scale as Nowlis were administered to 211 male and female students. The scores were then intercorrelated, followed by a factor analytic step involving Thurstone centroid extraction and varimax rotation. This and subsequent analyses using different sets of adjectives and oblique as well as orthogonal rotation have revealed the presence of four monopolar activation descriptive adjectives. Many validity and reliability studies have been conducted (Thayer, 1970, 1971a, 1971b; Thayer and Cox, 1968, 1969; Thayer and coworkers, 1970). The instrument developed from this work is called the activation–deactivation–adjective checklist (AD–ACL). The four factors are shown in Table 9.6.

The four main factors: deactivation–sleep (DS); general deactivation (GD); general activation (GA); and high activation (HA); are all monopolar. Thus the concept of a single bipolar factor, the phenomenological equivalent of the underlying hypothesized continuum of Duffy, would appear to be an oversimplification. In principle a decrease on one or both of the positive activation factors (GA, HA) could be accompanied by a decrease in one or both of the negative activation factors (GD, DS). As with the Nowlis studies, these independent changes in concepts thought to be mutually interdependent are opposed to the commonly held views of both scientist and layman. To account for this finding, Thayer (1967) stated that 'These factors roughly approximate four points on a hypothetical activation continuum.' The pattern of change we would expect if this were true is shown schematically in Figure 9.3.

Nevertheless, however sensible this may seem, the four factors must, due to the factor analytic procedures used, represent separate and independent continua. Elsewhere, Thayer (1971a) has stated that 'the use of the AD–ACL does not necessarily imply acceptance of the assumption that a single activation continuum underlies all behaviour . . .'.

Table 9.6. A summary table showing the activation factors found by Thayer in his original (Thayer, 1967) and subsequent studies

General Activation	High Activation
Lively[1]	Clutched up[1]
Active[1]	Jittery[1]
Full of pep[1]	Stirred up
Energetic[1]	Fearful[1]
Peppy	Intense[1]
Vigorous[1]	Tense[1,2]
Activated	Anxious[2]

General Deactivation	Deactivation–sleep
At rest[1]	Sleepy[1]
Still[1]	Tired[1]
Leisurely	Drowsy[1]
Quiescent	Wide awake[1,2,3]
Quiet[1]	Wakeful[1,2,3]
Calm[1]	
Placid[1]	

[1]Adjectives on short form. [2]Adjectives added in revised version. [3]Scoring of these adjectives reversed.

More recent work (Thayer, 1971a) reports that factors obtained from additional analyses using both orthogonal and oblique rotations differ in their stability and independence (see Table 9.6). In a recent amended and revised version of the AD–ACL (Thayer, 1975, unpublished) the deactivation–sleep factor has become bipolar. Since Thayer used the same four-point asymmetrical scale as originally used by Nowlis, his monopolar factors may have been caused by the scale. This possibly was tested by Meddis (1969, 1972). Using a similar list of adjectives, Meddis compared the original asymmetric scale with the new symmetric scale. The new scale provided bipolar factors, two of which corresponded (approximately) to a combination of general activation with deactivation–sleep, and high activation and general deactivation. This particular finding will be returned to later in more detail.

The AD–ACL has been used as a self-report measure of arousal in a number of studies. Olmedo, Kirk, and Suarez (1973) showed that variable combinations of light and white noise led to a decrease in general activation scores and an increase in general deactivation scores during a vigilance task. No correlations between AD–ACL factor scores and detection efficiency were found. Thayer and Carey (1974) showed that

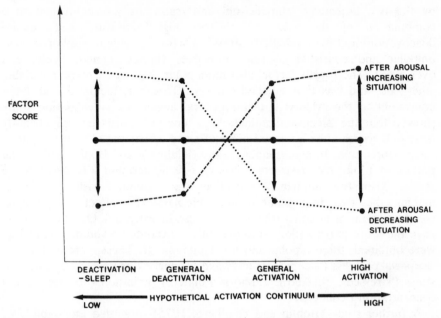

Figure 9.3   A schematic representation of the hypothetical activation continuum proposed by Thayer (1967) showing the effects of both an increase and a decrease in arousal on the four factor pattern

moderate increases in white noise had a significant effect upon high activation and general deactivation. M. Eysenck (1974) used the general activation score to discriminate between low and high activation level subjects. A complex interaction between activation level and noise exposure on the experimental task indicated that high activation facilitates recall of high dominance items from semantic memory. Here, what is supposed to be a 'state' measure is being used as a 'trait' measure, i.e. as a more enduring personality characteristic. Other studies with the AD–ACL have been carried out by Thayer and Moore (1972), Morrison and Walters (1972), Munz, Costello and Korabik (1975) and Wittmaier (1974).

The original AD–ACL has been used as a basis for the development of checklists in languages other than English. Bohlin and Kjellberg (1973) have described the development of a Swedish version of the AD–ACL. 27 activation descriptive words together with 25 with no activation content were given to 204 psychology students during a lecture period. The Nowlis asymmetric scale was used. After several analyses of the data, a four factor solution was adopted. Factor 1 represented a bipolar sleep–wakefulness continuum and was equivalent to the (revised) AD–ACL factor deactivation–sleep. The second factor was also bipolar, and was anchored by the two adjectives 'clutched-up' and 'calm'. It was equivalent to a combination of the AD–ACL factors high activation and general deactivation and was labelled 'stress'. Factor 3, called 'euphoria', was unipolar and consisted of four adjectives (peppy, elated, lively, and overjoyed). The fourth factor, also monopolar, had as its marker variable 'energetic; and was thus labelled 'energy'. Together, factors 3 and 4 are equivalent to the AD–ACL factor general activation. A validation study showed that the 'sleep–wakefulness' and 'energy' factors had significantly increased scores after a normal night of sleep as compared with a night of sleep deprivation. In a subsequent study (Kjellberg and Bohlin, 1974), the previously found factor structure was cross-validated and was shown to be stable. Also, the number of adjectives was extended with the aim of making the two monopolar factors bipolar. The effects of oblique, compared with orthogonal rotation were also investigated. Oblique rotation gave the more parsimonious solution. In the extended inventory six factors were obtained, three bipolar and three monopolar. These were as follows: sleep–wakefulness ('sleepy', 'wide awake'); energy ('energetic', 'apathetic'); stress ('stressed', 'relaxed'); euphoria ('elated'); irritation ('irritated'); and concentration ('collected').

A further study (Bohlin and Kjellberg, 1975) examined the stability of the revised instrument, in particular its factorial complexity at different levels of arousal. Three different situations were chosen: during the evening prior to bedtime; during a lecture; and during an examination. The six factors, previously described, were found in the lecture situation but were reduced to five in the examination group and four in the evening group. The authors conclude that the six factor solution is an appropriate one, but that in certain situations, one or perhaps two of the factors may become redundant.

Clements, Hafer, and Vermillion (1976) have similarly performed a re-analysis of Thayer's original list of adjectives with the aim of constructing a single, true activation continuum. These investigators found two major factors; a bipolar dimension consisting of the original deactivation–sleep adjectives (negative loadings) and the general activation factor (positive loadings); and a factor similar to high activation (but with two moderately loading negative adjectives). This was interpreted as an anxiety–tension factor. The first bipolar factor was chosen as that most consistent with a hypothetical arousal continuum. This showed a pronounced inverted U shape when administered at different times during the day, suggesting its sensitivity to circadian fluctuations in arousal.

The present writer has used the AD–ACL in a number of investigations but has, on occasions, experienced some difficulty in interpreting the results obtained. One possibility was that British populations experienced

Table 9.7. Adjectives loading on the two factors of the stress–arousal checklist (SACL)

Stress		Arousal	
Positive	Negative	Positive	Negative
Tense	Peaceful	Active	Drowsy
Worried	Relaxed	Energetic	Tired
Apprehensive	Cheerful	Vigorous	Idle
Bothered	Contented	Alert	Sluggish
Uneasy	Pleasant	Lively	Sleepy
Dejected	Comfortable	Activated	Somnolent
Uptight	Calm	Stimulated	Passive
Jittery	Restful	Aroused	
Nervous			
Distressed			
Fearful			

difficulty in responding to adjectives of a predominantly American orientation (e.g. 'peppy'). A re-analysis of a number of Thayer's adjectives (less the American words) and with new ones added was carried out on a large sample of male and female British undergraduates (Mackay *et al.*, 1978). Several analyses using both oblique and orthogonal rotation were performed on the data. After inspecting many of the solutions from the factor analyses, a two factor solution was adopted as the most satisfactory. The two factors have been labelled stress and arousal and the instrument has been called the stress–arousal checklist (SACL).* The adjectives loading on these two factors are shown in Table 9.7.

The 'stress' factor is interpreted as an internal response to the evaluation of the favourability of the external (and internal) environment. The 'arousal' factor has been thought of as a phenomenological representation or integration of ongoing autonomic and somatic activity. A number of studies carried out so far suggest that the two factors are differentially sensitive to a variety of environmental, task, and drug effects. Some representative data are shown in Figure 9.4. This shows changes over a 15 minute period during which the subject performed a psychomotor task under one of three noise conditions. SACLs were given before and after the task period. (For details of experimental procedures see Simpson, Cox, and Rothschild (1974).)

In this series of experiments we have consistently found the stress factor to be more sensitive to changes in noise level. The arousal factor, which

*Copies of the SACL, instructions, and scoring keys are available from the author.

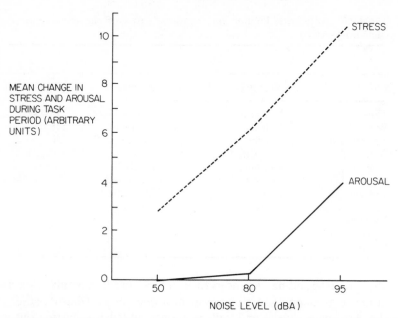

Figure 9.4 Effects of noise on the stress and arousal factors of the SACL. The data shown represent increases in both factors over the task period

corresponds more to the idea of a continuum representing sleep—wakefulness, is susceptible to longer term changes. For example, it is sensitive to circadian fluctuations and sleep loss.

3.2 Validity of self-reported arousal

Essentially, two approaches to the problem of validity have been adopted by those concerned with the development of self-reported arousal checklists. Since the concept of a unidimensional continuum representing arousal, at least as measured by physiological indices, has been discredited (Lacey, 1967), one approach has been to anchor the phenomenological concept of arousal to independent variables (hypothesized to alter arousal levels) rather than to examine intercorrelations (Kjellberg and Bohlin, 1974). Some of the changes in self-reported arousal have been discussed already. Nevertheless, however sensible and valid these changes may seem, it has been implicit in the development of such inventories that they should be related, at least partially, to orthodox physiological indicants of arousal. Thayer (1967) carried out several studies, as part of a validation exercise, using skin resistance and heart rate. He suggested that self-report measures would correlate more highly with physiological composites (combinations of physiological measures) than individual physiological measures would correlate amongst themselves, based upon the hypothesis that self-report measures are a more accurate reflection of overall general bodily activation than are individual peripheral systems. Thayer used a variety of mildly threatening situations (paced arithmetic task, loud buzzers, mild electric shocks) to induce an increase in activation. In all three situations, correlations between AD–ACL factors and either physiological composites or individual physiological measures were found. As hypothesized, intercorrelations between AD–ACL factors and physiological variables were higher than those between the physiological measures themselves.

Table 9.8. Correlations between the difference scores of the AD–ACL factors of Thayer (see Table 9.6) and individual psychophysiological variables or combinations of variables for physiological index A and index B (see text). Copyright © 1970 The Society for Psychophysiological Research. Reprinted with permission of the publisher from Thayer, R. E. (1970). Activation states as assessed by verbal report and four psychophysiological variables *Psychophysiology*, **7**, 86–94

Psychophysiological variables	AD–ACL factors			
	General activation	High activation	General deactivation	Deactivation–sleep
Index A				
SC	0.29	0.00	0.30	0.31*
HR	0.33*	0.34*	0.21	0.31*
BV	0.01	0.25	0.11	−0.09
MAP[a]	0.15	0.10	−0.03	0.13
SC–HR–BV–MAP[a]	0.46**	0.38*	0.39*	0.12
SC–HR–BV	0.53**	0.33*	0.46**	0.33*
SC–HR–MAP[a]	0.52**	0.20	0.36*	0.33*
SC–BV–MAP[a]	0.23	0.29	0.36	0.02
HR–BV–MAP[a]	0.34*	0.30	0.10	0.05
SC–HR	0.62**	0.21	0.48**	0.53**
SC–BV	0.36*	0.36*	0.42**	0.12
SC–MAP[a]	0.25	0.06	0.30	0.15
HR–BV	0.30	0.36*	0.23	0.14
HR–MAP[a]	0.33*	0.17	0.00	0.17
BV–MAP[a]	0.18*	0.31*	0.09	0.03
Index B				
SC–HR–BV–MAP[a]	0.47**	0.34*	0.36*	0.39*
SC–HR–BV	0.48**	0.44**	0.31*	0.44**
SC–HR	0.45**	0.35**	0.46**	0.22

[a]38 subjects were used in these correlations.
*$p < 0.05$.
**$p < 0.01$.

Overall, the general activation factor showed the greatest number of correlations. A second investigation extended this approach using a similar experimental paradigm but with two extra physiological measures; muscle action potentials (MAPs) and relative finger blood volume (BVs). As with the previous study a difference score was used as the basis for analysis (activation period scores minus control (pre) scores). Two types of physiological index were employed. Index, A, based upon the individual response specificity approach, used the single system showing the greatest change. Index B used all four physiological measures equally weighted in an additive model. The correlations between the AD–ACL factors and the various physiological indices are shown in Table 9.8.

The 'largest response system' model (index A) yielded higher correlations with AD–ACL factors than did simple physiological systems. The composite of skin conductance and heart rate gave the largest correlations. The additive model (index B) also yielded significant correlations, although they were generally lower than index A. Correlations between physiological variables themselves were generally low and insignificant. These findings have led Thayer (1970) to suggest that 'the results lend evidence to the contention that self report may be an integrative variable more representative of general status of bodily activation than any single psychophysiological variable'. Similarly, H. J. Eysenck (1975) has concluded that controlled verbal report may be in many ways the preferred method by which to measure arousal.

Bohlin and Kjellberg (1973) manipulated arousal levels by the use of one night's sleep deprivation (compared with normal sleep). After the period of sleep deprivation the effect of a passive habituation procedure on four physiological measures was investigated. These measures were body temperature, EEG (parieto-occipital), skin conductance, and skin conductance responses. The correlations between Bohlin and Kjellberg's four original factors and the physiological measures are shown in Table 9.9. No data on the effect of the habituation procedure on self-reported arousal were given. Similarly, no intercorrelations between physiological measures were presented.

Clements, Hafer, and Vermillion (1976) investigated the relationship between their revised activation factor in a 'passive' ('relax and remain motionless') and an 'active' (backward subtraction task) condition. Pulse rate (PR), respiration rate (RR), and skin resistance (SRL) were recorded continuously throughout the five minute experimental period. The revised AD–ACL was administered after the experimental phase. In the passive condition, the arousal factor correlated with both PR and RR ($p < 0.001$) but not with SRL, which remained unchanged during the experimental period. No intercorrelations between physiological measures were found. In

Table 9.9. Correlations between physiological variables and ratings made before and after an habituation experiment involving repeated auditory stimulation. Reprinted with permission of *Scandinavian Journal of Psychology* from Bohlin, G. and Kjellberg, A. (1973). Self-reported arousal during sleep deprivation and its relation to performance and physiological variables, *Scand. J. Psychol.*, **14**, 78–86

	Sleep–wakefulness		Stress		Euphoria		Energy	
	Before	After	Before	After	Before	After	Before	After
Initial SCL	0.462*		-0.023		-0.170		-0.009	
Initial number of spontaneous SCRs	0.162		-0.191		0.331		0.212	
Temperature before	-0.242		-0.174		0.388		0.733**	
Mean SCL		0.456*		-0.086		0.407		0.324
Total number of spontaneous SCRs		0.270		0.163		0.240		0.586*
EEG–alert		0.442		0.156		0.325		0.481*
Weighted sleep		-0.446		-0.242		0.389		-0.578*
Temperature after		0.630**		-0.074		0.606**		0.692**

*$p < 0.05$.
**$p < 0.01$.

the active condition the instrument correlated with all three physiological measures. A low but significant correlation between PR and SRL was found ($r = 0.36, p < 0.05$).

Bell (1973) (see also Bell, Christie, and Venables, 1975) carried out a detailed investigation of the changes in the original AD–ACL during the menstrual cycle. Subjects were relaxing in bed rest conditions. A variety of electrodermal and cardiovascular parameters were measured. Several low but significant correlations were found, mainly between the physiological measures and the factors deactivation–sleep and general deactivation (these two factors changed during the cycle, general activation and high activation did not). A high correlation between high activation and palmar K^+ did, however, emerge ($r = 0.648, p < 0.001$).

Dermer and Berscheid (1972) examined the validity of self-reported estimates of arousal using a simple rating scale approach. 51 subjects were asked to keep a diary hourly (whilst awake) for four consecutive days. Subjects were asked to record their estimate of subjective arousal on a scale running from -10 (extreme tiredness) to $+10$ (extreme alertness) using an integer number. Using a curve fitting technique (Halberg, Tong, and Johnson, 1965, COSINOR model) a circadian rhythm approximating to 24 hours was detected. The parameters of the fitted curve (reference acrophase values) correspond exactly to those obtained by Gunther, Knapp, and Halberg (1969) who used a 7-point semantic differential scale. The authors also reported extremely good agreement between the self-report acrophases and a number of published estimates of oral temperature acrophases. Of methodological interest is that subjects were asked specifically *not* to look at their previous ratings before making their new estimate, presumably in order that they would not be influenced by any pattern in the scores that may have been emerging.

The SACL has been used in a number of studies where it has been possible to correlate factor scores with a variety of physiological measures. In one study (Burrows, Cox, and Simpson, 1977) the SACL was used to assess the demands inherent in a sales training exercise. In this 'real life' situation the participants were required to give a ten minute talk to their colleagues and the training staff. This period was followed by a further ten minutes of critical appraisal of the content and standard of presentation. Over the period of the talk, changes in blood glucose level were correlated with both changes in self-reported stress and self-reported arousal. Between stress and arousal the correlations were positive, but between arousal and blood glucose levels and between stress and blood glucose levels the correlations were negative. The reason for these negative correlations is, at the moment, unclear. Correlations between self-reported stress and arousal, and blood glucose levels have also been shown in the laboratory experiments investigating the effect of noise and glucose

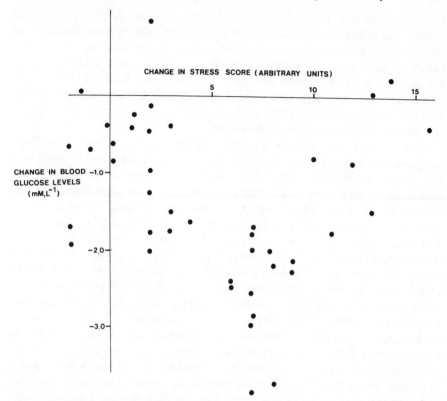

Figure 9.5 The relationship between changes (positive) in self-reported stress and changes in blood glucose levels over a fifteen minute period. Subjects had been given a glucose drink 30 minutes beforehand

preloading upon blood glucose levels and performance, mentioned earlier. Based upon a number of experiments a curvilinear relationship between changes in self-reported stress and changes in blood glucose level has been found. This supports the hypothesis of a two stage process in the regulation of blood glucose levels during stress (Cox and Mackay, 1975; Bradley, Cox, and Mackay, 1975). This curvilinear relationship is shown in Figure 9.5.

3.3 Self-reported arousal: summary and recommendations

A number of inventories for the measurement of self-reported arousal have been developed. Factors found in these studies have been shown to be sensitive to a variety of conditions traditionally used to manipulate arousal levels. Similarly, correlations between these factors and physiological indices of arousal have consistently been reported. After a decade of almost continuous development work, however, the precise structure of self-reported arousal remains unclear. Clements, Hafer, and Vermillion (1976) suggest that self-reported arousal can best be described by a single bipolar factor. At the other extreme, Kjellberg and Bohlin (1974) argue that a multifactorial approach is most appropriate. Even when rating scale artifacts were eliminated, these authors found six factors each describing a component of phenomenological arousal.

Recent work by Thayer (1978a, 1978b), using oblique rotations, suggests that a two bipolar, rather than four monopolar, factor solution is the most satisfactory. Thayer found that general activation and deactivation–sleep were negatively correlated, as were high activation and general deactivation. This is similar to the solution found by Mackay and coworkers (1978) which was used as the basis for the SACL. The reader will recall that the basic structure of mood was shown to be two dimensional (Section 2.5). It is suggested that the two clusters observed in almost all work on self-reported arousal are a reflection of, if not totally identical to, the two factor structure of mood. As well as checklist studies, some work with magnitude estimation rating scales has also found two dimensions. These have been labelled 'discomfort' and 'effort in performance' (Lundberg, personal communication). Even though the Kjellberg and Bohlin inventory has six factors, it is possible to discern two major groupings. The sleep–wakefulness and energy factors would appear to define the activation dimension whilst the stress, euphoria, irritation, and concentration factors would constitute the pleasantness dimension.

A two factor model has a number of advantages. One is its simplicity. Another is that it has close similarities to the formulations of Malmo (1959), Malmo and Belanger (1967), and Schachter and Singer (1962). There are two main determinants of arousal level. One is the physiological status of the individual. This is represented in the various studies by the following factors: vigour (Meddis, 1969); arousal (Mackay and coworkers, 1978); sleep–wakefulness and energy (Kjellberg and Bohlin, 1974); general activation–deactivation–sleep (Thayer, 1978a, 1978b) and the single activation factor of Clements, Hafer, and Vermillion (1976). Information about bodily activity is available from the cortex which acts as an integrating mechanism for information received from various physiological systems (H. J. Eysenck, 1975, p. 441), presumably via the reticular activating system. This would account for the high correlations Thayer found between the composite physiological index A and self-report measures, particularly general activation. Other aspects of consciousness no doubt contribute towards the selective processing of information from bodily systems (Brown, 1975). The second component that contributes indirectly towards arousal is the appraisal of the favourability of the environment and its consequences for the individual. Self-report factors related to this concept are as follows: hedonic tone (Meddis, 1969), stress (Mackay and coworkers, 1978); euphoria, stress, irritation (Kjellberg and Bohlin, 1964) and high activation–general deactivation (Thayer, 1978a, 1978b). On their own, changes in these factors do not necessarily imply a change in arousal. Under conditions perceived to be unfavourable, however, we would expect the two dimensions to be correlated, and in turn to be correlated with one or more physiological variables. This was the case in the Burrows, Cox, and Simpson (1977) study. It is possible that a more complex factor pattern may be necessary in future studies, but only further development work will show if 'fractionation' in factor scores occurs, and whether it is matched by equivalent changes in their physiological counterparts.

The studies reported have demonstrated the validity and usefulness of a phenomenological approach to arousal. They indicate that individuals are easily able to provide an accurate and reliable assessment of ongoing bodily activity. In many ways a self-report approach would seem to be preferable to physiological indices for measuring arousal, especially where only one or two variables can be recorded. Self-report would also seem to be advantageous when large numbers of people need to be tested simultaneously and in situations in which electrophysiological monitoring hardware cannot be used, for safety, or other reasons. A disadvantage is, of course, that a continuous record cannot be taken. Checklists such as the SACL have been shown, however, to be sensitive to quite rapid fluctuations in physiological activity in the order of a few minutes. Routine monitoring of checking behaviour may be necessary, especially if the characteristics of the population are unknown. For the same reasons, the use of a measure of social desirability may also be a useful precaution.

4. SCALES MEASURING SPECIFIC STATES

Apart from the checklists and questionnaires designed to measure a variety of states simultaneously, a number of scales exist for the assessment of moods and feelings associated with specific bodily states. The majority of these are concerned with infraradian, ultraradian or circadian rhythms. This section describes some of the more commonly used scales.

Hoddes and coworkers (1973) have developed the Stanford sleepiness scale (SSS). This seven item instrument is concerned with the onset of sleep. 52 items were subjected to Thurstone's method of equally appearing intervals. The seven item scale obtained is shown in Table 9.10.

Murray, Williams, and Lubin (1958) have produced a simple rating scale approach to self-reported sleepiness and fatigue. The four item sleepiness scale consists of the phrases: 'wide awake', 'getting sleepy', 'pretty sleepy',

Table 9.10. The subjective sleep scale

1. Feeling active and vital, alert, wide awake.
2. Functioning at a high level, but not at peak. Able to concentrate.
3. Relaxed, awake, not at full alertness, responsive.
4. A little foggy, not at peak, let down.
5. Fogginess, beginning to lose interest at remaining awake, slowed down.
6. Sleepiness, prefer to be lying down, fighting sleep, woozy.
7. Almost in reverie, sleep onset soon, last struggle to remain awake.

and 'trouble staying awake'. The fatigue scale also has four items: 'not tired', 'little tired', 'pretty tired', and 'dead tired'. Murray, Williams, and Lubin asked people to select one card that best described their feelings during a sleep experiment. Scores on both scales were significantly correlated (inversely) with body temperature. A similar 13-statement inventory is concerned with feelings of fatigue and well being. The instrument is known as the feeling tone checklist (Pearson and Byars, 1956). Increases in feeling tone score indicate decreasing fatigue. This instrument shows a marked circadian effect (Friedman and coworkers, 1977). Other, more specific scales for the measurement of fatigue have been advanced by Poffenberger (1928), McNelley (1966), and Yoshitake (1971).

One aspect of circadian rhythms that has attracted much attention is that of 'morningness' and eveningness'. These terms refer to the extent to which individuals rate themselves as being at their best at particular periods of the day; thus morning types feel active, lively, and generally at their best during the morning and so on. Some early attempts to devise a questionnaire for determining morningness–eveningness were made by O'Shea (1900) and Marsh (1906). Several Swedish language versions have recently been developed which appear to be able to distinguish between the two extremes (Öquist, 1970; Östberg, 1973a, 1973b). Based upon this work an English language version has been devised by Horne and Östberg (1976). The questionnaire consists of 19 items investigating such items as: ease of awakening, bed and rise times, appetite throughout the day and other daytime habits. The majority of the items consist of a four point choice scale, while the remainder consist of time scales in hours. These are subsequently divided into equal intervals and assigned numerical values from one to five. The item scores are summed and converted into a five point morningness–eveningness scale:

Definitely morning type	70–86
Moderately morning type	59–69
Neither type	42–58
Moderately evening type	31–41
Definitely evening type	16–30

48 subjects participated in a validation exercise based upon circadian variation in oral temperature. Morning types had a significantly earlier peak time in oral temperature than evening types. The questionnaire was a better predictor of peak time than sleep–wakefulness patterns suggesting that morningness–eveningness is not solely related to sleep habits.

Mood changes during the menstrual cycle have been particularly well examined. Moos (1968, 1969) has developed the menstrual distress questionnaire which includes a number of self-report items. Coppen and Kessel (1963) have also designed a questionnaire to assess mood changes during the menstrual cycle. Both these scales rely upon retrospective reports of feelings. According to May (1976), retrospective mood shifts during the menstrual cycle, as measured by the Wessman and Ricks (1966) 10-item 'elation-depression' scale do not correspond with actual mood variation. May therefore suggests that data from questionnaires that rely upon retrospective reports should be treated with caution. The Nowlis MACL has been shown to be sensitive to changes in mood during the menstrual cycle (Moos and coworkers, 1969).

A number of scales for the measurement of subjective stress have been constructed. Kerle and Bialek (1958) and subsequently Berkun and coworkers (1962) used Thurstone's method of equally appearing intervals to scale lists of adjectives denoting stress and discomfort. Many of the words used relate to extreme situations, since the scales were intended for use in a military context. The scale has subsequently been adapted by Jacobs and Munz (1968) for use in more normal circumstances. It is known as the perceived stress index (PSI). Each of the two scales consists of fifteen items. Scale 1 is used by the person to describe how he 'normally feels', scale 2 asks about feelings 'at this moment', and a score is computed as the difference between scales 1 and 2. One major advantage with this scale is its great simplicity and the speed with which it can be administered and scored.

5. SELF-REPORTED SOMATIC PERCEPTION

5.1 Introduction

The last two decades have seen an enormous growth in research concerned with biofeedback and self-regulation of physiological processes. Much of this work has been carried out within the context of operant conditioning and other behavioural paradigms. Often the response of the individual has been divorced from more global characteristics (see Shapiro, 1977, for a review). However, there has been a growing trend towards the study of the cognitive and perceptual aspects of these regulatory processes. One area of research has focused, in particular, upon the perception of bodily activity, its relationship to actual activity, and the acquisition of control of bodily

T

systems. Although the concept is a new one in the area of biofeedback (i.e. treated experimentally), it has had a long history elsewhere. The detection and labelling of bodily changes formed the cornerstone of the Jamesian view of the genesis of emotion. The view was partially discredited by Cannon and others, but the perception of bodily changes has remained an area of interest, particularly in regard to the generation of anxiety states. Many of the questionnaires available for diagnosing anxiety contain questions such as 'I often notice my heart beating', and 'I am seldom short of breath'. Brener (1978) has noted other manifestations of visceral perception. Reports on the intensity and quality of pain, and in location on or within the body form the basis for clinical diagnosis. Reorientation of behaviour contingent upon fluctuations in the *milieu interieur* suggests a powerful effect of the processing of visceral events. Experiments on diet selection by animals and changes in sexual behaviour due to hormonal shifts indicate that quite small variations in bodily activity exert marked effects on behaviour.

5.2 The basis for somatic perception

Information regarding bodily activity is available from numerous distinct sources. Proprioceptive receptor mechanisms associated with the striate musculature, tendons, joints, and non-auditory parts of the inner ear provide gross information about balance, posture, and movement as well as feedback concerning fine control movements. Visceral perception is based upon information from receptors which monitor the state of the *milieu interieur*. Chernigovskiy (1967) has divided these into four subtypes: mechanoreceptors, chemoreceptors, osmoreceptors, and thermoreceptors. Although there are some differences the visceral afferent system is not substantially different from the proprioceptive, or indeed, exteroceptive systems (Newman, 1974). However, only small areas of the cortex are devoted to the reception of visceral information. Moreover, the cortical projections of visceral afferents are not localized with respect either to topography or function (Brener and Jones, 1974). These factors conspire to militate against fine discrimination of visceral activity. Changes in proprioceptive information are also invariably linked to changes in the organism's external sensory environment either by gross changes in body movement or by fine changes associated with the movement of the sense organs, such as the eyes. It has also been suggested that perceptions based upon exteroceptive stimuli, refer to, and are identical with descriptions of the characteristics of the object; however, 'since individuals have not learned to label internal stimuli or localise interoceptors, visceral perceptions when they are expressed verbally tend to refer to states of the organism (Brener, 1978)'. This also implies the processing of information from a variety of sources. For example, the feeling of coldness is probably associated with information from thermoreceptors on the surface of the body, in the nasal passages and in the trachea, from localized piloerection from shivering, or from changes in skin coloration brought about by alterations in blood flow. These perceptions may also be augmented by exteroceptive cues in the environment. Thus the perception of visceral activity is not solely contingent upon interoceptive feedback, other indirect sources may be available. The resulting sensation is therefore an integration of information from various sensory modalities.

5.3 Self-report measures of visceral perception

Mandler, Mandler, and Uviller (1958) have described the development of an instrument, known as the autonomic perception questionnaire (APQ)* designed to assess the extent to which subjects are aware of, and can report on, visceral changes associated with states such as anxiety and pleasure. The APQ consists of three sections. In the first part, the subject is asked to describe his feelings when: (a) in a state of anxiety and apprehension; and (b) in a state of pleasure. The second section consists of 30 graphic scale items relating to the perception of body activity. Each scale consists of a question such as 'when you feel anxious, are you aware of increased muscle tension?' and 'when you feel anxious, do you get a sinking or heavy feeling in your stomach?' The graphic scale is a 14.5 cm line anchored at the endpoints by the words, 'always' and 'never'. For scoring purposes, the scale is divided into ten equal intervals. Items are then scored from 0 to 9. 21 of these scales refer to the state of anxiety and 9 relate to the state of pleasure. The scales deal with seven bodily systems: heart rate, respiration, temperature changes, perspiration, gastrointestinal disturbance, muscle tension, and blood pressure. The third part of the APQ consists of the 70 items from the MMPI. Fifty are from the manifest anxiety scale (MAS), and an additional 20 are taken from the MMPI as dealing with reports of internal bodily sensation. These 20 items plus 14 from the MAS form the 34-item body perception scale (BPS). Mandler, Mandler, and Uviller (1958) correlated the various parts of the Anxiety APQ, Pleasure, APQ, MAS, BPS test using 116 students. Apart from Pleasure APQ and BPS, all the intercorrelations was significant at, or greater than, the 0.01 level. As a validation exercise a variety of difficult cognitive tasks were used to induce the feeling of stress from ego-threat. Heart rate, psychogalvanic response, respiration rate, facial temperature, and blood volume (ear) were monitored throughout the experimental

*Available from: The Library of Congress, Photoduplication Service, 10 First Street SE, Washington, DC 20 540, USA, Document ADI-6764.

session. The 19 highest, and 14 lowest scoring subjects from the correlational study on the Anxiety APQ participated in the stress situation. The results from this study indicated that high perceivers showed significantly greater autonomic reactivity than low perceivers, and that the former tend to overestimate their autonomic responses, whilst the latter tend to underestimate them, based upon discrepancies between actual and reported activity. A further study using a more representative sample (Mandler and Kremen, 1958) than previously was undertaken. Identical tasks, procedures, and physiological measures were used. A weak but significant correlation between scores on the APQ and actual autonomic activity was found, replicating the earlier study. This study did not, however, replicate the earlier finding that high perceivers tend to overestimate autonomic activity, and vice versa. If anything, using the unselected population, the reverse was the case. When the top and bottom four scores on the APQ were selected, however, the trend, according to the authors, was in the direction found previously. This later study did show that subjects *low* in autonomic activity tended to overestimate this activity in their report, whilst subjects with high activity tended to underestimate it. A further study by Korchin and Heath (1961) showed distinct sex differences in mean APQ scores, women reporting more experience of bodily events than men. High APQ scorers, of both sexes, had significantly higher scores on the MACL anxiety and depression factors.

The APQ has been used in a number of studies in which objective tests of visceral perception have been employed. Many of these studies failed to find a significant relationship between APQ scores and objective indices of heart rate perception (Donelson, 1966; McFarland, 1975; Whitehead, Drescher, and Blackwell, 1976). Similarly, experiments on the acquisition of visceral control have produced conflicting evidence. Bergman and Johnson (1971) found that subjects with APQ scores in the middle range were better than high or low scoring individuals at controlling heart rate. This finding is similar to that of Fentz and Dronsejko (1969) who showed that those with midrange anxiety scores showed more adaptive autonomic responses. Studies that have reported significant correlations between APQ scores and autonomic control found negative relationships, Greene and Nielsen (1966), using GSR, and Blanchard, Young, and McLeod (1972) using heart rate. Donelson (1966) and Whitehead, Drescher, and Blackwell (1976) reported non-significant correlations between APQ scores and heart rate during biofeedback.

An instrument, however, that does correlate with visceral control is the locus of control scale (LOC) developed by Rotter (1966). Locus of control is a personality construct developed within the context of social learning theory (for a review see Throop and MacDonald, 1971). Those who have a high score on the LOC would tend to believe that events in life are due to chance and that it is difficult to influence one's destiny in any way. Those with low scores, i.e. those with internal locus of control, would believe that it is possible to influence events in life and that these are not due to chance. The LOC consists of 29 items, each of which has two parts. The respondent is required to choose those which most closely apply.

2a.   Many of the unhappy things in people's lives are partly due to bad luck.

   b.   People's misfortunes result from the mistakes they make.

In this example, checking of item 2a would count towards the score. Six items in the list are for filling purposes and they do not count towards the score. The scale runs therefore from 0 to 23. Correlations with the Crowne–Marlowe social desirability scale range from − 0.07 to − 0.35. A ten item short form of the LOC has been developed by Valecha and Ostrom (1974).

Fotopolous (1970) found that internal locus of control subjects produced greater heart rate increases than external locus of control subjects. When feedback was presented, however, no differences were apparent. Ray and Lamb (1974) instructed subjects both to increase and decrease heart rate. Internal locus of control subjects were better able to increase heart rate than externals; and externals were better able to decrease compared with internals. The external LOC subjects appeared to benefit more from external heart rate feedback. This study was extended by Ray (1974). All the findings in the earlier study were replicated. In addition, self-report data indicate that the two types of subject adopted different strategies for controlling heart rate. External locus of control subjects looked at 'objects in the room' more often than internals during the heart rate decrease task, whilst during the increase heart rate task internal locus of control subjects 'thought about feelings'. These findings have some correspondence with the intake–rejection hypothesis of Lacey and coworkers (1963) and the concept of 'levellers' and 'sharpeners' (Isreal, 1969).

Work with more 'objective' and direct techniques for gathering information has shown them to be much better predictors of subsequent autonomic control. These are discussed by Brener (1977, 1978) and Whitehead and coworkers (1978).

6. CONCLUDING REMARKS

This chapter has attempted to cover some of the currently available techniques for the measurement of self-reported mood, self-reported psychophysiological activity, and questionnaire methods for the assessment of visceral perception. The overall balance in favour of the first two topics reflects the author's own interests. It also reflects the considerable uncertainty existing in the area of visceral perception concerning the usefulness of paper and pencil tests such as the APQ. It is to be hoped that this approach will not be abandoned completely.

A number of approaches to the study of mood and self-reported psychophysiological activity have been described in this chapter. At the present time it is difficult to make any firm recommendations concerning the relative merits of checklists, rating scales, and questionnaires since no studies reporting comparisons have been made. The potential user is, therefore, left to draw his own conclusions from the available information on the usefulness of each technique.

It is often the case that methodological and conceptual advances are intimately related. This seems to be particularly apparent in mood research. Early research into emotions, feelings, and moods used simple models; advances in methodology eventually brought about more complex multidimensional approaches. However, the most recent research indicates that the multidimensional approach to mood may be replaced by a two-dimensional model. Although many will see this as an unjustified oversimplification, it is clear that when psychological considerations are involved, the multidimensional model becomes somewhat unwieldy and has led to a variety of *post hoc* methods for collapsing across factors.

Further work will indicate how useful for psychophysiology this approach is. The outcome may be that a multilevel or hierarchical framework for mood is the most satisfactory, analogous to some approaches to the structure of personality. This suggestion is, however, highly speculative and must await further investigation. Long standing and fundamental problems, many of a philosophical nature, remain to be solved. One concerns the nature of precisely what is being measured with an adjective checklist. Nowlis (1967) has divided mood research into three components: the phenomenological, the dispositional, and the somatic. If we are to follow Nowlis (see Section 2.2.2) then it is the second of these which is being investigated with adjective checklist responses. However, there is clearly a strong interaction between each of these three components, suggesting that checklists also collect information concerning phenomenological and physiological activity. In the future, it may be better to develop separate self-report methods in order to assess these levels individually.

Some have advocated the use of subjects who have been extensively trained in the use of verbal reports which denote specific components of autonomic and somatic activity. Comparatively little is known however about the extent to which such highly sophisticated language systems modify the perception and subsequent reporting of bodily changes. The work of Schachter and Singer (1962) and Valins (1970) in particular, has underlined the fundamental importance of cognitive and perceptual processes in mediating verbal report of emotional activity and bodily changes. It may be useful, therefore, to gather information about individual 'cognitions' as well as recording data about mood and bodily activity.

Little attention has been given in this review to clinical rating scales and inventories, many of which include items covering bodily functioning (although these are often of an abnormal nature). This area will however continue to play an important part in developing methodologies for investigating and analysing mood. For example, Nemiah, Freyberger, and Sifneos (1976) have described a syndrome often associated with those suffering from psychosomatic disorders; this they have termed 'alexithymia' (from the Greek meaning literally, 'without words for feelings'). It is characterized by an inability to describe feelings in detail, apart from simple labels such as sad or angry. Sufferers are also unable to localize affects within their body, and are unaware of the common bodily changes that accompany the experience of emotion. Clinical observations such as these will undoubtedly shed light upon the relationship between mood and bodily function and hopefully help to further ways in which they can be measured through self-report techniques.

One final note. Psychophysiologists, particularly with roots mainly in physiology have long distrusted 'subjective' techniques. However, psychophysiology has much to offer the study of mood and much to gain from such study.

REFERENCES

Aitken, R. C. B. (1969a). A growing edge of measurement of feelings. *Proc. R. Soc. Med.,* **62**, 989–96.

Aitken, R. C. B. (1969b). Measurement of feelings using visual analogue scales. *Proc. R. Soc. Med.,* **62**, 989–93.

Aitken, R. C. B. (1970). Communication of symptoms. *Psychother. Psychosom.,* **18**, 74–9.

Aitken, R. C. B., and Zealley, A. K. (1970). Measurement of moods. *Br. J. Hosp. Med.,* **4**, 215–24.

Allport, G. W. and Odbert, H. (1936). Trait names: a psycho-lexical study. *Psychological Monographs* 47, (1, Whole no. 211).

Arnold, M. B. (Ed.) (1970). *Feelings and Emotions: The Loyola Symposium,* Academic, New York.

Barton, K. and Cattell, R. B. (1974). Changes in psychological state measures and time of day. *Psychol. Rep.,* **35**, 219–22.

Barton, K., Cattell, R. B., and Connor, D. V. (1972). The identification of state factors through P-technique factor analysis. *J. Clin. Psychol.,* **28**, 459–63.

Barton, K., Cattell, R. B., and Curran, J. P. (1973). Psychological states: their definition through P-technique and Differential R (dR) technique factor analysis. *J. Behav. Sci.,* **1**, 273–8.

Bates, H. O. (1970). Frequency of affect adjective checklist endorsements as a function of item social desirability. *Newslett. Res. Psychol.,* **12**, 4–5.

Beck, A. T., Ward, C. H., Mendelson, M., Mock, J., and Erbaugh, J. (1961). An inventory for measuring depression. *Archs Gen. Psychiat.,* **4**, 561–5.

Bell, B. (1973). Psychophysiological studies of the menstrual cycle. *PhD. Thesis,* University of Birmingham, unpublished.

Bell, B., Christie, M. J., and Venables, P. H. (1975). Psychophysiology of the menstrual cycle. In P. H. Venables and M. J. Christie (Eds), *Research in Psychophysiology*, Wiley, London.

Bergman, J. S., and Johnson, H. J. (1971). The effects of instructional set and autonomic perception on cardiac control. *Psychophysiology*, **8**, 180–90.

Berkun, M. M., Bialek, H. M., Kern, R. P., and Yagi, K. (1962). Experimental studies of psychological stress in man. *Psychological Monographs* 76 (15, Whole No. 534).

Blanchard, E. B., Young, L. D., and McLeod, P. (1972). Awareness of heart activity and self-control of heart rate. *Psychophysiology, *9, 63–8.

Bohlin, G., and Kjellberg, A. (1973). Self-reported arousal during sleep deprivation and its relation to performance and physiological variables. *Scand. J. Psychol.*, **14**, 78–86.

Bohlin, G., and Kjellberg, A. (1975). Self-reported arousal. Factorial complexity as a function of the subject's arousal level, *Scand. J. Psychol.*, **16**, 203–8.

Bond, A. J., and Lader, M. H. (1974). The use of analog scales in rating subjective feelings. *Br. J. Med. Psychol.,* **47**, 211–18.

Borgatta, E. F. (1961). Mood, personality and interaction. *J. Gen. Psychol.,* **64**, 105–37.

Bradley, C., Cox, T., and Mackay, C. J. (1975). The effects of stress on the regulation of blood sugar levels. *Paper presented to The Psychophysiology Group, Bedford College, London, December*.

Brener, J. (1977). Sensory and perceptual determinants of voluntary visceral control. In G. E. Schwartz and J, Beatty (Eds), *Biofeedback: Theory and Research*, Academic Press, New York.

Brener, J. (1978). Visceral perception. In J. Beatty (Ed.), *Biofeedback and behavior: A NATO Symposium*, Plenum, New York.

Brener, J., and Jones, J. M. (1974). Interoceptive discrimination in intact humans: detection of cardiac activity. *Physiol. Beh.*, **13**, 763–7.

Brown, B. (1970). Recognition of aspects of consciousness through association with EEG alpha activity represented by a light signal. *Psychophysiology*, **6**, 442–52.

Brown, B. (1971). Awareness of EEG-subjective activity relationships detected within a closed feedback system. *Psychophysiology*, **7**, 451–64.

Brown, B. B. (1975). Biological awareness as a state of consciousness. *J. Altered States Consciousness,* **2**, 1–14.

Burrows, G. C., Cox, T., and Simpson, G. C. (1977). The measurement of stress in a sales training situation. *J. Occup. Psychol.,* **50**, 45–51.

Burt, C. (1950). The factorial study of emotions. In M. L. Reymert (Ed.), *Feelings and Emotions*, Chap. 46, McGraw-Hill, New York, pp. 531–551.

Bush II, L. E. (1973). Individual differences in multidimensional scaling of adjectives denoting feelings. *J. Personality Soc. Psychol.,* **25**, 50–7.

Cameron, J., Specht, P., and Wendt, G. R. (1967). Effects of meprobramate on moods, emotions and motivation. *J. Psychol.,* **365**, 209–21.

Cannon, W. B. (1929). *Bodily Changes in Pain, Hunger, Fear and Rage*, 2nd edn, Appleton, New York.

Cannon, W. B. (1931). Again the James–Lange and the thalamic theories of emotion. *Psychol. Rev.,* **38**, 281–95.

Cattell, R. B. (1943). The description of personality: 2. Basic traits resolved into clusters. *J. Abnorm. Soc. Psychol.*, **38**, 476–507.

Cattell, R. B. (1963). Personality, role, mood and situation-perception: a unifying theory of modulators. *Psychol. Rev.,* **70**, 1–18.

Cattell, R. B. (1973) *Personality and Mood by Questionnaire*, Jossey-Bass, San Francisco, California.

Cattell, R. B., Cattell, A. K. S., and Rhymer, R. M. (1947). P-technique demonstrated in determining psychophysiological source traits in a normal individual. *Psychometrika*, **12**, 267–88.

Chernigovskiy, V. N. (1967). *Interoceptors*, American Psychological Association, Washington, DC.

Christie, M. J., and Venables, P. H. (1973). Mood changes in relation to age, EPI scores, time and day. *Br. J. Soc. Clin. Psychol.*, **12**, 61.

Clark, W. C., Kurlander, K., Bieber, R., and Glassman, A. H. (1976). Signal detection theory treatment of response set in mood questionnaires. In Spielberger C. D. and Sarason I. G. (Eds), *Stress and Anxiety*, Halsted Press, N.Y. Vol. IV, pp. 313–24.

Clements, P. R., Hafer, M. D., and Vermillion, M. E. (1976). Psychometric, diurnal and electrophysiological correlates of activation. *J. Personality Soc. Psychol.*, **33**, 387–94.

Clyde, D. J. (1960). Self-ratings. In L. Uhr and J. G. Miller (Eds), *Drugs and Behavior*, Wiley, New York.

Clyde, D. J. (1963). *Clyde Mood Scale Manual*, University of Miami, Biometrics Laboratory, Coral Gables.

Coppen, A., and Kessel, N. (1963). Menstruation and personality. *Br. J. Psychiat.*, **109**, 711–21.

Cox, T., and Mackay, C. J. (1975). Stress and the regulation of blood glucose levels. *Joint meeting of The WHO Psychosocial Centre and Physiological Psychology Unit, Stockholm University. Stockholm. October.*

Cronbach, L. J., and Furby, L. (1970). How should we measure change or should we? *Psychol. Bull.*, **74**, 68–74.

Crowne, D. P., and Marlowe, D. (1964). *The Approval Motive*, Wiley, New York.

Crumpton, E., Grayson, H. M., and Keith-Lee, P. (1967). What kinds of anxiety does the Taylor MAS measure? *J. Consult. Psychol.*, **31**, 324–6.

Dana, C. L. (1921). The anatomic seat of the emotions: a discussion of the James–Lange theory. *Arch. Newd. Psychiat.*, **6**, 634–40.

Davitz, J. R. (1969). *The Language of Emotion*, Academic, New York.

Dermer, M., and Berscheid, E. (1972). Self-report of arousal as an indicant of Activation Level. *Behav. Sci.*, **17**, 420–8.

Donelson, F. E. (1966). Discrimination and control of human heart rate. *Doctoral dissertation*, Cornell University, unpublished.

Duffy, E. (1962). *Activation and Behavior*, Wiley, New York.

Eckman, G., Frankenhaeuser, M., Goldberg, L., Hagdahl, R., and Myrsten, A. L. (1964). Subjective and objective effects of alcohol as a function of dosage and time. *Psychopharmacologia*, **6**, 399–409.

Edgren, B. (1971). A model of relativity in the analysis of the magnitude of psychophysiological reactions. *Laboratory of Clinical Stress Research, Karolinska Hospital, Stockholm, Sweden, Report No. 22.*

Ewart, O. (1970). The attitudinal character of emotion. In M. B. Arnold (Ed.), *Feelings and Emotions*, Academic Press, New York.

Eysenck, H. J. (1975). The measurement of emotion: psychological parameters and methods. In L. Levi (Ed.), *Emotions—Their Parameters and Measurement*, Raven, New York. pp. 439–67.

Eysenck, M. (1974). Effects of noise, activation level, and response dominance on retrieval from semantic memory. *J. Exp. Psychol.*, **104**, 143–8.

Fenz, W. D. and Dronsejko, K. (1969). The effects of real and imagined threat on ASR and heart rate as a function of trait anxiety. *J. Exp. Res. Personality*, **3**, 187–96.

Fotopolous, S. (1970). Locus of control and the voluntary control of heart rate. *Paper presented at the Meeting of The Biofeedback Research Society, New Orleans.*

Freyd, M. (1923). The graphic rating scale. *J. Educ. Psychol.*, **14**, 83–102.

Friedmann, G., Globus, G., Huntley, A., Mullaney, D., Naitoh, and Johnson, L. (1977). Performance and mood during and after gradual sleep reduction. *Psychophysiology*, **14**, 245–50.

Fröberg, J. E., Karlsson, C-G, Levi, L., and Lidberg, L. (1975). Psychobiological circadian rhythms during a 72 hour vigil. *Förvarsmed.*, **11**, 192–201.

Goldberg, D. P. (1972). *The Detection of Psychiatric Illness by Questionnaire*, Oxford University Press, London.

Gough, H. G. and Heilbrun, A. B. (1965). *The Adjective Checklist Manual*, Consulting Psychologists Press, Palo Alto.

Green, R. F. (1965). On the measurement of mood. *Technical Report No. 10*, Rochester University, Research Project NR 171–342, Contract Nonr 668 (12), Office of Naval Research.

Green, R. F., and Nowlis, V. (1957). A factor analytic study of the domain of mood with independent validation of the factors. *Am. Psychol.*, **12**, 438.

Greene, W. A., and Nielsen, T. C. (1966). Operant GSR conditioning of high and low autonomic perceivers. *Psychonom. Sci.*, **6**, 359–360.

Guttman, L. (1954). A new approach to factor analysis: The Radex. In P. F. Lazarsfeld (Ed.), *Mathematical Thinking in the Social Sciences*, Columbia University Press, New York.

Günther, R., Knapp, E., and Halberg, F. (1969). Refereznormen der Rhythmometrie: circadiane Acrophasen von zwanzig KorperFunktionen. *Z. Angew. Bader Klimaheilk.*, **16**, 123–53.

Halberg, F., Tong, Y. L., and Johnson, E. A. (1965). Circadian system phase—an aspect of temporal morphology; procedures and illustrative examples. In H. Mayersbach (Ed.), *Cellular Aspects of Biorhythms*, Springer Verlag, New York.

Handlon, J. H. (1962). Hormonal activity and individual responses to stresses and easements in everyday living. In R. Roessler and N. S. Greenfield (Eds), *Physiological Correlates of Psychological Disorder*, The University of Wisconsin Press, Madison, Wisconsin.

Harlow, H. F., and Stagner, R. (1933). Psychology of feelings and emotions, II. Theory of emotions. *Psychol. Rev.*, **1933**, 184–195.

Hayes, M. H. S., and Patterson, D. G. (1921). Experimental development of the graphic rating method. *Psychol. Bull.*, **18**, 98–99.

Herron, E. W. (1969). The multiple affect adjective checklist: a critical analysis. *J. Clin. Psychol.*, **25**, 46–53.

Herron, E. W., Bernstein, L., and Rosen, H. (1968). Psychometric analysis of the Multiple Affect Adjective Check List: MAACL—Today. *J. Clin. Psychol.*, **24**, 448–50.

Hendrick, C., and Lilly, R. S. (1970). The structure of mood: a comparison between sleep deprivation and normal wakefulness conditions. *J. Personality*, **38**, 453–5.

Herbert, M., Johns, M. W., and Dore, C. (1976). Factor analysis of analogue scales measuring subjective feelings before and after sleep. *Br. J. Med. Psychol.*, **49**, 373–9.

Hoddes, E., Zarcone, V., Smythe, H., Phillips, R., and Dement, W. C. (1973). Quantification of sleepiness: A new approach. *Psychophysiology*, **10**, 431–6.

Horne, J. A., and Östberg, O. (1976). A self-assessment questionnaire to determine morningness-eveningness. *Int. J. Chronobiol.*, **4**, 97–110.

Hutcheson, F. (1728). *An Essay on the Nature and Conduct of the Passions*, Facsimile edn., Scolar Press, Menston, Yorkshire.

Isreal, N. R. (1969). Levelling-sharpening and anticipatory cardiac response. *Psychosom. Med.*, **31**, 499–509.

Jacobs, A., Kapek, L., and Meehan, J. P. (1959). The development of an adjective checklist to measure affective states. *Psychol. Newslett.*, **12**, 515–20.

Jacobs, P. D., and Munz, D. C. (1968). An index for measuring perceived stress in a college population. *J. Psychol.*, **70**, 9–15.

James, W. (1884). What is an emotion? *Mind*, **9**, 188–205.

Johansson, G. (1976). Subjective wellbeing and temporal patterns of sympathetic—adrenal medullary activity. *Biol. Psychol.*, **4**, 157–72.

Johnson, D. T. (1970). Response set and an Adjective Checklist: A second look. *J. Clin. Psychol.*, **26**, 88–90.

Johnson, M., and Hackman, H. (1977). Cross-validation and response sets in repeated use of mood questionnaires. *Br. J. Soc. Clin. Psychol.*, **16**, 235–9.

Joyce, C. R. B. (Ed.) (1968). *Psychopharmacology: Dimensions and Perspectives*, Tavistock Publications, London.

Kamiya, J. (1969). Operant control of the EEG alpha rhythm and some of its reported effects on consciousness. In C. Tart (Ed.), *Altered States of Consciousness*, Wiley, New York. pp. 489–501.

Katkin, E. S. (1966). The relationship between a measure of transitory anxiety and spontaneous autonomic activity. *J. Abnorm. Psychol.*, **71**, 142–6.

Kerle and Bialek, H. M. (1958). The construction, validation and application of a subjective stress scale. *Staff Memorandum*. US Army Leadership Human Research Unit, Monterey, California.

Kjellberg, A., and Bohlin, G. (1974). Self-reported arousal: further development of a multi-factorial inventory. *Scand. J. Psychol.*, **15**, 285–92.

Knapp, P. H., and Bahnson, C. B. (1963). The emotional field: a sequential study of mood and fantasy in two asthmatic patients. *Psychosom. Med.*, **25**, 460–83.

Korchin, S. J., and Heath, H. A. (1961). Somatic experience in the anxiety state: Some sex and personality correlates of 'autonomic feedback'. *J. Consult. Psychol.*, **25**, 398–404.

Lacey, J. I. (1956). The evaluation of autonomic responses: Towards a general solution. *Ann. NY Acad. Sci.*, **67**, 125–63.

Lacey, J. I. (1967). Somatic response patterning and stress: Some revisions of activation theory. In M. N. Appley and R. Trumbull (Eds), *Psychological Stress: Issues in Research*, Appleton, New York.

Lacey, J. I., Kagan, J., Lacey, B. C., and Moss, H. A. (1963). The visceral level: situational determinants and behavioural correlates of autonomic response patterns. In P. H. Knapp (Ed.), *Expression of the Emotions in Man*, International Universities Press, New York.

Lange, C. (1885). *The Emotions*. Copenhagen. (Translated by H. Kurella). Leipzig: Theodor Thomas, 1887.

Lazarus, R. S. (1966). *Psychological Stress and the Coping Process*, McGraw-Hill, New York.

Lazarus, R. S., Speisman, J. C., Mordkoff, A. M., and Davison, L. A. (1962). A laboratory study of psychological stress produced by a motion picture film. *Psychological Monographs* 76, No. 34 (Whole No. 553).

Lorr, M., Daston, P., and Smith I. R. (1967). An analysis of mood states. *Educ. Psychol. Measurement*, **27**, 89–96.

Lorr, M., McNair, D. M., Weinstein, G. J., Michaux, W. W., and Raskin, A. (1961). Meprobamate and Chlorpromazine in psychotherapy. AMA *Archs Gen. Psychiat.*, **4**, 381–9.

Lykken, D. T. (1976). The role of individual differences in psychophysiological research. In P. H. Venables and M. J. Christie (Eds). *Research in Psychophysiology*, Wiley, London.

Lynch, J. J., and Paskewitz, D. A. (1971). On the mechanisms of feedback control of human brain wave activity. *J. Nerv. Ment. Dis.*, **153**, 205–17.

McFarland, R. A. (1975). Heart rate perception and heart rate control. *Psychophysiology*, **12**, 402–6.

Mackay, C. J., Cox, T., Burrows, G. C., and Lazzarini, A. J. (1978). An inventory for the measurement of self reported stress and arousal. *Br. J. Soc. Clin. Psychol.*, **17**, 283–4.

McNair, D. M., and Lorr, M. (1964). An analysis of mood in neurotics. *J. Abnorm. Soc. Psychol.*, **69**, 620–7.

McNair, D. M., Lorr, M., and Droppleman, L. F. (1971). *Profile of Mood States*, Educational and Industrial Testing Service, San Diego, California.

McNelley, G. W. (1966). The development and laboratory validation of a subjective fatigue scale. In J. Tiffin and E. J. McCormick (Eds), *Industrial Psychology*, George Allen and Unwin, London.

Mahl, G. F. (1959). Measuring the patient's anxiety during interviews from 'expressive' aspects of his speech. *Trans. NY Acad. Sci. Ser.* II, **21**, No. 3, 252–7.

Malmo, R. B. (1959). Activation: A neurophysiological dimension. *Psychol. Rev.*, **66**, 367–86.

Malmo, R. B., and Belanger, D. (1967). Related physiological and behavioural changes: What are their determinants? *Proc. Assoc. Res. Nerv. Ment. Dis.*, **45**, 288–318.

Malpas, A. (1971). Sedation in man: a study of some effects of nitrazepam and amylo-barbitone. *Ph.D. Thesis*, University of London, unpublished.

Malmstrom, E. J. (1968). The effect of prestimulus variability upon physiological reactivity scores. *Psychophysiology*, **5**, 149–65.

Mandler, G. (1962). Emotion. In R. Brown, E. Galanter, E. Hess, and G. Mandler (Eds), *New Directions in Psychology*, Holt, Rinehart and Winston, New York.

Mandler, G., Mandler, J. M., and Uviller, E. T. (1958). Autonomic feedback: The perception of autonomic activity. *J. Abnorm. Soc. Psychol.*, **56**, 367–73.

Mandler, G. and Kremen, I. (1958). Autonomic feedback: a correlational study. *J. Personality*, **26**, 388–99.

Marsh, H. D. (1906). The diurnal course of efficiency. *Contributions to Philosophy and Psychology from the University of Columbia*, 14 *No.* 3.

Marshall, M. S., and Bentler, P. M. (1976). The effects of deep physical relaxation and low-frequency alpha brainwaves on alpha subjective reports. *Psychophysiology*, **13**, 505–16.

May, R. R. (1976). Mood shifts and the menstrual cycle. *Psychosom. Med.*, **20**, 125–30.

Meddis, R. (1969). The analysis of mood ratings. *Doctoral dissertation*, University of London, unpublished.

Meddis, R. (1972). Bipolar factors in mood adjective check lists. *Br. J. Soc. Clin. Psychol.*, **11**, 178–84.

Mefferd, R. B. (1976). Some experimental implications of change. In P. H. Venables and M. J. Christie (Eds), *Research in Psychophysiology*, Wiley, London.

Moos, R. (1968). The development of a menstrual distress questionnaire. *Psychosom. Med.*, **30**, 853.

Moos, R. (1969). Fluctuations in symptoms and moods during the menstrual cycle. *J. Psychosom. Res.*, **13**, 37.

Moos, R. H., Kopell, B. S., Melges, F. T., Yalom, I. D., Lunde, D. T., Clayton, R. B. and Hamburg, D. A. (1969). Fluctuations in symptoms and moods during the menstrual cycle. *J. Psychosom. Res.*, **13**, 37–44.

Morrison, B. J., and Walters, S. B. (1972). The placebo effect: I. Situational anxiety and model behavior. *Psychon. Sci.*, **27**, (2).

Munz, D. C., Costello, C. T., and Korabik, K. (1975). A further test of the inverted-U hypothesis relating achievement anxiety and academic test performance. *J. Psychol.*, **89**, 39–47.

Murray, E. J., Williams, H. L., and Lubin, A. (1958). Body temperature and psychological ratings during sleep deprivation. *J. Exp. Psychol.*, **56**, 271–3.

Nemiah, J. C., Freyberger, H., and Sifneos, P. E. (1976). Alexithymia: A view of the psychosomatic process. In D. W. Hill (Ed.), *Modern Trends in Psychosomatic Medicine (2)*, Butterworths, London.

Newman, P. P. (1974). *Visceral Afferent Functions of the Nervous System*, Edward Arnold, London.

Norris, H. (1971). The action of sedatives on brain-stem oculomotor systems in man. *Neuropharmacology*, **10**, 181–91.

Nowlis, D. P., and Kamiya, J. (1970). The control of electroencephalographic alpha rhythms through auditory feedback and the associated mental activity. *Psychophysiology*, **6**, 476–84.

Nowlis, V. (1963). The concept of mood. In S. M. Farber and R. H. Wilson (Eds), *Conflict and Creativity*, McGraw-Hill, New York.

Nowlis, V. (1965). Research with the mood adjective check list. In S. S. Tomkins and C. E. Izard (Eds), *Affect, Cognition and Personality*, pp. 352–389.

Nowlis, V. (1967). Invited commentary on chapter by Weybrew. In M. H. Appley and R. Trumbull (Eds), *Psychological Stress*, Appleton, New York.

Nowlis, V. (1970). Moods: Behavior and experience. In M. B. Arnold (Ed.), *Feelings and Emotion: the Loyola Symposium*, Academic Press, New York.

Nowlis, V., and Green, R. F. (1957). The experimental analysis of mood. *Technical Report No. 3. Office of Naval Research. Contract No. Nonr–668 (12)*.

Nowlis, V., and Green, R. F. (1964). Factor analytic studies of mood. *Technical Report, Office of Naval Research: Contract No. Nonr–668(12)*.

Nowlis, V., and Nowlis, H. H. (1956). The analysis of mood. *Ann. NY Acad. Sci.*, **65**, 345–55.

Olmedo, E. L., Kirk, R. E., and Suarez, E. M. (1973). Effects of environmental variation on arousal during vigilance performance. *Percept. Mot. Skills Res. Exch.*, **36**, 1251–7.

Osgood, C. E., Suci, G. J., and Tannenbaum, P. H. (1957). *The Measurement of Meaning*, University of Illinois Press, Urbana.

O'Shea, M. V. (1900). Aspects of mental economy. *Bull. Univ. Wisconsin*, **2**, 33–198.

Öquist, O. (1970). Kartlaggning av individualla dygnsrytmer. *Thesis*, Department of Psychology, University of Gothenburg, Sweden, unpublished.

Östberg, O. (1973a). Circadian rhythm of food intake and oral temperature in 'morning' and 'evening' groups of individuals. *Ergonomics*, **16**, 203–9.

Östberg, O. (1973b). Interindividual differences in circadian fatigue patterns of shift workers. *Br. J. Indust. Med.*, **30**, 341–51.

Pankratz, L., Glaudin, V., and Goodmonson, C. (1972). Reliability of the Multiple Affect Adjective Check List. *J. Personality Assessment*, **36**. 371–3.

Pearson, R. G., and Byars, G. E. Jr (1956). The development and validation of a checklist for measuring subjective fatigue. (*Rep. 56–115) Air University, School of Aviation Medicine, USAF, Randolph Air Force Base, Texas.*

Peper, E. (1971). Reduction of efferent motor commands during alpha feedback as a facilitator of EEG alpha and a precondition for changes in consciousness. *Kybernetik*, **9**, 226–31.

Plotkin, W. B. (1976). On the self-regulation of the occipital alpha rhythm: Control strategies, states of consciousness, and the role of physiological feedback. *J. Exp. Psychol. (Gen.)*, **105**, 66–99.

Poffenberger, A. T. (1928). Effects of continuous work upon output and feelings. *J. Appl. Psychol.*, **12**, 459–67.

Radloff, R., and Helmreich, R. (1968). *Groups under Stress: Psychological Research in SEALAB II*, Appleton–Century–Crofts, New York.

Ray, W. J. (1974). The relationship of locus of control, self report measures and feedback, to the voluntary control of heart rate. *Psychophysiology*, **11**, 527–34.

Ray, W. J., and Lamb, S. B. (1974). Locus of control and the voluntary control of heart rate. *Psychosom. Med.*, **36**, 180–2.

Roessler, R., Burch, N. R., and Childers, H. E. (1966). Personality and arousal correlates of specific galvanic skin responses. *Psychophysiology*, **3**, 115–30.

Roth, W. T., Tinklenberg, J. R., Doyle, C. M., Horvath, T. B., and Kopell, B. S. (1976). Mood states and 24-hour cardiac monitoring. *J. Psychosom. Res.*, **20**, 179–86.

Rotter, J. B. (1966). Generalized expectancies for internal versus external control of reinforcement. *Psychological Monographs*, **80**, (Whole No. 609), 1–28.

Ruckmick, C. A. (1936). The systematic position of emotion. *Psychol. Rev.*, **43**, 417–26.

Ryle, G. (1949). *The Concept of Mind*, Hutchinson, London.

Sacks, B., Fenwick, P. C. B., Marks, I., Fenton, G. W., and Hebden, A. (1972). An investigation of the phenomenon of autocorrelation of the alpha rhythm and possible associated feeling states using visual feedback. *Electroenceph. Clin. Neurophysiol.*, **32**, 461–3 (abstract).

Sarason, I. G. (1960). Empirical findings and theoretical problems in the use of anxiety scales. *Psychol. Bull.*, **57**, 403–15.

Schachter, S., and Singer, J. E. (1962). Cognitive, social and physiological determinants of emotional state. *Psychol. Rev.*, **69**, 379–99.

Seligman, L. (1975). Skin potential as an indicator of emotion. *J. Counselling Psychol.*, **22**, 489–93.

Shapiro, D. (1977). A monologue on Biofeedback and Psychophysiology. *Psychophysiology*, **14**, 213–27.

Sherrington, C. S. (1900). Experiments on the value of vascular and visceral factors for the genesis of emotion. *Proc. R. Soc. Lond.*, **66**, 390–403.

Siller, J., and Chipman, A. (1963). Response set paralysis: Implications for measurement and control. *J. Consult. Psychol.*, **27**, 432–8.

Simpson, G., Cox, T., and Rothschild, D. R. (1974). The effect of noise stress on blood glucose levels and skilled performance. *Ergonomics*, **17**, 481–8.

Singer, J. E., Lundberg, U., and Frankenhaeuser, M. (1974). Stress on the train: a study of urban commuting. *Reports from the Psychological Laboratories, University of Stockholm*, No. 425.

Sjöberg, L., and Svensson, E. (1976). The polarity and dimensionality of mood. *Göteborg Psychol. Rep.*, **6**, (12).

Spielberger, C. D., Gorsuch, R., and Lushene, R. (1970). *The State–Trait Anxiety Inventory*, Consulting Psychologists Press, Palo Alto, California.

Stagner, R. (1948). *Psychology of Personality*, McGraw-Hill, New York.

Stevens, S. S. (1972). *Psychophysics and Social Scaling*, General Learning Press, Morristown.

Strahan, R. (1970). A simple device for the polygraphic recording of judgements. *Psychophysiology*, 7, 135–7.

Strahan, R., and Gerbasi, K. C. (1972). Short, homogeneous version of the Marlowe–Crowne Social Desirability Scale. *J. Clin. Psychol.*, 28, 191–3.

Svensson, E. (1977). Response format and factor structure in mood adjective check lists. *Scand. J. Psychol.*, 18, 71–8.

Syz, H. C. (1926). Observations on the unreliability of subjective reports of emotional reactions. *Br. J. Psychol.*, 17, 119–26.

Thayer, R. E. (1963). Development and validation of a self-report adjective checklist to measure activation–deactivation. *Doctoral dissertation*, University of Rochester, unpublished.

Thayer, R. E. (1967). Measurement of activation through self-report. *Psychol. Rep.*, 20, 663–78.

Thayer, R. E. (1970). Activation states as assessed by verbal report and four psychophysiological variables. *Psychophysiology*, 7, 86–94.

Thayer, R. E. (1971a). Personality and discrepancies between verbal reports and physiological measures of private emotional experiences. *J. Personality*, 39, 57–69.

Thayer, R. E. (1971b). Studies of controlled self-reports of activation. *Terminal Progress Report, National Institute of Mental Health, Public Health Service, MH*-14248-01.

Thayer, R. E. (1978a). Towards a psychological theory of multidimensional activation (arousal). *Motivation and Emotion*, 2, 1–34.

Thayer, R. E. (1978b). Factor analytic and reliability studies on the activation–deactivation Adjective Checklist. *Psychol. Rep.*, 42, 747–56.

Thayer, R. E., Anderson, J., White, V., and Spadone, A. (1970). Stimulus-seeking behaviour and activation level as a function of white noise. *Paper presented at Western Psychological Association, Los Angeles*.

Thayer, R. E., and Carey, D. (1974). Spatial stimulus as a function of white noise and activation level. *J. Exp. Psychol.*, 102, 539–42.

Thayer, R. E., and Cox, S. J. (1968). Activation, manifest anxiety and verbal learning. *J. Exp. Psychol.*, 78, 524–6.

Thayer, R. E., and Cox, S. J. (1969). Performance in non-competitional paired associates as a function of anxiety, intelligence and general activation. *Paper presented at Western Psychological Association, Vancouver*.

Thayer, R. E., and Moore, L. E. (1972). Reported activation and verbal learning as a function of group size (social facilitation) and anxiety-inducing instructions. *J. Soc. Psychol.*, 88, 277–87.

Throop, W. F., and Macdonald, A. P. (1971). Internal–external locus of control: A bibliography. *Psychol. Rep.*, 28, 175–90.

Tucker, L. A., and Lewis, C. (1973). A reliability coefficient for maximum likelihood factor analysis. *Psychometrika*, 38, 1–10.

Tyrer, P. (1976). The role of bodily feelings in anxiety. *Institute of Psychiatry—Maudsley Monographs, No.* 23, Oxford University Press.

Valecha, G. K., and Ostrom, T. M. (1974). An abbreviated measure of internal–external locus of control. *J. Personality Assessment*, 38, 369–76.

Valins, S. (1970). The perception and labelling of bodily changes as determinants of emotional behaviour. In P. Black (Ed.), *Physiological Correlates of Emotion*, Chapter 11, pp. 229–43.

Venables, P. H., and Christie, M. J. (1974). Neuroticism, physiological state and mood; an exploratory study of Friday/Monday changes. *Biol. Psychol.*, 1, 201–11.

Walsh, D. H. (1974). Interactive effects of alpha feedback and instructional set on subjective state. *Psychophysiology,* **11**, 428–35.

Warr, P. B., and Knapper, C. (1967). Negative response and serial position effects on the adjective checklist. *J. Soc. Psychol.,* **73**, 191–7.

Wessman, A. E., and Ricks, D. F. (1966). *Mood and Personality*, Holt, Rinehart and Winston, New York.

Wendt, G. R., Cameron, J. S., and Specht, P. G. (1962). Chemical studies of behaviour: VI. Placebo and dramamine as methodological controls, and effects on moods, emotions, and motivations. *J. Psychol.,* **53**, 257–79.

Whitehead, W. E., Drescher, W. M., and Blackwell, B. (1976). Lack of relationship between autonomic perception questionnaire scores and actual sensitivity for perceiving one's heart beat. *Psychophysiology,* **13**, 177–83.

Whitehead, W. E., Drescher, V. M., Heiman, P., and Blackwell, B. (1978). Relation of heart rate control to heart rate perception. *Biofeedback and Self-regulation*, in press.

Winer, B. J. (1962). *Statistical Principles in Experimental Design*, McGraw-Hill, New York.

Wing, J. K., Cooper, J. E., and Sartorius, N. (1974). *The Measurement and Classification of Psychiatric Symptoms*, Cambridge University Press, Cambridge.

Wittmaier, B. C. (1974). Changes in arousal as a function of emotional or non-emotional appraisal. *Bull. Psychon. Soc.*, **3** (1B).

Wright, T. (1604). *The Passions of the Minde in Generall*. University of Illinois Press Urbana. Chicago. Reprint based on 1604 edition.

Wundt, W. (1905). *Grundriss der Psychologie*, Engelmann, Leipzig.

Yagi, K., and Berkun, M. (1961). Some problems in the reliability of the adjective checklist. *Paper read at Western Psychological Association, June*.

Yoshitake, H. (1971). Relations between the symptoms and feelings of fatigue. In K., Hashimoto, K. Kogi, and E. Grandjean (Eds), *Methodology in Human Fatigue Assessment*, Taylor and Francis, London.

Zealley, A. K., and Aitken, R. C. B. (1969). Measurement of mood. *Proc. R. Soc. Med., 62*, 993–6.

Zuckerman, M. (1960). The development of an affect adjective checklist for the measurement of anxiety. *J. Consult. Psychol.,* **24**, 457–62.

Zuckerman, M., and Lubin, B. (1965). *Manual for the Multiple Affect Adjective Checklist*, Education and Industrial Testing Service, San Diego.

Zuckerman, M., Persky, H., and Link, K. E. (1969). The influence of set and diurnal factors on autonomic responses to sensory deprivation. *Psychophysiology,* **6**, 612–14.

Part 2

General Aspects of Measurement and Analysis

Techniques in Psychophysiology
Edited by I. Martin and P.H. Venables
© 1980, John Wiley & Sons Ltd.

CHAPTER 10

On Setting Up a Psychophysiological Laboratory

ANTHONY GALE and DAVID SMITH

1 INTRODUCTION

In contrast with the more erudite and precise contributions to this volume, the present brief chapter has a gossipy, over-the-garden-fence air. When one of the authors was shown the outline proposal for the new edition of the *Manual* he observed that there is no published general guide to setting up a laboratory. An extensive literature search confirmed this suspicion. We decided that we must make a direct approach to those who had the expertise. This chapter was therefore compiled in an unusual way. We wrote to a large sample of members of the Society for Psychophysiological Research, in North America, Scandinavia, and Australia, and to members of the Psychophysiology Group in Great Britain. Respondents were asked for their views on the following key topics: soundproofing, electrical interference, air-conditioning and temperature control, access to computers, the psychosocial environment, and installations in special

565

locations. The chapter is therefore a distillation of expertise and, in the case of some respondents, of bitter experience. We are most grateful to all those who replied, many in considerable detail, enclosing references, reprints, and accumulations of sales material.

The construction of laboratories is a complex business involving collaboration with many professional groups, and often in ·a situation in which the individual psychologist has relatively little say. Expertise comes slowly and often too late. Few of us will have had the opportunity to construct one laboratory from scratch, never mind several. Many of us will inherit inadequate laboratories, which superiors will tell us were 'acceptable' to the previous incumbent. One simple mistake in construction can cost a great deal in time, expense, and frustration.

Readers will have had work done for them by contractors at their own homes. As a general rule, four things happen: (i) you do not get what you expected; (ii) the builder denies that you agreed that you would get what you expected; (iii) the work is not completed on schedule; and (iv) the final cost represents a considerable percentage increase on the original estimate. Although large institutions have the power to insist upon fixed price contracts, this in itself is no guarantee that the first three outcomes will be avoided. Indeed, it might operate to make things worse for you, since where resources are limited, the needs of the psychophysiologist may seem both to the institution and to your own colleagues as unnecessary and self-indulgent luxuries. Why should you be allowed additional space for waiting and preparation rooms, separate power supplies, an integral temperature and air-flow system, separate earthing, and costly deep-pile carpeting not only within the laboratory but on the adjacent floor surfaces? (You will have already carried off a good part of your Department's equipment grant for the apparatus installed in the laboratory or will be seen to make disproportionate use of computing facilities.) Several respondents complained of the lack of sympathy of both colleagues and the institution's administration for the special needs of the psychophysiologist. There is no doubt that these special needs are costly and represent a rather unique potential burden on capital budgets. We cannot emphasize too strongly the need for adequate documentation, explanation, and simple public relations exercises, and we hope that this chapter will help in this respect. Even where you have convinced other colleagues of your needs, there are many pitfalls between the original plan and the final product. Where an installation occurs in an existing building it is relatively easy to anticipate difficulties, Where a new building is evolved, a substantial level of vigilance is essential. You must ensure that architects, and soundproofing, heating, ventilation, and electrical engineers, are fully acquainted with your requirements and that the person or persons charged with coordinating and/or supervising their activities is fully *au fait* with the problems. This is no easy matter, since specifications alter continuously and variations in availability of essential items and even the weather conditions will alter not only the pace, but the sequence of work. Even though the specification for your own laboratory remains constant there might be changes elsewhere in the building, e.g. elevators, ventilation systems, location of noisy workshops, etc. which will influence the functional capacity of your laboratory. It would be foolish to assume that universities or hospitals are more efficient than any other large organization. As elsewhere, there are individuals whose sublime flexibility and indifference can create minor disasters for your laboratory. There is also an unfortunate tradition in the construction industry that the client does not have regular access to the site once the work has been set in motion. His representative (in Britain, the Clerk of Works) is responsible for ensuring that the work is carried out according to specification. It is essential that this person knows exactly what is required; indeed you are well-advised to insist upon the exchange of a written and agreed record of all your consultations. The hair-raising stories which circulate within organizations after buildings have been completed, give ample justification for this apparently paranoid advice. Remember, once a building, or part of a building has been erected, it is not easy to take it down and start again. Be vigilant!

The problems to be reviewed in the following sections are representative of much larger bodies of expertise. Since new techniques, special materials, and theoretical advances constantly appear within these separate specialities, the reader is advised not to accept our suggested solutions as the final word on the problems. Rather, the reader should use this chapter as a back-up or training ground before entering the fray. Most manufacturers have ample sales literature which they are eager to distribute and which usually defines the problem in question as well as providing technical specifications. There are also specialist organizations such as the Building Research Laboratories (in Great Britain) which produce straightforward information leaflets. The reader should acquire a literature of this nature and consult it before encountering the experts, thus avoiding communication failures and misunderstandings.

No psychophysiologist is likely to obtain an ideal laboratory. Cost must be a crucial element in making decisions, particularly nowadays where public expenditure on institutions of higher education and on research in particular, has been reduced. Psychophysiology, next to primate research is probably one of the most costly of research activities in psychology; it is a chastening exercise to compute relative costs per printed page of journal publication for your laboratory, taking into account staffing, building, equipment and recurrent costs. Psychophysiology probably costs several dollars per printed word! The researcher must have a clear idea of his building objectives, the relative costs and conflicting interests of different emphases in laboratory construction and location, and decide on priorities. For example, adequate temperature control may be more important than a high level of soundproofing (rather than mere damping). Sound-damping at source may be more effective than elaborate remedies within the laboratory area. It may be preferable to use the space allocated to you to create a single suite which is adequate for both teaching and research purposes rather than construct two cramped smaller areas, neither of which is wholly satisfactory. Since labour costs can represent some two-thirds of most building costs, you may well save money by adopting techniques which can be employed by existing staff (see below). At the same time, the researcher should be aware that the design of the laboratory reflects certain assumptions about the nature of psychophysiology itself. Several respondents expressed discontent with the 'artificial' nature of Pavlovian sound-proofed cubicles and the laboratory environment in general; they expressed the need for new skills, enabling the psychophysiologist to work in the field, sampling data in more naturalistic surroundings. If this view prevails over the coming years and if the appropriate technology is forthcoming, then much of the present chapter will prove to be an anachronism or achæological curiosity In fact, other than making observations concerning the relative merits of hospital and university environments, few of our respondents could offer advice on field installations. Our impression is that human psychophysiological ethology is some way off and will be dependent upon advances in other psychological disciplines. In the meanwhile, problems of soundproofing and temperature control are of some importance. Problems of electrical interference will probably multiply with field applications. Although some of the modern polygraphs are relatively impervious to interference in a stable laboratory environment, increased involvement with fieldwork will revive interest in strategies for reducing unpredicted interference.

2 SOUND INSULATION

Sound insulation is subject to the law of diminishing returns. A considerable reduction in transmission can be achieved by relatively straightforward techniques. However, complete and total reduction will involve elaborate precautions and few experts will be willing to guarantee complete success in advance. Luckily, none of our respondents expressed a need for total sound insulation. Indeed, several regretted the degree of insulation they had achieved, pointing out that the effect created could be quite disturbing for subjects, particularly for clinical populations (see below).

Principle sound sources which one wishes to eliminate are as follows: traffic external to the building (automobiles, aeroplanes, locomotives);

machinery (workshop tools, vacuum cleaners, floor polishers, elevators, ventilation motors, typewriters, telephone bells, telephone switchgear); voices (within and external to your laboratory); typical building noises (rain on roofs and windows, wind, doors slamming, footsteps, transmissions through heating and water pipes, flushing lavatories, wall mounted roller towels); howls and squeals from animal housing and child laboratories; computer, polygraph, slide projector, and stimulus programming devices within the laboratory. We assume that you do not have colleagues who play radio receivers in the building, but this can be a problem on a campus, particularly where there are halls of residence or student recreation facilities. If you prefer running subjects in the evening, you will find that radio, television, and record player sounds transmit beautifully on an otherwise silent campus.

Sound is transmitted both through the air and via the fabric of the building. To counteract both sources one needs a combination of mass and discontinuity of structure. Choice of location (perhaps the most crucial of your decisions) must depend on the characteristics of the building and its immediate environment and upon the activities of adjacent users. By adjacent, we mean above and below the laboratory as well as users on the same floor.

It is clear from the list set out above that no particular location in a building is ideal. For example, several respondents reported that their laboratories had been installed in basements, but that this was a mixed blessing. Remoteness from areas of heavy building traffic, reduction in window area and the ability to install heavy purpose-built cubicles without worrying about floor weight was a bonus. However, footstep sounds are transmitted from the floor above the laboratory and the bare walls and corridor floors typically found in basements serve as echo chambers for lift-shaft and stairwell noise. Such remote areas might also be unacceptable on psychosocial grounds (see below). If computing facilities are to be shared for on-line work, then there may be no alternative to meshing your laboratory in with a general laboratory suite used by your colleagues. Again, you may wish to have your own office and that of research staff close to the laboratory. Such a mixture of adjacent room functions, disruptive of modular constructional design, is not always popular with architects. Clearly then, choice of location is determined by several factors, of which sound attenuation is but one. However, given a reasonably large space for the laboratory, most sound insulation difficulties can be overcome by means of adequate construction of the subject chamber. Space is required because soundproofing techniques take up considerable horizontal and vertical space. Two 9″ walls occupy one-tenth of a 15 foot room. In a modern building with 8 foot ceilings, a cubicle, floating floor, and roof-mounted air baffle (for cubicle ventilation), can reduce usable height to only 6 feet. Moreover, the final dimensions are in terms of a completed cubicle; but initial construction and subsequent maintenance probably demand usable space both around and above the cubicle. The quality of finish in soundproof cubicles must be of a high standard (e.g. sealing off all airpaths) and this calls for easy access during installation. Standard prefabricated cubicles used in many laboratories are barely large enough internally for a standard laboratory couch and are therefore typically useless for social psychophysiological research involving recording from more than one subject at once, or for installing both the subject and elaborate displays, e.g. simulated cockpits or car seats. Generally speaking, on-site construction, if adequately supervised, will produce a more desirable outcome. We have found that given adequate consultation, very detailed drawings, modern materials, and a competent and willing carpenter, one can produce a pleasant and functional cubicle at less than half the cost of a cramped, prefabricated construction.

If cost and weight are no problem then there is probably no substitute for a 9″ solid brick wall, with an appropriate mortar mixture. But such expense is not necessary. Modern gypsum boards are used in housing projects, even as partition walls between dwellings and come in heavy-duty thicknesses quite suitable for cubicling. In sound transmission terms they can substitute for solid brick (Lee, 1967). They are certainly more efficient than light-weight building blocks, which should be avoided. We have found the following wall construction very satisfactory.

Solid and continuous 4″ × 2″ timber is firmly screwed to the floor, the air gap between timber and floor being caulked with special purpose mastic solution. A metal blind-E frame is then screwed into the timber flush to the near edge and vertical members are inserted at intervals compatible with plaster board widths. British Gypsum Ltd provide a special purpose non-reverberant galvanized frame. Additional framing should be installed where weight is to be borne, i.e. for supporting the ceiling, for shelves, around entry points of air ducts, windows, cable ducts, etc.. The heavy-duty plasterboards come in lengths of up to 3 metres and thicknesses of 12.5 millimetres. These boards can be screwed to the frame with an electrical screwdriver. Two layers of board should be fixed at overlapping intervals, so that the junction of two boards on the lower skin comes in the centre of the boards of the top skin. Outer boards can be purchased with a bevelled edge on one side, and a special sealing tape and plaster mixture allow for a smooth, paint-ready, virtually dry finish. The walls are constructed by having two vertical sections in parallel, leaving a minimum of 8″ air gap between. In this gap, special-purpose, heavy-duty fibre-glass quilting is suspended. Electrical cabling can be slipped into the gap before sealing off. Most cubicles require a light dimming system and the controls are typically in the external room at a vantage point which allows a sight of the cubicle illumination level, i.e. either through the door, or the observation or projection window.

The floor for the room is easily constructed. Wooden battens are fixed at 14″ intervals to heavy-duty chipboard sheets and these are then rested upon fibre-glass quilting, making sure that there is a small gap between floor and cubicle walls, up into which the quilting may be drawn. The floating floor can then be carpeted and the join between carpet and cubicle walls finished with plastic skirting board. Vibration pads are a good alternative to the quilting but they typically require slightly more vertical height. The ceiling is particularly difficult since one requires a frame adequate to carry a substantial weight, which may include an air baffle system. Ideally, the walls should be taken through the existing ceiling and a frame for the new ceiling built onto wall supports. Again, a sandwich arrangement of boards, air gap, and quilting is required; this time the quilting may be folded in zig-zag fashion and rested on the lower skin. At all points of construction (particularly at corners) air gaps must be sealed with deliberate care and junctions designed to minimize sound transmission. Working drawings and a flow diagram for the work must be produced *before* you begin and discussed at length with the craftsmen concerned if you are to achieve an air-proof, sound-deadened box. Unfortunately, one has to get access to the box for a number of reasons. People must get in and out, air must flow, cables must be fed in and out, and windows are required for observation and for presenting projected stimuli. Any of these points of access can destroy all the good work achieved in overall construction; every break in the fabric is a potential inlet for sound. For example a 9″ solid wall or 11″ cavity wall on a domestic building reduces external sounds by 50 dB. But by introducing an ordinary single sheet window, combined attenuation of wall and window is cut sharply to 20 dB. A major and worthwhile item of expenditure is the entry threshold and if possible, double doors, one opening inwards and the other, outwards. The door frame and doors should be constructed as a separate unit by a skilled carpenter. Cheap materials (e.g. softwoods) should be avoided. Standard domestic hardboard doors are not acceptable and heavy-duty doors should be constructed to give a tight fit against a rubber seal or neoprene rim. An adequate door frame, particularly if the opening is a foot deep and the doors solid, is likely to be heavy, and you should consult your institution's structural engineer about floor stress. We have found it sensible to locate the door towards the edge of the wall, rather than in the centre; this leaves more wall space available, e.g. for beds, projector screens, etc.

With the introduction of closed-circuit television, large observation windows are probably unneccessary. However, slide projectors and mechanical shutters are noisy and require a reasonable focal length to produce a large image; a small projection window is essential. We have found that two layers of glass can produce a blurred image; a single sheet of 3/4" glass is acceptable, but should only be inserted into a well-sealed frame *after* determining an appropriate beam angle for the projector. An image may be projected downwards from above and behind the subject's head and an adjustable angle solid screen is employed to reduce image distortion. This will mean that the projector is mounted rather high in the experimental room. Ensure there is plenty of space for obtaining access and inserting slide dispensers. The projector can be mounted on a deep shelf below the window frame, some 6 feet off the floor. The shelf needs to be deep to give adequate room for lens and shutter. Some slide dispensers move forward and project forward.

Several respondents referred to socket panels installed on external and internal walls for conveying cables in and out of the sound-deadened chamber. This is probably unnecessary. We have devised a hinged, baffled-box system which enables cables to be uninterrupted yet maintains sound-insulation, and are able to provide drawings on request. This enables us to remove equipment from the laboratory or install it without difficulty and without socket compatibility problems.

The major difficulties are undoubtedly the problem of air circulation, maintenance of a stable temperature, and humidity control. A decent system can be particularly costly, exceeding the price of the cubicle itself. Not only do air circulating systems break into the soundproofing of the chamber, they are themselves a potential noise and vibration source, apart from conveying sounds via the air inlet. A continuous background hum can provide an adequate masking noise and reduce the unpleasant subjective effects of total sound insulation but a thermostatically controlled system will be subject to irregular switching and sudden changes in background noise level. Wind noise and cold draughts are not compatible with subject comfort. The air-change rate and the appropriate fan capacity, taking into account the nature and length of the baffle system, cubicle volume, and most extreme patterns of use, should be carefully estimated with the ventilation engineer. The possibility of sound transmission from other parts of the building means that apart from cubicle temperature regulation, there are ready grounds for an isolated special purpose unit. Do not share the general building ventilation ducts or motors. At the same time, care must be taken in locating the air intake grille for the system. If your laboratory is some distance from the intake grille, then the inflow ducts are likely to pass through other laboratories.

Air circulation is essential. Cubicles can become intolerably hot, stuffy, and smelly. Temperature and humidity control are considered equally important by several of our respondents. Ax has a particularly elaborate arrangement and we reproduce here his very detailed description:

A troublesome source of noise is usually the air inlet. I avoided this and any draughts by a ceiling plenum of 2–4 feet high into which the cooled, dried, and heated air was discharged. Then it entered the room through tiny holes evenly spaced all over the ceiling tile. Air was exhausted all around the bottom edges of the room. Although the air was changed quite rapidly one could never sense any drafts. The final fine temperature control was achieved by a thermistor about 2 feet down from the ceiling which controlled an 1800 watt electrical heater, in the intake stream, on a continuous basis (the air being supplied a few degrees cooler than the final temperature desired). I should mention the sensing thermistor was also fitted with a tiny heating unit which mimicked the heating level of the main heater and thus served as an anticipator and dampened out all tendency to hunt. We achieved 0.1 deg.C constancy over several hours in a room about $10 \times 14 \times 8$ft high. Incidentally, there was no sound produced by this temperature control system. We controlled the humidity between 40% and 60% relative humidity.

Several respondents warned us that rooms with external windows can be subject to glare from sunlight and undergo uncomfortable variation in temperature. If you put your laboratory on the colder side of the building then only a *heating* system is necessary; however, on the warm side, you will need air cooling as well!

Many readers will have resources for a simple air-exchange system, but not for temperature and humidity control. A poor substitute is to have available a portable fan which can be used to vacate stale air from the cubicle in between testing sessions. However there must be an air inlet because an air sealed, soundproofed box can be lethal. Even so, always ensure that the door (or doors) can be opened from the inside as well as the outside. This is an appropriate point to mention fire safety. A person working away in an air conditioned, soundproof cubicle, will be the last person in the building to see smoke or flames, experience rising temperature or hear alarms or voices raised in panic. However inelegant alarms may be, it is worth considering installation in your cubicle of a small bell. Indeed, your local fire officer may well be required to approve your structure before you proceed with building.

Our description of general principles of construction has not included reference to electrical screening since this is dealt with in detail below (see Section 4). Nevertheless, we should warn that incorporation of a screen makes for excessive complication in construction and if done badly, can create more problems than if not done at all.

We have heard of, and visited, laboratories where ignorance of basic principles of soundproofing has led to ridiculous results. One laboratory has an expensive anechoic but sound transmitting chamber in which the subject may hear sounds from a nearby motorway! Soundproofing tiles and other fabric *inside* your laboratory are quite ineffective in reducing sounds emanating from *outside*. If you can afford only the simplest precautions remember the following simple rules. Dense materials in thin panels vibrate, and will therefore amplify noise rather then reduce it. Heavy, thick structures reduce sound transmission but their smooth surfaces can create echoic conditions. Soft linings reduce echo, but do not prevent noise passing through. Thus the ideal is a solid mass partition, with a soft lining on its surface. Given a limited budget, install soft linings at *source* (e.g. curtains, carpets, cork or polystyrene tiles) and this will reduce echo and transmission to adjacent rooms.

From this brief discussion it will be clear that the erection of an adequate experimental chamber involves considerable planning and preparation. Moreover, a laboratory which is large, well soundproofed and has temperature and humidity control, will cost a great deal of money. There are regrettably few laboratories in Great Britain which match the ideal specification. If you have the opportunity, visit colleagues' laboratories before you sit down to design your own. At least you will benefit from their mistakes.

3 COMPUTER INSTALLATION

Most computer manufacturers will provide customer assistance in all phases of site planning. After installation, various maintenance and service options are available for different systems.

Make sure that the route the equipment is to take to the designated area will facilitate delivery. Check the size of doors, passageways, ramps, etc. for height, width, and turning radius to see if there are any receiving or installation problems. Take into account the moving equipment and the pallet attached (if any). If a lift is to be used check its size and weight limitations.

Although each system may well differ, the following points should be considered:

(a) Space for the equipment, working and servicing area. Do not forget that to teach a group of students, you may need standing space for groups of six or more at any one time.
(b) Availability and location of adequate power (voltages, current, tolerance on voltage and frequency, provision of an adequate ground).
(c) Proper fire and safety precautions.
(d) Air conditioning and/or humidifying equipment.
(e) Location of cables and other equipment.

(f) Efficient work-flow pattern to other work areas, ease of visual observation of input/output devices.

(g) Sufficient storage space for supplies necessary to the operation of the system; most laboratories generate vast quantities of hard copy (computer or polygraph) within a short space of time.

(h) Further system expansion.

Proper fire and safety precautions should be carried out. All personnel working in the computer area should be trained in such emergency measures as:

(a) Proper method of shutting off all electrical power.

(b) Handling fire extinguishers in the correct manner (including an appreciation of the different uses of different types of extinguisher).

(c) Evacuating personnel and records and calling the fire service.

Special safeguards should be taken to protect vital data which are very expensive or impossible to duplicate. Adequate duplicate copies should be stored away from the computer area. In most cases, a regular program of updating the duplicate data is necessary to maintain the value of such back-up storage.

The reliability of a computer system is a complex function of the task it is expected to perform and its environment. The on-line laboratory computer may require complete error-free operation or several hours for scheduled downtime. Some of the non-environmental factors are:

(a) Time interval before data are irretrievably lost.

(b) Use of a small, independent subsystem for data capture.

(c) Significance of a data error.

(d) Significance of extended downtime.

(e) Partially or completely redundant system with manual or automatic system changeover.

(f) Graceful system degradation upon subsystem failure.

(g) Input/output device-independent software.

High temperatures increase the rate of deterioration of virtually every material. Temperature cycling and thermal gradients induce temporary and permanent microscopic changes in materials. High absolute humidity (dewpoint) causes moisture absorption and dimensional and handling changes in paper and plastic media (line printer paper, cards, paper tape, magnetic tape, etc.).

Low humidity allows the build up of static electricity. Lack of air cleanliness results in reduced life of tapes, excessive headwear and early data errors in all moving magnetic storage media (drums, discs).

The combination of static electricity and airborne dust is particularly detrimental to magnetic tapes. Vibration can cause slow degradation of mechanical parts and when severe, may cause data errors on discs and drums.

High-power radio-frequency pulses conducted through the power mains or radiated through space when severe, may cause hardware logic errors. Such pulses can come from radar installations, nearby broadcasting stations and welding operations, and from less obvious sources such as nearby arcing relay or motor contacts and the arcs which occur when static electricity is discharged. In extreme circumstances filtered or isolated power mains and/or radio frequency shielding may be required.

The recommended computer room environment has an air distribution system which provides cool, well filtered, humidified air. The room air pressure should be kept higher than the pressure of adjacent areas to prevent dust infiltration. (Think twice before linking this to the cubicle air system.) Central processor units operate under much wider temperature and humidity ranges than do paper cards, printer paper, and magnetic media. The system will thus be restricted to the limits which these impose. A factor that should be considered in equipment layout is that certain items of equipment (notably discs and drums) are sensitive to sudden changes in temperature like those produced by the cycling of certain types of air conditioning systems. Sensitive units should be located where they will not be subject to sudden changes in air temperature. Also, storage of supplies should be held at the same temperature as the computer room and isolated from sudden temperature changes.

Static electricity can be an annoyance to operators and can (in extreme cases) affect the operational characteristics of the equipment. Carpeting, if installed, should be of a type designed to minimize the effects of static electricity. Metal flooring or flooring with metal strip surrounds should be adequately grounded. Static resistant wax is commercially available.

Some peripheral devices (line printers, reader/punches, tape transports) have a high noise level. Acoustically damped rooms may reduce noise to a reasonable level (see Section 2).

If cathode-ray tube peripheral devices are to be employed, the surrounding illumination should be such that the user can conveniently observe the display; it might be sensible to have dimmer switches for lighting in the outer room as well as the subject cubicle.

4 ELECTRICAL INTERFERENCE

External electrical interference of severe nature should not be present in a well planned laboratory and the chosen site should be tested to confirm that this is so. It is difficult to evaluate the elctromagnetic fields that can occur in the laboratory. Detailed measurement is the only reliable method of evaluation, since analysis of the practical case in many buildings is almost impossible.

It is very important having purchased very expensive electrophysiological recording equipment that further time, money, and effort is not wasted getting the subject–equipment combination to perform adequately in what at first viewing appeared to be a suitable laboratory environment. It is a fact that no matter how sophisticated the signal conditioning/recording equipment is, superior results will be achieved with appropriate shielding.

The majority of electric potentials that may be recorded from tissues or organs of the body are to be found in the range from a few thousandths of a volt (mV) down to a few millionths of a volt (μV). This necessitates the use of amplifiers with gains from several hundred thousand to several million. By far the most common source of interference within the laboratory is that which emanates from the mains supply, which is unfortunately often in the subject area. When a subject is 'hooked up' with electrodes, one of the electrodes serving as the 'earth' electrode has a resistance which is effectively in series with the capacitive reactance (due to the capacitive coupling between a mains conductor and the subject's body). The potential due to this coupling is very small in comparison with the mains supply voltage, but may be extremely large in comparison with the potential of interest from the subject. If the subject is replaced by a 'dummy' subject (a resistor of about 10kΩ) and moved about the room, variations with location will become evident. It is imperative that any mains introduced into the subject area is electrically screened. This screening should not come into direct contact with the separately screened electrode leads to the amplifiers.

If, as is not uncommon, there are constraints on choice of location of laboratory and severe external interference is present, the laboratory may well have to be shielded. (It is possible to 'kill' the interference at source but this is not often the case.) Severe interference emanates from such sources as diathermy, radiographic and arc welding equipment; elevators, heating, and ventilation control systems; flickering neon lamps, fluorescent mercury-vapour lamp and dimmers; motors, relays, bleepers, etc..

Electrical shielding and grounding which is always necessary to some degree must be carried out properly and with utmost care. As already mentioned, the shielding of the input to high gain amplifiers is almost always required and therefore should be provided for. Shielding the subjects' room usually entails the construction of a complete iron 'cage' around it. A clear and concise article by Thomson and Yarbrough (1967) is very worthwhile consulting and making available to those in charge of the 'cage' construction. Ideally the 'cage' should be constructed to form a fully lapped and seamed 'ideal box' with a ground connection made at one point only. The ground conductor must be as large and as short as possible and be completely separate from any other building connections. Any departures from the 'ideal box' will start to degrade the shielding. The shielding must be completely insulated from any extraneous ground. Obviously a door, and ventilation ducts and maybe windows have to be introduced in the practical situation. These facilities must still maintain the integrity of the shielding system. Windows should be of wire reinforced glass which is connected to the shielding. The door shield must be connected to the wall shields, not by spring contact alone but by securely attaching braided buswires at as short a spacing as is possible between them. Even when great care has been taken to eliminate the interference with shielding, complications can still arise if a long ground line has been employed. This may well introduce interference by picking up radio frequencies (RFI). RFI can be a difficult problem to eradicate and might well involve enclosing the whole laboratory within a thin copper shield, connected to ground at one point only; that is, the ground connection to the 'cage'. As Thomspon and Yarbrough point out ' . . . as shielding against radio frequencies is a tricky business, engineering consultation may save time and money'.

Make sure that everyone concerned understands your shielding requirements from the outset. Get equipment in and make tests before, during, and after finishing the inside of the room.

Some guidelines are given below:

(a) Try to site the laboratory away from any 'heavy current' equipment and if possible get the laboratory supplied on its own mains distribution circuit.

(b) Keep to the ideal seamed box configuration as much as possible.

(c) Use a heavy conductor to ground the 'cage' at only one point. (Multiple grounds can be disastrous.) A copper stake driven deep into perpetually moist soils makes an ideal ground connection. Drastic changes in ground conditions, e.g. from summer to winter, can vary the resistance path between your earth stake and the building earth.

(d) Screen all input signal leads to input amplifiers. Keep electrode leads short. Ensure electrodes are properly fixed. Although notch filters can be used as a last resort, the proper remedy to eliminate 'hum' is to deal with the problem at source.

(e) Provide incandescent room lighting supplied via screened power wiring and transformer. If possible a d.c. supply (rectified and smoothed) should be used. Control of lighting is best done from outside the subject's room.

(f) Any motors installed for air conditioning control or other purposes should be sited well away from the laboratory.

(g) Do not violate the high quality ground when introducing ventilation ducts into the room. Insulate the ducting to prevent this. (Remember also that the introduction of a rigid fixing between the inside and outside walls of a soundproof room will have a detrimental effect on the soundproofing characteristics.)

(h) If carpeting is to be used in and around the laboratory, try and use the electrically groundable type. Electrostatic interference can be very disconcerting for both experimenter and subject and has also been known to destroy control logic and halt minicomputer processing.

One point that cannot be overemphasized too much is that of safety. Any ground introduced into the laboratory should provide the same degree of safety as the power line ground. Haphazard linking of equipment screening may produce circulating currents. Ground securely, and to one point only. All wiring, signal through to power, should be checked and maintained regularly.

Grass Instruments Ltd produce a special safety manual for polygraph users (1972).

5 THE PSYCHOSOCIAL ENVIRONMENT

Do we need to worry about the impression made by the laboratory upon the subject? The psychology experiment is after all a particular type of social interaction. The psychophysiologist, perhaps even more than other researchers, needs to have an explicit model of the psychology experiment. High levels of anxiety, induced by the subject's attributions to the laboratory, are likely to constitute an unnecessary source of error variance. Interactions with the experimenter involve physical contact, invasion of personal space, and application of electrical wires and a variety of transducers. Some respondents saw laboratory attendants as very much a part of the perceived environment and reported that they spend time training students in adopting the appropriate manner, just as psychometric testers are taught to establish rapport. They also reported that they had taken great care in the design of general layout, decorations, and furnishing. Our view is that it should not be necessary for subjects to see the apparatus and that therefore, access to the cubicle should not be via the experimenter's room. However, a problem associated with separating cubicle and apparatus room is that quite often the experimenter has to move back and forth between the two rooms to make minor adjustments. Some prefer to wire-up and clean up subjects in a separate room. Ideally there should be a waiting room and lavatory in the vicinity. Washing facilities, including hot and cold water, should also be provided.

The room from which one enters the cubicle should be pleasantly decorated in pastel shades; if possible have an external window to reduce the sense of enclosure, and have soft furnishings and carpeting. This is one of the areas from which sound might be transmitted to the cubicle and carpets may be justified as a means of reducing sound at source. Some of the commercially available cubicles have refrigerator-type doors with enormous chrome handles (and even submarine-type latch cover wheels) and are likely to provide more than a hint of claustrophobia. Recent critics of the psychology experiment (Silverman, 1977) have suggested that testing rooms are something like man-sized Skinner-boxes and that their use presupposes a view of man as a stimulus–response lump. As we have suggested above, the psychophysiologist is obliged to invade the privacy of the individual; it is therefore essential that he treats his subjects in a humane manner and within a friendly and relaxed atmosphere. Initial visits to the laboratory by psychiatric patients are unlikely to yield robust data. There is no reason to believe that 'normal' subjects are not made uneasy by racks of electronic gear on an atmosphere redolent of a Frankenstein cellar.

This is a short section compared with our treatment of earlier topics and one would think that the points we have made although of crucial importance are nevertheless rather obvious. Unfortunately, many of the laboratories we have visited look more like an adjunct to a physics laboratory than a drawing room. Perhaps this is an extension of the general rule that psychologists study those topics which reflect their own personal inadequacies; perhaps psychophysiologists have little personal understanding of emotion or the stimuli which trigger it!

6 TECHNICAL SUPPORT

Two general points are worth emphasizing in this respect. Firstly, the more you know about the equipment you are using, the less trouble you will have and the less dependent you will be on other people's help. Six months of intensive study of circuitry and computer systems could well prove to be an invaluable investment. Secondly, before you employ technical staff make sure what skills you need. Respondents referred to the danger of employing persons whose notions of specification for electronic devices were simply out-of-touch with the needs of the psychophysiologist. In simple terms, what the technician thought important was not what the psychophysiologist needed, and what the psychophysiologist needed just was not appreciated by technical staff. Again this is a matter of sitting down and clarifying the functional requirements and limitations of the systems you propose to use.

7 CONCLUDING REMARKS

A number of general principles emerge from this brief account of problems and solutions in the setting up of psychophysiological laboratories. The psychophysiologist must be skilful in making a case for his laboratory, because he will be competing for limited resources. Good psychophysiological laboratories are expensive. Although we have enumerated a number of general principles relating to location, soundproofing, ventilation, electrical screening, and computer installation, we have resisted the temptation to lay down specific rulings or judgements. It is clear that there can be no simple formula for determining even quite crucial aspects of design and layout. Your decision must be based on multivariate considerations. Materials, technology, and prejudice, alter rapidly. The reader is advised to familiarize himself with the issues we have raised, to visit other laboratories and to take as much professional advice as possible before embarking on elaborate schemes. The construction of an adequate laboratory cannot be sketched out on the back of an envelope; detailed planning and consultation are essential. We have emphasized repeatedly that mistakes can be costly and indeed irremediable. No matter how well you plan, there will always be unpredicted problems; but planning will reduce these to a minimum or help to anticipate the need for alternative solutions. Set out in a quite explicit fashion your research and teaching objectives since these, in the final analysis, will be crucial determinants of design. This specification will help you decide which characteristics of the laboratory are essential, rather than merely desirable. We can predict that you will be obliged to sacrifice a number of features, so have a list of these in reserve.

Unlike the authors of a cook's recipe book we cannot provide those explicit instructions which will inevitably lead to a perfect product. However, we can wish you the best of luck with your laboratory and many happy hours of experimentation. Do not hesitate to write to us if you find our advice misleading or inadequate.

ACKNOWLEDGEMENTS

We wish to thank the following colleagues who responded to our request for advice:
Bill Acker, Institute of Psychiatry, Maudsley Hospital, London.
John L. Andreassi, Department of Psychology, Baruch College, City University of New York.
Albert F. Ax, Behavioural Sciences Center, Nova University, Florida.
James Averill, Department of Psychology, University of Massachusetts.
Graham Beaumont, Department of Psychology, University of Leicester.
Richard Bloch, Department of Mental Health and Mental Retardation, Eastern State Hospital, Williamsburg.
Clinton C. Brown, Maryland Psychiatric Research Centre, Baltimore.
Monte S. Buchsbaum, National Institute of Mental Health, Bethesda.
James Allan Burdick, Box 65, Sanford, Manitoba.
Nicholas J. Carriero, Department of the Army, US Army Human Engineering Laboratory, Maryland.

Mike Clarke, Department of Psychology. Long Grove Hospital, Epsom.

Michael G.H. Coles, Department of Psychology, University of Illinois at Urbana-Champaign.

Robert Edelberg, Rutgers Medical School, New Jersey.

Ray Fuller, Department of Psychology, Trinity College, Dublin.

John J. Furedy, Department of Psychology, University of Toronto.

John Hinton, Department of Psychology, University of Glasgow.

David Hord, Department of the Navy, Naval Health Research Center, San Diego.

Wilfred Hume, Department of Psychiatry, University of Leeds.

Malcolm Lader, Institute of Psychiatry, Maudsley Hospital, London.

Vaman G. Lokare, Department of Clinical Psychology, West Park Hospital, Epsom.

Chris Mawson, Department of Psychiatry, University of Sheffield.

Cheyne McCallum, Burden Neurological Institute, Bristol.

Sarnoff A. Mednick, Social Science Research Institute, University of Southern California, Los Angeles.

O.D. Murphree, Research Laboratory, Veterans Administration Hospital, North Little Rock.

John O'Gorman, Department of Psychology, University of New England, Armidale.

T.W. Picton, Department of Medicine, University of Ottawa.

Georgina Rippon, Department of Psychology, University of Warwick.

Gary E. Schwartz, Department of Psychology, University of Yale.

David Shapiro, Department of Psychiatry, School of Medicine, University of California, Los Angeles.

John A. Stern, Department of Psychology, University of Washington, St. Louis.

Ian St. James-Roberts, Institute of Education, University of London.

Samuel Sutton, Psychiatric Institute, Department of Mental Hygiene, New York.

Sven Svebak, Department of Somatic Psychology, University of Bergen.

R.T. Wilkinson, MRC Applied Psychology Unit, Cambridge.

REFERENCES

Grass, E. R., and Grass, A. M. (1972). *Questions and Answers about Electrical Safety (Specifically Related to Electroencephalography)*, Grass Instruments Co., Quincy.

Lee, B. (1967). A shielded, sound-attenuating chamber. *Psychophysiology*, **3**, 255–7.

Thompson, N. P., and Yarbrough, R. B. (1967). The shielding of electroencephalographic laboratories. *Psychophysiology*, **4**, 244–8.

Silverman, I. (1977). *The Human Subject in the Psychological Laboratory*, Pergamon Press, New York.

Techniques in Psychophysiology
Edited by I. Martin and P.H. Venables
© 1980, John Wiley & Sons Ltd.

CHAPTER 11

Computers in Psychophysiological Research

M. D. RUGG, R. P. FLETCHER, and DAVID T. LYKKEN

1 THE LABORATORY COMPUTER

The power of a computer (general purpose digital computer) lies in its immense flexibility. A computer has only part of its ultimate structure installed at the factory, allowing it to accomplish a few rudimentary functions but, more importantly, facilitating its almost unlimited capacity to learn by receiving additional structure, i.e. to be programmed. A *program* is a specific set of instructions residing in the computer's memory; the computer's variability of function is determined by the variability of the programs which are fed into it. The organization of a typical laboratory computer is illustrated in Figure 11.1

The heart of a computer is its central processing unit (CPU). This can receive information — either program instructions or data — from an input device such as a teletype (although the word 'teletype' strictly refers to a particular device marketed by one manufacturer it will be taken in this chapter to mean any such device with the same function). Every computer incorporates a *machine language*, a set of elementary instructions which the

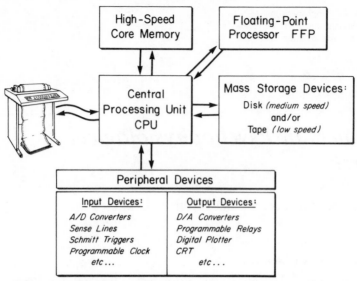

Figure 11.1   Organization of a typical laboratory computer

CPU can recognize and perform. Since computers deal only in numbers these instructions — program commands — are themselves coded as numbers and stored in *registers*. A register may be thought of as a row of switches each of which may be 'on' or 'off' as in Table 11.1. For example, a computer might have 12 switches per register and would then be said to deal in 12-bit words; a computer having 16 switches per register would be a 16-bit machine and so on. A 12-bit register can contain numbers ranging from −3777 to +3777 in octal notation (−2047 to +2047 in decimal) with the leftmost bit determining the sign (plus or minus) of the number. Typical basic commands in the computer's repertory might be commands to halt processing, to clear (set to zero) a particular register of the CPU or to fetch a number from some address (location) in memory and add it to the contents of a specified register in the CPU. Most commands, such as this last one, require the performance of some operation (fetching from, storing in, clearing, adding to) on a particular location in memory and the address of that memory location may be provided in the instruction word along with the operational command itself.

Although it is convenient to represent computer-related numbers in octal notation it should be noted that computers operate solely with binary numbers. The reason for this is that a single binary digit has only two forms, 0 and 1, and can therefore easily be represented in a machine by a switch, transistor, etc. which has only two states. A register consisting of 12 such switches can contain any 12 digit (12-bit) binary number — such a string of 0's and 1's is hardly amenable to easy manipulation by the human

Table 11.1. A 12-bit register can be thought of as a row of 12 solid-state switches each of which can be set either on (= binary 1) or off (= binary 0). As shown in the top of the table, the 8 possible combinations of 3 binary digits can represent the 8 digits of octal notation; therefore, binary and octal numbers are easily translated from the one form to the other. In the lower portion of the table, a 12-bit register is shown set to the binary number 010101100011. This is equivalent to octal 2543 which, in turn, can be translated by a more laborious process into its decimal equivalent, 1379

BINARY	OCTAL
000	0
001	1
010	2
011	3
100	4
101	5
110	6
111	7

bit number:	1	2	3	4	5	6	7	8	9	10	11	12
Register:	0	1	0	1	0	1	1	0	0	0	1	1
Octal		2			5			4			3	

brain. The octal representation of any 12-bit number requires only 4 digits and is thus considerably easier to deal with and remember and, moreover, is easily converted into its binary form as shown in Table 11.1

Referring once more to Figure 11.1, sequences of commands (i.e. programs) as well as data can be inserted into designated locations in memory from the teletype, the CPU acting as the coordinator of such operations. One reason for the computer's power in addition to its large memory and great speed, is its capability of treating any word in its memory either as data or as a command. This means that the computer is able to change its own program by modifying certain command words in the course of the execution of the program. A simple example of this is a situation in which a command to store a newly input number in a given location is incremented after each execution so that successive numbers will be stored in successive memory locations. This means that repetitive operations can be programmed such that the computer loops through the same sequence of commands any required number of times. This ability to modify its own program commands is what gives the computer its rudimentary 'intelligence', its ability to 'do A until X occurs but if Y occurs do B' and the like. The term *software* is a generic term used to describe all aspects of programming within a computer, i.e. the commands themselves and associated data. Conversely, the term *hardware* refers to the physical structure of the computer, e.g. the circuitry of the CPU or the 'chips' which make up the core memory.

The core memory of the computer is its 'working memory' and can be accessed at very high speed. Invariably core memory is a *random-access* type, i.e. every location can be accessed with equal facility, a word anywhere in core being fetched, stored or changed in a few microseconds. Most laboratory computers also have slower but more capacious supplementary memories known as *mass storage* devices. These allow information (in the form of programs or data) to be transformed into and out of core memory as required and for information to be stored in a medium separated entirely from the computer. Digital *magnetic tape* drives, using tape either on reels or cassettes, are relatively slow and may require several seconds to fetch or store information since the tape must spin from wherever it starts to wherever the specified information may be located. Tape media have the advantage however of being an economical means of storing large masses of data or 'back–up' programs which are required only infrequently. More expensive but also more convenient for most purposes are *magnetic disc* memories. Access time for disc memory is in the region of milliseconds, orders of magnitude faster than tape. Large interchangeable disc packs can store as much data as a 10 inch reel of tape.

For any computer system to be efficient it must incorporate some form of mass storage. A convenient arrangement might be the implementation of two disc drives and one magnetic tape drive. One disc can serve as the *system device,* housing regularly utilized programs and the software associated with the *operating system* (See Section 4). The other disc drive may be utilized for the storage of large amounts of data on discs unencumbered with programs and the like. The magnetic tape drive allows data and programs to be 'dumped' when they are no longer frequently required and this facilitates the most economical use of relatively expensive disc packs.

Most computers also incorporate a number of *buffers*. A buffer is a type of memory used for the temporary storage of information. They are often used in conjunction with input/output devices such as the teletype. For example, the printer section of the teletype contains an input buffer which accepts character code from the computer and stores it temporarily until the printer is ready to accept and print the character. Many operations involving computer *peripheral devices* (see Section 3) which are slow in comparison to the CPU's high speed of operation are therefore buffered so as to preserve maximum CPU efficiency. This is often achieved in conjunction with the computer's *interrupt facility*. Certain events (e.g. the completion of a read operation from a disc) can be made to interrupt the current operation of the CPU. After saving a record of the on-going operation the CPU shifts control temporarily to a service routine which determines the source of the interrupt and takes appropriate action (e.g. filling the teletype input buffer with appropriate characters), after which the previous activity is resumed. The *teletype* is in two-way communication with the CPU (via input and output buffers). As an input device it provides a means of manual entry of data or program commands. The computer can also output to the teletype, providing listings of programs, raw data or the results of data analyses. Modern teletypes can output information at rates of 30 characters per second or faster whilst line printers are available which can operate at 10 or 20 times that speed.

2 BASIC CONCEPTS IN LABORATORY COMPUTERS—BITS, BAUDS, AND FLOATING POINTS

A bit is the minimum unit of information recognized by a computer and is equivalent to a single binary digit, i.e. either 0 or 1. A *byte* is commonly referred to as the amount of memory required to represent a single character, although strictly it is the smallest memory addressable unit of information. On the same lexicon, a *word* is the number of binary digits treated as a single unit by the computer registers. Large computers have large registers capable of storing 36-bit words or larger (a 36-bit word could represent all the integers from $-34,359,738,379$ to $+34,359,738,379$). Laboratory computers have shorter words, e.g. 12 bits in the case of the DEC PDP/8 (capable of representing the integers from -2047 to $+2047$) and 16-bit words for the DEC PDP/11 ($-32,767$ to $+32,767$). It is clear from this discussion that the representation of very large or very small numbers or fractions cannot be achieved by the use simply of one memory register per number.

There are two approaches to the representation of the number continuum over an adequate range. One method involves using two or more successive registers as if they were tied end-to-end to form a single large register. This allows numbers to be represented in *double-precision* format and has the effect of converting a 12-bit machine, say, into a 24-bit one (and at the same time reducing its effective core memory by at least half). Representing real numbers involves the use of *floating-point* format. Floating-point notation separates numbers into two components, the *mantissa*, which gives the sequence of digits and the sign of the number, and the *characteristic*, which indicates where the octal or decimal point should be placed. Thus, in a 12-bit machine, the number 12,345.678 has a mantissa of 01234567 and a characteristic of 0005, i.e. two successive 12-bit words contain the mantissa and a third word contains the characteristic. The first digit of the characteristic determines in what direction the octal point should be moved (right in this case) and the first word of the mantissa determines the sign of the number (positive in this example). For instance the number -0.0012345678 would, in the format used above, have a mantissa of 11234567 and a characteristic of 1002, the first '1' in the mantissa indicating a negative number and that in the characteristic indicating a leftward-shifting octal point.

All real numerical data must be 'floated' before they are manipulated arithmetically and, perhaps, 'fixed' (the point returned to its original position) before the results are output. This can be achieved either by means of a software package (a program subroutine designed for floating-point manipulation) or else by means of a *floating-point processor* (FPP). An FPP is a hardware device which can accomplish floating-point conversions at high speed with little involvement of the computer's CPU. When running fairly complex programs in real-time an FPP, because of its great speed compared with that attainable by the equivalent software, may be a necessary investment. The term *baud* means, roughly, bits per second, and is used to rate capacity of information-transmission lines associated with computers. Teletypes and some other peripheral devices transmit data as 8-bit *ASCII* code (American Standard Code for Information Interchange). With this code data are transmitted serially, 6 bits being used to represent each of a set of standard characters and 2 extra bits marking where each sequential character begins and ends. A 30 characters per second teletype requires a line transmission rate of 300 baud from the computer. Recent technology permits the use of ordinary telephone lines with special *interface* devices or *modems* for transmitting at rates as high as 2400 baud. (An *interface* is a shared boundary, usually a hardware device linking the computer with a peripheral device.) Such devices allow the transmission of data between, say, a laboratory computer and a large, centralized one. The capacity to perform information transfers of this nature can be useful as it facilitates the transfer of raw or semi-analysed data to a machine more appropriate for sophisticated analysis than the laboratory computer which originally collected it.

3 PERIPHERAL DEVICES

In contrast to large centralized computers, specialized for 'data-crunching', possessing vast memories, and operating under complex multi-user systems, laboratory computers are valued principally for their ability to operate in *real-time*, i.e. to interact with events in the physical world. This interaction is accomplished by means of specialized *peripheral devices*, of which the teletype is an example. An important peripheral device in the psychophysiology laboratory is the analog-to-digital convertor (ADC), a device capable of sampling a varying input voltage (from, say, a polygraph) at specified time intervals and outputting to the CPU a sequence of numbers representing the voltage 'seen' at each sampling time. The sampling rate of an ADC is usually variable over wide limits, allowing the programmer to choose the rate which gives adequate resolution to the signal of interest without wasting valuable core memory by sampling too often. It is noteworthy that the choice of sampling rate is of some importance. As a rule of thumb it can be stated that the inclusion in a sample waveform of frequencies which are more than half the sampling frequency of the ADC will result in *aliasing*, i.e. distortion of the sampled signal with harmonics of the higher frequencies. This can be avoided by a suitable choice of sampling rate of the ADC and by low-pass filtering of the waveform to be sampled to remove unwanted higher frequencies. A detailed discussion of this and related problems will be found in Vaughan (1974).

Another useful peripheral device is some form of cathode ray tube (CRT). With a suitable graphics system this device is of enormous utility in the psychophysiology laboratory. A remote CRT mounted in an experimental room is, for instance, a useful means of presenting well controlled visual stimuli. The real power of the CRT, however, lies in the way in which it facilitates the editing and analysis of data. It is a relatively simple matter to program a computer such that waveforms of interest (e.g. skin conductance responses) can be displayed on the CRT. They can then be inspected, rejected on the grounds that they contain unacceptable artifacts, or subjected to further processing or analysis. Many analysis programs make use of moveable cursors, which can be positioned along a waveform so as to indicate areas of interest, e.g. the peaks of an evoked response, which the computer can quantify. In the case of an evoked response, for example, the quantification might be in terms of peak latency and peak-to-peak amplitude. The use of CRT displays of this kind obviates the need for the scoring by hand from polygraph paper records many of the commonly investigated psychophysiological parameters. A device similar to the CRT is the visual display unit (VDU). This consists of a CRT with a teletype keyboard attached to it and is an alternative to the more traditional teletype, displaying text on the CRT rather than a paper print-out. In addition to providing the facilities of a teletype many VDUs can perform the functions described above with respect to the CRT.

The types of operation performed by a laboratory computer clearly rely on accurate timing. This is most often provided by means of a *programmable clock*. The clock can be made to 'tick' accurately at a very high rate (e.g. 500,000 Hz) and to interrupt the CPU after a preset number of ticks for long enough to allow, say, a 'sample and store' operation to occur. The time in between interrupts can be utilized by the computer to perform other functions such as the analysis of previously sampled data. Many clocks are equipped with *Schmitt triggers*. These are analog inputs which generate an interrupt whenever an input signal rises above or falls below a variable threshold value. These devices can be used to detect transients such as trigger pulses or EKG R-waves and to initiate appropriate action on the part of the computer. For example, it is easy to calculate beat-to-beat intervals in EKG data by recording the times between successive firings of the Schmitt trigger by the R-wave of the EKG.

It is very useful for a laboratory computer to be able to sense and initiate events in the physical world. These functions may be accomplished by devices known respectively as *digital inputs* and *digital outputs*. A digital input consists of a switch which may be opened or closed by some event and a buffer in which such a change of state is registered. By arranging for the activation of a digital input to cause a 'program interrupt' accurate timing (in, for example, a reaction-time paradigm) may easily be achieved. Typically, a laboratory computer will possess a series of independent digital inputs allowing the detection of one or a combination of events to be achieved. The obverse function, that of initiating an event, is mediated by digital outputs. These consist simply of relays, switches, voltage levels, etc, which may be accessed and changed from a program. They may be used, for example, to perform functions such as turning on and off slide-projectors or tape-recorders, allowing such stimuli to be presented with a high degree of control. The digital-to-analog convertor (DAC) converts strings of numbers to a constantly varying analog signal. This device may be used to present, say, pure tone stimuli from a source consisting of one cycle of digitized sine wave or to synthesize complex waveforms such as speech stimuli. By generating these stimuli within the computer a high degree of control is possible over variables such as timing, amplitude, intensity, etc.

It is also useful for a laboratory computer to have some means of representing graphic material in 'hard-copy' form. One such device which achieves this is the *digital plotter*, this having the capability to draw curves, graphs, etc., and to label them with alphanumeric titles. Equipped with appropriate software many plotters can be made to work in reverse, i.e. to digitize and transmit to the computer graphic material, which can then be stored or processed. *Electrostatic printer-plotters* are now available at relatively modest cost and, in addition to being capable of producing hard copies of graphic material can double as high-speed printers, capable of operating at speeds well in excess of those of the usual teletype.

4 PROGRAMMING AND COMPUTER LANGUAGES

A computer program has previously been described as a sequence of commands that can be inserted into core memory in the form of binary numbers or 'words'. Such a list of number-coded instructions is known as a *machine language* program because it is written directly in a language that the machine understands without the need for further translation. Due to the impracticability of handling and remembering any more than a few of these number codes, even in their octal representations, most computers are equipped with a program called an *assembler* which is able to translate symbolic commands (e,g. 'ADD') into their binary, machine language equivalents. A program written in symbolic *assembler language* is just as detailed as its machine language equivalent but is more congenial to the human memory. Assemblers are usually provided in the form of software provided by the computer manufacturer. This software often not only performs the translation process described above but also provides facilities for program *editing*, i.e. the writing, changing, and correcting of programs. Facilities of this type are often provided in a software package known as the *operating system* (O/S). A good O/S will 'oversee' nearly all the operations of a laboratory computer. It will for example, allow the selection from mass storage of a specific program, execute it, and at the end of execution, regain control of the computer. It will contain many useful 'housekeeping' programs which facilitate the handling and storage of information both in memory and on mass-storage devices and will provide facilities which allow information easily to be transferred from one medium to another. In situations in which the computer is engaged in time-sharing operations, i.e. running more than one program at once, the O/S has the responsibility of coordinating all on-going operations so as to make maximally efficient use of available memory space and CPU time.

In the early 1970s most laboratory computers could be programmed only in assembler languages requiring one programming step per computer operation and hence a laborious and time-consuming exercise. It is now increasingly the case that *high-level* programming languages such as FORTRAN, PASCAL, and BASIC are available in versions designed for laboratory computer application. The use of these high-level languages greatly reduces the number of programming steps that need to be written, compared to those required in assembler language, to produce a given end result.

Languages such as FORTRAN and PASCAL are referred to collectively as *compiler languages* because they require a complex software package known as a *compiler* to translate the series of high-level statements of which they consist into machine code appropriate to the computer on which they are intended to be run. The most widely used compiler language is FORTRAN, a language oriented towards numerical analysis and written in an algebraic format. Most laboratory computer FORTRAN compilers allow the 'linking' of FORTRAN programs with special 'library subroutines', often written in assembler language, which perform specialized functions such as ADC input or clock initialization.

A number of languages exist which utilize *interpreters* rather than compilers, most notably DEC's FOCAL series of languages and the ubiquitous BASIC. An interpreter is effectively a 'core-resident' compiler, i.e. unlike a compiler, it is in core memory during the time that a program is executing. Thus, at the expense or the sacrifice of a (not inconsiderable) portion of core memory it is possible to converse *interactively* with the computer. The interpreter translates the high-level statements of, say, BASIC into appropriate machine code as the statements are input from the teletype, obviating the need to edit, store, and compile programs prior to execution. The principal disadvantage of interactive languages, other than their uneconomical use of memory, is that they are relatively slow, all commands having to be mediated by the interpreter prior to execution. These languages are, however, convenient and often of utility in the teaching of programming to novices, who can immediately see the results of any programming technique they apply.

Another means of producing machine code from a high-level language, and one which is particularly useful when developing programs on a large sophisticated computer for application on a smaller one bereft of an O/S, is the *cross-compiler*. Cross-compilers are programs which accept as their input a program written in a high-level language and produce as their output the equivalent program in a low-level format. A recent example of a cross-compiler is MODULA. This accepts programs written in a language format similar to PASCAL and outputs code in PDP/11 or LSI/11 (a microprocessor based on the PDP/11, see Section 5) assembler language.

5 A TYPICAL LABORATORY COMPUTER AND ITS CONFIGURATION IN A PSYCHOPHYSIOLOGICAL LABORATORY

In an effort to make the preceding discussions more 'concrete' and also to provide some guide as to the way in which a psychophysiology laboratory might typically employ a laboratory computer system, an existing system, based on the DEC PDP/11, will be described. The PDP/11, introduced in 1970 in conjunction with a broad range of compatible peripherals, is a machine very likely to be installed in a psychophysiology laboratory at the present time. It is a 16-bit computer with an extremely flexible instruction set which allows programming in assembler language to be accomplished with relative ease. It is also easy to implement a wide range of high-level languages, notably FORTRAN, PASCAL, and interactive BASIC.

The PDP/11 series differed from other computers existing at the time of its inception in the way in which the problem of servicing the peripheral devices was solved. The computer was designed around a high-speed bi-directional information-transmission system known as the UNIBUS. Essentially, the UNIBUS consists of 56 parallel lines along which information can be transmitted and which run through all the peripheral devices, core memory and CPU (See Figure 11.2). These lines carry data, addresses, and control signals, and operate asynchronously, i.e. they are not dependent for their operation on the influence of a timing device. For example, a word of data might be two letters to be typed on the teletype terminal, the address would in this case be the teletype and the control signals would signal to the CPU when the terminal was ready to accept the data and when it had done so. The UNIBUS system is configured in such a way that devices attached to it are associated in a variable hierarchy of priorities in which a device controller can only assume control of the UNIBUS and transmit or receive data if no device with a higher priority requires the use of the UNIBUS also. To return to the example, the transfer of a word from memory to the computer terminal would involve the following sequence of events. The terminal would first issue a signal, an interrupt, to the effect that it was ready to accept information. The CPU would then check a special word in memory, the processor status word (PSW), to determine whether the interrupt could be accepted. If no other devices operating at a higher priority required the use of the UNIBUS the interrupt would be accepted. Following acceptance the appropriate 'interrupt routine' would be entered and a 'read-from-memory cycle' initiated, during which the required word would be transferred to the UNIBUS along with the address of the terminal. The word would be transferred to the terminal buffer and a signal sent back 'down' the UNIBUS indicating receipt of the data and freeing it for further data transfer. The time taken for this process is around 400 nanoseconds.

A number of different O/Ss are available for the PDP/11 family of computers. The most common of these are 'RT-11', 'RSX-11M' and 'UNIX'. RT-11 is an example of an O/S designed for single-user environments, the mode of use most commonly found with respect to laboratory computers. In situations in which the computer is running

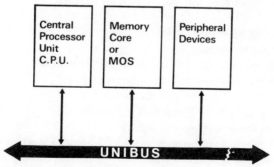

Figure 11.2 UNIBUS system of the PDP–11 series of computers

programs which require relatively little processing 'effort', e.g. occasionally sampling an ADC channel, it is possible using RT-11 to run in the 'foreground/background' mode. This allows two programs, one in the high-priority 'foreground' and one in the lower-priority 'background' to run simultaneously utilising different areas of memory. It is possible to arrange for such programs either to run independently or, if desired, to communicate with one another.

RSX-11M and UNIX are O/Ss designed for multi-user time-sharing situations. It is not common for a laboratory computer, the principal purpose of which is real-time operation, to be run in a time-sharing mode as such an arrangement makes it difficult to maintain time-critical functions, particularly if more than one user wishes to operate in real time. The use of a recently developed peripheral device, the *laboratory peripheral accelerator* (LPA) alleviates this problem. The LPA is a microprocessor based 'intelligent' peripheral interspersed between those peripherals required for real-time operation (the ADC, Schmitt triggers, etc.) and the computer's CPU. It is programmed in such a way that it acts as a coordinator, 'managing' the data being collected and transmitted in real-time by the use of temporary storage buffers and, when an opportunity arises, transmitting the data at high speed to the computer CPU and memory. As it allows multi-user real-time operation it is possible that its employment will result in an increase in the popularity of multi-user systems for laboratory computers. A recent development of the PDP/11 has been the LSI/11, a relatively cheap microprocessor based version of this computer, Its cheapness makes it an attractive proposition, particularly as it can service the peripheral devices originally designed for the PDP/11 and can be connected to a larger computer in a 'satellite/host' relationship, allowing it to be used in much the same way as the LPA described previously.

A particular PDP/11 installation currently installed in a psychophysiology laboratory is configured as follows:

An 11/40 CPU
2 RK05 exchangeable disc drives
24k words of core memory
2 serial input/output lines (for communication with teletypes etc.)
An LA-30 Decwriter (control terminal teletype)
A Decwriter III (fast matrix printer/terminal)
A VR-14 CRT with VT-11 graphics processor
A TS03 magnetic tape drive (6″ tapes)
A Hewlett-Packard digital graph plotter (4 pen colours)
A Hewlett-Packard fast decay phosphor oscilloscope
An LPS-11 laboratory peripheral system containing:
  8 ADC's
  2 DAC's

6 light emitting diode (LED) display
16-bit digital input/output
Programmable real-time clock with 2 Schmitt triggers and 2 normally open relays

The laboratory also possesses an LSI-11 microprocessor consisting of:

LSI-11 CPU
16k words of memory
4 serial input/output lines
16 bit digital input/output
A real-time clock as defined for the PDP/11 system described above.

The PDP/11 system is run under the RT-11 O/S. It is used most commonly for the analysis of data pre-recorded on FM tape and for 'real-time' experimentation. Data held on the PDP/11 can be transferred to the institution's DEC-10 system for further analysis if necessary, thus minimizing the amount of time dedicated to non-time-critical functions.

6 CONCLUDING REMARKS

It is hoped that this chapter will have given the reader some insight into the mode of operation of the modern laboratory computer, and its potential for application in the psychophysiological laboratory. Further discussion of many of the issues covered in this chapter will be found in Buchsbaum and Coppola (1974), Cooper (1977), and Donchin and Heffley (1975).

REFERENCES

Buchsbaum, M. and Coppola, R. (1974). Computer use in bioelectric data collection and analysis, In R. F. Thompson and M. M. Patterson (Eds), *Biolectric Recording Techniques: Part B*, Academic Press, New York
Cooper, R. (1977) "Do as I say" or a Guide to Programming. In A. Rémond (Ed.), *EEG Informatics. A Didactic Review of Methods and Applications of EEG Data Processing*, Elsevier, Amsterdam.
Donchin, E., and Heffley, E. (1975). Minicomputers in the signal-averaging laboratory. *Am. Psychologist*, **30**, 299–312.
Vaughan, H. G. (1974). The analysis of scalp-recorded brain potentials. In R. F. Thompson and M. M. Patterson (Eds), *Bioelectric Recording Techniques: Part B*, Academic Press, New York.
Reference notes:

Techniques in Psychophysiology
Edited by I. Martin and P.H. Venables
© 1980, John Wiley & Sons Ltd.

CHAPTER 12

Measurement Units in Psychophysiology

A. B. LEVEY

1 INTRODUCTION

It was originally the intention of the author that this chapter would examine some empirical and numerical characteristics of the measurement scales used in psychophysiology, discussing them in terms of contemporary scaling theory. In practice, this goal proved overly ambitious, and the literature review and formulation made it evident that apart from fascinating thoretical problems, questions of scaling in psychophysiology really give rise to only two practical problems. These are the problem of transformation of data, and the problem of the interdependence of tonic and phasic levels. In its present form, this chapter will discuss these two problems drawing on the published literature and illustrating the main points of the effects of alternative transformations on a set of psychophysiological data from a large sample conditioning study. Both of these problems are thorny, controversial, and difficult. No attempt will be made to provide final answers; rather the aim will be to review the issues and current practices in the field, and to provide a guide to the relevant sources for further consultation.

There are good reasons why both these problem areas should be difficult in the context of psychophysiological measurement. In most instances the measurement units are not derived directly from observations of behaviour or from self-reports, but from transducers linked to complex circuitry such that the measurement units reflect in part the physical characteristics of the measuring system. This fact of measurement is virtually unique to the field of psychophysiology. Most of the theoretical and practical formulations regarding scaling and measurement have grown up in the areas of psychometrics, attitude measurement and experimental design. These are areas in which the investigator is, in a sense, closer to the original units of observation. Most of us are neither mathematicians nor statisticians, and we have tended to rely heavily on the formulations from these direct areas of observation.

In most cases the measuring devices are applied to the detection of activity in physiological substrates, internal systems which are measured at the surface. In consequence the measurement units are influenced by sources of variance which are difficult to identify separately, derived as they are from electronic properties which are well understood and physiological properties which may be little understood. It is perhaps a mild historic irony that the early investigators in the field hoped to bypass the subjectivity of observation and report, together with the limitations of the behaviourist approach. In practice the discipline of psychophysiology has generated some of the most complex data forms, and has raised problems whose difficulties were probably not envisaged by the early investigators. This is not to say the scientific ideals of the field are tarnished, and we continue to believe that the complexities of the field also ensure a potentially rich yield of information.

Choice of measurement units, then, must be influenced by a number of factors. Some of these are discussed in the chapter on response detection. Apart from the considerations of wave form detection, and selection of interest points, there remains the problem of appropriate units determined by the characteristics of the effector system or systems being measured. For example, the increasing use of photoplethysmography illustrates one of the difficulties. While this method, or family of methods, can yield very accurate information a number of its measurement characteristics remain problematic. It is difficult and sometimes impossible to estimate the size and depth of the vascular beds which contribute to the numerical characteristics of the measures. As a consequence the choice of units, and the decision whether to transform, must be made in the absence of fairly essential information concerning the underlying process. A detailed examination of these problems is found in Chapter 2. A simpler example is found in the developing field of phallometry. How do we specify changes in penile activity? We can measure volume, length, circumference, turgidity or all of these. Each of these measures imposes explicit, though fairly simple, mathematical properties on the measurement scale. The psychophysiology of the cardiovascular system raises similar measurement problems. Measurements of pulse volume can be made very sensitively, but are known to be strongly influenced by baseline or tonic effects which reflect the current homeostatic balance of the system but which are difficult to recover. The controversy concerning beat or time based measurement units in the study of heart rate offers another example. These then are some of the measurement problems which make the choice of units in psychophysiological studies almost uniquely difficult. They dictate the necessity of finding answers to the two problems with which this chapter is chiefly concerned, the problem of data transformation and the problem of tonic-phasic relations.

The literature in this area suggests that these two problems together have constituted a source of chronic irritation for a very long time. The presence of this chronic irritant might by now have produced a pearl of exquisite truth and beauty. Conversely it might have produced a disfiguring or fatal neoplasm. Neither of these extremes has in fact been realized and the process remains what it was, a source of chronic irritation for which no definitive intervention has yet been found. In the remainder of this chapter some of the sources of the ideational friction are reviewed together with some of the ameliorative manoeuvres which have been attempted.

2 DATA TRANSFORMATION

A recent textbook of research methodology (Keppel, 1973) reserves its final chapter for the discussion of controversial issues. It treats of three topics concerning which there is 'no consistent agreement as to their usefulness'. One of these topics is data transformation. Most contemporary authors agree that the ideal basis for data transformation is the use of theoretical information about the system being measured. In the chapter mentioned the author points out that the kind of theory which specifies an appropriate transformation 'is as yet rare'. In this situation, most discussions of the transformation problem have been directed at statistical requirements including those of experimental design. Nevertheless, a review of the literature shows surprising disagreement among authorities. Statisticians are by nature givers of advice and most of us are used to contradictory advice. Keppel (1973) and Scheffé (1959) recommend transformations be avoided where possible. Cox (1958), Guilford (1965), and Winer (1971) recommend that transformations be used where possible. In fairness, this opposition of experts is more apparent than real and ignores for rhetorical purposes the complex arguments underlying the positions endorsed. Nevertheless, it serves to highlight the difficulty faced by the experimental investigator looking for authoritative direction, often in a state of mathematical demi-virginity, coupled with idealism in wishing to avoid merely quick and easy recipes.

The statistical literature has given rise to a number of classic papers. Bartlett (1947) is well known as having given the first definitive treatment of the transformation problem, and his paper laid the foundations for many subsequent treatments. Mueller (1949), Tukey (1957), Anscombe & Tukey (1963), and Box and Cox (1964) together with others, refined the issues and laid the foundations for modern theory and practice in the statistical aspects of tranformation. Most textbooks of experimental design give useful outlines of the issues, considered from a practical standpoint; and of these, Winer (1971) is probably the most complete. Other useful sources are Cox (1958), Edwards (1968), Guilford (1965), Keppel (1973), Kirk (1968), Myers (1966), and Snedecor and Cochrane (1973). All provide brief but useful discussions of the transformation problem and the list is not exhaustive.

2.1 Reasons for transformation

A review of the literature will disclose a large number of reasons for transforming raw data, but the consensus falls on half a dozen: (1) to provide a more useful and understandable description of the data; (2) to describe functional relationships in such a way that the transformation may aid in identifying the nature of the underlying processes; (3) to test or to conform to theoretical assumptions about the process being measured; (4) to satisfy the assumptions of statistical analyses; (5) to eliminate non-linearity in functional relationships, including interactions among treatment effects; (6) to minimize the contribution of deviant scores. Mueller (1949) was probably the first to point out that these goals, particularly (2), (3), and (4), are often incompatible. By implication the investigator must be alert to the properties of individual transformations and to the rationale underlying them. The consensus of current opinion is that the satisfaction of statistical assumptions is the least important of the goals listed. In summary, among the reasons for transforming data, two conflicting purposes stand out. One is to satisfy statistical concerns, that is to meet the assumptions of the analyses, and the other is to satisfy experimental concerns, that is to ensure sensitivity to treatment effects and interpretability of results (Box and Cox, 1964). For most investigators the latter is by far more important, and in a mildly cynical sense the object is to get 'significance' out of the data. Stated more objectively, the object of an experimenter is to detect for theoretical or empirical reasons real differences between contrasting treatments, and the role of data transformation is probably most important where is ensures maximum sensitivity to real effects. Needless to say, this must be balanced against the danger of producing spurious effects and this problem will be referred to again.

The statistical reasons for data transformation will be discussed first. Tukey (1957) describes the purely statistical bases of data transformation as 'bending the data nearer the Procrustean bed of the assumptions underlying conventional analyses' (p. 602). Conventional analyses usually refer to analysis of variance and the ideal requirements that distributions be normal, variances homogeneous, and effects additive. It is customary to point to the fact that the analysis of variance is robust in the face of departures from these assumptions, particularly the first two. The authority most often quoted for this statement is Box (1953) whose classic paper defined the issues empirically and theoretically. Subsequent writers have pointed to reservations which were contained in the original paper. Tests of significance achieve their greatest efficiency and sensitivity if their assumptions are met, and the sacrifice of efficiency must be considered when invoking this dictum.

Scheffé (1959) suggests that one solution is to choose the most robust test where a choice among tests is available. He suggests a number of useful guidelines. The problem of inequality of variance refers most importantly to error variance, and this problem is best handled by ensuring equal cell means. An approximate test for significant departure from this requirement, in the case of equal cell means, is given and is recommended as a preliminary analysis. He points out that departures from the normality assumption are least important in dealing with means, and suggests that the problem of normality can be ignored in the case where variances are approximately equal. This author also makes the important observation, referred to in a later section, that data transformations invariably affect the means as well as the observations, and that this may make the treatment means less interpretable.

Snedecor and Cochrane (1973) note that in spite of the loss of efficiency involved in departures from the assumptions, the danger of unequal *error* variance is in the opposite direction, that is that it can lead to too many significant F-tests. With regard to the additivity of effects these authors point out that additivity can and should be built into the data by choice of appropriate units and that the additivity assumption cannot hold when the measurements units are chosen such that the treatment by subject effects are multiplicative. Cox (1958) also discusses this problem. The difference between treatment means is additive if the difference can be expressed as the unit value minus the treatment value. If the difference between treatments represents the unit value multiplied by a treatment value the additivity assumption cannot hold. In considering this problem the definition of a unit may refer either to a unit of observation or to a unit activated in the physiological system underlying the observations. If within a single observation unit, for example a subject, the process measured depends upon a number of similar units which are independently activated, for example individual sweat glands, the treatment effect will represent multiplicatively the number of units activated by each treatment. Both the authors cited note that this situation gives rise to the common practice of 'logging' the data and justifies it.

The problem of the normality of distributions is the one which is probably most frequently discussed in the statistical context of data transformation, and the one which is most likely to give rise to misunderstanding. A brief review of the issues may be useful. The assumption of normality, as already noted, refers most rigorously to the normality of within cell distributions. This is a mathematical problem, but the issue of normality is considerably wider. Two sources of non-normality must be kept separate. A distribution may depart significantly from normality as a consequence of sampling variation. For this reason, non-normality is chiefly of importance in random effects designs (Scheffé, 1959). Many investigations of psychophysiological variables necessarily rely on small samples. In this case the apparent non-normality may be due simply to the size of the sample, and increasing the sample size will ensure normality, if the underlying distribution is normal. It should be remembered that the assumption of normality, in the statistical sense, refers to the distribution of the means of successive samples drawn at random from the same population. The central limit theorem ensures that the random sample size will tend to increasing normality with increase in N. Edwards (1968) offers a proof of this theorem. Of more interest to the practical investigator is his empirical demonstration, by tables, that the three common departures from normality, that is a U-shaped distribution, a rectilinear distribution, and a skewed distribution, all progress towards normality with increase in the number of cases. As a general rule this increase is limited to between 15 or 20 cases and this is convincingly demonstrated.

In this connection it should also be noted that the practice of grouping data, less common today than in the era of hand calculation, makes the apparent normality of the distribution dependent upon the frequency intervals. In this case a monotonic transformation cannot be applied since several subjects exhibit the same score value and the transformations can only be applied to continuous data. The foregoing arguments suggest that it is a waste of time to attempt a normalizing transformation on distributions involving very small number of subjects, as well as on those involving discrete data. Nevertheless a certain uneasiness is generated in most of us by visibly non-normal distribution and this source of *angst* can be referred to the second major source of non-normality, that is to the scale itself.

Most of the analyses undertaken in experimental work involve interval scales, that is scales in which the numerical differences between equidistant observations are constant throughout the regions of the scale. The analogy to an elastic yardstick is often made and its implication is that the scaling units at one end, or in one region of the scale may differ from those in another. It is important to remember that in this context the term 'scale' refers to a hypothetical continuum based on differences which can be detected by the measuring instrument. For most psychophysiological variables the differences detected represent the interaction of several sources of variation, each of which may separately explained. The resulting 'scale' is merely a convenient means of summarizing these differences. Regardless of sample size, inequalities of the units in differing regions of the scale will result in non-normality of the observed distribution. The most difficult case, and the rarest, is that in which selected regions of the scale differ in a non-linear way. More commonly the scale is stretched out at one or the other end. In either case the variance for treatment groups located at mean values distributed along the scale will bear a systematic relation to the means. The nature of this relation provides the rationale for choice of a normalising transformation, and this was first systematically examined by Bartlett (1947). Most of the recipes for normalizing distribution have followed from this definitive approach to stabilizing the variance, and this approach will be considered more fully in the section on methods of transformation.

Non-normality due to inequality of the scaling intervals cannot be dismissed on the same grounds as non-normality due to sampling variation. Figure 12.1 presents an example of the effects of a simple transformation on data for 15 subjects, a case in which sampling variation can be virtually ignored. As the figure shows, a highly skewed distribution, together with highly correlated means and variances has been transformed to a normal distribution with uncorrelated means and variances. This type of example, not uncommon in practical experience, is probably one of the compelling reasons why the issue of normality bothers most investigators.

To summarize, the use of an interval scale satisfies both the intuitive and mathematical requirements of measurement. Siegel (1956) defines an interval scale in terms of transformation properties. Thus a scale which has equal interval properties is said to be unique up to the linear transformation ($Y = AX + B$). By implication a suitable transformation can ensure that the underlying scale is based on equal intervals, with the numerical advantages of linearity and additivity which this implies.

A further problem introduced by non-normality due to inappropriate scaling, which is more subtle than the effect just discussed, is the production of spurious interactions. This topic is rather more complex and its details lie beyond the scope of this chapter. However there are clear guidelines in the literature. Kruskall (1965) describes in detail a transformation technique involved in eliminating interactions of this sort. He also refers to computer programmes which accomplish this aim and

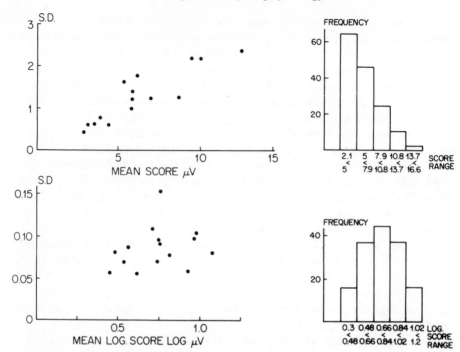

Figure 12.1   Plots of relationships between the mean and standard deviation of alpha abundance for 15 subjects calculated from the scores of ten 5-s epochs. Above: before transformation (correlation = 0.88); below: after log transformation ($r = 0.18$). The corresponding frequency histograms are shown on the right. (From Cooper, R., Osselton, J. W. and Shaw, J. C. (1974), *EEG Technology*, Butterworth & Co., London. p. 242. (Reproduced by permission.)

provides scaling models on which attention can be confined to main effects, with increased interpretability. Cox (1958) discusses the problem of 'removable ' interactions, that is those which result from scale differences at one ot more treatment levels, and provides an objective criterion for detecting them where detection is possible. This emphasizes the important point that measurement scales are themselves subject to treatment effects. This is particularly true of psychophysiological variables for which the scaling 'units' are generated by a complex of factors many of which are unstable.

   The fact that an interval scale is mathematically and intuitively desirable in its properties does not guarantee that such scales exist in Nature. The remaining source of misunderstanding in the application of data transformations designed to achieve normality is the assumption that normality best represents the behaviour of natural phenomena. The normal distribution is the final distribution for a number of generating functions, and this fact has been used to argue that normality is a property of natural events. A number of investigators, considering the problem from a practical standpoint, have noted this fallacy (e.g. Lykken and Venables, 1971). Useful discussions of the problem of normality are provided by Edwards (1968) and by Snedecor and Cochrane (1973). However the most informative discussion of the 'normality fallacy' is due to an author whose goal is to defend distribution-free statistics. Bradley (1968) presents a witty and informative discussion of the history of the normality concept which can be recommended for its good humoured treatment of a rather ponderous subject which it would be inappropriate to summarize here.

However, one remaining issue, discussed in the reference just cited, is relevant to data analysis. The increasing popularity of nonparametric statistics should not obscure the fact that the conventional parametric analyses are in general more powerful if they can be applied. Guilford (1965) argues in opposition to some authors, that the assumption that the *real* scale is normal is not necessary to the application of tests of significance. If a transformation can achieve normality, the investigator need not worry that he has failed to represent the real underlying distribution. Tests of statistical transformations cited by Guilford show that the conclusions from treatment effects hold equally for the natural phenomenon whether the underlying distribution is normal or not.

In considering the statistical grounds for applying data transformation one further problem deserves mention. A number of authors point out that any transformation that alters the values of the observations must necessarily also alter the values of the treatment means. This statement contains the most compelling arguments both for and against the use of transformations, and is consequently a controversial area. Scheffé (1959) discusses with some delicacy the advantages of applying or witholding transformations where the results may interfere with the observed means. The argument hinges on making an informed judgement, usually on theoretical grounds, as to whether the effect of the transformation on the means distorts their interpretation. This includes both the possibility that the transformation can be witheld in the interests of interpretability and the possibility that the transformation can be applied, and the conclusions regarding significance of differences sustained, but the results interpreted in terms of the original means. Cox (1958) argues against this point of view and insists that when transformations are applied differences are estimated on a new scale which cannot be referred directly to the original. A startling example of the hazards of transformation in this context is provided by Myers (1966). Table 12.1 shows a hypothetical set of data presented first in raw form then as a square root transformation. As the table shows, the effect of the transformation is to reverse the direction of the differences between treatments! A few minutes of the reader's time

Table 12.1. Hypothetical data for two treatment groups, raw and transformed scores compared (adapted from Myers, 1966)

Treatment	Raw data		Square root	
	a_1	a_2	a_1	a_2
	4	25	2	5
	64	36	8	6
Means	34.0	30.5	5.0	5.5

will suffice to show, by trial and error, that this manufactured example is somewhat unique. However it demonstrates rather dramatically the problems involved in deciding whether means are interpretable under transformation.

The remaining reasons for data transformation offer issues which are considerably less clear-cut. Mueller (1949) discusses the rationale for a choice of transformations where the goals of transformation are incompatible. Keppel (1973) discusses the desiderata of transformations which provide a more useful or understandable description of the raw data. Snedecor and Cochrane (1973) discuss the desirability of removing non-linearity in the data and this is an issue which lies well beyond the scope of the present chapter. What is involved in providing a useful description of the data or a description which reveals the underlying functional relationships is closely linked to the substantive characteristics of the data and to the system under observation. The purely substantive literature abounds with discussions of these individual issues and it would not be a useful exercise to attempt to summarize them across widely differing physiological systems.

A number of authors (e.g. Guilford, 1956; Haggard, 1949a; Scheffé, 1959) urge selection of transformation techniques on theoretical grounds. The latter author points out that the preliminary role of theory should be in the design of the experiment, leaving the transformation problem in a secondary role. The theoretical reason for applying a transformation is usually to make the data conform to some model or expectation based either on theory or assumptions about the variables involved and the system measured. The 'normality fallacy' represents one such general model, under the assumption that most biological variates are inherently normal in their distributions. Another general model, to be discussed later, uses the assumption that pre and post stimulus values are independent of one another and that any observed relationship between them should be attenuated. However, it is not enough to assert that 'most biological variates are normally distributed' or that 'many biological functions are logarithmic' and so on. Regrettably, for most variates the underlying physiology is not sufficiently explicit. This problem will be considered again in discussing methods of transformation.

The final reason for applying transformations which occurs with sufficient frequency in the literature to be regarded as a consensus view, is the elimination of the contribution of deviant or extreme observations to the scale. In spite of the popularity of this issue, its importance in the context of data transformation is probably minimal. Given the issues discussed above, the likelihood that a given transformation will eliminate the effect of extreme scores, and still serve one of the more important goals of transformation is remote. Objective criteria for excluding deviant observations have long been used in the physical sciences (e.g. Chauvenet's criterion, Parrat, 1961) but have tended to be discouraged in the biological sciences. This problem has been closely considered (Anscombe, 1960; Anscombe and Tukey, 1963). On the whole it seems preferable to exclude the few cases falling well outside the main distribution rather than attempt to find the transformation which will draw them in toward the mean, at the expense of seriously distorting the bulk of the observations.

Statistical criteria for identifying outliers have been proposed by Grubb (1969) who considers in detail the bases for their application. Gentleman and Wilk (1975) noting that the use of modern computer techniques often makes the raw data 'invisible' to inspection techniques, recommend the use of computer algorithms which will *detect* the outliers before deciding whether to discard them. The well known program package GENSTAT allows the user to inspect deviant observations which occur in the data. Outliers may represent errors of measurement, but the possibility must always be given serious consideration that deviant observations result from sampling from a population other than the one of interest. Snedecor and Cochrane (1973) recommend that if a deviant observation is removed from one treatment cell, the most extreme observation in each of the remaining cells should also be removed. This satisfies both mathematical and intuitive requirements but is probably less preferable than replacing the deviant observation with a freshly drawn sample. Winer (1971, pp. 51–4) provides the most extended discussion of the problem of outliers to be found in a basic text.

The formulations just discussed offer guidelines for the choice of a data transformation, and the references cited provide detailed discussions of the issues. In practice, however, these ideal principles encounter difficulties. The transformation which produces the most elegant scale may not be the one which is most sensitive to treatment effects. As was noted earlier, the measurement scales are themselves susceptible to treatment effects and to the conditions of observation. This can be illustrated by reference to a set of

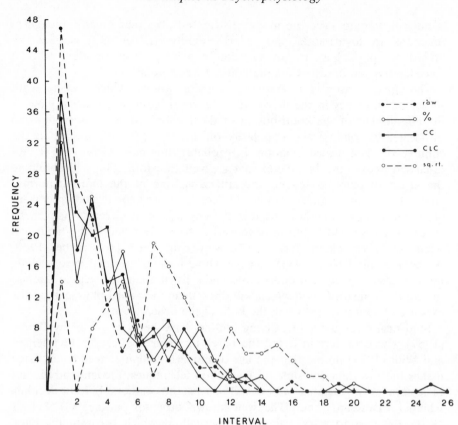

Figure 12.2   Frequency polygons for distributions of raw and transformed response amplitudes of electrodermal responses of 144 subjects to the first of a series of three corneal airpuffs. Raw resistance (raw), change in resistance (%), change in conductance (cc), change log conductance (clc) and square root transformation (sq. rt.), based on standardized ranges

real data, taken from an eyelid conditioning study in which a number of concomitant psychophysiological variables were measured in order to assess their influence on conditioned response emergence and maintenance. The study was a large sample factorial experiment ($N = 144$) designed to observe the influence of personality on conditioning (Eysenck and Levey, 1972) and the psychophysiological variables were analysed separately. One series of analysis used the data to examine empirically the effects of data transformation. Figures 12.2 and 12.3 show the results of alternative data transformations on the measurement of electrodermal responding to the first unpaired corneal airpuff (Figure 12.2) and the third (Figure 12.3) of a series of test trials prior to conditioning. In figure 12.2 the subjects have

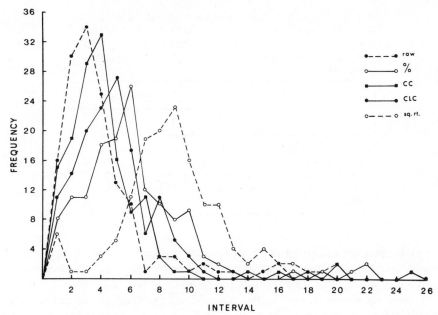

Figure 12.3 Frequency polygrams for distribution of raw and transformed response amplitudes of electrodermal responses of 144 subjects to the last of a series of three corneal airpuffs (legend as in Figure 12.2)

responded to the first salient stimulus of the experiment (resting level). In Figure 12.3 the same subjects have responded a moment or a two later to the same stimulus which has now acquired an altered significance (activated level).

In the first instance the transformation which gave the nearest approximation to normality was the square root, though it is far from satisfactory. In the second, the percentage change gave a reasonable approximation, and in fact showed no significant departure when the outliers were discarded. Interestingly, none of the transformations had the effect of reducing outliers, and the tendency was to produce a marginal increase. It is clear that the activated and resting conditions involve differing scales of measurement.

The corneal airpuff was presented at two levels of intensity, dividing the subjects into two groups at random. Table 12.2 shows the p values for analysis of variance of the two intensity levels for each of the test trials. On the first trial the square root transformation which came nearest to normalizing the data also provided the most sensitive test of the experimental effect. For the third trial, however, the normalizing transformation was the least sensitive, and none of the transformations improved on the raw data. This example serves to illustrate the importance

Table 12.2. Probability values for analysis of variance of raw and transformed electrodermal response amplitudes to two levels of intensity of a corneal airpuff (3 and 6 psi) on the first and third trials of a test series

	Test trials	
	1	3
Raw resistance	0.065	0.194
% change	0.182	0.344
Change in conductance	0.211	0.295
Log change conductance	0.195	0.318
Square root	0.034	0.295

of examining the effects of any transformation chosen. In practice, the final choice must rely on the investigator's judgement. The 'best' transformation is the one which most nearly fulfils the purpose of the investigator.

It may be useful to review the main issues involved in the reasons for transforming data. Data transformation is most frequently urged in the literature for statistical reasons, but this reflects a certain bias from texts concerned with statistics and experimental design. The methods of transformation arise in psychometric observations and the data of psychophysiological measurement differ from psychometric data in important ways. The problem of sampling is paramount in the psychometric field, and less important in the field of psychophysiology for reasons outlined earlier. The basic problem in psychophysiology is the nature of the scaling procedures, and their intimate relation to electronic and physiological sources of variation which are less well understood than the mechanics of sampling. Consequently the statistical reasons for data transformation are less interesting to the psychophysiologist than those concerned with scaling, and with theoretical models of the underlying process. Nevertheless the statistical limitations should be regarded with respect, and the reader has been referred to discussions of these limitations. The problem of normality, in the field of interest, hinges not on sampling normality but on the influence of scaling on the distribution.

2.2 Methods of transformation

The most general family of transformations takes the form $Y = f(X + C)^p$. Depending on the nature of the function (f) the transformation will be monotonic or linear. Non-linear transformations are more complex and will not be considered (see Box and Cox, 1964, for an analysis of the issues).

In this formula it is usually expected that p will be a real value equal to or less than 1 and in practice this is usually the case. The sum of X the original variate and C the constant is expected to be greater than zero and again this is usually the case empirically. If C takes the value zero it disappears from the formula, and if p takes the value 1 it also disappears; that is these constants are unit factors. Examples are the square root and log 'traditions' (Lykken and Venables, 1971). There seems little doubt that the simpler transformations are sometimes applied as an unthinking ritual though this practice is disappearing and the evidence just presented may suggest that its disappearance is a good thing.

In the following sections the methods available for choosing a transformation will be reviewed at a descriptive level. There are several substantive fields, notably EEG and cardiovascular response in which the transformation problem is complex and the reader is referred to the respective chapters on these areas. The purpose of this section is to provide an overview of the general principles in largely non-mathematical terms, as a perspective for the more specific treatments. In the light of the discussion of the preceding section it is convenient to regard transformation methods under three headings: mathematical, empirical (*ad hoc*), and substantive or theoretical. These will be considered in reverse order of importance.

2.2.1 Mathematical methods

In his classical formulation of the transformation problem, Bartlett (1947) specified four *desiderata* of the transformed variate. The variable after transformation should: (1) exhibit variances which are unrelated to the treatment means; (2) be normally distributed; (3) provide a scale in which the arithmetic average is the most efficient measure of level; (4) provide a scale for which real treatment effects are linear and additive. These represent the mathematical rationale for transformation and they have been discussed previously. It will be seen that the last two requirements refer to the problems of scaling which are particularly relevant to the concerns of psychophysiology. The methods of choosing a trans- formation were referred by Bartlett to the relationship between variances and means for treatment groups and they have constituted convenient rules of thumb ever since (Maxwell, 1958). They will not be reviewed here but are presented in tabular form in Table 12.3, together with the common transformations.

Tukey (1957) discusses in detail the objective methods for selecting a transformation on mathematical and statistical grounds and provides charts for estimating the parameters of the transformation and the power functions for the most general set of transformations. He also provides a

W

Table 12.3. Commonly used data transformations. T, transferred variate; x, original observation; P, observation as proportion; a, b, c, constants; p, power exponent; SD, standard deviation

Formula, $T =$	Transformation	Effect	Criterion
$\sqrt{x + c}$	square root	stabilize variance correct skew	SD equal to $\overline{X}$
$\dfrac{1}{x} + c$	reciprocal	stabilize variance normalize data	SD proportional to $\overline{X}^2$
$a + b\log(x - c)$	log	stabilize variance normalize skew	SD proportional to $\overline{X}$
$\log_e(-\log_e P)$	log log	normalize proportions	skewed proportions
$\arcsin(P + C)$	arcsine	stabilize variance	upper limit constrained
$\sin^{-1}(ax + b)$	inverse sine	stabilize variance	lower limit constrained
$\sin^{-1} P + c$	inverse sine proportion	stabilize variance of proportions	skewed proportions
$f(x + c)^P$	general form	empirical	empirical
$a + b(c + x)^p$	Dolby family	empirical	empirical

method for estimating the 'strength' of transformations by comparing the differences in the interval characteristics at selected regions of the scale. Similarly Box and Cox (1964) discuss in detail the objective methods for selecting transformations on mathematical grounds and provide graphs for interpreting their effects.

Most textbooks provide one or more refinements of the basic rules of thumb, and Scheffé (1959) offers a number of valuable shortcuts. An interesting proposal by Winer (1971) offers a convenient shortcut for the choice of transformation in practical data analysis. He recommends that as a first step those transformations which appear appropriate to the investigator should be compared in terms of the range of transformed observations within treatment groups, selecting the 'best' transform on the basis of greatest similarity and uniformity of range. The effect of this strategem is to select the set of transformed data which most nearly correspond to a scale of equal intervals. This uses the property of the range in reflecting more complex facets of a distribution. It has been noted earlier that the purely mathematical requirements of transformation are regarded by most authors as secondary to other concerns and this brief discussion, together with the references given earlier, will suffice for the present purpose.

2.2.2 Empirical methods

Where there is no obvious or easily recognizable theoretical basis for transforming a variate, and where the concern of the investigator is to approximate to equal interval scaling, it is common practice to employ an *ad hoc* manipulation of the units of measurement. The method most frequently used is to employ a rank transform which can be referred to tabled values of the normal equivalents of ranked data given by Fisher and Yates (1948). A number of rank statistics are available and they are described in detail by Bradley (1968). The use of the Fisher and Yates tables and the application of tests based on non-normality effects are discussed at length and procedures given in detail. In particular, rank tests for identifying the scaling parameters themselves are provided and serve as a useful adjunct to the more general forms of transformation.

While the method of ranking is popular and easy, it suffers limitations which should be emphasized. The original formulation of transformation methods by Bartlett (1947) defended the use of rank methods but pointed out that other methods should be adopted wherever possible. The important reason is that the original measurements are discarded if the data are ordered and transformed. In consequence all the mathematical properties of the original scale are discarded and cannot be recovered. Since an important part of the underlying rationale for transformation may be to disclose the operation of more than one source of variation, if the rank transform is applied then the information necessary to consider alternative further transformations has been lost. The question of successive transformations will be referred to again.

Another approach to empirical transformation is to generate a family of transforms and adjust their parameters to achieve an appropriate scale. It should be emphasized that the term appropriate refers both to the mathematical properties of the data as such, and also to their sensitivity to treatment effects. The desirability of maximising treatment effects has been mentioned earlier and is a highly desirable goal of transformation. Dolby (1963) has provided a general transformation to which constants can be fitted and the use of computer technology makes it possible to do this iteratively. The resulting set of transformations includes those commonly used; viz. square root, log, reciprocal, exponential, and quadratic, as well as others.

In summary, while authors advocate the use of theoretical considerations in the choice of transformations, it remains the case that they are often hard to come by. The use of *ad hoc* transformations is fully justified, provided the investigator is satisfied that he has not overlooked a possible theoretical basis. If an ad hoc transformation is applied it precludes the use of further transformations to get at hidden sources of variance, for example the appearance of interaction artefacts in the transformed data.

2.2.3 Theoretical methods

Where something is known of the nature of the underlying process and a theoretical model is available, transformations can take advantage of this knowledge to achieve greater simplicity or parsimony of description. For example, it is known that the perception of pitch bears a logarithmic relationship to the physical units of the pitch scale and this dictates the appropriate transformation for judgements of pitch. Similarly simple reaction time measures provide an example of a physiologically determined non-normal distribution, since they have a floor effect, and are susceptible to the standard textbook transformation. Many physiological processes generate spontaneous or random responses which follow a Poisson distribution for rare events. In this case the variances are equal to the means and the square root transformation can be expected to secure a normal distribution. Interestingly, an entirely unrelated transformation ($Y = \log X + C$) provides an equally good transformation for which there is no obvious rationale (Tukey, 1957). Another simple case in which the transformation is determined by the nature of the data is the treatment of measures resulting from counts of the number of occurrences of a given event from epoch to epoch or trial to trial. This type of observation has a built in ceiling which may obscure treatment differences. By converting the observations to proportions and applying the arcsine transform (Table 12.3) the ceiling effect can be partly removed. In the study mentioned previously, the effect of CS-UCS interval (400 or 800 ms) showed a consistent but non-significant advantage in response frequency for the longer interval over trials. Figure 12.4 shows that the application of the appropriate transformation resulted in the exhibition of a 'real' treatment effect in terms of a significant difference in linear trend, concealed by the ceiling effect.

In the area of psychophysiology, transformations should ideally be based on known physiology, where available. Possible mechanisms have been discussed by Lacey (1956) in connection with heart rate, and by Darrow (1964), and Lykken and Venables (1971) in connection with palmar skin conductance. Lader (1970) has provided a cogent rationale for transformation of SRR data based on the assumption that sweat glands are acting independently and in parallel. He recommends the change in log conductance as the appropriate unit of measurement on this basis.

The measurement of electrodermal phenomena, that is SCL and SCR,

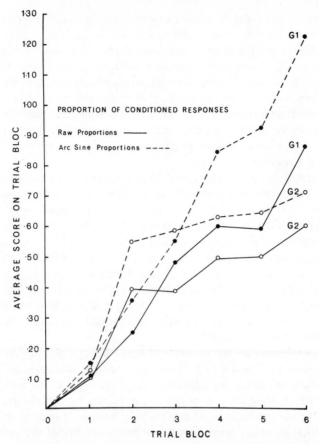

Figure 12.4   Raw and arcsine proportions of frequencies of
conditioned eyelid responses to short (400 ms, Group 1,
$N = 72$) and long (800 ms, Group 2, $N = 72$) CS durations

SPL and SPR, SRL and SRR, is an area which has attracted much
attention in terms of theoretical justification of transformation and choice
of units. The most widely accepted view is that skin conductance levels are
the result of two main processes, one arising in changes in permeability of
the corneum and underlying layers of the epidermis, and the other from the
activity of the sweat gland. A more complicated model of sweat gland
activity is required to encompass response phenomena. A chain of
mechanisms seems to contribute to the SCR, and recent evidence has
implicated the role of ductal mechanisms and the diffusion of sweat.

It is thought that sweat glands provide relatively low resistance current
pathways through the epidermis, and that they can change individually in
value. The well known paper by Lykken and Venables (1971) considers

the problem of appropriate measurement units in detail for electrodermal activity. These authors argue that conductance measures bear a simpler and more linear relationship to the underlying processes of psychological interest than do resistance measures and they advocate the use of conductance measures in the context of constant voltage measurement systems. They suggest that the strategy of range correction is preferable to other forms of transformation in the first instance, and provide evidence that it effectively eliminates irrelevant sources of variation. The authors argue that an ad hoc scalar transform can then be applied to achieve normality 'if necessary'.

The argument for range-corrected scores (Lykken and coworkers, 1966) is that a substantial proportion of the variance in any distribution across subjects of SCL or SCR values must be attributable to physiological differences which are essentially unrelated to the psychological processes in which we are primarily interested. They argue that until some such method of analysis is actually applied to real data there will be no adequate substantive grounds for specifying the function relating the corrected measures of tonic level to the underlying variable of interest. The approach clearly recognises the necessity of specifying a theoretical function as the precondition for rational choice of transformations which will meaningfully represent the data.

Finally, in considering the theoretical bases for transformation, reference should be made to Tukey's (1957) observation that investigators are likely, by the nature of their assumptions about the data, to build in scale properties which they do not intend. This relates to the choice of scaling units prior to the application of any transformation. It is apparent that this outcome when it occurs must have paradoxical results. If the original scale units are inappropriate in some sense, the subsequent transformation may either bring the transformed variable closer to or farther away from the 'real' underlying measurement scale. It is also apparent that this dilemma can only be avoided by very critical examination of scaling units. Happily, the tendency to use conventional or arbitrary units is diminishing in frequency and more attention is being paid to scaling properties in psychophysiological measurement.

None of the procedures just reviewed is able to meet a problem which occurs frequently in real data. Just as the investigator may build in scale properties by choice of units, the necessity to apply the same units to all subjects cannot account for the fact that the scale properties may differ in subsamples of the population. In the conditioning project mentioned earlier, the subjects were divided into a group of 'good' conditioners ($N = 67$) and a group of 'poor' conditioners ($N = 77$) according to their frequency of responding. They were then compared on the basis of oral temperature taken prior to the conditioning session. The two groups

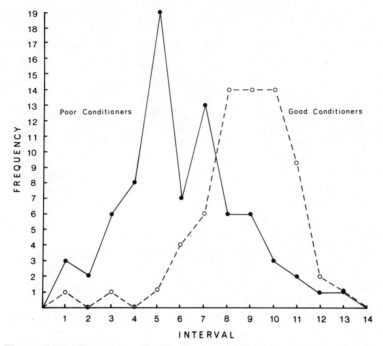

Figure 12.5 Frequency distributions of oral temperatures prior to conditioning for good conditioners ($N = 67$) and poor conditioners ($N = 77$). Scale interval = 0·2 °F

differed significantly and this is in agreement with observations of metabolic influences on conditioning made by Russian investigators (Ol'anynskaya and Fedorov, 1959). Figure 12.5 shows that the two groups, whose parent distribution was normal without transformation, were skewed in opposite directions. In short the two groups not only represented different populations with respect to body temperatures, but the physiological units of the temperature scales are different for the two populations. If such a difference were extreme, how would we justify the choice of a transformation? Any transformation which reduced the skewing in one subgroup would increase it in the other. In this case, the argument is strong for applying non-parametric statistics without benefit of transformation (Bradley, 1968) since there is no possibility of comparing the two sets of data if they were transformed separately.

3 TONIC–PHASIC RELATIONSHIPS

In studies of psychophysiology the problem of tonic–phasic relationships is usually referred to the law of initial values (LIV). It is probably fair to say that this 'law' has become a fetish which is in danger of obscuring the complex processes associated with 'baseline' properties of psychophysiological measurements. As with the problem of data transformation the issues are extremely difficult and no satisfactory answer is in view. Again, the psychometric literature has paid careful attention to the problems associated with the measurement of change (e.g. Harris, 1962) and to the measurement of 'true' change scores (Lord, 1969). The theoretical and statistical issues lie well beyond the scope of this chapter, and of psychophysiological measurement generally. The LIV formulation is merely one of a number of instances of base-related change, though it has been allowed to dominate the field . It should be remembered that the original formulation of the 'law' (Wilder, 1958) drew attention to the different *meaning* of responses arising from differing baselines. In the transformation sense this implies that the units measuring change at one end of the base scale are larger than those at the other, hence the problem is to define a function which will equalize the units. This does not imply that it is necessarily desirable to eliminate baseline effects or to achieve independence of pre and post stimulus measures. The implication of such a view is that in getting rid of baseline effects we are getting rid of noise in the system. It can equally well be argued that there is almost certainly a relationship between pre-stimulus activity and response activity, and that the nature of the interaction depends upon the response system, the experimental conditions, individual differences, and the position of the response in the stimulus series, as has been demonstrated empirically (Block and Bridger, 1962). This alternative formulation argues for identifying the contribution of the pre-stimulus level without discarding it.

The use of regression methods (Lacey, 1956; Benjamin, 1963) has been widely advocated and practised. If the object is genuinely to remove the effect of tonic values these procedures may be justified. This amounts to asking the question: what would the phasic response have been if all subjects had had the same pre stimulus level? However, if it is assumed that a meaningful relationship exists between pre-stimulus levels and responses other techniques such as discriminant analysis or multivariate analysis of variance can be used to assess the contribution of tonic levels under each experimental condition. The assumptions underlying regression techniques are discussed in Chapter 3.

In fact, the relationship between tonic and phasic levels represents several distinct situations. The relationship differs, for example in a SCR habituation series, from early trials to late trials. Characteristically in the early trials a high level of tonic resistance gives scope to large amplitude responses simply because there is 'room to move'. In late trials a high level of resistance tends to be associated with low amplitude responses through the habituation process itself. Further, this is true only on average, since for some unresponsive subjects a high initial resistance level is associated with meagre responding in the early trials. In addition, changes in the tonic level alter its relationship with response levels. Indeed, it is useful to distinguish at least two tonic levels; the resting level prior to any stimulation, and the active level during interstimulus intervals. It is common to observe a sharp decrease in resistance from high resting levels to low active levels following the first stimulus presentation. In this situation it is difficult to imagine a single standard procedure which will represent the data meaningfully.

Some authors advocate the application of separate normalizing transformations to the distributions of both tonic and response levels and when this is done any relationship between them frequently disappears or is attenuated. However, if the goal of transformation of each of the variable sets is to rationalize or normalize the scale then transformations need not result in complete independence of the two sets of measures. Indeed, a desirable effect of transformation may be to stabilize the linear relation between dependent and independent variables, for example in applying multiple regression analyses to the data (Box and Cox, 1964). Alternatively the application of a transformation to each of the variables may distort results in the dependent variable, and this problem is discussed by Bergman (1972).

Where independence is the only requirement, and the investigator is sure of this, regression and covariance techniques are probably more appropriate. However a number of precautions need to be observed, and the nature of regression analysis needs to be considered. The usual regression formulae result in residual measures of the extent to which a subject's responses depart from some expected level. The prediction may be derived from responses of a group of subjects, in which case the individual is described in terms of his departure from the group. Alternatively, it may be derived from individual pre-stimulus levels in which case the resultant measures describe the extent to which the subject has departed from the responses he was expected, on the best information available, to give. The important point is that the investigator should know what he is after.

In particular, it must be fully appreciated that the effect of most regression units is to discard the common variance between two measures. This means that a good deal of the most reliable information is lost. Table 12.4 shows the intercorrelations of transformed and untransformed variables with the raw and transformed baseline measures for the data presented earlier in Table 12.2. The two variables which approached or reached significance in the analysis of variance in that table show appreciable correlations with the baselines. By contrast the change in log conductance, which removed the correlation with the baseline, also

Table 12.4. Correlations of raw and transformed values of electrodermal response amplitudes to the first presentation of a corneal airpuff with the tonic level prior to stimulation

	Base level	
	kohms	Log kohms
Raw resistance	0.345	0.377
% change	0.028	0.010
Change in conductance	−0.270	−0.266
Log change conductance	−0.045	0.071
Square root	0.225	0.282

obliterated the difference between treatments. Interestingly, none of the correlations was affected by transformations of the baseline.

If removal of the tonic influence results in the disappearance of an experimental effect it is difficult to know what conclusion to draw, other than that some important information has been thrown away. The use of part-correlation, which removes the effect of common variance from only one of the variables may deserve attention in specific situations (Dubois, 1965).

Lykken and Venables (1971), in the definitive paper quoted earlier, address themselves to the problem of tonic–phase relationships and suggest that the LIV interpretation is probably only appropriate to ceiling effects. They point out that the use of conductance units in electrodermal measurement can eliminate tonic–phasic dependence though they also point out that this is not necessarily a desirable goal in itself. The implication, however, is that inappropriate choice of units in itself may generate a linear relationship between tonic and phasic levels. A

Table 12.5. Hypothetical example of the effect of resistance and conductance units on tonic–phasic relationships in electrodermal responding. The correlation of phasic with tonic levels for resistance units is 0.998 while that for conductance units is zero. (After Lykken and Venables (1971, p. 669).)

Trial	1	2	3	4	5	6	7
Tonic SCL (mho)	10	11	12	13	14	15	16
SCR (mho)	1	1	1	1	1	1	1
Tonic SRL (kohm)	100	91	83	77	71	67	62
SRR (kohm)	9.09	7.57	6.41	5.49	4.76	4.17	3.68

hypothetical example is offered in which the use of resistance units in electrodermal measurement would produce nearly perfect correlation between tonic and phasic levels within an individual subject, while the use of conductance units would produce zero correlations (see Table 12.5). Interestingly, early papers by Haggard (1949a, 1949b) suggest that this result would not apply across groups and the authors make it clear that their example is hypothetical.

In view of the earlier discussion of regression techniques it is probably preferable to determine first whether a transformation will remove unwanted baseline effects. Figure 12.6 shows a comparison between the well known autonomic lability score (ALS) based on regression (Lacey,

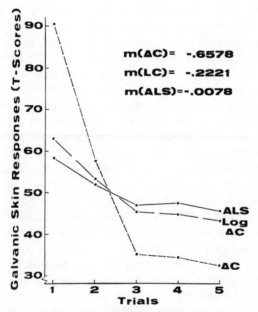

Figure 12.6   Mean SCR amplitudes of seven subjects to five presentations of 1000 Hz, 75 db tone treated as change in conductance (ΔC), log change conductance (log ΔC) and autonomic lability score (ALS). Each of the measures is in standard form. Slope values (m) are shown in the upper right hand corner. (Copyright © 1968, The Society for Psychophysiological Research. Reprinted with permission of the publisher and author from Germana, J. (1968). Rate of habituation and the law of initial values. *Psychophysiology*, **5**, 31–6)

1956) and log change conductance. The two scores are very similar, but the transformation is grounded in theoretical considerations drawn from the underlying process, while the regression technique merely discards the baseline. There is a real sense in which the investigator might feel happier if the transformation failed to dispose of the baseline, since he would thereby know that the baseline information was relevant.

The use of covariance analysis is common practice in the treatment of pre and post-stimulus configurations. Cox (1958) points out that the adjustment of treatment means should parallel the concomitant variable, that is, the treatment groups should not differ on the concomitant variable for this type of analysis. In this situation, however, subjects may advantageously be grouped by levels of basal response (Cronbach and Furby, 1970) and compared without sacrifice of information. Evans and Anastasio (1968) give examples of spurious significance tests due to the confounding of variance and covariance and point to the danger of this sort of error if these precautions are ignored. Benjamin (1967) advocates the use of difference scores derived from covariance. This method has been widely advocated and is certainly to be preferred to the use of raw difference scores in most situations. Overall and Woodward (1975) derive from conventional test theory the finding that the reliability of difference scores varies inversely as the correlation between pre and post measures. This gives rise to the paradox that difference measures having zero reliability can contribute the largest amount of information on change.

Finally, there is another approach available: a multivariate conception for the problem of measurement of change. This approach has been advocated by Cronbach and Furby (1970) who suggest that 'change is multivariate in nature' (p. 76). At different stages in the presentation of a series of stimuli, different processes can be expected to affect the dependent variables, as noted earlier. Figure 12.7 illustrates this process in the conditioning data already referred to. The two distributions, limited to the group of good conditioners, show by their form that the underlying scale units are different for the first and last third of the acquisition series.

Cronbach and Furby imply that it is fallacious to regard changes as being due to a unitary psychological process and suggest that some processes drop out, others vary in level, and so on. The approach is exemplified in a study of psychomotor scores at successive stages of practice, but the underlying rationale is equally applicable to serial measures of psychophysiological variables. A similar argument and examples, together with an appropriate methodology, have been proposed by Tucker (1964, 1965) in the form of three mode factor analysis, for which computer programs are available.

At a simple level, this was demonstrated in the conditioning study. A principal components analysis of all the autonomic measures yielded separate factors for baseline and response measures, together with a third

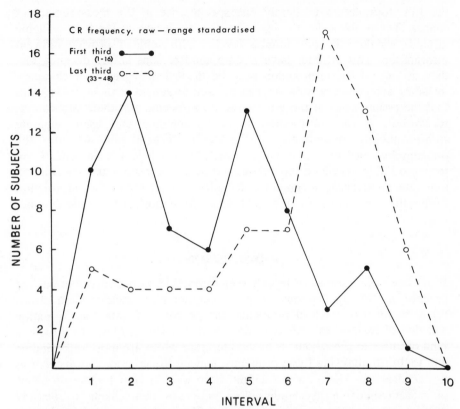

Figure 12.7   Frequency polygons for response occurrence during the first and last third of a series of eyelid conditioning experiments, based on subjects giving responses in both ($N = 67$)

factor containing high and equivalent loadings from both. In other words, a hypothetical variable was identified which was a joint function of the relationships between baseline and response. A comparable finding has recently been reported by Jennings and Wood (1977) for HR data, in which principal component analysis satisfactorily separated the contributions of pre and post response data, and provided a measure of initial values independent of these. The relevant techniques have been reviewed by Van Egeren (1973) in the context of psychophysiological measurement. It is to be expected that the increased availability of multivariate techniques of analysis will lead to their wider application in the field of psychophysiology.

In summary of this section, the measurement of change is the most thorny problem in measurement theory, and one for which a dogmatic attitude is least appropriate. With this proviso, it has been suggested that the LIV formulation is merely one special case in the measurement of change. The problem for the investigator is to decide on the best available grounds whether the pre-stimulus levels of his subjects provide relevant information. This includes having some good reasons before deciding that they do not. If the information is to be discarded, regression techniques, including analysis of covariance, can be used to get rid of them, taking care that the assumptions of these methods are respected and their implications recognized. If the information is to be retained and used, separate transformations can be applied to the pre- and post-stimulus measures, the pre-stimulus measures can be grouped by level and their effects on response levels examined separately, and so on. A more appealing solution is to use multivariate techniques of analysis which retain the information from both sources and provide additional information on their interaction.

4 DISCUSSION

It has been the purpose of this chapter to provide a brief survey of current practice in the applications of psychophysiological measurement which relate to its two practical problems: the problem of data transformation and that of tonic–phasic relationships. A further aim has been to provide a kind of index to those sources in the literature which are most authoritative and useful in attacking these problems, leaving the user to consult them as the need arises. There are no definitive answers in view for the problems of measurement in psychophysiology, nor are there likely to be any lurking just over the immediate horizon. The author has implied that his own predilection is for the exploration of multivariate methods of scaling and analysis. However, the word 'exploration' is chosen advisedly, in preference to 'application' or even 'advocacy'. It is one thing to assert, perhaps blandly, that multivariate techniques hold great promise for psychophysiology. It is quite another to specify the appropriate techniques. The methods have largely been developed in fields whose data properties are quite different from those of psychophysiology; for example, in test theory, attitude measurement and the description of personality. With a few exceptions, notably in EEG analysis, multivariate techniques have not been developed with the specific problems of psychophysiology as the major concern. Nevertheless the arguments in favour of this approach are compelling. We know from our experience in the laboratory, that we are dealing with complex interrelated processes. It becomes apparent when we have to choose an 'appropriate' measure from among several possibilities, each of which has given or can be expected to give, a different result. This complexity is particularly evident when we consider measures of change. Inherently, then, we are dealing with multivariate processes.

It is understandable that in the field of psychophysiology whose flavour has always been empirical rather than predominantly theoretical, the development of measurement theory should have lagged behind the investigation of substantive problems. It is noteworthy that none of the major formulations in the literature on data transformation, for example, has originated in the field of psychophysiology. The literature is chiefly concerned with experimental design and statistical analysis in fields far removed. Notably the literature is concerned with problem areas in which sampling is the major concern. One is reminded that modern techniques of data analysis originated in agriculture where the problems were those of random variation.

Indeed it is only recently that texts devoted to data analysis in the behavioural sciences have appeared. Winer (1971) notes that the problems of interdependence of measures, almost univeral in the various disciplines of psychology, but scarcely noticeable in the observation of random variation, are not yet solved. It may not be too far fetched to suggest that the apparatus of classical statistics, which begins to creak when it is extended to behaviour, simply will not stretch far enough to encompass psychophysiology.

Apart from rhetorical exaggeration, there are sound reasons for this breakdown, It may be useful to review them though they are very familiar if not always explicit. The concern of psychophysiology is with an integrated organism which we observe in activity as a working system. Most often we are concerned with serial measures of multiply determined processes which we can only examine at sites remote from their origin inside the system. To do so we must employ measurement devices which are themselves complex and subject to their own constraints. The time constants, band filters, and spectral densities of these measurement devices are not artifacts, but intrinsic aspects of the measurement process. It is not surprising then, that the techniques of analysis developed in other fields fall short of our requirements. This is not a counsel of despair. It was observed at the outset that psychophysiology gives rise to some of the most complex data forms in the study of behaviour. The yield of information from this data is potentially enormous. Furthermore, it is matched by the information processing capacity available in contemporary computer technology. Three developments can be observed within the past decade. The measurement and analysis of data have become immensely more sophisticated. There has been a move away from reliance on standard formulae and sanctioned rituals towards a critical examination of measurement concepts and methods of analysis, some of which have been reviewed earlier. Finally, as the other chapters of this volume will show, there is an increased reliance on techniques which are specific to the field and this may partly reflect the successful solution of problems of instrumentation which tended to dominate the work of the previous decade.

A final point of interest stems from the literature which has been reviewed. It is noteworthy that there have been no important recent developments and it is no accident that the references appended to this chapter tend to centre on the past. The problems of data transformations were formulated and largely solved in the field of psychometrics and experimental design in the post war period. The problems of measuring change are still in the 'age of brass' and the Augustan era is yet to come. Consideration of this fact may suggest that the field of psychophysiology, falling somewhere between, is ready to find its own solutions.

REFERENCES

Anscombe, F. J. (1960. Rejection of outliers. *Technometrics*, 2, 123–47.

Anscombe, F. J., and Tukey, J. W. (1963). The examination and analysis of residuals. *Technometrics*, 5, 141–60.

Bartlett, M. S. (1947). The use of transformation. *Biometrics*, 3, 39–52.

Benjamin, L. S. (1963). Statistical treatment of the law of initial values (LIV) in autonomic research: A review and recommendation. *Psychosom. Med.*, 25, 556–66.

Benjamin, L. S. (1967). Facts and artifacts in using analysis of covariance to "undo" the law of initial values. *Psychophysiology*, 4, 187–201.

Bergman, L. R. (1972). Linear transformation and the study of change. *Reports from the Psychological Laboratories of the University of Stockholm, No. 352.*

Block, J. D., and Bridger, W. H. (1962). The law of initial value in psychophysiology: A reformulation in terms of experimental and theoretical consideration. *Ann. NY Acad. SCI.*, 98, 1229–41.

Box, G. E. P. (1953). Non normality and tests of variance. *Biometrika*, 40, 318–35.

Box, G. E. P., and Cox, D. R. (1964). An analysis of transformations. *J. Roy. Statist. Soc.*, 26, 211–43.

Bradley, J. V. (1968). *Distribution——Free Statistical Tests*, Prentice-Hall, Englewood Cliffs, New Jersey.

Cooper, R., Osselton, J. W., and Shaw, J. C. (1974). *EEG Technology*, 2nd Edn, Butterworths, London.

Cox D. R. (1958). *Planning of Experiments*, Wiley, London.

Cronbach, L. J., and Furby, L. (1970). How should we measure 'change'—or should we? *Psychol. Bull.*, 74, 68–80.

Darrow, C. W. (1964). The rationale for treating the change in galvanic skin response as a change in conductance. *Psychophysiology*, 1, 31–38.

Dolby, J. L. (1963). A quick method for choosing a transformation. *Technometrics*, 5, 317–26.

Dubois, P. H. (1965). *An Introduction to Psychological Statistics*, Harper and Row, New York.

Edwards, A. L. (1968). *Experimental Design in Psychological Research*. 3rd Edn, Holt, Rhinehart and Winston, New York.

Eysenck, H. J., and Levey, A. B. (1972). Conditioning, introversion–extraversion and the strength of the nervous system. In V. D. Nebylitsyn and J. A. Gray (Eds), *Biological Bases of Individual Behaviour*, Academic Press, London.

Evans, S. H., and Anastasio, E. J. (1968) Misuse of analysis of covariance when treatment effects and covariance are confounded. *Psycho. Bull.*, 69, 225–34.

Fisher, R. A., and Yates, F. (1948). *Statistical Tables for Biological, Agricultural and Medical Research*, Oliver and Boyd, London.

Gentleman, J. F., and Wilk, M. B. (1975). Detecting outliers. II. Supplementing the direct analysis of residuals. *Biometrics*, **31**, 387–410.

Germana. J. (1968). Rate of habituation and the law of initial values. *Psychophysiology*, **5**, 31–6.

Grubb, F. E. (1969). Procedures for detecting outlying observations in samples. *Technometrics*, **11**, 1–21.

Guilford, J. P. (1965). *Fundamental Statistics in Psychology and Education*, 4th Edn, McGraw-Hill, New York.

Haggard, E. A. (1949a). On the application of analysis of variance to GSR data: I. The selection of an appropriate measure. *J. Exp. Psychol.*, **39**, 378–92.

Haggard, E. A. (1949b). On the application of analysis of variance to GSR data: III. Some effects of the use of an inappropriate measure. *J. Exp. Psychol.*, **39**, 861–7.

Harris, C. W. (1963). *Problems in Measuring Change*, University of Wisconsin Press, Madison.

Jennings, J. R., and Wood, C. C. (1977). Principal component separation of pre- and post- response effects on cardiac interbeat-intervals in a reaction time (RT) task. *Psychophysiology*, **14**, 89–90.

Keppel, G. (1973). *Design and Analysis: a Researcher's Handbook*, Prentice-Hall, New Jersey.

Kirk, R. E. (1968). *Experimental Design: Procedures for the Behavioural Sciences*, Brooks-Cole, Monterey.

Kruskall, J. B. (1965). Analysis of factorial experiments by estimating monotone transformations of the data. *J. Roy. Statist. Soc.*, **27**, 251–63.

Lacey, J. I. (1956). The evaluation of autonomic responses. Toward a general solution. *Ann. NY Acad. Sci.* **67**, 123–64.

Lader, M. (1970). The unit of quantification of the GSR. *J. Psychosom. Res.*, **14** 109–10.

Lord, F. M. (1969). Statistical adjustments when comparing pre-existing groups. *Psychol. Bull.*, **72**, 336–7.

Lykken, D. T., Rose, R., Luther, B., and Maley, M. (1966). Correcting psychophysiological measures for individual differences in range. *Psychol. Bull.*, **66**, 481–4.

Lykken, D. T., and Venables, P. H. (1971). Direct measurement of skin conductance. *Psychophysiology*, **8**, 656–72.

Maxwell, A. E. (1958). *Experimental Design in Psychology and the Biological Sciences*, Methuen, London.

Mueller, C. G. (1949). Numerical transformation in the analysis of experimental data. *Psychol. Bull.*, **46**, 198–223.

Myers, J. L. (1966). *Fundamentals of Experimental Design*, Allyn and Bacon, Boston.

Ol'anynskaya, R. P., and Fedorov, V. K. (1959). Basic metabolic rate and typological features of the nervous system in mice. *Dokl. Akad. Nank. SSSR (Biol. Sci.)*, **124**, 121–4.

Overall, J. E., and Woodward, J. A. (1975). Unreliability of difference scores: A paradox for measurement of change. *Psychol. Bull.*, **82**, 85–6.

Parrat, L. G. (1961). *Probability and Experimental Errors in Science*, Wiley, New York.

Scheffé, H. (1959). *The Analysis of Variance*, Wiley, New York.

Siegel, S. (1956). *Non-parametric Statistics for the Behavioural Sciences*, McGraw-Hill, New York.

Snedecor, G. W., and Cochrane, W. G. (1973). *Statistical Methods*, Iowa State University Press, Ames, Iowa.

Tucker, L. R. (1964). The extension of factor analysis to three-dimensional matrices. In N. Fredrickson and H. Gulliksen (Eds), *Contributions to Mathematical Psychology*, Holt, Rhinehart and Winston, New York.

Tucker, L. R. (1965). Experiments in multi-mode factor analysis. In *Proceedings of the 1964 Invitational Conference on Testing Problems*, Educational Test Service, New Jersey.

Tukey, J. W. (1957). The comparative anatomy of transformations. *Ann. Math. Statist.*, **28**, 602–32.

Van Egeren, L. F. (1973). Multivariate statistical analysis. *Psychophysiology*, **10**, 517–32.

Wilder, J. (1958) Modern psychophysiology and the law of initial value *Amer. J. Psychother.*, **12**, 199–221.

Winer, B. J. (1971). *Statistical Principles in Experimental Design*, 2nd Edn, McGraw-Hill, New York.

Techniques in Psychophysiology
Edited by I. Martin and P.H. Venables
© 1980, John Wiley & Sons Ltd.

CHAPTER 13

Response detection and measurement*

L. N. LAW, A. B. LEVEY, and IRENE MARTIN

1 INTRODUCTION

This chapter has two main concerns, firstly with response detection techniques, and secondly with methods of analysing a response once it has been detected. The approach illustrates a strategy for examining

*Acknowledgements. We gratefully acknowledge the support of the Bethlem Maudsley Hospitals Research Fund (to I. Martin and L. N. Law) during the period of development of the computer programs. We also thank Christine Eysenck, Gertrude Frcka and Kieron O'Connor for allowing us to use their data reproduced in Figure 13.9, Figures 13.1–13.8, and Figure 13.10 respectively.

psychophysiological data which concentrates on the 'response' within the context of an S–R paradigm. It derives from experience obtained in the transition from hand-scoring data to the use of computer methods, experience which has raised many questions about how we look at responses and how we can define them by operations which can be specified with minimum ambiguity. We define the problem in general terms as the measurement of consistent features of the response waveforms obtained from a particular instrumentation system operating within a particular experimental context.

The problem of response detection has been dealt with in most of the preceding chapters in the context of specific response systems. In some instances, for example skin resistance and eyeblink responses, the response is 'visually obvious' from chart recordings obtained via the standard types of instrumentation, and problems of detection have centred on an amplitude criterion and onset latency limits. What is meant by 'visually obvious' must however be considered carefully since what is obvious to the human eye is not necessarily obvious to a computer.

Many responses are not easy for the eye to detect when data presentation is in its usual form. This is particularly true when analysis is required in terms of the frequency characteristics of the waveform, since it is not easy to visualize changes in a spectrum. Again, cortical evoked potentials may be barely visible in an EEG record, and further processing is necessary, e.g. averaging, in order to emphasize the pattern of the response and make it suitable for visual presentation. By averaging and by careful control over experimental conditions a representative response may be obtained and a 'typical' cortical evoked potential defined.

In the case of the cardiac response the problem of detection is very considerable. There is too much variation arising from immediate pre-stimulus activity, from recurring physiological rhythms, and from differences between individuals and experimental conditions. The contributions in Chapter 3 illustrate the variety of methods which have been applied to cardiac activity with a view to determining the occurrence and the shape of the cardiac response curve.

In this chapter we are concerned to draw together and discuss response detection methods *per se*, and to consider the general problems, assumptions, and rationale underlying the application of the techniques. No attempt has been made to give a completely general definition of the term 'response', apart from the literal one of being the 'answer' to the stimulus, but it must be stressed that a definition is always implicit in any detection method. At the operational level a response is whatever is recognized as such, whether by a person or a machine. The judgement 'by eye' that a response has occurred implies that a set of criteria is employed in the acceptance or rejection of a response. The introduction of computer methods in general requires that rigorous operational definitions of the task to be undertaken by the computer must be provided. If the task is to be the detection of responses then the set of criteria used in 'by eye' detection must be made explicit before a program can be written.

Once a response has been detected, the problem passes on to the identification of a response shape which can be termed 'typical' (though preferably not 'idealized') in the sense that it can be reproduced within a specifiable set of experimental conditions. Investigators have been concerned to delineate a 'typical' shape in order that meaningful measurements of its features can be made, e.g. onset latency, rise time, amplitude, recovery, and duration, under given stimulus conditions. In the case of some fairly straightforward responses (like the skin resistance response) such an approach has been possible.

Many authors have pointed, however, to the difficulties in specifying response shape, and the need for a standard presentation of data. Chapter 2 emphasizes how the appearance of the plethysmographic waveform on the polygraph depends on basic characteristics of the particular measurement technique employed. Time constants, sensitivity levels, filters, sampling rates, etc., all contribute to the observed response shape.

Cardiovascular and EEG activity both illustrate another problem. In a certain sense we are considering a different kind of response when it occurs against a background of ongoing activity, as it does with these variables. The problem is not only that of response detection in terms of signal to noise, but of meaningful changes in the background activity. We are also faced with a terminology which may be well established in specific response systems but which has not been used in any overall rational way, e.g. tonic and phasic, signal and noise, background and foreground.

For many response systems, however, a typical shape can be defined, and its major features identified. We go on to examine how response features can be defined, in such a way that accurate measurements can be made of them. An example will be discussed of a feature extraction program, based on the measurement of changes in slope, which comprises both response detection procedures and the measurement of individual response elements.

The final part of this chapter takes up the question of the meaningfulness of response measurements. It considers the information which is contained in a response considered as a waveform, and the decisions which have to be made concerning how much of this information is to be retained, how it is to be selected and summarized, and the fidelity with which the summary of the data reflects what has happened.

Can computer analysis assist with these problems? The introduction of computer techniques can undoubtedly take over more reliably some of the work of hand-scoring. In the following sections we attempt to show that it can also contribute to our understanding of psychophysiological data by clarifying the problems of response detection and measurement.

2 RESPONSE DETECTION

The detection of a stimulus related response occurring in some psychophysiological variable, whether by means of a skilled observer examining a chart record, or by an automated method, may conveniently be considered as a problem of pattern recognition. Computer techniques which come under the heading of pattern recognition are often concerned with the automation of some human skill such as reading the figures on a cheque or counting the number of white cells in a sample of blood, and a skilled human observer provides the standard by which the performance of the automated technique may be judged. For instance a cheque reading machine should ideally be capable of reading handwritten figures, although in practice it may be restricted to reading specially printed figures which provide more easily recognizable patterns. Thus the existing theory of pattern recognition may be used to provide a set of unifying concepts applicable to a variety of response detection methodologies.

While it is not yet practical to design a completely general purpose pattern recognition technique it is possible to describe a general strategy for the design of a recognizer for a specific pattern. Such a strategy will consist of the following stages.

(a) The data to be analysed for the presence or absence of the pattern will be presented is some standard form. In the case of a psychophysiological variable this could be a chart recording for the human observer, or in digital form as a sequence of discrete measurements spaced at intervals of time in the case of an automated method.

(b) As much information as is available must be obtained about the characteristics of the data when the specified pattern is known to be present.

(c) As much information as is available must be obtained about the characteristics of the data when the specified pattern is known to be absent.

(d) Using the information obtained in the previous two stages, an algorithm will be derived for a decision function which, when applied to the data, will generate a measure maximizing the difference between data where the pattern is present and data where the pattern is absent.

(e) A threshold or criterion will be defined for the decision function. If the value obtained from the decision function when applied to a given set of data exceeds the criterion then the specified pattern is considered to be present, otherwise it is considered to be absent.

An immediate problem with such a very general description of the strategy as given above is that it may appear to be too vague to provide a recipe for a practical method of detecting psychophysiological responses. It is hoped that its practical application will become clearer when related to the descriptions of specific response detection techniques given below, while at this point we proceed with a little more theory.

Firstly it should be noted that while the above strategy relates to the recognition of a single pattern it may be extended to the classification of a number of different patterns which may be present in the data.

Secondly the strategy must be considered as implying a considerable amount of feedback control (i.e. trial and error!) since there may not be initially sufficient information available to allow the design of an efficient recognizer. The testing of a less than adequate pattern recognizer may then be used to provide information that will allow improvements to be made in the recognition algorithm.

Thirdly, and arising partly from the previous point, the question of how to measure the performance of a pattern recognizer must be considered. Testing will usually be by comparison with the results obtained by one or more skilled human observers. For any given set of data together with the corresponding decision by the recognizer the result will be either a hit, a miss, a correct rejection or a false alarm.

The performance of a particular pattern recognition technique may sometimes be given only in terms of hits and will be considered to be satisfactory if it can be demonstrated to be capable of recognizing the pattern when present. A more meaningful measure of performances can be given in terms of the 'hit rate' and the 'false alarm rate' (the hit rate being the ratio of hits to total of hits and misses, and the false alarm rate the ratio of false alarms to total of false alarms and correct rejections). These two ratios are often found to be interdependent, so that an increase in the hit rate can only be made at the expense of increasing the number of false alarms. Any trade-off between the two will depend on the purpose for which the recognizer is being used and the penalty incurred by a miss as opposed to any penalty incurred by a false alarm. If sufficient statistical information about the data is available, signal detection theory (Egan, 1975) provides techniques for the design of an optimum recognizer.

The following examples of specific response detection methods will be described in relation to the theory of pattern recognition outlined above. Although many of the methods are closely connected with the analysis of a particular psychophysiological variable and may be included as part of the technology of that variable in other chapters of this book, they are collected together here both for comparison and also because the underlying theory is quite general and may find a use in the analysis of other variables.

One problem of such a comparison is that of varying terminology. In one case a pattern may be being recognized against a background, in another a signal may be being detected in the presence of noise, or a feature extracted from a dataset. In more psychophysiological terms phasic activity must be separated from tonic, and responses distinguished from ongoing spontaneous fluctuations. All such formulations should be considered as equivalent.

2.1 Visual methods

This is the traditional method of response detection and consists simply of careful examination of polygraph chart records, using the human visual system in its role of efficient if idiosyncratic pattern recognizer to detect the presence of responses. Visual methods provide both the starting point for most automatic methods and the standard by which their performance may be judged. They also provide certain problems when used for either of these purposes. Visual methods are essentially subjective, relying on the skill and experience of a particular observer. Agreement between even skilled observers is rarely complete and sometimes non-existent.

All this makes it very difficult to obtain operational definitions of the visual characteristics of a response as observed in the polygraph record. Textbooks usually refer to an illustration of the particular response in an idealized form, which is of little use to the computer programmer attempting to extract responses from long tables of numbers.

Some clues are available however. Descriptions of the appearance of chart recordings using terms such as 'slow waves' or 'fast activity' suggest that the scale factor used for the time axis is important, since 'slow' and 'fast' are not used in any absolute sense but can only be relative to the time scale used for a particular variable. More or less standardized time scale factors have become established in practice for the variables commonly used in psychophysiology, although considerable variations may occur between different laboratories. It should be noted also that while the amplitude scale factor is as important as the time scale in the standardized visual presentation of responses, amplitude changes in the record are not the most significant factor in response detection, even though an amplitude criterion (such as greater than 1 mm deflection) may be given. Thus amplitude changes much greater than the criterion may occur, but are considered to be changes in basal level if they are 'slow', or artifacts if they are 'fast', compared to the conventional time scale for the variable.

Consideration of the above leads to the suggestion that what is being observed in the visual detection of responses may not be changes in the amplitude of the response variable, but changes in the relative slope of the chart record. That is, the eye looks for distinct changes of direction in the ink line of the chart record and recognizes responses in terms of a sequence of such changes. If this is the case then it is equivalent to approximating the chart record as a sequence of straight line segments.

[The term slope is used here to mean the observed angle between a segment of the response variable plotted on the chart record and the time axis. At any given point on the record the slope can be measured as the angle between the tangent at that point and the time axis, and can therefore be computed by taking the first differential of the response record considered as the plot of a function. Relative slope is used to stress that what is important for the visual presentation is not the actual rate of change of the variable (for instance in $k\Omega/s$ for a SRR recording) but the observed rate of change in cm/cm of the ink line on the chart for particular values of amplitude and time scale factors.]

The analysis of visual detection methods as given above may seem a little forced. Its justification lies in its use as the theoretical basis for a practical automatic response detection method to be described later. As far as purely visual methods are concerned it may be worth suggesting that consistency of response scoring between different observers and different laboratories could possibly be improved if common standards for the amplitude and time scale factors of chart recordings could be achieved, or at least if the standards in use were quoted.

2.2 Averaging

There are several variables, for instance EMG and ECG, which are too complex in their 'raw' state to allow easy visual detection of responses and require further processing before they are suitable for visual presentation. Processing such as the rectification and integration of EMG and the conversion of ECG to heart rate represent relatively simple transformations of the original data. The method of averaging involves a much more complex treatment of the original response variable data, and raises questions about the definition of a response similar to those raised by an automatic detection method. A brief look at the theory of averaging may therefore be useful.

The technique of averaging was developed for use with EEG waveforms when the response to be detected—an evoked potential or a CNV—is too small in comparison with the background EEG to be reliably detected visually for a single stimulus. It represents an automation of the first four stages of the standard strategy given above. That is, it uses an automated method which seeks to maximize the difference between the response data and the non-response data, with the final stage of response detection usually achieved by visual inspection of the average.

The information available about the response is that it is assumed to have a fixed time relationship to the stimulus and has a stable amplitude and waveform when evoked by a sequence of identical stimuli. The background EEG activity is assumed to have no fixed time relationship to the stimulus and to have a random variation of amplitude and waveform. If then sections of EEG waveform of fixed duration following each of a number of stimuli are obtained and the sections of waveforms summed, the responses will add algebraically while the background EEG activity will add statistically. That is, the amplitude of the sum of the responses will increase in proportion to the number of stimuli, whereas it is the variance of the random background EEG waveforms which will increase in this proportion. Since the amplitude of a random waveform is measured by its standard deviation, the amplitude of the random component of the sum will increase in proportion to the square root or the number of stimuli. Thus if a true average is taken the amplitude of the background EEG will appear to have been decreased, and if a large enough number of stimuli are used can be decreased sufficiently for any responses present to become visible.

A less condensed description of averaging will be found in the chapter on evoked potentials. The emphasis here is on the assumptions made about the nature of the response and the nature of the background from which it is to be distinguished.

2.3 Wiener filtering

The technique of averaging assumes that the background data set from which the responses are to be extracted is a truly random variable of time as well as having a random time relationship to the stimulus. This is manifestly not true in the case of the EEG and may well not hold in the case of other variables where averaging techniques are used. While a lack of true randomness in the background data does not invalidate the use of averaging, it does reduce its efficiency. A two stage procedure may then be devised which uses an initial averaging to obtain information about the response and non-response data and then uses this information to improve the efficiency of a second averaging of the data. In the case of Wiener filtering the desired information is the power spectrum of the response and non-response data. This can then be used to construct a filter which is applied to the original data prior to a second averaging. Analysis takes place in stages as follows.

(i) An initial average response is obtained in the usual way and converted to a power spectrum by Fourier transformation. This will give the best available estimate of the true spectrum of the response.

(ii) The power spectrum of each segment of data entered into the average is obtained individually and the resultant set of spectra averaged. Since a power spectrum removes all information about the phase (i.e. time relationships) of the frequency components of the spectrum, the averaging in this case will not reduce the contribution of the non-response data.

(iii) The spectrum of the average is subtracted from the average spectrum. The result will be an estimate of those frequency components present in the non-response data but not in the response data. This spectrum is used to compute the filter.

(iv) The filter is applied to each segment of the original data and a new average taken of the filtered data to obtain an improved average response.

Wiener filtering seeks to improve on simple averaging by making use of a more realistic model of the background against which the response must be recognized. Whether the improvement is worth the considerable amount of extra computation will depend on the facilities available and the overall needs of the analysis.

2.4 Template matching

The use of averaging, with or without Wiener filtering, has the major disadvantage that it is not possible to say whether the response was present or absent for any particular trial. What averaging does provide is the best available estimate of the form of the response that can be expected as the result of each trial. Since this represents an increase of information about the response, it should be possible to utilize it to improve the detection of responses. Template matching is one way of doing this.

The term 'template' is used to refer to an ideal or typical response available in the same form as the data being tested for the presence of responses. Conceptually, the template could be drawn on graph paper for visual comparison with a chart record, but in practice is more likely to be stored in a computer as an array of data points. The array representing the template can then be cross-related with a corresponding array representing the data to be tested, and a criterion value for the magnitude of the correlation coefficient used to distinguish the presence or absence of the response in the data.

Template matching has been used mainly for the detection of single trial evoked potentials (Weinberg and Cooper, 1972) with the template obtained by averaging, but again we would stress the generality of the technique. Template matching could be used with variables other than EEG, the template could be constructed theoretically, or obtained from actual data by means other than averaging and comparison of template and data could be made by techniques other than correlation.

2.5 Autoregressive model

In terms of the general strategy, template matching makes use of information about the response, comparing the template with the data and inferring a response if the match is sufficiently close. It is a simple matter to invert this technique by using a template representing a segment of data where a response is assumed to be absent, comparing this with the data and inferring a response if the mismatch is sufficiently great. The use of an autoregressive model is one of the more elaborate ways of achieving this. The autoregressive model is built using a segment of data immediately preceding a stimulus. The model then allows a prediction to be made of the form of the data succeeding the stimulus if the stimulus had not been applied. The predicted data are then subtracted from the observed data and any difference is assumed to be a response.

The full use of an autoregressive model requires a considerable amount of computer processing and raises questions about the accuracy of the model and the reliability of the prediction made from it. It has however been used to construct a model of the EEG (Fenwick and coworkers, 1971) and for the analysis of heart rate in an attempt to disentangle the heart rate response from the ongoing sinus arrhythmia (see Chapter 3). A simpler form of the method avoids the use of the autoregressive model by taking the pre-stimulus data as non-reponse template and comparing with the post-stimulus data using cross-correlation (Wicke and coworkers, 1978). As with the standard form of template matching only an indication of response present or absent is given, with minimal information about the exact form of the response.

2.6 Discriminant functions

The response detection techniques described so far have been in increasing order of complexity of processing and of the distance between the experimenter and the data. This is taken a stage further in the case of the use of discriminant functions (Donchin and Herning, 1975). In this case the definition of the characteristics of a response, or of several types of response, is left entirely to a computer program. A 'training' set of typical responses (i.e. a set of templates) is supplied to a discriminant analysis program which generates a corresponding set of discriminant functions. Applying the discriminant functions to the observed data will then classify them into responses types (including non-response data).

At this high level of statistical manipulation a number of techniques such as factor analysis or cluster analysis could be used. It is possible however that such methods are oversophisticated for most purposes and that simpler and more robust methods might be more practical. It is such simpler methods that we consider next.

2.7 Feature extraction

Feature extraction is often used as an umbrella term to describe a miscellaneous collection of pattern recognition techniques devised on an *ad hoc* basis to meet the requirements of a particular problem. Any available information about the response or responses to be detected is used to define a set of 'features' which typify the response. Selection of features is often somewhat arbitrary, but provided an operational definition is given for each selected feature then together they form an operational definition of the response.

The detection of each feature is in itself a small problem of pattern recognition, but features can be chosen and defined so as to simplify detection. Sequential search methods may also be used, an initial search of the data being made for some key feature using a simple detection method which will maximize hits while probably also allowing an unacceptable number of false alarms. Provided that there are not too many false alarms this initial search should considerably reduce the amount of data. Further more detailed searches can then be made of the remaining data to confirm the hits and reject the false alarms obtained from the previous search.

The automatic detection of epileptic spikes and slow waves (Gotman and Gloor, 1976) provides a good example of sequential search techniques and also of a general approach to response detection problems. An initial analysis of visual methods is used to identify those features of the EEG waveforms which imply epileptic activity. This information is then used to derive a hierarchical set of precise operational definitions for the features. Once the definitions have been obtained then computer implementation is a relatively straightforward technical problem of programming. Finally, the performance of the automatic method is compared with the traditional visual scoring of the EEG record (Gotman, Gloor, and Schaul, 1978).

Feature extraction is also the major response detection technique used in the system described in the next section.

2.8 A practical system

A package of computer programs developed by the authors under the title of SARA (stimulus and response analysis) adopts the same philosophy as has been expressed in this chapter, generalizing analysis methods across variables. It has been used for eyelid conditioning, heart rate, skin resistance, evoked potentials, and contingent negative variation among

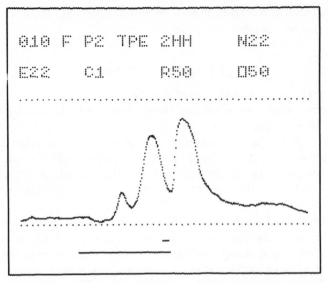

Figure 13.1 Computer plot of stored data for one trial of an eyelid conditioning experiment. 500 measurements of eyelid position taken at 5 ms intervals over 2.5 s of time. The two dotted lines represent the limits of full scale deflection of the blink amplifier output. Information on the stimulus conditions is also stored and shown plotted below the lower dotted line. The longer lower stimulus line indicates the occurrence and duration of the conditioned stimulus (a tone) and the shorter line above this indicates the occurrence and duration of the unconditioned stimulus (airpuff). The 500 measurements of eyelid position and stimulus condition comprise the data available for computer analysis

others. The package contains programs for performing standard computer operations such as analog to digital conversion of psychophysiological data. These techniques are discussed briefly in the appendix to this chapter and will be assumed here, as will programs for performing operations such as averaging. Thus the data to be analysed will be in the form of a vector of numbers representing a sequence of measurements taken at uniform time intervals. Figure 13.1 shows a computer plot of such data representing 2.5 seconds of eyeblink activity.

The discussion of visual methods suggested that what the eye is observing is changes in the slope of the chart record, or equally, that the eye analyses the waveform of the chart record into a sequence of straight line segments which meet at a sufficiently sharp angle for the slope of one to be clearly different from that of the next. It is such sequences of straight line segments which are the basic features detected by the SARA analysis programs.

For the purposes of the SARA programs, three types of straight line segments are defined. These are:

(1) An upward sloping line with a slope greater than some specified criterion value. Such a line indicates a time period during which the system generating the response variable is active and producing an increase in the observed level of the response variable.

(2) A downward sloping line with a negative slope greater than the criterion value. Here the activity is such as to cause a decrease in the level of the response variable.

(3) A line whose slope may be positive or negative (or zero) but is less than the criterion value in either direction. Such a line defines a time period during which the response system is inactive.

The criterion value of slope used to distinguish active from inactive segments of the response record is a variable which may be altered by the user of the SARA programs. A second criterion is also provided which specifies the minimum length of a line segment. That is, a segment of the response must satisfy the definition for a particular type of line segment for more than a specified time duration if it is to be accepted as a separate line segment. Adjustment of these two parameters by the user allows some control over the rejection of artifacts and slow changes of basal level that may be present in the response record.

A straight line segment can be defined in terms of the Cartesian Coordinates of its endpoints. The effect of dividing the response record into a sequence of straight line segments is thus to reduce the data to a sequence of endpoint coordinates, each point marking the end of one segment and the beginning of the next. Figure 13.2 shows the same data as Figure 13.1 with markers added to identify the endpoints of the sequence of 'straight line' segments and in Figure 13.3 the original response data are replaced by actual straight lines connecting up the marked points to allow a comparison with the original data.

So far only a sequence of straight line segments has been extracted from the data, but once this has been achieved it is relatively easy to produce a realistic definition of a response in terms of straight line segments. In the SARA system four different markers are used to identify the endpoints of the straight line segments (see Figure 13.2 and 13.3). Each marker identifies one of the following four transitions:

(1) A transition from low or zero activity to high positive activity. (It is assumed that the instrumentation for a particular response variable is arranged so that an upward deflection represents an increase in activity.)

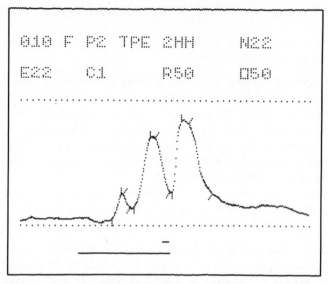

Figure 13.2   The data of Figure 13.1 to which the automatic scoring program has added markers indicating the beginning and end points of the 'straight line' segments extracted from the data set

(2)   A transition from high positive to low activity.
(3)   A transition from low to high negative activity.
(4)   A transition from high negative to low activity.

Responses may now be defined in terms of a set of transitions related in time to a given stimulus. For example, in the relatively simple case of an eyeblink or SRR a response will be observed as an initial transition from low to high positive activity with a short or zero segment of low activity at the peak of the response and then a segment of high negative activity returning the response to the initial low level. Definitions of more complex responses shapes may be set up in a similar way.

The minimum information about the response provided by a response detection method is simply the presence or absence of the response, but in general more information than this will be required. Obtaining this extra information we have distinguished as a question of response measurement as opposed to response detection although in the case of the more informative detection methods there may be a considerable overlap. Feature extraction in particular provides considerable information about the response and if some or all of the features are also the desired measurements a worthwhile reduction in processing can be obtained.

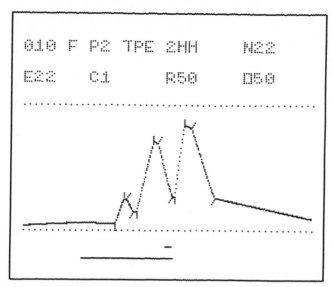

Figure 13.3 In this plot the original eyelid position data of Figure 13.1 have been replaced by straight lines joining the scoring markers shown in Figure 13.2. Comparison with Figure 13.1 shows the extent to which the shape of the response waveform has been retained while reducing the measurement points from 500 to 14. (12 marked points and the first and last points of the original data)

Taking the measurement of eyeblink as an example, measurements are required on the timing of the response in relation to the stimulus, and of the size and shape of the response. The detection method used in the SARA package can provide measurements for all three aspects of the response since the markers provide a set of reference points which locate the response in time and level. However, problems arise in the relation of these reference points to the traditional concepts of onset, peak, and recovery associated with hand scoring by visual methods.

The most difficult of these problems is the concept of response onset. No guidance on how to determine where a response starts appears to be available in the literature. Attempting to trace a response backwards to its source by increasing the sensitivity of the instrumentation simply results in the onset being placed earlier and earlier in the development of the response. In terms of the response detection method used in the SARA package this is equivalent to reducing the slope criterion used. Since a criterion which gives adequate detection places the first marker later on the response than is considered appropriate by an experienced observer a

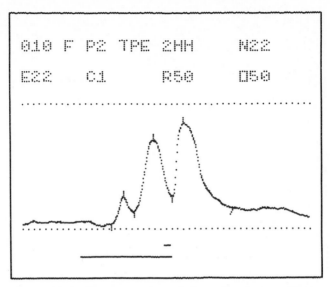

Figure 13.4 Computer plot of the same data as Figure 13.1 but here the automatic scoring program has used the marking shown in Figure 13.2 to identify the more conventional points of interest of onset, peak, and recovery

second and lower slope criterion is provided. Once a response has been detected its development is traced back in time and the onset defined as the first point to exceed the second criterion.

Once an onset has been determined the definitions of peak and recovery present fewer problems. Peak is defined as the highest point on the response and recovery as a return to below a level which is some defined percentage of onset to peak amplitude. Responses scored for onset, peak, and recovery are shown in Figure 13.4 and may be compared with the original scoring shown in Figure 13.2.

That the system is capable of handling large quantities of data while giving consistent results is indicated by Figures 13.5 to 13.7. These illustrate the use of the programs to obtain data on the distribution of onsets, peaks and recoveries of detected responses as a function of time within the trial. Each distribution is derived from upwards of 4000 responses, all scored entirely automatically.

Figures 13.8–13.10 show further data scored using the SARA system. Figure 13.8 illustrates data from a single trial, whereas the evoked potential and CNV data have been averaged.

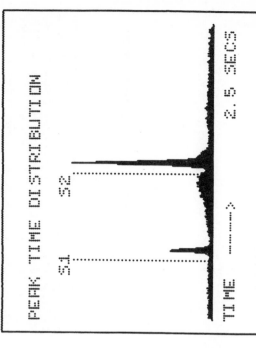

Figure 13.5 The automatic scoring program was used to score data from a conditioning experiment consisting of 60 stimulus presentations to 100 subjects. No manual editing of the scoring was used. The computer plot shows the distribution of onsets of all detected responses as a function of time within the trial. S1 = CS (tone); S2 = UCS (airpuff). Responses following S1 indicate orienting responses and following S2 unconditioned responses; pre-S2 responses are anticipatory conditioned responses

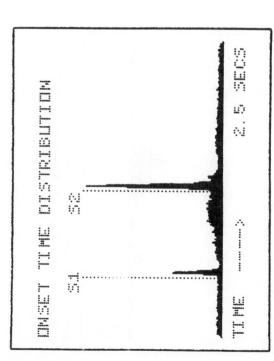

Figure 13.6 Distribution of response peaks derived from the experiment described in Figure 13.5

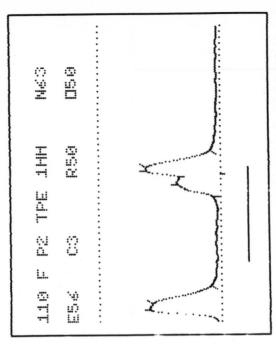

Figure 13.8 Computer plot of extinction trial data from an eyelid conditioning experiment illustrating computer scoring of eyelid responses. Lower horizontal line indicates duration of CS. The program has scored a 'spontaneous' response and a CR/UCR blend occurring to the CS

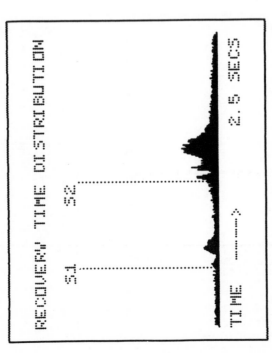

Figure 13.7 Distribution of response recovery corresponding to the onset and peak distributions of Figure 13.5 and Figure 13.6

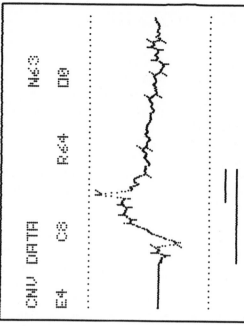

Figure 13.10   Computer scoring of CNV data

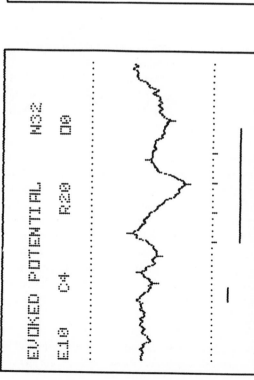

Figure 13.9   Computer scoring of evoked potential data

3 RESPONSE MEASUREMENT

The measurement of waveform characteristics is of paramount interest in psychophysiology, and in this section we shall attempt to look analytically at the problems of measuring waveforms. In choosing our measurements we will want to consider how well they match the visual characteristics of the record, the physiological interpretation and the extent to which they represent the psychological situation in which the response was observed. We may be interested in a number of differing aspects of responding, or may focus attention on some particular aspect of the response.

We must also bear in mind that while it is natural to think of responses in terms of their standard forms, a chart recording can only be a partial record of observations made through the window of a particular instrumentation system applied in a particular way within a particular experimental context. The window may be wide or narrow, transparent or opaque, but in any event the view will always be restricted. It is therefore important not to reify the chart recording by thinking that measurements made on the chart or within a computer are other than at least one stage removed from measurements of the response itself.

Here as elsewhere in this chapter problems of definitions must be considered. Terms such as onset, slope, peak, inflexion, and even response itself are normally used in a descriptive sense to refer to widely understood concepts in psychophysiology. This is perfectly adequate when we are considering what it is we wish to measure, but less adequate when we use the same term to refer to the measurement itself since the method of measurement implies a narrower definition. Problems of definition in the measurement of onset have been referred to in the previous section. In the remainder of this section terms will be used in their wide sense unless a specific definition is given.

The simplest measurement is a count of the number of responses which has occurred in response to some stimulus, or has failed to occur. We may be interested in the magnitudes or amplitude of each response, and in the way in which this or some other feature changes across a series of stimuli, for example in the study of habituation. The response of interest may consist in a change in rate, for example in the analysis of heart rate data or respiration. Similarly, as in the case of EEG or EMG, we may be concerned with the appearance of phasic features against a background of tonic activity. Alternatively, as in the analysis of eyelid conditioning data, SRR responding or penile plethysmography we may be interested in measuring a series of discrete waveforms.

Our strategy is to divide the measurements into response elements, response derivatives, and response composites. Response elements are the simplest points of interest such as those which, as has already been discussed, a computer might extract for the purpose of response detection. Response derivatives are those measures which can be obtained by simple algebraic summation of the response elements, for example the definition of response amplitude as the difference in level between onset and peak. We use the term response composites to refer to more complex combinations of measures designed to reflect some aspect of the behaviour of the response which is imposed on it by the interest of the observer.

3.1 Response elements

These are the basic features of the response, some of which will have been used in response identification. They include the time and amplitude at the response onset, the time and amplitude at response peak, and the point of return to zero activity. In selecting the elements of interest we are concerned with the information available and the information to be retained, and these will be considered separately.

When we talk about points of interest it is not immediately obvious that we are invariably talking about inflexions of the waveform. These inflexions represent the significant changes of acceleration in the level of activity of some system represented by the waveform. The concept has been discussed earlier in describing the use of line segments in the program of response identification. The response itself is a segment of continuous activity bounded by an onset and termination which identify the limits of the response. Within this segment any change in level of activity, together with its associated time coordinates, may be potentially of interest.

These changes in acceleration are dictated by the nature of the waveform, though they may not be of interest to the observer. It is important to note that each of these points has a time value and a level, each of which can be represented numerically. Thus no matter how complex the response, the waveform itself can be specified as a vector of values whose ordinal positions represent the discrete time points of the response. It is in this form that the computer program uses the information to select and store the response features.

While it is evident that this type of analysis makes available more information than is needed, it serves to remind us that in looking at responses we are interested in changes of activity of the system under study. Any other method is likely to be some variant of this form of analysis. The use of a template will superimpose another set of coordinates whose distances from the points of interest can be measured. Similarly, a discriminant analysis would work by taking these points of interest and exaggerating or weighting the distances between them. From an analytic viewpoint, the two essential pieces of data are the paired values of the coordinates.

It has been noted already that not all of the available information is likely to be used. Indeed, the selection of points of interest has already discarded some of the information in the waveform. In deciding which points of interest are to be retained three major considerations are implied in the analysis: their relevance, their significance, and their fidelity to the data. The interest of the observer is likely to determine what is relevant to a particular response system given a particular observational paradigm. For example, onset latency, that is the time coordinate of the first inflexion, may be the principle measure of interest in studies concerned with speed of reactivity. The use of onset and recovery measures as monitors of electrodermal activity has been fully discussed by Venables and Christie (1973); similarly, other points of interest may be used in isolation depending upon their relevance to the interest of the observer.

The problem of summarizing data, that is of retaining what is relevant and eliminating what is irrelevant, is concerned with defining and unitizing the best and most appropriate samples of behaviour. This is true of psychological testing, for example, and of other experimental investigations, but in psychophysiology the fact that we are usually dealing with a waveform raises additional problems, for example, the possible non-independence of statistical analysis and sampling.

The decision to retain a particular response feature will depend on its relevance to the observer, and this must also involve some judgment as to its physiological significance. In the past these decisions were often imposed by the necessity of economy, but the present era of widespread availability of computer facilities has lifted many of these restrictions. There is an argument for reconsidering the significance of individual data points, and there has been a recent spate of interest in retaining more information on the topography of the response.

In these terms, the fidelity of the measurements retained to the waveform as a whole has assumed increasing importance. There is a sense in which a waveform is a unique type of data, as distinct from other kinds of numerical data, and it may be this uniqueness which interests the investigator. For example, in studies of habituation or conditioning in autonomic systems, we are interested in the progress of a change, which is represented in relatively minor differences in the successive responses. While we have often been satisfied in the past with measures of peak amplitude, the techniques of data analysis available at present allow us to study much more intricate changes. Thus selection of interest points to be retained and stored must be influenced by considerations of the extent to which they faithfully represent changes in the response from beginning to end and from occasion to occasion.

Finally, the selection of data, in terms of the fidelity to the overall form, will determine the usefulness of derived and composite measures to be discussed next. As psychophysiologists we select points of interest and we hope that these points of interest have captured the representative aspects of the data.

3.2 Response derivatives

Response derivatives, or derived measures, are defined as those which arise when the response elements are algebraically compared. This way of looking at physiological data is derived from the methods used in computer analysis. It is not immediately apparent that when one has defined points of interest as pairs of coordinates, the form of data used by the computer, one is already talking about derived measures. The SARA program first identifies the points of interest and then generates a series of measures derived from them separately. For example, in order to define response amplitude it is necessary to subtract the amplitude of the waveform at the onset or point of first inflexion, from the amplitude at peak or maximum level of zero velocity. Again it is convenient to discuss this area in terms of information available and the information to be retained.

Apart from the maximum amplitude of a response the available information includes the amplitude at other points during its time course. These may include amplitude at the presentation of some second stimulus, for example in conditioning or CNV studies, or the amplitude of local minima or peaks in the course of a multiple response. Whether these local minima are of significance is likely to be determined by their consistency from response to response. For example, the identification of the P300 segment in ERP studies is based on the consistency of the waveform, often within individual laboratories.

The common derived measures are response amplitude, response duration, and rise time. Others are the area under the waveform, or the mean level of the waveform, particularly useful when a waveform is complex, duration of the recovery limb, and duration to 50% recovery, which avoids the problem of spurious activity immediately following a response. A derived measure which we have found useful in the study of eyelid conditioning is the time from half amplitude to half recovery, which is sensitive to changes in stimulus intensity and interstimulus interval.

The use of rise time, that is the time from onset to peak activity, has a rough approximation to the slope of the response which can now be readily measured by software differentiation. Similarly the area under the waveform is most efficiently measured by integration, and these numerical analyses represent more complex forms of derived measurement. One advantage of the computer analysis of waveforms, and of the strategy of detection and measurement presented here is that it enables the investigator to formulate derived measures which would not be immediately apparent on the chart record and which may be found to have significance for the system under observation.

The decision as to which of the possible derived measures are to be retained and further analysed is influenced by the factors discussed earlier, namely their relevance, significance and fidelity to the waveform and to the system under observation. For many response systems the duration of the response may not be important, while for responses like CNV and EMG it is of crucial interest. The slope of an eyelid conditioned response is important in determining the sensitivity of the response system and in defining 'voluntary' responding, while the slope of a heart rate segment is usually of trivial interest. It should be noted that the derived measures are equally applicable to averaged responses and to isolated responses, and indeed averaging may be necessary to detect the response elements necessary in computing derived measures. Multiple waveforms introduce special problems. Depending upon the nature of the transducer, the respiratory waveform may show multiple response features which are of little interest. For example, the use of a strain gauge may introduce skeletal components attributable to rigidity of the thorax, while the use of a thermistor may introduce inflexions due to flow turbulence which momentarily influence the ambient air temperature. Although these are consistent, they are of little interest when we are concerned chiefly with the depth and rate of inspiration and expiration. By contrast, some aspects of multiple responding may be of interest, for example SRR measurement in the context of autonomic conditioning.

Recent interest in the recovery limb of the SRR response, while controversial, illustrates the heuristic value of analysing derived measures other than those of amplitude (Edelberg, 1970, 1973; Edelberg and Muller, 1977). The work of Mednick and Schulsinger (1968) in applying this type of measure to pathologies of development has attracted wide interest. A further example is the identification of the alpha blink in eyelid conditioning by Grant and Norris (1947). This identification was made from histograms of onset latencies and amplitudes which revealed a separate subpopulation of low amplitude, short latency responses which had previously been regarded as conditioned responses, but which were shown to be a form of orienting response. The same author's identification of medium latency beta responses as being due to light sensitization (Grant, 1945) enabled significant clarification of the nature of conditioned responding in subsequent studies.

The argument of this section is that modern computer oriented methods of data detection and analysis enable us to define measures which give a summary of the waveform which increases the information available. They provide measures of change in the response and also provide measures of change between responses. As such they may be sensitive to individual differences or to experimental conditions or both, and they may have heuristic and theoretical value in describing the underlying physiological properties. The introduction of these methods has led us away from the laborious task of hand scoring chart records and potentially opens new areas for investigation.

3.3 Response composites

A composite measure is a combination of response elements and derivatives into holistic patterns which reflect activity of interest to the investigator, and is likely to arise from some theoretical consideration in the study of a particular response system. In discussing measures of this type reference will be made to some eyelid conditioning studies, in which we have found them singularly useful. First, however, a description of their historical origins will be outlined.

The type of composite measure used most frequently has been the derivation of a ratio reflecting the relationship between two or more response derivatives which are held to have significance for the system under study. Probably the earliest example of a composite measure was the inspiration/expiration ratio used in studies of respiration in the 1940s. While crude, this measure was used by earlier investigators to study patterns of attention and aesthetic preference among others. Before the days of information theory the hypothesis underlying this measure was that inspiration represents intake of stimulus content, and the assumption was made that increased duration of inspiration relative to expiration represented increased willingness to absorb information from the environment.

Work on eyelid conditioning among American investigators has been much influenced by the distinction between voluntary (V) responses and conditioned responses, and an extensive literature has grown up regarding this distinction in response type. The practice has been to identify the V form response by its visual characteristics of short latency, rapid rise time, and long duration. Subjects who exhibited a proportion of V form responses over some conventional criterion were discarded from the analysis on the assumption that they had failed to condition and had substituted voluntary closure of the eyelid.

Subsequently Hartman and Ross (1961) offered a criterion for classifying V form responses which was essentially a composite measure. They selected the average maximum slope of the UCR on the first few trials preceding the appearance of a conditioned response as the criterion slope for that subject. This averaged peak derivative was then used to form a ratio with the peak derivative of each conditioned response as the numerator. Classification of the frequency histograms for these values resulted in the identification of V form responses as those having greater than 50% of the criterion peak slope. Subsequent work, using this objective classification, has shown that V form responding is probably not simply a voluntary response but shows characteristics which can be related to hemisphere dominance and to linear or global modes of information processing (e.g. Grant, 1972; Hellige, 1974) which are of considerable theoretical interest to the physiology of the response system. Thus the use of a composite measure provides an objective criterion for separating responses into the two types which resulted in an important clarification of the nature of the underlying processes.

3.3.1 Measurement of composites

The rationale of composite measures in the sense used here is to examine some aspect of responding which is of interest for the topography of the response, independently of some measure which represents one of its basic characteristics. For example, in conditioning studies the amplitude of the UCR on a particular trial may be taken as representing the maximum response energy available on that trial, and the amplitude of the conditioned response (CR) may be examined independently of that maximum as a function of changes over trials, to reflect the topographic development of the response. We have chosen to use ratio measures in this way because they are intuitively satisfying in terms of the physiological processes underlying the response, but a similar goal may be achieved by using covariance techniques to examine statistical independence of the response features of interest. It is reassuring that when the latter method is applied (Martin and Levey, 1969) the results are not in contradiction while the ratio measures are more easily interpreted.

Our work on the 'efficiency' of the conditioned eyelid response serves to illustrate this approach. Interest in the concept of response efficiency arose from observation of changes in the developing response which appeared to reflect an underlying learning process which was not represented in the usual frequency curve of response acquisition. In order to examine these changes objectively all possible aspects of the CR and UCR were measured, including onset latency, peak latency, peak amplitude of both responses, and also the amplitude of the CR at the moment of impact of the UCS and at the onset of the UCR. Derived measures generated by these data included rise time, rate of rise, proximity of CR peak latency to unconditioned stimulus (UCS) onset, and so on. The question asked of the data was whether there are response elements or response derivatives and composites which show consistent trends either linear or curvilinear during the course of acquisition for individual subjects. The argument is that those measures that show consistent changes during acquisition reflect the aspect

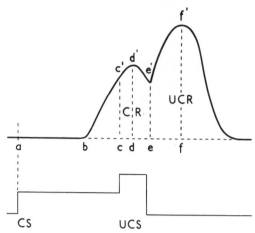

Figure 13.11 The major parameters of the conditioned and unconditioned response: (a) CS onset; (b) CR onset; (c) UCS onset; (d) point of maximum CR amplitude; (e) UCR onset; (f) point of maximum UCR amplitude. CS = 1000 Hz tone; UCS = airpuff. CS–UCS interval = 400 ms

of responding which the subject is optimizing or maximizing in the course of learning the response, and in this sense describe what the CR accomplishes for the organism.

Examples of response composites are given in Figure 13.11. If the amplitude of the CR at the moment of onset of the UCR is taken as a ratio of the amplitude of the UCR (ee′/ff′) the resultant measures show significant linear increase during acquisition. These changes discriminate among experimental conditions which are not identified by differences in response frequency, with which this measure is virtually uncorrelated. We have described this measure as performing part of the physiological work of the UCR and have labelled it the 'work ratio'. It represents the extent to which the CR and UCR are integrated, such that the lid is partially closed when the UCR begins. If the same amplitude is taken as a proportion of the CR itself (ee′/dd′) a different measure results. This measure rapidly maximizes and tends to remain stable. It appears to represent the efficiency with which the CR itself is employed, that is, the extent to which it is used or wasted in relation to the goal of integration and this measure we have labelled the 'utility ratio'. Another measure uses the area under the response (Figure 13.12) and represents essentially a combined function of peak amplitude and rise time which appears to reflect the amount of energy expended in responding. Pennypacker (1964)

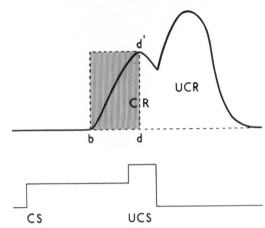

Figure 13.12 The 'response area' of the CR (bd.dd') derives from CR amplitude and duration

has used a similar measure calculated by direct measurement of the actual area. He found significant differentiation amongst experimental conditions using the average value summed across trials and this measure also was independent of response frequency.

One implication which follows from the use of composite measures is

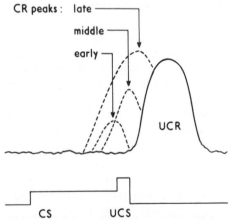

Figure 13.13 Schematic representation of changes in response amplitude and latency early, middle, and late in the course of CR acquisition. The increase in amplitude and efficiency necessitates a compensatory decrease in latency, following an initial increase

that some subtle balance among response elements, onset latency, amplitude, etc., must occur in order that the CR be shaped in an effective response topography. That response elements can be integrated in many different ways to form alternative CR shapes is shown in Figure 13.13. In order to maximize amplitude, rise time or latency must be adjusted and vice versa. The figure shows how variable response amplitude can be achieved either by varying onset latency or rise time. This work has suggested that these changes in response topography are sensitive to stimulus conditions, to personality variables, and may have significance for understanding the fundamental nature of classical conditioning.

The physiological processes underlying the conditioned response must subserve adaptive ends for the organism and measures of this type may show what is accomplished by the CR. In particular, they can be used to determine objectively whether, or under what circumstances, the classical eyelid response is an avoidance response, and to what extent the underlying mechanism is independent of the reward conditions of the experiment. Evidence to date suggests that the integration of the CR and the UCR represent some fundamental property of conditioning, but that UCS intensity beyond some maximum also introduces an instrumental reward component, or instrumental overlay.

This type of composite topographical analysis of waveform has also been applied to electrodermal data (Kimmel, 1965; Martin, Levey, and Slubicka, 1975) to describe in detail the changes in the response topography brought about by conditioning. The conditioned behaviour of the nictitating membrane response has been studied in relation to progressive change in the shaping of this response with convincing evidence being produced for some intrinsic physiological mechanism other than reward (Smith, 1968; Gormezano, 1972). Barr and McConaghy (1973) have applied this type of composite measure to the study of penile plethysmography and have shown that similar changes occur.

3.3.2 Theoretical problems

The use of composite measures involves some theoretical problems which are relevant to the problems of response measurement. The physiological significance of response topography, and of changes in response topography, is as yet little understood. Measures of response topography have not been widely applied, for example to the EMG or EEG, though their use in CNV analysis has been advocated by Loveless (1979). It is in the nature of these measures that they make assumptions about the underlying nature of the process and it is possible that these can be self-confirming if the measures are not derived objectively and used with reasonable care. It must be asked whether there is a point at which the investigator superimposes a concept on the waveform which may insult the real nature of the response.

On the other hand, the usefulness both practical and theoretical of this approach has been reasonably well established. The use of range correction in SRR measurement (Lykken and coworkers, 1966) is an example of a composite measure in which response amplitudes are defined as a proportion of an agreed maximum response which has proved to be useful in response measurement. On the theoretical side an example can again be cited from eyelid conditioning literature where a controversy concerning the law of effect can only be answered by reference to response topography, and where objectively defined measures of topography are essential (Gormezano and Kehoe, 1975).

In summary, the use of composite measures, whether in the form of relatively simple ratios or in more complex mathematical forms seems to offer a tool for studying changes within the response and between responses which may have considerable heuristic and theoretical promise. The use of computer analysis of response elements, derivatives and composites has made possible a range of investigations which would not be practical in terms of hand scoring.

4 SUMMARY AND IMPLICATIONS

This chapter has described in a general way some of the problems and methods in response detection and analysis. It has aimed to bring together the general methods, of which specific examples will be found in the substantive material of other chapters dealing with specific response systems. We have concentrated on the measurement of waveforms to the neglect of other measures of response systems. These include the analysis of frequency data for response systems such as heart rate in which the problems of change in response frequency are paramount. The analysis of beat by beat or second by second heart rate changes introduces problems which are not directly related to the concepts of response detection and analysis employed in the previous discussion. A detailed examination of these problems is to be found in Chapter 3. To summarize, we have presented a method of response detection and analysis which begins with the criteria for detecting a response as an objective event, and have reviewed the available methods. We have outlined an approach to the selection of interest points and the measures derived from them which is appropriate to the use of computers and can be readily implemented. It remains to discuss some implications of this approach.

The past decade has seen an increase in detailed analysis of responses in a number of psychophysiological fields. From an era in which psychophysiology was concerned chiefly with the frequency and amplitude of responding in a variety of autonomic systems, we have entered an era in which the details of response topography are beginning to yield new information. It is to be hoped that one of the outcomes of this development will be a move away from stereotyped concepts of what the response does and towards a re-examination of the essential features of responding in the physiological systems in which we are interested. Such an approach offers the possibility of generating testable models of physiological processes which take account of an optimum amount of the available data. The application of simulation techniques to the testing of such models is entirely feasible, and may offer a new approach to the understanding of psychophysiological data.

In the last analysis, however, it is essential to remember that we are studying physiological systems and their activity, and that the data which we analyse are merely representations of this activity. There is a pardonable tendency in the laboratory to reify the record generated by a transducer and to regard it as primary data. We must continue to match methods of analysis to these data, examining critically the match of the analyses to visual characteristics of the data, to its physiological significance, and to the sense in which it represents the psychological milieu in which measurements are recorded. We must also bear in mind that our ultimate interest is in describing and understanding the physiological responses themselves.

APPENDIX: COMPUTER PROCEDURES

In computer terms, the analog representation of a variable as length across a polygraph chart is replaced by a measurement of an analog voltage, stored within the computer as a number in a table of such numbers. Analog voltages are normally readily available, being the usual representation of any variable during processing by a polygraph amplifier. An analog to digital convertor is used to make a measurement of the voltage presented at its input, on command from the computer, and transfer the numerical value of the voltage to the computer for storage. As with a length analog, a scale factor is required which relates voltage as measured to the true value of the variable. This scale factor also depends on the sensitivity settings of the polygraph amplifiers and is normally supplied separately to the computer by the user.

The equivalent of the chart paper speed control is provided by the rate at which measurements of the analog voltage are being made and entered into the table. As with chart speed, an appropriate measurement rate for any given variable may be found by experience, but with some help from information theory. A minimum measurement rate is two measurements per cycle of the highest frequency component present in the variable being measured, including any noise content. The noise must be taken into account so as to avoid the transformation of high frequencies into lower ones that would distort the measurements. When measurements are being taken at the minimum rate each measurement will be independent, that is there will be a low serial correlation between measurements and the number of degrees of freedom in the data will be equal to the number of measurements. At higher rates consecutive measurements will be correlated and the number of degrees of freedom will be less than the number of measurements. A higher than minimum rate is desirable for good graphic displays and the quality of the displays may be used as a check on the measurement rate. For skin resistance, measurement rates between a minimum of 5 per second up to about 20 per second have been used, depending on the accuracy required for the measurement of time. Taking a measurement rate of 10 per second as typical, a table of 500 measurements will be required to represent within the computer a 50 second segment of a polygraph chart recording.

Since a slope criterion is to be used, the initial operation will be to obtain from the table of measurements a second table of the corresponding slope values, that is the rate of change of the measurements, or in mathematical terms to differentiate the measurements with respect to time. A problem that must be considered at this stage is that the operation of differentiation can be considered as equivalent to a high pass filter, increasing the level of the high frequency components of the measured variable in relation to the lower frequency components. Since the high frequency components tend to be associated with noise and artifacts, differentiation will tend to increase any noise present in the data. It is therefore important that differentiation should be combined with a smoothing operation to reduce the noise level, and these two operations will be considered together.

SMOOTHING AND DIFFERENTIATION

In the particular implementation used to develop the automatic scoring programs, three stages of smoothing were used, the first stage being combined with the measurement program. In taking a stored table of discrete measurements as representing a continuous variable it is assumed that each measurement is a good estimate of the level of the variable over the time interval between the measurement points. If only a single measurement is taken during the interval it may well coincide with a noise peak, and thus not provide a good estimate of level. It is therefore better to take measurements at a faster rate than required and to take an average of the measurements made over the required interval as an estimate of level for entry into the stored table. The averaging process is equivalent to a smoothing filter, reducing the noise level of the stored data.

The second stage of smoothing that was provided was a specific smoothing operation that could be applied to the data as many times as required by the user. A running weighted average was used, averaging over 5 measurements with weights of 1/16, 1/4, 3/8, 1/4, and 1/16. That is, given a table of measurements M with M_i as the ith entry in the table, then a new table of smoothed measurements (SM) was formed, where

$$SM_i = 1/16*M_{i-2} + 1/4*M_{i-1} + 3/8*M_i + 1/4*M_{i+1} + 1/16*M_{i+2}$$

Provision was made for graphic displays which allowed the smoothed data to be compared visually with the original data, so that the effect of smoothing could be assessed.

The third stage of smoothing was combined with the computation of the slope values. Given a table of measurements M (smoothed as required), then a table of slope values S was formed where–

$$S_i = M_{i+2} - M_{i-2}$$

This is equivalent in terms of geometry to taking the slope of the chord of a segment of the variable as being equal to the slope of the tangent at the mid-point of the segment. The approximation involved is equivalent to a smoothing operation on the slope data. Again, graphic displays were provided which allowed the slope data to be compared visually with the measurement data.

REFERENCES

Barr, R. F., and McConaghy, N. (1973). A general factor of conditionability: a study of galvanic skin responses and penile responses. *Beh. Res. Therapy*, **10**, 215–27.

Donchin, E., and Herning, R. J. (1975). A simulation study of the efficacy of stepwise discriminant analysis in the detection and comparison of event related potentials. *Electroenceph. Clin. Neurophysiol.*, **38**, 51–68.

Edelberg, R. (1970). The information content of the recovery limb of the electrodermal response. *Psychophysiology*, 6, 527–39.

Edelberg, R. (1973). Mechanisms of electrodermal adaptations for locomotion, manipulation, or defense. In E. Stellar and J. M. Sprague (Eds), *Progress in Physiological Psychology*, Vol. 5, pp. 155–209. Academic Press. New York.

Edelberg, R., and Muller, M. (1977). The status of the electrodermal recovery measure. *A caveat. Paper presented at the 17th Annual Meeting of the Society for Psychophysiological Research, Philadelphia, October, 1977.*

Fenwick, P., Michie, P., Dollimore, J., and Fenton, G. (1971). Mathematical simulation of the electroencephalogram using an autoregressive series. *Biomed. Comput.*, **2**, 281–307.

Egan, J. P. (1975). *Signal Detection Theory and ROC Analysis*. Academic Press, New York.

Gormezano, I. (1972). Investigations of defense and reward conditioning in the rabbit. In A. H. Black and W. F. Prokasy (Eds), *Classical Conditioning II: Current Theory and Research*, Appleton–Century–Crofts, New York.

Gormezano, I., and Kehoe, E. J. (1975). Classical Conditioning: some methodological–conceptual issues. In W. K. Estes (Ed.), *Handbook of Learning and Cognitive Processes*, Vol. 2, Wiley, New York.

Gotman, J., and Gloor, P. (1976). Automatic recognition and quantification of interictal epileptic activity in the human scalp EEG. *Electroenceph. Clin. Neurophysiol.*, **41**, 513–29.

Gotman, J., Gloor, P., and Schaul, N. (1978). Comparison of traditional reading of the EEG and automatic recognition of interictal epileptic acitivity. *Electroenceph. Clin. Neurophysiol.*, **44**, 48–60.

Grant, D. A. (1945). A sensitised eyelid reaction related to the conditioned eyelid response. *J. Exp. Psychol.*, **35**, 393–402.

Grant, D. A. (1972). A preliminary model for processing information conveyed by verbal conditioning stimuli in classical differential conditioning. In A. H. Black and W. F. Prokasy (Eds), *Classical Conditioning II: Current Theory and Research*, Appleton–Century–Crofts, New York.

Grant, D. A., and Norris, E. B. (1947). Eyelid conditioning as influenced by the presence of sensitised beta-responses. *J. Exp. Psychol.*, **37**, 423–33.

Hartman T. F., and Ross, L. E. (1961). An alternative criterion for the elimination of 'voluntary' responses in eyelid conditioning. *J. Exp. Psychol.*, **61**, 334–8.

Hellige, J. B. (1974). Hemispheric processing differences revealed by differential conditioning and reaction time performance. *PhD Thesis*, University of Wisconsin, unpublished.

Kimmel, H. D. (1965). Instrumental inhibitory factors in classical conditioning. In W. F. Prokasy (Ed.), *Classical Conditioning*, Appleton–Century–Crofts, New York. pp 148–71.

Loveless, N. (1979). Event-related slow potentials of the brain as expressions of orienting function. In: H. D. Kimmel, E. H. van Olst, and J. F. Orlebecke, (Eds) *The Orienting Reflex in Humans* (in press).

Lykken, D. T., Rose, R., Luther, B., and Maley, M. (1966). Correcting psychophysiological measures for individual differences in range. *Psychol. Bull.*, **66**, 481–4.

Martin, I., and Levey, A. B. (1969). *The Genesis of the Classical Conditioned Response*, Pergamon, Oxford.

Martin, I., Levey, A. B., and Slubicka, B. (1975). Response relationships in SRR conditioning. *Psychophysiology*, **12**, 83–9.

Mednick, S. A., and Schulsinger, F. (1968). Some pre-morbid characteristics related to breakdown in children with schizophrenic mothers. In D. Rosenthal and S. S. Kety (Eds), *The Transmission of Schizophrenia*, Pergamon, New York. pp. 267–91.

Pennypacker, H. S. (1964). Measurement of the conditioned eyelid reflex. *Science*, **144**, 1248–9.

Smith, M. C. (1968). CS-UCS interval and US intensity in classical conditioning of the rabbit's nictitating membrane response. *J. comp. Physiol. Psychol.*, **66**, 679–87.

Venables, P. H., and Christie, M. J. (1973). Mechanisms, instrumentation, recording techniques and identification of responses. In W. F. Prokasy and D. C.

Raskin (Eds), *Electrodermal Activity in Psychological Research*, Academic, New York.

Weinberg, H., and Cooper, R. (1972). The recognition index: A pattern recognition technique for noisy signals. *Electroenceph. Clin. Neurophysiol.*, **33**, 608–13.

Wicke, J. D., Goff, W. R., Wallace, J. D., and Allison, T. (1978). On-line statistical detection of average evoked potentials: Application to evoked response audiometry. *Electroenceph. Clin. Neurophysiol.*, **44**, 328–43.

Glossary

acceleration

(i) An increase in the rate of change of a variable with respect to time. When applied to heart rate, this implies an increase in heart rate or if expressed as heart period, a shortening of the interbeat interval.

(ii) An increase in rate, with deceleration being a decrease in rate. Mathematically, deceleration is usually expressed as a negative acceleration. The terms velocity and acceleration in their usual meaning are derived as the first and second differentials of position with respect to time. By analogy they may be used for the first and second differentials of any variable with respect to time.

agar-agar (New Zealand)

A substance derived from sea-weed, useful as an electrolyte medium. To be distinguished from nutrient agar-agar which is used as a culture medium.

algorithm

A specified procedure for performing a particular calculation. A general recipe for a mathematical operation.

aliasing

The phenomenon of the reflection of frequency values with respect to half the sampling frequency (in computer analysis of electrophysiological signals in the frequency domain) or with respect to frequency zero. The effect is termed aliasing since unwanted frequencies appear under the alias of wanted frequencies.

ambulatory devices

Means of recording signals from freely moving subjects over comparatively short distances; they may involve radio telemetry or recordings on portable miniature tape recorders.

amplitude/magnitude of SCR

Mean amplitude: the mean size of response calculated over all occasions on which a response is present.

Mean magnitude: the mean size of response calculated over all occasions on which a response might be given, i.e. over all times when a stimulus is presented.

analog to digital convertor

Analog records are continuous records of changing voltage level. Computer analysis requires that voltage levels be converted to a series of discrete numerical values coded in computer bits, i.e. to digital form. This involves two steps: defining the length of the temporal period separating successive voltage samples, and converting the sampled voltages to numbers. The first step defines the sampling rate. For example, if the temporal period is 10 ms the sampling rate is 100/s. An analog to digital convertor is an electronic device for accomplishing this process.

anti-aliasing filters

A low pass analog filter used to eliminate any frequencies higher than the Nyquist or folding frequency.

apocrine

One of two types of sweat glands (*see* Eccrine) of limited importance in electrodermal measurement.

artifact

Unwanted electrical signals which impose 'noise' on the signal of interest. One common source is electrical interference from the alternating mains supply; another is high electrode resistance. When artifacts are caused by movement of the subject, this usually arises from a fluctuation in voltage arising from mechanical disturbance of the skin/electrolyte/metal juncture.

auto-correlation

Correlation between a waveform and the same waveform shifted in time, for all possible time shifts. When expressed as a function of the time shift gives the autocorrelation function. By definition will be symmetrical about the zero time shift axis and have unity value for zero time shift.

autoregression

A technique used in time series analysis to construct a statistical model of a set of sequential observations with respect to time. An autoregressive model expresses the current observations in terms of the current disturbance and all the past observations.

autospectrum

See Spectrum

averaging

The process whereby the sum of many measurements (or sets of measurements) is divided by the number of measurements in order to form the mean value or average. This technique can be used to distinguish a small signal that is unrecognizable in other activity. If the signal is consistently related to a stimulus and the background activity quite random in relation to that stimulus, averaging the responses to many stimuli will leave the signal quite constant but will cause the background activity to decrease in amplitude. 'Square root averaging' is a term that may be used to describe the process whereby the sum of a series of measurements is divided by the square root of the number of measurements.

backing-off

The operation of opposing a potential (possibly representing another value, such as conductance) by an equal and opposite potential so as to suppress a tonic level and hence enable phasic responses to be measured at greater gain. (Synonymous with bucking, suppression.)

bandpass filter
band selective filtering
See Filter.

bandwidth

In the EEG, bandwidth is used to refer to a clustering of frequencies, e.g. 0.5–4 Hz or 8–12 Hz.

beamwidth

A measure of the width of a beam of light or other radiation. Since the edges of a beam are seldom clearly defined the width is taken between points where the power has fallen to half its value in the centre of the beam. Usually expressed as an angle relative to the source.

bias potential

Potentials inherent in electrodes appearing as error in measurement.

bi-spectrum

A statistical technique applied in time-series analysis and used to compute the degree of interaction of component waves making up a single trace.

bit

Contraction of binary digit. In the binary system of numbering only the digit values 1 and 0 are used. Also a unit of information when the two values correspond to true and false.

blood glucose
Principal energy yielding carbohydrate.

blood plasma

Natural liquid medium in which cellular elements of blood are suspended.

boundary conditions

In optics, a boundary condition occurs when the light passes through media of different refractive indices. At the optical boundary, the distribution of light in space may be altered.

bucking

See Backing-off.

byte

A group of eight adjacent bits that can represent one alphanumeric character, two decimal digits or two hexadecimal digits.

cadmium selenide

A semiconductor material whose resistance varies with level of illumination, used in the measurement of light. Similar to the more widely used material cadmium sulphide but having a faster response to changes in light level. Both have relatively slow response times (tens of milliseconds) compared with less sensitive devices based on silicon (microseconds).

calibration

Methods for defining an accurate and known relationship between the input and output of a system. Usually involves inputting a known quantity (e.g. a known resistance) and noting the response of the system.

capacitive reactance

See Reactance

cardiotachometer

A device for measuring heart rate and heart period. Strictly, an accurate measure of heart rate can only be obtained by counting the number of beats produced in one minute (or 30 secs. or 15 secs. if less accuracy is required), but a cardiotachometer usually measures interbeat interval (i.e. interval between R wave components). This time is either displayed directly, in which case a non-linear calibration in terms of rate is required, or converted to reciprocal form to give a linear rate scale.

cartesian coordinates

Coordinates from any N-dimensional space such that the axes from this space are mutually orthogonal and the absolute values of any unit length are the same. The familiar X, Y plane is cartesian if one unit along the X-axis is the same as one unit along the Y-axis.

cascading

The filtering of data by using two or more filters. The output of one filter is the input to the next.

catecholamines

Family of organic compounds with endocrine and transmitter functions, principally Dopamine, Noradrenaline and Adrenaline.

cluster analysis

A mathematical technique of allocating objects into groups such that all objects in a given group have similar properties and all objects with similar properties are in the same group.

coherence spectrum

See Spectrum.

coherence averaging

The computation of average coherence values over several coherence spectra.

collimated illumination

Illumination in which the individual rays of light (or other radiation) have been made parallel. Hence the source of the illumination appears to be located at infinity.

common mode rejection

The efficiency of the common mode rejection is described by the discrimination ratio of the amplifier; it relates to the discrimination of in-phase (e.g. unwanted 50 Hz interference) over anti-phase (e.g. biological) signals.

computer

An instrument designed to perform mathematical calculations and logical operations according to instructions programmed by the operator. An *analog* computer is one that uses continuous variables and performs its calculations by modelling equations in electronic components. A *digital* computer is one that uses discrete numerical values for its arithmetical and logical operations. A *general purpose* computer is one that can be used either for handling large amounts of data independently of any supervision, or for handling smaller amounts of data in continuous interaction with an operator. A *hybrid* computer is one that combines both analog and digital processes. A *special purpose* computer is a small computer that is designed to do one particular function, such as signal averaging.

constant current methods

A method of measuring skin resistance where the current through the skin between two electrodes is maintained at a constant value.

constant voltage methods

A method of measuring skin conductance where the potential across electrodes on the skin surface is maintained at a constant value.

Cooley–Tukey fast Fourier transform algorithm

A method, first published in 1965, that drastically reduced the amount of time required to perform a Fourier transform on a set of data. The data length must be 2^N, where N is an integer, for maximum efficiency. For a data series length of 1024, the speed advantage for the fast Fourier transform is 30 to 1.

covariance (analysis of)

An extension of the method of analysis of variance: (i) to reduce experimental error; (ii) to analyse the effect of independent variables on the covariance of two dependent variables.

cross-correlation

The correlation between two signals of similar pattern but occurring at different times.

cross-spectrum

See Spectrum.

deceleration

A decrease in the rate of change of a variable with respect to time. When applied to cardiac data, this implies a decrease in heart rate or if expressed as heart period, a lengthening of the interbeat interval.

demodulation

A process by which the carrier frequency is removed and the modulation frequencies retained.

dicrotic notch

A small oscillation on the falling phase of the arterial pulse wave. It is due to vibrations generated by closure of the aortic valve.

digital voltmeter

A device for measuring voltage with the result being produced as an actual number rather than a pointer position relative to a scale.

dipole

A dipole generator may be thought of as a source of electrical potential whose length is small relative to the extent of the medium in which it is situated and whose poles are of equal magnitude but of opposite polarity, one positive and the other negative. An alternating dipole is one in which these polarities are constantly reversing. When such a dipole is embedded in a conducting medium, it gives rise to an alternating potential field which extends throughout the medium and causes alternating current to flow in it.

discriminant analysis

A statistical process whereby two or more groups of measurements are most effectively distinguished. This is usually done on the basis of a discriminant function that describes the most important differences between the groups of measurements.

Drohocki amplitude integrator

A time series analyser in the frequency domain. A continuous processing method in the frequency domain which has a minimum time resolution of 1/400 of a second and displays the summed amplitudes of the primary waves as a proportional number of simple spikes per unit time.

eccrine

One of two types of sweat glands (*see* Apocrine) of major importance as a mechanism in electro-dermal measurement; distributed all over body but with maximum density on palms of hands and soles of feet.

EEG frequency bands

Conventionally divided into:
   alpha (8–13 Hz)
   beta (18–24 Hz)
   delta (0.5–4 Hz)
   fast beta (21–24 Hz)
   slow beta (13–20 Hz)
   spindling activity (12–14 Hz)
   theta (5–7 Hz)
also kappa, lambda waves, K complexes.

electrodermal activity

General term for the electrical activity of the skin which covers both skin conductance and skin potential activity (*q.v.*).

electrode

A device providing a connection between an electrical circuit and an electrolyte. A probe for allowing the passage of electrical activity. This may be for recording or for stimulation. Usually a medium (cup, disk, needle, pad) used to transmit electrical activity between an electric conductor or source to a recording or display instrument.

electrodes, bipolar

Electrodes placed over two electrically active sites.

electrodes, reversible

Electrodes consisting of a metal in contact with a solution containing its own ions.

electrodes, silver/silver chloride

Electrode consisting of pure silver with an electrolytic coating of silver chloride; the most commonly used reversible electrode in current use by psychophysiologists.

electrodes, 10–20 system

A standardized guide to locating EEG electrodes on the scalp, based upon measurements from nasion to inion and from right to left pre-auricular points. Designed to ensure equal interelectrode spacings along any anteroposterior or transverse line.

electrolyte

A substance (usually a salt, acid or base), which in solution dissociates wholly or partly into electrically charged particles known as ions; more commonly in a psychophysiological context the term is also used to denote the solution itself which has a higher electrical conductivity than the pure solvent.

electrolytes

Elements capable of existing in ionized form, principally sodium, potassium, chloride and calcium.

electrolyte medium

A substance used to 'bulk out' an electrolyte to render it viscous or paste-like.

electromagnetic field

Every electrical circuit carrying an alternating current radiates a certain amount of electrical energy in the form of electromagnetic waves. Each radiator has directional characteristics resulting in a pattern of stronger and weaker waves known as the electromagnetic field.

electromagnetic spectrum

The entire range of frequencies of electromagnetic radiation from very low frequency through radio frequencies to visible light and gamma rays.

electrostatic potentials

Non-physiological electrical activity induced in a subject by such things as friction in clothing caused by movement.

endosomatic

Measurement of electrodermal activity due to changes in potential and resistance inherent in the skin itself.

epidermis

The outer layer of the skin containing aspects of importance in electrodermal measurement.

epsilon

An index of the homogeneity of a variance–covariance matrix.

epsilon correction

Statistical technique used in the analysis of variance, when repeated observations from the same subject have been obtained. This situation usually gives rise to unequal variance–covariance matrices which violate assumptions underlying the analysis. Epsilon provides a correction factor for the number of degrees of freedom associated with significance testing of repeated measures factors.

event-related potentials (ERP)

Changes in electrical activity, most frequently recorded from the surface of the scalp and occurring in response to physical stimuli.

ERP components

Aspects of the ERP whose identification most commonly involves visual recognition of 'peaks' in the waveform. These peaks can be named: (i) according to sequence and polarity; (ii) according to polarity and peak latency; (iii) through principle component analysis. Another type of classification depends on the relationship of the component to external stimuli; viz. exogenous, endogenous and mesogenous responses, related respectively to physical characteristics of external stimuli, psychological demands of a situation and a mix of both.

erythrocytes

Non-nucleated red blood cells responsible for oxygen/carbon dioxide transport.

exosomatic

Measurement of electrodermal activity by the use of an externally applied potential resulting in activity measured as skin conductance, resistance, admittance or impedance.

extracellular body fluids

Fluids maintained within the body but not within its cells.

fiducial points

The limit points on either side of a representative statistic giving the width of variation of the statistic on either side of the mean for given probabilities (usually $p = 0.05$ or 0.01).

filters

  band-pass
  Ability to pass a specific frequency band.

  band-reject
  Ability to reject any band of frequencies.

  high pass
  Pass only high frequencies with low frequencies filtered out.

  low pass
  Pass only low frequencies with high frequencies filtered out.

  single frequency
  Can be passed and by cascading (placing in series) of filters the bandpass roll-off can be made sharper.

  see also *notch filtering*

flux

Flow of physical entities, e.g. the flow of charge or radiation across a given area. In EEG, refers to the activity as a mixture of frequencies, each having a specified amplitude, centre frequency, and phase delay with reference to a specific epoch of time beginning at an arbitrary starting point. Primary data are trains of waves.

incident

The flow of energy from a source of electromagnetic radiation. Radiant flux and radiant power are synonymous terms in SI radiometric measurement where the energy unit is watts.

steady state

Constant average value of radiant flux over the time interval of interest. Potentials evoked by stimuli of sufficiently high repetition rate that there is an overlapping of responses to form a continuous waveform with constant amplitude and phase relationship to the repeating stimulus.

folding frequency

The principal folding frequency is equal to half the sampling rate but other folding frequencies appear at the zero frequency axis and at all multiples of the principal folding frequency. The term gives a useful visualization of the effect of aliasing as a folding of the frequency spectrum of a waveform about the folding frequencies. Sampling a 6 Hz sine wave at a sampling rate of 10 Hz will produce a single fold and an alias frequency of 4 Hz. Sampling a 12 Hz sine wave at the same rate will produce a double fold and an alias frequency of 2 Hz.

Fourier analysis

Any analysis where the data are represented as sums of sines and cosines of various frequencies.

Fourier series analysis

The analysis of signals that are repeated exactly at regular intervals. Periodic signals of this type can be expressed as the sum of a series of sine waves whose frequencies are harmonically related to the repetition frequency of the signal. The components have amplitudes and phases determined by the signal pattern. A power spectrum analysis provides a 'picture' of the relative power, which depends on the amplitude of the component sine waves, at various frequencies.

Fourier integral analysis

A mathematical technique for dealing with signals which are not periodic but which recur with exactly the same waveshape and size. These aperiodic or transient signals can be expressed as a continuous function of frequency. Amplitude and frequency of the components are illustrated by the spectra.

Fourier transform

See Fourier analysis.

frequency analysis

A mathematical technique applied to signals which never recur exactly. Such signals are termed random or stochastic signals: they cannot be uniquely described by a set of parameters, but only in statistical terms. The component amplitudes are often expressed as mean square values. The result of analysis is called a power spectrum (*q.v.*).

frequency domain

When waveforms are analysed in terms of their spectra, the analysis is said to be in the frequency domain (as opposed to time domain for analysis in terms of time relationships). In EEG, analysis of time series data which describes the frequency of primary interest.

frequency modulation

A method of superimposing information on a carrier frequency from a lower frequency or d.c. signal source by varying the carrier frequency above and below its central value.

gain

The ratio of input to output amplitude of an amplifier (often expressed in db).

galvanic skin response (GSR)

Term (now superseded) denoting exosomatically measured phasic electrodermal activity.

Y

galvanometer

An instrument for detecting or measuring small electrical current by means of the interaction of magnetic fields.

Gaussian

One of several terms for the normal curve; from Carl Friedrich Gauss who derived the formula in the 19th century to quantify errors of observation in astronomy.

haemolysis

Contamination of serum or plasma with haemoglobin liberated from damaged erythrocytes.

hardware

A general term to describe the electronic instrumentation part of the computer as opposed to the software programs which provide the sequence of steps in which the various parts of the instrumentation are used. (*See* Software.)

heart rate

Strictly, this refers to the number of heart beats produced in one minute. However, the term is usually applied to the reciprocal transformation of the interbeat interval.

heart period

The time between successive QRS (*q.v.*) complexes of the cardiac cycle, i.e. the duration of the interbeat interval.

hydrostatic pressure

Pressure arising from the gravitational pull on a liquid at a certain position in space.

hysteresis

The ability of magnetic material to maintain its own magnetic state.

hybrid systems

See Computer, hybrid.

hypothenar eminence

The pad of flesh on the palm at the base of the little finger; useful as an electrode site for electrodermal measurement.

impedance

A quantity analogous to resistance in direct current circuits but complex as it relates to alternating current circuits where capacitors or inductors have both a resistive and reactive component. The impedance of a circuit is equal to the ratio of the effective voltage to the effective current.

inductive reactance

See Reactance.

inflection

Point at which slope changes in direction, e.g. positive to zero or negative to positive.

input resistance (or impedance)

The resistance which a measuring device (e.g. a polygraph input) presents to the measured input potential.

interface

A shared boundary; in computer usage a hardware device which links the computer with peripheral devices.

intracellular body fluids

Fluids compartmentalized within body cells.

Korotkoff sounds

Sounds that can be heard through a stethoscope placed distally to a deflating occlusion cuff. The sounds vary in quality as the pattern of blood flow under the cuff changes, and criteria characteristic of the systolic and diastolic pressure can be identified.

latency

onset
The time from the onset of a stimulus to the beginning of a detectable change in ongoing activity.

peak
The time from the onset of a stimulus to the maximum amplitude of a phasic response.

window
The temporal gap into which latency values normally fall so that apparent responses having latency values outside this window may be considered as non-specific responses (*q.v.*).

'law' of initial values (LIV)

As proposed by Wilder, the LIV states that the magnitude of a physiological response to a stimulus is related to the prestimulus level according to the following rule: given a standard stimulation and a standard period of measurement, the response defined as the change from the initial (pre stimulus) level will tend to be smaller when the initial value is higher.

light emitting diode (LED)

Semiconductor device which produces light when an electrical current is passed through it. Of low efficiency, it will only produce small quantities of light, but has the advantage of a very high speed of switch-on (microseconds) and of producing well defined narrow bandwidth (i.e. pure colour) light.

light history effects

The recovery time of a photoconductive cell (light dependent resistor) after exposure to a change of illuminance; an effect in which observed output values depend on prior storage in light or dark.

log scales

See Scales.

magnitude

See Amplitude.

mercury strain gauge

A column of mercury sealed in an elastic tube; resistance of the mercury is a function of the length of the tube.

metabolite

Compound resulting from the biochemical modification of a parent compound.

mho

The unit of conductance most commonly used in psychophysiological work, now superseded by the siemen. Conductance more conveniently expressed in terms of micromhos.

microprocessor

A complete central processing unit for a computer built on a small piece ('chip') of silicon. When combined with other devices, forms the basis of a microcomputer.

module

A self-contained unit; generally connected with others to make a large system.

moving average

A method used to smooth data points whereby a data point is replaced by a linear combination of adjacent data points and the original data points. It is, in effect, a digital low-pass filter.

multiplexing

A process by which two or more signals are transmitted simultaneously over a single channel or stored on a single recording channel.

non-specific responses

Changes in physiological activity which may have the appearance of elicited responses but which cannot be associated with an identifiable stimulus; also called spontaneous fluctuations.

notch filtering

Selective filtering to reject energy occurring over a narrow bandwidth, and typically at a single frequency. This is accomplished with active filters utilizing operational amplifiers which enable sharp attenuation of energy occurring over a narrow frequency range(s). Notch filtering is most commonly used to reject energy at the power-line frequency and its harmonics.

Nyquist criterion

$f_n = 1/(2\,\Delta t)$, where Δt is the sampling period. It is necessary to sample at least twice per cycle to resolve that frequency.

Nyquist frequency

One-half the sampling frequency. The frequency about which aliasing (q.v.) takes place. Also known as the folding frequency (q.v.) because frequencies higher than the Nyquist frequencies are folded into the range 0Hz to the Nyquist frequency.

Nystagmus

The general term for a large class of eye movements of an oscillatory or unstable nature; includes both smooth and saccadic components. Normally a repetitive eye motion comprised of a slow moving progression followed by a rapid return period. This type of movement may be elicited by a stimulus moving with respect to the head (whether the observer is rotated or the object is moved) or by direct stimulation of the vestibular system.

off-line, on-line

The terms 'on-line' and 'off-line' denote whether data analysis does or does not proceed apace with data recording. On-line analysis means that data are analysed as they are recorded (such analyses generally utilize a computer). On-line analyses are typically used in biofeedback techniques requiring immediate reduction of data in order to provide the subject with feedback based on analysis of his last response or last series of responses. Off-line analysis means that data are not analysed during recording, but the term off-line is generally used only when the data analysis being described could conceivably be carried out on-line.

one-shot multivibrators

A digital logic module whose output goes from 0 to 1 (or false to true) for a specified period of time whenever the input goes from 0 to 1 (or false to true).

optoelectronic

A term used to describe a range of devices which either emit or detect light when used in an appropriate electronic circuit configuration.

'outlier'

A deviant observation; that is, a measurement which falls outside the range of variation of a series of observations.

period

Duration between specific amplitude points usually measured on a baseline. The reciprocal of period gives wave frequency.

period analysis

A method of display of the total count of waves during an epoch per unit of time. The baseline crossing is used to determine the periods.

intermediate period
The intermediate period is derived from the first derivative of the primary EEG trace.

major period
The major period is the time relationship between points of inflection and the baseline cross of the primary EEG.

minor period
The minor period is derived from the mathematical second derivative of the primary trace. The minor periods are 'wiggles' superimposed on the primary EEG.

pH

Standard measure of the acidity or alkalinity of a solution expressed as the negative logarithm of the hydrogen ion concentration in moles/litre; values lying below 7.0 are acid, above 7.0 alkaline.

phalanges

the divisions of the fingers — distal, medial and proximal. Useful as electrode sites in electrodermal measurement.

phase shift

Displacement of a waveform in time measured in degrees (or radians) as phase lag or lead. Measurement of phase implies comparison of two waveforms, one serving as a reference. The sign given to the phase shift (lag or lead) is determined by which waveform is chosen as reference. If t is the displacement of a waveform in time and T

is the period of the waveform (time for completion of one cycle), phase shift is calculated as: $0 = t/T$ (360°). For example, if a 5 Hz sinusoidal waveform were displaced 0.05 s forward in time relative to a reference waveform, the phase lead would be:

$$\frac{0.050\ s}{0.200\ s}(360°) = 90°$$

phasic

When applied to psychophysiological responses, the term 'phasic response' usually refers to a short-term change in physiological activity, often following an identifiable stimulus, which can be distinguished against a background, ongoing ('tonic') level of activity. The response would typically have a relatively rapid onset and a return to baseline within a period which is characteristic for different response systems.

photodiodes

bipolar semiconductor devices in which irradiation of the p–n junction ($q.v.$) liberates electrons from the material of which it is composed and makes them available for conduction.

photomultiplier

A device in which electrons released by photoelectric emission are successively multiplied by dynodes that produce secondary emission.

Photometry

Quantification of analytes by study of the incident light absorbance characteristics.

Plasma cortisol

Principal adrenal glucocorticoid. Steroid hormone having major effects on carbohydrate metabolism, salt and water balance, and inflammation.

Platelets

Circulating non-nucleated element of the blood active in the clotting process.

p–n junction devices

Devices made from semiconductor materials formed such that one region has donor atoms and an adjacent region acceptors. Donor material has extra electrons and is known as n-type (n representing negative); acceptor material has vacant holes that can accept electrons and is known as p-type material (p representing positive). When biased properly flow can be bidirectional.

Points of inflection

Points at which there is a change in the direction of a wave (*see also* Inflection).

polarization potentials

Potentials which are developed due to the passage of current and arise at the interface between electrode and electrolyte.

power

A term used to refer to electrical energy of an EEG spectrum, computed by multiplying frequency times amplitude. Some prefer the term 'intensity' to 'power'.

power, radiant

See Flux, radiant.

power spectrum

See Spectrum.

prostaglandins

Family of compounds derived from arachidonic acid having a wide variety of hormone like actions.

psychogalvanic response (PGR)

Superseded term denoting exosomatically measured phasic electrodermal activity.

pulse code modulation

A process by which one or more analog signals are converted into binary numbers and recorded on tape or transmitted via telemetry as the presence or absence of a pulse for 1 or 0. The advantage of this system is the high immunity from noise interference.

pulse wave velocity (arterial)

The rate of propagation of the pressure pulse through the arterial system; related to the resting dimensions of the vessel and varying inversely with arterial distensibility. Permits an estimation of pressure change on each cardiac cycle.

pulse width modulation

A process by which the logic states to which an analog signal is converted (as in pulse code modulation) are represented by alteration in pulse width. More immune from interference than pulse code modulation.

Purkinje image

When light waves are incident upon a boundary between two media in which the velocity is different they divide into reflected and refracted trains. Light waves that are incident to the eye encounter four boundaries each of which divides them. Purkinje images are the reflected components.

QRS complex

Refers to part of the EKG waveform and represents ventricular depolarization and contraction.

radio frequencies

electromagnetic radiation in the frequency band 40×10^3–30×10^6 Hz.

reactance, capacitive

A practical capacitor operating in an alternating current circuit is considered to consist of two parts. One part through which the voltage and current flow together (in phase) is named the 'real' or resistive part. The other part through which the current flow leads the voltage by 90° is called the 'imaginary' or reactive part. The reactive part (the reactance X_c) is expressed in ohms and has a value

$$\frac{1}{2\pi fC}$$

where f is the frequency in hertz and C is the capacitance in farads.

reactance, inductive

Similar to the capacitive reactance above but in the inductor case the current lags the voltage by 90°. The reactance (X_L) is expressed in ohms and equals $2\pi fL$ where f is the frequency in hertz and L is the inductance in henrys.

readiness potential

a negative shift of cortical potential occuring before a self-initiated movement in the absence of any external stimulus.

recovery rate (of SCR)

The number of micromhos lost per second during the half recovery time.

recovery time (of SCR)

The time taken for the post peak amplitude value of the SCR to recover to half the peak amplitude value (half recovery time) or to 37% of its peak value (recovery time constant).

recruitment (of SCR)

The number of micromhos gained per second during the rise time of the SCR.

rectification

A means of obtaining a unidirectional flow of current either in the positive or negative direction from a zero reference from an alternating source of current, i.e. a waveshape that traverses a zero point. *Half-wave* rectification takes place when current is permitted to flow only during unidirectional half-cycles of the a.c. source. *Full-wave* rectification takes place when in addition one half-cycle is inverted so that each half cycle of the a.c. wave becomes unidirectional.

resistance

(i) A quantity expressed in ohms that determines the opposition to the flow of current in an electrical circuit. The current in a resistive circuit is always in phase with the applied voltage.
(ii) A property of material which obstructs the flow of electricity. One component of impedance.

'ringing' frequency

The frequency of the damped oscillation that can be generated when a step function is applied to some mechanical or electrical systems. It can also be considered as a frequency where the proximity to a resonance can create a rise in electrical output in a system that is less than critically damped.

rise time (of SCR)

The time from the commencement of the SCR to its peak amplitude.

saccades

Saccadic movements are quick (20–700°/s) jumps of the eye to change the locus of fixation, i.e. to shift the gaze between two points in the field of view. Saccadic movement is nearly conjugate, i.e. the direction, amplitude, and latency of the eyes' movements are very nearly identical. Saccades are the most common eye movements; they occur when we explore our surroundings and when we read.

sampling rate

Any quantity which varies with time must have a value at all times, but measurements of it can only be made at specific times. Such measurements therefore represent only a sample from the infinite number of possible values and the number of measurements made per unit of time is the sampling rate. The unit of time will often be a second, in which case the sampling rate may be given in Hz.

scale

An ordered series of measurement units expressing degrees of difference within a range of quantities.

nominal
A scale whose units reflect typological differences; e.g. male, female.

ordinal
A scale whose units reflect only the relative magnitudes of a series of observations, e.g. rank order.

interval
A scale whose units express equal degrees of difference between adjacent quantities, without reference to an absolute zero point; e.g. temperature in degrees centigrade.

ratio

A scale whose units express proportional differences between quantities referred to an absolute zero point, e.g. length.

logarithmic

A scale whose units constitute a logarithmic series, e.g. pitch.

Schmitt trigger

A circuit device for converting an analog input voltage into a two level digital signal. If the input voltage is above some chosen value, the 'upper trigger point' (UTP) the output is at logic 1. If the input voltage is below a second value, the 'lower trigger point' (LTP) the output is at logic 0. Between UTP and LTP the device exhibits hysteresis and provides a degree of noise immunity.

semiconductor

A material that has a resistivity approximately halfway between that of a good conductor and that of a good insulator. A term commonly used to describe small electrical devices such as transistors that are made from a semiconducting material such as silicon or germanium.

semiconductor diode

(i) A two terminal electrical device possessing asymmetrical conductive characteristics and made from semiconducting material often in the form of a p–n junction. (*See* p–n junction devices.)
(ii) A semiconductor p–n junction device designed to conduct electricity in a single direction.

serum

Supernatant liquid produced following the clotting of blood.

signal averaging

See Averaging.

signal generator

A device which produces electric signals of accurately determined waveform and amplitude. Used for testing instrumentation, or for generating a stimulus of known properties.

signal to noise

This is an expression implying a wanted electrical variation containing an unwanted component. The unwanted component can be due to external sources, circuit compromises or internal sources. External sources which cause noise are electric and magnetic fields or microphony. Circuit compromise arises when, say, a demodulation circuit is designed to strike a balance between modulation frequency range and efficient residual carrier frequency elimination. Signal and noise from the above two sources of unwanted component can be thermal (source) noise or 'shot' and 'flicker' noise. Thermal noise is due to the carriers within a circuit element having electrical resistance being in a constant state of thermal agitation. Shot and flicker noise is also a feature of the movement of carriers (electrons or positive holes) within a discrete device or amplifier. The internal noise performance measures adopted for input devices or amplifiers are the NEP (noise equivalent power) or NF (noise factor).

silicon chip

Material that is basic structure of semiconductors; appropriate treatment creates p- and n-type materials.

sinus arrhythmia

(i) Variation in heart rate with a cyclicity which is related to respiration.
(ii) A general term to describe any rhythmic or cyclic fluctuation occurring in the pattern of resting cardiac activity. More specifically respiratory sinus arrhythmia refers to fluctuations in HR which are associated with the breathing pattern.

skin admittance

The analogue of skin conductance measured by an impressed alternating potential taking account of the capacitive elements in the skin.

skin conductance

Exosomatic electrodermal activity measured as conductance of the skin to impressed potential, directly measured by constant voltage techniques (*q.v.*).

skin impedance

The analogue of skin resistance measured by an impressed alternating potential, taking account of the capacitive elements in the skin.

skin potential

Endosomatically measured electrodermal activity, usually appearing as a tonic level negative at the palm with respect to a neutral reference point and a phasic response having one, two or sometimes three components.

skin resistance

Exosomatic electrodermal activity measured as resistance of the skin to an imposed current, directly measured by a constant current technique (*q.v.*).

smoothing

The effect produced by a low-pass filter (*q.v.*)

smooth movements (of the eyes)

Slow (1–30°/s) sweeping rotations of the eye which serve to maintain fixation on an object moving with respect to the head. They are called pursuit if elicited by movement of the object and compensatory if elicited by head or body movement.

software

The distinction between hardware and software is made in the context of computer analysis. Hardware is equipment like the computer, printer and analog to digital convertor. Software refers to programs used to instruct computers to perform specific functions (*see* Hardware).

solid state filters

An active analog filter that does not use vacuum tubes.

somnogram

A comressed spectral array, used to portray the EEG intensity in the various frequencies during sleep.

source resistance (or impedance)

The resistance inherent in the measurement of a potential; at the skin surface appearing as a resistance in series with the source of potential.

spectral intensity

See Power spectrum.

spectrophotometer

Analytical instrument designed to measure the amount of monochromatic light absorbed by a solution.

spectrum

  autospectrum
  A spectrum reflecting EEG periodicity obtained by correlating different parts of the same curve which leads to extraction of periodic signals. Sometimes referred to as autocorrelation analysis.

  bispectrum
  In contrast to cross and coherence spectra (*q.v.*) where the comparison is between two simultaneously recorded traces, bispectra present the degree of interaction of component waves making up an EEG trace.

  coherence spectrum
  Measures the linear relationship between two time series at various frequencies.

  cross-spectrum
  Measures the in-phase and out-of-phase relationship between two time series at various frequencies. Generally not of interest in itself, but is ussed to calculate coherence and phase shifts between time series.

  power spectrum
  The representation of how the variance of a time series varies over frequency. If the power spectrum is represented by a graph, the abscissa varies over frequency and the ordinate represents the spectral intensity in microvolts. Some prefer the term 'intensity' to 'power'. In addition to the quantitative analysis of brief epochs,

the spectra over long time periods can be compressed to highlight changes in spectral components over time (*cf.* somnogram).

sphygmomanometer

A device for measuring blood pressure, consisting of an inflatable bag connected to a pressure monitor (usually a mercury manometer). The bag is enclosed within a non-distensible cuff, so that the air pressure (measured by the manometer) compresses the limb. As air is released from the system, changes in the blood flow under the cuff can be detected, and the blood pressure can be read from the manometer.

stationary (stationarity)

A time series is stationary if the mean and the variance of the time series remains constant over time.

strain gauge

A device for measuring the mechanical strain in a material resulting from the application of mechanical stress. Often a semiconductor device which, when pushed, pulled, bent or twisted produces an output proportional to the degree of push, pull, bend or twist.

stratum corneum

The outer layer of the epidermis composed of non-living cells acting as a sponge for the retention of water and electrolyte.

stratum lucidum

A barrier layer in the epidermis of palmar and plantar surfaces possibly acting as a membrane involved in the determination of tonic electrodermal activity.

suppression

See Backing-off.

template

A model of a waveform or standard used to measure waveform characteristics.

thenar eminence

The pad of flesh on the palm at the base of the thumb, useful as an electrode site for electrodermal measurement.

time constant

Mathematically, the constant T in the exponential equation $y = Ae^{-t/T}$. In psychophysiology most commonly met in relation to simple RC filters. The time taken for the voltage or charge in a capacitor to either fall to 36.8% of its initial value or rise to 63.2% of its final value. The time constant (T) measured in seconds is equal to the product of the resistance (R) in ohms and the capacitor value (C) in farads.

time domain

Systems of analysis which abstract and emphasize a description of time series data which use the temporal sequence of the data as an important element of the descriptive process; single waves or half-waves are treated as primary. No assumptions are made concerning the nature of the underlying process.

time series analysis

A descriptive term used to group a variety of statistical techniques concerned with the modelling, evaluation, and forecasting of changes in serial observations collected with respect to time.

tonic

Refers to ongoing physiological activity, which may show slow changes, i.e. 'slow' relative to the speed of shorter-term 'phasic' responses (*q.v.*).

toposcopy

A method of EEG analysis which emphasizes phase relations between more than two derivations. The display shows the typology and spreading of EEG potentials.

transducer

A device whereby energy in one form is converted to energy in another form frequently into electrical signals which vary as a function of variation in input energy. Common applications are devices converting to or from electrical energy, for example microphones and loudspeakers. Another example is a strain gauge which changes (transduces) movement into an electrical signal which can be measured.

Tucker 3-way factor analysis

Statistical technique, based on factor analysis, which evaluates changes in the factor structure with respect to another variable, usually time.

Unibase

A proprietary substance used as an electrolyte medium.

Valsalva's manoeuvre

(i) A respiratory exercise in which inspiration is followed by forced expiration against a closed glottis. It leads to rapid and dramatic changes in heart rate and blood pressure.
(ii) A forcible attempt to breath out with glottis closed. Thought to reduce venous return leading to decrease in pulse and blood volume.

vascular bed

Complex network of small vessels: arterioles, capillaries, and venules.

vasoconstriction

Narrowing of the diameter of blood vessels.

vasodilation

Expansion of the diameter of blood vessels.

vergence (of the eyes)

A disjunctive movement involving slow (6–15°/s) rotation of the axes in opposite directions to maintain binocular fixation on an object approaching or moving away from the eyes.

Wiener filter

A statistical technique to define the optimal filter weights by looking into the ratio between signal spectrum (EEG) and noise spectrum (artifacts).

word length

The size of a unit of storage within a computer expressed as a number of bits (*q.v.*). It normally indicates the maximum amount of information that can be processed in a single elementary operation by the computer. In general the more powerful the computer the larger the word length, microprocessers using 8-bit words, minicomputers using 12- or 16-bit words and larger computers using from 32- up to 60-bit words.

Abbreviations

A	ampere
mA	milliampere
μA	microampere
a.c.	alternating current
ACh	acetylcholine
ACL	adjective checklist
ACTH	adrenocorticotrophic hormone
AD–ACL	activation–deactivation adjective checklist
ADC	analog to digital convertor
ADH	antidiuretic hormone
AG	'and' gate
Ag/AgCl	silver–silver chloride
AM	amplitude modulator
ANCOVAR	analysis of covariance
ANOVAR	analysis of variance
ANS	autonomic nervous system
APQ	autonomic perception questionnaire
BAL	blood alcohol level
BP	blood pressure
bpm	beats per minute
CFP	corneofundal potential
CLEMS	conjugate lateral eye movements
CNS	central nervous system
CNV	contingent negative variation
CO	cardiac output
CPG	clock pulse generator
CPU	central processing unit
CRC	cardiac response curve
CRT	cathode ray tube
CSF	cerebrospinal fluid
DA	driver amplifier
DAC	digital to analog convertor
dB	decibel
DBP	diastolic blood pressure

d.c.	direct current
DF	degrees of freedom
drl	differential reinforcement of low rates
ECF	extracellular fluid
ECG	electrocardiograph
ECR	evoked cardiac response
EDA	electrodermal activity
EDL	electrodermal level
EDR	electrodermal response
EEG	electroencephalograph
EKG	electrocardiograph
EMG	electromyograph
EOG	electrooculograph
ERP	event-related potential
FFT	fast Fourier transform
FM	frequency modulation
FPP	floating point processor
GaAs	Gallium arsenide
GSR	galvanic skin response
HP	heart period
HR	heart rate
Hz	hertz
kHz	kilohertz
I	Current
IBI	interbeat interval
IC	integrated circuit
ICF	intracellular fluid
IR	reverse current
K^+	potassium
$k\Omega$	kilohm
KCl	potassium chloride
LED	light emitting diode
LIV	law of initial values
LOC	locus of control scale
MAACL	multiple affect adjective checklist
MACL	mood adjective checklist
MANOVA	multivariate generalization of analysis of variance
Maps	muscle action potentials
MAS	manifest anxiety scale
MMPI	Minnesota multiphasic personality inventory
MPI	Maudsley Personality Inventory
ms	millisecond
ml	millilitre
$M\Omega$	megohm

Na^+	sodium
NaCl	sodium chloride
NS	non-specific response, e.g.
Ns.SCR	non-specific skin conductance response
PCM	pulse code modulation
p.d.	potential difference
PDF	probability density function
pF	picofarad
PGR	psychogalvanic response
POMS	psychiatric outpatient mood scale
PPT	pulse wave propagation time
PR	pulse rate
PT	phototransistor
PWV	pulse wave velocity
RE	variable resistor
rec.t	recovery time
rec.t/2	recovery half time
rec.tc	recovery measured in terms of the time constant
REM	rapid eye movement
ris.t	rise time
RR	respiration rate
RT	reaction time
SA	sinus arrhythmia
SACL	stress-arousal checklist
SBP	systolic blood pressure
SCL	skin conductance level
SCR	skin conductance response
SD	standard deviation
SI	Système International
SN	signal to noise
SNS	sympathetic nervous system
SPL	skin potential level
SPR	skin potential response
SRL	skin resistance level
SRR	skin resistance response
SSS	Stanford sleepiness scale
STAI	State–trait anxiety inventory
SYR	skin admittance response
SYL	skin admittance level
SZL	skin impedance level
SZR	skin impedance response
TC	time constant
TSF	transcellular fluid
TSH	thyroid stimulating hormone
TT	transit time (pulse transit time)
V	volt
VDU	visual display unit

mV	millivolt
μV	microvolt
VAS	visual analog scale
VF	forward voltage
VHF	very high frequency
VR	reverse bias voltage
Z	impedance

Index

695